EUROPEAN POLITICS AND

A Comparative Approach

GOVERNMENT

CLIFFORD A. L. RICH
Oklahoma State University

ROBERT O. GIBBON
Wisconsin State College

LOWELL G. NOONAN
San Fernando Valley State College

HELMUT BADER
El Camino College

KAREL HULIČKA
University of Buffalo

Edited by Clifford A. L. Rich

THE RONALD PRESS COMPANY • NEW YORK

Library of Congress Catalog Card Number: 62–10835

PRINTED IN THE UNITED STATES OF AMERICA

Preface

This textbook is for the undergraduate course in comparative European politics and government. The aim is to analyze the causal determinants of political behavior and institutions instead of leaving it to the student to conjecture why certain phenomena occur. The editor has collaborated with persons who are specialists on a particular country and who have an intimate knowledge of its language, history, culture, and thought patterns, as well as being familiar with the country's political and legal literature and source materials.

The book is divided into six parts. Parts I to V present the major countries of Europe that have made the most outstanding contributions to the development of political techniques and institutions. Great Britain, France, Germany, Italy, and the U.S.S.R. are included because each represents a principal facet of Europe's culture. Part VI summarizes the politics and institutions of European union.

In the country by country approach to the study of comparative politics and government, the student is acquainted with the political institutions as an integrated whole stemming from a particular national culture, history, and social environment. After making a composite study of diverse national political institutions, the student will have some basis for drawing comparative conclusions. Before comparative evaluations can be made intelligently, however, the student must have a firm grasp of the characteristics and significance of national politics and institutions.

Over one-third of the treatment of each country is devoted to the sources of political behavior and the political process. Instead of presenting a summary of the historical background, the nation's political environment is analyzed and interpreted in the light of historical traditions, social environment, economic system, and the general culture pattern. It is hoped that this will provide a better understanding of the motivations, drives, and particular value systems that produce political behavior. The organization of politics is thoroughly described along with the techniques of political action. The governing process is given in great detail; legislative organizations and procedures, the role of the executive, the administrative system, local government, and the treatment of individual liberty are dealt with systematically. The rather elaborate treatment of the governmental structures and procedures is intended to provide the student with a comprehensive understanding of how the major European systems compare to that of the United States.

A selected reading list follows each chapter, and a more comprehensive bibliography of selected materials for further consultation is provided. A number of charts and tables are included together with maps showing the principal political and administrative subdivisions of each country.

CLIFFORD A. L. RICH

Stillwater, Oklahoma
February, 1962

Contents

Dal

Part I
POLITICS AND GOVERNMENT OF GREAT BRITAIN
by Robert O. Gibbon

Part II
POLITICS AND GOVERNMENT OF FRANCE
by Lowell G. Noonan

Part III
POLITICS AND GOVERNMENT OF ITALY
by Clifford A. L. Rich

Part IV
POLITICS AND GOVERNMENT OF GERMANY
by Helmut Bader

Part V
POLITICS AND GOVERNMENT OF THE U.S.S.R.
by Karel Hulička

Part VI
POLITICS AND INSTITUTIONS OF EUROPEAN UNION
by Clifford A. L. Rich

I

POLITICS AND GOVERNMENT OF GREAT BRITAIN

UNITED KINGDOM
Showing cities of more than 100,000 population
Scale of Miles
0 25 50 100
ATLANTIC OCEAN
North Sea
Irish Sea
English Channel
SCOTLAND
NORTHERN IRELAND
WALES
ENGLAND
IRELAND
FRANCE
ZETLAND (SHETLAND IS.)
ORKNEY ISLANDS
SUTHERLAND
CAITHNESS
ROSS & CROMARTY
NAIRN
MORAY
BANFF
ABERDEEN
Aberdeen
INVERNESS
KINCARDINE
ANGUS
Dundee
ARGYLL
PERTH
KINROSS
CLACKMANNAN
FIFE
STIRLING
DUMBARTON
W. LOTHIAN
Edinburgh
E. LOTHIAN
MIDLOTHIAN
RENFREW
Glasgow
BUTE
LANARK
PEEBLES
BERWICK
SELKIRK
ROXBURGH
AYR
DUMFRIES
KIRKCUD BRIGHT
WIGTOWN
LONDON-DERRY
ANTRIM
TYRONE
FERMANAGH
ARMAGH
Belfast
DOWN
ISLE OF MAN
NORTH UMBERLAND
Newcastle
South Shields
Sunderland
Gateshead
CUMBERLAND
DURHAM
WESTMORLAND
Middlesborough
N. RIDING
YORK
York
E. RIDING
CITY OF YORK
Hull
W. RIDING
Leeds
LANCASHIRE
Liverpool
Sheffield
ANGLESEY
CAERNARVON
DENBIGH
FLINT
CHESHIRE
DERBY
NOTTINGHAM
LINCOLN
LINDSEY
Derby
Nottingham
KESTEVEN
HOLLAND
MERIONETH
Stoke-on-Trent
STAFFORD
LEICESTER
RUTLAND
SOKE OF PETERBOROUGH
NORFOLK
Norwich
MONTGOMERY
SHROPSHIRE
Wolverhampton
Walsall
Birmingham
Leicester
ISLE OF ELY
CARDIGAN
RADNOR
Coventry
WARWICK
NORTHAMPTON
HUNTINGDON
Northampton
CAMBRIDGE
SUFFOLK
W. SUFFOLK
E. SUFFOLK
Ipswich
HEREFORD
WORCESTER
PEMBROKE
CARMARTHEN
BRECKNOCK
GLOUCESTER
OXFORD
BUCKING HAM
BEDFORD
Luton
ESSEX
Swansea
Rhondda
GLAMORGAN
Cardiff
MONMOUTH
Newport
Bristol
HERTFORD
BERKS
Reading
MIDDLESEX
London
LONDON
Southend-on-Sea
WILTS
SOMERSET
HAMPSHIRE
SURREY
KENT
DEVON
DORSET
Bournemouth
Southampton
SUSSEX
W. SUSSEX
E. SUSSEX
Brighton
Portsmouth
ISLE OF WIGHT
CORNWALL
Plymouth
Blackpool
Preston
Blackburn
Bradford
Leeds
YORK
W. RIDING
LANCASHIRE
Bolton
Oldham
Huddersfield
Wallasey
St. Helens
Salford
Manchester
Liverpool
Stockport
Sheffield
Birkenhead
CHESHIRE
DERBY
HERTFORD
BUCKING-HAM
MIDDLESEX
Enfield
ESSEX
Edmonton
Walthamstow
Hendon
Tottenham
Harrow
Leyton
Ilford
Hornchurch
Wembley
Willesden
W.Ham
E. Ham
Dagenham
Ealing
Heston & Isleworth
London
LONDON
Twickenham
SURREY
Croydon
KENT

1

Backgrounds of British Government

British government has evolved slowly from the time of the Anglo-Saxon kings (sixth to the eleventh centuries) to the present. This evolution was not always peaceful or without painful periods of backsliding; but the outcome has been a curious yet practical blending of old and new ways of governance and the emergence of a stable, democratic society. When compared with the frailties of democracy in Germany and Italy and with the uncertainty of democracy in France, Britain does stand as a "rock." Part of the explanation for this successful establishment of stable political institutions is found in the evolutionary pattern of British development.

Embryonic ideas of limited, representative government were in existence even in Anglo-Saxon times. The king was elected by his chief lords who, in turn, advised the king in council. The king did not make law but merely revealed law by his "dooms" (orders or decrees). When the Normans conquered the Anglo-Saxons in the eleventh century (1066), these ideas were not vanquished but reinforced. Magna Carta of 1215 is evidence that even the new Norman lords refused to allow an uncontrolled monarch. The Norman kings benefited English development by their early centralization of government. The feudal system in England never became as decentralized or entrenched as in the continental countries. The capriciousness of local lords was limited by the king's justice,[1] and the lords, by threatening to withdraw their support, limited the capriciousness of the king. The ancient liberties of the people were protected by this continual balancing of the power forces. Although a civil war and a revolution were needed to delineate the rules of the game, the victors of these

[1] The king instituted a system of royal courts presided over by royal justices.

seventeenth-century revolutions did not attempt to establish a new set of rules; they adjusted the old rules to fit a new situation. Such has been the pattern of British development—a modern welfare state with an ancient monarchy, a representative democracy with a semihereditary second chamber of its legislature, religious toleration with an Established Church and a required Protestant monarch.

Another important clue to the understanding of British political stability is the apparent ease by which new social groups have gained political influence. There have been remarkably few "stormings of the Bastille" in Britain. The ruling groups have managed to give in to the demands of new power-seeking groups in sufficient time to prevent a complete collapse of social and political order. The medieval kings brought in the lesser gentry (knights of the shires) and representatives of the towns (the commercial class) to give them support against the nobility. The Tudor monarchs often had the political support of the merchant class during the period of the commercial revolution (*ca.* 1350–1700). The lesser gentry and commercial classes joined forces in the House of Commons. During the reign of the Stuarts, many of the gentry joined forces with the middle class, and this combination secured the supremacy of Parliament over the king. In this struggle even the lower middle class tasted of political power through the position of the Army, but it did not secure representation in Parliament.

The restoration of the Stuart monarchy in 1660 and the Glorious Revolution of 1688 slowed down the growth of political consciousness in the lower classes. Political power, whether in Whig or Tory hands, was the power of the propertied interests. Propertied interests in England between 1688 and 1832 basically meant land ownership. England became a landed aristocracy and rule by the "gentlemen of England" was accepted.

The impact of the Industrial Revolution was felt in the nineteenth century. The non-propertied middle class was the first group to awaken politically. The Reform Act of 1832 extended the suffrage and therefore representation to the new middle class. The Reform Act was also revolutionary in that it promoted the union of the new industrialists with the old Whigs to form the Liberal party. The Tories (Conservatives) counter-attacked this new Liberal alignment by becoming the champions of the new industrial workers. However, the new class of industrial workers was not enfranchised by the Reform Act of 1832. Factory legislation alleviated the worst aspects of the industrial system and helped to prevent the growth of militant socialism among the industrial workers. The history of the extension of suffrage from 1832 to 1918, when universal manhood suffrage was achieved, is a history of the gradual absorption of new groups into the political society. Benjamin Disraeli could talk of "Tory democracy" with some validity, and William Gladstone could speak of the "Liberal reforms" toward more democracy.

As the new groups achieved political recognition, the two major parties managed, until the twentieth century, to find room for the intruders and still preserve social distinctions. The Conservatives formed Conservative Workingmen Clubs and kept their Carlton Clubs socially pure.

The arrival of the Labor party did not change the basic patterns. From its inception the party was dominated by trade-union officials and middle-class intellectuals. Neither group was interested in the promotion of a class struggle, nor were they convinced of any necessity to overthrow the existing economic and political institutions. Advocates of gradual reform to be accomplished within the democratic framework, the Laborites could become one of the major political parties and be accepted by the other parties as either Her Majesty's Government or Her Majesty's Loyal Opposition.

The long, historical development and the relatively easy acceptance of new groups to political power indicate another fundamental of British politics—its pragmatic character. The cartoons of John Bull "muddling through" express the practical, often illogical, British approach to political problems. Edmund Burke could attack the leaders of the French Revolution for their glorification of logic and reason and their failure to recognize the importance of tradition in preserving political stability. All major political groups have accepted the idea of compromise, which is the prerequisite for political democracy.

GEOGRAPHIC AND DEMOGRAPHIC BACKGROUNDS

Geographic characteristics have also played a part in the development of modern Britain. Close yet unattached to the European mainland, the British Isles (about the size of Oregon) have been free of invasion except for the Norman Conquest and the thwarted invasion by Hitler. Because of her fortuitious location, Britain has had the opportunity to develop her institutions without continual political crisis and material damage to her own resources. Britain's geographic location promoted her historic role as the holder of the balance of power in European affairs.

As an island people the British early turned to the seas and became a trading nation. With the advent of the Industrial Revolution, manufacturing was added to trade. Britain is a trading nation and its economic life depends upon external trade. Agriculturally, Britain depends upon imports for about half of her food supply and her population is not large enough to absorb her industrial production.

With the exclusion of Northern Ireland, Great Britain comprises about 87,812 square miles. The main isle is a little under 600 miles in length and 300 miles across at its widest part. Because of river bays and inlets, no part of Britain is more than 75 miles from tidal water. The island lies on the continental shelf and the waters are shallow around the isle. This has aided in fishing and also in increasing the warming effect of the North Atlantic current upon the climate. The greater parts of Scotland, Wales, and northern England are highland plains, mountains and valleys. Soil in these areas is poor and most of the land is suitable only for grazing. Lowland Britain, which includes most of the eastern and southern portions of England, is rolling plains land. The soil is above average and is arable.

Climate is temperate. The prevailing winds are from the southwest and bring in the warm air of the North Atlantic current. Freezing temperatures are rare but do occur; extreme high temperatures are infrequent. Mean monthly temperatures in the north are 39° F. for winter months and 53° F. for summer months. In the south 43° F. is the mean winter temperature and 63° F. for the summer. Annual rainfall is over 40 inches and is fairly evenly distributed throughout the year. The even climate and rainfall make sheep and cattle grazing available twelve months of the year.

The last official census was taken in Britain in 1951.[2] The population was 50,225,000. The 1957 estimate was 51,455,000 (Northern Ireland included). The population density is one of the higest in the world; in 1957 the estimated density was 546 persons per square mile. Regional distribution of population in 1957 was as follows: England, 42,296,000; Wales and Monmouthshire, 2,611,000; Scotland, 5,150,000; and Northern Ireland, 1,398,000.

The population of Britain is predominantly urban. Over 75 per cent of the population lives in urban areas, and approximately 40 per cent of the population lives in one of the seven large metropolitan areas. Only in Northern Ireland does a fairly equal distribution between urban and rural population exist. The heavy concentration of population becomes more striking when it is noted that five out of the seven metropolitan areas are located in an area about forty miles wide that extends from Liverpool on the west coast to London. The total population of these five areas—London, Leeds-Bradford, Manchester, Birmingham and Wolverhampton, and Liverpool—is 16,013,000. The other two metropolitan areas are Newcastle upon Tyne and Glasgow. Greater London has a population of 8,251,000. The high urbanization creates a multitude of problems for government. Housing, slum clearance, sanitation, and unemployment are only a few of the problems that are magnified by urban concentration.

The age distribution of the population is significant to government. In Britain 23.2 per cent of the population is under fifteen years, 65.3 per cent between fifteen and sixty-four, and 11.5 per cent over sixty-five. If death rates continue to decline and if the birth rate increases or remains constant, Britain will have both an increase in people of productive age and an increase in the number of older people. Both developments present major problems for government. Britain must maintain a growing economy to

[2] *Britain: An Official Handbook* (London: Her Majesty's Stationery Office, 1959).

absorb the new employables and to provide for a satisfactory retired life for increasing numbers.

SOCIAL STRUCTURE

A century ago Benjamin Disraeli wrote of the "two nations" in Britain and of the impenetrable gulf between the rich and the poor. Alan Sillitoe, in *The Loneliness of the Long-Distance Runner,* makes the same contention for the present century. Has not the advent of the welfare state modified the class structure of Britain, either as a leveling up, or down, or both? Obviously, changes have occurred since the time of Disraeli; and these changes have blurred the rigidity of the class structure. But a class structure does exist although the social mobility is about 20 per cent at the present time. Wealth continues to be a criterion of social stratification; but education, family background, and occupation are as important, if not more so, than wealth in the modern social system.

The upper class in Britain is a composite of the nobility, the landed gentry, industrialists, top managerial people, and the more successful professional people. Such a listing is somewhat misleading as these are not mutually exclusive groups. A large percentage of the nobility today is of recent origin, as about half of the peerages have been created in the twentieth century and only about one in fifteen dates from 1689. In recent years many leaders of industry and commerce have been given titles, a fact that the Labor party deplores. Industrialists have become landed gentry either by purchase or marriage.

By the measurement of wealth the upper class varies tremendously. Some landed gentry are in reality land poor with relatively small current income. Some of the older nobility are not only land poor but live in genteel poverty. Others have commercialized their ancestral homes to make them income producing or have allowed the government to take their estates in lieu of tax payments. Some of the landed gentry and nobility have diversified their income sources, married wealth, or have entered the business world. The older industrial and commercial families are probably the wealthiest segment of the upper class. These families acquired their fortunes before the advent of the welfare state. But as the family fortune is passed to the next generation, the government now materially reduces the net inheritance. Estate taxes are progressive and run from 1 to 80 per cent of the capital value, depending upon the amount involved. Extremely wealthy families and individuals are scarce in Britain today. Millionaires find it difficult to retain their wealth, and potential millionaries find it even more difficult to become one. Not only do heavy estate taxes work their leveling goal, but the regular progressive income tax, personal or corporate, is heavy enough to prevent huge accumulations of wealth. The income tax reaches at the higher levels a rate of about 93 per cent. Britain taxes unearned income (interest, dividends, and the like) at a higher rate than earned income (salaries and wages). The figure £6,000 ($14,800) income after taxes is a maximum even for the upper class.

Education is a clearer measure of upper-class status than is income. The educational background will invariably include one of the "better" public schools such as Eton or Harrow and a degree from Cambridge or Oxford. Education in one of the public schools is not a matter of prestige alone. It has been long recognized that the public schools have provided the best education in Britain not only in academic subjects but also because of their strong emphasis upon duties and obligations, the development of fair play, and the desirability of public service. Since World War II, education has been democratized in Britain. More students are achieving higher education as a result of government subsidization of the universities. The government has also provided scholarships to individual students. Approximately half of the students at Oxford and Cambridge have government scholarships. Even the famous public schools are accepting more scholarship students from the lower and middle classes. But class emphasis upon "proper" education is prevalent and is not likely to disappear quickly. However, the right to wear an old school tie or to call oneself an Oxonian will not guarantee upper-class status. It must be coupled with other criteria.

The upper class may also be distinguished from the other classes by its way of living. Materially, the upper-class families are the two- and three-car families. A Rolls Royce, Bentley, Jaguar, or at least a Talbot or Sunbeam will be garaged along with a smaller Austin, Morris, or Ford. For those who can afford the luxury, a chauffeur drives the Rolls or Bentley. The upper class is housed on large or small country estates, in the walled-in large single houses, or in fashionable flats in the metropolitan areas. The employment of resident domestic sevants, i.e., housekeepers, butlers, and nannies, is often a characteristic feature of upper-class life.[3]

The upper class tends to belong to the Church of England and not to a Nonconformist sect. Membership in the exclusive private clubs is another criterion of acceptance into the upper class.

At its best the upper class has provided much of the government leadership in Britain. Reared in an atmosphere of *noblesse oblige*, the aristocracy has approved of positions in the foreign service, military establishments, and in home governmental service. This sense of duty has been

[3] Resident domestic servants have declined in number since the 1940's. It is estimated that in England and Wales there were 706,800 such servants in 1931. By 1951, the number was reduced to 178,000. The upper middle class has felt the loss much more than the upper class.

transmitted to the new arrivals in the upper class. This tradition of service is still present in the upper class, but it should not be overexaggerated. The upper class has its full share of misfits, playboys, alcoholics, and those who are interested primarily in their own economic advancement.

The Conservative party attracts the upper class and, with exceptions, the party may count upon the financial and voting support of the class. Although individual industrialists may complain of the Conservative party's statism, certainly the party is a better friend of the free-enterprise system than is the Labor party. The Conservative party's traditional program of "God, Monarchy, and Empire" still has an appeal to large sections of the upper class.

Middle Class

The middle class is the most difficult to describe. It has less cohesion than either the upper or the lower class and a greater variety of characteristics. The upper level of the middle class is composed of the great bulk of professional people; the managerial group of medium-sized business; the lower managerial people in large business; and the more successful owners of independent plants, businesses, and farms. The middle class extends downward to include the small shopkeeper and greengrocer, the tenant farmer, and scores of white collar (in Britain, the "black coated") workers in all types of occupations.

Except for the upper reaches, the middle class depends upon current income for its livelihood. Savings for the most part are small and are placed in the British equivalents of savings and loan institutions or into various insurance company plans. The disparity of income is greatest in the middle class. Net income ranges from approximately £1,500 ($4,200) to £350 ($980) per year. The lower levels may receive less income than the working class. Attachment to the middle class is psychological for many of its members.

The pressure for educational status is intense for many of the middle class. Attendance at a public school is preferred over a council controlled school even though the public school is not one of the better known schools. More of the children of middle-class parents attend universities, particularly the regional universities such as Bristol, Liverpool, Glasgow, and Edinburgh. For those of the middle class who cannot afford a public school and university background, completion of the secondary level and some training in a technical institute will provide sufficient status.

Emulation of the upper class in style of living is common among the upper middle class. Not capable of owning a Rolls or Bentley, the upper middle class will often have a Rover or Sunbeam and if possible a smaller car. The majority of the middle class have one car, and it is usually one of the smaller cars. The middle class is housed in detached bungalows, semidetached housing units, and flats. The more fortunate have part-time domestic help, although this has become a luxury and not a commonplace practice.

Religious affiliation is scattered among the Church of England, Roman Catholic, and Nonconformist churches. No real pattern of church membership exists as it does for the upper and lower classes.

Much of the British "floating vote" is found in the middle class. Traditionally, the class voted the Liberal party; and today the real strength of the Liberal party is still in the middle class. The decline in the Liberal party has been accompanied by a shift in the middle-class vote. The shift has tended to favor the Conservative party in recent elections but went to Labor in the immediate postwar period.

The middle class as the salaried class has felt the pressure of postwar British economic problems more than the other classes. Salaries have not increased at a rate equal to the wages of the working class. Inflation has increased the cost of living at a faster rate than increases in salary have occurred. The obvious result has been a decreased standard of living for many of the middle class. The lower middle class has seen the working class become materially better off. Increased resentment toward the working class and a growing sense of insecurity has been the result. Despite benefits from the state's welfare services, the lower middle class feels that its position is in jeopardy.

The middle class has played the traditional role of supplying the bulk of the professional and managerial posts. The incentives of the middle class have been monetary award and advancement within the business and professional worlds. Economic security and independence, proper education and legacies for their children, plus a feeling of being a "gentleman" have been the goals of the middle class. The achievement of these goals has been frustrated in postwar Britain.

Working Class

The lower class or working class comprises the wage earners, the unskilled, semiskilled, and skilled working groups. To this must be added some non-manual workers, junior clerks and others in the lower levels of the black coated positions. The working class constitutes about 60 per cent of the British population.

Income alone is not a safe criterion to judge the working class. In general the working class receives less than the other classes. Exceptions to this generalization are no longer rare. Some skilled workers may have incomes as high as £1,000 ($2,800) per year; but, as a group, incomes range from approximately £600 ($1,680) downward. The actual income of working-class families may be higher than these figures indicate as the greater proportion of married women gainfully employed come from the working class.[4] The gross income of the working class is diminished less by income tax rates than any other class.

Prior to the Education Act of 1944, the education of a working-class child normally ended upon completion of the primary school or upon reaching the age of fourteen. Secondary education was almost closed to the working class as fees were charged by the public authorities for attendance. Some democratization of the educational system occurred as a result of the Education Act of 1944. Today, the school leaving age is fifteen. The working-class child attends a council school (often called a "county school"). During a child's eleventh year, examinations (called "eleven plus examinations") are given to determine the kind of education the child will receive at the secondary level. Three general directions are available: college preparatory, general education with an orientation toward vocational training, and pure vocational training. This secondary education may be given in separate schools or in comprehensive schools. Secondary education continues until the child is fifteen or sixteen. The majority of students are assigned to the general education program. With an increasing number of state scholarships available for university training, the more talented working-class youth now has the opportunity of a complete education. Technical colleges for craft and technical training have been established by many governmental authorities. The working class has virtually no access to the public preparatory or grammar schools. Most children leave school at fifteen and enter a trade.

In their way of life a rather wide gulf separates the working class from the other classes. Bicycles, public busses, and trams are the chief means of transportation. Small flats in the dreary sections of the cities or flats in the council housing developments are normal for the working class. Recreation is found at the trade-union quarters, at Saturday afternoon football matches or greyhound races, at the cinema, and at the local pubs. Television is fairly evenly distributed among all classes in Britain with over one-half the families owning a television set.

Although church membership varies, the working class tends to belong to the Nonconformist churches such as Methodist or Baptist.

As expected, the Labor party draws its main support from the working class. The trade-unions have a membership of over nine million. About eighty of the trade-unions, including the seventeen largest, have political funds that are used to support the Labor party. The working class votes the Labor party for its labor orientation and not for its Socialist constitution. Doctrinaire socialism has made little penetration into the ranks of

[4] About one-half of the female labor force is under thirty-five years of age, and about 35 per cent of the working married women are under twenty-four. These figures imply that in the working class, women tend to be gainfully employed during the early years of marriage when the husbands are receiving beginning wages.

the working class in Britain. The class supports the welfare state. The trade-unions are essentially practical in their approach to political issues.

Britain still has a class conscious society, but the effect of the postwar years has been to eliminate certain major distinctions. Income differentials are much less today than they were in prewar Britain. Personal income after taxation is concentrated in the £250 to £1,000 ($700 to $2,800) bracket. Less than 1 per cent of the incomes after taxes are over £2,000 ($5,600). A greater proportion of income today is from gainful employment and less from rent, dividends, or other forms of unearned income. The government-supported programs of medical insurance, child benefits, unemployment compensation, and other social welfare benefits have aided in raising the economic level of the lower classes. The educational opportunities for the working class and the lower middle class are better today.

GREAT BRITAIN TODAY

Great Britain has been in a period of rapid change since the beginning of World War II. The changes are occurring not only in relationship to the class structure and the acceptance of the welfare state but also in relationship to Britain's economic and world position. Britain emerged from the war with a weakened economy; foreign assets, particularly dollar assets, were greatly reduced and her shipping supremacy was destroyed. In the immediate post-war years, India, Ceylon, and other parts of the empire gained their independence and Commonwealth status.

Britain's economic recovery has been slow and has relied upon American assistance and an "austerity" approach. Rationing and a reduced standard of living became an accepted part of British life in the immediate postwar years. The government adopted neomercantilistic policies in an attempt to restore a favorable balance of trade. The adoption of welfare programs increased the expenditures of government funds. Inflation, both in Britain and abroad, further complicated recovery. Nevertheless, Britain has increased her national gross product between 1948 and 1957 by 85 per cent; with price change allowance, the increase has been about 30 per cent. Britain has managed to regain a small favorable balance of trade, but as yet it is insufficient to meet what the British government believes are Britain's overseas obligations. These obligations are the repayment of postwar loans and the extension of investments.

Britain has recovered economically but her economic position is precarious. Increased competition from Germany and Japan and the success of the European Common Market have forced the British to review their traditional trade orientation toward the Commonwealth and to seek participation in the European Common Market. Britain must continue to increase her export trade in order to continue her economic growth. The costs of defense and welfare programs constitute about one-half of government expenditures. To prevent these commitments from becoming a burden upon the internal economy, further export expansion is needed.

Politically Great Britain remains a stable, democratic country, committed firmly on the side of the Western world in the current ideological and power struggle with the Soviet Union. British political institutions are not perfect, either as working institutions or as applications of theoretical models. But the British may rightfully be proud of their political institutions and the influence these institutions have had on governmental systems throughout the world.

SELECTED READING

BARKER, SIR ERNEST. *Britain and the British People.* Fair Lawn, N.J.: Oxford University Press, 1955.

BOWEN, IAN. *Population.* Cambridge: Cambridge University Press, 1954.

BROGAN, D. W. *The English People.* New York: Alfred A. Knopf (a division of Random House, Inc.), 1943.

SMELLIE, K. B. *The British Way of Life.* New York: Frederick A. Praeger, Inc., 1956.

WORSWICK, G. D. N., *et al. The British Economy, 1945–50.* Fair Lawn, N.J.: Oxford University Press, 1952.

2

Political Ideologies

Various conceptions of the state and government are found in the value systems of a society. The democratic ideology is dominant in Britain. A few fringe groups espouse the ideology of authoritarianism, but they represent a very small minority within the country. Often, individual members of the Communist party have a difficult time in behaving and thinking as Communists rather than as traditional Britishers. Democracy and the political concepts of democracy developed slowly in Britain. The gradualness of democratic development allowed both the traditional holders of political power and the masses to accommodate themselves to the democratic concepts. The Britisher speaks of his "ancient liberties" and often includes in the list of "ancient liberties" innovations of the nineteenth and twentieth centuries. Thus, a political myth has been created; and the Britisher thinks of his present day democratic ideology as part of the British tradition.

The acceptance of democracy by the major ideological groups has meant that the dominant ideologies have many similarities and that the differences are not sharp and incompatible. In fact, the ideological groups have borrowed from one another as they have matured. Another characteristic of British ideologies is that they are not perfect systems of philosophical thought. They tend toward the practical and have been constructed as much upon experience as upon logic. Also, the exercise of political power by the groups has modified and molded the ideologies. In this way the ideologies have been brought closer together.

British ideologies may be classified for examination as liberalism, conservatism, and socialism.

LIBERALISM

As a political ideology, liberalism developed during the power struggle between the monarchy and Parliament in the seventeenth century. The

Stuart rulers believed in the divine right of kings. They argued that Parliament was an instrument of the monarch. The parliamentary forces denied the divine right theory. They contended that political supremacy belonged to Parliament as the representative body of England, or at least that Parliament shared political supremacy with the monarchy. As the struggle continued, justifications and rationalizations developed; and out of these justifications emerged the basic doctrines of early British liberalism. Many writers and active participants in the struggle contributed to the formation of liberalism. Mention can be made of the levellers of Cromwell's Army, John Milton, James Harrington, and others. The "bible" of liberalism was John Locke's *Treatise on Civil Government.* Some familiarity with Locke's writings is necessary to understand early British liberalism.

Locke began his political analysis with the simple question, "Why does man enter into a political society?" In order to answer the question, Locke attempted to describe life and the condition of man prior to the existence of an organized society. Locke, in common with other seventeenth- and eighteenth-century writers, called this presocietal state the state of nature. It is pointless to condemn or condone Locke for his partial belief that man had really lived in such a condition. The state of nature must be viewed essentially as an abstract concept in Locke's thought. In the state of nature, man lived under the conditions and laws of nature. Man was free, equal, and reasonable. Each individual possessed the natural rights of life, liberty, and property. Life was fairly decent in the state of nature; but certain inconveniences, such as the lack of certainty in the interpretation of natural law and the lack of a definite enforcement medium, made it desirable to organize civil society.

Because of these inconveniences and because man was reasonable and desired to improve his lot, he agreed to organize into a political society. The instrument or method of organization was a social contract among the members of the community. The interpreters of Locke divide on the nature of the contract and whether government was created contractually or as a trust. The significant ideas for liberalism are that government was based upon consent, that it was essentially representative government, and that the governed had the right to change their governors either by peaceful or revolutionary methods.

Lockian liberalism included the idea of a limited or constitutional government. The organs of government were responsible to the governed (at least to the electorate). Furthermore, government was instituted for the express purpose of preserving the natural rights of man. Its authority was only legitimately used to protect natural rights. Although Locke's concept of liberal government did not contain the separation of powers concept as developed in America, Locke did argue for a division of governmental power with legislative supremacy.

Early liberalism stressed the right of private property. Locke included property as one of the natural rights of man. Historically, the rise of liberalism is associated with the rise of the commercial middle class in Britain. It is often charged that early liberalism and, in particular, the writings of Locke are mere rationalizations to insure the protection of the new propertied class. Such a generalization is only partially true. It is true that many passages in Locke's writings produce the feeling that the pocketbook was the most sacred right of an individual. However, early liberalism was not a creed of the absolute, unlimited rights of private property. Early liberalism was preindustrial and, at least in the writings of Locke, had the germ of the medieval and Aristotelian idea of property. The use of property, not its mere possession, was implied as important.

Locke's concept of liberalism emphasized the individual and his natural rights. Natural rights tended to be identified with the ancient rights of the English.

Locke's liberalism was dominant in liberal thought until the Utilitarians and the early classical economists made their appearance in the eighteenth century. The eighteenth century may be called the period of middle liberalism in Britain. Jeremy Bentham, John Mill, David Ricardo, John Austin, and Adam Smith were the principal purveyors of the new liberal doctrines. The Utilitarians claimed to reject the natural rights theory and to substitute the hedonistic law of pleasure and pain. Bentham declared that the master of man is his desire to seek the pleasurable and to avoid the painful. From a social viewpoint, the desired goal was the greatest amount of pleasure for the greatest number of people. The individual was considered rational enough to determine degrees of pleasure and pain. Bentham believed the greatest happiness principle was subject to mathematical analysis.

The function of government was negative, and governmental intervention was designed to protect the individual from pain inflicted by other members of the community. Before government acted, however, it was necessary to prove that the lack of governmental action would result in more harm than good. Utilitarianism continued to emphasize individualism and the concept of freedom expressed in early liberalism.

The Utilitarians emphasized the right of private property, but it was Adam Smith who elevated the science of economics to a creed of middle liberalism. Smith's denunciation of governmental control of economic activity and his plea for free enterprise (laissez faire) became the gospel of economic liberalism. Smith justified his individualism by an appeal to natural law and the unseen hand that guided selfish individuals to benefit the entire community. The commercial and industrial middle class thus found through Smith a rationalization for the use of both fair and foul means in the accumulation of wealth. With the development of the Iron Law of Wages (wages tend to seek the lowest level necessary for human existence) by David Ricardo, economic liberalism became the creed of the new middle class.

The transition from middle liberalism to modern liberalism was prompted by the changing character of society and in particular the economic reorganization of society. The transition was gradual, and the greatest change in ideology was in the concept of governmental functions. John Stuart Mill exemplified the confused state of liberalism during the transitional period. Mill had been carefully nurtured in utilitarianism. In much of his writing he expounded utilitarianism, but his exposition was hesitant and full of doubts. Mill accepted individualism. His argument for freedom of thought has become classical. However, in his acceptance of individualism, Mill advocated a number of reforms designed to extend the concept of individualism. Among his reform ideas were proportional representation, woman suffrage, and the extension of male suffrage. Mill began as a laissez-faire economist, but in later life he admitted the need for positive intervention by government in economic activity. In his *Autobiography*, Mill toyed with socialism and admitted his concept of liberty needed state action in the economic area to provide for equality of opportunity.

During the late nineteenth and early twentieth centuries another school of thought was added to British liberalism, that of German idealism. German idealism, primarily Platonism, was molded into British liberalism through the writings and teachings of T. H. Green, Bernard Bosanquet, L. T. Hobhouse, and others. German idealism rejected the natural rights individualism of Locke and the hedonistic individualism of the Utilitarians. Idealism viewed the state not as a contractual, mechanistic association but as an organism capable of moral judgment. Furthermore, the state had the moral obligation to provide a social environment to allow for the betterment of the individual. Individualism and rights were placed within the framework of society. The stigma against governmental interference was removed. Government became a positive force, not a negative factor in social organization.

Present-day liberalism is an eclecticism of the three main streams of British liberal thought plus borrowed ideas from Fabian socialism. Sir William Beveridge, Maynard Keynes, and R. J. Cruikshank are representative contributors to modern liberalism. Liberalism continues to accept the ideas of constitutional government and representative democracy. Individual rights are stressed not as natural rights but as conditions necessary for the moral and ethical development of the individual. These rights include the freedom of worship, speech, writing, assembly, association, occupation, and management of personal income. The right of assembly and association includes the right to bring about a peaceful change of the governing authority.

The greatest difference between modern liberalism and early and middle liberalism is in economic thought. Modern liberalism rejects the concepts of laissez-faire capitalism. Liberals now argue that competition is not a sufficient regulator of the economic system and that too much inequality and lack of opportunity exists in a free-enterprise economy. Also, liberals reject the early stress on the importance of the profit motive and the idea that economic value is individually produced. Modern liberals point out that the role of the owner has changed with the rise of the corporation, and hence the owner's right to returns has been diminished. The modern liberal's economic views are collectivistic, and the concept of a mixed economy is accepted.

With the rejection of laissez-faire capitalism, liberalism assigns to the state a significant role in economic activity. Most of the actual production would be left in private hands, but the state would regulate to insure industrial responsibility to the community and to prevent exploitation of the community and its resources by private industry. The state must provide a progressive tax system as one method to prevent gross inequality in wealth and income. The state must attempt to prevent the cyclical fluctuations of the business cycle and to be the compensating factor in the economy to insure prosperity. Social services in the fields of education, health, retirement, maternity benefits, and similar areas are an obligation of the state. Subsidization of segments of the economy is a standard belief of modern liberalism. Some nationalization may be desirable if it is necessary to protect the public interest. Liberalism also expounds the idea that partial nationalization of an industry may provide a healthy competition within the industry.

The social service state or welfare state is the present credo of British liberalism. Liberalism is essentially a middle-class ideology as it was in its earlier periods. It has been reinterpreted to fit the needs of the twentieth-century middle class in Britain. The middle class is no longer the class of rising industrialists and the lesser gentry. The middle class is composed of clerks, small shop and farm operators, skilled workers, technicians, managers of small and medium-sized companies, and much of the professional class. The modern middle class does not feel secure under an unregulated free-enterprise system and for this reason demands the social service state and regulated capitalism. Yet the middle class does not favor a complete Socialist system. The middle-class British believe their mobility, standard of consumption, and chances of improvement would be forfeited under socialism. Socialism, in their estimation, would bring a leveling down of their social position, not a leveling up.

CONSERVATISM

In its early context conservatism was the ideology of the nobility and landed gentry. Its major political expression was voiced through the power of the monarch and the nobility. The monarch was obligated both by God and by custom to rule for the benefit and protection of his subjects. Even in early conservatism the rule of law, based upon custom, was recognized. The Coronation Oaths of the Anglo-Saxon kings stated that the king was to rule justly and for the benefit of his subjects. This idea of rule by an aristocracy obligated to the masses provided the foundation stone of British conservatism. As the country expanded and developed, conservatism's creed became the preservation of the monarchy, church, and empire. These three concepts are still basic to conservative thought. Modern conservatism found its ideological father in Edmund Burke (1729–1797). A brief account of Burke's thought is essential in order to understand British conservatism. It is characteristic of British political thought that Burke, the founder of modern conservatism, was one of the main organizers of the Whig party, the forerunner of the present Liberal party.

Burke's entire political thought is derived from his intense belief in the providential design of mankind and man's society. Religion is the basis of all authority and all obligation. God's design is unfolded in society throughout its history. Tradition, custom, and prescription, based upon the conventions and usages of successive generations, tend to contain or reveal providential design. A major task of government becomes the conservation of these traditions and prescriptions. Society, Burke informed us, is a contract between the visible and the invisible world, between the lower and higher natures of man and God. Society is a "contract of the dead, the living, and the future living."

To conserve the traditional did not mean to Burke the mere perpetuation of the status quo. Change, betterment of humanity, and the extension of liberty were necessary and desirable. Change should be gradual, and the pattern of change should be fitted into the traditional patterns in order to preserve the best of tradition and to provide continual linkage with the past. Burke believed complete reform and revolution to be destructive. Both man and society demanded the stable influence of tradition.

Burkian conservatism placed less emphasis upon man's ability to reason and more emphasis upon knowledge gained through experience and prejudice or intuition. Government was a contrivance of human wisdom to provide for human wants. Wisdom meant more than mere reason. Wisdom required the additions of experience, prejudice, and prescription.

Wisdom, so necessary to government and society, was not found in every individual. Burke accepted the idea of a natural aristocracy. Burke defined an aristocracy as "the wiser, the more expert, and the more opulent." The aristocracy was not a separate interest in society but was the group of individuals capable of governing in the interests of the whole society. The aristocracy had an obligation to rule, and the masses had an obligation to obey the rule of the aristocrats. Only in this manner could a selfless government endure. Burke's aristocracy was not to be composed of only the rich. In several letters Burke flailed out against the moneyed person who thought he was an aristocrat merely upon the grounds of wealth. Partly because of his belief in an aristocracy, Burke was not greatly interested in the extension of suffrage and did not believe that the existing holders of suffrage could or should mandate their elected representatives. Burke's theory of virtual representation made the member of Parliament a representative of all England, not the delegate of a particular constituency.

Burke accepted private property as a natural and a prescriptive right. By its very nature, property was unequally divided in a society. Government needed to protect this inequality. Burke's concept of property rights was not in agreement with the concepts of economic liberalism. There was no *a priori* argument against any state intervention in the economic system or any statement that property rights were absolute. Property was necessary to individual development, and the unequal distribution of property was necessary to society's development. The possessors of property were morally obligated to use their property in socially desirable ways. Government should and could intervene if the possessors of property used their property in ways destructive to society.

British conservatism today is still essentially Burkian. As a practical political ideology, however, it has been watered down with liberalism and has accepted the more conventional concepts of mass democracy. Benjamin Disraeli, Tory Prime Minister from 1874 to 1880, taught the conservatives the need to believe in tradition but also that conservatism needed "the invigorating energies of an educated and enfranchised people." According to Disraeli, the old landed aristocracy was not an adequate bulwark to preserve the true England from destruction by industrial capitalism. Territorial representation of the masses was needed to restore the balance in support of traditional England. Conservatism must truly represent the interests of all sections of the English people. A conservative workingman was as needed as a conservative nobleman. Modern writers such as Quentin Hogg have continued to stress the essential concepts of conservatism and to tie these concepts to a democratic base.

Quentin Hogg defends the conservative belief in private property on the grounds that the possession of private property is a right of the individual, that private property is a safeguard for the family, that private property provides a moral incentive for work, and that private property is a bulwark of liberty. Mr. Hogg further argues that the possession of property creates a responsibility, a duty to use property wisely and justly.

A few conservative writers have urged the formation of a new Conservative party that would repudiate modern aberrations and reaffirm Burke's basic tenets. Government by the people is considered destructive to society and its betterment. The crass materialism and selfishness of the wealthy classes are as bad as rule by the masses. True conservatism demands a return to the belief in providential order, a moral society, and a state governed in the best interests of the country. A harmonious community of interests should replace the conflict of classes. Private property must be respected.

A third strain of thought that is often labeled conservatism attempts to make modern conservatism into eighteenth- and nineteenth-century liberalism. H. Bennett in his book, *Must England Fall* (1946), makes the state a monster and glorifies business and unregulated competition. Such ideas are not truly a part of conservative ideology but are often expressed by sections of modern conservatives.

SOCIALISM

The historical foundation of British socialism is found in innumerable movements. Mention may be made of the Chartists, the Owenites, the Guild Socialists, the Social Democratic Federation, the Independent Labor party, and trade-unionism. Critics of capitalism and the evils of a capitalist society may be found in the eighteenth century (William Wordsworth, Samuel Taylor Coleridge, and William Godwin are examples), but it was in the nineteenth century that modern socialism developed. The word "socialism" became part of the English language in 1832 to designate the espousal of an ideology.

The nineteenth century was the century of the Industrial Revolution with the rise of the factory system and urbanization. Liberal laissez-faire economics provided a ready explanation and rationalization of the evils of the Industrial Revolution. The industrial workers, exploited and apparently doomed to a subsistence life, had two possible solutions. The workers could accept socialism and its aim to destroy capitalism or they could band together in trade-unions. By accepting socialism the workers would demand the abolishment of the market economy of capitalism, the profit motive, and private ownership. To replace capitalism the Socialists advocated schemes of communal ownership, more equal distribution of income and wealth, and cooperation not competition as the guiding principle of the economy. If the workers accepted the solution of trade-unionism, then the workers would attempt to control the labor supply and to bargain collectively with the employers within a capitalist system.

British workers followed the path of trade-unionism, and by the 1850's trade-unions were firmly established in Britain. The early trade-unions rejected political action and relied upon the economic tactic of collective bargaining to improve the condition of the workingman. It was not until the late nineteenth century that socialism and political action made inroads into trade-unionism. Certain unions backed particular candidates for the House of Commons who were often called the "Lib-Labs" (Liberal party members from within the ranks of labor or who were sympathetic to labor).

In 1888 a Scottish Labor party was formed in Glasgow. James Keir Hardie became the secretary of the party. The Scottish Labor party called for partial nationalization, but the party was not committed fully to socialism. It did call for the election of labor representatives to Parliament, and it sent delegates to the meetings of the Second Socialist International. Out of the Scottish Labor party and other local Labor parties came the creation of the Independent Labor party in 1893. Again the new organization refused to adopt the term socialism, and it refused to limit its membership to Socialists. The ILP leadership was Socialist, but it placed the political desire for a working-class party above its Socialist beliefs. Keir Hardie was the recognized leader of the new party; and he emphasized the emotional, non-doctrinaire approach to socialism. The ILP was influential as a Socialist agitation group within the trade-unions and in particular the Trades Union Congress. Gradually the trade-unions recognized the need for a labor party, and in conjunction with several Socialist groups the Labor Representation Committee was formed in 1900 to increase labor representation in Parliament. In 1906 the name was changed to the Labor party. The Fabian Society was an association member of the Labor Representation Committee as it is of the present Labor party. Bernard Shaw and E. R. Pease served as Fabian representatives on the committee to work out the organizational details of the Labor Representation Committee. Fabians have continued to influence the Labor party out of all proportion to their membership.

Among the Socialist groups in Britain, the Fabian Society is responsible for the ideology of British socialism. The Society was formed in 1884 and soon included some of Britain's outstanding scholars and literary figures. The Society probably took its name from a verse by John Gay, "Let none object my lingering way: I gain, like Fabius, with delay." The verse well describes Fabian socialism. British socialism is not a revolutionary credo *for* or *of* the working classes. It rejects Marxian revolutionary tactics for a practical approach to economic and social reform. Politically, Fabianism has its origins in liberalism. British Socialists accept the assumptions and concepts of British democracy. The existing political institutions (with some questions over the structure and representational base of Parliament) are sufficiently democratic to meet the demands of socialism.

Economically and socially, the Fabians condemn British capitalism. They argue that the economic and social institutions must be democratized in order that all individuals may enjoy equality of opportunity. To provide for the goal of greater equality, some degree of socialization is necessary.

Fabian socialism may be divided into the early Fabianism and modern Fabianism. The early Fabians viewed the state as the guardian or trustee of the people. Through a benevolent representative state, the Socialists' goals of equality and justice could be established. Nationalization of basic industry, state economic planning, progressive taxation, and state guaranteed social services were considered the programatic method of achieving socialism.

With the advent of the Labor government (1945–1951), much of the program of the early Fabians was enacted. The Labor party had adopted a Socialist platform in 1918. Although the Labor party held governmental power with the support of the Liberals in 1923, no attempt was made to implement its Socialist program. Again in 1929, the Labor party formed a government with the support of the Liberals with no attempt to change basic domestic policies. Ramsay MacDonald created a coalition or national government previous to the elections of 1931; and, as a result of the 1931 elections, he remained Prime Minister until 1935. No attempt was made to implement socialism. In 1945 the Labor party won an overwhelming victory and considered the victory a mandate to implement its Socialist program.[1]

The Labor government nationalized the banking system by purchasing the Bank of England. In addition the coal, steel, transportation, gas, electricity, and overseas cable and wireless companies were nationalized. The entire nationalization program brought about 20 per cent of the economy under direct ownership and control by the state.

In the areas of social welfare, an extensive social security program was adopted. It provided for old age assistance, unemployment compensation, industrial sickness and accident compensation, family allowances, maternity benefits, and death benefits. A nationalized health insurance plan was also created.

The Labor party believed that a progressive tax system would aid in the redistribution of wealth. The tax program the Labor government adopted was not substantially different from the old tax system; but it did increase the progressive rates on both earned and unearned income, estate taxes, and inheritance taxes.

Labor legislation provided for economic planning and control of the economy to provide for full production and full employment. The Distribution of Industries Act, the Town and Country Act, the Borrowing Act, the Anti-Monopoly Act, and the Industrial Organization Act were all designed to give government full control over the allocation of economic

[1] This interpretation of the 1945 election has been questioned by Socialists. According to G. D. H. Cole, the election was only a mandate for more welfare capitalism and an extension of the social service state. Part of the program adopted during Labor's control of government had been agreed upon in principle by the Labor and Conservative party leaders who served in the coalition government.

resources. The powers were used sparingly and planning often gave way to liberty.

Labor's agricultural policy was a subsidization program coupled with a land-use policy. Farmers were guaranteed a market for their production at government guaranteed prices. To participate in the subsidy, the farmer had to abide by the decisions of the local agricultural board as to the proper use of the farm and to practice good husbandry.

During the period of Labor's rule and since that time, Socialists and Fabians in particular have attempted a reconsideration of their programs and their ideology. No new ideology has been developed, but a number of questions in regard to the old have been raised.[2]

Modern Socialists retain the early Socialists' belief in democracy. The goal is the recognition of the individual as a unique entity and a social system that permits the individual's development. Freedom, the area of voluntary choice, must be expanded to achieve socialism. Unlike the early Fabians with their belief in the innate goodness of man, modern Fabians accept the idea of individual morality and immorality. Social institutions are only moral if man makes them moral. Social morality is always subject to degeneration through the desires for special privilege and the apathy of the masses. A moral elite is required to be the Socratic gadfly if freedom and morality are to exist and develop together.

Modern Fabians believe that the "Keynes-plus modified-capitalism-plus-Welfare-State" (the phrase of C. A. R. Crosland) has not achieved Socialist goals. The present system is better than the old capitalism, but inherent dangers to individual freedom may be found. The main danger of the semi-Socialist state is that economic power is still concentrated in an elite—the elite of civil service managers. What is needed is the decentralization of economic power. This could be accomplished by techniques such as worker participation in management, cooperatives, and individually owned and operated establishments. Continued nationalization as a policy is under serious question. Modern Fabians question the need for any further extension of social services. In fact the Fabians see the need to allow the individual greater choice in the expenditure of his personal income. The emphasis is on the preservation of the existing social services but with no great increases.

Contemporary Fabians stress the need for greater equality in the economic and social system. Britain is still a class society.[3] The class structure is based upon wealth, education, birth, and occupation. Fabians recognize that individual differences tend to produce a hierarchial social system but insist that the criterion of class should be based upon ability.

[2] R. H. S. Crossman (ed.), *New Fabian Essays* (New York: Frederick A. Praeger, Inc., 1952).

[3] See Chapter 1.

To have such a class system requires the creation of equality of opportunity. Education is of prime importance in achieving the desired equality. Socialists believe that the British educational system must be democratized, but they do not want the democratized educational system to become the mass education they believe exists in the United States.

British socialism is essentially practical. If there are any dominant value concepts in British socialism, the concepts of democracy and equality would be considered of primary importance.

SELECTED READING

CECIL, LORD HUGH. *Conservatism.* London: Butterworth & Co., 1912.
CROSSMAN, R. H. S., *et al. New Fabian Essays.* New York: Frederick A. Praeger, Inc., 1952.
HOBHOUSE, L. T. *Liberalism.* New York: Holt, Rinehart & Winston, Inc., 1911.
SHAW, G. B., *et al. Fabian Essays.* New York: Doubleday & Co., Inc., n.d.
WHITE, R. J. (ed.). *The Conservative Tradition.* London: Adams & Charles Black, Ltd., 1950.

3

Political Organizations

In a democratic country the citizenry needs avenues of communication with its government. Political parties and pressure groups have become two of the most effective means of such communication. Through parties and pressure groups individuals have found the techniques to control their government, or at least to influence their government.

CHARACTERISTICS OF THE BRITISH PARTY SYSTEM

British parties, in a general sense, originated during the period of struggle between the Stuarts and Parliament. The Cavaliers (supporters of the Stuarts) and the Roundheads (supporters of Parliament) were the forerunners of today's political parties. Historically, then, parties owe their origin to a natural pro and con issue. The immediate result was the beginning of a two-party system. Gradually through its influence on the growth and formation of British institutions and political processes, the two-party system not only perpetuated itself but became an integral part of British life. Disraeli stated it succinctly when he said, "Without party, parliamentary government is impossible." The two-party system results in another characteristic of British parties; namely, that they are mass parties that must appeal to the majority of the electorate. Neither party may become so ideologically oriented and doctrinaire that it antagonizes the bulk of the voters. The major parties do have definite points of view based upon different philosophical principles, but they must accommodate their immediate programs to the voter. Thus, the differences between the parties are not so great in Britain as many Americans believe.

A third characteristic of British parties is that they are definitely national parties. Although variations exist in party strength based upon geography, occupation, and economic status, the British system does not have "one-party areas" to the same degree as is found in America. The parties are national in the sense that the national or central organization is the center of power, not the regional and local organizations. A few regional parties exist (the Welsh Nationalist party and the Scottish Nationalist party are examples), but they are doomed to remain minor parties.

British parties are also characterized by the degree of discipline that the party leaders exert over the rank and file. Despite support from the local organization, a candidate seldom seeks election without endorsement by the central party organization. Since the party extends its endorsement to only one candidate in a constituency, the need for party primary elections comparable to those in the United States does not exist. Party discipline within Parliament may be carried to the point of expulsion from the party. This does not mean, however, that the party can force a member of Parliament to resign his seat. The decision to resign and stand for re-election is the prerogative of the member and cannot be dictated by the party.

PARTY ORGANIZATION

Outside of Parliament both the Conservative and Labor parties are organized on a dual basis.[1] One organizational structure represents the popular organization of the party (i.e., the rank and file members of the party) and draws its membership from the great mass of volunteer political workers. The other organizational structure represents the professional organization of the party and is composed of a group of full-time professional party workers, in essence, the "civil service" of the party.

Conservative Party

The Conservative party consists of the National Union of Conservative and Unionist Associations (known as the National Union) and the Central Office under the direction of the Leader. The National Union is the popular and voluntary organization of the Conservative party. The Central Office represents the professional organization of the Conservative party.

The National Union was formed in 1867 as a federation of local constituencies. Structurally, the National Union consists of the local constituency associations, the area councils, the annual party conference, the central council, and the national Executive Committee. See Figure 3–1 for an organizational chart of the Conservative party.

Local constituency associations are the basic organizational unit of the National Union. They are organized to parallel election districts, although

[1] The organization of the party within Parliament will be considered in Chapter 5.

the number of local associations may be more or less than the number of election districts. Membership in a local is open to anyone who is a resident or "connected with" the constituency. The applicant must naturally be willing to support the aims of the association and to contribute to its finances. Associations are admitted into the National Union by approval

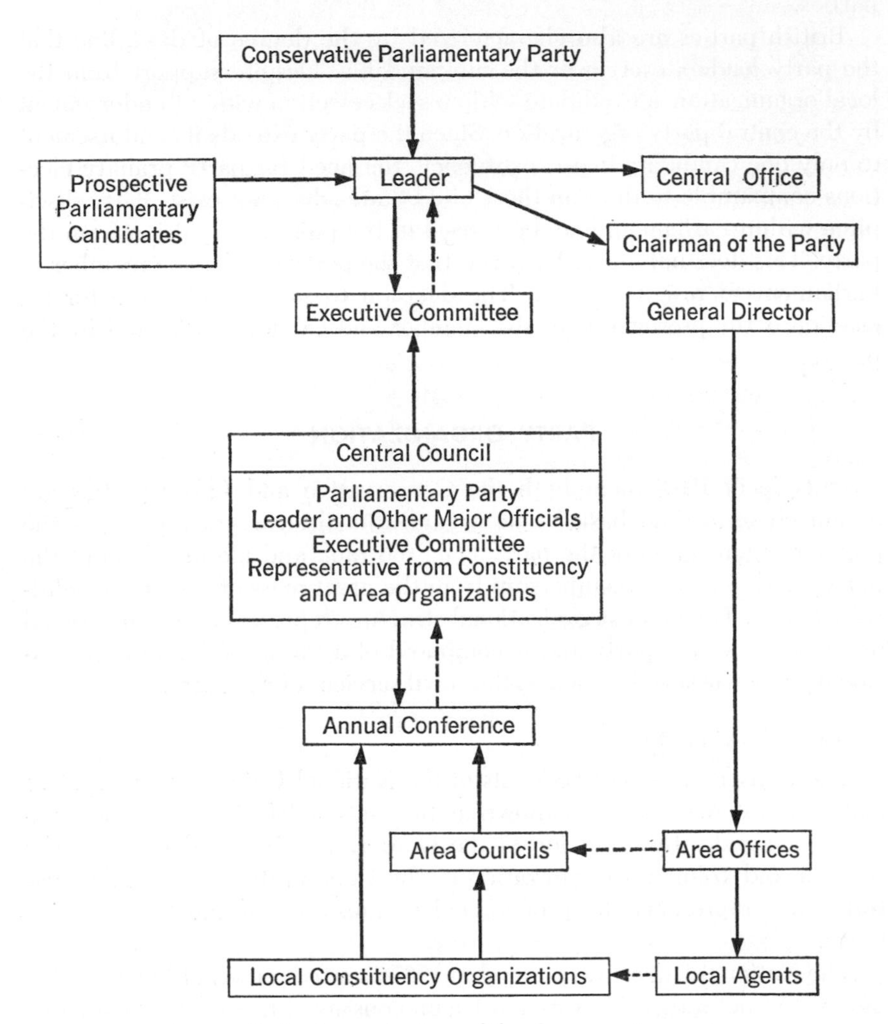

Figure 3–1. Organization of the Conservative party.

of the executive committee and may be expelled by the executive committee. In practice, the local associations are virtually autonomous bodies and the Conservative party takes pride in this fact. Autonomy does not signify that the locals strongly influence party policy, but rather that the locals are free to manage their own affairs.

The local associations are governed by an executive council composed of the chairman, treasurer, secretary (a paid political agent who has been certified by the Central Office), chairmen of standing committees, and representatives of the polling districts within the constituency. In addition, representatives of the Young Conservatives and the Conservative Clubs serve as members of the executive council. The local association campaigns, raises funds, chooses parliamentary candidates (with the approval of the Central Office), and selects delegates to the central organs of the National Union.

Area or regional councils are composed of representatives from the local associations. They serve as additional sounding boards for rank and file recommendations to the National Union. They also function as electioneering units during campaigns. The area councils select the area officers except for the secretary who is the senior official of the Central Office's area organization. The chief area officer is the chairman. He is responsible for bringing the views of his area and the local associations within it before the national executive committee. Also, the chairman is charged with the general supervision of the party campaigns in his area. How well the area chairman performs his duties depends upon the caliber of the person chosen, or who is willing to serve, and upon his personal relationship with the Central Office's agent in the area.

The annual party conference has become a massive gathering of party faithfuls. The average attendance is over 3,000. Party members gather to express party enthusiasm and party unity. The conference may be attended by all members of the central council as well as representatives of the local associations. The conference hears reports from the central council and the executive committee. It may discuss these reports but rarely does so with any great seriousness. The conference debates resolutions upon party and public policy. Often, these resolutions are simply devices to invite a party leader to address the conference. Resolutions may be critical of party leadership. Such resolutions are warning signs to the party leaders that the rank and file members desire a change in party policy. Resolutions of the conference are not binding upon the party leadership, but often the leaders will "accept" a resolution of the conference.

The central council, which meets annually, is the governing body of the National Union. Its membership includes representatives of the local and area organizations, members of the Parliamentary party, Conservative candidates, and the major officers of the Central Office. The council elects the president, chairman, and vice-chairman of the National Union. The council conveys motions and resolutions on party policy to the Leader of the Conservative party. On occasion, the council has attempted to instruct the party leadership but such attempts have been rejected. Nevertheless, the Leader of the party cannot totally ignore such resolutions without jeopardizing his own position of leadership.

The national executive committee meets every other month and functions as the control organ of the National Union between meetings of the central council. The executive committee is composed of area representatives, senior party officers, and representatives of the Parliamentary party.

The National Union has a varied and flexible advisory committee system. Some committees, such as the Women's National Advisory Committee, are responsible to the executive committee. Others, such as the Standing Advisory Committee on Parliamentary Candidates, are responsible directly or indirectly to the Leader of the party even though the committee has representation from the National Union.

As previously noted, the Central Office represents the professional organization of the Conservative party outside of Parliament. The Central Office is the backbone of the Conservative party, and executive responsibility for the operation of the party's political machinery is centered here. It operates Abbey House in London and Area Offices (comparable to branch offices) throughout the country. Activities of the Central Office are divided on a departmental basis, and the departments correspond closely to the national advisory committees of the National Union. The Central Office's activities include the supervision of party finances, approval of Parliamentary candidates, management of party publicity and speakers' engagements, organization of Trade Union Councils and Labor Advisory Committees, assistance to the local constituency associations and Conservative members of local governments, direction of election campaigns and coordination of the youth organizations of the party. Adjunct to the Central Office are the Research Department and the Political Center. These agencies devote their energies to policy research and political education.

The Central Office is presided over by the chairman of the party, the vice-chairmen, and the honorary treasurers. All these officers are the personal appointees of the Leader of the Conservative party. The chairman of the party supervises the work of the Central Office and Area Offices and maintains diplomatic contact with the officers of the National Union. It is his responsibility to eliminate or reduce any unrest within the party and to inform the Leader of any party dissatisfaction. The detailed management of the Central and Area Offices is performed by the general director who is directly responsible to the chairman. The Area Offices provide direct contact with the local constituency associations and the area councils.

Numerous references have been made to the Leader of the Conservative party. The Leader is the matrix of Conservative party organization. Formally, he is elected by the Conservative members of Parliament, parliamentary candidates, and the executive committee of the National Union. On an informal basis, the Leader has usually been acknowledged for some time by the members of the Conservative party. The Leader is held responsible for party policy by both his own party and that of the opposition. It is obvious, however, that he cannot and does not formulate party policy by himself. Major policy thrusts upon the Leader may come from the Parliamentary party, the National Union, the Central Office, or any of the subsidiary groups. Nevertheless, the final decision must be made by the Leader.

The Conservative party has been criticized for the aristocratic role of the Leader. Certainly it is true that the Leader's powers are subject to very few formal restraints. But it must be remembered that the weight of his responsibilities dictates the immensity of his powers and that he retains his position only by the consent of his followers. If he proves unable to bear the responsibilities of leadership, the party may withdraw its consent and support. This has in fact occurred.

Labor Party

Outside of Parliament, the Labor party's national organization is composed of local constituency parties, regional councils, the annual conference, the national executive committee, and the head office. See Figure 3–2 for an organizational chart of the Labor party.

The constituency parties are of varying forms, and only a generalized sketch will be given. A constituency is divided into wards, and the individual party members belong to a ward committee. A woman's section and a youth section may be organized on a ward basis. Representatives of the wards are elected by the individual members to serve on a General Management Committee at the constituency level. These representatives are joined by delegates from affiliated bodies to make up the General Management Committee. Affiliated bodies may include a local trade-union or unions, perhaps a local Fabian Society, or a cooperative society. The General Management Committee is the governing body of the local constituency party subject to control by the national executive committee. The local committee has the power to expel a member, to conduct election campaigns, and to select the constituency candidate (subject to the approval of the national executive committee). If the constituency is large, the General Management Committee may elect an executive committee to serve as a smaller administrative group. The secretary of the local party is elected by the General Management Committee. If the local party employs a paid political agent, the agent is more often than not elected as secretary. The secretary is often the central figure in the local organization. It is the secretary who becomes responsible for the day-to-day "nursing" of the constituency.

The first regional councils were formed in 1938 in order to establish and support the constituency parties. They also serve the purpose of coordinating labor policy among the various affiliated labor organizations within the region. It is significant that the regional councils are limited in their discussions to matters of regional interests only and cannot concern themselves with national and international issues. This limitation has been protested on both regional and national levels, but thus far no change has been effected. The membership of a regional council consists of represent-

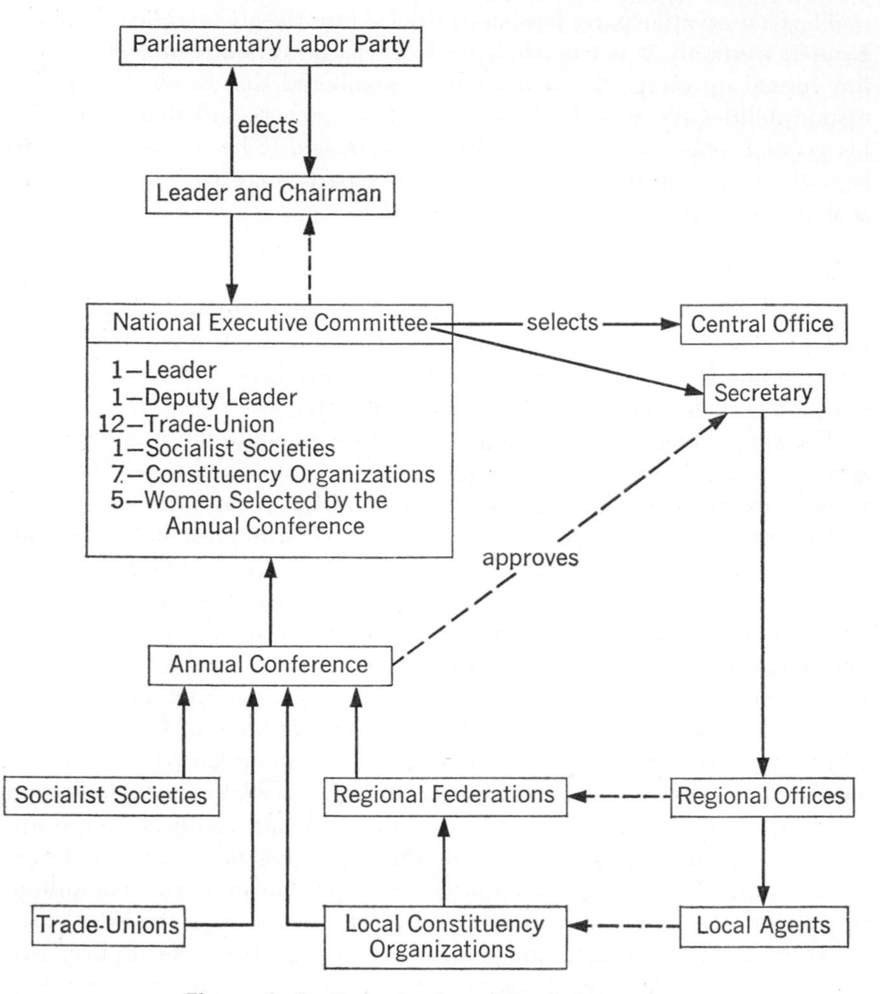

Figure 3–2. Organization of the Labor party.

atives from constituency parties and regional affiliated bodies such as trade-unions, Socialist societies, cooperatives, and the Leagues of Youth federations. The regional councils meet annually to elect an executive committee, which in turn carries out the work of the councils during the remainder of the year.

The annual conference is composed of delegates from the constituency associations and the aforementioned affiliated groups. Ex-officio members of the conference include members of the Parliamentary party, the national executive committee, prospective candidates, and the party secretary. The distribution of delegates is based upon the membership of the local or affiliated group. Potentially, the conference would have about 2,500 members but the average attendance is about 1,500. The trade-unions seldom send the number of delegates allotted to them. The explanation of this failure to send delegates is that voting is not done on a basis of one delegate, one vote, but rather upon the total membership of the group represented by the delegation. The trade-union groups control about five-sixths of the votes.

The annual conference hears the usual party speeches of the party leadership and receives and debates the policy program outlined by the national executive committee as well as the report of the Parliamentary Labor party. The various groups may propose resolutions and amendments to the Constitution and lively debate is likely to occur at this point of the conference. Although the party leadership is normally able to control the important votes at the conference, the annual meeting does provide an effective avenue of communication between the membership and the leadership. The latter must certainly listen carefully to the signs of protest and criticism. Also, the party's Constitution may be changed only by the annual conference.

The national executive committee is composed of representatives from four major groups within the Labor party. The trade-unions elect twelve members, the constituency associations elect seven members, and the Socialist and cooperative societies elect one member. Five women are elected by the annual conference. In addition, the treasurer is elected by the annual conference and he is a member of the executive committee. The Leader and Deputy Leader of the party are ex-officio members. The secretary of the party is also a member, but custom denies him the privilege of voting. Actually, the national executive committee is usually composed of a majority of members who are also Labor Members of Parliament.

The national executive committee is the power center of the national organization. It has the general responsibility of directing the work of the party at all levels of organization. Although changes in the Labor party's Constitution, policies, and programs are submitted to a vote of the annual conference, the initial development of these changes takes place in the executive committee. The committee has the power to expel individual members from the Labor party and may follow the same procedure with regard to contituency associations and affiliated groups. The committee must give its approval to all Labor candidates for the House of Commons.

The head office of the Labor party, unlike the Central Office of the Conservative party, is formally controlled and directed by the national executive committee.

The executive committee makes use of a number of subcommittees in order to facilitate its work. The three most important subcommittees relate to policy, organization, and international policy.

Transport House in London is the home of the head office of the Labor party. As previously noted, the head office is directly responsible to the national executive committee. It serves as the central administrative office of the Labor party, and its staff constitutes the professional administrative organization of the party. Under the direction of the secretary, the head office is divided into departments roughly correspondent to the subcommittees of the national executive committee. Transport House has both regional and local offices that aid the regional councils and local constituency parties.

Originally, the Leader of the Labor party had the title of Chairman.[2] The term "Leader" was used in official reports for the first time in 1923. The change in title indicates the evolution of the position. Today, the Leader of the Parliamentary party is more than a chairman; he is the director, the leader of the party. His role, when Prime Minister, is not unlike his counterpart in the Conservative party. When the Labor party is in opposition, the Leader's role may be more circumscribed; but even then the Leader exercises a greater influence than is customarily associated with the term "Chairman."

The structure and constitutional principles of the Labor party have led to a serious question of the relationship of the national organization to the Parliamentary Labor party and, in particular, to the Labor party leaders when they constitute the government. In brief, can the annual conference and the national executive committee dictate policy to the Parliamentary party and to a Labor Prime Minister? Based upon the experience of the Labor government from 1945 to 1951, the answer to the question is no. As Prime Minister, Clement Attlee chose his own Cabinet and made it clear to the executive committee and the annual conference that the responsibility of governing was the Cabinet's and that it could not be divided. Mr. Attlee (now Lord Attlee), as would a Conservative Leader, agreed that the party should be consulted and listened to but that the national party could not dictate.

PARTY FINANCES

For the student interested in a detailed accounting of income and expenditures, the British parties are singularly deficient. Candidates are re-

[2] The Leader of the Labor party is elected annually by the Labor members of the House of Commons.

quired by statute to declare their expenses, and their expenditures are limited by law. The parties, however, are not subject to such a declaration; and there is no legal limitation placed upon party expenditure. The Labor party does publish some financial statements, but the Conservative party seldom reveals any details of party finance. In both parties, the local organizations raise funds of their own and collect dues for the national organization. Locals make use of dues, dinners, benefit dances, and the usual fund raising techniques of American parties. The Labor party collects dues from the individual members of the trade-unions affiliated with the party. These dues are automatically collected by the union unless the individual worker "contracts out" (signs a statement that he does not want Labor party dues taken out of his wages as part of his union dues). The unions make additional payments to the party and supply funds for individual candidates. Although the Labor party does not have many wealthy contributors, it would be a mistake to believe that the party does not receive large contributions from individual members. In 1950, the annual income of the Labor party was given as approximately £232,000 ($650,000) and the financial resources at approximately £689,615 ($1,930,920). Comparable figures are not available for the Conservative party.

Traditionally, the Conservative party has relied upon large contributions from wealthy individual members. As the party base has broadened and as the tax structure in Britain has reduced the number of really wealthy individuals, the Conservatives have attempted to find new sources of income. The national organization has increasingly pressured the local organizations to send in their quota contributions. Similarly, larger and more frequent donations have been solicited from business and professional groups. In addition to these sources, the Conservative party has capital funds or endowments that provide some annual income.

PARTY PROGRAMS

The programs of the parties are partial reflections of the ideologies of socialism and conservatism.[3] The obvious goal of a major political party is to win elections and to control the government. To achieve this goal, the programs of the parties must appeal to the electorate and must be concerned with immediate issues, not theories of government. Both major parties are capable of a pragmatic approach. However, differences in the programs of the parties do exist; and these differences reflect the ideological basis of the parties.

Labor Party

The Labor party is a Socialist party. Labor insists that the ethical, social, and economic principles of socialism are the true guides to the

[3] See Chapter 2.

establishment of social justice and peace. If the principles of socialism are the guides, the welfare state is the method by which the Labor party would establish social justice and peace.

Domestically, the Labor party is proud of the program it implemented during the period of 1945–1951. Labor insists that the Conservatives have done nothing to extend the reforms of 1945–1951, and that in some areas the reforms have been sabotaged.

Today, the Labor party is still committed to a program of nationalization of industry; but it has toned down its demands for further government ownership.[4] In 1959, the party advocated renationalization of only two segments of the economy, namely, long distance road haulage and the steel industry. In the field of education, Labor believes that the national government should allocate more funds for school construction, school operation, and student scholarships. The party claims that if it were returned to power, the present eleven plus examinations would be abolished.[5] The party manifesto of 1959 called for extension of benefits for old-age assistance, unemployment compensation, medical benefits, and aids to widows. The party advocated an extension of government's role in the housing industry and believes in the desirability of extensive local government ownership of rental housing. Private ownership would be encouraged by lower interest rates.

The Labor party's foreign policy emphasizes the need for a workable disarmament system; complete cessation of nuclear tests; and the destruction of nuclear, chemical, and biological weapons. The party also urges greater British participation in aid programs for underdeveloped countries. While the party recognizes the need for alliances based upon strength, it advocates a constant search for methods that would replace power politics with the rule of law.

Finally, the Labor party's colonial policy is designed to give Commonwealth status to any of the present colonies that desire it and to eliminate racial discrimination throughout the colonial system.

Conservative Party

In its 1959 manifesto, the Conservative party gave as its policy the promotion of prosperity and peace. Prosperity involves a doubling of the British standard of living within the lifetime of the present generation. To achieve this goal, the Conservatives stress the need to expand production, develop new technology, and increase trade. Reliance on private inititative with governmental assistance was chosen as the best means of accomplish-

[4] Mr. Hugh Gaitskill, Leader of the Labor party, is fighting for a change in the party's Constitution on the point of nationalization. Mr. Gaitskill believes that less emphasis should be placed on nationalization as part of the Socialist creed.

[5] See page 11.

ing this goal. Conservatives are against any further nationalization and believe in decentralization of the existing nationalized industries. Instead of government ownership of depressed industries, the Conservative party advocates governmental grants and loans to private industry.

The Conservative party has accepted the welfare state in terms of government controlled programs in medicine; old-age assistance; unemployment compensation; and categorical aid to widows, dependent children, and handicapped persons. The major difference in party approaches seems to be the proportion of total benefits to be borne by the government.

Instead of the abolishment of the eleven plus examinations in education, the Conservatives would prefer to raise the standards and curriculum of the vocational schools. In addition, the Conservatives agree with the Labor party that increased funds should be provided for school construction and operation.

Internationally, the Conservative party desires disarmament, international control of nuclear weapons, and a continued search for patterns of coexistence. Until these are achieved, the Conservatives wish to maintain their present alliances and to negotiate through strength with the Soviet Union. Conservative colonial policy is committed to the idea of eventual commonwealth status for the present colonies. The transition would be slower than that desired by the Labor party.

MINOR POLITICAL PARTIES

As in American politics, a variety of minor political parties exist in Britain. The most notable difference is that one of the British minor parties, the Liberal party, was once a major party and continues to operate in the hope of reachieving that position. In the postwar elections, the Liberal party has made an effort to increase the number of its candidates. The Liberal party's appeal is primarily to the middle-class electorate. Liberals charge that the Conservative party is controlled by big business and that the Labor party is under the domination of the trade-unions. Liberals insist that they provide a progressive party for all people who believe in a non-Socialist (against nationalization) democracy.

Britain also has three sectional parties; the Welsh Nationalist party, the Scottish Nationalist party and the Irish Nationalist party. As would be expected, these parties directly appeal to these national areas; and their programs emphasize greater freedom and home rule for themselves.

The Communist party, established in 1920, has never won but a handful of seats in Parliament; and since World War II, it has steadily declined in popular membership. In the elections of 1951, 1955, and 1959, the party was unable to elect a single member to the House of Commons and failed in most districts to poll enough votes to secure a refund of the candidate's deposit. At times, the Communist party has attempted infiltration of the Labor party; but these attempts have not been very successful. The party is opportunistic and follows the Moscow line, although it has been slow in making adjustment to the new word from Moscow.

Other minor parties are the Cooperative party and the Commonwealth party.

Minor parties have little chance of influencing Parliament. They do provide an outlet for doctrinaire individuals who desire to espouse a particular creed. The three nationalist parties exert influence more as pressure groups than as parties.

PRESSURE GROUPS

British pressure groups are well organized and, although their methods differ somewhat from American techniques, they are quite effective.

The Federation of British Industries, the Trade Union Congress, the British Medical Association, The Cooperative Union, the National Farmer's Union, and a myriad of other organizations in Britain are interested in politics and in particular governmental policy. These groups make use of modern communications and methods of propaganda to influence the general public.

More frequently than in America, British pressure groups manage to sponsor their own members for election to the House of Commons. Although these members are normally back-benchers, at least the pressure groups have direct access to the party leadership and are assured that the group's views are expressed within the party. Particularly, these members can exert influence when the Commons, or a committee of Commons, is discussing a technical question related to the member's interest group. Also, the member may be effective in the functional committees of the parties.

Little attention is given by the British pressure group to the individual member of Parliament. The pressure groups know that policy decisions are made by the leaders of the parties rather than the rank and file. Attention devoted to the rank and file is for the purpose of indicating to the party leaders that there is interest on a particular question.

The major efforts of pressure groups are concentrated upon the responsible ministers and the Cabinet. The task of influencing the Cabinet is difficult; and only the large, well-organized pressure groups have much chance for success. The Cabinet knows it is responsible to the electorate, which is larger than any single pressure group. Yet the Cabinet is aware that the well-organized pressure group may influence a large segment of the electorate, so the group's demands are given consideration.

SELECTED READING

BIRCH, NIGEL. *The Conservative Party.* London: William Collins Sons & Co., Ltd., 1949.
BULMER-THOMAS, IVOR. *The Party System in Great Britain.* London: Macmillan & Co., Ltd., 1953.
CRUIKSHANK, R. J. *The Liberal Party.* London: William Collins Sons & Co., Ltd., 1948.
HALL, W. G. *The Labour Party.* London: William Collins Sons & Co., Ltd., 1949.
McKENZIE, R. T. *British Political Parties.* New York: St. Martins Press, Inc., 1955.

4

Elections

The democratic ideals of representation and universal suffrage are nowhere more effectively utilized than in Great Britain. This fact is perhaps the most striking feature of the British electoral system.[1] How the Englishman achieved the right to vote and the right of representation in government is a fascinating tale of success and failure. From the beginning the king found it prudent to consult his lords and clergymen before initiating a new law or decreeing a new tax. Once the invitation list to these "talks" (the word "parliament" originally meant talk) was enlarged to include not only lords and bishops but two knights of each shire (county), two citizens of each city, and two burgesses of each borough, the institution of a representative Parliament was founded.[2] Similarly, the idea of suffrage gained impetus since the new members were to be elected. The spread of suffrage and the development of election rules and regulations paralleled the struggle of Parliament to win supremacy over the king. Once the House of Commons became established as a separate body from the House of Lords, the question of elections became even more important. Theoretically, at least, members of the House of Commons represented the common people and were elected by them. What were the qualifications for voting? The answer would involve a detailed examination of the rules and customs of each county and town. In some cases, residence was necessary; in others, possession of title to a piece of land or a house was sufficient. In reality, these apparent qualifications meant little. An infinite variety of legal loopholes rendered them meaningless, and those who could substantiate their right to the franchise were usually quite willing to sell their vote to the highest bidder. Seats in the House of Commons were bought and sold with alacrity, and until 1832 a small group of wealthy and powerful men controlled the elections. The lack of standard-

[1] Membership in the House of Lords, however, is not subject to the electoral process.
[2] Initiated in the Model Parliament of 1295.

ized laws and uniform regulations throughout the country abused the concept of representation and made a mockery of the franchise.

The Reform Act of 1832 did not eliminate bribery and corruption, but it did reduce the opportunities and incentives for such acts. Uniform qualifications for voting were established for the county and borough electors. The rapidly growing middle class, which had long chafed at its lack of representation in government, was enfranchised and soon became the dominant group within the House of Commons. Election districts were reorganized, and seats were redistributed in order to eliminate the most glaring abuses of unequal representation. The Act also provided for the registration of each qualified voter and resulted in the extension of suffrage to approximately three quarters of a million persons. In 1885, plural-member districts were eliminated and the system of single-member districts was adopted. In 1918, limited female suffrage was gained and in 1928 women achieved the full franchise. The last vestiges of plural voting and university representation were abolished in 1948.

PRESENT QUALIFICATIONS AND REGULATIONS

The only national elections held in Great Britain are the elections for the House of Commons. According to law, the election must be held every five years. In practice, however, the fourth year seems to be the most propitious time for the Prime Minister to call for the dissolution of Parliament and a new election. If a government loses the confidence of Commons, then elections are held earlier than usual. For example, elections were held in 1950, 1951, 1955, and in 1959. By-elections are held to fill vacancies in the House of Commons. The rules are similar to those for a general election except for the period relative to the filing of nomination papers. By-elections are viewed with tremendous interest by the major parties as an expression of public opinion. They sometimes serve as a weather vane in forecasting the next general election.

For election purposes, Great Britain is divided into single-member election districts known as county or borough constituencies.[3] The number of constituencies is determined by law (the Redistribution of Seats Acts of 1949 and 1958) as applied by Parliamentary Boundary Commissions. The present number of districts is 630. England has 511; Scotland, 71; Wales, 36; and North Ireland, 12. The Boundary Commissions must review the distribution of seats during the interval of ten to fifteen years. Seats are distributed according to population.

The qualifications for voting are few: residency in the voting district, twenty-one years of age, a citizen, properly registered, and subject to no

[3] A single-member district means that only one candidate from that district will be elected to the House of Commons.

legal limitation. Among the legally excluded are peers (who are members of the House of Lords), aliens, persons of unsound mind, persons convicted of an election crime (within the previous five years), and felons who are serving a sentence of more than one year (except in Scotland). The British make use of impersonal registration. The registration officer in each constituency (normally the clerk of the county, borough, or district) is responsible for preparing an annual Parliamentary Register of those eligible to vote. To accomplish this task, the registration officer canvasses the area and then publishes a provisional list. The provisional list is posted in public buildings from November 28 to December 16. During this period, the potential voter must check the list and lodge a formal complaint if he believes there is an error. The final list or Register is published not later than February 15 and becomes effective February 16. Provision is also made for registration as a Service voter. Any member of the Armed Forces, Crown civil servants in overseas duty, and wives of the members of the Armed Forces and civil servants may register in their own constituency and vote either by proxy or by mail. Absentee voting is permitted either by mail or in some cases by proxy for those registered voters who for specified reasons are unable to vote in person.

A candidate for the House of Commons must be an eligible voter, properly nominated, and not disqualified by the House of Commons Disqualification Act of 1957 and other pertinent acts. As contrasted to the American practice, a British candidate does not need to be a resident of the district in which he files for election. Nomination consists of the filing of the legal nominating paper with the local returning officer (usually the sheriff of the county or mayor of a borough). The paper must state the candidate's name, place of residence, and occupation. It must be "subscribed" by two electors as proposer and seconder, and by eight electors as assentors. The candidate must deposit £150 ($420) to attest to his seriousness of intent to run for office. Most candidates are chosen by the political parties, but independent candidates may file nomination papers.

Certain classes of people are prohibited by law from becoming candidates for the House of Commons. Clergy of the Church of England, the Church of Scotland, the Church of Ireland, and the Roman Catholic church are barred from candidacy. In addition, a general category of persons holding offices of profit under the Crown are prohibited candidacy. For years the definition of offices of profit was not clearly defined, and the laws upon the subject were not codified. In 1957, the Commons passed the House of Commons Disqualifications Act to codify and clarify the problem. The Act is specific in its listing of disqualified persons; but, in general, the following groups are prohibited from candidacy: civil servants, judicial officers, certain local government officials, police, members of the regular Armed Forces, members of public corporations and commissions, and holders of specifically listed government offices.

ELECTION PROCEDURE

Election procedure is regulated by the Representation of the People Act, 1949. Once the Royal Proclamation is issued to dissolve Parliament, Writs of Election are issued to the returning officers who are responsible for the conduct of the election. The returning officers publish official notices of election. Nominating papers are filed not later than eight days after the Royal Proclamation, and nine days later is polling day.[4]

Each constituency is divided into polling districts with an assigned polling station under the direction of a presiding officer. A poll card is mailed to each eligible voter to inform him of the hours of voting and the location of his station. The polls are open from 7:00 A.M. to 9:00 P.M.

Balloting is secret in Britain. Each qualified voter is handed an officially stamped ballot. The ballot contains the names of the candidates in alphabetical order, but no party designations are on the ballot. The voter marks the ballot, folds it with the official stamp to the outside, and deposits it in the ballot box in the presence of the presiding officer or one of his subordinates. The candidate's polling agent may be present at the polling station. At the close of the polls, the presiding officer seals the ballot box and returns it to the returning officer. Unlike American elections, the count is not done at the polling station or precinct level but is centrally done in the constituency. The count is done in the presence of the returning officer and the candidates, their election agents, or counting agents. Recount is made upon request of a candidate if the returning officer approves. In cases of a tie vote, the election is decided by lot. The returning officer endorses a writ of certificate to inform the Clerk of the Crown the name of the successful candidate.

British elections are closely supervised. Corrupt and illegal practices are specifically prohibited. Corrupt practices are of course illegal and include such acts as bribery, voting under a different name than one's true name (known in Britain as "personation"), and false declarations of election expenses. Examples of illegal practices are the wrong hiring of conveyances and illegal payments. Persons who are convicted of either corrupt practices or illegal practices are subject to fine or imprisonment.

Election expenses are regulated only for the candidates and not the political parties in Great Britain. Each candidate must name an individual or himself as an election agent. The election agent is responsible for all acts committed in behalf of the candidate. The election agent is the sole person authorized to make payments of election expenses and is responsible for a declaration of expenses after the election. A candidate cannot spend more than £450 ($1,260) plus 1½*d.* (pence, or about 4¢) for each

[4] Sundays and certain holidays are not counted.

elector in a borough constituency or more than £450 plus *2d.* (about 5¢) for each elector in a county constituency.

Each candidate is permitted to send free of postage one communication to each elector. The national parties are allotted radio and television time for both annual political broadcasts and for election broadcasts by the government owned British Broadcasting Corporation. The private Independent Television Authority also allows the parties time for broadcasts. These broadcasts are party broadcasts and not those of the individual candidates. All printing and advertising for a particular candidate must be paid for by the candidate. In short, there cannot be advertising "paid for by the friends of Bill Smith" under British campaign laws.

Disputed elections and questions of violation of the election laws are decided by the Queen's Bench of the High Court of Justice in England and Wales and by the Court of Session in Scotland.

ELECTION CAMPAIGNS

The official period of campaigning is a little over two weeks; however, potential candidates and the national parties may "nurse" the constituency before Parliament is dissolved and the official Writs of Election are issued. Even when this practice is followed, British campaigns are of short duration compared to American campaigns. Despite this fact, British elections and election campaigns are similar to those in America. The American student of politics may miss the use of the superlative, the parades and bands, and the use of Hollywood stars; but beneath the surface he would find many of the same processes. The political agent is comparable to the campaign manager but is often more of a highly trained specialist than the latter. Variations do exist in qualifications of voters and of candidates, but the same basic pattern is found in both countries. The administration of elections and the regulations upon candidates are different in detail but are derived from the same premise, an intent to have an honest election. A British candidate does not violate the financial limitations as is common in America; however, it should be remembered that party expenditures are not subject to limitation. The candidate's dependency upon party funds underscores the power of the party in elections. The British candidate usually appeals to a smaller constituency both in area and population. Billboards, posters, pamphlets, and even sound trucks are in evidence in Great Britain during a campaign. The national parties, through their national staff and the local constituency organizations, make use of most of the techniques of modern communication. The party and the candidate attempt a door-to-door campaign. Personal contact with the voters is as important in Britain as it is in America. Handshaking in the local pubs, during a tea "break" at a factory, and on the street corners helps to establish personal contact with the voters. Open meetings with speeches by the candidate and shrewd comments from hecklers continue to be evident, but studies of recent elections indicate that this form of campaigning has lost its popular appeal.

In doubtful constituencies, a party candidate may be aided by the appearance of one or more of the party leaders. The potential Prime Minister takes to the "hustings" and travels the "whistle stop" route of the country.

A difference often noticed is that the cult of personality is not as well developed in Britain as in America. Issues are emphasized at the national level more than personalities. When there are no great issues, the election is often dull and uninspired. This difference is important but it should not be stressed too much. To convey the impression that personalities of candidates are of no significance in a British election is misleading. Recent studies of elections and voting behavior in Britain indicate that the average voter is interested in the personality and behavior traits of the candidate. The intensity of the campaign is dependent upon the nature of the constituency, the candidates, and the general political climate at election time.

ELECTION PROBLEMS

By American standards, a high percentage of British voters turn out to vote in the national elections. In 1951, 82.6 per cent of the eligible voters cast ballots; in 1955, 76.8 per cent voted; and in 1959, almost 79 per cent. There were about 35,000,000 registered voters in 1959. The British political system is not troubled by voter lethargy to the same degree as the American system. What problems are found in the British system? The determination of election districts and the relationship of popular support to parliamentary representation constitute two of the major problems in Britain.

As noted, the British use single-member election districts. For years the drawing of district lines has been a source of conflict between the parties. Under present law, the districts are to be drawn on the basis of equal population subject to local government boundaries. The electoral quota for England is about one representative for every 55,670 people. However, when redistricting was implemented in 1955, the districts varied in population from about 40,000 to 80,000 in England. The average Scottish district was about 48,000 and in North Ireland over 70,000.

The problem has been partially solved by the creation of Boundary Commissions and the requirement for a revision at least every fifteen years. The Boundary Commissions are four in number—one each for England, Wales, Scotland, and North Ireland. Each commission consists of the Speaker of the House of Commons (ex-officio chairman), a judge (deputy chairman), and two members appointed by a designated minister. No member of the House of Commons may sit as a commission member. The ministerial appointments are made by common agreement among the parties.

The two-party system and the single-member district have produced the second major problem in the British electoral system. What is the relationship between party representation in the House of Commons and the party strength among the electorate? The single-member district and two-party system tend to create a disproportionate strength in the House of Commons for the major parties. If Table 4–1 is examined closely, one

Table 4–1. Election Statistics

Parliamentary Representation	1945		1950		1951		1955		1959	
	Seats	% of Seats	Seats	% of Seats	Seats	% of Seats	Seats	% of Seats	Seats	% of Seats
Conservatives	213	33.3	297	47.5	321	51.4	345	54.8	365	58.0
Labor	393	61.4	315	50.4	295	47.2	277	44.0	258	40.9
Liberal	12	1.9	9	1.4	6	1.0	6	0.9	6	0.9
Others	22	3.4	4	0.7	3	0.4	2	0.3	1	0.1

Percentage of Popular Vote	1945	1950	1951	1955	1959
Conservatives	39.9	41.7	48.0	49.8	49.4
Labor	48.0	46.4	48.8	46.4	43.9
Liberal	9.0	9.1	2.5	2.7	5.8
Others	3.1	2.8	0.7	1.1	0.9

can note that the popular vote of the third and other minor parties is not reflected accurately in the distribution of seats in the House of Commons. Also, the tendency is to exaggerate the majority of the dominant political party even at the expense of the minority party.

The major parties do not consider this situation a problem, but it does present to the minor parties an argument for some form of proportional representation. The present-day Liberal party forcibly argues that PR is the only remedy that would provide for a truer reflection in the Commons of the party's voting strength and of public opinion. It is also contended that PR is necessary for the existence of strong minor parties, which would in turn provide the voter with a real choice. The two major parties, despite their ideological differences, must appeal to a widely divergent electorate if they are to achieve a majority or near majority vote. To appeal to such a diverse electorate, the majority parties tend toward similarity in programs and thus, say the proponents of PR, do not offer the voter any real choice.

The major parties and, apparently, the voters reply that the stable working of Cabinet government depends upon the dominance of two parties. The single-member district and plurality election aid in the perpetuation of the two-party system and stable government.

The third major problem of the election system involves the question of the meaning of representation. Whom does Parliament represent? What is the relationship of a member to his constituency? These questions may be answered in a variety of ways, and there is no single theory of representation applied in Britain. The historical origins of Parliament and the writings of leading political thinkers provide the answer for Britain.

Parliament, as we will note in detail later, originated in the medieval period.[5] The concept of representation accepted by the medieval lawyer and political theorist was that Parliament represented not individuals or territorial divisions, but rather the entire realm and all the people in their corporate or societal capacity. Parliament was called to advise the king, and the king in his Parliament represented the highest wisdom of the realm. In short, the will of Parliament was the will of the people as an organic body. This concept of representation has never been lost in British thought or practice despite the infusion of majority rule and individualism. Yet even in the medieval period, the idea of territorial representation was applied as a practical way of selecting representatives. The early writs provided for the selection of knights from each shire and burgesses from the towns. However, medieval theory did not include the idea that the knights or burgesses were bound by the immediate wishes of their constituents.

In the period of early liberalism and the English civil war, the ideas of territorial representation and representation based upon wealth were given approval in the writings of John Locke. Locke also declared that the legislature was restricted in its powers by the social contract. Representatives were not bound by the wishes of their constituents, but rather by the laws of nature.[6]

Even after the Glorious Revolution, the idea of representatives instructed as delegates had not gained appreciable acceptance. In 1745, a minister explained in Parliament that a member was not obligated to follow the advice of his constituents.

Probably the most elequent expression of the organic concept of representation was made by Edmund Burke in his *Letter to the Sheriffs of Bristol* in 1777. Burke explained that a representative had an obligation to visit his constituency, to aid it and its membership in specific requests of

[5] See Chapter 5.
[6] See Chapter 2 for an explanation of Locke's views on the laws of nature.

a non-legislative nature, but that the representative was not and could not be bound on matters of policy. To Burke, the representative was not a territorial representative except for purposes of election. He was a representative of the whole nation and must represent past and future generations as well as the present one.

With the growth of political parties, a modification occurred in the theory and practice of representation. A member of Parliament was first obligated to the party that secured his election. The party, in turn, was responsible to the electorate. Only in this sense is there a mandate on Parliament, and this is not a constituency mandate.

SELECTED READING

BUTLER, D. E. *The British General Election of 1955*. London: Macmillan & Co., Ltd., 1955.

———. *The Electoral System in Britain, 1918–1951*. Fair Lawn, N.J.: Oxford University Press, 1951.

POLLOCK, J. K., *et al. British Election Studies*. Ann Arbor: University of Michigan Press, 1951.

ROSS, J. F. S. *Elections and Electors*. London: Eyre & Spottiswoode, Ltd., 1955.

5

The Legislature

The British claim to have one of the oldest parliamentary governments in the world. Certainly, it is true that the origins of the present-day legislature may be traced to at least Norman times, and many historians insist the origin is to be found in Anglo-Saxon institutions.

The Anglo-Saxon Witenagemot and the Norman Great Council (*Magnum Concilium*) are the forerunners of the House of Lords and the House of Commons. These bodies were not legislatures in the modern sense of the term but were called at the king's pleasure and were to advise the king and to give consent to certain of the king's proposals. They did not make law but consented to law made by the king. Even today the fiction of this medieval idea is used in the statutes, "Be it enacted by the Queen's most Excellent Majesty, by and with the advice and consent of the Lords Spiritual and Temporal, and Commons, in this present Parliament assembled, . . ."

The term "parliament" began to be used with regularity during the reign of Edward I (1272–1307), although the term may be found in some of the chronicles of the reign of Henry III (1216–1272). During Edward's reign, there developed a standardization of these conferences or parliaments called by the king. Edward's "Model Parliament" of 1295 provided for representation of the spiritual and temporal nobility, the lesser clergy, knights of the shires, and the cities and boroughs. The Model Parliament was truly a national assembly. At this time the clergy, nobility, knights, and commoners met as separate groups; but by the middle of the fourteenth century, a consolidation into two main groups had occurred. The spiritual lords sat with the temporal lords (the House of Lords), and the knights joined the burgesses (the House of Commons).

Initially, the commoners occupied an inferior position within the Parliament. They might request or petition the king to grant or amend a law;

but, unlike the Lords, neither their advice or consent was sought by the king. Gradually, the Commons was recognized as coequal with the Lords. The power and prestige of the Commons was further enhanced when the king accepted the principle that all money bills must originate in the House of Commons. But of greater importance in the development of Parliament was the struggle between the parliamentary force and the monarchy for supremacy in power. The struggle reached its climax in the seventeenth century with the defeat of the Stuart kings. Parliament won the power to govern and, despite difficulties, effected a strong and workable form of government. Thus, the modern concept of parliamentary government came into existence. The subsequent growth of political parties and the Cabinet system served to consolidate and perpetuate Parliament's control of government.

COMPOSITION OF THE BICAMERAL LEGISLATURE

As noted, the two-house legislature was not developed by design but evolved out of historical circumstances.

The House of Lords still represents the nobility, but the lineage is for the most part of recent origin. The eighteenth century marks the beginning of the lavish bestowal of peerages. Today, peerages may be hereditary or for life (title ceases upon the death of the individual and cannot be inherited by descendants); both types are eligible for seats in the House of Lords. Hereditary peerages are granted by a writ of summons or by letters-patent. Peerages by writ signify a family inheritance of long standing and may apply to female descendants as well as male. Letters-patent is merely a more formal way of conferring a peerage; its literal meaning refers to a document not sealed, but open. Such peerages are usually of more recent origin and customarily apply only to male descendants. An individual may refuse a hereditary peerage; but once granted, no heir may refuse to inherit the peerage. Since 1800, only peerages of the United Kingdom (Great Britain and Northern Ireland) have been granted; although peerages of Great Britain, England, Ireland, and Scotland still exist. Life peerages began in 1876 with the creation of the Lords of Appeal in Ordinary, known as the Law Lords.[1] In 1958, Parliament passed the Life Peerages Act, which provides that the Queen may by letters-patent confer a life peerage on any person. There is no limit on the number to be granted or, more significantly, with regard to the sex of the individual. Women may now sit in the House of Lords. New peerages are normally granted on the Queen's birthday and on New Year's Day. They are granted by the Queen upon the recommendation of the Prime Minister.

[1] For an explanation of the duties of the Law Lords, see pages 101 and 103.

Hereditary and life peerages also include royal peers, Scottish and Irish peers, and spiritual peers. Royal peers (princes of royal blood) by custom do not vote or participate in discussion. The holders of Scottish peerages elect sixteen representatives to sit in the House of Lords. The Irish peers may elect twenty-eight of their own to be representative Irish peers. However, no election has been held since 1921; and at present, only two Irish peers sit in the House of Lords. Spiritual peers include the Archbishops of Canterbury and York; the Bishops of London, Durham, and Winchester; plus the twenty-one senior Bishops of the Church of England. Approximately 850 peers are eligible to attend the sessions of the House of Lords, but the working membership seldom totals more than 100.

The composition of the House of Lords has been a source of conflict in modern Britain. It is inconsistent for a democratic government to have a legislative chamber whose membership is based upon heredity and appointment. Although in recent years more peerages have been granted to members of the Labor party, there is no doubt that the House of Lords is a stronghold of the Conservative party. In no way does its composition reflect a cross-section of popular opinion. One answer to this anomaly of a democratic country has been to curtail the power of the House of Lords, but this answer has never been completely satisfactory to all groups.[2] Some people, especially those who are members of the Labor party, have demanded outright abolishment of the House of Lords. This proposal has never been taken too seriously; perhaps it is too great an affront to tradition.

Various attempts have been made to find a suitable change in the composition of the House of Lords. The preamble of the Parliament Act of 1911 declared an intention to make the selection of the second chamber elective, but the preamble also noted such a change was not immediately practical. With the advent of World War I, serious consideration of the problem was postponed; but in 1917 the Prime Minister appointed a committee under the chairmanship of Lord Bryce to examine the powers and composition of the House of Lords. The Bryce Report was issued in 1918. The committee found agreement on the powers and functions of the second chamber much easier to reach than agreement on the composition. The recommendation of the committee called for the election of 218 members for twelve-year terms. The election was to be effected by means of panels chosen from the membership of the House of Commons. The panels were to be territorial in representation. In addition, 81 members with twelve-year terms were to be chosen by a joint standing committee of the two houses; the Lord Chancellor, ex-Lord Chancellors, and the Law Lords were to be selected by the Cabinet. Nothing developed in the way of a concrete reform from the Bryce Report.

[2] See pages 59 and 60.

In 1948 the leaders of the Labor and Conservative parties reported agreement upon the general basis for reorganization of the membership of the House of Lords, but they could not agree upon the extent of the House's powers. No action was taken on the report. The agreement did provide that no one party should have a permanent majority in the Lords, that the "Lords in Parliament" should be selected from hereditary peers and commoners on the basis of public service, and that women should have equal rights with men to be "Lords of Parliament."

The latest reform proposal was made by the Conservative government and enacted in the Life Peerage Act of 1958.[3] Eventually, some reform in the composition of the House of Lords will emerge, either as a result of conscious deliberation or by customary change. Today, those persons who attend the sessions regularly are interested in the conduct of governmental affairs and have often performed public service. The level of debate is admittedly high, and its membership is not harried by either a real or an imagined demand of a constituency. It may be that democratic systems need some form of check upon the popular rule of the majority, and that the House of Lords now partially performs this function in Great Britain.

The House of Commons is composed of 630 members who are elected by popular vote from single-member districts. It is not a cross-section of the population but, like American legislative bodies, has a large number of the legal profession as members.[4] With the rise of the Labor party, more workers, or at least trade-union officials, have been elected to the Commons. Within the House may be found lawyers, workers, businessmen, teachers, farmers, housewives, journalists, etc. The educational background of the members is considerably higher than that of the electorate. This is true of both major political parties.

PRIVILEGES AND IMMUNITIES

Members of both houses enjoy certain privileges and immunities equally, yet there are some differences between the two houses. If salary may be counted as a privilege, members of the House of Lords receive no compensation except for travel and expenses while attending sessions. Members of Commons receive an annual salary of £1,750 ($4,900) plus an attendance allowance and a tax deduction for expenses incurred in attendance.

Neither the Lords nor the Commons are provided with the office conveniences and staff that American legislators enjoy. Nor do they have free postal service and telephone and telegraph privileges. In fact, most members do not even have a permanent desk, only a locker.

[3] See page 50.

[4] For example, following the 1955 elections, there were 113 out of 630 members who gave their profession as law.

In earlier days, a member of the House of Lords had the privilege of being tried only by the House of Lords; but this privilege has been gradually curtailed.

After centuries of struggle, members of both houses enjoy freedom from civil arrest during parliamentary sessions and also in their travel to and from these sessions. The members are free from suits for any words spoken within Parliament. The Bill of Rights of 1689 provided that "the freedom of speech, and debates on proceedings in Parliament, ought not to be impeached or questioned in any court or place out of Parliament." The House of Commons has the right to decide any question of eligibility of its members. Both houses may punish their membership.

POLITICAL AND PARLIAMENTARY ORGANIZATION

The organization of the national parties has been discussed in Chapter 3. Reference was made to the Parliamentary party and its relationship to the national party. Because British government is party government, the organization of the parties in Parliament is extremely important, particularly in the House of Commons. There is party organization in the House of Lords but its use is limited. The main party organization is found in the House of Commons.

The Parliamentary Conservative party has a rather informal organization in the House of Commons. We have already noted how the Leader of the Conservative party is chosen.[5] The Leader is the most important member of the Parliamentary party. He appoints the party chief whip and assistant whips. The whips serve as liaison officers between the party leaders (front-benchers) and the rank and file members (back-benchers). The chief whips are responsible for working out procedural agreements between the two parties. They also are responsible for the presence of members when a crucial vote is eminent. The Leader appoints or selects his Cabinet when in power, and this group serves as the shadow Cabinet when the party is in opposition. On occasion, the Prime Minister has designated another member of the party as the Leader of the House of Commons but this is not a regular practice.

The back-benchers have an organization called the "1922 Committee." The more formal title is the Conservative Private Members Committee. In 1922, the Committee was formed in response to national party pressure for more communication between the leaders and the rank and file of the party. The Leader does not have control of the 1922 Committee. Except for the party whips, the front-benchers do not attend the meetings of the 1922 Committee. The Committee discusses policy, is often critical of the party leadership, and serves as a useful device for back-benchers to present their views to the party leaders.

[5] See page 30.

The Conservative party has a number of functional committees to discuss policy on a particular subject. The number of these committees varies, but usually there are fewer than twenty. When the party is in power, the chairmanships of these committees are filled by back-benchers; the shadow Cabinet members become the chairmen when the party is in opposition. The committees also serve as checking devices upon the ministers.

The Parliamentary Labor party is not as different from that of the Conservative party as Labor sometimes proclaims. Annually, the Labor members of Parliament elect a party leader and chairman (the same individual when the party is in opposition but two individuals when the party is in power). Labor insists that this annual election makes their party more democratic. It must be noted that re-election is the rule. The Labor party does meet as a body much more frequently than the whole Parliamentary Conservative party. When the Labor party is in opposition, the Labor leaders are subject to more rank and file control than are their Conservative counterparts.

The Parliamentary Labor party has an executive committee composed of twelve or more members who are elected by the rank and file. The executive committee meets at least once a week to discuss pending legislation and party policy. Unlike the Conservatives, the chief party whip is elected by the Labor membership; but the junior whips are appointed by the chief whip. The Parliamentary Labor party makes use of "subject groups." The subject groups are similar to the functional committees of the Conservative party.

Both parties within Parliament exercise discipline over their members. A party may "withdraw the whip" from a member and by this action exclude the member from all party proceedings within Parliament. A member may himself initiate such action by declaring his independence of the party and refusing to receive the whip's instructions. In either event, the member's seat in Commons is jeopardized. The party organization may refuse to endorse the candidate for re-election or may even officially expel the member from the party.[6]

The parliamentary organization is sufficiently different in the two houses to justify individual treatment. The presiding officer of the House of Lords is the Lord Chancellor. The Lord Chancellor, who receives his appointment from the Prime Minister, may be a commoner; usually, however, he is a peer. As presiding officer of the House, he forgoes the privilege of participating in debate and casting a vote. The Lord Chancellor does not have the power to make rulings on points of order or to recognize members who wish to speak. These are matters settled by the House itself.

[6] As noted in Chapter 3, the party cannot force a member to resign his seat in Parliament.

The chief duties of the Lord Chancellor are to serve as moderator and to act as the government's spokesman in the House of Lords. In addition to the Lord Chancellor, minor positions include record clerks and the Gentleman Usher of the Black Rod and the Yeoman Usher, both of whom serve as sergeants of arms.

The Lords do not have an elaborate committee system but make extensive use of the Committee of the Whole. A standing committee on the revision of bills and sessional committees for the consideration of private bills constitute the major committees. The Lords meet Monday through Thursday in formal session each afternoon.

The House of Commons requires more organization than the House of Lords. Like the Lords, the Commons has the usual number of clerks, parliamentary secretaries, and other minor positions.

The Speaker of the House of Commons is chosen from its own membership at the beginning of each Parliament. Custom rules that a Speaker, once elected, is re-elected until his retirement. Furthermore, he is not contested in the district in which he stands for Parliament.[7] Once a member is elected Speaker, he becomes non-partisan, a servant of the House, not a party man. The Speaker is definitely a presiding officer with the power to recognize members, interpret rules, reprimand members (in effect this may go so far as suspension for a period of time), appoint committees, and put questions to vote. The Speaker also has the power to decide which bills are money bills.[8]

The committees of the House of Commons are either standing committees, select committees, sessional committees, or private-bill committees. In addition to the Committee of the Whole, the Commons has six standing committees. Unlike the American committees, these are not functional by name; the committees are designated simply A, B, C, D, E, and the Scottish Committee. The standing committees consist of fifteen to twenty members each, with representation divided according to the party ratio in the House. Members are selected by a sessional Committee on Selection (the Scottish Committee is composed of only Scottish representatives). The standing committees may add additional members of the House who have expressed an interest and knowledge of a particular bill under consideration. Often a committee will actually consist of a group of forty to fifty members. The chairman of a standing committee is appointed by the Speaker from a list prepared by the Committee on Selection. The chairman, as often as not, is a member of the minority party. The chairmanship is an important position, and the chairman normally has the power of closure of debate and of kangaroo (the power to determine which proposed amendments will be discussed). Bills that con-

[7] The Labor party contested both of these customary practices but was unsuccessful.
[8] See page 59 for the importance of this power.

cern Scotland are referred to the Scottish Committee. Although there are no standing orders to functionalize Committees A, B, C, D, and E, the practice is growing to assign similar bills to the same standing committee.

Sessional or select committees are those created for each session of Parliament to perform a particular task. A select committee may be nothing more than a committee on refreshments; on the other hand, it may be a very important committee. Select committees may be created to examine a particular public bill. If so, the examination is made prior to the normal committee stage. Certain select committees are formed for every session and constitute major committees. Such select committees are the Committee on Selections, the Committee on Public Accounts, the Committee on Standing Orders, the Committee on Privilege, the Committee on Statutory Instruments, and the Committee on Estimates.

The private-bill committees, sometimes called groups, are committees of four members who hold public hearings and deliberate on the acceptance of a private bill and who report their considerations to the House. Members of private-bill committees are selected by the Committee on Selection and must agree that they have no personal interest in the private bill and that they will regularly attend the meetings of the committee.

A fourth kind of committee infrequently used is a joint committee of the two houses. In theory, and partially in practice, a joint committee is a joint meeting of separate select committees to discuss a particular bill.

The House of Commons' committee system is not as elaborate as that found in the American Congress. The tradition of British parliamentary practice has been that the entire membership of the houses, either as a House or a Committee of the Whole, deliberates upon legislation. The pressures of modern government with its increased areas of specialization have caused the House of Commons to resort to committees. Although Cabinet government in Britain would prevent the growth of committee power equal to that of American committees, it may be expected that the use of committees will continue to develop in British parliamentary practice and organization.

LEGISLATIVE PROCEDURES

The legislative procedure varies in accordance with the kind of bill. Bills are either public bills, private bills, government bills, or private-member bills. This classification is overlapping inasmuch as government bills may be either public or private and private-member bills may be either public or private. A government bill is a bill introduced by the Cabinet. A private-member bill is one introduced by an individual member and may or may not have the Cabinet's approval. Public bills are bills that affect the general public. Private bills are those that do not concern the general public but which grant special powers to companies, corporations (including local units of government), and private persons.

Public bills usually originate in the House of Commons, although they may originate in the House of Lords. The major exception to this practice is a money bill, which must begin in the House of Commons and also be a government bill. A member of the House deposits a bill (sometimes a dummy) with the proper clerk and it is titled, recorded, and printed. The recording constitutes the first reading of the bill. The time for the second reading of the bill is determined by the majority party after consultation with the opposition. Often, this consultation is referred to as a ruling "behind the Speaker's chair." During the second reading, the general principles of the bill are debated. A negative vote on the second reading kills the bill. If the bill is approved on the second reading, it is referred to a committee or to the Committee of the Whole House. The Committee of the Whole House is used for money resolutions, ways and means (financial bills), supply or expenses of the public service, and for selected ordinary public bills. The committee stage provides opportunity for a discussion of the details of a bill and for the proposal of amendments. After the committee has deliberated, the next stage is the report stage. The chairman reports the bill with or without amendment. Debate follows the order for consideration, and amendments may be made during the report stage. Following the report stage (often on the same day), the third reading of the bill occurs. Debate is permitted, but no amendments except for textual revision are allowed. If the bill passes the third reading, it is sent to the House of Lords.

Procedure in the House of Lords is similar. Three readings of a bill are required. The Lords may or may not refer a bill to committee. The Lords may amend the bill subject to the restrictions of the Parliament Act of 1949.[9] If the bill is approved in the Lords, it is prepared for the Queen's assent. If the bill is rejected or amended, it returns to the Commons. The Commons may either accept the amendments made by the Lords, invoke the procedure of the Parliament Act of 1949, or begin negotiations with the Lords to achieve a compromise.

A private bill is initiated by the affected person or group. Not many private bills are introduced (about thirty-five in a year) since Parliament has provided delegated legislation to empower ministers to make many of the decisions formerly acted upon in private bills. Every effort is made to settle any opposition to the bill before it is introduced. Public notice must be given of the intent and contents of the proposed bill. The group or individual represented in the private bill petitions Parliament usually through a parliamentary agent. A parliamentary agent is a legal practitioner who is registered with Parliament. The examiners of petitions con-

[9] See page 59.

sider the petition to ascertain if the conditions of notice have been met. If so, the examiners report the bill to both Houses. The bill is then presented to one of the Houses and has its first reading (recording only), and a date is assigned for the second reading. Second readings of private bills usually require only a few minutes, but occasionally a full scale debate is allowed. Private bills that are opposed in debate are sent to a select private-bill committee. If the bill is unopposed, it is referred to the Unopposed Private Bill Committee. If the bill has been opposed, semijudicial hearings take place in the committee stage. After the committee reports, the bill follows the usual procedure. The report of the committee is generally accepted by the House. If one House approves the private bill, it is rarely contested in the other House.

Passage of private-member bills has become almost a rarity; but, although difficult to achieve, some important legislation has had its beginning as a private-member bill.

Individual members draw for the privilege of introducing a bill. This lottery is often called "drawing a turkey." Occasionally, a private member will receive Cabinet support of his bill; and if this occurs, the chances for passage are greatly improved. Normally, private-member bills and resolutions are considered on Wednesday and Friday in the first twenty weeks of a session, unless the Cabinet demands part of this time for its bills. Most private-member bills never survive the second reading. If they do, the procedure is the same as for any public bill. The major problem, other than the draw and short time for consideration, is that the guidance of the bill through all the legislative hurdles is left to the proposer of the bill.

As might be expected, the Cabinet dominates the legislative time. Over one-half of the debate time is devoted to Cabinet-sponsored legislation.

As in most modern legislatures, the number of bills deemed important makes some restrictions upon debate necessary. In the House of Commons, there are several ways to limit or close debate. Most frequently, time limits debates; and the division of time between the parties is determined by the party whips "behind the Speaker's chair." Closure may be achieved by "moving the previous question." The Speaker must consider the feeling of the House if he allows the motion to be put. A majority, including at least 100 members, must approve the motion. If the motion is approved, debate ceases. Closure may be by "guillotine," or closure by compartment. This technique, adopted by motion at the beginning of the consideration of a bill, creates a timetable for each stage of a bill's passage. At the end of the allotted time, any debate or consideration automatically ceases. The "guillotine" is not liked by the opposition, but government parties have used it increasingly in recent years. The "guillotine" prevents the use of delaying tactics by the opposition.

Another method of closure is the "kangaroo." The Speaker and the chairmen of standing committees have the power to "jump over" proposed amendments if they do not consider them representative of the opinion of the House.

The procedural arrangements in the House of Commons do provide for debate and for the opposition party to express its views. Private members also have some opportunity to be heard, although not as much as they desire.

LEGISLATIVE FUNCTIONS

Although the term "legislature" denotes a policy-making body, modern legislatures do not have exclusive power to make governmental policy. In Britain, as in the United States and elsewhere, the charge is often levied that the legislature has forfeited its traditional function of law making. A wiser judgment might be that the role of the legislature in the law-making process has been modified. As we have stated, most important legislation is initiated and prepared by the Cabinet in Britain. Furthermore, the government party usually has a sufficient majority in the House of Commons to insure passage of its proposed legislation. If viewed superficially, the House could be labeled a "rubber stamp" for the Cabinet. At times this charge is true. But more often Commons does give careful consideration and debate to a Cabinet bill before granting approval. Valuable amendments may be made by the House of Commons or by the House of Lords. The Cabinet is sensitive to the opinions of the Commons, as these opinions are one expression of the popularity of the government. Although Parliament does not initiate and determine the general policy proposals that are ultimately incorporated into law, it does have the power to review and approve such proposals. If the House of Commons expresses disapproval of a general policy proposal either by resolution or vote, the Cabinet must reassess its position on the proposal or face the possibility of losing control of the government to the opposition party.

As a legislative body, the House of Lords is even more restricted than the House of Commons. The Parliament Acts of 1911 and 1949 substantially limited the Lords as a coequal upper chamber. The provisions of these acts make it possible for the House of Commons to pass legislation over the opposition of the Lords. Any money bill that has been approved in Commons must be approved by the House of Lords within a month's time after its receipt. If default occurs, the bill is sent to the Queen for her signature as if it had been approved by the Lords. Ordinary legislation becomes law over the opposition of the House of Lords if it has passed by Commons in two successive sessions and if one year has elapsed between the first second reading and the final passage. Actually, the Parliament Acts of 1911 and 1949 are seldom invoked (three times to date and one of those times was to make the 1949 changes in the Act itself). The Lords have basically agreed to the Acts' provisions and rarely attempt total obstruction to a bill. Legislatively, the House of Lords is useful as a delaying and revising body. The Lords, free from time limitations and an immediate responsibility to the electorate, may freely discuss a bill. Amendments (some technical) that are acceptable to the Commons may be proposed by the Lords and thus the quality of a bill is improved. The Lords also relieve the Commons of the examination of many private bills and noncontroversial public bills.

A major function of modern democratic legislatures is that of control over the executive branch. British parliamentary organization and procedure provide several methods by which control is exercised. Major debates such as the debate on the Queen's Address at the opening of a Parliament give an opportunity for criticism of major governmental proposals.

The question time in the Commons is the best opportunity that individual members have to raise pertinent questions about specific governmental policy and programs. Approximately an hour of each sitting (except Fridays) is set aside for questions. A member who desires to ask a question of a minister hands to a clerk the written question. He may indicate whether he wants a written or oral answer. The clerk examines the question to see whether it is in order, and, if so, it is recorded and listed on the Order Paper of the day it is to be asked. The question is forwarded to the proper minister in order that he and his subordinates may prepare a reply. From 60 to 200 questions are listed each day. The Speaker recognizes the member of Commons and he puts the question to the minister. After the reply, the Speaker will usually recognize a supplementary question and even several if time permits. Those questions not answered orally in a sitting have written replies that become a part of the Hansard. The question time is an effective method of control. If the question and the supplementary questions are skillfully worded, a minister is clearly made to defend his action. Although different in method, the result of question time is similar to the American practice of having administrative officials quizzed before Congressional committees. It is possible for the Cabinet to refuse to answer certain questions on the grounds of public security, but any attempt to abuse this privilege creates dissatisfaction in the House.

Debate upon the motion to adjourn is another technique to provide both for general debate and for individual members to raise questions of the government bench. Occasionally, by previous arrangement between the whips and the Speaker, a Cabinet member will move the adjournment immediately following question time. Then a general debate may take place upon a subject previously agreed upon by the parties. Unless there is important public business, the House usually devotes the last thirty minutes of a sitting to debate a motion to adjourn. During this time, individual members are given the opportunity to speak on whatever subject the member is interested in. Often, the debate is a continuation of a member's question put earlier to a minister.

Certain select committees perform a control function in behalf of the House of Commons. The Committee on Statutory Instruments examines executive orders issued under delegated legislation to see whether any order requires parliamentary action. The Committee, as part of its function, reports any irregularities or abuses of the executive power to issue orders, rules, and regulations to Parliament.

The Public Accounts Committee in the House of Commons examines the detailed reports of the Comptroller-General and Auditor and makes a report to the House. The Committee serves as an effective restraint upon irregularity in expenditures by the executive departments. The Estimates Committee of Commons performs a similar function in regard to current expenditures.

Parliament has an investigative function, and often select committees are formed in either House to make a study of a particular subject. However, select committees of investigation are not the main method in Britain of attaining a study of a controversial subject. The British make extensive use of Royal Commissions for this purpose. Royal Commissions are created by the executive and are executive committees rather than parliamentary committees. A Royal Commission Report usually results in legislation designed to implement the recommendations of the Commission.

Parliament acts as a purveyor of public opinion to the government and as a molder of public opinion. The Cabinet is able to feel the pulse of the public by listening to the comments, debate, and criticisms of the backbenchers of its own party as well as the comments and criticisms of the opposition party. Often, debates in Commons focus the Cabinet's attention upon areas of popular discontent. Conversely, Parliament and its actions are widely covered in the British press and, hence, act as a molder of public opinion.

Parliament, if not dominated, is certainly led by the executive in modern Britain; and it is the executive that will be examined in the next chapter.

SELECTED READING

Bailey, S. D. (ed.). *The Future of the House of Lords.* New York: Frederick A. Praeger, Inc., 1954.

Ilbert, Sir Courtenay. *Parliament.* 3d ed. Fair Lawn, N. J.: Oxford University Press, 1950.

Jennings, Sir Ivor. *Parliament.* 2d ed. Cambridge: Cambridge University Press, 1959.

Mackenzie, K. R. *The English Parliament.* Baltimore: Penguin Books, Inc., 1950.

Taylor, Eric. *The House of Commons at Work.* Baltimore: Penguin Books, Inc., 1955.

6

The Executive

After years of struggle to achieve parliamentary supremacy over the king, the needs of modern government have forced a reversal in British development, and once again the center of governmental power is found in the executive branch. A strong executive branch responsible to Parliament is one of the major characteristics of the British system. The major component parts of the executive branch, excluding administration, are the Monarchy, the Privy Council, the Cabinet, and the Prime Minister.

THE MONARCHY

From the Bretwalda of Anglo-Saxon days to the reign of Elizabeth II (1952–   ), the role of the monarch has had a fascinating and vacillating development. Much of the history of England and Great Britain can be written in terms of an attempt by the British to define the role of the monarch. Republican movements have flourished from time to time and such ideas may still be heard, but with the exception of the period of Cromwell the monarchy has outlived its critics. In many ways the monarchy is stronger today than it has ever been, and its prestige position is almost unquestioned. How may this be explained in an age of republicanism throughout most of the world? The answers are found in the unique role that the British monarch plays in British life and government. The monarch is above politics, and under normal conditions is a ceremonial head of state. Removed from the political arena, the monarch is also removed from the stigma of responsibility for political decisions. As the ceremonial chief of state, the monarch performs a convenient, colorful, and useful function in the British system.

The monarch has become a unifying element in British society. The government and the opposition may hurl charges and countercharges at one another across the floor of Commons, in the newpapers, and in election oratory; but the Queen, the fountain of government, remains unsullied. Not only is the monarchy a unifying factor within Great Britain, but it is also the major visible tie that binds the British Commonwealth. The coronation of a new monarch is as important in Canada as it is in Britain.

The monarchy answers the need for personalization of government and for color in the modern world. It also serves to provide a sense of historical continuity. No one can watch the crowds gather around Buckingham Palace and along the Mall to Westminster (Parliament) and then witness the ceremonial drive of the Queen without sensing a feeling of continuity; the past lives into the present and the future. In a world dominated by the struggle to satisfy material needs, the royal family and the ceremonial attached to it provide a welcome relief and add warmth and color to the lives of most Britishers.

As the ceremonial chief of state, the monarch frees the political head of government from burdensome and time consuming activities. The Queen, not the Prime Minister, lays cornerstones, acts as the honorary chairman of charitable organizations, and makes public appearances at the opening of a new play. Perhaps more important, the monarch does much of the formal entertainment of foreign diplomatic representatives and visiting dignitaries from abroad. This function should not be underrated; and when comparison is made with the American President, who functions both as a ceremonial head and political head of state, the advantages of a dual executive become apparent.

But what of the monarch's governmental powers? Walter Bagehot's description is still valid after almost 100 years; namely, that the monarch has "the right to be consulted, the right to encourage, the right to warn." Bagehot added that no good king would desire more power. Normally, the monarch follows the advice of his ministers. Legally, the monarch is the supreme executive and has coordinate power with Parliament. The latter can be dismissed with the statement that Queen Anne (1702–1714) was the last monarch to refuse assent to a legislative enactment. The question of right was argued as late as 1913 over the Home Rule Bill for Ireland. The king exercises his right to convene, prorogue, and dissolve Parliament on the advice of the Prime Minister. The monarch delivers the Address of Parliament, but the speech and its content is the work once again of the ministers.

As supreme executive, the monarch makes appointments; and, theoretically, the civil servant serves at the pleasure of the Crown. The monarch appoints the Prime Minister. However, the appointment is usually predetermined; and the monarch has no choice if a political party has a clear majority in the House of Commons and if there is a clearly established leader of the majority party. It is possible that the monarch might exercise a real choice in certain rather exceptional cases. If the majority party leader (Prime Minister) resigns or dies and there is no known second in command and if the majority party is unable to name its new leader, then the monarch could name the new leader or Prime Minister. Even in this situation, the monarch would consult with members of the majority party to aid in determining which person would be most acceptable. This may have been the case in the appointment of Harold Macmillan as Prime Minister instead of R. A. Butler at the time of Anthony Eden's resignation in 1957.

A second situation has and can develop in which the monarch exercises a true choice in the selection of the Prime Minister. Such a situation occurs if there is no clear majority party in the House of Commons and the present government has been defeated or has resigned. The monarch is then free to consult with whomever he wishes in order to work out a solution either in the form of a coalition, as with Ramsay MacDonald in 1931, or in the formation of a minority government.

The examples above are exceptional. The monarch appoints the other ministers upon the advice of the Prime Minister and accepts their resignations in the same way. His political acts are in reality the acts of his responsible ministers.

Yet the monarch must be consulted and can influence by his counsel. The monarch has meetings with his Prime Minister and other ministers but does not attend Cabinet meetings and has not since the reign of George I (1714–1727). However, the agenda and the minutes of Cabinet meetings are regularly sent to the monarch. In addition, the monarch receives communications and reports from the Foreign Office and other important ministries. The monarch's influence is largely personal and depends to a large extent on his personality and ability to establish a proper rapport with his ministers. A monarch who attempts too much and actually interferes is headed for rebuke.

The monarch makes appointments and grants titles and honors. Twice yearly, New Year's Day and on the monarch's birthday, an Honors List is published. With certain exceptions, such as awards of the Royal Victoria Order, the Honors List is prepared by the Prime Minister. The sovereign may resist and press but usually accepts the list. There is still a debatable question on the creation of peers for the purpose of packing a House of Lords in order to achieve passage of a measure already adopted in the House of Commons.[1] The generally accepted view is that the monarch cannot be compelled to make the peer appointments until he is convinced the people are in favor of the proposed legislation. He may insist upon an election as proof on this question.

[1] With the Parliament Act of 1911 as amended in 1949, this question is not too important. For a discussion of this Act, see pages 59–60.

For the functions performed, the monarch and members of the royal family receive both financial and privilege awards. The revenues from the Duchies of Cornwall and Lancaster are revenues of the Crown, and the government provides additional income.

We Americans are prone to question the monarchial system of government and to suggest that the cost is not justifiable in terms of functions performed. Certain benefits of the monarchy have been suggested. These benefits cannot be measured in terms of cost accounting, and all governmental activity should not be thought of in terms of efficiency. The British find in the monarchy tremendous satisfaction. A head of state above the political level adds dignity and prestige to government and acts as a stabilizing and unifying force. Inasmuch as the dual executive system relieves the political head from ceremonial and social functions, certainly the political head has more time and energy to devote to affairs of the state. Obviously, a dual executive system can be constructed in a republican form of government and perhaps at less cost than the present British monarchial type. But to attempt this in Britain would mean a sharp break with the traditions and heritage of the centuries. To the Britisher, such an idea is almost inconceivable.

PRIVY COUNCIL

The Privy Council is an outgrowth of the Great Council of the Norman kings. A small council or *Curia Regis* developed out of the Great Council and became the principal advisory body to the king. The Privy Council developed as a committee of the *Curia Regis.*

Membership in the Privy Council is by appointment by the Crown for life. The qualifications for such an appointment are varied, and there are no rules governing the appointments. The Privy Council's membership includes past and present Cabinet members, high administrative officers, the Law Lords, religious leaders such as the Archbishops of Canterbury and York, ambassadors, and distinguished citizens.

The Privy Council seldom meets as a plenary body except for ceremonial functions. A quorum is three and the usual practice is that four or five members in the presence of the monarch conduct the business of the Privy Council. The Privy Council is no longer a deliberative political body. Its political power has been transferred to the Cabinet; but, according to custom, certain actions of the Cabinet must have approval of the Privy Council. Its most important political function is the issuance of "Orders in Council" or, to use American terminology, certain kinds of "executive orders." Its power to issue Orders in Council is derived from both statute and royal prerogative. Important executive orders such as declarations of war are Orders in Council. Some delegated legislation or administrative orders must be formally issued by the Privy Council. In actuality, such orders are the work of the Cabinet circuited the route of the Privy Council.

The Privy Council also issues city charters and confers the oath of office upon ministers and "pricks" sheriffs. "Pricking" simply means the investing of the insignia of the office. From time to time, the Privy Council appoints committees from its own membership or outside to make special studies of political and social problems.

The judicial function of the Privy Council will be examined later. By a statute of 1833, there is a standing Judicial Committee of the Privy Council that is authorized to act as the final appeal court in a limited variety of cases.

Historically, the Privy Council has been the source of a number of executive departments. The Board of Trade is still termed a committee of the Privy Council, and the Ministry of Education began as a special committee of the Privy Council.

If the Privy Council no longer holds any real power, why is the body kept in existence? Why not by statute transfer its legal functions to the bodies that actually hold political power? Again an anomaly of the British system presents itself. The Cabinet is not a legally recognized body and has no legal powers. It operates through previously existent or posteriorily created legal bodies. The British recognize and accept the idea of government by custom, not rational design; and since the system is operative, the British see no need to simplify and clarify the governmental pattern.

THE PRIME MINISTER

The Office of Prime Minister is the most important office in British government today. The Prime Minister is the chief political leader of his country and one of the free world's most powerful governmental officials. The office has grown and developed with the Cabinet, although the idea of a "chief-minister" predates the development of the Cabinet. These "chief-ministers" were responsible to the king, and their position depended upon their personal influence with the king. For this reason, they should not be thought of in terms of a modern Prime Minister. In part, however, these early "chief-ministers" provided stepping stones in the growth of the office. Lord Godolphin exercised considerable control over appointments and the direction of the Cabinet in the reign of Queen Anne. Sir Robert Harley, who succeeded Godolphin, was described as a "prime minister" by Jonathan Swift. During Anne's reign, both the Whigs and Tories were beginning to develop party organization, which aided the movement toward ministerial responsibility to Parliament.

Sir Robert Walpole was the first prototype of the modern Prime Minister, and by 1729 the position of Prime Minister was clearly established. Sir Robert denied he was a Prime Minister, although he established precedents that constitute some of the major characteristics of the office. For example, he clearly understood that his power was based on party power and Parliament. He resigned when defeated in the House of Commons. Walpole's twenty-one years in the House of Commons served to foster the idea that the Prime Minister must be a member of the House of Commons.

From Walpole to the present, the Office of Prime Minister continued to develop, although not in a straight and progressive manner. Like most British positions, the office is regulated by custom and by power factors more than by statutory provisions.

The Office of Prime Minister is now legally recognized; and, in accordance with the Ministers of the Crown Act of 1937, the Prime Minister is also the First Lord of the Treasury. The latter position is a sinecure post and carries no responsibilities. The Prime Minister may, if he desires, hold another office, since there is no rule to prevent this. Occasionally, Prime Ministers have also served as Foreign Secretaries, Ministers of Defense, and even as Chancellors of the Exchequer. Generally, most Prime Ministers have felt that the occupancy of another governmental office proved too burdensome. As a result, either the departmental obligations or the obligations as Prime Minister suffered. The Prime Minister's duties as leader of his party in the House of Commons have been reduced by the creation of a separate office, the Leader of the House of Commons.

The Prime Minister is selected by the monarch; but, as noted, the leader of the majority party in the House of Commons is chosen.[2] The custom that the Prime Minister must be a member of the House of Commons has been clearly accepted since 1923. Actually, the year 1902 was the last time that a Prime Minister was chosen from the House of Lords. The reason for this limitation is quite simple. The Commons has legislative supremacy; it is the elected legislative organ; and it is, far more than the House of Lords, the body of political parties. Government revolves around the House of Commons, and it is only good judgment that the leader of the government be a member of the Commons. The Prime Minister's official headquarters is 10 Downing Street.

Statistics can be misleading, but it is possible to delineate certain general characteristics that have consistently appeared in the lives of the Prime Ministers. The Prime Minister generally will have the advantage of a higher education and probably possess a university degree. The university degree is more likely to be from Oxford or Cambridge than from a regional university. This pattern of higher education has been slightly modified with the rise of the Labor party. Ramsay MacDonald had only an elementary education, but Clement Attlee was a university graduate. Until a university education becomes normal for labor political leaders, it

[2] See pages 63–64.

is quite possible that formal academic training will be less than in previous years.

The occupational background of previous Prime Ministers provides no real basis for generalization. Law, business, party organization, and trade-unionism have all been part of the occupational background. Winston Churchill served as an army officer and journalist.

The Prime Minister's age will be approximately sixty years when he first takes office. The youngest Prime Minister since 1894 was Lord Rosebery, who took office at the age of forty-three. Churchill's statement, "I am a child of the House of Commons," explains the relatively late rise to the position of Prime Minister. A man must make a name for himself in Commons as well as in his party before he can aspire to the leadership. As a rule, most members of the House of Commons begin as back-benchers and move slowly to the front benches. In addition, a Prime Minister has usually had experience as an administrative officer, both in junior ministerial positions and in Cabinet positions, although such experience is not mandatory.

With the exclusion of Lord Salisbury and Lord Rosebery, the Prime Ministers from 1894 to 1959 have had an average of twenty-five years' service in the House of Commons before becoming Prime Minister. Ramsay MacDonald's fourteen years is the shortest membership and Winston Churchill's thirty-eight years the longest one. With the exception of Ramsay MacDonald, all the Prime Ministers have had some administrative experience. The Office of the Chancellor of the Exchequer and the Foreign Office tend to be the final steps toward the Prime Ministership. This path is not a fixed one and a number of examples can be found as exceptions. For instance, Winston Churchill was First Lord of the Admiralty just before he became Prime Minister. Local governmental experience is of little importance in the background of Prime Ministers.

Unlike the United States and the selection of the President, geographic location does not play a significant role in the selection of the national party leader and the Prime Minister. The public does not vote directly for the Prime Minister. There are no doubtful areas of such magnitude as New York or California that exercise a disproportionate vote. Prime Ministers have come from England, Scotland, Wales (only Lloyd George), and even from Canada (Bonar Law).

Religion is a relatively insignificant factor in modern British politics; it is even difficult to determine the religious affiliation of parliamentary candidates. It is true that no Roman Catholic has ever been Prime Minister, and it is an open question whether a Roman Catholic would be acceptable to the people as the Prime Minister.

Family and class lines have played an important role in politics, but they are becoming less significant. A contrast can be made between the

Prime Ministers of 1832–1894 and those since 1894. Between 1832 and 1894, Disraeli, Peel, and Gladstone were the only Prime Ministers who were not descendants of the nobility. Since 1894, most of the Prime Ministers have been of middle-class origin except for Lord Salisbury, Lord Rosebery, Arthur Balfour, and Winston Churchill who had connections with the aristocracy. Ramsay MacDonald is the only Prime Minister of definite lower-class origin. Although family and class background are receding in importance, they cannot be dismissed. Social position may not make a Prime Minister, but it often opens the door to a political career.

Other factors should be noted in the selection of a Prime Minister and head of the party. The man must be acceptable to the party as a loyal party man. Winston Churchill is the only Prime Minister of the twentieth century who has successfully crossed party lines. The leader must be of an agreeable personality, he must get along well with the press, and he must appeal to the electorate. As in any country, it is difficult to know what personal characteristics will appeal at a given time to the electorate. Dynamic personalities such as Winston Churchill may be passed over for quieter types such as Clement Attlee. Unimpeachable moral character is still a necessity in Britain with its semipuritanical standards. Anthony Eden is the only divorced man who has risen to the Prime Minister's position. The facts of the case produced public sympathy for Eden. High public integrity is another characteristic normally required of political leaders in Britain. Non-rational factors are also important; for example, a pipe smoker may have more appeal than a cigarette or cigar smoker.

Lord Bryce once wrote that the American system of selecting a President tended to produce men of second-rate ability while the British system produced leaders of first-rate ability. Such a comparison is misleading, for certainly not all American Presidents have been second rate or all British Prime Ministers first rate. The difference in the system does make it less feasible for a political unknown to become Prime Minister than for the same to become President. The future Prime Minister is more likely to have national political experience with a longer period before the public than the potential President. Inasmuch as this factor would aid in allowing the public and the party to acquaint themselves with the competency or incompetency of a candidate, it is less likely that a second-rate person would achieve the Office of Prime Minister. However, lack of political experience on the national level does not necessarily give validity to Lord Bryce's opinion. He would have scored more heavily had he referred to our system of electing a Vice-President and his possible succession to the Presidency.

Once selected, the first task of the Prime Minister is the selection of his Cabinet and the ministerial positions not of Cabinet rank. The monarch legally appoints, but the Prime Minister names the individuals to be appointed. Again the monarch may advise and warn, but the Prime Minister must decide whether he wants to accept the advice of the sovereign. There is no prescribed number of ministerial positions, but the usual number is about thirty-five. The degree of control exercised by the Prime Minister in filling subordinate positions below ministerial rank will vary in accordance with the character and desires of the individual Prime Minister. One may allow ministers complete freedom, while another may insist on the selection.

The Prime Minister has one major objective in his selection of the major governmental officials. He wants to build as strong a government as possible. Yet he is not free to select anyone whom he chooses. He must consult party leaders and, if he is wise, will seek the advice of the chief whip of the party. The chief whip has direct contact with the party backbenchers, who constitute the rank and file of the party. The custom of choosing outstanding members of the Parliamentary party to fill the Cabinet and other ministerial posts further limits the Prime Minister's freedom of selection. However, the Prime Minister does retain some discretion relative to the exact positions these "self-chosen" men will occupy.

The size of the Cabinet is dependent upon the decision of the Prime Minister within the limits of tradition and necessity. He decides, again with the advice of his party and friends, how large the Cabinet will be and what offices and departments will be included. Normally, this choice is limited by the tradition and the necessity of certain departments to have Cabinet rank. The Ministries of the Treasury, Foreign Affairs, Defense, Home Affairs, and others are considered to be "Cabinet" ministries. Often a few sinecure posts will be included in the Cabinet in order to insure Cabinet rank to a number of men with no specific assignment. The Chancellorship of the Duchy of Cornwall is such a sinecure position.

It is difficult to describe the role of the Prime Minister in relationship with his Cabinet. He has been called a "first among equals" and a "star among lesser moons" but any phrase is inadequate. The relationship must depend upon the character and personality of the Prime Minister and his Cabinet members. The Prime Minister may dominate his Cabinet and, hence, the policy of the government. If the Prime Minister is of a concilatory nature, he may allow the Cabinet to make policy. As it is in the American presidency, Prime Ministers may be strong or weak.

Regardless of the exact relationship with his Cabinet, the Prime Minister must bear the main responsibility for the formation of government policy. As head of the government of his country, the electorate, parties, and Parliament all look to the Prime Minister for leadership. May the Prime Minister make policy without Cabinet consent or even consultation? Yes, if he can get away with it. It is conceivable but not likely. Usually, the Prime Minister will consult with his Cabinet and a consensus will be reached. It may be that the Prime Minister will have to decide what the consensus is or use his influence to arrive at a consensus. If the Cabinet is seriously divided, the Prime Minister must determine what action to take. He can ask for the resignation of those opposed, he can decide to take no action on the policy contemplated, or he can decide the Cabinet should resign and request new elections. If the Prime Minister wishes the principle of collective responsibility to operate, he must necessarily develop policy with the members of his Cabinet.

The Prime Minister must also perform an over-all administrative function. As head of the government, he is held responsible for the administration of all ministries and departments. He must keep in touch with his departments and agencies and know in a comprehensive manner what is being done in each. Primarily, however, the Prime Minister's administrative role is that of coordinator and conciliator.

The Prime Minister is the leader of his party in the House of Commons. At times another party man has been given the title of Leader of the House of Commons, but the Prime Minister cannot escape the final responsibility of answering for the government in the House of Commons. He does not have to attend every "sitting" or participate in every debate, but he must be available for debate and for answering questions on major policy.

Finally, the Prime Minister is responsible to the electorate. A Britisher casts his vote for the parliamentary candidate of his residential district, but he is really casting a vote for the party or the potential Prime Minister. The Prime Minister must sense the will of the populace and act in accordance with it if he and his party are to remain in power. Party history and the governmental practices of parties in power indicate that the parties act less on principle and more on political expediency.

THE CABINET

In Britain the Cabinet, under the leadership of the Prime Minister, operates under the principle of collective responsibility. As a group the members of the Cabinet are directly responsible to Parliament and indirectly responsible to the electorate for the formation and execution of public policy. This concept of collective responsibility serves as a fairly effective check on the power of the Cabinet inasmuch as it tends to produce compromise within the Cabinet and also compromise with Parliament. It is a rare occurrence when a Prime Minister has a Cabinet that accepts without question all of his policy ideas. Although the Prime Minister holds the power of his threatened resignation and the power to make adjustments in the personnel of the Cabinet, any major split in the Cabinet will often lead to its own resignation and the dissolution of Parliament.

The Cabinet's primary function is the formulation of public policy to present to Parliament for adoption. The Cabinet may reasonably expect Parliament to pass proposed legislation substantially as the Cabinet has written the proposal. This normal expectancy has led to the charge that Parliament is subservient to the Cabinet and that British government is Cabinet government. The major fact that diminishes the absolute character of Cabinet dominance is that the Cabinet members are also Parliament members and have been nurtured in Parliament. Informal traditions and the recognition that although a Cabinet today they may become the shadow cabinet of the opposition tomorrow are effective checks upon arbitrary action by the Cabinet. Also, the question period in the House of Commons and the debate of adjournment provide avenues for Parliamentary criticism of Cabinet action.

The second major function of the Cabinet, collectively and individually, is the administration of the executive branch. The Cabinet must make the basic internal management policies, resolve certain interdepartmental differences, and be in constant touch with the day-to-day decisions made by the permanent civil servants. The wide discretionary powers granted the agencies under delegated legislation make this function one of major importance. The problems involved in the administrative function will be discussed in Chapter 7.

As the Cabinet has evolved, a permanent organization has developed to make Cabinet work more efficient. Cabinet meetings may be called at any time by the Prime Minister. Ordinarily, two meetings a week while Parliament is in session and one a week when Parliament is not in session are adequate. The Cabinet meets at 10 Downing Street, the official residency of the Prime Minister. The Prime Minister sits in the center of the conference table with his back to the fire (a priority of warmth). Votes are rarely taken, but the Prime Minister attempts to take a consensus of the viewpoints discussed. The meetings are secret as are the minutes of the meeting. The latter are protected both by custom and the Official Secrets Act of 1920.

Since 1916, the Cabinet has had a secretary with a staff. The secretariat for the Cabinet was created by attaching the existing secretariat of the Committee of Imperial Defence to the War Cabinet. The secretariat has the following functions: (1) issues notices of Cabinet meetings and meetings of the Cabinet committees; (2) prepares the agenda of the Cabinet meetings and of the Cabinet committee meetings; (3) records, files, and circulates the minutes of the Cabinet meetings and of the committee meetings; and (4) distributes memoranda required for Cabinet meetings and committee meetings. The secretary and at times one or two deputy secretaries attend the Cabinet meetings. At the close of the meeting, the secretary prepares the minutes (not detailed but summary statements of issues discussed and the conclusions). These are sent to the ministers, and one copy is retained for the official files. Legally, disclosure can be made only by the Queen, who acts upon the advice of the Prime Minister.

Within the secretariat, two offices are of sufficient importance to be mentioned. The Central Statistical Office and the Economic Section were created during World War II and have remained as part of the permanent organization of the secretariat. The Central Statistical Office has the primary responsibility of gathering and reporting statistical information for use by the Cabinet, the ministries, and other interested groups and persons. The Economic Section makes studies and reports on the progress and problems of the British economy.

The Cabinet also makes use of committees. The number of committees varies with the Cabinet in power and the problems that arise. Committees may be standing or *ad hoc,* the former to handle more or less permanent problems and the latter to handle transient problems. There is no formal committee system. The committees function like the Cabinet, and a member of the secretariat is assigned to be the secretary for the committee. Committees perform two functions: they discuss and report on problems to be decided upon by the Cabinet, and they actually decide matters delegated to them by the Cabinet.

The Cabinet is in a sense an extension of Parliament. The great majority of the Cabinet members will be members of the House of Commons. Such a situation has resulted in a valid question; namely, if too many of the leaders of the majority party are in ministerial positions, does this not weaken parliamentary control of the executive? The ministers are expected to support governmental policy under the idea of collective responsibility. The seriousness of the problem is increased by the fact that in addition to ministers, a number of parliamentary undersecretaries are also members of the House of Commons. The question has been the subject of parliamentary inquiry. At present, the rule is that at least three ministers in addition to the Lord Chancellor must be members of the House of Lords. The only prescription for the House of Commons is that no more than twenty undersecretaries may be members of Commons. The possibilities of arbitrary action are limited by the accepted "rules of the game" and by the fact that the Cabinet knows it must keep the party together. The circle is completed by the knowledge that election returns favorable to the party depend upon public reaction to Cabinet actions.

In addition to membership in Parliament, what other qualifications are required of a Cabinet member? Honesty and integrity are obvious requirements. Experience in Parliament and in administration are desirable.

Party loyalty is a definite consideration. Ability to develop new ideas, to compromise, and to lead is necessary. These are political requirements. Various Cabinets have adopted rules to govern such questions as ministers engaging in private law practice, holding directorships in companies, and similar situations. These "rules of obligation," as they were called by Mr. Asquith, generally prohibit a minister from continuing in private business relationships if such action produces a conflict of interest between public and private affairs.

The Cabinet under the leadership of the Prime Minister constitutes the working executive. Under the Cabinet is the administration, and it is the administration that is considered next.

SELECTED READING

Carter, B. C. *The Office of Prime Minister.* Princeton, N.J.: Princeton University Press, 1956.

Hankey, Lord. *Diplomacy by Conference.* New York: G. P. Putnam's Sons, Inc., 1946.

Jennings, Sir Ivor. *Cabinet Government.* 3d ed. Cambridge: Cambridge University Press, 1959.

Keith, A. B. *The British Cabinet System.* 2d ed. London: Stevens & Sons, Ltd., 1952.

Wheare, K. C. *Government by Committee.* Fair Lawn, N.J.: Oxford University Press, 1955.

7

Administration

The British administrative system almost defies description. The labyrinth of administrative powers and responsibilities is equaled only by the maze of offices, ministries, departments, boards, commissions, and committees. There are hundreds of authorities, and each exercises an administrative function with either complete autonomy or some degree of autonomy.

Administration in Britain is a typical product of English historical growth; custom, practice, statutes, and personal whim have all contributed to its multiheaded character. A unified, comprehensive plan of organization does not exist. Yet some unifying force or factor must exist if a government is to execute successfully its laws and policies. The "unity" of the British system develops from the political control of the Cabinet over its ministers and from the Cabinet's direct access to the legislative authority of Parliament. The Cabinet's role in administration will become more apparent as we discuss the basic administrative problems, i.e., organization, coordination, personnel, legislation, adjudication, and devolution.

ADMINISTRATIVE ORGANIZATION

Administrative agencies in Britain may be classified as ministries or single-headed departments, boards and commissions, and government corporations. This classification does not mean that each of these types is independent or unrelated to each other. A corporation may be found within a ministry, or a board may actually function as a single-headed ministry. The classification merely serves as an approach to the study of the British system.

As the name implies, a single-headed agency is one that is the responsibility of a single individual. Examples of such ministries or Departments of State, as they are sometimes designated, are the Ministries of Home Affairs, Treasury (although technically the Treasury is headed by a board), Commonwealth Relations, and Foreign Affairs. The number varies in accordance with the needs of the time and the desires of the Prime Minister. The Prime Minister has the authority to transfer ministers from one ministry to another and to abolish and create ministries.

These ministries have a varied internal structure but some generalization is permissible. The minister, who is appointed by the Prime Minister, is responsible for the operation of his ministry. He is directly accountable to the Cabinet and indirectly accountable to Parliament via the Cabinet's relationship with Parliament. The minister has a political staff composed of a private secretariat and a parliamentary secretary who is a junior minister. There may be other ministers who head subordinate departments or divisions within the ministry. Each ministry has a career civil servant who is known as the permanent secretary. The primary duties of the permanent secretary are to inform the minister of the operation of the department and to advise him in the making of top-level decisions. Theoretically, all subdivisions and their heads report to the permanent secretary; but in practice some may have direct access to the minister.

Below the office of the permanent secretary, the ministry is divided and subdivided into units for the performance of specific tasks (Figure 7–1). The names of these units and subunits do not follow a standard nomenclature. Each is headed by a responsible career officer, usually with the title of deputy or assistant secretary. Each subunit is under the direction of an officer responsible to the deputy or assistant secretary. In this way, a hierarchy of command is achieved within the ministry. This chain of command is not perfect inasmuch as both formalized and informal deviations occur. Furthermore, the Treasury's control over fiscal administration tends toward the establishment of a multiple chain of command. A multiple chain of command normally exists whenever a single officer is responsible to two or more superiors. The major problem in multiple chains is that conflict may develop between orders from the two superiors.

In addition to ministries, the British administrative system makes use of autonomous or semiautonomous bodies. These agencies are autonomous to the degree that they are independent of ministries and ministerial control. Such agencies are similar to our own government corporations and independent boards and commissions. Examples are numerous; for instance, there are the National Coal Board, the British Broadcasting Corporation, and the British Overseas Airways Corporation. The growth of these independent authorities has been accelerated with the advent of nationalization in Britain. Some of these agencies are within ministries and subject to ministerial control. Exceptions occur in those matters in which

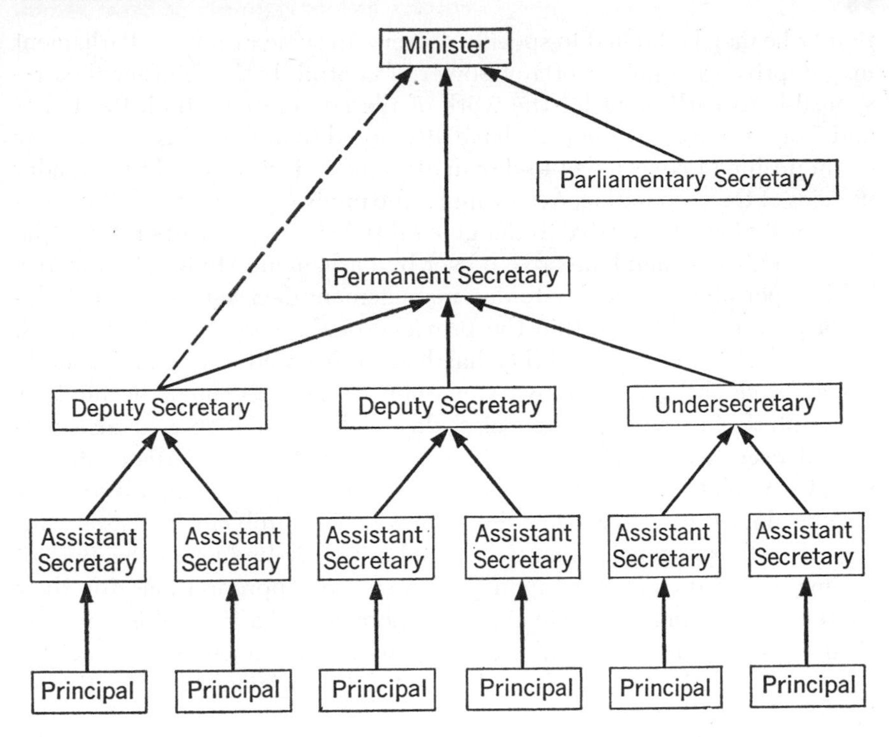

Figure 7–1. Organization of a ministry.

Parliament has clearly given the agency power to act without the consent of a minister. Other agencies are within a ministry in terms of organization but are independent in terms of operation and control. Most of these agencies have been created as government corporations. The corporate device is useful for agencies of a business-like nature, since government corporations are usually endowed with the legal characteristics of a private corporation. Thus, the government corporation may sue and be sued without prior consent; it may buy and sell property and securities; it may borrow and possess assets and liabilities. The government corporation has no more power than the government wishes to give it, but normally it has greater freedom of action than an ordinary ministry.

The freedom of action of these independent authorities has been the subject of considerable discussion in Britain. To whom and how are they responsible? The obvious answer is that they are responsible to Parliament. Only an indefinite answer may be given as to how they are responsible to Parliament. Most of the boards of directors of the corporations are appointed by either the Prime Minister or an appropriate minister. The minister may be given the power of general direction of the corporation or he may be limited to specific powers. In some instances, Parliament may deprive the minister of any power of control. Is the minister then responsible to Parliament for the work of the corporation? Both the Labor and Conservative governments have attempted to answer this question by distinguishing between day-to-day management decisions and the broader policies of the corporation. Accordingly, the minister must answer the questions in Parliament relative to the general policies of the corporation if he has been given general directive power by Parliament. He is not, however, held responsible for the day-to-day management decisions, since such decisions are considered within the province of the corporation's directors.

This division of responsibility has had both an adverse and favorable effect. From the administrative viewpoint, it has prevented the minister from interfering with the agencies' day-to-day operation and also prevented excessive criticism from individual members of Parliament. Adversely, much of the work of the agencies is beyond Parliament's scrutiny via the device of questioning the minister. The problem increases with regard to those agencies that do not submit their budget in the Budget Estimate and do not rely upon parliamentary appropriations for their continued operation. In the final analysis, however, Parliament is supreme. If an independent agency abuses its powers, Parliament may enact restrictive legislation as readily as it enacted the original authorization of independence.

The internal organization of autonomous agencies is quite variable. Some are highly centralized and others decentralized. The common form of decentralization is organization upon a regional or territorial basis.

In addition to the ministries and government corporations, the British administrative system has a number of miscellaneous agencies that defy classification. Advisory councils and "working bodies" are frequently employed in the nationalized industries, and they may also be found in ministerial organization. A few essentially private professional societies such as the Law Society and the Pharmaceutical Society discharge statutory administrative duties. There are a number of administrative tribunals such as the Patents Appeal Tribunal that perform quasi-judicial functions but are independent of the regular administrative hierarchy.

In many ways British administration resembles American administration. Both are products of trial-and-error evolution. Both have developed with little adherence to administrative principles. Neither system has a coherent pattern of responsibility and control.

ADMINISTRATIVE COORDINATION

Administrative agencies are responsible to political officers who may or may not be members of the Cabinet. The Cabinet, in turn, is responsible to Parliament for the administrative agencies. But how may a degree of unity be achieved in the large bureaucratic structure of the modern administrative state? This question is as valid for the United States as it is for Great Britain. On the basis of trial and error and expediency, a number of devices have been developed in Britain to aid in the harmonious operation of administrative agencies.

The Prime Minister functions as a coordinating agent. The Cabinet and its committees frequently resolve administrative conflicts. The head of a ministry serves as a unifying force within his department.

In addition to these methods, the British make extensive use of the Treasury as the major coordinating body. The Treasury performs the usual treasury functions comparable to the United States Treasury Department. But in order to visualize the scope of the British Treasury, it would be necessary to add the United States Bureau of the Budget and part of the United States Civil Service Commission. In Britain the Treasury acts as a coordinator in several ways.

First, the Treasury has the responsibility of budget preparation and execution. To fulfill these functions, it has the authority to eliminate the overlapping and duplication of functions in the line departments. The Treasury is better suited than any other administrative agency to gain an over-all view of the entire administration.

Second, the Treasury has an Organization and Methods Division that functions as an efficiency staff to suggest improvements in the methods and techniques of the operating departments.

Finally, the permanent secretary of the Treasury is also the head of the civil service. Thus, the Treasury has control over personnel and personnel policies and can use this control to promote administrative coordination.

Interdepartmental committees are used as another coordinating device. Winston Churchill is reported to have remarked that administrative committees in Britain breed faster than Australian rabbits. Regardless of the accuracy or the authenticity of the remark, coordination has been attempted by the committee technique. These committees operate both at the departmental and subdepartmental levels. Composed of ministers, junior ministers, or permanent civil servants, they meet to discuss mutual problems and to determine solutions that will prevent duplication and conflict

THE CIVIL SERVICE

Historically, the civil service was dominated by the patronage concept so familiar to Americans. Unlike the American spoils system, however, the British civil servant, once politically appointed, could expect a lifetime employment. Reform began in 1853 with the publication of the *Trevelyan-Northcote Report,* which recommended the selection of civil servants by competitive examination. In 1855 the reform idea was partially introduced, and by 1870 selection by open competition was permanently established in almost all departments.

A Civil Service Commission performs the recruitment, examination, and certification functions. The permanent secretary of the Treasury is the head of the civil service. He is responsible for those aspects of the personnel program that are not performed by the Civil Service Commission. A special Treasury section, the Establishments Department, is charged with the management of the civil service. The Establishments Department works closely with an establishment and organization officer in each government department. The Treasury also represents the government on the National Whitley Council (a joint council of civil servants and officials that considers personnel problems) and performs the same role with regard to wage and salary claims before the Arbitration Tribunal.

The British civil service is divided into general or Treasury classes; a scientific or professional service; and, in some cases, a number of departmental classes. The Treasury classes are (1) the administrative class, (2) the executive class, (3) the clerical class, (4) the clerical assistants, and (5) the typing and manipulative class.

The administrative class is a small group of officials who hold the most important permanent positions. The class is recruited primarily from university graduates between the ages of twenty and a half and twenty-four by means of stiff competitive examinations. Only about 100 candidates are appointed yearly. There is a two-year probationary period, and advancement is dependent upon industry and talent. Within the administrative class are the grades of assistant principal, principal, assistant secretary, undersecretary, deputy secretary, and permanent secretary. Training is on-the-job training in most cases. Rotation from department to department is part of the training program. Theoretically, a member of the administrative class is a generalist and is capable of performing in any department. For years, the administrative class was drawn almost exclusively from the upper classes of British society, and recruitment was outside of the civil service. Today, a slight modification has taken place. As the middle and lower classes gain university training, they become eligible for the administrative-class competition. Also, limited promotion from the ranks of the executive and the scientific classes is now possible.

The executive class is the middle management group who occupy positions of responsibility just below those held by the small administrative class. The executive class is recruited by open competitive examinations held for young persons between the ages of seventeen and a half and eighteen and a half, for university graduates, for those who are completing their military service, and for former regular service people below the age of forty-five.

The clerical class is a large class composed of two main grades; the clerical officer and the higher clerical officer. Persons in this class do not have a great deal of administrative responsibility, but they perform the great bulk of the governmental paper work. The clericals are recruited in open examinations from persons between the ages of sixteen and a half and seventeen and a half and for ex-service people below the age of fifty. Normally, the examinations are written for the level of a person possessing at least four years of secondary education.

The clerical assistants perform routine office tasks. The class is limited to women and is recruited between the ages of fifteen and sixteen. The minimum education requirement is an elementary education.

The typist class is reserved for women between the ages of eighteen and thirty-three. It is divided into a number of grades dependent upon the nature of the stenographic work performed. The manipulative class performs manipulative tasks other than typing and shorthand.

The scientific service was created in 1945 to recognize the professional classes (lawyers, accountants, engineers, medical officers, and others) as a distinct part of the civil service. The scientific service is divided into grades, and recruitment is largely by a review of the candidate's record and by oral interview.

We have noted that personnel policies are a function of the Treasury. To assist and advise the Treasury and the individual ministries, a series of councils were established in 1921. These councils are the departmental and national Whitley Councils. The Whitley Councils are composed of equal representation from the government and the civil servants. They concern themselves with personnel problems that affect civil servants below the administrative class. Functions of the Whitley Councils are to (1) foster further education and training, (2) improve office organization, (3) utilize staff ideas and experience, (4) include the staff in consideration of conditions of employment such as hours and wages, and (5) help prepare basic civil service legislation. These functions are advisory; but, since the government is represented, the proposals of the Councils often become operative. The departmental Whitley Councils vary in influence on personnel policy decisions. The National Council has been an important factor in solving most of the problems of the civil service.

Civil servants may organize into unions; and, except for the years 1927–1946, these civil service unions may affiliate with private enterprise unions. Strikes are not forbidden, but any civil servant who participates in a strike is viewed as having refused to perform his duties and may be punished if the government chooses to do so.

Political neutrality of the civil servant has been an accepted part of the British system. The Act of Settlement of 1701 prohibited parliamentary membership to anyone who held a place of profit under the Crown.

Treasury and departmental rules have interpreted and enforced the idea of the Act of Settlement. Lower civil servants and some political theorists have long insisted that such restrictions were a denial of the political rights of the civil servant. In 1949, a Treasury Committee (the committee membership included private citizens) proposed that all civil servants in the typing class or above should not be allowed parliamentary candidature. Civil servants below the typing class (manipulative and industrial grades) should be allowed to be candidates for Parliament with reinstatement provisions. The right to hold local public office was to be liberalized for all classes. The proposals of the Treasury Committee were adopted and are still in effect. The British believe in political neutrality and do not consider a limited loss of political rights too great a price to pay in order to achieve it.

The personnel policies are designed to promote a career service integrated with the educational system. The service is noted for its honesty, integrity, and responsiveness to the demands of the ministers and parliament. Scandals are rarer than among American administrative personnel; and when they do occur, they are usually of a minor variety.

ADMINISTRATIVE LEGISLATION

That the modern state is a public service state is commonplace knowledge. The welfare state necessitates an expansion of governmental authority, and the repository of this increased governmental power is the executive branch of government. The source of most of this expanded power in Britain has been Parliament and its passage of delegated authority to the executive branch. "Delegated legislation" is a term used to describe the rules, regulations, and orders that are issued by the government as Orders in Council or as ministerial orders. These rules and orders amplify and apply statutes passed by Parliament. Since 1946, (the Statutory Instruments Act) the term "statutory instrument" is employed to cover the variously named delegated legislation. Delegated legislation has resulted in a vast expansion of administrative law. Almost any volume of British statutes will reveal innumerable examples of delegation. In addition, the Cabinet may issue Orders in Council and other rules and regulations based on the royal prerogatives.

The extent of delegated authority by each particular statute may be limited or virtually unlimited. For example, the British Air Navigation Act of 1947 provides that ". . . His Majesty may by Order in Council make such provisions as appears to Him to be requisite or expedient (a) for carrying out the Chicago Convention [Convention on International Civil Aviation, Chicago, Illinois, 1944] . . . (b) generally for regulating air navigation."[1] The statute does provide standards for His Majesty, but

[1] 10 and 11 George VI, c. 18.

these do not deny the broad grant of authority. Other statutes may delineate specific limitations upon the grant of authority. For example, The Summer Time Act, 1947, provides that an Order in Council may determine the beginning and ending dates for summertime, but that during this period summertime shall be two hours in advance of Greenwich mean time.[2] Although rarely used today, some statutes have what is termed the "Henry VIII clause" (named after the absolutist tendencies of Henry VIII). These clauses empower the executive branch to modify the provisions of the enabling act if it is felt necessary to implement the act.

Parliamentary control over delegated legislation is almost as varied as the extent of the power granted. The Summer Time Act, 1947, provided that Orders in Council became effective only after confirmation by Parliament. Other statutory instruments are effective upon issuance but may be annulled by either House within a specified period of time. Statutory instruments are laid before the Select Committee on Statutory Instruments, and the Committee may call Parliament's attention to any irregularity.

Unless Parliament has specifically provided otherwise, statutory instruments are reviewable by the courts. The British courts have no power of judicial review as in America, but they do have the power to declare a statutory instrument *ultra vires* (outside or beyond the authority granted). The courts have no power to pass upon the reasonableness of the administrative legislation.

Eminent British jurists have protested against the enlargement of administrative authority without an accompanying enlargement of legislative and court control. Lord Hewart in the *New Despotism* (1929) may be cited as one of the leading writers among the critics of administrative legislation. The criticism did achieve the appointment of a Committee on Ministers' Powers in 1929. The Committee (often referred to as the Donoughmore Committee) published its report in 1932. The report is still the outstanding study of the problem of delegated legislation. The Committee recognized the need for delegated legislation and in effect stated that the critics were alarmists. However, the Committee noted the grave dangers inherent in delegated legislation, especially what the Committee termed "exceptional grants of authority" (the power to impose taxation, the power to amend the enabling act, and similar types). The recommendations of the Committee have been accepted in part by both the executive and parliamentary branches.

ADMINISTRATIVE ADJUDICATION

Administrative adjudication refers to the administrative agent's power to judge the rightness of an administrative act if an individual or group has questioned the administrative decision. Instead of the affected party

[2] 10 and 11 George VI, c. 17.

taking his case to a regular court, he appeals to some higher level within the administration. This type of adjudication has developed rapidly since the beginning of the century. The areas of public health, social insurance, utility regulation, and town and country planning constitute the principal areas in which an extensive use of administrative adjudication is found.

Parliament bestows the power to adjudicate to ministers; administrative tribunals under a minister; or, in certain cases, to an independent administrative tribunal. Provisions may be made for appeal to a higher administrative officer or tribunal, or to the regular courts. In some instances, no appeal provision is provided; in which case, the decision of the minister or tribunal is final. For example, the Gas Act, 1948, which established the nationalized gas industry, created a Gas Arbitration Tribunal (appointed by the Lord Chancellor) to determine questions or disputes. The arbitration tribunal was a court of record. The Act provided that certain rules of procedure were to be followed and that the tribunal's findings were appealable to the Court of Appeal on questions of law and in certain situations on questions of fact. A similar situation is found in the Veterinary Surgeons Act, 1948, in which the Disciplinary Committee (five members, one of whom is named by the government) of the Council of the Royal College of Veterinary Surgeons is given the powers of suspension and removal of names from the register of licensed veterinarians. The Act provides for appeal to the High Court by the aggrieved individual. However, the Town and Country Planning Act, 1947, provides that questions of compensation may be brought before the Central Land Board. Appeals may be made from the Central Land Board to the minister, whose decision is final.

The agencies of administrative justice do not make use of all regular court procedures and are marked by more informality than the regular courts. Critics have charged that personal liberties have been violated by the development of administrative adjudication and that these personal liberties are no longer protected by the concepts of natural justice as developed and applied by the regular courts. Complaint is made that the defendant's rights of notice, knowledge of charges, right to counsel, and right to proper hearings are violated. Many examples of arbitrary action have been cited by the critics.[3] The Donoughmore Report dismissed the charge of despotism by the administrative tribunals. It did note that safeguards should be provided, such as the use of plural bodies instead of a single ministerial officer, and that questions of law should be appealable to the regular courts. Much has been done in recent years to prevent arbitrary action, but the question is still the subject of debate.

[3] See Bernard Schwartz, *Law and the Executive in Britain* (New York: New York University Press, 1949); C. K. Allen, *Law and Orders* (London: Stevens & Sons, Ltd., 1945).

The courts' role when appeal is allowed is not sufficiently clear. The courts may declare the administrative legislation *ultra vires* and in this way quash the decision of the tribunal. Or, if the tribunal has not followed the procedures required in the enabling act or the rules based upon the act, the decision of the tribunal is quashed on the ground of procedural *ultra vires*. But what of the twilight zone in which the statute has provided no procedural provisions or the language of the grant of authority is so general that precise terms of reference do not exist? The courts have wavered in their position. At one extreme, the courts have quashed administrative decisions on the grounds that the decisions and the procedures used in reaching the decision violated natural justice. At the other extreme, the courts have stated essentially that they have no right to dictate to a tribunal on procedure if Parliament has made no provisions. Between these extremes, most cases have been decided.

Administrative adjudication is necessary in the modern state. The question is one of organization to perform the task both democratically and efficiently. Several countries have established a system of administrative courts to hear cases that arise out of administrative decisions. Britain and America have resisted the establishment of a separate court system. The result is an exceedingly piecemeal approach to adjudicatory organization and the existence of areas of uncertainty in regard to appeal to the regular court system.

DEVOLUTION

Although Britain is a unitary state, British government has had to recognize the differences in the historic environments of the cultural areas within Great Britain. As in most political developments in Britain, the problem of devolution has been treated in a pragmatic, evolutionary manner.[4] The central government has adopted policies as the demand and need became urgent. No over-all plan has been accepted, although a Conference on Devolution (1920) presented general schemes in both a majority and minority report.

Since England first conquered Ireland in the twelfth century, antagonism early developed. The Act of Union of 1800 attempted a solution to the relationship, but in 1921 Ireland (except for Northern Ireland) gained commonwealth status. It ceased to be a member of the Commonwealth in 1949 and became the independent state of Eire. Northern Ireland (six counties) remained a part of the United Kingdom. Home Rule for Northern Ireland was approved by Parliament in 1914, but its implementa-

[4] Devolution means the delegation of authority downward. As used in Britain, it refers to the delegation of authority to regional units from the central government. Most devolution has been administrative and, thus, included in this chapter.

tion was delayed until after World War I. Northern Ireland has its own bicameral parliament and administration. The Northern Ireland Parliament has jurisdiction over most domestic policies with the provision that its legislation must not conflict with the legislation extended to Northern Ireland by the British Parliament. Certain activities, i.e., judiciary, postal services, income taxation, and others, are reserved for the Parliament in London.

From the time of the Act of Union in 1707, Scotland retained its own established church, legal system, educational institutions, and local government. Unlike Northern Ireland, Scotland has no separate legislature; but the British Parliament usually passes separate bills on a particular subject—a bill for England and Wales and a bill for Scotland. Legislative bills related to Scotland are examined by the standing Scottish committee in the House of Commons. Although this is not legislative devolution, the system does allow for the recognition of differences between the areas.

Devolution for Scotland has had its greatest development in administration. In 1885, a Secretary for Scotland was established. This position was enhanced in 1926 when the Secretary became a Secretary of State for Scotland. The Secretary of State for Scotland is responsible for the general administration of the statutes as they pertain to Scotland. The administrative offices are located in Edinburgh with only a small staff, known as the Scottish Office, maintained in London. Directly responsible to the Scottish Secretary of State are four major administrative departments: Home, Health, Agriculture, and Education. These departments perform the day-to-day execution of national statutes. The Scottish Home Department's areas of jurisdiction include a variety of functions, such as police, administration of prisons, legal aid services, fire and civil defense, local government, fisheries, and highways. The Department of Health is not only responsible for the administration of the national health insurance program but also administers the central government's programs in town and country planning, housing, and the development of new towns. The Education Department's major function is defined by its name. The Education Department also has control over the Royal Scottish Museum. The Agriculture Department administers all laws related to Scottish agriculture.

In addition to the major departments for Scottish administration, the Lord Advocate's Department and the Crown Office aid in drafting Scottish legislation, supervise the court system, and provide the prosecution in criminal proceedings. Other Scottish departments or offices with varying relationships with the Scottish Secretary of State include the Scottish Information Office, the Scottish Record Office, and the Department of Registers for Scotland. Central ministries have established special field offices in Scotland under controllers to administer their functions in keeping with Scottish needs.

Wales is the third principal region in the United Kingdom that differs from the original England. The central government has never recognized the need for as much devolution for Wales as it has for Northern Ireland and Scotland. In 1957, a Minister of State for Welsh Affairs was appointed with offices in Wales, and a Minister of Welsh Affairs continues within the London government. Those men are not responsible for administration as is the Secretary of State for Scotland but serve more as coordinators and advisers on Welsh affairs. A little time is allotted in the House of Commons for debate and questions upon Welsh matters, but there is no special Welsh committee.

Both in Scotland and Wales, demands are made for more devolution. The Scottish Nationalist party and the Welsh Nationalist party are the most vocal in this demand. Some of these groups advocate an extreme and desire Commonwealth status. Others would like to have a federal system adopted, and still others simply want greater autonomy within the existing pattern. This demand for more autonomy is not confined to the ardent nationalists but may be heard in almost any group when the question arises.

Both major political parties have agreed to more autonomy in principle if not in fact. Given the propensity of British government to evolve solutions to recurring problems, more devolution may well take place.

SELECTED READING

BRIDGES, SIR EDWARD. *Treasury Control.* London: University of London Press, 1950.
CAMPBELL, G. A. *The Civil Service in Britain.* Baltimore: Penguin Books, Inc., 1955.
CHESTER, D. N., *et al. The Organization of British Central Government, 1914–1956.* London: George Allen & Unwin, Ltd., 1957.
GLADDEN, E. N. *The Civil Service.* London: Staples Press, Ltd., 1948.
ROBSON, W. A. (ed.). *Problems of Nationalized Industry.* Fair Lawn, N.J.: Oxford University Press, 1952.

8

Local Government and Administration

Alexis de Tocqueville wrote that democratic governments arrive at centralization by instinct and only by reflection do they arrive at their local institutions. Ever prideful of the vitality of local government, the British have reached de Tocqueville's point of reflection. Not since the nineteenth century has so much concern been expressed over the fate of local government; and, interestingly enough, many of the current problems are analogous to those of the last century. Historically, local government has followed the national government; and, in so doing, it has fallen heir to many of the central government's headaches. The trend toward centralization of functions has increased on the local level as well as the national level. The increase of special authorities, joint commissions, and committees has made local government more and more complex. These facts coupled with the transfer of certain local functions to the national government and the increasing subsidization of local units by national grants have produced many reactions in Britain. Opponents of centralization and increased social services have charged that if the trends continue, local governments will become "picturesque anachronisms" or at the most mere agents of the national government. Others believe that if the local units are made more equal in area and population and if certain functional changes are effected, most of the immediate problems will be solved. In any event, a typically British approach has been made to the problem in the establishment of three Local Government Commissions. The Commissions (one each for England, Wales, and London) are required to make recommendations for changes in the pattern of local government structure and local government functions provided such changes will secure more effective and convenient local government. The Commissions are expected to take at least five years to complete their task.[1]

HISTORICAL BACKGROUND

Like Parliament, British local government can trace many of its features to Anglo-Saxon and medieval forms of organization. Historically, the oldest and perhaps most influential unit of government was that of the parish. The parish priest and his parishioners met together in the vestry to discuss both church and civil matters. Because of its democratic organization, the ancient parish meeting is often viewed as the direct forerunner of modern local government by elected councils. In addition to the parish, boroughs (towns with royal charters), counties (independent kingdoms before the Norman Conquest), sheriffs, and justices of the peace are examples of early civil institutions and offices that have survived to the present.

Until the latter part of the nineteenth century, local government suffered from a plethora of authorities. The Industrial Revolution had created new demands (better highways, street lighting, public health, sanitation improvement), but the existing local authorities were either unable or unwilling to shoulder these additional administrative responsibilities. Instead of consolidating these demands under the jurisdiction of one principal local authority, special units of local government were created to deal with each new need as it arose. The resulting confusion in functions and administrative areas led to the passage of the Local Government Act of 1888. This act together with the Acts of 1894 and 1899 established the basic system of local government that exists today. Sixty-two administrative counties were created, a majority of which broadly corresponded to the boundaries of the ancient counties. These new administrative counties were formed solely for purposes of local government; the ancient counties continued in existence primarily as areas for the administration of justice. In addition to the administrative counties, the Act of 1888 established units known as "county boroughs." County boroughs were towns with a population of 50,000, a figure deemed large enough at the time to entitle the inhabitants to administer their own local government services.[2] These county boroughs were given powers equal to those of the administrative county (in certain instances, the county boroughs' powers exceeded those of the county), and their independence of administrative county authority continues in the present. The subsequent local government acts divided the administrative counties into three types of districts: non-county bor-

[1] The England and Wales Commissions were established in 1958; the London Commission in 1957.

[2] Today, a town must have a population of at least 100,000 before Parliament will consider granting county borough status.

oughs (which are more easily identified by the term "municipal borough"), urban districts, and rural districts. Rural districts were further subdivided into approximately 11,000 parishes.

As may be surmised by the delineation of the county districts, the municipal borough is considered to be one step above the urban and rural districts. Incorporation as a municipal borough is accomplished by the grant of a royal charter from the Crown. A population of at least 20,000 is a prerequisite for incorporation. The distinction between a municipal borough and an urban district lies primarily in the traditional definition of the term "corporation." As a legal entity, the municipal borough may do any lawful act that is not prohibited by its charter; on the other hand, an urban district may do only what Parliament has given it power to do. At present, there are 318 municipal boroughs, 563 urban districts, 474 rural districts, and roughly 11,000 parishes.

ORGANIZATION

Before the passage of the reform acts, administration of local affairs was carried out by the sheriffs and justices of the peace in the historical counties and by a small group of men, known as the corporation, in the boroughs. The sheriffs and justices of the peace received their appointments from the Crown; the borough administrators were either elected by the enfranchised voters of the borough or, as frequently occurred, perpetuated themselves in office without regard to the wishes of the electorate.

By 1888, a majority of the British people had won the right to vote in parliamentary elections. This extension of suffrage broadened the democratic base of the House of Commons and manifested itself in the provisions of the Local Government Act of 1888. Parliament not only created new administrative areas, but it expressly provided that each unit be governed by a popularly elected council.[3] The councils in administrative counties, county boroughs, and municipal boroughs are composed of elected councilors and co-opted aldermen (co-option means that the councilors choose additional members to serve with them on the council). Usually about one-third of the council consists of aldermen. Councilors are elected for three-year terms and aldermen are co-opted for six-year terms. Councils of urban and rural districts and the parishes are all elected for three-year terms. In all cases, the councils choose a presiding officer called a chairman, mayor, or lord mayor. The presiding officer has no special power other than that of a chairman. In most cases, the presiding officer is the ceremonial head of the local unit.

To facilitate their work, most councils make use of a committee system. The committees are functional, i.e., committees for education, health, etc.

[3] Small rural parishes may meet in a parish meeting and not elect a council.

The committees operate much as committees do in American weak-mayor–strong-council cities. The committees develop basic policy, subject to council approval, and closely supervise the work of administrative officers in the area concerned. In many instances, the administrative officers look upon the committee members as their immediate superiors.

The principal administrative officer of the units is the clerk. Technically, the clerk is not a superior officer over other administrative officers; but he is looked upon as the coordinator by both the council and the other administrators. In many cases, the clerk is a solicitor and is the officer who has the best general knowledge of the actual powers of the local unit as granted by Parliament. The clerk keeps the minutes of the council and the council committees and is usually the person who knows what is going on in all council matters as well as within the departments.

The size and organizational structure of local administration depends upon the size of the area served as well as the level of the unit. Most larger units will have several departments such as health, education, and finance. The departments are headed by an officer who is responsible to the council and the council committee that supervises the particular function. The qualifications for administrative officers are often prescribed by the central ministry in charge of the over-all direction of the specific function. In certain cases, the central minister must approve the appointment. A National Joint Council for the Administrative, Professional and Technical Staffs of Local Authorities was established in 1945. The National Joint Council is composed of representatives of the local councils and representatives of the local civil service.[4] The National Joint Council made a number of general recommendations in regard to salaries and conditions of service for local personnel. These recommendations are referred to as the "scheme of service." The scheme of service has been adopted by most local councils. By order of the central government, all local units must provide pension plans for their civil servants. Although local civil servants do not have permanent tenure, dismissals for political reasons are rare. The quality of the civil service is high. Local government employs some one and a half million people (teachers included).

FINANCE

Local units now spend about 1.5 billion pounds (about 2.7 billion dollars) annually. Four sources of funds are available: income from rates; grants from the central government; fees, fines, and income from local governmental enterprises; and loans.

Rates are the English equivalent of the American real property tax.

[4] In addition to the National Joint Council, there are several other joint councils for special groups such as manual workers.

Unlike the American property tax, the rate is paid by the occupier of the property either as a rentor or as owner. The rate is a percentage levy on the annual rental value of the property. Rates account for about one-fourth of the local revenue. The levying and collection of rates is the responsibility of the county boroughs, municipal boroughs, urban districts, and rural districts. The administrative county and the parish receive their portion of the rates from the collection units. The actual assessment of property is done by officers of the national Board of Inland Revenue.

About 30 per cent of local revenues are provided by the central government. Most grants are of a general nature to the county boroughs and administrative counties and are intended to aid in the cost of specific services, i.e., education, police, town planning, and others. In addition to the general grants, the central government makes percentage grants for police and roads, unit grants for housing subsidies, and rate deficiency or equalization grants to the poorer rateable areas. Certain national license fees are turned over to the local units. These include the fees for pawn brokers, hawkers, and a few others.

Revenue from local fees, fines, and enterprises comprises about one-fourth of the total revenue. Most of this revenue is the result of municipal enterprises such as transportation, public housing, and water supplies. These enterprises are not operated for profit, and the revenue from them may or may not cover expenditures.

Loans, or in American usage, borrowing, are used extensively by local units to finance capital expenditures. Borrowing must be approved by the Minister of Housing and Local Government. The central government finances the Public Works Loan Board, which makes loans available to local governments. The councils may borrow by the issuance of stock on the stock exchange, or they may borrow from private sources.

FUNCTIONS

In a unitary government, the local units' functions are determined by the central government. The central authority may allow the local units extensive powers and functions, it may provide an area of freedom in choosing functions to perform, or it may narrowly define the powers.

Parliament has clearly designated certain functions to be performed by the local units and has allocated these functions among the levels of local government. In addition to the required functions, Parliament has granted permissive powers to the local units; the local unit may exercise its privilege to perform or not to perform the function. Finally, the local units may request by the instrument of the private bill a grant of a specific power from Parliament. In granting powers to the local areas, Parliament normally designates a ministry to whom the local areas are held accountable.

The functions performed by the local units are quite similar to the functions performed by American counties and municipalities. Protective services such as police, fire, and civil defense are a primary responsibility of local government. Educational, cultural, and recreational facilities; public housing, and many aspects of public health and welfare are important local functions. The usual activities of sewage, streets and roads, lighting, abatement of nuisances, sanitation, and the recording of vital statistics are as much a part of British local government as their counterpart in America. Local units may operate publicly owned enterprises such as water supply, markets, dock and harbor facilities, public transportation, public baths, and restaurants. The Town and Country Planning Acts delegate much of the responsibility for planning to the local councils.

CENTRAL CONTROL

The tendency toward central control of the local units has been strong in Britain in the present century. This control has not been the result of a deliberate effort to diminish the importance of local government. The increased complexity and scope of government functions, the need for greater central financial support, and the necessity of minimum uniform standards are the major explanations for greater national control.

The central government employs several techniques to accomplish its control function. These techniques are similar to those employed by American states over their counties and other units of local government.

Fiscal control is an obvious method used by the central government. Prior approval for local borrowing must be granted by the Minister of Housing and Local Government. The central government requires an audit of all financial records of the local units. In most instances, the auditors are appointed by the Minister of Housing and Local Government.

Before enactment, bylaws (local ordinances) must be submitted to the appropriate central minister for confirmation. Ministers often determine the standards of administration and have the power of inspection to insure compliance with the standards. These standards may establish the requisite qualifications of the personnel employed and may also stipulate ministerial approval of appointments.

Parliament has a further control over local government by its power to approve or reject private bills. In the passage of a private bill, Parliament may provide supervisory power to a central governmental department.

The national courts control local government in at least two ways. The courts have the power to declare a local act *ultra vires* if a suit is brought by an individual. Also, the regular courts may act to protect a citizen against arbitrary and unjust acts of administrative officers.

Finally, the central government exercises control through its power to determine what functions shall be performed by the local units. The central government may transfer a function of local government directly to itself. An example of this occurred during World War II when the National Fire Service was organized to assume the responsibilities and direction of the local fire departments.[5] Similarly, the Electricity Act of 1946 and the Gas Act of 1948 transferred municipally owned electricity and gas services to the appropriate public corporations of the central government. Sometimes a local function may be transferred to specially created authorities. An instance of this occurred with the passage of the National Health Service Act of 1946. This Act transferred the public hospitals of the local governments to the jurisdiction of new regional authorities. In other cases, the local units may be reduced to the status of agents for the performance of services administered by the central government.

THE GOVERNMENT OF LONDON

Local government in London differs from the rest of England and Wales by virtue of its position as the capital city and as the largest metropolitan area both in population and territory. An Administrative County of London was created by the Act of 1888, and its powers and duties were consolidated in the London Government Act of 1939. The London County Council is composed of 147 members (126 elected councilors and 21 aldermen) and is divided politically between the majority party and its opposition. The City Corporation and the metropolitan borough councils complete the formal administrative structure. The City (of London) Corporation has unique powers and duties and is in most respects independent of the London County Council.[6] The metropolitan borough councils are corporations comparable to the municipal boroughs outside of London. There are many special authorities, boards, and commissions within the London area; and it is not uncommon for the operations of these special bodies to extend well beyond the county of London.

SCOTTISH LOCAL GOVERNMENT

Scottish local government has been built upon medieval institutions. Burghs were created in the twelfth century as trading monopolies. Gradually the collection of local taxes and the performance of local services were entrusted to the burghers. In much the same way, the Crown extended local functions to the medieval sheriffdoms or to special committees of land owners within a sheriffdom.

[5] The Fire Services Act of 1947 dissolved the National Fire Service but returned the function only to counties and county boroughs. Thus, municipal boroughs and districts were eliminated as units for the administration of fire functions.

[6] Unlike the council of a county borough, the City Corporation is not an all-purpose authority. Some services, *e.g.*, education, within the city are administered by the London County Council.

The present system of local government was created by a series of Parliament acts from 1845 to 1929. In 1929, the Local Government (Scotland) Act was passed; and since that date, the structure of local government has been unchanged. The units of local government are 33 county councils, 198 town councils, and 199 district councils. Town councils are of three kinds: (a) city-counties of Edinburg, Glasgow, Aberdeen, and Dundee; (b) large burghs, i.e., cities over 20,000; and (c) small burghs, i.e., cities under 20,000.

County councils are composed of elected representatives of the rural areas of the counties and of representatives of the large and small burghs within the county. Representatives of the burghs are chosen by the burgh councils. County councilmen hold office for three years. The council selects from its membership a convener who is the presiding officer.

Town councilmen are elected from wards within the burgh for three-year terms; one-third retire each year. If the burgh is small, wards are not used and election to the council is at large.

District councils are composed of the members of the county council chosen from the rural areas within the district and of elected members from the district itself.

All councils are the governing bodies of their respective units of government. As in England and Wales, a committee system is employed to supervise the administration of local functions. Some committees such as education are required by statute; other council committees are voluntary. The councils have the power to appoint administrative officers with much the same central control as for England and Wales.

The functions of the local units are basically the same in Scotland as in England, although the distribution of the responsibility for functions varies. City-counties are all inclusive as are the English county boroughs. County councils share their responsibilities with the town councils. District councils are dependent upon county councils for grants of authority.

Central control of Scottish local government is a responsibility of the Secretary of State for Scotland and his major departments for Education, Home Affairs, Health, and Agriculture.

CONCLUSION

The most pressing problems of British local government today include the status and boundary extensions of local units, the increase in expenditures and search for additional revenues, the availability of private citizens who have both the time and knowledge to serve as elected councilors, and the problem of incentives (salaries and status) with regard to the recruitment of personnel in the local civil service.

These problems are easily recognized as being not unique to the British system. We, in the United States, face similar if not identical problems. Our metropolitan areas have difficulty in coordinating services and regularly seek boundary enlargements by annexation. Since the beginning of the century, local expenditures in America have increased several hundred per cent, principally because of the demand for new services and higher standards. Local revenues have not been able to keep up with expenditures, with the result that higher units of government (both state and national) have supplied both moneys and controls. As for personnel, the shortage of both voluntary and paid local government officials is readily acknowledged in the United States.

Many solutions have been offered in both countries. It as almost certain that the British will ultimately find a workable answer to most of their problems, the solution will not be one of extremes. The democratic traditions inherent in British local government are unlikely to be sacrificed; and, as in the past, the friendly cooperation of all units of government will continue.

SELECTED READING

Jackson, R. M. *The Machinery of Local Government.* New York: St. Martins Press, Inc., 1958.

Jackson, W. E. *Local Government in England and Wales.* Baltimore: Penguin Books, Inc., 1951.

Morrison, Herbert. *How London Is Governed.* London: Barrie Books, Ltd., 1949.

Smellie, K. B. *A History of Local Government.* London: George Allen & Unwin, Ltd., 1950.

Warren, J. H. *The English Local Government System.* London: George Allen & Unwin, Ltd., 1953.

9

The Judicial System

The British have long been proud of their judicial system. English courts and justices have played a significant role in the development of the constitutional monarchy and in the protection of the liberties of the citizen. The courts, as much as any institutional force, have perpetuated and implemented the supremacy of the rule of law.

The British legal system rests upon statutory law; equity law; common law; and, to a lesser degree, administrative law.[1] The oldest law is common law and it is judge-made law. From the reign of Henry I (1100–1135), the king's judges rode circuit throughout England. As they decided cases in each locality, the judges applied the same concept of law; and gradually a law "common" to the land developed. A decision in one case became a precedent for decisions in like cases. Students of law, in the Inns of Court, studied the decisions and precedents. From the particular cases, a common law developed that contained both civil and criminal law.

At times, an individual could not achieve redress or justice under common law. The law simply did not cover or protect the individual in certain matters. The person then sought a remedy from the king. The king, as the source of all justice, had the authority to grant equity (that which is fair) to the individual. At first, these petitions for equity were handled by the Chancellor, and then by the Court of Chancery. As the court made its decisions, a body of judge-made law developed, distinct from common law, to fill the gaps in the common law. This was and is the law of equity.

Neither common law nor equity, both based upon precedent, was fully able to provide satisfactory answers to all questions of government. The

[1] Scotland has a separate system of law derived primarily from Roman Law. The material presented above pertains to England and Wales, but much of it is applicable to Scotland as well.

king made or discovered law. Slowly the power of the king to make law was transferred to Parliament. Thus, the acts of Parliament became the chief source of statutory law. Today, statutory law has precedence over common law and equity. Yet common law is used to interpret statutory law, and statutory law is often based upon common-law principles.

Administrative law consists of the body of administrative rules and regulations made under delegated legislation or under the prerogative of the Crown. Quasi-judicial tribunals and high administrative officials interpret the myriad of administrative regulations (commonly referred to as statutory instruments). The decisions of these tribunals or ministers are normally either appealable or reviewable by the ordinary courts. Britain has not developed a separate court system for administrative law as have France, Italy, and Germany.

Out of common law, equity, and statute law, Britain has achieved a system of law designed to protect the individual in his relationship with other individuals and with his government. Certain characteristics of this legal system are essential if the rule of law is to prevail.

First, the court system and the judges are independent and free from control by either the legislature or the executive. The judges, except for the justices of the peace, are drawn from the barristers and are appointed for life (legally, during good behavior). Regular judges may not be members of the legislative or executive branches. The internal administration of the courts and the basic determination of the rules of procedure and evidence are left to the courts.

Second, the courts have control power over acts of the other two branches of government. Britain does not adhere to the idea of judicial review; and, thus, British judicial control is not as extensive as it is in America. In limited application, the courts may issue writs of mandamus, prohibition, and certiorari to compel or quash administrative action. Declaratory judgments may be rendered by the courts in regard to an administrative decision. The courts also have the power to declare an administrative action *ultra vires*. The use of *ultra vires* may be both substantive and procedural. The interpretative powers coupled with the high prestige of the judges and their decisions permit the courts a circumscribed control over the acts of the legislature and the executive branches.

Third, the British legal system accepts the innocence of the accused until guilt is proven. The burden of proof is upon the prosecution; and the accused is protected by a trial and decision in open court, the laws of evidence, and a right to counsel.

Finally, at least one appeal is available in a legal dispute upon questions of law; and in many kinds of disputes, an appeal is permitted upon questions of fact.

LEGAL ADMINISTRATION

Administration of the court system is divided among the Lord Chancellor, the Home Secretary, the Prime Minister, and committees of the judges.

The Prime Minister appoints the Lord Chancellor, the Lords of Appeal in Ordinary (the Law Lords of the House of Lords), and the Lords Justices of Appeal.

The Lord Chancellor appoints the justices of peace, the recorders, stipendiary magistrates, County Court judges, and the judges of the High Court of Justice. He shares jointly the administrative business of the Supreme Court of Judicature with the judges themselves.[2] The Lord Chancellor is a member of the Rule Committee of the Supreme Court, and he also appoints the Rule Committee of the County Court system. With the aid of advisory committees, the Lord Chancellor is responsible for making proposals for legal reforms.

The Home Secretary has administrative control over all Magistrate Courts, and he appoints the clerks of such courts. The Home Secretary is also responsible for the police systems in England and Wales.

COURT ORGANIZATION

The present system of courts is largely the product of the Judicature Act of 1873. Prior to the reform of 1873, the English court structure was extremely complicated and confused. The Act of 1873 produced a simplified court organization divided into civil and criminal courts (Figure 9–1).

The lowest civil court is the County Court. Over 400 County Courts are located in convenient cities throughout England and Wales. Sixty-nine judges travel circuit to conduct the courts in three sessions each year. A County Court judge must be a barrister with at least seven years of experience. Attached to each County Court is a recorder who is a qualified solicitor.[3] The County Court has general jurisdiction in common-law cases involving not more than £400. The court has specific jurisdiction over particular kinds of civil suits (rent restrictions, hire purchase agreements, and similar cases); and in such suits, there are no limits as to the amount of money involved. Appeals, usually on questions of law, go directly to the Court of Appeal. The recorder often attempts a settlement of a dis-

[2] The Supreme Court of Judicature is not an entity in the same sense as the United States Supreme Court. The High Court of Justice and the Court of Appeal compose the Supreme Court of Judicature, a general term used to refer to both courts.

[3] For an understanding of the differences between a barrister and a solicitor, see pages 105–6.

pute out of court and, in this way, reduces the number of cases actually tried in the court.

The High Court of Justice is the lower court of the Supreme Court of Judicature. The High Court is an original jurisdiction court divided into three divisions: The Queen's Bench; the Probate, Divorce, and Admiralty Division; and the Chancery.

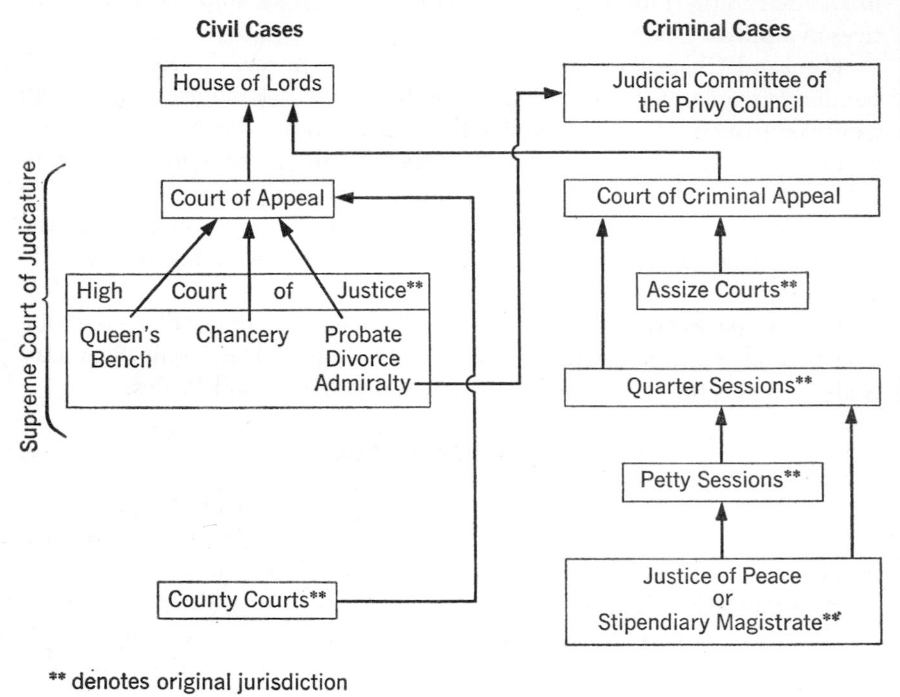

Figure 9–1. Organization of the courts.

The Queen's Bench is presided over by a Lord Chief Justice and is composed of the Lord Chief Justice and twenty-four puisne judges (judges without a special office of their own). The Queen's Bench is primarily a common-law court and hears cases involving sums of money over the limited amount permitted in County Courts. It also has limited appellate jurisdiction, primarily from administrative tribunals. Depending upon the nature of the case, the judges sit singly or in groups of three. Jury trials are available but their use is extremely limited.

The Probate, Divorce, and Admiralty Division is sometimes called the "court of wrecks" (wrecked wills, marriages, and ships). Its name indicates its jurisdiction. The court consists of a president and seven puisne judges.

The Chancery Division of the High Court is nominally headed by the Lord Chancellor, but for all practical purposes the court consists of seven puisne judges. The Chancery is basically an equity court and hears cases such as bankruptcy, partnerships, and administration of estates.

Technically, any of the three divisions of the High Court may take any of the cases; but they tend to stick to their own specialties. A judge of one division may sit in any other division.

Appeals from the High Court and the County Courts are heard by the Court of Appeal, the upper court of the Supreme Court of Judicature. Most appeals are on questions of law, although some questions of fact are appealable. The Court of Appeal is composed of the Master of the Rolls and eight Lords Justices of Appeal.[4] Usually, appeals are heard by three members of the court. The Appeal Court normally does not hold a trial but hears the record of the lower court. The Appeal Court may sustain the verdict of the lower court, sustain the verdict and change the amounts rewarded, or reverse the decision of the lower court.

Upon questions of law, and with the permission of either the Court of Appeal or the House of Lords, further appeal may be made to the House of Lords. When the House of Lords sits as a court, the case is heard by at least five of the Lords of Appeal in Ordinary.[5] The Lord Chancellor and any member of the House who has held "high judicial office" may sit with the Law Lords. The House of Lords is the highest civil court of appeal in Great Britain.

The criminal court system has both summary jurisdiction courts and regular trial courts. The lowest courts are the Justice of Peace and Stipendiary Magistrate Courts. Justices of the peace are usually unpaid laymen appointed by the Lord Chancellor. Stipendiary (paid) magistrates are used in place of justices of the peace in the larger towns and cities. Stipendiary magistrates usually have had legal training. Both Justice of Peace and Stipendiary Magistrates Courts have limited criminal jurisdiction. They also may determine bail in other offenses and bind over a suspect for trial in a higher court.

The Court of Petty Sessions consists of two, and not more than seven, justices of peace in a county. In London and certain other large cities, a Stipendiary Magistrate Court is used in place of the Petty Sessions Court. Minor offenses and less serious indictable offenses are tried in this court without recourse to a jury trial. The Petty Sessions Court also may indict

[4] There are a number of ex-officio members of the Court of Appeal, but they do not sit with the court.

[5] The term "in Ordinary" merely means in actual service or attendance. Such judges are paid professional judges with life peerages.

and bind over a suspect to a higher court. Most convictions are made in the Petty Sessions Court.

The lowest trial court is the Court of Quarter Sessions. Most of these courts, located in each county and in the major boroughs, hold sessions four times a year; although a few, such as in London and Lancashire, sit in continuous session. The courts are composed of the justices of peace in the county, presided over by a chairman or deputy chairman who must be a qualified barrister. A recorder (salaried barrister) presides as a single judge in most borough Quarter Sessions Courts. Quarter Sessions Courts use the jury trial and may try for any crime except the most serious (those subject to life imprisonment or the death sentence).

Assize Courts are held three times a year in the counties and large cities. The Assize Courts are under the jurisdiction of the Queen's Bench division of the High Court of Justice. Judges of the Queen's Bench travel circuit to hold the Assize Court. While usually a criminal court, the Assize Courts may try a civil case referred to it by the Queen's Bench. Any indictable offense may be tried in the Assize Court. Jury trial is used.

The primary criminal appeal court is the Court of Criminal Appeal. It consists of the Lord Chief Justice and a number of judges from the Queen' Bench. Three judges usually hear the appeal; no jury is employed. Appeal may be brought on a point of law that has been approved by the lower court; on any other grounds, the Criminal Appeal Court must give its consent to hear the case.

Rarely, and only with the permission of the Attorney-General, may appeal from the Court of Criminal Appeal on questions of law be taken to the House of Lords. The Attorney-General must certify that an important legal question is involved.

In addition to the general courts, a number of special courts have been created. Courts such as the Central Criminal Court (Old Bailey) in London and the Crown Courts in Liverpool and Manchester act in lieu of an Assize Court in those areas. In civil cases, the County Courts are supplemented by the City of London Court, the Liverpool Court of Passage, and a few other medieval courts still in existence. Coroner's Courts are held upon the decision of the coroner to hold an inquest in regard to the cause of death of an individual. The coroner may also hold inquests with a jury to determine cases of treasure-trove.

A number of justices selected from the personnel of the Petty Sessional and Magistrate Courts sit as Juvenile Courts in England and Wales. When sitting as a Juvenile Court, the number of justices is restricted to three, and both sexes must be represented. Similarly, Domestic Proceedings Courts are subject to the same limitations as those of the Juvenile Courts.

A unique court in Britain is the Judicial Committee of the Privy Council. At present the Judicial Committee may hear appeals on a limited variety of cases from the legal systems of New Zealand, Australia (dependencies included), Ceylon, Malaya, and all dependent territories of the United Kingdom. The kind of legal problem appealable is determined by statutes, Orders in Council, or by special leave of the Monarch in Council. When the Judicial Committee acts as a court, at least three or five members (depending upon the nature of the case) must sit and additional members may do so. Only certain qualified persons are invited by the Lord Chancellor to participate in the judicial proceedings. Among the qualified are the Lord Chancellor, the Law Lords, ex-Lord Chancellors, Lords Justices of Appeal, and others of high judicial experience.

CRIMINAL COURT PROCEDURE

Criminal charges against an individual may be made by a private citizen, police officer, a public prosecutor, or by a government official in the administrative services. Police officers and administrative officials make the most charges. Alleged offenses may be tried summarily (without a jury) or tried before a jury. The lines of demarcation between summary and indictable (jury) cases are not precisely drawn and some overlapping exists. Usually, petty cases, i.e., small thefts, violations of traffic laws, and similar cases, are tried by summary courts. If the offense is punishable by more than three months' imprisonment, the accused may demand a jury trial or he may choose a summary trial. A third category of cases may be tried in either summary courts or jury courts dependent either upon the wishes of the defendant or the decision of the magistrates of the summary courts. Serious crimes must be tried in jury courts.

Most cases start with a charge brought in a summary court (Justice of Peace, Magistrate, or Petty Sessions). The accused is notified of the charge and is requested to appear by summons. Failure to appear may result in the court's issuance of a warrant for arrest.[6] In many cases, an arrest has been made beforehand; and the accused is brought before the summary court out of custody. If the accused is held in custody, he must be informed of the reason; if he has not been informed, he may apply for a writ of habeas corpus to force the giving of charges.

In summary cases as well as in jury cases, the accused has the right to counsel. The substance of the charge is stated and the defendant may plead guilty. If this is the plea, the prosecutor summarizes the case, and the defendant may address the court and present witnesses in his behalf. Next, the court pronounces the sentence. If the plea of the accused is not guilty, then the summary trial continues with both the prosecution and the defense having the right to call witnesses. Both sides to the case may

[6] In minor cases, such as traffic violations, appearance of the accused is not required; payment of the fine by mail is easier.

cross-examine witnesses. Rules of evidence and procedure are supposed to be followed and are designed primarily for the protection of the defense. After the judge or judges hear the presentation by both sides, the judges usually retire to their chambers to consider the case. The judges may acquit the accused or find him guilty. If guilty, the sentence is pronounced. About 95 per cent of all convictions are made in summary courts.

If the case is indictable, the summary court holds a preliminary hearing to determine if the charges warrant a trial. The preliminary hearing takes the place of the grand jury used in many states and by the federal government in the United States. Witnesses for the prosecution give statements (depositions); and the accused may, if he chooses, give evidence and call witnesses. The court then decides if the accused should be committed for trial.

During the time interval between the preliminary hearing and the trial, the accused may be kept in custody or released upon a "recognizance" with or without bail. The law provides that bail must not be excessive. If bail is refused by the court or if the defendant believes the bail excessive, he has the right to apply to a judge of the High Court of Justice for relief. Little use is made of this protection.

Persons committed for jury trial are actually indicted by the clerk of the trial court. The person is committed either to a Quarter Sessions Court or an Assize Court. Determination of which court will hold trial depends upon the nature of the alleged crime (for example, offenses involving either life imprisonment or death must go to the Assize Court) and upon the decision of the summary judges. The procedure followed in a jury trial is similar to that found in a summary trial. The judge sums up the evidence as presented; the jury decides the question of guilt, and the judge pronounces sentence.

Appeal from summary courts may be made in two ways. Both the prosecution and the defense may appeal a case on a question of law to the High Court by the process of "case stated," in which the High Court (three judges) interprets the law and then orders the summary court to apply its interpretation. Appeal by this method is used more by the prosecution than the defense. The defense usually appeals from a summary court to the Quarter Sessions Court on either questions of fact or law. Further appeal from the Quarter Sessions Court may be made by the process of "case stated" to the High Court.

Appeal from an Assize Court or appeal from original jurisdiction of the Quarter Sessions Court is made to the Court of Criminal Appeal. Prosecution cannot appeal an acquittal. The defense may appeal on points of law or on point of fact if either the trial court or the Court of Criminal Appeal permits. If the Court of Criminal Appeal gives permission, an appeal may be made on the grounds of wrong sentence. The Court of

Criminal Appeal may dismiss the appeal, reverse the decision of the lower court, or modify the sentence imposed by the lower court.

The House of Lords is the final appeal court. As noted, the Attorney-General must certify that the appeal is on a question of law that is of sufficient public importance to merit further appeal.[7]

SCOTTISH COURTS

By the Act of Union of 1707, Scotland retained its own legal system. Scottish law is derived in part from Roman law and is characterized by its reliance upon broad principles of law. English common law with its strict observance of judicial precedent did not penetrate the Scottish border. However, since 1707 the two systems have grown closer together because of the increase in statutory law applicable to both England and Scotland.

Similarly, the Scottish court system varies from that of the English courts. The lowest civil courts are Justice of the Peace Courts (cases involving not more than £5). Sheriff Courts compare with the English County Courts, although there are no limits upon the amount of money involved in a case. Scotland also has special Land Courts with civil jurisdiction over particular agricultural matters. The high civil court is the Court of Session. It is divided into the Inner House, the civil appeal body, and the Outer House, a court of original jurisdiction. Appeals from the Inner House may be taken to the British House of Lords.

Criminal courts of summary jurisdiction in Scotland are the Justice of the Peace Courts, Police Courts in burghs, and the Sheriff Courts. The Sheriff Courts, functioning with a jury, may try indictable offenses. The High Court of Justiciary is both a court of first instance and an appeal court in criminal cases. Scottish criminal cases cannot be appealed to the House of Lords.

THE LEGAL PROFESSION

The legal profession is almost an autonomous body in Great Britain. The profession, through its legal societies, controls the licensing of new members, scrutinizes the professional conduct of members, and may effect the dismissal of a member. Lawyers in England and Wales are divided into solicitors and barristers. This division results in different regulations governing training, control by different legal societies, and a considerable differentiation in functions.

Although the line of demarcation between the work of a solicitor and a barrister is not precise, the general distinction is that a solicitor is an

[7] See page 102.

office lawyer who gives advice to lay people and who prepares legal cases; a barrister advises clients through a solicitor and is a courtroom lawyer.

To become a solicitor, a person must have at least one year of training in a law school, serve as an articled clerk to an established solicitor for a period of three or five years, and be able to pass the examinations given by a committee of the Law Society. Solicitors are now allowed to plead cases before the lower courts.

Barristers must be members of one of the four Inns of Court (Gray's Inn, Lincoln's Inn, the Middle Temple, and the Inner Temple), have passed the examinations given by the Council of Legal Education, and have read law for a specified period of time in a barrister's office. The Inns prescribe the legal training necessary for a barrister and offer courses of instruction. Also, they serve as clubs for practicing barristers. Many barristers have had training in a regular law school. Barristers are the only lawyers permitted to appear before the higher courts. They are divided into junior barristers and Queen's Counsels. Queen's Counsel is a title given to a barrister who has "taken silk." To take silk means that the barrister has applied to and been granted by the Lord Chancellor an appointment as a legal counselor to the Queen. Queen's Counsels are entitled to higher fees and, perhaps more important, are recognized as outstanding barristers.

CHARACTERISTICS OF BRITISH COURTS

British courts have a world-wide reputation for fairness and dispatch. Appointments to judgeships are free from political influence; and, except for the lower courts, all judges are barristers of recognized standing in their profession. The barrister, as judge, brings to the bench a thorough knowledge of the law and court procedure. The judge, wigged and robed as are the barristers, conducts trials with solemnity and dignity. British courts are less hampered by technical wrangles by the attorneys over technicalities of proceedings than are American courts. The judge has considerable control, and as a result the average trial is brief.

In recent years, criticisms have been levied against the regular courts. Appointment to the higher courts usually comes after a barrister has established a reputation. By this time, the barrister is usually in his late forties and more likely, well into his fifties. This fact coupled with the lack of a compulsory retirement age has led to a criticism analogous to F. D. Roosevelt's criticism of the American Supreme Court, i.e., too many tired old men. The charge is not directed against the judges' energy outlay but rather against the failure of the judges to keep their legal thinking abreast of the social and political thinking of the community. The validity of such a criticism is apparently open to question.

A second criticism relates to the requirement that higher-court judges be barristers. It is alleged that the judges have a class bias inasmuch as barristers either come from or soon enter the wealthy class. This charge tends to ignore the growing number of barristers who are members of the Labor party and that wealth does not bar a person from membership in the Labor party. Sir Stafford Cripps was a highly successful barrister who joined the Labor party and served in its government.

A long standing criticism involves the high cost of British justice. The loser in a civil case must pay all court costs plus the fees for legal service to him. If appeals are part of the case, the cost increases. For criminal cases, the fees for legal services are borne by the defendant. Court costs and legal service are expensive in Britain—sufficiently so that a person of moderate income may prefer to forget his problem rather than press charges in a court.

By the Legal Aid and Advice Acts (1949 to the present), a system of government aid in court costs and government aid for legal advice has been introduced. The system is administered by the Law Society under the direction of the Lord Chancellor. As of 1959, the aid did not apply to the lower courts; but the Conservative party stated that it intended to extend the application of the Acts to all courts. A means test is applied to determine eligibility for government assistance, and whenever possible some of the cost is borne by the individual.

Counsel for defendants in criminal cases has always been available in some form (a court-appointed attorney). Attempts to improve the availability were made in 1907, 1930, and 1933. The Legal Aid and Advice Acts continue the availability of free legal aid. The main innovations are that the central government assumes greater financial responsibility (transfer from local funds) and that the attorneys receive fair and reasonable compensation.

Although by no means perfect, the British legal system serves the British citizen well in its efforts to implement the rule of law.

SELECTED READING

ARCHER, PETER. *The Queen's Courts.* Baltimore: Penguin Books, Inc., 1956.

DENNING, LORD. *The Changing Law.* London: Stevens & Sons, Ltd., 1953.

FRIEDMANN, W. *Law and Social Change in Contemporary Britain.* London: Stevens & Sons, Ltd., 1952.

HOLDSWORTH, SIR WILLIAM. *The Elements of English Law.* Fair Lawn, N.J.: Oxford University Press, 1959.

JACKSON, R. M. *The Machinery of Justice in England.* Fair Lawn, N.J.: Oxford University Press, 1960.

II

POLITICS AND GOVERNMENT OF FRANCE

UNITED KINGDOM
English Channel
BELGIUM
WEST GERMANY
LUX.
SWITZERLAND
ITALY
SPAIN
ATLANTIC OCEAN
Bay of Biscay
MEDITERRANEAN SEA
PAS DE CALAIS
NORD
Roubaix
Lille
SOMME
SEINE MARITIME
Le Havre
Rouen
AISNE
ARDENNES
OISE
MANCHE
CALVADOS
EURE
SEINE
Paris
Reims
MARNE
MEUSE
MOSELLE
BAS-RHIN
Brest
FINISTÈRE
CÔTES DU NORD
ORNE
SEINE ET OISE
SEINE ET MARNE
Nancy
Strasbourg
MEURTHE ET MOSELLE
Rennes
ILLE ET VILAINE
MAYENNE
EURE ET LOIRE
AUBE
HAUTE MARNE
VOSGES
MORBIHAN
Le Mans
SARTHE
LOIRET
YONNE
HAUT RHIN
BELFORT
LOIRE INFÉRIEURE
MAINE ET LOIRE
Angers
LOIR ET CHER
CÔTE D'OR
Dijon
HAUTE SAÔNE
Nantes
INDRE ET LOIRE
CHER
NIÈVRE
DOUBS
VENDÉE
DEUX SÈVRES
VIENNE
INDRE
SAONE ET LOIRE
JURA
ALLIER
AIN
CREUSE
HAUTE SAVOIE
CHARENTE MARITIME
Limoges
PUY DE DÔME
RHÔNE
CHARENTE
HAUTE VIENNE
Clermont-Ferrand
LOIRE
Lyon
SAVOIE
St. Etienne
CORRÈZE
ISÈRE
Grenoble
DORDOGNE
CANTAL
HAUTE LOIRE
Bordeaux
GIRONDE
LOT
ARDÈCHE
DRÔME
HAUTES ALPS
LOZÈRE
LOT ET GARONNE
AVEYRON
TARN ET GARONNE
LANDES
GARD
VAUCLUSE
BASSES ALPES
ALPES-MARITIMES
TARN
GERS
Toulouse
HÉRAULT
BOUCHES DU RHÔNE
Nice
VAR
BASSES PYRÉNÉES
HAUTE GARONNE
HAUTES PYRÉNÉES
AUDE
Marseille
Toulon
ARIÈGE
PYRÉNÉES ORIENTALES
CORSICA
FRANCE
Showing cities of more than 100,000 population
Scale of Miles
0
50
100

10

Foundations of French Politics

I do not believe in Liberty (we are dying of its idolatrous cult), and am ready to accept many a constraint; but I cannot bow before certain iniquitous decisions, give even a tacit consent to certain abominations.

—André Gide[1]

A NATION OF PARADOXES

Many French indulge in constant grumbling about the inadequacies of their government, its system of taxation, and the "deepening moral crisis" within their society. Yet they continue to affirm their conviction that individual happiness is possible only in France, a testimony to their attraction to the "French way of life." Some Frenchmen cherish representative institutions, and some are receptive to authoritarian forms of political organization. Some Frenchmen proclaim their internationalism, proud of the fact that France is the collecting place for political and religious refugees from all parts of the world; and some militantly assert their nationalism and the conviction that the country is being "taken over" by "foreigners." Some Frenchmen subscribe to doctrines of the Left; others support those of the Right—yet it usually matters little whether French governments are dominated by leftists or rightists because their orientation is almost always conservative, and few consciously attempt to solve some of the society's most persistent problems.

In probably no other country in the world are social and civic responsibilities so broadly discussed, written about, and practiced so little. In few other countries do individuals so blatantly claim their own rights and ignore the rights of others. In few other countries are individuals so doc-

[1] André Gide, *The Journals of André Gide* (New York: Alfred A. Knopf, a division of Random House, Inc., 1951), iv, 114.

trinally conscious of "societal needs" and so rabid in pursuance of their own individual happiness at the expense of friends and neighbors. In few other countries are public bureaucrats as contemptuous of the citizens they theoretically "serve."

THE REVOLUTIONARY LEGACY

The Revolution of 1789 added new cleavages to a divided social order and paved the way for intense conflict between church and state. It bequeathed to French society a form of political organization different from anything it had previously experienced; that form was based on certain ideas inherent in the Revolution itself—the rights of men, the extension of political liberty to commoners, and dependence on rationalism instead of Catholicism as a means of solving the problems of society. Many of these ideas had reached refinement in the eighteenth century when certain Frenchmen called on society to accept scientific progress, to apply its findings to problems of social organization, and to seek salvation only in the world it knew.

Jean Jacques Rousseau's thought permeated all aspects of the Revolution. Particularly influential was his idea that men are capable of organizing themselves on a conscious rather than a traditional basis in order to cooperate in the attainment of common objectives. His belief that sovereignty resides in and not outside of the people was fundamental to the spirit of the Revolution. Various of his views concerning property influenced Jacobin theory and the egalitarian principles of the Declaration of Rights of the Constitution of 1793 (which abolished special rights for nobility and clergy and declared property not inviolable but secondary to the general welfare).

Despite the Revolution's ideals and achievements, the postrevolutionary social order remained divided. Some Frenchmen favored the Revolution, and others remained unalterably opposed to it. New societal divisions subsequently emerged in this nineteenth century when great industrial revolutions swept the country and created an industrial working class whose material condition was characterized by low wages and the poorest working conditions. Louis Napoleon Bonaparte's program of industrialization did much to convince the workers that the revolutionary ideals of Liberty, Equality, and Fraternity were meant only for middle-class application. Certain of the divisions he inflicted on the French social order persist to this day.

The Revolution was directed against the church, and as a result the church fell into the habit of denouncing some of the republics created subsequent to 1789. For years after 1789, the church clung to cherished visions that had their origin in the prerevolutionary era; and much of the history of France came to consist of real and theoretical conflict between church and state over the control of sovereignty. In 1864, Pius IX condemned liberalism, republicanism, and the spirit of free inquiry. In 1877, the French bishops demanded that the Republic recognize the temporal authority of the Pope and his government, an act that gave rise to considerable republican reaction and fear that it would lead ultimately to conflict between France and Italy. As a result, the Republic created new laws and invoked old ones in order to suppress various Catholic congregations (yet it allowed church schools to continue to exist). The great rupture came in 1904 when the Republic withdrew recognition of the Vatican, an act that intensified the internal conflict already raging within the nation. Extremists on both sides succeeded in shaping the major outlines of the controversy, overcoming the efforts at reconciliation undertaken by liberal Catholics and liberal secularists. Ideological warfare existed between church and state schools. Instruction in the former emphasized the moral aspects of Catholicism, and the latter taught secular republican morality. Church schools portrayed themselves as havens from "atheistic republicanism," and state schools proclaimed themselves democratic citadels free from "clerical reaction." Only after World War I did church-state controversies settle down to oral controversies over the control of education and the allocation of tax moneys. The issue was never solved, but as the years progressed both learned to live side by side without periodically declaring war on each other.

WORKERS, PEASANTS, AND MIDDLE CLASS[2]

France has two working classes: one is property owning and "integrated"; the other is propertyless and "alienated." France has two farming classes: one owns its land; the other is composed of workers, tenants, and sharecroppers. France has two middle classes: one is modern, relatively prosperous, and "on the make"; the other is archaic, poor, and on the decline. There are two Frances: one looks to the future, the other to the past; one stands for progress, the other for regression.

The industrial working force consists of approximately 6,500,000 people, of which a great number have been "alienated" from French society. President de Gaulle stated in 1960, "We must continue to lower social barriers, providing . . . greater opportunities for advancement for all classes, greater worker participation in the conduct of business, and a greater participation by labor and technical organizations in the regional and national

[2] The *Bulletin hébdomadaire de Statistique*, April 2, 1955, gives as the structure of the active population of France: 3,984,000 farmers, 1,153,000 farm hands, 2,296,000 businessmen, 554,000 executives, 1,139,000 supervisory staff, 2,074,000 white collar workers, 6,443,000 manual workers, and 1,529,000 others.

responsibilities of the French economy—the objective being to put an end to the outdated consequences of the former class struggle, to interest directly in the country's development all those who contributed to it, and to accelerate progress by this general participation." If that can be achieved, communism will become less than what it presently is, and France will enoy a more stable political atmosphere.

After the Russian Revolution of 1917, some French workers found in communism their symbols of the future and an "answer" to their subordinate position in French society. This group increased in size during the great depression of the thirties. The Socialist party (SFIO) was unable to alleviate its condition, and the Communist party was fully prepared to proclaim its willingness to do so. It succeeded in stealing from the SFIO considerable worker support. Then—primarily as a consequence of its leadership of the resistance in World War II—in the postliberation era, the Communist party was able to dominate most of the unions affiliated with the General Confederation of Labor (CGT). Today, the Communist party recruits the support of the majority of unionized, non-salaried workers. (It enjoys less success with salaried workers and technicians. Integrated more fully in society, this group shows few "secessionist" tendencies.)

Paradoxically, the material condition of the non-salaried workers is superior to what it was one decade ago. It is far from approximating "the growing pauperization of the working class," one of the persistent themes of French communism. Nevertheless, the reasons for which many workers are attracted to communism and not to the economic system within which they work and live are easy to understand. The worker knows that he is better off than workers in other European countries, but he continues to feel that the French economy yields him less than what he should justly derive from it. He wants an earning power that is not inferior to that of the average bourgeois, a respectable position in the society in which he lives, equality of opportunity for himself and his children, better housing, and a system that will protect him against the menace of runaway inflation. The French economy has failed to provide him with many of these things. He is convinced that it is concerned only with furthering middle-class interests and that he is "victimized" by it.[3] "The whole tone of [his] life is one of complete frustration."[4]

[3] Hadley Cantril and David Rodnick, *On Understanding the French Left* (Princeton, N.J.: Princeton University Press, 1956), p. 15.

[4] *Ibid.*, p. 24.; see also *French Workers: Their Problems, Their Morale, Their Hopes* (English ed., Paris: French Institute of Public Opinion, 1956). This study, based on interviews that took place between October and November, 1955, was confined to 1039 factory manual workers, 396 white collar workers, and 221 middle-rank industry staff workers—all eighteen years of age or more. They were asked detailed questions concerning the family and the home, employment experience and attitudes, labor union membership, participation in politics, their outlook on life, and their symbols of the future.

Approximately 25 per cent of the total population is engaged in agriculture (the figure is closer to 35 per cent if one counts the thousands of small communes that comprise people who live both in and off the agricultural areas). Approximately 3,000,000 peasants own their land, some 750,000 are tenants, and almost 200,000 are share croppers. Middle- and large-scale farmers are generally the rule (by French, not American standards). Approximately 25 per cent own 60 to 65 per cent of the land, approximately 5 per cent own more than 100 acres each, and more than half of all the farmers own fewer than 10 acres each. Employed by the peasant proprietors are 1,200,000 agricultural workers whose material condition of life is substantially inferior to that of industrial workers.

French agriculture is presently in a state of crisis. Peasant incomes have increased only 25 per cent during the past decade in contradistinction to non-peasant incomes that increased 50 per cent in the same period. The farmer has never been able to regain the prosperity he enjoyed in the period between 1944 and 1948 when he had no difficulty in selling his products at a price that allowed him some measure of profit. His decline began after 1948 when he continued to find a ready market for his products but not a ready profit. Farm prices declined even further after the beginning of the great inflation in 1952, and during the following year peasant demonstrations broke out in the Midi and in forty departments of the nation. Agricultural workers demonstrated, too, under the direction of their National Federation of Unions (FNSEA). The state responded by providing temporary agrarian relief. Demonstrations began again in 1955; road blocks were established and some violence occurred. The state resorted again to temporary measures and further action was averted. In 1960, approximately 300,000 peasants and workers assembled in Amiens and other agrarian centers to protest their plight. This time the state told them that their major problem was overproduction and that they should not expect the newly formed Common Market to accommodate all their surplus. Nevertheless, the state turned almost immediately to the consideration of a new agrarian law in order to modify existing tension. Peasant discontent reached a new peak in 1961, resulting in acts of violence and the creation of road-blocks in different parts of the nation. The underdeveloped Brittany demanded its own "Plan of Constantine" and in one of its towns a mob seized the *sous-prefecture* and held it for three hours. Premier Debré sought to quell the disturbances by promulgating new laws that increased state aid to the peasants, causing some of his critics to contend that he was confirming the conviction of some peasants that violence does pay.

The state generally regulates agrarian production, sets minimum prices for products, and resorts from time to time to piecemeal legislation in order to pacify various agrarian groups. It acknowledges the existence of a serious agrarian crisis and is searching for ways to remedy it. It hopes that its program of industrial decentralization will act as a partial corrective and reduce the total number of people engaged in agriculture. It hopes that those who leave will find employment in newly created industries within their own departments (and not flow into the predominantly urban and industrial departments of the Seine, Pas-de-Calais, Nord, Rhone, and Lorraine). It hopes that the program will aid and advance the poorer rural departments of central, western, and southwestern France and Corsica.

Only recently did the state turn to re-examination of its agrarian policy in areas in which it has long exercised favoritism. Now it has finally started to come face to face with the problem of agrarian subsidies, their allocation, and to question whether there is a legitimate rationale for producers of wheat and sugar beets to receive in excess of what other farmers consider as their fair share of subsidies. It concedes that perhaps there are other ways of elevating a farm income that now accounts for not more than 11 per cent of the total national income. It seeks now to convince some of the peasants that many of their methods are archaic (particularly those of the south), to overcome their suspicion and distrust in order to get them to adopt new ones, to increase substantially the number of advisers who provide instruction in scientific farming, to create agricultural machine pools that will allow for more efficient utilization of manpower, and to acquire the cooperation of peasants who have resisted its agrarian proposals by giving their support to Poujadism.[5] It hopes to develop complementary programs of agriculture and industry and thereby contribute to the improvement of the social, economic, and political situation.[6]

Approximately 50 per cent of the 2,500,000 people who work in commerce are self-employed; they belong to the social category known as the *petite bourgeoisie,* noted for its entrenched position and resistance to social change. They constitute that sector of the French economy that is generally regressive and which holds little promise for future progress. Even cursory examination of the Fourth Republic's legislation reveals that it was dominated by representatives of this regressive sector and that many of their laws sought to freeze the economic status quo in order to protect inefficient small- and middle-size enterprisers.

Far too many of these enterprisers cling to pre-twentieth-century methods that detract from effective realization of the nation's potential. They shield archaic methods of distribution, keep prices artificially high,

[5] See page 156 for an explanation of this term.

[6] The state hopes that industrial decentralization will modify the agrarian problem—it knows that it will not solve it, and that in its initial stages the program will further the belief that industry and agriculture are competitive and even create certain tensions between them; at this time, 65 per cent of all the industrial enterprises are still situated in the department of the Seine.

and inflict the heaviest economic punishment on elements of the society who can afford it least. They encourage the economy to grow at a disproportionate rate, widening the gap between its progressive and regressive sectors. This social category constitutes one of the true "reactionary" forces in modern France and exercises a divisive effect on both her economy and politics.

Within thousands of French communes are hundreds of thousands of small shopkeepers in whose establishments is accumulated the debris of at least two republics. Their commodities—instead of being moved by being sold at cost or below cost—become part of a seemingly unscalable mountain whose price increases with the passing years. These enterprises, instead of failing or readjusting to a market on the move, live on in a condition of marginal existence—to the detriment of all, including themselves. Many are handed down from father to son, and many a son would be better off if he closed his shop and took other employment. Few of them do it; generally they prefer the status that goes with ownership to the non-status of a more materially well-endowed worker. Whenever a volume enterprise such as Prisunic or Monoprix moves into their neighborhoods, the economy of the entire area is threatened. In 1959, a group of Grenoble's enterprisers descended on such a store and reduced it to a shamble in order to "safeguard" themselves against financial obliteration. Elements such as these convert the Jeffersonian dream of a nation of small property owners into a living nightmare.

THE HOUSING SHORTAGE

The severe housing shortage constitutes a social problem with important political implications. Even before World War II, France was far behind in construction. The average age of buildings in the capital was seventy-six years (most were constructed before 1859). In rural communities, the average exceeded one hundred years. At least 10 per cent of all French housing was destroyed in World War II. Today, France has the highest average rate of population increase in western Europe (approximately 800,000 per year), and its housing crisis is more profound than ever. Housing adequate to meet this rise must average 750,000 new units each year over the next thirty years. The state admits that it will be more than one hundred years before housing needs can be met in the heavily congested department of the Seine, which is the locale for 14 per cent of the total national population. Approximately 300,000 families—each averaging six persons—live there in single rooms!

Private capital has shown little interest in housing investments. Consequently, the state has tried to stimulate construction through grants, subsidies, and low-interest loans. Progress was made in the period 1954-1957;

but during 1957-1958 shortages in materials, the interruption of construction because of the requisition of materials for the Algerian War, and runaway inflation increased housing costs almost 20 per cent. Fewer units were begun and finished, and the housing program fell even farther behind. In 1961, construction was proceeding at the rate of 330,000 new units per year, a pace that falls far short of meeting the needs of French society. Considering all the demonstrations that take place each year in the capital, it is indeed surprising that there has not been one in behalf of the demand for housing.

THE QUEST FOR EXTERNAL SECURITY

France searches continually for ways to increase her national security. This quest is the result of an exposed geographical position, many wars, and numerous invasions. Between 1870 and 1940, France was invaded three times by Germany. The Franco-Prussian War resulted in loss of lives and the territories of Alsace and Lorraine. World War I destroyed 2,000,000 of her citizens, World War II caused the death of 160,000 of her men in combat, the destruction of 100,000 of her citizens at home, and the deportation and subsequent death of 200,000 others in Germany.

After her defeat by Germany in 1870, France sought to revise her diplomacy. She thought that she could protect herself more fully by entering into coalitions with other European powers. She searched for these in eastern Europe, thinking that future German aggression would be deterred by confronting that country with the threat of war on at least two fronts. Pacts were also concluded with Great Britain, 1904 being the date of the *entente cordiale*. World War I demonstrated the futility of this policy. After the war, France concentrated on the acquisition of a punitive treaty designed to render Germany impotent. She sought from her allies guaranties calculated to prevent the re-emergence of German industrial and military power, thinking that this would allow her to remain in advance of Germany for years. Seeking to transform the Rhine into a pillar of French strength, she proposed its annexation or her permanent ownership of its left bank. When these efforts failed, she sought its isolation, neutrality, or autonomy in order to keep it beyond the reach of Germany. Nevertheless, when the peace was concluded, the most she could obtain were promises for its permanent demilitarization.

The destruction in 1918 of the Tsarist regime destroyed the Franco-Russian alliance. France attempted to fill this gap by concluding new alliances with the small states of eastern Europe. She hoped that these alliances—supplemented by other guaranties from her allies—would serve as a check on Germany. Seeking to maintain herself as the dominant power on the continent, she concentrated on consolidating the status quo.

That policy failed and war came again in 1939. The country was stripped of its productive facilities, and it entered the liberation era perilously close to bankruptcy.

The postwar reconstruction of Germany and her emergence as a great power free from imperial designs shifted the threat to French security from Germany to the Soviet Union. After the announcement in 1946 of the Truman doctrine, France and the United States entered various joint military and financial treaties. France became a secondary and frequently reluctant partner in the mutual defense effort. Her importance in world affairs had diminished, and internal divisions paralyzed her consensus and prevented her from taking too many clearly defined positions. Moreover, her own empire was fragmenting. She went to war again in 1946, this time in Indo-China, in what was from the first a distinctly hopeless conflict. That experience lasted until 1954 when the defeat at Dien Bien Phu ended French hegemony in that part of the world. Within a year's time, elements of her Moslem population were in revolt, and approximately half a million French troops were sent to Algeria to combat the insurrection.

Contemporary French diplomacy is still committed to the quest for security. France's foreign policy is still similar to the policy that the country adhered to in the years between both world wars. It remains shaped by the idea of a balance of power. Today President de Gaulle favors the development of Europe and its leadership by France, who would act as an arbital and power-shaping force between the rival power blocs of the United States and the Soviet Union. He wishes to build Europe into a real "Third Force," which—under French direction—would modify and "humanize" the world situation. He stated in his speech of December 31, 1960, "In 1961 . . . We shall help to build up Europe, which, by confederating its nations, can and must—for the sake of mankind—become the greatest political, economic, military and cultural power that has ever existed. We shall help this assembled Europe and its daughter, America, to reorganize their alliance in order to better defend the free world and to act together in all parts of the earth." He seeks this by the implementation of agreements on the national rather than the international level. Therefore, he seeks to avoid commitments dictated by the United Nations, an organization that he views as being under the domination of "Anglo-Saxons." [7] He demands that France have within NATO policy-making

[7] De Gaulle's criticisms appear in his memorandum of September 24, 1958, addressed to Eisenhower and Macmillan. Although "secret," its contents are well known and have been described in *Le Monde,* November 11 and 13, 1958. In his speech of Grenoble, October 7, 1960, De Gaulle emphasized the disintegration of the United Nations and the necessity for safeguarding France's "liberty of action." He said that France wants to "maintain" and "reinforce" NATO but that France must "guard its own personality," its "own methods of defense," and its own "methods of atomic dissuasion." The address merely confirmed publicly what was in his "secret memorandum" of September 24, 1958.

powers equal to those of the United States and Great Britain, and he wants to transform the organization so that it can be employed in both regional and global capacities. To secure his objectives, he bargains with weapons of considerable diplomatic weight—having already reserved for the French naval contingent within NATO the right to act independently in time of war, for the French Air Corps an autonomous status, and for American missile positioning outside of French soil.

SELECTED READING

BROGAN, D. W. *France Under the Republic.* New York: Harper & Bros., 1940.
LUETHY, H. *France Against Herself.* New York: Frederick A. Praeger, Inc., 1955.
MORAZÉ, C. *The French and the Republic.* Ithaca, N.Y.: Cornell University Press, 1958.
THOMSON, D. *Democracy in France, The Third and Fourth Republics.* 3d ed. Fair Lawn, N.J.: Oxford University Press, 1958.
WERTH, A. *France, 1940–55.* New York: Holt, Rinehart & Winston, Inc., 1956.

11

From the Fourth to the Fifth Republic

The last year of the Fourth Republic was characterized by frequent Cabinet crises, the suspension of certain traditional political rights and the violation of others, numerous strikes in both public and private enterprises, increasing inflation in the economy, demonstrations against the regime by leftist and rightist political groups, and revolutionary threats by some militarists to take matters in their own hands in order to end the Moslem rebellion in Algeria. The regime ended on May 13, 1958 when Premier Pierre Pflimlin capitulated to the military revolt in Algiers, an event that heralded the end of the Fourth Republic and the coming of the Fifth. "May 13" was the consequence of the inability of the Fourth Republic to terminate the war in Algeria and to halt the constant degradation of the state after 1956.

GOVERNMENTAL INSTABILITY

Governmental instability increased greatly during the last two years of the Fourth Republic. On May 23, 1957, Guy Mollet was forced to resign as Premier when he lost the support of sixty-seven Independents. Bourgès-Maunoury was defeated on October 10, 1957 when sixty-three Independents voted against him; more than two months elapsed before the legislature was able to produce another government. Félix Gaillard fell in April, 1958, after one hundred Independents withdrew their support from him. As each coalition government collapsed, it became increasingly difficult to find a successor. Moreover, the lengthy constitutional crises were accompanied by strong waves of hostility against the political parties that circulated among the populace during the last months of the

Republic. This sentiment reached stunning proportions after the defeat of the Gaillard government, and it tended to be very much in tune with General de Gaulle's criticism of the "regime of parties." Absenteeism from the polls underwent a sharp increase, as was illustrated in the special election that was conducted in 1958 in the second district of the Seine for the purpose of filling the seat vacated by the death of Marcel Cachin, the eighty-seven-year-old dean of Communist deputies. In that election absenteeism rose to 51 per cent.

INFLATION AND STRIKES

Although economic and social reconstruction increased considerably in the decade after the liberation, the material condition of workers was constantly jeopardized by rising inflation and successive devalutions of the franc. Various studies describe the hostility with which they came to view the Fourth Republic.[1] Similar trends were evidenced among a number of lower middle-class enterprisers; some sought refuge in Poujadism, an extraordinary *mélange* of nineteenth-century economic tendencies and twentieth-century political reaction that sought the destruction of the existing regime. Finally, numerous strikes occurred in the period 1957–1958. They increased substantially in the public service as employees displayed their discontent with the regime's financial policy. Residents of Paris witnessed frequent interruptions in the nationalized gas, electricity, and transport services. In March, 1958, an unprecedented breakdown occurred when some 7,000 members of the Paris police force assembled at the office of the prefect for the purpose of demanding an increase in salary. After the prefect ordered them to disperse, the demonstrators converged on the National Assembly, where they sought to petition the deputies. Deputies Le Pen and de Marquet, both Poujadists, attempted to turn the demonstration into an attack on the National Assembly; nevertheless, the police ignored their plea to "throw the deputies into the Seine." The Republican Guard subsequently arrived, order was restored, and two days later Paris installed a new prefect of police, M. Papon. Although the police had not attempted to seize the Assembly, a substantial segment of the entire force had walked off the job that day, which illustrated the seriousness of the situation. Finally, on yet other occasions during 1957 and 1958, huge crowds of civil servants and workers assembled on the Rivoli and in some of the great squares of Paris to demonstrate against the financial policies of the different governments of the Fourth Republic.

[1] See *French Workers: Their Problems, Their Morale, Their Hopes* (English ed.; Paris: French Institute of Public Opinion, 1956); Hadley Cantril and David Rodnick, *On Understanding the French Left* (Princeton, N.J.: Princeton University Press, 1956); and Hadley Cantril, *The Politics of Despair* (Princeton, N.J.: Princeton University Press, 1958).

THE DETERIORATION OF INDIVIDUAL RIGHTS AND LIBERTIES

After the outbreak in 1954 of the Moslem rebellion in Algeria, the National Assembly passed special laws designed to curtail the publication and expression of views detrimental to or defamatory of the program of military pacification undertaken by the Republic in Algeria. Enforcement of these laws resulted in police seizures of issues of some newspapers, books, and periodicals; suppression of numerous political meetings; and arbitrary detention of many individuals. Issues of the leftist *France-Observateur,* the Communist *Humanité* and *France-Nouvelle,* and the Mendès-France oriented *Éxpress* were seized. The Left Catholic *Témoignage chrétien* established something of a record by submitting to sixty-eight seizures in 1957–1958. This confiscatory policy forced many of these organs of public opinion to undergo heavy financial losses. Monetary contributions by private citizens and established publishing houses provided compensation to newspapers, which helped them to survive. In one case, the leftist *France-Observateur* received thousands of francs from the conservative publishing house of Gallimard. During 1957–1958, the Paris police and the Republican Guard prevented or interrupted meetings of leftist political groups whenever they sought to express opposition to the war in Algeria. Units of the Republican Guard regularly patrolled those parts of the Latin Quarter where student associations met frequently for the purpose of voicing their criticisms. Rightist-groups meetings held in the vicinity of the Arch of Triumph and the Place de la Concorde in order to express their conviction that "Algeria is French" generally were less well supervised by the public authorities.

In December, 1957, the parliamentary committee for the Protection of Individual Rights and Liberties confirmed that the French police had arbitrarily detained a number of French citizens and Algerians who were critical of the war. It cited examples of torture practiced by the police on Algerians and Algerian sympathizers in Metropolitan France. It also made public examples of torture practiced by the French military. It refused, however, to identify its witnesses and stated that it sought to shield them from what it described as possible "acts of reprisal"—an indirect although obvious reference to the police and the army. The Catholic *La Croix* commented that "France is faced with an unprecedented national and human disaster . . . such abuses are less the fault of men than of the system." "All silence is complicity," declared 150 university professors who met on the inviolable grounds of the Sorbonne on January 12, 1958, to protest the war, the tortures, and the mysterious disappearance of M. Audin, a French citizen who was last seen being interrogated by the army in Algeria.

YEARS OF WAR: INDO-CHINA AND ALGERIA

After 1954, some militarists expressed the conviction that the French defeat in Indo-China was the result of weak support given to the army by faltering governments at home. The retired Marshal of the Armies, Alphonse Juin, fell into the habit of attributing to "those rotten politicians" responsibility for that collapse and blame for a war that had lasted nine years.

Although French rule in Indo-China had become untenable by the close of World War II due to the growth of a powerful resistance force, Chinese hostility, and French colonialism, France made a desperate effort to preserve her power and prestige in that part of the world. American aid enabled France to divert manpower and supplies to Indo-China. The United States stated that it was "important to the security of the United States that Indo-China remain among the free nations of the world [because its fall] would complete Communist domination of Asia east of India."

France's failure to resolve the colonial issue was one of many factors that contributed to her defeat in Indo-China. The Viet Minh opposition included many nationalists and non-Communists who joined forces with the Communists because of inadequacies in French policy. The French could not induce these people to shelve their nationalism and join them in sustaining colonialism in the struggle against communism. In other words, the French appeal always had a very weak basis. It united Communists and non-Communists more than it separated them; it also created between the French and their Vietnamese "allies" a relationship that was based on mutual suspicion. General Marcel Carpentier once announced that he would resign within twenty-four hours if any direct aid went to the Vietnamese. Tran van Huu announced in 1948, after he had left the premiership of Vietnam, that "If we had independence, the people would have no more reason to fight." Moreover, France's recognition of Bao Dai ("the nightclub Emperor") as the ruler of Indo-China helped to drive away good men who otherwise might have given its government their support. This was one of the reasons why the Catholic leader Ngo Kinh Diem refused the premiership in 1948. Finally, Bao Dai's lack of support was reflected in the fact that he had to wait for more than five years before he could order the full Vietnamese mobilization of July, 1951.

In 1950, France sought to give the impression that the Vietnamese had been granted their independence; what they did give were less limited spheres of internal freedom. In the conference participated in that year by France, Vietnam, Cambodia, and Laos, France reserved the right to influence all decisions while they were in the "study phase." The Laon delegation submitted that it was caught between the old imperialism of the French and the new imperialism of the Soviet Union and that it supported the former only because it considered it as "the most endurable form of oppression." The Cambodian delegation asked for "true independence." The French waited. Finally, they promised it in their policy note of July 3, 1953; months later, the Saigon Congress still sought its arrival.

While these events transpired, various French Premiers came to acknowledge the futility of the war. Laniel argued that it had to be terminated if the economy of France was to be saved. Pleven admitted that force was useless. The war ended in 1954 with the disaster at Dien Bien Phu. France then withdrew its forces from what was once the richest part of the French Empire. The war had lasted nine years. Within a year, the French Army was back in the field again, this time in Algeria, in a conflict far costlier in money and lives than Indo-China. By then, the military had been in the field for years and its members came to resemble those Roman legionaires who had been away from Rome for so long that they no longer knew what was going on at home. Many of its members now believed that the politicians of the Republic engaged them in wars that the politicians did their best to keep them from winning. Plans were already under way to terminate the life of the Fourth Republic.

France contended until very recently that Algeria is an extension of Metropolitan France and not a colony.[2] Nevertheless, there she introduced and sustained over many years practices normally associated with colonialism, implementing first the policy of "assimilation" and subsequently that of "association." The former prescribes standards to which the native population can "rise" and qualify thereby for French citizenship. The latter goes beyond the granting of citizenship and involves taking the native population into partnership in the administration.[3]

After the beginning of the Moslem rebellion in Algeria, various governments of the Fourth Republic sought to end the conflict. During his premiership of February 1, 1956 to May 21, 1957, Guy Mollet attempted to apply to the insurrection not one but three overlapping policies. He was

[2] Algeria covers 850,000 square miles and has a population of approximately 10,000,000. About 8,600,000 are Moslems (Arabs and Berbers); 1,200,000 are of European extraction. Some 2,000,000 Moslems are in agriculture, and 500,000 are in trade and industry. Almost 400,000 live in Metropolitan France. Algeria has a 600-mile coastline and is bounded by Morocco on the west and Tunisia on the east. It has a Mediterranean zone of 53,000 square miles with 8,500,000 people, a steppe zone of 73,000 square miles with 670,000 people, and a Sahara zone of 724,000 square miles with 630,000 people.

[3] David Thomson, *Democracy in France, The Third and Fourth Republics* (3d ed.; Fair Lawn, N.J.: Oxford University Press, 1958). If Algeria was never a colony, French practices there were colonial. See pp. 163–69 for description of French overseas activities.

receptive to (1) a solution through negotiations based on prior contacts with important leaders of the rebel Algerian Front of National Liberation (FLN); (2) a solution based on long-term reforms in Algeria; and (3) a solution based on military "pacification" of Algeria, with the defeat of Egypt's Nasser as one of its preconditions.

Mollet attempted to establish communication with the FLN on different occasions in 1956. He sent the late Pierre Commin in July and September of that year to meet with FLN representatives in Belgrade and Rome. These contacts proved fruitless. During that same period, he told the French nation that he favored his famous *triptyque* of "cease-fire, elections, negotiations." Yet he did not define the kind of elections that would take place in Algeria except to say that they would be "free." He said that he would accept "friends and representatives of foreign countries" as observers, but he did not define the number or state whether they would observe during the elections or in the period preceding the electoral campaign. Finally, during this same era, Mollet had at his disposal a plan that called for creation of an Algeria administered by a parliament that would have one of its houses elected by universal suffrage and the other by functional representation and a minister, designated by the parliament, who would be responsible to the French government. It is said that the plan amounted to a federal reorganization of French power, that it was approved by Morocco's late Mohammed V and Tunisia's Bourguiba (men whose cooperation was needed if the war was to end), and that some of Mollet's associates were convinced that its implementation would have ended the insurrection. That plan died on October 22, 1956 when five Algerian rebel leaders were kidnapped by the French while in route to Tunis over the territory of a non-belligerent. Mollet refused to view this act as a violation of international law. When he appeared before the National Assembly, he hinted that he might have liked to have received credit for it. By then it was obvious that he had come to rely primarily on military "pacification" as a solution to the Algerian problem—a policy whose inadequacy is attested to by events subsequent to 1956 and which include the collapse of a Republic.

Unreceptive to Algerian independence, Mollet's fear of its possibility probably increased his willingness to apply to the insurrection measures that he had previously rejected. André Philip contends that Mollet's trip to Algiers in February, 1956, produced a psychological transformation in his character, particularly after he was attacked by an angry crowd composed of workers and civil servants who were drawn from social categories that contributed to the composition of his own Socialist party in Metropolitan France. This critic concludes that Mollet was then thrown into a state of panic and confusion, which made it psychologically impossible for him to apply to the Algerian problem measures other than those based on force.

Although undoubtedly he made the defeat of Nasser a precondition of the Algerian solution, Mollet contends that he intervened in Suez in 1956 because of his unwillingness to compromise with a dictator's expansionism and a Pan-Arabism that was not "just a dream." He describes Nasser's nationalization of the Suez Canal as a "violation of international law" and his own intervention as an act of "socialist morality"—"Marx and Engels," he states, "always taught that in a conflict the socialists must be on the side of the people who are the most progressive. Between Nasser and Ben-Gurion I had to choose. Israel was going to be attacked. We made short work of a conflict that would have had the gravest consequences." The point is that he did not make short work of the conflict—the intervention failed, and almost overnight Nasser was transformed from a tottering fifth-rate military dictator to the status of a hero in the Middle East. Mollet than changed his line again and argued that the plan had failed as a consequence of being "unable to go through with it to the end"—an obvious allusion to the United States' failure to support France in Suez. To this day, various of Mollet's associates contend that he made the Suez decision without prior consultation with any of his Cabinet ministers. Finally, when Mollet had finished with Suez, the position of the Algerian FLN was more secure than it was prior to the beginning of the invasion.

The Mollet government was succeeded by the Bourgès-Maunoury and Gaillard governments. Both attempted to introduce new "framework laws" as a basis for the gradual establishment of new political structures in Algeria subsequent to the termination of hostilities. These laws were rejected by the Moslem rebels who contended that they declined to recognize full French citizenship for the Moslem population and that they merely prescribed standards of compliance for Moslems and exceptional privileges for Euro-Africans. Moslem leader Ferhat Abbas rejected the Gaillard "framework law" as an article of colonial reconquest that sought to annex a country without effectively annexing its inhabitants. The inability of the governments of Mollet, Bourgès-Maunoury, and Gaillard to terminate the rebellion hastened the death of the Fourth Republic. During the tenure of these governments, various militarists fell into the habit of announcing publicly that they were being "sold out" by Premiers who looked forward to a "soft policy" in Algeria, negotiations, and subsequent compromise with the rebels. In 1958, a number of high-ranking officers went unchallenged by Premier Gaillard when they charged that he and other politicians were withholding from the army funds that would have enabled it to end the rebellion in short order. The 105-billion franc slash in military expenditures recognized by the budget of the same year contributed to the further alienation of Generals Challe, Ely, Martin, Massu, and many of their subordinate field officers. That budget called for a reduction by 150,000 men of the nation's armed forces and cancellation of naval plans for construction of an aircraft carrier and two escort warships.

After the bombing of the Tunisian village of Sakhiet by the French Air Corps in February, 1958, it became evident that military policy in Algeria was no longer under the guidance of the civil authority in Paris. It was soon known that the decision to cross the frontier of the neighboring sovereign state had been unauthorized by the Gaillard government. The air strike resulted in the deaths of a number of Tunisian citizens and the destruction of a Red Cross station. Gaillard's reaction to it illustrated the powerlessness of his government. He first disclaimed all personal responsibility, admitting that the decision had been determined unilaterally and implemented by the military without the knowledge of Paris. Nevertheless, he assumed—within a matter of hours—the position that came so easily to Premiers during the last days of the Fourth Republic, which was defending in the National Assembly a major policy decision that had been made outside that body. That was when some of the Republic's politicians acknowledged that it was only a matter of time before the army asserted full control over the political system. His government fell in April, 1958.

"MAY 13"

On May 13, 1958, thousands of French settlers descended on the government headquarters building in Algiers and ransacked its offices. Later that afternoon, they entered the office of the United States Information Service and destroyed books and furniture and littered the streets of Algiers with United State's government literature. They also inflicted heavy material damage on the office of the daily *Journal of Algiers,* which was accused by some of the settlers of favoring termination of the rebellion through compromise with the Moslem opposition. The crowd increased to almost 50,000 by early evening. Its members chanted "The army to power" and "Algeria is French," and they proclaimed their opposition to Pierre Pflimlin who had been invested that day as Premier of the Republic by the National Assembly in Paris. Despite his reputation for timidity, one rumor had it that the handsome Premier and leader of the Popular Republican party favored a compromise solution to the conflict between France and the FLN.

Early during the afternoon of May 13, the revolt of the settlers was under the direction of an eleven-man Committee of Public Safety headed by the paratroop general, Jacques Massu. The Committee broadcast the following communique: "It is a committee and not a government which we have constituted. Now we await news from Paris. We have good reasons to believe that we have won the battle." General Massu told the homeland, "The Committee of Public Safety is now with you. It will not quit the scene until a council of safety has been formed in Paris." He appealed to General de Gaulle to take power in Metropolitan France.

His Committee of Public Safety included three militarists close to him and his policy and civilians drawn from the local veteran's association, which was the most militant of the French groups opposed to compromise with the Moslem rebels. Leadership of the Committee of Public Safety passed that evening to General Raoul Salan, Commander of the French Army in Algeria. Salan told the Algerian populace, "Having the mission to protect you, I provisionally take in my hands the destiny of French Algeria. I ask you to have confidence in the army and its chiefs and to show this through your calm and determination." Within hours the Algier's radio began a campaign calculated to increase tension in Metropolitan France; it beamed home such mysterious messages as "The palm tree is in the desert" and "The star is shining."

Paris was the scene of great confusion on May 13 as Parisians queued up at newsstands in order to get the latest news. Units of the Republican Guard (under the jurisdiction of the Ministry of Defence) were deployed at major points throughout the city; and it was some time before people knew who the Guard was supporting, the government or those sections of the army then in revolt. It supported the government. The government shortly thereafter imposed tight censorship over organs of public opinion and information. Paris remained relatively calm despite occasional demonstrations by rightist groups in behalf of General de Gaulle, which were confined to the Étoile, the Place de la Concorde, and the Place de la République, those "political playgrounds" on which political displays occur. Some days later an English reporter cabled home the information that thousands of refugees were in full flight from the capital and that Highway 20 was the scene of great traffic jams. It was, but not because of the political crisis—the reporter did not know that the crisis had not deterred thousands of Frenchmen from driving south on their vacations before the beginning of the Pentecostal holidays.

General de Gaulle maintained strict silence until May 19. On that date, he announced that he was ready to assume the premiership if the National Assembly would entrust him with exceptional powers and the mandate to prepare a new Constitution for the Republic. General Massu told the settlers in Algiers on the following day that he and De Gaulle would soon march together "up the Champs Élysées." The Algier's radio stated that the Committee of Public Safety would be satisfied with nothing less than the abolition of the "regime of parties," or the Fourth Republic itself, and the installation of General de Gaulle as the head of state. These dramatic announcements were answered by the National Assembly when it gave to Premier Pflimlin, by a vote of 475 to 100, emergency powers to deal with the insurrection.

The cautious Pflimlin was a master of coalition politics and had a highly developed knowledge of situations in which a successful politician should not find himself. If he had a Republic to guard, he also had his political future to protect. With one eye on the Fourth Republic and with his best eye trained on the Fifth, he told the National Assembly that there was "a certain measure of truth in the criticisms made by De Gaulle in his news conference of the previous Monday."

The revolution became an accomplished fact when Pflimlin announced on May 27 that he was delegating some of his emergency powers to General Salan, who appeared to be in full revolt against him! Pflimlin stated that the situation in Algeria was ambiguous, but that "the military chiefs who exercise authority, confronted with extraordinary difficulties, have obeyed the necessity of protecting national unity, public order, and republican legality." While Pflimlin was praising Salan, the latter was telling a huge crowd in Algiers that General de Gaulle had given France "an immense hope of greatness and national unity" and that "in Paris, the man who in other hours crucial for the country was able to point out the path to salvation, affirmed yesterday, publicly, with force and without ambiguity, that he understood your trouble and your driving force." On the night of May 27, Pflimlin told the National Assembly, "Tonight you must choose between me and De Gaulle. Tonight the Assembly must decide the fate of the Fourth Republic." The Assembly again voted him its support, but it was obvious that it was in no position to control the "fate of the Republic." He resigned the following day. General de Gaulle announced almost simultaneously, "I undertook yesterday the regular procedure necessary for the establishment of a republican government capable of insuring the unity and independence of the country." Although his words lacked legal authority, observers realized that shortly he would come to power. President Coty told the nation on May 30 that it was confronted with the threat of civil war, that he was offering De Gaulle the mission of forming a new government, and that he intended to resign if the Assembly declined to invest the General as Premier. Before it invested De Gaulle, the National Assembly decided to dispense with some of its unfinished business; and so it turned its attention to a bill pending for constitutional reform! A Poujadist rose to speak. He managed to complete one sentence, "I am a man of the streets." Shouts of "who gives a damn" filled the chamber, and he was forced to relinquish the floor. The Assembly then invested a Premier who had the army on his side.

A GOVERNMENT WITHOUT AN ARMY IS A POOR OPPONENT FOR AN ARMY WITHOUT A GOVERNMENT

Minutes after he resigned the premiership, Pflimlin was approached by a deputy who told him, "M. Pflimlin, power has deserted you; you have not deserted it." Many months later, he told his party that he had recognized the weakness of his government when the warship he had sent to recapture Ajaccio, capital of Corsica, refused to carry out his orders. He said that he had then reported to President Coty that General de Gaulle was the only person who could bring the army under control. He knew very well that a government without an army is powerless before an army without a government. It was subsequently revealed that the fate of the Fourth Republic was decided on the night of May 27 when De Gaulle met with some high-ranking members of the military and succeeded in deterring them from occupying Paris with their forces. Four of the nine military commanders in the Paris region were prepared to throw in with the rebels. On Highway 7, main route from Paris to Lyon, military command cars were placed 15 to 20 miles apart in constant radio communication with each other. That portion of the army then on maneuvers in Germany was prepared to re-enter France and proceed to the capital.

These facts were not known by approximately 200,000 people who congregated in the Place de la République on the night of May 28 to proclaim their opposition to what they considered as the illegal means employed by De Gaulle to come to power. Mendèsists, Socialists, Communists, and Republicans of different sorts denounced his maneuvers as bold Bonapartist gestures. Nevertheless, the hollowness of the occasion was not hidden by the manifesters' enthusiasm. They proclaimed republican virtues that for many years had not been identified with the institutions of the existing regime. It was almost as if the speakers were generalizing about what the Fourth Republic might have been; for in the eyes of an apathetic public, it was the regime of inflation, war, suppression of public liberties, and divided and demoralized political parties.

During the crisis, there was much talk of impending civil war. It was subsequently realized that rebel sections of the army and certain Gaullist elements had sought to profit by emphasizing the threat of future civil conflict. Many rumors circulated in the capital—one had it that Marseilles had been invaded by paratroopers and that the government was suppressing the information. Several minor riots took place in Paris, but the crisis confirmed that the France of 1958 was very different from the France of 1848. Most French workers were too concerned with maintaining their daily wages to take the time to express their opposition to General de Gaulle—that is, if they were opposed to him. They stayed on the job lest absenteeism from work remove the food from their dinner tables, and most of them returned to their homes at the end of each day's work—as men are likely to do if they have homes to which they can go. Thus, the crisis furnished evidence of the highly exaggerated importance of the Communist party as a revolutionary force in contemporary France. These weeks also demonstrated the fragility of all the classical French political parties and their inability to sustain the Fourth Republic. After May 27, their deputies in the National Assembly had come to realize that they had but two alternatives to which they could turn: (1) they could heed the demand of President Coty and invest De Gaulle as Premier, thereby allowing him to recast French political institutions in the form of extreme presidentialism; or (2) they could reject De Gaulle and thereby expose the government to military seizure and the country to military dictatorship. They accepted De Gaulle.

THE DEATH OF THE FOURTH REPUBLIC: SUICIDE OR REVOLUTION?

Scholars will debate for some time the exact date of the death of the Fourth Republic. Some contend that it died in 1946, in the flush of the liberation when the body politic reverted to its old divisions and habits. Others argue that the end came in 1952 when Antoine Pinay became Premier and re-established the strong influence of corporate and agricultural interests on governmental policy. Others insist that the final death thrust was administered when the French Army cast aside civil restraints and crossed the border of another sovereign state for the purpose of bombing one of its villages. They argue that Premier Gaillard "institutionalized anarchy" when he demonstrated that the politicians of the Republic were afraid of its generals. One of his critics described him as "too old to believe in Santa Claus, and too young to know any better." On the other hand, it is said that Gaillard realized the futility of the entire situation and had sought to leave the premiership after his first month in office. Some of his associates admit to his indecisiveness, but they concede that only another Clemenceau could have curbed the army at that late date. There is a rumor that General Salan telephoned Gaillard from Algiers on May 13—after the latter's resignation but before the investiture of Premier-designate Pflimlin—for the purpose of seeking instructions relative to dealing with the angry crowd then storming the government buildings, and that Gaillard replied, "Why ask me? It's not my problem. I'm not the President of the Council." In a broader sense, "Why ask me? It's not my problem" became an attitude that was particularly noticeable among citizens, politicians, and Premiers alike during the last days of the Fourth Republic. Mendès-France concludes that the Fourth Republic's death was self-inflicted and that it became its own worst enemy. Walter Lippmann states, "A regime . . . is rarely overthrown by a revolutionary movement; usually a regime collapses of its own weakness and corruption and then a revolutionary movement enters among the ruins and takes over the powers that have become vacant . . ." Many years ago, Paul Reynaud concluded that, "If regimes rarely reform themselves, it is chiefly because the abuses are so delicious." It was "delicious" as long as it lasted—at least it was for the deputies.

THE TRANSITION TO THE FIFTH FRENCH REPUBLIC

The De Gaulle government was invested by the National Assembly on June 1, 1958, by a vote of 329 to 224. On the following night, the Premier told the Assembly that "indispensable changes" would be proposed to the populace in the form of a national referendum and that Parliament would be sent home on a four-month "vacation." He requested and secured from the Assembly emergency powers that would allow him to rule by decree for a period of six months. His entire address took but six minutes and four seconds, and he left the chamber immediately after he delivered it. The deputies were speechless. The new government received on the following day from the Assembly, and on June 3 from the Council of the Republic, authorization to prepare a draft Constitution for a new Fifth Republic. The final draft was adopted by the government on September 3. It was submitted to a referendum on September 28, which was participated in by qualified voters in Metropolitan France, Algeria, and the Overseas Departments and Territories. All citizens twenty-one years of age or over who were registered on the electoral rolls, including members of the armed forces, were eligible to vote. They were asked to vote *oui* or *non* on the question: "Do you approve the Constitution that is being proposed to you by the Government of the Republic?"

The referendum had not the same meaning in the metropole and the overseas areas. In effect, it asked the Metropolitan French: (1) if they approved the Constitution proposed by the government of the Republic and its new arrangement of public powers; (2) if they were willing to assert their belief in General de Gaulle's ability to solve the Algerian problem with a policy that was then undefined; (3) if they were willing to "legitimize" De Gaulle's coming to power by revolutionary means, thereby assuring him that they wished him to remain chief of state; and (4) if they were in favor of a new Franco-African Community. For the French of the metropole, the referendum generally defined the nature of what the *oui* voter could subsequently expect and offered the *non* voter the opportunity of committing the society to subsequent alternatives that ranged from anarchy to military dictatorship. In turn, the referendum asked the Moslems of Algeria if they wished to be French and asked the Africans of the South Sahara if they were willing to enter an African-Franco Community. Finally, the Overseas Territories were given the option of forming a new Community with France or of breaking every tie with her.

The Constitution was endorsed by 83 per cent of those who voted; and it was accepted everywhere except in the African Territory of Guinea, which thereby declined membership in the French Community. No department in Metropolitan France returned a negative majority. The percentage of *oui* votes exceeded 70 per cent in all but five departments.

One of the most conspicuous features of the referendum was that almost two-thirds of the French working class voted *oui* despite the *non* campaign undertaken by the Communist party, almost one-half of the Socialist deputies, Daladier, Mendès-France, the General Confederation of Labor (CGT), and at least two other union organizations. Approximately 1,500,000 Communist electors voted for the Constitution, which was subsequently admitted by the Communist party itself.[4] This defection was particularly apparent in the *ceinture rouge* of Marseilles, Grenoble, Lille, and Paris (Jacques Duclos' constituency of Montreuil could muster a *non* vote of only 17,473); and in the *citadelles rouges* of Ivry, Saint-Denis, and Vitry. In all of France, only the town of Bagnolet voted down the Constitution (8,586 to 6,636).

THE FIFTH REPUBLIC AND THE PROBLEM OF ALGERIA

The Algerian insurrection is France's number one problem. Premier Michel Debré on January 15, 1959, said, "Algeria has absolute priority among the nation's concerns." The fate of the Fifth Republic, like that of the Fourth Republic, can still be decided on the other side of the Mediterranean.

General de Gaulle noted with enthusiasm the response of the Moslem population in Algeria to the 1958 constitutional referendum. He said that "the massive participation of the Algerians in the voting laid a psychological foundation, which had never existed before, for the political, economic, social, and cultural evolution of their country; and on this foundation, it is now possible for the Algerians and the French of Metropolitan France to build the future together." Stating that its results "mutually and forever pledge" France and Algeria to each other, he set forth in his 1958 speech of Constantine important aspects of his Algerian policy. In it he introduced plans for Algeria's modernization, free access of Moslems to government positions in Algeria and Metropolitan France; distribution of 617,500 acres of land to Moslem farmers; establishment of new industries; new educational opportunities for Moslems; construction of roads, ports, and housing; and employment for 400,000 new Moslem workers.

Shortly after the introduction of the Constantine Plan, Maurice Duverger wrote that "Some commentators see in the words of General de Gaulle

[4] *Le Monde*, October 7, 1958. See for report of Marcel Servin to the Communist party Central Committee.

signs of liberalism relative to Algeria, and distaste for integration. But the good people who judge *en gros*, who see only the grand lines, have stated that the men of May 13 have never been disavowed . . . that the discourse of Constantine commenced the application of integration. For a number of voters the views of the men of May 13 and of M. Soustelle are those of the General.[5] Interviewed in November, 1958, by the German weekly *Der Spiegel*, Soustelle stated that his "conception of integration consists of recognizing the Algerian personality," and that "This corresponds to the Five Year Plan that General de Gaulle announced in Constantine. I had recommended the same thing myself since 1955, in a proposition that was formerly called the Soustelle plan . . . It is inconceivable that I could ever find myself in opposition to General de Gaulle. Those who seek to set up a supposed difference between us do the General and myself and France a great disservice." On October 9, 1958, the Committee of Public Safety in Algeria and the Sahara declared its satisfaction with the speech of Constantine and that, without having pronounced the word integration, De Gaulle sought new economic, social, and political measures, "which are the equivalent of complete integration." Almost simultaneously, the extremist Marshal Alphonse Juin admitted that De Gaulle seldom pronounced the word integration but that he had "the greatest confidence in him." He concluded that, "We can build with the Algerian electors the form of integration judged the most suitable." And Roger Frey, then secretary-general of the UNR, stated, "The solidarity of all is . . . complete. The policy of France, it is the Charter of Constantine which has defined it."

If at that time De Gaulle's Algerian views were based on those of the men of May 13, his public statements did not reveal it. In fact, they revealed very little concerning Algeria. He remained secretive and referred only to the "Algerian personality" and used the word "integration" on only one public occasion. Indirectly, however, he did acknowledge that the war evaded a military solution; and by early 1959, he had essayed measures to which weaker governments of the Fourth Republic never dared resort. His clemency measures for some Moslem opponents were boldly proclaimed and he commuted to life imprisonment the death sentences of 180 Algerian prisoners and reduced by 10 per cent the sentences of others. Approximately 7,000 suspects were freed from prison camps, and the rebel leader Ben Bella and his associates were granted virtual prisoner-of-war status. De Gaulle's address of January 16, 1959, employed the word "pacification" as a means for discovering a solution to the conflict and not as an objective in itself.

By September 16, 1959, it appeared that De Gaulle was finally willing to publicize his views concerning the relationship between Algeria and

[5] Maurice Duverger, "Le Feu rouge," *Le Monde*, November 28, 1958, p. 2.

Metropolitan France. He announced on that date that the termination of hostilities would be followed by a referendum in which the Algerians would be allowed to express their will to remain with France or exercise self-determination and thereby cut all ties with her. The declaration infuriated rightists and Algerian "ultras"; and on January 24, 1960, insurrection broke out in Algiers—at just the time when it was suspected that preliminary talks were in progress between French and FLN representatives. The revolt was put down within two weeks. The army remained faithful to the orders of De Gaulle, and it appeared that the time was then propitious for the initiation of full discussions. Nevertheless, De Gaulle then went immediately to Algeria and told the unhappy settlers *Je vous ai compris*, emphasizing that pacification efforts would be renewed in an effort to end the Moslem rebellion! The integrationists who had revolted were given the impression that they were being welcomed back into the household with a status that was in some ways superior to what they had enjoyed prior to the beginning of their insurrection. Several days later, De Gaulle told the same settlers that the referendum would be held but under the supervision of the French Army. The FLN shortly announced that it was receptive to a referendum; that it, too, was prepared to go along with the ability of Algerians to choose self-determination; but that army supervision would result only in electoral manipulation and fraud. De Gaulle replied by re-extending to them his offer of "the peace of the brave" and contended that the war could come to an end only if the rebels would lay down their arms and submit to an amnesty—only then, he said, could France get on with the business of the referendum.[6] And so the insurrection continued.

ALGERIA AND THE REFERENDUM OF JANUARY, 1961

On December 20, 1960, President de Gaulle announced that the French people would be asked to express their views on Algerian self-determination in a referendum that was to be held in January, 1961. Passed first by the Council of Ministers in the form of a decree, the following question was put to the population of Metropolitan France, Algeria, and the Overseas Departments and Territories. "Do you approve the Government bill submitted to the French people by the President of the Republic concerning the self-determination of the Algerian populations and the organization of public powers in Algeria before self-determination?" The voters were asked to vote *oui* or *non*. The government bill stated that as soon

[6] De Gaulle defined the "peace of the brave" in 1958. See *Le Monde*, October 23, 1958, p. 2: "I have spoken of the peace of the brave. What is it? Simply this: that those who opened fire cease and that they return without humiliation to their families and their work."

as security conditions permit, the Algerian people will be allowed to determine by universal suffrage whether they wish to remain with France or break every tie with her. The bill also stated that until this is achieved, the Council of Ministers will determine by decree the organization of public powers in Algeria. The bill foresaw the creation of an Algerian executive and Algerian assemblies with jurisdiction over all the Algerian departments and the establishment of Algerian executive and deliberative organs within the various regions and departments.

The referendum was held in Metropolitan France and the Overseas Departments and Territories on January 8, 1961, and in Algeria on January 6, 7, and 8. In Metropolitan France, prereferendum campaigning was restricted to those political parties organized in the Senate and National Assembly who had applied to participate in it. Those who took part were the Communist party, the Socialist party (SFIO), the Radical Socialists, the MRP, the Independents, and the UNR. Jacques Soustelle's National Regroupment was allowed to campaign in Algeria but not in Metropolitan France. Nevertheless, the parliamentary group *Unité de la République,* with thirty-two deputies and favoring *Algérie francaise,* changed its name to the *Regroupment national pour l'unité de la République* in order to allow Soustelle to participate in the prereferendum campaign. Each party was granted radio and television time between December 26 and 30, 1960; a total of twelve broadcasts were held. Each party was limited to one eight-minute telecast and one ten-minute radiocast. Party posters were restricted to certain official locations, and only eligible parties were allowed to hold public meetings. In Algeria, a decree of the Ministry of State in charge of Algerian Affairs qualified nine parties and groups to participate in the prereferendum campaign. They were the National Association for the Support of General de Gaulle's Action, the National Regroupment, the Movement for the Community, the UNR, the SFIO, the MRP, the Independents, the Radical Socialists, and the Coordination Committee for the Support of the Policy of the Chief of State. Between December 26 and 30, each eligible party and group was allowed one five-minute radiocast and one five-minute telecast.

Voting in the referendum was by white and purple ballots; the former signified *oui* and the latter *non.* Balloting in the Algerian and Saharan departments was supervised by a central control commission situated in Algiers and by commissions in each of the departments. The results of the vote are given in Table 11–1.

DISTRIBUTION OF THE VOTE

The *oui* vote was the strongest in the western and eastern parts of the nation, which is country that is traditionally conservative and religious.

Table 11–1. Results of the Referendum of January 8, 1961, Issued by the Constitutional Council

Area	Basic Data	% of Registered Voters	% of Valid Ballots
METROPOLITAN FRANCE			
Eligible voters	27,184,408		
Votes cast	20,791,246		
Yes votes	15,200,072	55.91	75.26
No votes	4,996,474		
Abstentions	6,393,162		
ALGERIA			
Eligible voters	4,470,215		
Votes cast	2,626,689		
Yes votes	1,749,969	39.14	69.51
No votes	767,546		
Abstentions	1,843,526		
SAHARAN DEPARTMENTS			
Eligible voters	291,692		
Votes cast	193,018		
Yes votes	168,563	57.78	89.88
No votes	18,970		
Abstentions	98,674		
OVERSEAS DEPARTMENTS (French Guiana, Guadeloupe, Martinique, Réunion)			
Eligible voters	398,099		
Votes cast	241,174		
Yes votes	211,376	53.09	90.13
No votes	23,157		
Abstentions	156,925		
OVERSEAS TERRITORIES (Antarctica, Comoro Islands, French Somaliland, French Polynesia, Miquelon, New Caledonia, St. Pierre)			
Eligible voters	175,819		
Votes cast	134,786		
Yes votes	117,688	66.95	90.01
No votes	11,628		
Abstentions	41,033		

SOURCE: *French Affairs,* CXII, January, 1961 (French Embassy, Press and Information Division, New York, 1961), 8.

In thirteen departments of the west and in eight of the east, it exceeded 60 per cent of the total vote cast. However, it also surpassed 60 per cent of the total vote in the industrialized departments of the Nord and Pas-de-Calais, areas that are generally regarded as Socialist bastions. In two distinct parts of the country, negative votes and abstentions outnumbered *oui* votes. One was formed by the departments of the Indre, Cher, Nièvre, Saone-et-Loire, Allier, Puy-de-Dôme, Corrèze, Creuse, and the Haute-Vienne. The other consisted of the Var, Bas-Alpes, Isère, Vaucluse, Bouches-du-Rhône, Gard, Herault, Aude, Pyrenées Orientale, Haute Garonne, Tarn-et-Garonne, Lot-et-Garonne, Gers, and Ariège. Parts of these two areas are economically regressive; some are traditionally of Left orientation. Although the *oui's* won a majority of the vote cast in the department of the Seine, many of its *non* votes came from the Communist party. In twelve communes of the famous *ceinture rouge,* the *non's* received an absolute majority of the total vote, which enabled the Communist party to regain a considerable amount of the support it had lost in the referendum of 1958. Finally, the conservative vote went solidly to De Gaulle; and those rightist leaders who campaigned against the referendum met with little success, particularly in their own geographical areas. Jacques Soustelle's *non* campaign did not prevent three out of every four voters in the Rhone from voting *oui.* Roger Duchet, mayor of Beaune (Côte-d'Or) and a strong supporter of a *non* vote, saw his hometown outvote him by five to one.

POLITICAL ASPECTS OF THE REFERENDUM

The referendum was designed to appeal to the entire population. Francois Mitterand stated that it was based on a series of contradictory promises to elements of the populace in deep disagreement with each other. It urged the Metropolitan French to express their confidence in De Gaulle's ability to achieve peace. It asked the loyal Moslems of Algeria to vote *oui* for the purpose of subsequently obtaining Algerian executive and legislative organs. It asked the European settlers to vote *oui* in exchange for future French protection. It appealed to the army for its support; De Gaulle stated prior to the referendum that the military would serve as the "educator and protector" of the new Algeria. Finally, it suggested that a *oui* vote would make possible De Gaulle's promised "round table"—one which would embrace all shades of Algerian opinion, including the FLN—as one of the instruments by which peace can be sought.

The question put to the public in the referendum was such that few could vote on it without experiencing some degree of frustration. Those who wished to vote *non* because of De Gaulle's exercise of personal power could not do so without voting against Algerian self-determination. Those who wanted to vote *oui* could not be sure that their vote would shorten the war, that it would lead to the cessation of hostilities or to Algerian self-determination. They could express only their belief in De Gaulle's ability to achieve these feats. Those who wanted to vote *non* to register their contempt for Algerian self-determination knew, however, that even if they did win a majority that De Gaulle would not adopt *Algérie francaise*. Many of those who wanted to could not abstain without passing up an opportunity to express themselves on an issue on which they entertained deep convictions. The Unified Socialist party (PSU) and several other minor organizations, for example, wanted to vote against De Gaulle's personalism and for Algerian self-determination. They abstained, however, and announced prior to the referendum their moral support of the Moslem mass and their reasons for not balloting.

The results of the vote in the referendum clearly indicated that many Metropolitan French believed that they were paving the way for an environment in which De Gaulle will be freer to negotiate with the rebel provisional government of the Algerian Republic (GPRA). Now it is obvious that an increasing number of citizens have come to believe that the conflict can be settled only by negotiating with their adversary and not by continuing the war. For more than seven years, the Republic and its adversary have fought each other to a standoff. These people know that the Republic cannot vanquish its opponent and that the latter cannot banish it from Algeria. They feel that the negotiation of mutual guaranties can bring the fighting to an end and that the alternative is to go on fighting for years to come. The conflict offers a striking example of how a modern state and its army can find itself involved in a stalemate with a small guerilla force that has the weight of Moslem public opinion on its side. For a long time, the French asserted that the Moslem masses were for De Gaulle and opposed to the FLN. They created that fiction, and it appears that they even came to believe it. For a long time, the Moslem masses were relatively silent; and it appeared that their great intimidator, the FLN, prevented them from expressing their sympathy for the French. That illusion ended in December, 1960, when thousands of Moslems poured out of the Algier's Casbah waving the green independence flag and demanding the ouster of the French. Similar demonstrations occurred in Oran and other centers. The *Algérie de Beni-oui-oui* was then as dead as the *Algérie de papa*. The picture was clear. Algeria was never French, it was never Gaullist, it is Algerian. Moreover, its conception of an "Algerian Algeria" is strictly an Algerian one.

THE REVOLT OF THE GENERALS—APRIL 21, 1961

If the question put to the public in the referendum offered very few clear choices, it did acknowledge that the government felt that *Algérie francaise* is dead and that there is no way in which it can be revived. Premier Debré laid to rest the very idea that he had once held dear when he described integration as "an impossible solution." In his press conference of April 11, 1961, President de Gaulle candidly said that Algeria costs France "more than she is worth to us" and that France would consider with "the greatest calm a solution whereby Algeria would cease to be a part of France." He admitted that the Moslems obviously do not "wish to become a part of the French people," that Algeria will be a sovereign state, and that "France will raise no obstacle to this." He acknowledged that the Moslem insurrection merely confirmed his own thoughts on self-determination, ones to which he had subscribed since the conference of Brazzaville! This admission was the final insult to many of the men who had been instrumental in bringing him to power in 1958—men who stood for *Algérie francaise* and who had thought erroneously that he then endorsed all of their own beliefs.

In his press conference, De Gaulle said that if Algeria wishes to become a sovereign state "associated" with France, France will then be willing to "lend her economic, administrative, financial, cultural, military, and technical aid." He stated, however, that the conditions of "association" rest on France's acquisition of preferential conditions for economic and cultural exchange and the "bases and facilities necessary for our defense."

On the afternoon of April 20, 1961, Colonels Godard, Gardes, Broizat, Argoud, and Lacheroy completed their plans to revolt against President de Gaulle and retain Algeria under French domination. They were joined within hours by Generals Challe, Zeller, Jouhaud, Salan, and Gardy. All of these men had been involved in the revolt of May 13, 1958, which brought De Gaulle to power. That evening the First Paratroop Regiment of the Foreign Legion left its base at Zeralda to capture Algiers, and paratroop commandos left their bases at Staoueli and Blida to join them. By two o'clock the following morning, the Algier's *Palais d'Éte* had been occupied; and Jean Morin, delegate of the government in Paris, had been put under detention with Robert Buron, Minister of Public Works and Transport, who had just arrived in Algiers on an official visit. By 4:00 A.M., the rebellious Tenth Parachute Division had moved to take the city of Constantine. Oran fell when General Pouilly proclaimed both his fidelity to De Gaulle and his inability to fire on French soldiers, even if they were rebels. Those elements already engaged in the rebellion were subsequently joined by the paratroops of the Twenty-Sixth Division, the Thirteenth Brigade of the Foreign Legion, and the Second and Third Infantry Regiments. All of these units constituted a small percentage of the total military force based in Algeria.

The rebel generals and colonels announced their attachment to the principle of *Algérie francaise* and that they had taken "power in order to save France from the danger of communism." Their "anti-Communist mission" was emphasized in statements that were relayed in English on the Algier's radio by an announcer of the National Broadcasting Company. They told of General Challe's determination to strengthen NATO and to integrate French forces in it if his rebellion succeeded. While Challe was begging for American support, American diplomatic representatives in Paris were assuring De Gaulle that he could count on American aid if an invasion of Metropolitan France took place.

By April 25, it was obvious that a majority of the French Army, Navy, and Air Corps stood by the Republic. The insurrection ended when the rebels tried to capture the naval base of Mers-el-Kébir. They were repulsed when loyal warships fired several warning shots over their heads as they stood on the heights of the city. Order was restored rapidly. Generals Challe, Jouhaud, and Zeller were returned to Paris for trial; and Generals Salan and Gardy took flight.

What were the "lessons" of the insurrection? First, most of the Army, Navy, and Air Corps remained loyal to the Republic. In fact, few of the military men of "May 13" were in Algeria on April 21, 1961. General Massu was elsewhere, relieved of his command (his wife was on hand to tell *les Algerois* that her husband would still be the "saviour of France"). Activists such as Chateau-Jobert, Thomazo, Ducasse, Gigeard, Mirambeau, and Trinquier were no longer on the scene. Those "heroes" of 1958 who had since defected from De Gaulle were given very little opportunity to be traitors in 1961. Second, the insurrection gave the appearance of being strictly a military action from beginning to end. Settlers who were anxious to give the army rebels their support were kept in the background by the officers. Such professional "ultras" as Lagaillarde, Ortiz, Perez, Ronda, and Susini found that their direct participation was not wanted. Third, the speed with which the rebellion was put down (or collapsed) helped to clear the way for President de Gaulle to enter rapidly into negotiations with the GPRA. Shortly after the end of the revolt, he announced that future peace talks at Evian-les-Bains would seek to settle the conditions under which the Algerian referendum will take place; that they would establish "if possible, an agreement between the government and these same elements on a solution of constructive association between France and Algeria"; and that if the talks prove fruitless, the Republic will then "hasten and advance on the spot the accession of Algerians to all responsibilities, including those of their government, so that, in spite of everything, the new Algeria may be built." The peace talks were held at Evian and subsequently at Lugrin, and both meetings failed to bring an end to the conflict.

Contemporary French policy accepts an "Algerian Algeria" that may ultimately proclaim its sovereign existence and rupture all ties with France. Why, then, does the war continue when only one solution appears to be inevitable? First, the conflict will not end until the Republic and the GPRA exchange mutual guaranties concerning the fate of the

European settlers now in Algeria. It is obvious that De Gaulle will not abandon them to complete Moslem domination (although the resignation of M. Jacomet, secretary-general of the Algerian administration, in November, 1960, was due in large part to what he construed as De Gaulle's willingness to make few demands from the FLN concerning the future of settlers who may wish to stay in Algeria and remain French). Second, the war continues because an immediate peace—at the price of exorbitant French guaranties to the FLN—might destroy the prospects for a future "associated" Algeria and lead to its unassociated independence. De Gaulle does not hesitate to admit that Algeria is a nation—yet he cannot conceive of its destiny as being separate from that of France. He thinks instead of an "Algerian Algeria" that will associate with France and preserve with her certain indispensable ties. One day—after the termination of hostilities—its people will participate in another referendum in which they will decide once and for all whether they wish to associate with France or break every bond with her. De Gaulle finds it impossible to believe that Algeria could or should vote for any alternative other than the former. Third, the war continues because De Gaulle still clings to the belief (feebly now) that by some miracle the insurrection will end and the Moslems will assert their willingness to remain with France. Because he believes so strongly in France, he has difficulty recognizing that there are others who do not believe in her at all. Fourth, the war continues because the FLN wants Algeria to attain full sovereignty prior to concluding certain important agreements with France. In turn, the Republic is determined to secure these agreements from the FLN prior to granting Algeria her sovereignty. Fifth, the war continues because of disagreement between the Republic and the FLN over the future of the Sahara. In his press conference of September 5, 1961, De Gaulle demanded future access to the Sahara for exploitation of its gas and oil, the right to establish airfields there, and transit through it for communication with other parts of Africa. He stated that it will be necessary to create "something special" out of the Sahara (possibly a condominium) if these opportunities are denied France and if "association" fails. The FLN considers the Sahara a natural part of a future independent Algeria and contends that the French must recognize this before both parties can discuss other aspects of the peace.

AN "ASSOCIATED" ALGERIA

In 1957, an astute political observer argued that if France decides "to integrate Algeria in the Republic, it will cost as much in terms of yearly investments as the cost of maintaining Metropolitan France."[7] However,

[7] Raymond Aron, *La Tragédie algérienne* (Paris: Plon, 1957), p. 22.

now it matters little if integration would be financially prohibitive; it is not the present policy of the Republic, and its subsequent adoption appears to be out of the question. Nevertheless, it matters a great deal that an "associated" Algeria will demand great financial outlays by the Republic. The Moslem population is growing at so fast a rate that it will number approximately eighteen million by 1980. In his address of December 20, 1960, President de Gaulle stated that "in order to live, to develop, and to become prosperous and modern, Algeria must have help." During 1960, France invested in Algeria more than $800,000,000. The country cannot continue to remain in the neglected condition in which it has existed for so many years. The Constantine Plan is only the beginning, and it will require more than an outlay of $800,000,000 per year to modernize the country and to provide social services and real employment for a Moslem population that is now so badly in need of assistance.

THE FUTURE?

Prior to De Gaulle's announcement of an "Algerian Algeria," various private plans were proposed relative to its future status. One argued for the resettling of the majority of French settlers in a belt ranging from Algiers to Oran, which would constitute a "French Republic" in the interior. This plan suggested that Moslems live there according to predetermined percentages and enjoy civil rights and, eventually, political rights. It would have made the remainder of the country an Algerian Republic in which the French would enjoy equal rights, although as foreigners. Another plan proposed that Tunisia annex the oriental part, Morocco the occidental part, and the center would constitute the French departments. Yet another plan argued for the creation of two separate republics, each of different sovereignty. The shortcoming of this scheme is that it would not solve the real problem; moreover, it would further the "Balkanization," or "Bao-Daization" of North Africa. A "Middle East solution" is apt to be no solution at all. Finally, in speeches delivered during 1961, De Gaulle alluded to another plan that would partition Algeria into two separate communities; the settlers of European stock and those Moslems wishing to remain French would be regrouped around Algiers and Oran (when asked why they would be regrouped around these two centers, De Gaulle replied, "It's easier to protect two departments than thirteen"). He admitted that partition is not a "preferable solution" and only a "last resort," but that it will become a distinct possibility if peace negotiations fail and if "association" does not materialize. He added that partition would be a temporary expedient, and yet he failed to define its duration.

Achieving a rapid peace in Algeria is imperative for the French. Each day of war drives Algeria farther away from France and endangers the stability of the Fifth Republic. Perhaps, future discussions will reach the stage where both the French and the FLN will be able to proceed to a negotiated peace.[8] Perhaps, it could have happened in 1955 when moderates on both sides were close to the situation, and it might be possible in the future if De Gaulle remains in the driver's seat. It will never be possible if the extremists of Algiers and of the FLN reacquire the upper hand in their respective camps. On the other hand, the war can continue for a long time to come. The FLN knows that time and history are on its side. The final decision in the Algerian affair may not be of France's making if the nation remains afflicted with a paralysis of waiting.

SELECTED READING

BRACE, R. and J. *Ordeal in Algeria.* New York: D. Van Nostrand Co., Inc., 1960.
DUVERGER, M. *The French Political System.* Chicago: University of Chicago Press, 1958.
MACRIDIS, R., and BROWN, B. *The de Gaulle Republic, Quest for Unity.* Homewood, Ill.: The Dorsey Press, 1960.
MATTHEWS, R. *The Death of the Fourth Republic.* London: Eyre & Spottiswoode, Ltd., 1954.
TILLON, G. *Algeria: The Realities.* New York: Alfred A. Knopf (a division of Random House, Inc.), 1958.
WILLIAMS, P. *Politics in Post-war France; Parties and the Constitution in the Fourth Republic.* New York: Longmans, Green & Co., Inc., 1958.

[8] Numerous contacts have taken place between representatives of both forces, e.g., in Cairo, April 12, 1956; in Belgrade, July 2, 1956; in Rome, September 2–3, 1956; in Tunis, July 5–10, 1957; and in Switzerland, in 1958–1959. Meetings were held in Metropolitan France in June and July, 1960, but the discussions never got off the ground. More meetings took place in 1961 in Evian-les-Bains and Lugrin.

12

Political Ideologies

THE "LEFT" AND THE "RIGHT"

Segments of French society subscribe to diverse conceptions concerning the organization of society and government. Some conceptions predate the French Revolution; others are postrevolutionary in character. All have undergone varying degrees of change since their origin. New doctrinal modifications and reinterpretations have preceded or emerged in the wake of each political crisis. Finally, although independent of each other, these doctrines occasionally overlap.

French political doctrines are labelled "Left" or "Right." Those of the Left—while differing from each other—generally favor the separation of church and state, the subordination of clerical to civil power, the subordination of property to the general welfare, popular sovereignty, and liberty to authority. Doctrines of the Right—while also differing from each other—may or may not favor separation of church and state and the subordination of clerical to civil authority. They may or may not subordinate property to the general welfare; if they do, it is to a lesser extent than the doctrines of the Left. Right-wing doctrines may or may not include the principle of popular sovereignty; if they do, they subject it to far greater limitations than doctrines of the Left. Right-wing doctrines may or may not prefer liberty to authority.

As the years progress, terms such as Left and Right become less meaningful. Until the twentieth century, the Left was synonomous with the position of those who supported the republican tradition and its commitment to the separation of church and state. Nonetheless, since then the clerical issue has lost much of its relevance; and until the Gaullist adventure of 1958, the republican issue was all but solved. In the ninteenth century, the church spent much of its time affiliating with antirepublican issues and movements; this is hardly analogous to the position that it occupies today. Although some militant anticlericals still speak of the church as being part of the Right, that generalization has more to do with where the church once stood than with where it now stands. The church has spoken out against the war in Algeria, and it has taken a position against various inequities practiced by both state and society. If it supports the army, it has not rushed blindly to the defense of that "sacred ark" as it did in the time of Dreyfus. Its contemporary social views are moderate; and some of them are not too far removed from those that characterize the outlook of Pierre Mendès-France, a Frenchman of the moderate Left.

Contemporary Radical Socialists offer yet another example of the way in which the terms "Right" and "Left" fall short of adequate application. Up to the beginning of the present century, the Radical Socialists were the party of the Left. They fought an intense struggle to separate church and state, and they won it. Their statesmen were highly critical of the political and social privileges that could be purchased by money. Although in a historical sense the doctrine of radicalism is still considered "Left," now its men are generally identified with upper- and middle-bourgeois interests; and their approach to property renders somewhat ludicrous any effort to link them with the Left. If their inspiration once came from Gambetta or the young Clemenceau, their inspiration now comes from such moderates as Gaillard or Edgar Faure.

If the terms "Left" and "Right" now mean less than they once did, the fact remains that they still mean something. There is today a Left and a Right that are as divided among themselves as they are opposed to each other. There is a Communist Left, a pro-Communist Left, an anti-Communist Left, a Left that is neither pro nor anti-Communist, a Gaullist Left, an anti-Gaullist Left, and a Left that is neither pro nor anti-Gaullist! There is a liberal, republican Right, a conservative, republican Right, and a Right that is antirepublican and Fascist. There is a center, too; but its strength and importance is considerably inferior to anything that exists to either side of itself. It does influence somewhat the more moderate Left and the more liberal Right, although not to the extent that English liberalism influences conservatism and laborism.

FRENCH DEMOCRACY AND AUTHORITY

Many Americans interpret democracy as that system that seeks an equilibrium between the individual and society, so that one does not brazenly declare its precedence over the other; many Frenchmen do not see it this way. In France, the democratic tradition generally is interpreted in a way that is decidedly "French." Frequently, it is friendlier to broader dashes of authority than is the case with Anglo-American democracy. Consequently, French society often comes up with versions of "Bonapartized democracy" that are little concerned with balancing the conflicting claims of the majority and the minority. Today, for example, some undeniably democratic Frenchmen are receptive to De Gaulle's frequent rhetorical references to the popular will and are concerned less with his Bonapartism and his contempt for the minority.

In times of crisis, the democratic tradition recedes everywhere; nevertheless, democratic recession is usually more profound when it occurs in France. No simple explanation can be given for this phenomenon; perhaps one reason is that France was a monarchy for so many years and a democracy for not so many. Although the monarchical tradition gave way to the democratic nearly a century ago, many of the habits and practices generated by the former survive. Contemporary French politicians profess almost to a man to adhere to the democratic tradition, but many aspects of their behavior are influenced by predemocratic and monarchical roots. The political parties make numerous representations in behalf of democratic doctrines, but their maneuvers resemble those of groups "arrayed around the court" rather than those of the great political formations of the modern state. Despite the republican form of the modern French state, many of its societal tendencies predate it. One of the ways to better understand the workings, practices, and habits of France's government, politics, and "democracy" is to familiarize oneself with the practices and habits of monarchical France.

THE DOCTRINES

Socialism

Socialism is a phenomenon of the historical development of France and originated in the reaction to the social inequities of the industrial revolutions of the nineteenth century. From the time of its emergence, it was not one but many doctrines, all of which were critical of capitalism.

There is a type of socialism that adheres generally to an optimistic view of man's "nature" and his capabilities and which rejects class warfare and the idea of irreconcilable classes. It seeks without scientific pretence the emancipation of all social classes from exploitation because it considers that achievement to conform to its conception of justice. It emphasizes primarily its "moral" orientation. Another type seeks to synthesize its moral convictions and Marxism. A third type is Marxist, which favors rigorous systematization of thought and claims to be founded strictly on empiricism and holds to the belief that certain immutable laws govern all human phenomena.

Socialist thought developed during the latter half of the nineteenth century. Its acceleration was particularly great during the era of Louis Napoleon Bonaparte, who supported the new industrialism with scant regard for its social consequences, who did much to intensify antagonisms between bourgeois and worker elements, and who remained unconcerned with worker's representation in government (like Guizot, he thought that the way to acquire the vote was to go out and make some money). Socialism increased its influence under the Third Republic when the latter extended representation to the working class. Consequently, the Socialist movement underwent transition; it entered the political arena and became more practical and less theoretical. Moving closer to the established political order, it acquired a new "respectability," a transformation for which one Socialist was primarily responsible. That person was Jean Léon Jaurès, who succeeded in orienting a part of the movement in the direction of the parliamentary tradition. Doctrinally, he sought to reconcile the materialist conception of history with the political traditions of liberal bourgeois democracy. His emphasis was primarily on what he considered the moral aspects of socialism, and he was convinced that the state of the future could evolve only in the direction of what he called "the ideal of humanity."

Jaurès believed that education would make the workers aware of their newly acquired electoral strength and lead them to collaborate in effecting a peaceful transformation of the status of private property. He sought to distinguish between "evolutionary revolution" and those doctrines that preached the conflict of irreconcilable classes and the forceful overthrow of bourgeois regimes. He was an active political participationist and served in the Chamber of Deputies until his assassination in 1914. There he supported the quest for the adoption of an eight-hour workday, a weekly day of rest, a minimum-wage law, a progressive income tax on all revenue, and participation in elections by Socialists—a position that some of his Socialist opponents rejected on the grounds that it was indefensibly bourgeois. In 1899 when Waldeck-Rousseau chose the Socialist Millerand for Portfolio of Commerce, Jaurès defended the appointment against the attacks of Jules Guesde and the Marxian Socialists.

If Jaurès was convinced that socialism could achieve its ends by peaceful, evolutionary means, the orthodox Marxian Socialists continued to believe that only revolution could turn the trick. While Jaurès asserted that "The democratic Republic . . . heralds socialism, prepares for it, contains it implicitly to some extent, because only republicanism can lead to socialism by legal evolution without break of continuity," Guesde and his followers argued to the contrary when they contended that the democratic republic was a purely bourgeois form. They continued to attack all methods that advocated cooperation with the middle class and favored abstention from politics and repudiated the feasibility of bourgeois electoral methods. By the beginning of the twentieth century, the issue of reformism versus revolutionary Marxism had become acute in Socialist ranks. The doctrinal quarrel continued and it still exists today—although it must be recognized that there is often a wide gap between the revolutionary doctrine and non-revolutionary behavior of many contemporary Marxian Socialists.

French socialism has changed considerably since the time of Jaurès. No longer are there very many supporters of the Jaurès-Blum legacy or the humanist interpretation of socialism; yet it cannot be said that the latter has been entirely extinguished. It continues to exist and views socialism as a force that will result in the moral regeneration of mankind. It attempts, as Blum said, to develop and satisfy the religious urge in men; and it asks that men base their behavior on ideals that transcend them. Concerned with both moral values and material necessities, it contends that both are dependent upon each other. It believes that the extinction of material wants is not purely a material end and that higher wages, better working conditions, and security in old age are factors that are as moral as they are material. It professes to measure progress by what Jaurès called the "yardstick of humanity" and holds mass welfare to be one of its essential ingredients. It emphasizes the superiority of the individual over the economic and social factors that oppress him, and it regards economic democracy as the precondition of political democracy. It views the contemporary established social order as but a privileged substitute for the economic and social oligarchy of prerevolutionary France.

While the Jaurès-Blum legacy has receded in recent years, the Guesdian interpretation of socialism has grown stronger. It professes to be Marxist and rejects humanism, which it views as a defect rather than an advantage. It considers it sentimental, if not clerical. This type of thought is particularly prevalent in the Socialist bastions of the north, in the departments of the Nord and Pas-de-Calais, and in those areas sometimes described as "Guesde country." Guy Mollet, secretary-general of the Socialist party (SFIO), adheres to this tradition and professes his Marxism whenever the opportunity presents itself. At the same time, his behavior is more that of a Conservative than anything else—so much so that segments of the moderate Right take delight in accusing him of frequently practicing the politics that the Right itself would never dare to undertake! When Mollet "justified" his intervention in Suez with quotations from Marx and Engels, the spectacle was nothing short of ludicrous. The humanists contend that he is not a Socialist, the Marxists argue that he is not a Marxist, and some of the men who have worked closely with him insist that he does not believe in anything except Mollet.[1]

[1] André Philip, *Le Socialisme trahi* (Paris: Plon, 1957), p. 8. Philip insists that there is little difference between Mollet's thought and conservatism. He describes it as pitting the little against the big in vulgar fashion. Curiously enough, after the liberation, Philip played a considerable role in getting Mollet to take a more active part in politics. Philip remembers when he criticized Mollet for being "too timid." The "timid" Mollet was instrumental in arranging Philip's expulsion from the SFIO in 1958.

Liberalism

The Constituent Assembly of 1789 broke with France's monarchical and clerical past by proclaiming the Declaration of the Rights of Man and Citizen. It expressed the conviction that "ignorance, forgetfulness, or contempt of the rights of man are the sole cause of the public miseries and of the corruption of governments." It declared "natural, inalienable, and sacred" such rights as property, liberty, security, and resistance to oppression—adjudging them to be of universal character. It defined sovereignty as vested in the nation—not in anything outside of it—and law as the expression of the general will before which all citizens were equal. It prohibited *ex post facto* laws and accessibility to employment on grounds other than capacity. It upheld freedom of opinion and religious belief and recommended the adoption of a general tax apportioned equally among the citizens according to their means. It coined the revolutionary word "citizen" and indicated that members of the society had a legal right to determine the course of their own destiny and that they were no longer the manipulatable subjects of the monarchy and the church. The principles set forth in the Declaration constitute one of the clearest expressions of French liberalism, which have reemerged in many constitutions subsequent to 1789. In 1946, the Preamble of the Constitution of the Fourth Republic reaffirmed "The rights and freedoms of man and of the citizen consecrated by the Declaration of Rights of 1789."

One of the major difficulties of French liberalism is that it has changed so little since 1789. Dedicated initially to the winning of a republic, it continued that struggle long after the Republic became a fact. It stood staunchly by a little-changing doctrine while the world around it changed. It came to be associated almost exclusively with sentiments that favor liberty from governmental interference. Stressing individual rights more than individual responsibilities, it became affiliated more with the cause of property holders than with the interests of the non-propertied categories of society. It opposed authority and defended popular sovereignty, and in doing so created for itself paradoxes that it was never able to resolve. It professed to speak for society, but very often it spoke only for some individuals in society. Its individualism ran so deep that it became almost antisociety. When the Republic made certain inroads on property, French liberalism became a highly negative doctrine concerned with blocking state action. Today, its view of "liberty, equality, and fraternity" fits the historical scene far less effectively than it did in the France of 1789. Its present conception of "liberty, equality, and fraternity" is class dominated and historically dated.

While liberalism contributed to its own decline by failing to adjust to the demands of a changing world, perhaps that decline was inevitable. An individualism so exaggerated helped to divide rather than unite French society. Liberalism across the channel played a decidedly different role; it broke away from anarchic individualism and united rather than fragmented English society. There, after a bloodless revolution and long evolution, it triumphed—so much so that today Tories and Laborites alike readily acknowledge that they have been "liberalized." When early nineteenth-century French monarchists such as Benjamin Constant and Chateaubriand exhibited a definite interest in liberalism, it was not by accident that they turned their attention primarily to the English scene in order to examine it as a developed thing. They lamented France's inability to profit by the English experience; and Constant, in particular, decried the unwillingness of his contemporaries to even understand—let alone appreciate—this very important source of English strength. But the reaction of Constant's contemporaries was also understandable, inasmuch as French liberalism was born of bloodly revolution and secured only after the application of the most painful procedures. No wonder liberalism was able to find a happier home in England than in France.

Catholicism

The French nation became Christian during the sixth century. Catholicism was proclaimed the official state religion in 1516. Although the church distinguished between the spiritual and temporal powers, it clearly emphasized the supremacy of the former over the latter. More than a few of its spokesmen declared dogmatically that a Pope could admonish a monarch whenever temporal power jeopardized spiritual authority. Education was entrusted solely to the church by the state. Both church and state were so closely linked that the revolutionary movement of 1789 necessarily was as anticlerical as it was antimonarchical.

The Revolution divested the church of its prerevolutionary prerogatives. Education was reclaimed from it by the state. Its lands were confiscated, and it was no longer allowed to hold the power that it had legally exercised over the individual. Nevertheless, with the termination of the revolutionary era, various privileges were restored to the church. Church schools made their reappearance, and in 1850 the Falloux Law reinvested the church with supervision of elementary education and authorized clerics to teach without having to meet state educational qualifications. Louis Napoleon strengthened the church to the point where it became again a potent influence in national affairs. Had he pursued a wiser course, he might have averted much subsequent conflict between church and state.

The church entered the Third Republic clinging to certain cherished visions that had their origin in the old regime. Some Jesuits played a role analogous to the one now played by some Communists, that is, conspiring against the Republic and doing whatever they could to bring it down.

Their objective was restoration of Catholic primacy over the state. They sought a Catholic monarchy and the abolition of parliamentarism, which they equated with "Judaism, Englishism, and Protestantism." For a time, they concentrated on the army and attempted to use it as a vehicle by which they could implement their ends. Simultaneously, they sought the protection of certain republican prerogatives calculated to assure their own position within the Republic, should it fail to fall. For some years, they were strengthened by a Republic whose shortcomings were only too apparent and by such supporters of their cause as Édouard Drumont, Leo Taxil, and others. Their activities overshadowed those of a relatively uninfluential minority Catholic element whose views were best represented in the writings of Jean Baptiste Henri Lacordaire, Compte Charles de Montalembert, and Marc Sangnier. These Left Catholics differentiated between spiritual and political authority and sought a definite separation of church and state. They pledged themselves to freedom of expression and viewed secular education as a state obligation.

The church withheld its recognition of the Third Republic until 1880, and then it waited another decade before acknowledging that Catholics could uphold it. Much of the history of the Third Republic between 1875 and 1920 revolved around the conflict between church and state. Various governments began in the 1890's to systematically reduce church power, and complete separation of church and state was achieved in 1905. Diplomatic relations between the state and the Vatican were terminated until 1921. Church properties were confiscated (their use by the church was not prohibited) except for those that performed certain charitable activities on behalf of the needy. Church gifts were limited and collections were restricted. Not until after World War I did the church-state controversy slow down noticeably. Today, the conflict is by no means solved, but it has been resolved. More than twelve million French citizens have signed a petition protesting against the Gaullist regime's grant of subsidies for parochial schools, and yet thus far the dispute has remained free of violence and that type of controversy that goes to the very roots of society. Seemingly endless verbal exchanges have become the residue of what was once a fierce struggle—and this, in itself, constitutes some measure of progress.

French society still regards itself as Catholic; approximately 80 per cent of France's citizens were baptized in the Catholic church. Nevertheless, there is a difference between practicing and non-practicing Catholics; politically, the former tend to be more Conservative than the latter. There is a small Protestant minority that politically tends to be less Conservative than both types of Catholics. This Protestant minority is predominantly peasant and its votes are largely Socialist or Communist. Its Left orientation has much to do with the terrible persecutions waged against it by the

Catholics in the sixteenth and seventeenth centuries and sometimes little to do with the appeal of socialism or communism.

Conservatism

Some types of French conservatism are lukewarm to republican parliamentarism, others are hostile to it, and none cherish it. All types exhibit a base that is religious, although religion is greater in some than in others. If all are bound up with nationalism—some more than others—this was not always the case. For years after the Revolution, nationalism was associated more with the Left than with the Right. Boulangerism, for example, had its birth among leftist workers in the industrialized areas of Marseilles, Toulon, and St. Etienne; and only later did it become a movement of the Right, antiparliamentary, and racist. Midway through the nineteenth century, some conservatives realized that nationalism afforded a tool with which they could strike back at republican doctrines. They accused the republicans of ignoring the very thing that had made France great and condemned them for refusing to use nationalism to rebuild French prestige.

An example of conservatism that is militantly nationalistic is found in the thought of Paul Déroulède and Maurice Barrès. Déroulède was a Boulangerist who sought revenge against Germany. Barrès condemned reason and wanted a Napoleonic Republic that would restore French strength and grandeur. He viewed all individual considerations as distinctly secondary to "the nation" and believed that the entity overshadowed all else in importance. During the Dreyfus trial, it mattered not to him that Dreyfus was innocent, but only that the nation and its instrumentalities (particularly the army) would suffer as a result of his acquittal. It was preferable that an innocent Dreyfus should go to prison than to allow his exoneration and the consequent devaluation of French institutions.

An example of conservatism that goes back all the way to God and the Pope was that of Joseph de Maistre. God, said De Maistre, is the only legitimate repository of authority, and all of the efforts of man to rationalize human authority are meaningless. His thought was clerical, monarchical, antireform, and contemptuous of human reason. Close but not identical with it was the conservatism of Louis de Bonald, which favored Catholicism, the superiority of "divine will" to human will, and a political system presided over by a monarch responsible to and restrained by God.

Examples of conservatism that are anti-Bonapartist, decentralized, and individualistic are found in the thought of Hippolyte Taine and Alexis de Tocqueville—one a historian and the other a social critic—who were equally opposed to popular democracy and monarchism. De Tocqueville argued that popular rule is limited by morality and the slow evolution of lasting societal forms.

Contemporary French conservatism is associated mainly with the frugal outlook of many people possessing small and large savings who are militantly opposed to both socialism and communism. They are particularly against Socialist financial policies and contend that "the Socialists do to the franc what a drop of water does to a cube of sugar." They are generally lay in outlook, although they have occasionally cooperated tactically with the church. It is customary for them to refer frequently to the Christian legacy, although they generally seek not to equate it solely with Catholicism. They stress the importance of national defense and view French political life primarily along military lines and identify themselves often with defense of the army and varying degrees of adherence to the idea of *Algérie francaise.* Their dislike for the Soviet Union is usually reflected in most of their pronouncements, and their distaste and contempt for the British—a widespread French sentiment—often shapes their views. They sometimes picture the Englishman as "that double-crosser" who is behind most French diplomatic problems. Lately, their pronouncements suggest that the Englishman has been replaced to a considerable extent by the American, particularly in Strasbourg, Tours, and Lille, once strongholds of pro-Americanism in France.[2] Finally, they take great pride in their "empiricism" and "realism," and they like to boast that they are the ones who have on hand the "real men" to bail France out of the mess in which they almost always accuse the men of the Left of putting her. One notable exception to the latter is Socialist Guy Mollet, who served as President of the Council in 1956–1957, whose foreign policy they often agreed with.

Fascism

French fascism, like most everything else in France, is divided and lacking in leadership. First, there exists still today remnants of the fascism expressed by Charles Maurras around the first decades of the twentieth century in his *Enquête sur la Monarchie* and in his articles in *Action francaise.* Maurras viewed politics as a science devoid of all moral considerations and justice. He described it as an "organized empiricism." He condemned democratic doctrine as being of Protestant and Jewish origin. He felt that the Protestant Reformation was a disaster because it opened the way for free inquiry and destroyed the unity of Catholicism. He urged France to return to those institutions that were "exclusively of French origin"—decentralization, hereditary monarchy, and the re-establishment of intellectual and moral "order" under the supervision of the Catholic church. Under his inspiration, the group known as the *Action francaise* became concerned less with its original monarchical goals and more with intense nationalism and racism—so much so that eventually the Count of Paris condemned it as being a disgrace to monarchy. As the years progressed,

[2] This statement is based on a study of 802 cases conducted by the French Institute of Public Opinion in December, 1957.

Maurras urged the use of violence against the existing political order and various minority groups. He was excommunicated from the church in the 1930's. Another type of fascism is represented by Pierre Dominique who is critical of the French economy and seeks the establishment in France of corporate institutions modeled after those of Portugal, whose dictator he admires. Dominique has enjoyed very little success in France. He has been unable to sway Fascist-oriented French youth, many of whom contend that he is "too restrained."

The most highly publicized French fascism in recent years was the comic-opera movement of Pierre Poujade, stationery supplier of Saint-Ceré. Poujadism had its origins in the difficult plight of numerous small proprietors who were caught in the squeeze between high taxation and the great inflation that set in after 1956. Poujadism represents an extraordinary mixture of numerous restraints on trade in behalf of small proprietors and twentieth-century political reaction. In its southern strongholds, it recommends that the tax collector be sent back to Paris with a bloody nose and that certain deputies be thrown into the Seine. Poujade is antiparliamentary, anti-Semitic, and favors *Algérie francaise*. Although his influence has waned, the social conditions that contributed to his rise persist. At one time, Poujade attempted to extend his movement beyond the French borders; and it met with limited success in southern Belgium and in the south of England. His movement won forty parliamentary seats in the national elections of January 2, 1956; and he announced that his deputies would enter Parliament "as paratroopers descending on enemy territory." He ordered them to maintain strict discipline, live under one roof in a special Poujadist hotel, and contribute part of their legislative salaries to him. They entered Parliament, participated in its sessions, and eventually dismissed many of his demands. The Poujadists were deprived of parliamentary representation as a result of the legislative elections of November, 1958. Poujadism may survive among the lower middle class until there is considerable improvement in the material conditions of many of the small-income people who flocked to it. Today, Poujade boasts that he can count on the support of at least 800,000 followers, a figure which is undoubtedly exaggerated.

The Young Nation has been particularly active in the department of the Seine ever since it was founded in 1949 by the four Sidos brothers. Its symbol is the Celtic Cross, which appears frequently on the walls of Paris buildings—chalked there usually by young *lycée* students. Its themes are anti-Semitism, antiparliamentarism and antiforeignism. The *Mouvement Populaire du 13 Mai* was founded in May 1958 and is led by Robert Martel. Its leader in 1958 was General Chassin, one of the noisiest individuals associated with the great movement of that year and who often appeared dismayed because many Gaullists were not inclined to take him too seriously. The movement dwells on the theme that the leaders of the Fifth Republic have betrayed the revolution of 1958 and have diverted it from what they consider as its "natural course." The *Parti Nationaliste* was created on February 6, 1959, at the instigation of the Young Nation. It comprised members of *Le Mouvement Populaire du 13 Mai* and was led by Francois Sidos, Ferdinant Ferraud, and Dominique Wenner. It was officially dissolved by the regime subsequent to the Algiers uprising of February 12, 1959, after various of its members had demonstrated against De Gaulle and Debré. Robert Ortiz, one of the leaders of the 1960 insurrection in Algiers and now a fugitive from French law, participated in its founding. Its charter called for "direct action" whenever the government's policies did not adhere to its own views (which was almost always). *Le Front National des Combattants* was founded in 1957, and was dissolved by the regime on April 29, 1961. It advocated *Algérie francaise* and brooked no criticism of the army. It was founded by Deputies Le Pen and Demarquet, after they broke with Poujadism. Both men, attired in paratrooper berets with tricolor wrapped around their waists, have delighted in leading demonstrations. Both have claimed heroic records while serving with the *paras,* but there is no evidence that either of them ever saw any action with their units. They have been so noisy and crude that most Gaullists appeared distressed whenever their names were associated with them. In the revolution of May, 1958, Le Pen was ordered back to Metropolitan France from Algiers by the men he had gone there "to aid." After 1959, he came into opposition to De Gaulle and became one of the most severe critics of the Gaullist regime. Finally, the *Mouvement Restauration Nationale* has been led by Olivier de Roux and has worked closely with the *Centre d'Études supérieures de psychologie sociale* to establish various civic committees to deal with immediate issues. It has sought to be on hand whenever Russian political leaders have visited France in order to instigate civic disorders. Some of its leaders were deported temporarily to Corsica during Khrushchev's visit to France in 1960.

SELECTED READING

Bodley, J. E. C. *The Church in France.* New York: The Macmillan Co., 1936.

Einaudi, M., Domenach, J. M., and Garosci, A. *Communism in Western Europe.* Ithaca, N.Y.: Cornell University Press, 1951.

Mayer, J. P. *Political Thought in France from the Revolution to the Fourth Republic.* London: Faber and Faber, Ltd., 1949.

Scott, J. A. *Republican Ideas and the Liberal Tradition in France, 1870–1914.* New York: Columbia University Press, 1951.

Soltau, R. *French Political Thought in the Nineteenth Century.* New Haven, Conn.: Yale University Press, 1951.

Thomson, D. *The Democratic Ideal in France and England.* New York: Cambridge University Press, 1940.

13

Political Organizations

THE LEFT

The Communist Left is organized in one political party. The non-Communist Left is disorganized and distributed among many parties and alliances. Jacques Fauvet describes it as forming a "political mosaic" that is predominantly urban and whose influence outside the large cities is generally limited to the departments of the Lot-et-Garonne, Allier, Creuse, and Corrèze.[1] It draws its membership from intellectuals, civil servants, workers, small proprietors, merchants, and members of the liberal professions; its beliefs range from doctrinaire Marxism to Catholic leftism. Within it are revisionists who seek to extract from Marxism elements adaptable to contemporary circumstances and the latest findings of science, Socialists of diverse kinds, different types of Christian leftists, Christian and non-Christian pacifists, syndicalists, and nonconformists. Usually, these components are in deep and lively controversy with each other.

If the Communist and non-Communist Left were to unite, the Left might succeed in achieving a majority in the country and Parliament. Some members of both forces argue that such a union is possible but unlikely as long as the leaders of the Socialist party (SFIO) continue to oppose it. In turn, the Socialist leaders argue that the Communist party seeks a regrouping purely for the purpose of eliminating the Socialist party and that it is less concerned with the realization of any of the advantages that might result from joint action. Despite these contentions, studies show noticeable differences between the political attitudes manifested by the Communist and non-Communist Left and how significantly they detract from possible common action. They show that both groups

[1] Jacques Fauvet, *Les Forces politiques en France, Étude et Géographie des divers Partis* (Paris: Éditions Le Monde, 1951). The author wishes to express his indebtedness to Fauvet's excellent treatment of the non-Communist Left.

take different positions relative to different problems. For example, the Communist Left is more concerned with existing problems, such as the economic condition of the workers and the operation of colonialism, while the non-Communist Left tends to be more sensitive to problems of principle. The Communist Left is more inclined to action, whereas the non-Communist Left is likely to verbalize about those problems that confront it. Undoubtedly, both forces see and interpret the social order in different ways.[2]

The Communist Party

Before the end of World War I, most of the diverse tendencies in French socialism could be found in the Unified Socialist party. After the armistice, at least three different tendencies competed for control of the party's apparatus. The Right faction, which was led by Renaudel, upheld reformism and cooperation with the bourgeois Radical Socialist party. The Center faction, led by Faure and Longuet, controlled the party machinery and pledged the organization to the policy of the Socialist Second International. The Left faction, under the direction of Souverine, sought to subdue the Right and Center factions. Leninist in orientation, it sought to commit the party to the revolutionary program of the Communist Third International. The final break came in 1920 when doctrinal and tactical differences relative to ministerial participation in government, collaboration with Radical Socialists, and relations with the Second and Third Internationals led to the separation of Leninist and non-Leninist Socialists. The Left wing of the Unified Socialist party voted at the Congress of Tours its subordination to the Communist Third International and became the Communist party of France (*Section francaise de l'Internationale communiste*). The Right and Center factions seceded or were expelled; they subsequently united to form a new Socialist party (*Section francaise de l'Internationale ouvrière*), which proclaimed its accreditation to the Socialist Second International. Since that rupture of four decades ago, Communists and Socialists have maintained separate identities and have engaged in constant conflict with each other.

The newly created Communist party adhered to the "Twenty-One Points" for admission to the Third International. In doing so, it surrendered unconditionally to bolshevism. The party then sought to control the whole of the French labor movement. That effort was thwarted by the conflicting policy of the General Confederation of Labor (CGT), whose

[2] See "La Gauche," *Les Temps modernes,* CXII–CXIII, Numéro special (1955), 1576–1625 for studies of French Institute of Public Opinion to determine Left and Right opinions. Two hundred and eight persons of all social catagories, ages, and sex were interrogated by projective tests and direct questions. They were presented with ten photographs designed to solicit Left and Right reactions and nine stories posing a definite problem that permitted the taking of Left or Right positions.

charter was oriented more toward syndicalism than partyism, and the competition of the Socialist party (SFIO). The Third International, unable to inflict its designs on the CGT, turned then to the creation of its own organization—the Red International of Labor Unions (RILU).

It was soon apparent that the rupture of 1920 had divided the working-class vote, which resulted in a reduction in the total number of Communist votes and frequently led to the success of conservative candidates. Beginning with 1922, such Communist militants as Pierre Brizon, Raoul Verfeuil, Henri Favre, and others began to emphasize the theme of unity and eradication of the split in the working class. They argued that the fusion of Communist and Socialist parties was desirable from the Communist point of view. They contended that the Tour's schism was a mistake and embarked on a program designed to secure mutual participation of Communists and Socialists in a "United Front."

In the years between 1922 and 1934, the Communist party made repeated attempts to form a "United Front" with the Socialist party. All such efforts were characterized by strong Communist conditions and reservations. In 1924, for example, the Communists demanded a complete break by the Socialists with the Radical Socialists and subsequent fusion of the Communist and Socialist trade-unions. In 1927, when the Socialists rejected the latest set of Communist conditions, the Communists retaliated by utilizing rivalry on the second ballot as an effective propaganda weapon—claiming that various Left losses were the result of the Socialist refusal to enter the "United Front." After 1932, the Communists adopted the theme of "united action against war," and made the threat of impending fascism the necessity for collaboration between the two parties. Simultaneously, they sought to convince the electorate that they were a "legal" party, parliamentary, and in the tradition of the French Revolution. The Communist party adopted a façade of "respectability" and made a concerted bid for the support of traditionally bourgeois electors. At the same time, its tactical policy was in agreement with the 1935 directive of the Third International, which ordered all Communist parties to come to terms with Socialists and democrats in a "common front against fascism." When the Seventh Congress of the Comintern convened in August, 1935, Georgi Dimitrov praised the French Communist party for its adherence to this policy and cited it as an example for other Communist parties to follow.

Communist tactical policy identified the Socialist party as the primary obstacle to the formation of an undivided Left against fascism. The time approached when the Socialists could no longer decline Communist "United Front" invitations without damaging their own following. Communist party leader Maurice Thorez said himself that the Communists had "devoted themselves to making the United Front, as Léon Blum's phrase puts it: 'not only inevitable, but dangerous any longer not to accept it.'"

In 1934, the Communist and Socialist parties entered into a united front that fell short of organic unity and systematic recourse to violence. That agreement served subsequently as the basis for the Popular Front government of 1936, which was composed of Socialists and Radical Socialists and was supported in the Chamber of Deputies by the Communist party. Despite its cooperative appearance, the Popular Front government was characterized by continued competition between Socialists and Communists. The government fell in 1937 after it was reversed by the Senate, and after that both Socialists and Communists returned to their traditional relationship.

The Communist party's chance came after 1940, after the Socialist and Radical Socialist parties had become identified with scandal and broken promises and after many Communists had played leading roles in the Resistance movement. It captured 166 seats in the legislative elections of 1946, 106 in 1951, and 150 in 1956. It fell to 10 in the elections of 1958. That decline was due primarily to an electoral law that was directed against it and not to a sharp decrease of its support in the country. In the elections of 1956, it won approximately 26 per cent of the total vote. In 1958, it received approximately 19 per cent of the vote on the first ballot and 21 per cent on the second.

The Communist party still refuses to accept the idea that it is impossible for it to recapture the bulk of the working-class vote. It continues to make overtures to workers affiliated with other parties to join it in a broad movement that would be instrumental in taking it to power. It is, nevertheless, now farther from that possibility than at any other time during the last decade and a half.

The Communist party is the type of association that can be anything at any time—revolutionary or non-revolutionary, parliamentary or non-parliamentary. Its tactical behavior is determined by the pursuance of certain fixed objectives, namely, the acquisition of power and its consolidation. In its desire to transform the existing order, it endorses the use of any methods—even legal ones.

The leaders of the French Communist party are more "Sovietized" than the leaders of any of the other Communist parties in the Western world. Disagreement between them and the Soviet Union is seldom heard of, and their defense of Russian nationalism is something that can be taken for granted. Disagreement among them is fairly common, however, but it expresses itself in terms of tendencies rather than individuals. In 1961, the Thorez-Rochet tendency crushed the Servin-Casanova tendency concerning tactical policy relative to the Gaullist regime. Servin, Casanova, and Kriegel-Valrimont were accused of wishing to compromise with Gaullism.

In the May, 1961, Communist party Congress of Saint Denis, Servin was charged with playing down "the importance of the role of the party as an *avant-garde* of the working class" and seeking to push the party in the direction of "false economic analysis" (distinguishing between Gaullist and Pinay capitalism). Kriegel-Valrimont was accused of encouraging dissension within the party and seeking to put in opposition the theses adopted by his own party and those evolved by Khrushchev at the Twentieth Congress of the Communist party of the Soviet Union. Today, the Thorez-Rochet tendency dominates the French Communist party and views the regime as "the expression of the direct domination of monopolies on the nation" and describes its foreign policy as "imperialistic" and aligned with "American imperialism."

The Communist leaders boast that among the 3,882,304 Communist voters there are approximately 407,000 militants who think as they do and respond immediately to their commands. It appears that this figure is exaggerated; calls to the militants are often followed by considerable abstention. During May, 1958, the Communist leadership called on its followers to resist the Gaullist revolution by waging a general strike. The movement failed; there was less than 5 per cent absenteeism recorded in the entire nation. In November, 1958, the party told its followers to vote against De Gaulle for the presidency; and approximately a million and a half voted for him, a fact that was acknowledged by the party executive in its meeting the following month.

It should be recognized that numerous individuals frequently vote for the Communist party for reasons that are indigenous to the French socioeconomic scene. Many of these people are discontented with the existing order and vote Communist as a way of reacting against it, not because they are Communists or because they have any sympathy for communism itself. Some workers vote Communist because they feel that they cannot cast their vote in any other way without setting the stage for decreases in their own wages. The Communist party hold over the CGT makes some workers feel that they must vote for Communist candidates, even if they find this type of voting behavior to be psychologically grating. There are other workers who may not wish to vote for Communist candidates but who also feel that they cannot vote against them.

It is common knowledge that a bloc of lower middle-class citizens vote Communist because they believe that in this way they can inflict the greatest damage on the existing order. Its destruction is their objective, not communism; and on certain occasions they have no difficulty in switching their votes from communism to fascism—the legislative elections of January 2, 1956, reflected this fact. Some Poujadist gains were at the expense of the Communist party, as a surprising number of votes came from former Communist electors.

Some intellectuals vote Communist because they feel that only in this way can they manifest and consistently sustain "systematic opposition" to the existing order. They argue that there is no other party of such relentless opposition to which they can give their support. Finally, some electors who once voted Socialist now vote Communist because they feel that there is now no true Socialist party to which they can give their vote. They argue that they would rather vote for a "Sovietized" party that stands for socialism than for a bureaucratized and corrupt party whose only resemblance to socialism is in its title and mythology. This source of Communist strength has its origin in the weakness of the Socialist party.

THE SOCIALIST PARTY (SFIO)

Although the Socialist party is opposed to capitalism, its representatives in government frequently subscribe to financial policies less daring than those favored by representatives of orthodox political parties. It is anticlerical and yet it often concludes electoral alliances with the Popular Republican party (*MRP*) that ultimately result in the furtherance of clerical objectives. It is anticolonial but it often decides that the alternative to colonialism would be "worse" than colonialism itself. It is opposed to militarism and yet its deputies usually find it "necessary" to vote moneys for the armed forces. Jacques Fauvet observes that although it is "anti" most things, in the National Assembly its deputies vote frequently for most anything.

Socialist leaders continually prescribe the dominance of reason, justice, and the "inevitable" orientation of democracy in the direction of socialism —seldom, however, do they seek to convert their dreams into national realities. As Yvan Craipeau states, "Paralyzed by their integration in the bourgeois parliamentary regime, obsessed by their panicky horror of the Communist party, the leaders of the SFIO have given up all political reflection. The leaders are installed in the system and they believe in it . . . They no longer study the problems of capitalism for subsequent adjustment to socialism."[3]

Doctrinal tendencies range within the SFIO from that which is to the right of rightist Jacques Soustelle to that which is not to the right of Communist Jacques Duclos. These tendencies can be traced back to 1904 when Jaurès attempted to synthesize diverse interpretations of humanism and Marxism in the Unified Socialist party. They were not eliminated when centrists and rightists withdrew or were expelled from that organization in 1920 and subsequently created the SFIO. Today, there are at least four definite tendencies within the Socialist party; Roger Racier

[3] Yvan Craipeau, *La Révolution qui vient* (Paris: Les Éditions de Minuit, 1957), p. 15.

describes these as social patriots, social Europeans, social republicans, and social revolutionaries.[4]

The social patriots are dedicated to parliamentary political forms, the orientation of society in the direction of full republicanism, and retention of the Overseas Territories. The social Europeans are Guesdists who concentrate their activities in the Pas-de-Calais, the Nord, the Haute-Vienne, and adjacent departments. They endorse the "European idea" and compromise with middle-class elements. They are secular and yet they frequently collaborate with the MRP in the movement for adoption of a "united states" of Europe. The social republicans form the party's antischism bloc and vote sometimes with the social patriots and at other times with the social Europeans. Finally, the social revolutionaries are almost always in deep disagreement with each other on interpretations of the class struggle that range from anarchosyndicalism to Trotskyism.

The leader of the SFIO, Guy Mollet, finds his condition of existence in working closely with the two large Federations of the Nord and the Pas-de-Calais, which account for many of the votes cast in the annual party Congress. When these Federations and those of the Bouches-du-Rhône and the Haute-Vienne work with each other, it is practically impossible for dissident Federations to place their delegates on the executive committee of the party. Today, that committee, or the *comité directeur*, is dominated by the Mollet "machine."

Mollet has sought to minimize the divisive effects of the tendencies and to unite the party as an organization of "realists." He came to his post in 1946. Early in his career he secured considerable support from the militants as the "man of the Left" who could best combat the "archaic humanism" and orthodoxy of Secretary-General Daniel Mayer. Mollet demanded that the party adopt a stricter application of Marxist thought in order to implement the demands of the working class. He told the party that it "could be a party of revolutionary Socialist democracy." He said that the "idealism" of various of his associates was a detriment to the party and that it had no real role within it.

Joseph Barthelemy observed that "Political life is a strong movement which is born on the Left and dies on the Right." Mollet's current version of "realism" exhibits the following characteristics. First, he has modified his "Marxism" and now concedes that contemporary capitalism is more aware of its contradictions than it had been previously and that a paternalist theme of "management-labor interdependence" is evolving. He describes French capitalism as "the worst in the world," and yet he is receptive to types of capitalism practiced elsewhere. After his return from

[4] Roger Racier, "Quatre tendances," *France-Observateur,* February 3, 1955, pp. 8–9; Lowell G. Noonan, "Some Political Aspects of the French Fifth Republic," *Western Political Quarterly,* June, 1960, pp. 469–72.

the United States, he is said to have told his associates that American capitalism has in it "more socialism than those people know they have." Second, he continues to deplore humanism because of what he describes as its "clerical tendencies," but he finds no difficulty concluding electoral alliances with the clerical MRP in the Nord and Pas-de-Calais. Third, he now appears relatively unaffected by the question: "How little socialism can a Socialist get along with when in government?" Soon after assuming the secretary-generalship, he began justifying Socialist ministerialism on the basis of programs that he described as being not "uniquely Socialist, but applicable and acceptable for all republican moderates." He states that he entered the Gaillard government in 1957 because "it was necessary for France to have a government at any price, provided it was Republican." In 1958, he entered Premier de Gaulle's post-May 13 emergency Cabinet on the grounds that it was his responsibility to do so "after turning the country from civil war and saving the Republic." He was, in fact, the one who made it possible for De Gaulle to come "legally" to power after the events of May 13, 1958. "Saving the Republic" has become for him a frequently articulated reason for Socialist exercises of ministerialism. Finally, he continues to assert that "The Socialist party must combat all forms of imperialist exploitation, aid the peoples of the territories of the *outre-mer* in their struggle for emancipation, and guide them on the road to social revolution." Nevertheless, in 1957, he considered Algeria not as a problem in colonialism but as an insurrection in a legitimate part of France and criticized the conservative Raymond Aron for "encouraging rebellion" there after the latter had questioned the intelligence of French policy (and Mollet's) in that part of the world.

Mollet and his machine have inflicted an ironlike discipline on the SFIO. In the face of his "Socialist realism," the humanist element within the party has become impotent; various members have resigned or have been expelled from the party by its *comité de correction.* Many of these people subsequently entered the Unified Socialist party (PSU).

Not until 1956 was the SFIO able to inflict strong discipline on its parliamentary group. Many of its deputies defied discipline in the period between 1952 and 1954. Eighteen of the twenty deputies who voted against the National Assembly debate of February, 1952, which proposed to implement a European Defense Community, were subsequently disciplined by the party. Thirty-three Socialist deputies voted against the Defense Community Treaty when it was finally put before the Assembly on August 30, 1954; various disciplinings again occurred, and Charles Lussy was removed from the presidency of the parliamentary group. Later that year, seventeen of the eighteen deputies who expressed their opposition to German rearmament by voting against the Paris Agreements were expelled from the party. After the party resolved the crisis of the EDC, it was then confronted with the crisis of Algeria. In 1956, a number of SFIO members criticized the use of force in Algeria and requested the Mollet government to take the "initiative in negotiating with the representatives of different tendencies of Algerian opinion, including the leaders of the insurrection." Their views were very close to those expressed by the Mendèsists, with whom they were in close collaboration. They also contended that Secretary-General Mollet had supplied misinformation to the party members and that his government of 1956 had converted press, radio, and television into instruments of propaganda. Dissident André Philip charged that the rise of "collective clericalism" was destroying the individual conscience within the party and that a movement based on power alone could easily lead to the "democratic centralism" of the Communist party. He compared his controversy with Mollet to the pre-World War II conflict between the "realist" Paul Faure (who later became a Vichyite) and the "idealist" Léon Blum. He described Mollet as "the image of Paul Faure" and he equated his "realism" with moral cynicism and hatred for things intellectual.[5] Philip's criticisms received considerable support from many intellectuals and such journals as *Ésprit, France Observateur,* and *Les Temps modernes.* He was expelled from the SFIO in March, 1958. After the national crisis of May 13, 1958, he and other SFIO expellees and resignees united in the newly created Unified Socialist party (PSU).

The SFIO slipped to 13.8 per cent on the second ballot in the national elections of 1958.[6] Defeated were Defferre, Gazier, Pineau, Moch, Ramadier, and Lacoste (Resident Minister in Algeria for the Mollet government in 1956). Only forty Socialist deputies were returned to the National Assembly. After considerable intra-party disagreement, the SFIO decided to uphold De Gaulle's candidacy for the presidency, although it soon announced its opposition to the economic and financial policies of the Debré government. With reference to Algeria, it states that negotiations with qualified representatives of the Algerian people remain the sole method of producing a political solution to the conflict. Now it extends a priority to "negotiations" at any time and in any place, and contends that results are the important thing. And, concerned with the lowly role now played by the Parliament, Francis Leenhardt has advised his Socialist parliamentary group to seek the acquisition of new parliamentary prerogatives stronger than those conferred on the National Assembly by the Constitu-

[5] André Philip in an interview with the author, Paris, December 17, 1957.

[6] See *Le Monde,* November 25, 1958, pp. 4–13 for complete results of first ballot, and *Le Monde,* December 2, 1958, pp. 3–13 for results of second ballot. The Socialists refused on the second ballot to support common candidates with the Communist party. Communist candidates deferred in thirty instances on the second ballot to Socialists who had voted *non* in the referendum—all of these "gifts" were fatal.

tion of the Fifth Republic. "The Constitution permits the parliamentary game, and this must triumph," states Leenhardt.

Today, the SFIO represents higher wages for the civil servant, occasional membership in the government, and a doctrine that is based on "workerism" but which is unsupported by those non-salaried workers who constitute a majority of French organized labor. It depends primarily on salaried workers who are employed by the nationalized industries or by small private industries situated in the small communes of the nation. Their "workerism" is essentially bureaucratic and provincial, and they constitute but a small minority of French labor.[7] Moreover, the party is unable to compete successfully with the Communist dominated unions; in the mining areas, it is incapable of imperiling the hold maintained over the CGT by the Communist party. And although it is usually associated with the Worker's Force (FO), this is largely a "paper" organization; among its components, only the civil servants of the Post, Telephone and Telegraph (PTT) are strongly attracted to the SFIO. Finally, recent studies confirm that only some 8 per cent of the peasant proprietors and 6 per cent of the agricultural workers vote for it.

Thus, this "party of tradition with a revolutionary vocabulary" now proclaims its opposition to "Gaullism," the authoritarianism" of the Communist party, the "confessionalism" of the MRP, and the "reaction" of the radicals. It lives in a regime in which political parties now mean very little, and to its own limitations it has added others inherited from a generally impoverished political party system. It is now but one of many nineteenth-century political associations incapable of coping with the political and economic problems of the twentieth century.

The Unified Socialist Party (PSU)

After the crisis of May 13, 1958, various expellees and resignees from the SFIO constituted the Autonomous Socialist party (PSA). It comprised Édouard Depreux, Robert Verdier, Alain Savary, Orestes Rosenfeld, Dan-

[7] Pierre Rimbert, "Le Parti socialiste *SFIO*," in Maurice Duverger, *Partis politiques et Classes sociales en France* (Paris: A. Colin, 1955), pp. 195–207. Rimbert surveyed approximately 400 sections of the SFIO comprising 14,519 party members in 81 of the 90 departments. He estimated that 90 per cent of all Socialist electors lived in cities inhabited by fewer than 100,000 people, 42 per cent in cities of fewer than 2,000, 22 per cent in cities of 5,000 to 20,000, and that fewer than 10 per cent lived in Paris and its suburbs. Rimbert concluded that 58 per cent of all the interrogees were salaried and 22 per cent non-salaried, and that 24.9 per cent were civil servants; see Joseph Klatzmann, "Comportement éléctoral et Classe sociale," in Maurice Duverger, Francois Goguel, and Jean Touchard, *Les Élections du 2 janvier 1956* (Paris: A. Colin, 1957), pp. 272–75. He estimates that for every ten workers who exercised the suffrage in Paris and elsewhere in the department of the Seine in the national elections of 1956, one voted Socialist; seven, Communist; and two, for other lists. He concludes that the Communist party is the sole "worker's party" in this department.

iel Mayer, André Philip, Andrée Vienot, and many other well-known names in Socialist circles. It condemned Guy Mollet for being "the first to go to Canossa-les-deux-Églises"—that is, for having made it possible for De Gaulle to come "legally" to power—and Robert Lacoste, Mollet's Resident Minister in Algeria in his government of 1956.

The Autonomous party was created partially because of the inability of the former SFIO minority to capture the apparatus of the parent organization. Its existence constituted admission of the defeat of the anti-Molletists. Its members had been unable—when they were within the SFIO—to terminate Mollet's highly successful policy of lying back, watching the Socialist Federations closely, and attaching himself to the shoulders of an existing majority after it had clearly and safely defined itself. They had lost out to a secretary-general who knew that one of the first lessons of sovereignty consists of commanding what already exists.

In April, 1960, the Autonomous Socialist party (PSA) joined the Union of the Socialist Left (UGS), the Tribune of Communism, and the Mendesists to form a new political party—the Unified Socialist party (PSU). It aspires to become a Socialist party situated between the SFIO and the Communist party. Its membership includes radicals, liberal radicals, Trotskyites, syndicalists, progressive Christians, Communists opposed to Maurice Thorez, former members of the Young Republic and the UDSR, former members of the SFIO minority, and many of the Mendèsists with whom they had so closely worked. In other words, the new party includes all known Left tendencies. It states that it is open to all those who wish to substitute for the capitalist system a collectivist one that is Socialist or Communist (not pro-U.S.S.R.); that all other beliefs have no place in it; that it will work closely with the labor unions; and that it will seek the independence of colonial peoples, peace in Algeria, and realization of a "united worker's front." The party is opposed to the Gaullist regime; however, its internal differences of opinion run deep. The majority wish to recruit around the working class, while the minority seek to recruit around the middle class. Divided as it is, the party is held together, however, by the opposition of its groups to the Algerian War.

Because of its diverse internal tendencies, its members are likely to spend much of their time combatting each other. It is no secret that Mendès-France would like to dominate the new organization, a possibility that many members oppose because they regard him not as a Socialist but as a kind of welfare state "new dealer." He has already expressed the idea that he wishes to see socialism abandon its doctrinaire orientation and that he views socialism as consisting of full employment, full utilization of natural resources in the public interest, support for the Common Market, and nationalization of certain areas of the economy with retention of broad areas of private enterprise. "I am for the principles of Bevan," he states. Because of the difficulty presented by his adherence to the party, both he and his opposition saw to it that he remained simply a militant and not a member of its executive council.

The party also includes André Philip, who was among the first of its members to announce that it must not be a totalitarian party, that it must reject the use of violence, and that it must correspond to the realities of the twentieth century by being non-ideological. Other members refuse to reject the use of violence and emphasize that they must employ force if "fascism obliges them to use it"; they also want the party to be equipped with a clear doctrine. Finally, the conservatively oriented Daniel Mayer views the party as a vehicle of protest against "the treason of socialism and the sclerosis of the parties of the Left."

The party's executive committee contains nineteen former PSA members, twenty-two former UGS members, and five former members of the Tribune of Communism. Some of those who come from the PSA are former deputies, which causes some of the party's less conservative members to fear that it will eventually become no more than an association of former parliamentarists.

It remains to be seen if the party can unite both Marxists and Christians and convince them that they should be united on the lay issue; whether it can acquire a worker's base; and if it can reconcile such diverse personalities as Henri Longeot, Édouard Depreux, Laurent Schwartz, Gilles Martinet, Jean Poperan, Charles Hernu, Maurice Klein, Robert Verdier, and Jean Verlhac. It remains to be seen if the party can increase its membership—estimated now as 20,000—to the extent of becoming one of the important parties of the Left. It has no Jean Jaurès or Jules Guesde to guide it, and so much will depend on its ability to strengthen its leadership. Finally, its future is likely to be affected by the evolution of the SFIO and its control by the "Mollet machine." If the Molletists should lose control of the SFIO's apparatus, and should the latter reorient itself to the Left, many PSU members might be willing to return to it.

Smaller Parties of the Left

The Democratic and Socialist Union of the Resistance (UDSR) originated in the Resistance movement. Constituted in 1945 as a non-party organization, it sought to reflect various non-Communist Left tendencies. It worked with the SFIO in the first of the postliberation electoral campaigns and then with the Radical Socialists—breaking with the SFIO after it rejected the draft constitution of 1946. Later that same year, it altered its status and transformed itself into a political party. Today, it is a collection of parliamentary "generals," which lacks mass support and organization. Nevertheless, for years it was perhaps the most important of all the minor parties and occupied a central position in the parliamentary politics of the Fourth Republic and supplied the Socialists, Radical Socialists, and Gaullists with members in Parliament. Jacques Soustelle went from it to the Rally of the French People (RPF); Francis Leenhardt left it to enter the SFIO and become the leader of its parliamentary group. With the formation of the RPF, the UDSR suffered a great blow when many of its deputies defected to it. Later, the UDSR worked with the Radical Socialists within the Rally of the Republican Left (RGR), although in 1950 its parliamentary group opposed Radical Socialist Premier Queuille and supported the Conservative Pinay Ministry. The RGR, in turn, was not a party but an alliance of Radical Socialists, the UDSR, and some smaller parties. It served a coordinating function and existed under the Fourth Republic. The smaller parties were the Republican Socialists, the Democratic Alliance, the Republican and Social party of French Reconciliation, and the Democratic Socialists (which included former Pétainists discredited after the last war).

The Union of Democratic Forces (UDF) is not a party but another alliance that in 1958 included the Autonomous Socialist party (PSA), the Young Republic, the Mendèsists, the Francois Mitterand wing of the UDSR, and the Union of the Socialist Left. It campaigned against the constitutional referendum of that year and opposed De Gaulle's candidacy for the presidency. Members Claude Bourdet states that it viewed the national elections as lacking true competition and ideas and that "The speeches of the General furnished some commodious citations which took the place of platforms for the most diverse people." It was all calculated, he states, and in keeping with the mysterious, ambivalent, and elliptical attitude of the General—allowing any candidate to thereby maintain pace with any change and making it possible for him to say that he was always "in line." Bourdet views this as a return to infantilism, which abandons the destiny of adult citizens into the hands of an all-powerful and resolved "father."

The Center for Republican Reform (CRR) is an alliance that was created after May 13, 1958, and describes itself as consisting of "Gaullists of the Left." Shortly after it made its appearance, Assistant Secretary-General Servan-Schreiber assured the public that "There is no internal contradiction here. We are new men. We are realists. We wish to destroy this traditional superstition of French democracy which, by an inferiority complex, identifies an illustrious man with the candidate for dictatorship. For us, there is no incompatibility between the liberty for which tomorrow we are willing to give our lives, and authority, without which the Republic is no more than a caricature and France a decadent nation."[8] Servan-Schreiber's views have since changed. Now he considers De Gaulle Bonapartist and dictatorial.

[8] Jean Servan-Schreiber, "La Gauche avec de Gaulle," *Le Monde,* November 19, 1958, p. 2.

By this time, the reader is undoubtedly aware of the fact that the French Left exhibits a tendency to form innumerable groups and alliances and that some last for a long time while others are of very short duration. Following are examples of this. In the 1950's, the Democratic Revolutionary Rally (RDR) included orthodox Marxists, socialists affiliated and unaffiliated with the SFIO, secular militants, leftist intellectuals, and some members of the Christian Left. It favored a revolutionary socialism opposed to both capitalism and Soviet communism. Most of its membership came from the Revolutionary Socialist Action (ASR), which was created in 1948 by Yves Dechezelles (a former assistant secretary-general of the SFIO), Socialist David Rousseau, and Trotskyites Louis Dalmas and Paul Parisot. The Unitary and Democratic Socialist Movement (MSUD) constituted yet another group that worked frequently with the Communist party and its fellow travelers; although it differed with the Communist party from time to time, particularly on the issues of Stalinism and Yugoslavia. The Independent Socialist Left originated through the efforts of three members of the MRP who sought to synthesize some elements of Marxism with certain values associated with the Christian Left. For a time, it enjoyed the support of the former Trotskyite Jean Rous and Yves Dechezelles. Finally, the Union of Progressives was created of fellow travelers who reserved for themselves, nevertheless, liberty of expression on issues in the arena of party politics. While it seldom disagrees with the Communists, it does reserve the right to do so. Its most famous member is the brilliant orator and Soviet apologist Pierre Cot.

The Radical Socialist Party

Once the largest party of the Third Republic, the Radical Socialists have declined to the status of one of the lesser parties of the Fifth Republic. The party professes to draw its inspiration from the principles of 1789, particularly those that assert the preferability of personal liberty. It claims Georges Clemenceau, Louis Blanc, and Leon Gambetta as its doctrinal fathers. Prior to the present century, it attracted politicians who exhibited an affinity for what was then "the Left." Clemenceau was one—early in his career he announced that "The conservative republicans demand of the Republic a minimum; us, its maximum." He defined his goal as the "accomplishment of the grand renovation of 1789, begun by the French bourgeoisie and abandoned by them after their achievement." He advised that, "You will always be strong if you govern with the country; you will always be weak if you govern against it." He founded *La Justice* and another famous Radical by the name of Camille Pelletan served as its editor. Clemenceau helped to shape the party's early program and demanded among its objectives abolition of the Senate, revision of the Constitution of the Third Republic by an Assembly elected by universal suffrage, and individual and collective responsibility of ministers to the majority in the Chamber of Deputies.

The Radical Socialist's first party Congress of 1901 marked the beginning of an anticlerical campaign that sought to enlist the aid of republicans of all types. The issue itself served for a time as one of the few on which most of the Radicals were truly united. It remained until 1907, however, before the party was able to draft a program, and until 1913 before it was able to achieve loose internal unification by eliminating various of its most difficult dissidents.

Some Frenchmen contend that the Radical Socialist party never had a definite doctrine; others argue that it has one but that it has not succeeded in clarifying it to the country. For many years, it consisted of simply "thinking little"; and it is said that the philosopher of radicalism, Alain, conducted a series of conferences in which he taught his disciples how to avoid "thinking big." Throughout the years, it was always associated with the defense of certain segments of the middle class. Jacques Fauvet describes the party as the most bourgeois of bourgeois parties, one that is concerned primarily with the support of small property holders situated in the small cities.[9]

The party's great decline was accentuated by the slowing down of the controversy between church and state, by the passage in the 1930's of many of its electors to the Socialist party (SFIO), and by its economic views that became less supportable when the country entered the great depression. During the same era, various of its representatives became involved in numerous financial scandals. The party's decline was pronounced after 1934. Then its ministries remained in office only with the support of the Socialist party. They gravitated around the latter, for any other tactical policy would have hastened further their defeat by the expanding Left.

After 1934, the traditional Radical Socialist game of darting back and forth between the Right and the Left in the party arena came under careful restriction. Prior to that year, the party's support—whenever it was in government—depended on Socialists or conservatives but seldom on the simultaneous support of both. After 1934, it was forced to bargain for Socialist support alone. It entered Cabinets that the Socialists supported but into which they refused to enter. In this way, the Radical Socialists gained momentary assurance of their own nominal dominance.

After 1934, the Radical Socialists found that they could no longer play the parliamentary game by appealing at different times to different sides of the Chamber of Deputies. They were then lodged in a position from which they were unable to extricate themselves. Nevertheless, they did find consolation in the fact that they were at least able to remain in office.

[9] Jacques Fauvet, *La France dechirée* (Paris: Arthème Fayard, 1957), p. 130.

Like the British Liberal party, they came to pay the price demanded of parties who have frequently wielded power—namely, a reduction in their own power. They were forced to pay for years of unfulfilled promises and constant involvement of their ministers in practically all of the great scandals that rocked the state during the years when they were prominent.

Within the Radical party, diverse tendencies produce distinct types of radicalism. One kind professes to be a way of life based on internationalism, tolerance, and progressive nationalism. It is confined primarily to the Rhône, Drome, Vaucluse, and to the southwest and east of the Champenois. It was associated for a time with the views and sentiments presented by the former Radical Socialist Pierre Mendès-France, who tried to rejuvenate the Radical Socialist party by thinking that he could create a modern political movement that would push both Marxism and conservatism into the background. He failed, but only after he had caught the imagination of many citizens. In appealing for the introduction of a modern capitalism, he sought the support of many Radical Socialist electors who were concerned not with modernism but only with the interest of merchants, farmers, small industrialists, and artisans—the very interests who hide behind various protective devices—who cannot afford a modern capitalism because they live in what is essentially an economically underdeveloped part of the nation. But Mendès-France's great mistake was to believe that the party could be rejuvenated and that it could be reoriented toward his doctrine. It would be reasonable to say that he wasted far too many years on it. Another type of radicalism comprises different and mutually contradictory tendencies. In the Côtes-du-Nord the radicalism of René Pleven is none other than conservatism, as is the case in the Seine-Maritime and the Eure-et-Loir with André Marie and Maurice Violette. In the Charentes, former Premier Felix Gaillard articulates the "European outlook" and practices "cognac politics." Another type of radicalism gained strength after the end of World War II and is concentrated primarily in the Seine-et-Oise, Alpes-Maritimes, Indre, Bouches-du-Rhône, Nantes, and the right bank of Paris. It emphasizes its anticommunism and antisocialism. It is antireformist and its views are well represented in the pages of *Le Figaro* and *L'Aurore*. It rejects—unlike the type of radicalism first discussed—electoral and parliamentary alliances with the Socialists and seeks them instead with more conservative parties. It has considerable financial power, and consequently various pressure groups are at its disposal. For years, its arguments were articulated by Jean Paul David, former deputy of the Seine-et-Oise. Finally, a type of radicalism based in North Africa reflects an outlook sympathetic to *Algérie francaise*.[10]

[10] See Alain Gourdon, "Le Parti radical," in Duverger, *op. cit.*, pp. 219–39 for a good discussion of different kinds of radicalism to which the author expresses his indebtedness. See also Felix Gaillard, "La Place du Parti radical dans la nouvelle République," *Le Monde*, November 22, 1958, p. 2.

The Popular Republican Party (MRP)

Although the MRP is not a Catholic party—according to its charter—its membership is composed predominantly of Catholics who are concerned with the introduction and preservation of various Catholic principles. It is the closest thing to a Catholic political party in a country that has never had one.

The origins of the MRP can be traced back to those Left-wing Catholics who first affiliated with the *Action liberal* during the latter part of the nineteenth century and which, in turn, was succeeded by the Popular Democrat party that returned thirteen deputies to the Chamber in the elections of 1936. Some party members worked during World War II with the Socialist Movement of National Liberation (MLN); in 1943, after participating in discussions in Paris and Lyon, they decided to create the Popular Republican party. The leaders of the new party were progressives who wished to make it into a new, large Socialist party of mass appeal, divorced from reactionary Catholicism, Maurrasianism, and the convictions of *Action francaise.* They favored nationalization of different enterprises and societal proposals calculated to keep pace with the demands of Left elements. They hoped to collaborate with the Socialist party in the realization of certain social objectives, both in the country and in the legislature.

The MRP received over 5,500,000 votes and 28 per cent of the total vote cast in the elections of June, 1946. Its show of electoral strength was amazing and not characteristic of one area or region; it was strongly represented in Normandy, Champagne, Alsace, Brittany, in some of the departments of the south, and in various of the large cities. Many of the 160 MRP deputies triumphed in the elections because of their assertions that they sympathized with the sentiments of General de Gaulle. In some ways, the situation resembled subsequently the one that was created in November, 1958, when many deputies of the newly created Union of the New Republic (UNR) rode to seats in the National Assembly by holding onto the tail of the General's white horse. Unlike the UNR, however, in 1945 the MRP was not a Gaullist party, and it did not demonstrate its willingness to become one in 1947 when De Gaulle issued the call to join him in his new Rally of the French People (RPF). The only MRP leaders who defected to him were Edmond Michelet and Louis Terrenoire, "old faithfuls" who had to wait another eleven years before they were rewarded with ministerial portfolios in the first government of the Fifth Republic. The other MRP leaders stayed with Bidault, André Colin, and Pierre-Henri Teigen. However, in the municipal elections of 1947, many electors broke away from the MRP to vote for the RPF. The party became a secondary force in French politics only one year after its great victory of

1946. If it had gone up faster than any of the other parties, its descent was just as rapid.

There are many reasons for the decline of the MRP. First, Christian democratic parties often are artificial creations—political sieves through which individuals flow in route to their true party destinations. God seldom holds people together when their pocketbooks and interests are opposed. Some of the most intense conflicts in history have been fought by Christians among themselves. There is no reason to believe that Christians will live in one party as one big family simply because they belong to the same religious faith. In fact, they seldom do. Numerous MRP electors found that to be so. Second, the party was never able to evolve a doctrine that was truly satisfactory to most of its factions. It was not able to achieve that measure of internal cooperation that would have allowed it to propagandize effectively in its own behalf. Its diminishing Left wing continued to see it as a vehicle of moral regeneration and welfare policies, while its mass saw it as an expression of their conservative tendencies and a pillar against communism. As a result, it stood still and soon became little more than a very ordinary political party. As the years progressed, it lost more of its Left intellectuals and militants and many mass supporters who found greater satisfaction in casting their votes for a more durable party of conservative orientation. Finally, it would be very difficult to discuss the MRP without noting the transformation undergone by Georges Bidault, its former leader. A former Resistance leader, he evolved—in the years between 1945 and 1958—from "full republicanism" to what might be described as "full reaction." The reasons for his transition remain a great mystery, one which even the present leaders of the MRP find themselves at a loss to explain. By 1958, Bidault emerged as one of the working partners of Jacques Soustelle, and he and the MRP parted company. His current tendencies are now carried on in the MRP by Christian Bonnet, a man of rightist inclination, and resisted by Rombault and Lambert, men of progressive orientation.

THE RIGHT

The Union of the New Republic (UNR)

The UNR was created in 1958. It emerged from the elections of November, 1958, as the largest party in the National Assembly.[11] It is a giant formation that harbors many tendencies; its electoral plank appears to consist solely of fidelity to General de Gaulle. Its former Secretary-General

[11] See Noonan, *op. cit.*, pp. 467–69. More than three years after its creation, the party still suffers from organizational problems. Its recruiting program is ineffective, and its militants few—even in those geographical areas in which it has won its greatest electoral victories. In its three-day meeting in Arcachon in October, 1960, the party admitted that it is still not a "mass party."

Roger Frey declares that its goals consist of "renewing and moralizing" French political life, "in the sense that these men intend to follow the example of General de Gaulle." Frey states that one of the party's fundamental responsibilities is to bring to French political behavior a new kind of moderation that, thus far, it has lacked. Its mission, less parliamentary than national, is to be that of a renovator—"to restore the spiritual, intellectual, and moral values which have always been the endowment of our country." Frey concludes that the party will strive "To remain ourselves, neither to the Left nor the Right, to avoid engaging in superannuated quarrels, to be faithful to the social and national philosophy of Gaullism, these are the lines along which the General must guide us." At the same time, he also explains that the future will hold no "splendid isolation" for the UNR and that its behavior will conform closely to the function that it is to perform—that of serving as the indispensable bond between Right and Left, "the meeting place of ideas and men." Finally, he acknowledges that the party may be compelled to move to the Left because of the near destruction of the representation of the non-Communist Left in the National Assembly

One of the UNR's highly publicized objectives is to destroy the representation of the Communist party on the national and municipal levels. During the elections of November, 1958, the party went out of its way to combat Communist candidates and announced that it was free on the second ballot to make deferments to its Right and to its Left without sacrificing any aspect of its doctrine. During the municipal elections of 1959, it announced that it sought "to chase the Communists from all the mayorships where they have installed themselves to the great misfortune of the country." After its founding, one of its stated objectives was to maintain "French Algeria"; and it declared that it would do so by founding its methods on directives referred to it from time to time by De Gaulle.[12] When De Gaulle pronounced in favor of an "Algerian Algeria," the UNR revised its position in order to conform with his. Sentiments relative to going it alone in Algeria have been expressed by some of its members—ones that the leadership has gone out of its way to play down. It is obvious that they are trying very hard to make the organization appear more responsible and respectable than some of its members wish it to be. The party has already undergone some crises and witnessed the defection of some deputies from its parliamentary group; nevertheless, it has developed a fair amount of internal cohesion.

What is the social composition of the UNR? Claude Estier writes that "a rather great number of these new deputies are of military origin, or 'old soldiers.' They are not Gaullists in the way in which we defined that adjective during the war. They are militarists of the classical type, indis-

[12] *Le Monde,* November 15, 1958, p. 3.

putable colonialists, characterized by a certain contempt for politics and politicians." There is the Biaggi type, admittedly Fascist, and the type represented by Colonel Bourgeoin, pure Gaullist and extreme nationalist. There is the Lucien Neuwirth type—gentle and often blindly obedient to the dictates of the General. There is the type that is conservative on the social plan without being specifically nationalist. Others are liberals, and some are adventurers. Georges Izard states, "There is everything in the UNR; we know that some men have taken this ticket because it offers them more chances, men who would have been radicals in a different context—and there are others, this we also know, who are pure Fascists." Étienne Borne writes that the party's only "common denominator is nationalism, felt more than it is thought . . ." Conservative André Stibio is convinced, however, that "This nationalism is not fascism." And Jacques Soustelle, before he was expelled from the party, felt that in the sense in which it favored political and social progress, the UNR had as much right as any political formation to be called "a party of the left."[13]

Nationalism and repetitious references to faith in De Gaulle serve as the UNR's common bonds. Nevertheless, its nationalism differs considerably from the classical nineteenth-century nationalism of the Independents, for many of its important members are willing to combine a strong nationalist policy with broad social change. Albin Chalandon, for example, argues that French capitalism must respect its responsibilities if it wishes to conserve its rights.

UNR members proclaim themselves staunch believers in "Gaullism," and yet they experience difficulty in identifying its doctrinal outlines. Their plight is understandable; to believe in "Gaullism" is to believe in Charles de Gaulle—one cannot be distinguished from the other. "Gaullism" is revealed by De Gaulle to the followers on a day-to-day basis, and a good Gaullist follows without question all the dictates of the General and endorses everything that he articulates. If the General contradicts tomorrow what he said yesterday, a good Gaullist does likewise. It is obvious that "Gaullism" cannot possibly outlive Charles de Gaulle.

In 1951, the Gaullist Rally of the French People (RPF) was one of the most important parties in the National Assembly; but its leader was out of power. The Gaullist UNR is now the most important political formation in the National Assembly, and its leader is the President of the Fifth Republic. In 1956, the widening gap between De Gaulle and the RPF contributed to the collapse of that party; Jacques Fauvet states that without De Gaulle, "the UNR will probably know the same decline."

[13] See "L'*UNR* telle qu'elle est vue de Claude Bourdet à André Stibio," *Le Monde*, December 9, 1958, p. 3 for views of the UNR expressed by Claude Bourdet, Claude Estier, Jean Ferniot, André Stibio, Georges Izzard, Étienne Borne, and Jacques Soustelle.

The Independents

In 1952, Maurice Duverger stated that "Except under unusual circumstances there does not exist in France—at least to the Right of the Radicals—political parties worthy of the name. This normal state of affairs ceases only when there is a serious threat to national security or when some other compelling concern creates an ephemeral coalition around one man."[14] Today, two important political parties exist to the Right of the Radical Socialists and they are worthy of consideration. The Independent party is one of these. Another is the UNR, that "ephemeral coalition" around President de Gaulle.

After the liberation, the conservative forces re-emerged in three different groups—the Republican Party of Liberty (PRL), the Independent Republicans, and the Republican Group of Peasant and Social Action. The National Center of Independents was created in 1948 for the purpose of coordinating their activities. It came under the guidance of Roger Duchet, Independent senator of the Côte-d'Or. (Duchet was succeeded by Camille Laurens in May, 1961, after considerable opposition from the Independent deputies and a reputation for being close to the insurgent generals in April, 1961). During the legislative elections of 1951, it managed to conclude various electoral agreements with the RGP, MRP, RPF, and some of the Third Force groups. On no occasion did it attempt to conclude such agreements with the Socialists because its program was and is as opposed to socialism as it is to communism. In fact, it has always taken particular exception to Socialist financial policy.

During the last two years of the Fourth Republic, the Independents behaved in the National Assembly in a way that was not greatly different from the activities of Communist deputies who sat in that body. They did their best to block practically all proposals for constitutional reform. Moreover, various of the governmental crises that occurred during that period might have been averted had the Independents played a constructive parliamentary role. Unwilling to make concessions, they tenuously defended a tax system that derived more than 70 per cent of its revenue from consumers by shielding it from legislative changes that would have shifted part of the tax load to producers. On the floor of the National Assembly, they specialized in the art of turning certain issues away from serious legislative scrutiny by employing various techniques—parliamentary, of course—that allowed them to pluck the life from many proposals. Although they were (and remain) militantly anti-Communist, they did not hesitate to coordinate their votes with those of the Communist party in order to bring down various governments. Guy Mollet was forced to resign the premiership on May 23, 1957, when he lost the support of sixty-

[14] Maurice Duverger, "Public Opinion and Political Parties in France," *American Political Science Review*, December, 1952, p. 1072.

seven Independents; Bourgès-Maunoury was defeated on October 10, 1957, when sixty-three Independents voted against him; Gaillard fell in April, 1958, after one hundred Independents withdrew their support from him.

The Independents started off the Fifth Republic by playing a constructive game and giving full support to President de Gaulle. Antoine Pinay, "Mr. Conservative" himself, became Minister of Finance in the Debré government. Soon it was apparent, however, that Pinay and other Independents were not greatly pleased by the financial policy of the new regime. Pinay resigned his post early in 1960 after disagreeing with at least four of his ministerial associates on financial policy and with President de Gaulle on foreign policy. He then announced that he was retiring from political life and that he did not intend to go into opposition to the regime. He is nonetheless still far from retirement and maintains with other Independents what they have described as "watchful vigilance" over the course of contemporary events. Of all the large political parties, only the Independents refused to condemn the militarists of Algiers after their insurrection of April, 1961. They said only that they "disapprove of all illegal acts."

Lately, there have been indications that many Independents are not taking kindly to the devaluation of parliamentary institutions—not because they manifest genuine affection for parliamentarism, but because they often find in it various opportunities to satisfactorily pursue their own ends. The Parliament of the Fourth Republic was chaotic and divided, but it did dominate the legislative scene. It afforded the Independents the ability to block certain types of legislation, ones that would have affected adversely the status of the very interests that they represent. They found it convenient to play their negative role within the periphery of a badly divided Parliament that allowed them to block and counter and even paralyze the parliamentary process, whenever that was necessary. Today, there is a different regime and they have begun to complain that very few of their men are able to get close to the decision-making process; they generally resent De Gaulle's increasing tendency to depoliticize the government and those committees in which important decisions are made. Finally, they know that De Gaulle has very little affection for them because he views them as speaking more for partisan interests than for the general public. They know that he knows that they are the true "realists" and that if they are with him today, they can be his greatest enemies tomorrow.

PARTY ORGANIZATION

The Communist party's basic unit is the cell, which consists of three to thirty members. Organized on an occupational or geographical basis, some cells exist in various places of work, others according to living districts or communes. The bureau of each cell is responsible to both the cell and the section, the next highest organizational unit. The sections supervise the cells, form the departmental federations (90), and send delegates to the Communist party Congress, which is supposed to meet once every two years. The Congress elects its large Central Committee, which comprises approximately seventy-five members and is supposed to constitute the highest organizational authority in the party but in fact has become secondary to the Political Bureau (14), the Finance Control Committee (8), the Secretariat (4), and the Control Committee (6). Only the Political Bureau may speak for the party; it controls the Secretariat and the Control Committee, which is entrusted with maintaining party "purity." All party members who gain political office must assure the party in advance that they will resign their posts when ordered to do so, vote according to the dictates of the party executive, and pay a percentage of their monthly salaries to the party. In Parliament, as elsewhere, their responsibility is to the party before all else; and a vote based on "freedom of conscience" is not permitted.

The basic unit in the Socialist party (SFIO) is the section. The party is organized on a geographical basis, not an occupational one. All of the sections in a department form the departmental federation. The national Congress consists of the delegates of those federations that comprise at least five sections or one hundred members. Each federation is represented in the national Congress in proportion to its membership. In recent years, the Congress had diminished in importance to the National Council, which consists of one delegate from each departmental federation. The real power in the party lies in the *comité-directeur*, or executive committee, which consists of thirty-one members elected to it by a majority of all the delegates to the Congress. This method of voting is of great significance inasmuch as the four large federations of the Nord, Pas-de-Calais, Bouches-du-Rhône, and Haute-Vienne account for at least one-third of all the votes cast in the annual Party Congress. As SFIO member Max Lejeune once said, the election of a delegate to the *comité-directeur* "is practically impossible . . . if he has not obtained the agreement of the delegates of these important federations." The party's conservative organization and structure are now in the tight grip of Guy Mollet and his "machine." The largest federations sustain him in the secretary-generalship. It was understandable when in 1957 an exasperated SFIO minority leader exclaimed, "If the Radical party lacks organization, the SFIO has too much of it."[15] The party speaks reverently of freedom of expression and tolerates little in the party's ranks when it conflicts with party policy. Finally, the control of the party over its parliamentary group is tight,

[15] André Philip in an interview with the author, Paris, December 17, 1957.

which results in an ironlike discipline that is matched only by that of the Communist party.

The Radical Socialist party has its local committees, federations, and national Congress. Its National Council presides between national party meetings. In one sense, the party has not come far from what it was when it was first organized. It is still an association of diverse groups held loosely together, and it continues to live up to the description given of it late in the nineteenth century by Ernest Picard, "The Radicals are not a party, they are a coalition—they represent a means of attainment." The party has little control over its parliamentary group. In fact, under the Fourth Republic, Radical deputies created considerable anguish for governments that included ministers drawn from their own party. Some of the party's critics contend that Radical deputies act this way because of their individualism. Others argue that their constant shifts derive only from the fact that they just cannot be trusted. Whatever the merits of such arguments, Radical deputies do inspire suspicion; and their record is generally less than commendable. One of their factions was led by André Morice (he withdrew from the party in 1956); another faction is led by Edgar Faure, and one is led by Felix Gaillard. Mendès-France and his faction left the party in 1959. These factions usually communicate in order to combat each other.

The MRP's basic unit is the section; its sections form federations. Its Congress meets annually to elect its president and secretary-general. Candidates are endorsed by the National Executive Committee, which is controlled by the top party lights. Party discipline is implemented by its executive.

The Independents belong to the National Center, a committee composed of deputies and senators that seeks to coordinate the activities of various of its conservative groups. In turn, the National Center maintains ineffectual ties with the departmental centers. The disunity so characteristic of the Independents is not as great now as it was one decade ago. Its executive stated in 1951 that, "It is not a classical party with a pyramidal organization and a politically rigid doctrine. It is the only group which leaves total liberty to vote to its members, who vote according to their convictions and their conscience." Now, under the Fifth Republic, the Independents enjoy greater internal discipline and even resort occasionally to expulsions from their ranks.

The UNR lacks organization and mass support. It has its departmental federations that are dominated by committees staffed with many of the party's founders and its annual Congress, which elects its Central Committee. This party born of General de Gaulle probably will not outlive him. It has failed to develop any political roots among the many divergent social classes and interest groups of the French nation.

PRESSURE GROUPS

A pressure group is an association of individuals that employs various methods in order to induce government to satisfy certain objectives. France embraces numerous associations of this type. Nevertheless, French public opinion classifies only those associations that seek to implement their own partisan and exclusive ends as pressure groups; ones that are considered as furthering the general welfare are not placed in this category. The reasons for this distinction are undeniably moral in nature.

Pressure groups are a means of representation. They exist because the political parties do not implement certain interests as fully as they would like. They tend to increase as parties come to appeal to more and more interests. They influence parties, although the extent to which they do varies from group to group. They seek to influence the administration; if their success with it is generally less than with Parliament, it is because the former is more closely identified with the public welfare and because it offers them fewer opportunities than the latter. The pressure groups seek to influence newspapers and other organs of public opinion. Their success depends greatly on the amount of money that they are able to raise, as well as on their ability to deploy it successfully.

Pressure groups seek to influence governments by having direct access to a minister or ministers sympathetic to or dependent upon the services of that particular group. While conservative ministers are by tradition receptive to the pressures generated by partisan economic groups, "Left" ministers—particularly Socialists—engage in essentially similar practices. Socialist Premier Guy Mollet's 1956 government made concessions to civil servants that were nothing less than scandalous.

The relationship between a pressure group and a political party is usually dependent upon the degree of discipline that the latter is able to exercise over its membership. A highly disciplined party is usually a poor target for a pressure group—that is, providing that its demands do not coincide precisely with theirs. A less disciplined party with a membership more susceptible to outside pressures offers a pressure group more promising game. Parties that bid for the support of all classes fall also in this category. Parties that are tied to one class risk becoming the captive of a particular pressure group and domination by it.

When Parliament is truly of importance—as is not the case under the Fifth Republic—pressure groups usually concentrate on the committees and seek to induce their members to enact their demands into law. This is often one of the surest roads to success. But when Parliament is not important and when a government rules on the basis of emergency powers —as is the case with the government of Michel Debré—then some pressure groups may find themselves cut off from their ability to implement their ends. This has happened under the Fifth Republic to various veteran and family groups whose privileges have been trimmed by the Debré government. On the other hand, this did not happen to certain wine and wheat producers who were successful in getting through to the ministers and getting them to sustain their privileges.

Labor interests are represented by various trade-unions who act as pressure groups. These unions first regarded political parties with suspicion and refused to enter into close collaboration with them. The CGT's Charter of Amiens (1901) prohibited institutional working arrangements with the parties—although in fact various of its members did belong to the Socialist party (SFIO) and occasionally held posts in both organizations. Today, the relationship between the trade-unions and the parties is much stronger than it was many years ago, even if it still remains unofficial.

After the beginning of the twentieth century, the CGT was the major trade-union. After World War I and the split in the Unified Socialist party that led to the creation of the Socialist party (SFIO) and after the reconstitution of the Unified party as the new Communist party, the latter sought to create its own union, the General Confederation of Labor (CGTU). During the twenties, it remained basically weak, as did the French Confederation of Christian Workers (CFTC). The CGT dominated the situation and continued to maintain its apoliticism, although it paused occasionally to support Herriot's Radical Socialist government of 1924 and his prosecution of the Riff War. The CGT and the CGTU merged in 1936, and the Communists became a minority in it. During the liberation the Communists forged into the majority and succeeded in capturing the central apparatus. After the liberation, a number of anti-Communists broke with the CGT in order to form their own organization, the Worker's Force (FO). Today, it is largely a paper organization that does not have roots among those non-salaried workers who constitute the majority of organized labor. It has strong ties with certain categories of civil servants who affiliate primarily with the Socialist party (SFIO) and who are concentrated primarily in the Post, Telephone and Telegraph (PTT) services.

Today, the Communist party dominates the CGT, the Socialist party influences the FO and vice versa, and the MRP maintains a relationship with the CFTC. The relationship between the CFTC and the MRP is, with reference to the latter, almost exclusively with its Left wing and not its other wings, whose members are conservative and not in great sympathy with the worker's advancement.

In a sentence, the pressures generated by French trade-unions are not very strong because the movement itself is very divided. The CGT makes a great many demands, but it is not in a postion where it can implement them effectively. The strength that it does enjoy can be attributed to the Communist party—however, many of its weaknesses can be traced to the same organization. It has difficulty negotiating with the state because the latter views it as its enemy. The FO and the CFTC cannot negotiate effectively because they cannot break the monopoly of the Communists over labor and because they receive weak support and assistance from the Socialist party and the MRP. If the parties of the Left should ever unite, this would probably eliminate the divisions in the trade-union movement and put it in a position where it would be capable of holding both the government and the society to its demands.

French employers also have their pressure groups. The National Confederation of French Employers (CNPF) is composed primarily of large enterprisers. The Confederation of Small and Middle-Size Enterprises (PME) is what the name implies, but within it exists a certain amount of resentment against middle-size businessmen. These associations suffer from certain internal divisions and an inability to pull together or to attract people to membership in them.

The peasantry also has its pressure groups. Before World War II, the two major agricultural associations were the National Union of Agricultural Syndicates and the National Federation of Mutuality. The former was of conservative orientation; the latter predominantly Radical Socialist. Less than these were the National Peasant's Confederation, which was of Socialist orientation; the Communist General Confederation of Peasant Workers; and the Group of Peasant Defense. The picture was completed by certain syndical organizations concerned with the production of sugar beets, wheat, wine, milk, etc. After World War II, the General Confederation of Agriculture (CGA) and the National Federation of Agricultural Worker's Syndicates (FNSEA) were created. The former lacks real power; the latter eventually attained a membership of approximately 700,000 adherents. After a time, it became concerned more with enlarging its membership than with taking a position on various agricultural problems. It is often charged with extending certain privileges to various of its internal groups and ignoring the requests of others. It lacks strong control over the behavior of its adherents, as was revealed in some of the peasant demonstrations that took place in 1960 and 1961. Its Federations are autonomous. One short look at the peasantry should convince the observer that most farmers are not enthusiastic about organization for political action.

SELECTED READING

Duverger, M. *The French Political System.* Chicago: University of Chicago Press, 1958.

Ehrmann, H. *Organized Business in France.* Princeton, N.J.: Princeton University Press, 1957.

LORWIN, V. *The French Labor Movement.* Cambridge, Mass.: Harvard University Press, 1954.

MICAUD, C. A. "French Political Parties: Ideology, Myths and Social Realities." In *Modern Political Parties,* S. Neumann (ed.). Chicago: University of Chicago Press, 1955.

WILLIAMS, P. *Politics in Post-War France; Parties and the Constitution in the Fourth Republic.* New York: Longmans, Green & Co., Inc., 1958.

WRIGHT, G. "Peasant Politics in the Third French Republic," *Political Science Quarterly,* LXX (1955), 75–87.

14

Elections

Qualifications for voting in France are citizenship, at least twenty-one years of age, registration, and full civil and political rights. The voter may ballot only in the one electoral district in which he is registered. Absentee ballots are available for those unable to be at the polls for legally permissible reasons, as are proxy votes for citizens, servicemen, and officials of the Republic who reside outside the country or are absent from it on election day.

Candidates are elected to political office by methods prescribed in one or more laws adopted prior to the election. Most laws are favorable to the parties who have played a leading role in their drafting. Some provide for variations of majority voting, some prescribe variations of proportional representation, and some utilize elements extracted from both systems.

Most of the general elections conducted in the Third Republic used majority voting without lists. The electoral district was the administrative division known as the *arrondissement.* Candidates were elected on the first ballot if they received an absolute majority of the vote cast and if their vote exceeded a predetermined fraction of the entire vote. If no candidate was elected on the first ballot, the seat subsequently went to the candidate who received a relative majority on the second final ballot. The first ballot yielded so few absolute majorities that candidates could campaign on it without too much risk. Candidates usually waited for the interval between the first and second ballots to enter alliances with each other for the purpose of supporting common candidates on the second ballot. The second ballot reflected the strength of these electoral coalitions rather than the strength of each candidate and party.

Majority voting without lists had the effect of encouraging localism; it made the deputy more the creature of his district than of his party. It also encouraged interparty agreements and the subsequent formation of great electoral coalitions of the Left and the Right, more because of necessity than choice. It attracted parties of similar tendencies to each other. Their electoral agreements sometimes carried over to the parliamentary level, which helped to produce a majority in Parliament. It should be observed that when parties approach the second ballot allied in great coalitions of the Right and Left, the multiparty system transforms itself at the polls into something that resembles the two-party system. If the Right unites and the Left fails to do so, this usually results in victory for the former and defeat for the latter–and vice versa.

Under the Third and Fourth Republics, only three elections relied on a voting system that was completely proportional. Proportional representation uses the multimember electoral district. It seeks for parties and groups representation in the legislature that is directly proportionate to what they earn at the polls. It enables the legislature to reflect very clearly all the tendencies found among the voting public. It is the fairest system of representation. Some observers contend, however, that it furthers the existence of many parties, which, in turn, detracts from the formation of a possible legislature majority with results that are disastrous to effective and stable government.[1] Whatever the merits of this argument (and it hasn't many), no system of representation–majority or proportional–has easily produced coherent majorities in French legislatures. France is basically a multiparty state, and it is unlikely that any kind of *representative* system could succeed in changing this phenomenon.

The political parties favor the type of electoral law that advances their own interests. The Communist party is generally favorable to proportional representation; under the majority system, its opponents usually enter into electoral agreements that reduce Communist representation in the legislature to the point where it is only a shadow of the party's real strength in the country. The Socialist party (SFIO) usually wavers between proportional representation and the majority system. Its sentiments are sympathetic to the former, and its interests are often advanced by the latter. Lacking nationwide strength, it is favored normally by the majority system, which throws the election into the laps of the constituencies. Despite the fact that this system was used in the legislative elections of November, 1958, a "May 13" atmosphere and a set of unusual circumstances encouraged some voters to abandon some of their most cherished habits. Consequently, the SFIO did not benefit from that election. The MRP lacks local strength; therefore, it favors proportional representation. The Radical Socialists and the Independents favor the majority system. Their candidates draw their strength from local following and not from endorse-

[1] Some political scientists attribute to proportional representation responsibility for all kinds of dire consequences. With several, the preoccupation is not less than monomanic.

ments given to them by their executive committees. In 1958, the UNR favored the majority system, even if few of its candidates enjoyed strong local support (it won many of its seats in the November, 1958, elections because it was the "party of May 13," not because of the mode of election employed). The party had no alternative than to accept the method of election preferred by the leader of the nation who, it is said, designated the majority system with the idea of preventing too many "Gaullists" from colonizing the National Assembly! The precursor of the UNR, the RPF, was an ardent enemy of proportional representation and supported majority voting by list on the departmental level. Its strategy was to win large numbers of seats on the first ballot and strengthen itself on the second ballot through alliances concluded with other parties on a basis that was almost purely anti-Communist. It thought that this strategy would pave the way for emergence in the National Assembly of a coherent majority, one which would operate to its own profit. Its successor, the UNR, joined with the Independents to form a coherent majority in the Assembly after the legislature elections of November, 1958; but by that time, the Assembly had been devalued and reduced to a relatively insignificant legislative role!

Following are examples of specific electoral laws used by the Third, Fourth, and Fifth Republics and the results they helped to achieve.

THE THIRD REPUBLIC AND THE ELECTORAL LAW OF 1919

The electoral law of 1919 created a limited number of election districts; each sent more than one representative to the Chamber of Deputies. All candidates of a party or coalition were voted for on one ticket, and all were elected to the Chamber if their ticket received an absolute majority. There was no second ballot. If an absolute majority was not received, the seats at stake were distributed on the basis of proportional representation. The ticket with a plurality received a number of seats in the Chamber—the number varying from one-third to one-half—according to established voting ratios. The law had the effect of encouraging the emergence of party coalitions. The ticket that headed the polls had a definite advantage, and individual candidates sought to get on it by forming alliances with other groups. The conservative groups and parties united on a great coalition ticket that elected many of their candidates to the Chamber. The Left parties generally put up independent tickets; as a consequence, they suffered heavy losses. That experience exercised a tremendous influence on the subsequent electoral behavior of the Left. For some time after 1920, the electoral law remained essentially unchanged; and the newly created Socialist party (SFIO) came to realize that it was confronted with the choice of fighting an independent campaign and surrendering control of the Chamber to the conservatives or preventing this by entering into electoral alliances with the Radical Socialist party. As Léon Blum stated, "If we did not enter a bloc of the Left, which had absolutely no chance of success without our support, it was practically certain that the National Bloc (the conservatives) would have a majority in the next chamber. . . . That is why we consented to enter the coalition."[2] Socialists and Radical Socialists concluded an interparty electoral agreement; this, in turn, led subsequently to an interparty parliamentary agreement.[3] The latter gradually transformed the tactical orientation of both parties, which drew them closer together.

THE FOURTH REPUBLIC AND THE ELECTORAL LAW OF 1946

The electoral law of October, 1946, regulated the first general election held in the postliberation era. It used the department as the electoral district. The seven largest departments were divided into additional constituencies. Each department was allotted one deputy for each 100,000 people who resided in it. Each department was entitled to a minimum of two deputies. Each district returned generally fewer than six deputies. The method of election was proportional representation with list voting. The parties submitted their departmental lists that contained the names of their candidates, and each voter could vote only for one list. The lists were compelled to name as many candidates as there were seats at stake in the district. The list receiving the greatest number of votes received the first seat. The remaining seats were distributed on the basis of lists that showed the highest average number of votes. This law of 1946 was calculated to strengthen party discipline and to favor the government parties. For this reason, cross-voting was not tolerated. After the elections of 1946, however, a break occurred in the coalition of Communists, Socialists, and MRP—the balance of power in the legislature shifted to the Right, and new circumstances made the law a threat to the center parties. Communism and Gaullism were on the rise, and their future electoral victories threatened to be at the expense of the center. As a result, the center parties collaborated to create a new electoral law for the elections of 1951. It allowed all electoral districts (with the exception of the department of the Seine) to give all of the seats available to any party capable of winning

[2] Léon Blum, "The Socialists and the French Elections," *The Living Age,* CCCXXI (April 26, 1924), 838.

[3] Soon the Socialist party modified its behavior, despite its contention that it was a collectivist party that had little in common with the bourgeois Radical Socialists. In 1924, Blum said that, "Socialist support will not be wanting for a Government of the Left which acts vigorously against the Right, except insofar as such a government begins to lack reforming energy." For reproduction of other of his views, see "Elections and Socialist-Liberal Collaboration, *Labor Monthly,* VI (August, 1924), 508.

an absolute majority of the votes cast in them. The department of the Seine used proportional representation with ticket-splitting and preferential voting (voters were allowed to rearrange the order in which candidates appeared on each list). Nonetheless, these practices received legal recognition only on those lists that attained majority status.

The center parties succeeded in injecting in the electoral law the device known as the "alliance system." Parties were allowed to enter into alliances if they filed their intention to do so with the prefect of each department a designated number of days before the date of the election. This possibility was open, however, only to those parties capable of submitting lists in thirty or more departments. The qualifying allied parties campaigned separately, and on the day of election put up their lists on a separate basis. Nevertheless, if all the votes received by the allied parties equalled or exceeded an absolute majority of the votes cast in the department, then all of the seats went to the allied parties—being distributed among them on the basis of proportional representation. The law also stated that proportional representation would govern if no alliance or party secured an absolute majority in each department.

The center parties entered alliances in the majority of electoral districts that allowed them to restrain the Communists and the Gaullists who were unable to conclude such agreements with other parties. The Communists stood alone. Although they received 26 per cent of the national vote, they obtained fewer than 100 seats in the National Assembly. The Gaullists were able to enter only twelve alliances. Although they won 22 per cent of the vote, they were able to secure only 107 seats in the National Assembly. In other words, the Communists and Gaullists won 48 per cent of the total vote and 204 of the 627 seats at stake. The center parties won 38 per cent of the vote and 253 seats! In the departments of the Seine and Seine-et-Oise, proportional representation allowed the smaller center parties to hold the extremist parties to 60 per cent of the total number of seats at stake.

Although the "right kind" of electoral law in the hands of the center parties produced both a "safe" distribution of Assembly seats (and a travesty of the representative system), it did not produce the desired majority in the National Assembly. It served again, however, as the basis for the general election of January 2, 1956, the last one conducted under the Fourth Republic. Originally, the deputies hoped to get around to producing a new law for the elections of that year and were considering one founded on majority voting with two ballots; but before it could be prepared, the country was confronted with the necessity of holding new elections. When the vote was concluded, forty new Poujadist deputies were added to the Assembly and subsequent governments became even harder to maintain.

THE FIFTH REPUBLIC AND THE ELECTORAL LAW OF 1958

During November, 1958, 475 deputies were elected in Metropolitan France and the Overseas Departments, and seventy-one in Algeria, which constituted the total membership of the National Assembly at 546. In Metropolitan France, voting took place in single-member constituencies; two ballots were necessary if no candidate was elected by a majority on the first, a plurality sufficing on the second. The election districts were constituted on the basis of one deputy for every 93,000 inhabitants. A minimum of two deputies was elected from each department—the Basses-Alpes was entitled to two, the department of the Nord to twenty-three, and the department of the Seine to fifty-five. The total area of each election district varied from department to department according to population density. Districts larger than those used in previous elections allowed for a smaller number of deputies to be returned from Metropolitan France.

Electoral regulations prohibited filing new candidacies between the two ballots—in order to minimize "deals" among candidates of parties likely to oppose each other in the National Assembly lest they endanger the subsequent formation of a stable governmental majority. The Ordinance of October 13, 1958, stipulated: (1) no one could be a candidate in more than one election district, (2) no one could be a candidate on the second ballot unless he ran on the first ballot and received at least 5 per cent of the total votes cast, (3) each candidate had to deposit 100,000 francs ($238), and (4) candidates not receiving 5 per cent of the total vote cast forfeited their deposits. Those people who were ineligible for candidacy included persons deprived of civil rights due to conviction for a crime as well as certain categories of civil servants and certain appointed officials whose prestige in an election district "might exert pressure on the voters." Reimbursement for campaign expenditures and equal radio and television time was made available to all parliamentary groups running a minimum of seventy-five candidates; groups that combined to form election coalitions were not obligated to present seventy-five candidates each—that figure sufficed for the entire coalition. The minimum age for candidacy was twenty-three. All candidates had to be French. Both sexes were eligible. Punishment for violation of campaign regulations ranged from fines of 300,000 to 800,000 francs or imprisonment from fifteen days to three months, or both.

The electoral law of 1958 introduced a new twist by requiring all candidates for political office to name substitutes who would replace them after their election under circumstances such as death; resignation; acceptance of paid employment as an official of a professional association; or appointment to the Constitutional Council, the government, or a government mission in excess of six-months duration. Thus, the voter balloted for both the candidate and his substitute.

In Algeria and in the two Saharan departments, seventy-one deputies were elected by direct universal suffrage—four by the Saharan departments of the Oases and the Saoara, and sixty-seven by Algeria. The method of election was by list voting with one ballot. The lists contained as many names of candidates for deputy as there were seats to be filled in each election district in Algeria and in each department of the Sahara. The list that won the most votes received all the seats at stake in the election district. Ticket-splitting and preferential voting were prohibited in order to encourage the uniting of candidates of North African and European origin on a single list in proportion to the relative size of these communities. It was assumed that this would prevent the election from becoming a contest between the two communities. The eighteen Algerian election districts were drawn up on the basis of the geographical distribution of the different groups. Nevertheless, two-thirds of the elected representatives had to be Moslem (forty-six), and twenty-one had to be of European origin. Civil servants and ex-soldiers separated less than one year from the military were ineligible for candidacy. Otherwise, the rules of eligibility and ineligibility and the regulations relative to conduct were identical with those of Metropolitan France. Campaign expenses were assumed by the Algerian Budget. The powers of the Central Control Committee and subordinate Control Committees were defined in the letter of October 22, 1958, of General de Gaulle to M. Hoppenot, President of the Committee, urging freedom of candidacy, speech, assembly, vote, and regularity of the count. Despite this, the campaign was marred by frequent interventions by the military.

The Overseas Departments of Guiana, Guadaloupe, Réunion, and Martinique were divided into single-member constituencies, one for Guiana and three for each of the others. They enjoyed the same electoral procedure and rules as Metropolitan France.

POLITICAL ASPECTS OF THE ELECTORAL LAW OF 1958

Majority voting with two ballots was favored by General de Gaulle as the method of electing deputies to the National Assembly in Metropolitan France. He asserted that it would give more clearness, simplicity, and continuity to French politics than had existed under other types of electoral systems. The law sought to bring about a direct relationship between voters and deputies. It sought to make the deputies more representative of their new electoral districts by cutting substantially into the control that normally would be exercised over them by the political parties. It sought also to take advantage of the Communist tendency to concentrate its votes in geographical pockets, and the election districts were so constructed as to drastically reduce Communist representation in the National Assembly. At the same time, the electoral system was of the type that might have favored the Socialist party (SFIO), the party of the small communes; and it might have returned more Socialist deputies to the Assembly if the French had decided not to rebel against voting habits to which they had clung for so many years.

Three-fourths of a century ago, adoption of majority voting with two ballotings attenuated the threat of Boulangerism, thereby establishing the system's "republican virtue." The Boulangerist's inability to put up in the 600 election districts candidates with sufficiently local reputations proved disastrous to the industrial and urban phenomenon that was concentrated in the mining country of the north and in the suburbs of Paris, Marseilles, Toulon, and St. Étienne. Unlike the elections of 1889, however, the elections of 1958 resulted in an overwhelming victory for the Right.

RESULTS OF THE 1958 ELECTIONS TO THE NATIONAL ASSEMBLY

In Metropolitan France, twelve important political groups participated on the first ballot and elected thirty-nine deputies by absolute majority; postfirst ballot electoral maneuvers reduced to seven the number of important political formations participating on the second ballot. The second tour witnessed the failure of the Communist and Socialist parties to support common candidates on a broad basis, unlike various of their adversaries who did enter electoral coalitions that enabled them to elect a large number of deputies to the National Assembly.

The electoral results were surprising in that the Gaullist UNR exceeded all that had been expected of it. In five departments, it captured all the seats; in the Gironde, eight of ten; in the Alpes-Maritime, four of six; in the Maine-et-Loire, five of six; in the Nord, twelve of twenty-three; and in the Paris region, more than 50 per cent. Its success was great in the former MRP territory of Alsace, and only some victories in other regions previously unfavorable to it saved the MRP from disaster. In instances when the UNR and the Independents competed with each other, it was the former who usually won. The Radical party, now the residue of the Third Republic, suffered one of its greatest electoral defeats; it accounted for only 2.5 per cent of the total votes cast on the second and final ballot. Its former hold on the southwest was reduced by 75 per cent, and few of its leaders survived; Felix Gaillard, Maurice Faure, and André Marie were the only ones to return to the National Assembly. The Socialist party (SFIO) slipped to approximately 14 per cent on the second ballot; defeated were Defferre, Gazier, Pineau, Jules Moch, Ramadier, and Lacoste. Heavy losses were suffered by the party in the departments of the

Nord and Pas-de-Calais, as well as in the southwest and in the Massif central. In instances when Communist candidates deferred on the second ballot to Socialist candidates who had voted "no" in the referendum, such "poisoned gifts" were less than helpful. The Communist party restricted itself to thirty such deferments. Although it received approximately 21 per cent of the total votes cast on the second ballot, its tendency to store up its votes in geographical pockets placed it at the disadvantage of the electoral system; and so its representation in the National Assembly was reduced to ten seats.

Voting in the elections of 1958 tended to gravitate around one man, as the candidates and the parties generally sought to avoid the competition of ideas and platforms. The Count of Paris observed that "the candidates and the parties, with the exception of the Communists, articulate approximately the same propositions, refer to the same principles, announce the same promises." One observer concluded that since De Gaulle proclaimed for no one, the voters proclaimed for De Gaulle by voting for those who most loudly proclaimed for him. Paradoxically, the voters on the first ballot rejected Mendès-France, that man who had announced his personal opposition to De Gaulle, even though some of the views held by the two men are very similar.

If the results of the elections of 1958 represented the victory of one man, they also reflected the failure of the classical party system that—with the exception of one of its components—entered the contest with a status that was less than significant. The one exception was constituted by the Independents. It was an understandable one, too, in view of the fact that they had been instrumental in toppling two of the last three governments of the Fourth Republic. Among the traditional parties, the Independents were able to profit from the elections. Its vote on the first ballot exceeded even that of the UNR. The electoral results are given in Table 14–1.

Table 14–1. Electoral Results of the 1958 Elections to the National Assembly

Parties	Seats	Second Ballot		First Ballot	
		Number	%	Number	%
Communist	10	3,741,384	20.7	3,882,204	18.9
Diverse Left	2			347,298	1.4
Socialist	40	2,484,417	13.8	3,167,354	15.5
Radical	13	362,784	2.5	983,201	4.8
Center Left	22	1,035,625	5.5	1,364,788	6.7
M.R.P. and Christian Democrats	44 + 13	1,365,064	7.5	2,378,788	11.6
U.N.R.	189	4,769,052	26.4	3,603,958	17.6
Independents and Peasants	120 + 12	4,250,039	23.6	4,092,600	19.9
Extreme Right	1			669,518	3.3

SOURCE: *Le Monde,* November 22, 1958, p. 5.

THE ELECTORAL LAW OF 1958 AND THE SENATE

The Senate of the Fifth Republic comprises 307 members—255 for the departments of Metropolitan France, 7 for the Overseas Departments, 32 for Algeria, 2 for the Sahara, 5 for the Overseas Territories, and 6 for French citizens who reside abroad. The term of office is nine years, and one-third of the membership is elected every three years. Senators must be at least thirty-five years of age, they may not serve simultaneously in the government (in May, 1959, Senators Jean Berthoin, Edmond Michelet, and Roger Houdet resigned their seats in order to remain ministers in the Debré government), and they must also name their substitutes.

The members of the Senate are elected indirectly by an Electoral College composed of members of the National Assembly, the General Councils, the Territorial Assemblies, and representatives of the Municipal Councils:

1. *The National Assembly.* All deputies to the National Assembly are senatorial electors.
2. *The General Councils.* Each department has an elected assembly called a General Council that is responsible for assisting the prefect in administering the department. The term of office for each general councilor is six years. All are divided into two categories that become vacant alternately every three years. Fifty per cent of the membership of the General Councils was elected in April, 1958. The next election took place in April, 1961. All general councilors are senatorial electors.
3. *The Territorial Assemblies.* Each Overseas Territory has an Assembly that is elected by universal suffrage and whose members are senatorial electors.
4. *The Municipal Councils.* The municipal elections of March 8 and 15, 1958, were a precondition of the senatorial elections. In cities whose populations number fewer than 9,000 people, the Municipal Councils elect to the Electoral College delegates from among their own membership. The number of delegates is as follows:

   a) One for Municipal Councils having nine to eleven members
   b) Three for Municipal Councils having thirteen members
   c) Five for Municipal Councils having seventeen members
   d) Seven for Municipal Councils having twenty-one members
   e) Fifteen for Municipal Councils having twenty-three members

   In all cities of the department of the Seine and in those whose populations exceed 9,000 people, all municipal councilors are delegates ex officio. In cities whose populations exceed 30,000, the Municipal Councils elect delegates from lists of candidates. Elections are conducted on the basis of proportional representation. One additional delegate is elected for every 1,000 inhabitants in excess of 30,000.

After the Electoral College is assembled, each of its members is restricted to one vote. If an elector is both a deputy and a general councilor, he must have a substitute appointed for him by the President of the General Council. If he happens to be a deputy and a muncipal councilor, he must have a substitute appointed for him by the mayor.

There are two methods of election to the Senate. The first is by majority vote with two ballots, and the second is by proportional representation according to the rule of the highest average in those departments entitled to more than five senators. The majority vote with two ballots is used in the Metropolitan departments entitled to from one to four senators and in the Overseas Territories (each of which may elect one senator). Election on the first ballot may be acquired only if a candidate receives an absolute majority of the votes cast and if the number of votes received is equal to one-fourth of the eligible voters. A relative majority suffices on the second ballot. Proportional representation is used in the departments of the Bouches-du-Rhône, Nord, Pas-de-Calais, Rhone, Seine, Seine-Maritime, and Seine-et-Oise; all of these departments are entitled to five or more senators.

The electoral law governing the election of senators has its conservative aspects. The proportion of senatorial electors is greater for small cities than for the large ones. The majority come from small villages of fewer than 1,500 people, ones that represent but one-third of French society. Cities with populations in excess of 10,000 and which constitute approximately 42 per cent of the total population of France are entitled to 22 per cent of the senatorial electors. This unequal distribution of senatorial electors works to the advantage of the rural and less heavily populated departments—so much so that the Senate has already earned the name of "the Chamber of Agriculture." In fact, the method of election to the Senate was calculated to give that body a conservative orientation. In the heavily populated urban departments, it is proportional and so it gives representation to the rural minorities. In the non-densely populated departments, the method of election is based on the majority system, which accentuates the underrepresentation of the cities. The method of election sought to continue the immobilism of the second chamber.

Nevertheless, if the elections to the National Assembly produced a great victory for the "new men" of the Fifth Republic, the Senate elections of April, 1959, did result in great success for the "old men" of the Fourth Republic despite the conservative electoral law. Elected were such perennials as Edgar Faure, Francois Mitterand, Jacques Duclos, and Edouard Bonnefous. As the *Manchester Guardian Weekly* stated, "The Assembly looks as though the only event in French history was last year's *coup* of May 13; the Senate looks as though the *coup* had never taken place." The Senate comprises eighty-five Independents, forty-eight Socialists (SFIO), fifty-one Radical Socialists, twenty-nine MRP, twenty-seven UNR, fourteen Communists, and one member of the non-party Left.

THE ELECTION OF THE PRESIDENT OF THE REPUBLIC

The President of the Republic is elected for a term of seven years by an Electoral College comprising the members of Parliament, the departmental General Councils, the Assemblies of the Overseas Territories, and the elected representatives of the Municipal Councils as follows:

1. The mayor for communes of fewer than 1,000 inhabitants
2. The mayor and first deputy-mayor for communes of 1,000 to 2,000 inhabitants
3. The mayor, first deputy-mayor, and one muncipal councilor selected according to order of appearance on the council lists for communes of 2,001 to 2,500 inhabitants
4. The mayor and first two deputy-mayors for communes of 2,501 to 3,000 inhabitants
5. The mayor, the first two deputy-mayors, and three municipal councilors selected according to the order of appearance on the council lists for communes of 3,001 to 6,000 inhabitants
6. The mayor, the first two deputy-mayors, and six municipal councilors selected according to the order of appearance on council lists for communes of 6,001 to 9,000 inhabitants
7. All the municipal councilors for communes of more than 9,001 inhabitants
8. Additional delegates in communes of more than 30,000 inhabitants at the rate of one delegate for every 1,000 inhabitants exceeding 30,000, elected by the municipal councilors by proportional representation based on the rule of the highest remainder

The Electoral College met on December 21, 1958, to elect the President of the Republic and the Community. Only those persons nominated by fifty or more members of the Electoral College could be candidates for the presidency. The candidates were General de Gaulle, Albert Châtelet, and Georges Marranes. The Union of Democratic Forces (UDF), non-Communist Left, supported Châtelet, the *doyen* of the Faculty of Science of the University of Paris; while the Communists supported Marranes, a Communist deputy and mayor. General de Gaulle received approximately 79 per cent of some 80,000 votes cast. Marranes and Châtelet received 12 and 9 per cent of the vote. Only one ballot was taken, and General de Gaulle received an absolute majority on it.[4] It should be noted that the

[4] If a second ballot is undertaken, election is by a relative majority. The Constitution says nothing about presidential qualifications. The President is eligible for re-election. The President of the Fourth Republic was elected for a seven-year term by the Parliament, and he was eligible for re-election only once. Although not required by the Constitutions, all Presidents of the Third and Fourth Republics had served previously in Parliament.

college that elected De Gaulle is similar to the one that elects the Senate and that in it the weight of authority is thrown to electors who come from communes comprising fewer than 300 people each—in other words, to the mayors of the small villages.

SELECTED READING

CAMPBELL, P. *French Electoral Systems and Elections, 1789–1957.* New York: Frederick A. Praeger, Inc., 1958.

DUVERGER, M. *Political Parties.* New York: John Wiley & Sons, Inc., 1955.

GOGUEL, F. *France Under the Fourth Republic.* Ithaca, N.Y.: Cornell University Press, 1952.

MIDDLETON, W. *The French Political System.* New York: E. P. Dutton & Co., Inc., 1933.

NICHOLAS, H. G., *et al.* "The French Election," *Political Studies,* No. 4 (1956), 139–282.

WILLIAMS, P. *Politics in Post-War France; Parties and the Constitution in the Fourth Republic.* New York: Longmans, Green & Co., Inc., 1958.

15

The Legislature

THE ORIGINS OF PARLIAMENT

The modern French Parliament's precursor was the medieval organization known as the States-General. Prior to 1789, it met infrequently and performed advisory functions to the monarchy. Its membership consisted of clergy, nobility, and non-commoners. In 1789, it convened at the request of Louis XVI, primarily because of the great financial crisis that confronted the regime. Soon it was in defiance to him, and its three estates combined in a National Assembly that—despite its still medieval character—proclaimed various modern sentiments. It asserted the sovereign will of the people and the separation of executive, legislative, and judicial powers. Only two years later, yet another arrangement of public powers was instituted (one somewhat suggestive of De Gaulle's revolutionary Constitution of 1958). The monarch chose his ministers (not from the Assembly), and once appointed they were responsible to him. The initation of legislation was vested in the Assembly, but the King could request that it consider proposals to which he was sympathetic.[1]

After the abolition of the monarchy in 1792, the separation of powers was eliminated and complete authority passed to the Assembly and its Committee of Public Safety; two years later yet another Constitution was adopted and the powers were again separated. Two legislative chambers were created—the Council of the Five Hundred and the Council of the Ancients. Initiation of legislation belonged to the Five Hundred; the Council of Ancients could accept or reject it. Executive power was vested in a Directory that consisted of five individuals recommended by the Five Hundred and approved by the Ancients. Between the Directory and the legislature existed a carefully defined division of power; they had no

[1] For a good discussion of early legislatures, see David D. S. Lidderdale, *The Parliament of France* (New York: Frederick A. Praeger, Inc., 1952).

control over each other, and membership in one precluded simultaneous membership in the other. Despite these constitutional barriers, almost immediately they set out to subdue each other. Paralysis set in and that spectacle of government was resolved by the Napoleonic coup of 1799, forceful exclusion of the deputies from the Five Hundred, and provisional vestment of the government in the hands of the Consuls Siéyes, Bonaparte, and Roger-Ducos. The legislature went home, the Revolution was finished, and the country adjusted to a Consulship of the Republic. Before long three Consuls became one, and ultimately an emperorship under Napoleon.

Constitutional monarchy made its way into France after Napoleon's defeat, and then it was dictated by the allies. Its principles were embodied in the Charter of 1814, which created a legislature that consisted of a Chamber of Peers and a Chamber of Representatives; both were seated on an elective basis. Also created was an independent executive and a pooling of legislative power by the King and the Chambers. Initiation of legislation was reserved to the monarch, as was the promulgation of all bills as law. Legislators were allowed to suggest to the King what they wanted, but they were not endowed with the means to enact it. The ministers belonged to the King, although they could be impeached by the Chamber of Representatives and tried by the Peers.

The Charter of 1814 was the result of outside intervention rather than the result of internal choice. The pressures that led to its adoption were English, not French. In no way did its limitations contribute to modification of the subsequent rule of Louis Philippe (1830–1848). After his abdication, a new provisional government called for an elected National Assembly and the introduction of universal manhood suffrage. The Assembly promulgated a Constitution that called for a one-house legislature—a President elected by the people who, with the deputies, initiated legislation and promulgated as law bills passed by them. That came to an end when Louis Napoleon Bonaparte, the Republic's first President, introduced his own Constitution and subordinated the legislature completely. His regime ended in 1870 when France was defeated by Prussia and a revolutionary uprising in Paris proclaimed a Government of National Defense and elections to a new National Assembly. Acting as a constituent assembly, it framed a Constitution for the Third Republic, one which lasted for more than sixty years.

The Constitution of the Third Republic created a Senate and a Chamber of Deputies of coequal powers. Nevertheless, the realities of politics seldom permit two chambers to recognize each other as equals. If they find that they are unable to devour each other, they nibble away and hope to accomplish the same end. The Constitution designated the Chamber of Deputies as the place of origin for finance bills; the Senate was given the right to amend such bills. Sometimes the Chamber refused to accept its changes. It tried over the years to reduce the Senate's financial power and sought to amend the Constitution so that the Senate would have to accede to a second vote by the Chamber on a finance bill—thereby reducing its power to a suspensory veto. The Senate was able to resist such attempts because any constitutional amendment required its majority approval. Although the conflict resulted in the appointment of a committee satisfactory to both houses that concerned itself with producing a compromise, the controversy continued for years.

The Constitution of the Third Republic allowed both the Senate and the Chamber of Deputies to exact ministerial responsibility from the Cabinet. Both chambers sitting together elected the President. According to the Constitution, the President was able to dissolve the Chamber of Deputies with Senate consent. Nevertheless, what the Constitution prescribed and the way the system subsequently functioned were soon two different things. In 1877, President MacMahon failed in his attempt to dissolve the Chamber of Deputies. Subsequent Presidents became generally servants of Parliament. The Cabinet was put in a position where it stood defenseless before two houses, without a weapon that it could utilize in its own behalf. Thus, leadership and authority passed finally to the chambers, particularly to the popularly elected Chamber of Deputies.

The Fourth Republic's legislature was composed of two houses, the National Assembly and the Council of the Republic. The most conspicuous characteristic of the system was that it concentrated authority in the former, which created what the French call "government by Assembly." Practically, the powers of the President and Cabinet were few. The National Assembly voted the laws, and the President was compelled to adopt them ten days after the adopted text had been sent to the government; the time could be reduced to five days in the event of a national emergency. The President had the power to ask the Assembly to reconsider a bill within a limit of five or ten days. His refusal to promulgate a bill as law presented the Assembly with no particular difficulty inasmuch as the President of the National Assembly was then capable of promulgating it. The Assembly had control of finance, and all budgets were submitted to it for its approval. To its members was reserved the right to initiate expenditures.

The second chamber, the Council of the Republic, was endowed with prerogatives of slight consequence. Bills originating in it could not be received by the secretariat of the National Assembly if their passage would have resulted in the reduction of revenues or in the creation of new ones. It could check the National Assembly, but only momentarily, and had the power to examine bills voted by it and the right to ask the Assembly for a second reading in the event that it disagreed with it. It could bring to the attention of a weak President of the Republic any act of the National Assembly that it felt was unconstitutional. It was described very accurately by members of the constituent assembly as a "Council of Reflection." Its existence was guaranteed, however, by a constitutional article that prohibited any revision relative to its existence without its agreement or resort to a referendum.

THE LEGISLATURE OF THE FIFTH REPUBLIC

"Government by Assembly" died with the Fourth Republic. The National Assembly of the Fifth Republic is restricted in its powers. It does not dominate Cabinets; it does not dominate anything—it is dominated. It appears almost as the successor to the Council of the Republic, the weak second chamber of the Fourth Republic. The powers of the Senate are almost the same as those of the Assembly, with the exception that, unlike it, the Senate may not reverse a government and thereby bring about its downfall. Both chambers vote the laws of the Republic, but narrow limitations are placed by the Constitution on that which falls by definition within the domain of law. If the former is consistent with the legislative tradition of the Third and Fourth Republics, the latter was utterly foreign to them.

Members of Parliament have certain rights and obligations. Their freedom from civil and criminal prosecution is confined to what they say and do inside of Parliament and not outside of it. During a parliamentary session, a legislator may be prosecuted for illegal activities only if the chamber of which he is a member lifts his immunity and thereby releases him for trial (Pierre Lagaillard's immunity was lifted December 8, 1960, after his participation in the Algier's insurrection of January, 1960; Marc Lauriol lost his immunity June 23, 1961, after being involved in the *putsch* of April, 1961). When the chamber is not in session, he may be arrested with the permission of its bureau. At the request of the chamber of which he is a member, he may be released from custody or his prosecution suspended. Occupations that exclude an individual from assuming a legislative position are those that involve making legal representations in behalf of enterprises carrying an action against the state, those by which an individual serves as director of a state subsidized or nationalized enterprise, or as director of an organization involved exclusively in the execution of state contracts.

According to the Constitution, members of Parliament may not receive specific instructions on voting. Intended originally to undercut the Communist party's life-and-death grip over its legislators, this provision appears incapable of implementation. Thus far, the regime has ignored it and it appears that it will continue to do so. If applied, it could spell the end of any party that is characterized by some measure of internal discipline—that is, truly a party. The control of the Socialist party (SFIO) over its parliamentary group is no less than that of the Communist party, and rigid pursuance of this article would bring Socialist deputies within its meaning.

Members of the legislature must vote in person and not by proxy. This is a sharp departure from the practice of the Fourth Republic, which allowed the deputies to hand their ballots over to one or several proxies (with the allowance that they could subsequently rectify any abuse in the exercise of their vote). The Constitution states that a legislator may authorize "the delegation of his right to vote in exceptional circumstances"; and those circumstances that come within this meaning are illness, accident, excused absence due to a government mission, military service, or other plausible reasons. There is, however, no opportunity for subsequent rectification of a voting abuse by a proxy. A proxy may serve not more than one other associate at a given time.

Regular attendance is requested of members of Parliament, another departure from the practice of the Fourth Republic. Today, legislators are supposed to be on hand, even if in this regime they do relatively less than they did under preceding ones. They receive in addition to their base pay an additional salary that is based on attendance. A legislator who is absent from more than one-third of the balloting in one month is supposed to forfeit one-third of his attendance salary, two-thirds if he misses more than half, and all of it if he is not on hand for the month. Absence from three consecutive committee sessions is supposed to amount to dismissal of a deputy from the committee and one-third reduction in his additional salary until the commencement of the session the following October. Valid absence from balloting and committee hearings is permissible, although the privilege is subject to great abuse. Deputy absenteeism has become chronic.

Each of the chambers has its bureau. The National Assembly's consists of the President of the Assembly, six vice-presidents, twelve secretaries, and three *questeurs*. The bureau of the Senate includes its president, four vice-presidents, eight secretaries, and three *questeurs*. The bureaus deal with the administration of the legislature. They are elected each October session, with the exception of the President of the Assembly who serves for the entire Parliament and the President of the Senate whose tenure extends to the next partial renewal. Election of the Presidents is by an absolute majority on the first or second ballots, or by plurality on the third. The vote is secret. The Presidents must be "consulted," according to Article 16 of the Constitution, by the President of the Republic before he takes emergency "measures required by circumstances." The President of the Assembly may refer to the Constitutional Council any proposed constitutional amendment or private bill for an interpretation of their constitutionality. The President of the Senate replaces the President of the Republic in the event of his disability (determined by the Constitutional Council) instead of the President of the Assembly, as was the case under the Fourth Republic. However, the President of the Assembly is the presiding officer whenever both the Assembly and the Senate convene as a Congress for the purpose of amending the Constitution. Both Presidents chair their respective chambers.

The powers of Parliament are as follows: There are areas in which it may legislate fully and in detail, areas in which it must confine its legislation to principles and not to details, and areas in which it may not legislate at all. Those in which it may legislate fully and in detail are described in Article 34 of the Constitution; they include civil rights, the electoral system (parliamentary and local), creation of the judiciary and the status of judges, currency, marriage contracts, inheritances and gifts, nationality, the creation of public institutions, nationalization, and eminent domain. Areas in which it must confine its legislation to principles and not to details include local administration, labor legislation, civil law, property rights, education, social security, and the organization of national defense. Subjects that fall outside of those stipulated here may be handled by the government by executive orders. In the event that the Parliament should seek powers denied to it by the Constitution and allowed to the government, the latter may alter by executive order such bills as the Parliament may seek to pass—providing that the Constitutional Council verifies that the Parliament has sought to overstep its constitutional bounds. "In the event of disagreement between the Government and the President of the Assembly concerned, the Constitutional Council gives a ruling, at the request of either party, within a week" (Article 41). It should be noticed that the government has no difficulty keeping the legislature from encroaching on its own domain; at the same time, the government has not hesitated to introduce decrees that the legislature often construes as invading its own law-making area. With respect to this matter, thus far the Constitutional Council has ruled consistently in favor of the executive power. Particularly is this reflected in its decisions of August, 1960, relative to the disputed Ordinances of 1958—the one of December 30, dealing with the finance, and that of December 31, dealing with war damages.

The Constitution states that there are kinds of legislation that must be enacted as "organic laws" (in other words, not as ordinary legislation). "Organic laws" are those passed by Parliament or realized as a result of ordinances in fulfillment of a constitutional article or articles. They are not debated or voted on in the chamber in which they are introduced until two weeks after their initiation, and they are reviewed by the Constitutional Council in order to determine their constitutionality. The procedure adhered to for government and private-member bills governs their passage. In the event that the two chambers disagree, they must be passed by an absolute majority of the members of the National Assembly. Any organic law that refers in any way to the Senate must pass both houses by the same kind of majority.

Bills may originate in either chamber. Most originate with Cabinet members—a normal trend but one even more characteristic of the Fifth than of the Third and Fourth Republics now that the Cabinet so thoroughly dominates Parliament. Government bills may be presented first to either of the two chambers. Government bills and private-member bills favored by the government are discussed by priority in the legislature. The agenda is fixed by the government. Finance bills are submitted first to the National Assembly.

A government or private-member bill once introduced finds its way to a legislative committee within whose competence it falls. If the government is willing, it goes to one of the permanent or standing committees of Parliament. It may decide, however, to send it to a special committee created by it for this very purpose. Bills sent to standing or special committees must find their way to the floor of Parliament before three months elapse. Once a bill attains the floor, it is subject to discussion. If the committee recommends that it be killed, it dies. Sometimes it is returned to committee for additional scrutiny. It may be subjected to amendments proposed by ministers or members of Parliament; although the Constitution states that once the debate has begun, the government may object to the discussion of any amendment that has not been submitted previously to committee. Moreover, whenever the government requests it, the house of Parliament involved must accept or reject by a single vote "the whole or part of the Bill or motion under discussion, together with such amendments as have been proposed or accepted by the Government," a requirement for which there is no precedent insofar as the Third and Fourth Republics were concerned.

During discussion of a bill, each of its articles is inquired into separately and amendment or abolition of each is possible, providing that the government allows this. When this process has been completed, the bill has undergone its first reading. It goes then to the other house of Parliament in identical form. After its passage there, it is sent to the government and subsequently promulgated as law by the President of the Republic or vetoed by him. In some instances, it may go first to the Constitutional Council, in which case its disposition will depend on a ruling as to its constitutionality.

When the National Assembly and the Senate are in disagreement on a bill, it may be re-referred to the two houses for a second reading; if it continues to fall short of their agreement, the government may then send it to a special committee created by it and staffed with an equal number of representatives from both houses of Parliament. However, it may be sent to the special committee only after the first reading if the Premier decides that it requires "urgent consideration." The committee reworks the bill and the government receives it again and again refers it to the two houses with no amendment possible unless it is willing to agree to it. If both houses still refuse to vote the bill, they may be asked by the government to give it further consideration; failing agreement, the government can ask the National Assembly to make a final decision relative to the adoption of the bill—in other words, to rule definitively on it. The Assembly may accept the special committee version, its own, or its own plus the amendments made by the Senate.

Although the right to initiate legislation belongs to members of Parliament and the government, and although the legislators may introduce finance bills, they may not introduce private ones, resolutions, or amendments that would result in the diminution of public financial resources or in the creation or increase of public expenditures. These restrictions do not apply to finance bills that are introduced by the government and which must be submitted first, states the Constitution, to the National Assembly. Thus, legislators are restricted in their ability to vote laws in the area of finance.

Article 47 of the Constitution facilitates the government's guidance through the legislature of bills for revenues and expenditures whose acquisition it seeks. If the finance bill determining revenue and expenditures for the financial year has not been introduced in time to be promulgated before its beginning, the government may ask Parliament for authorization to levy by decree the taxes voted and allocation of "the sums necessary for estimates already approved." This means that the government may ask it to make the endorsement in the light of what it had accepted previously in the way of estimates.[2]

If the National Assembly has received a finance bill but has not completed its first reading within forty days, the government may request the Senate to submit it to a first reading within a period of two weeks. If seventy days elapse and a finance bill remains unvoted by the Senate, the government may then implement it as an ordinance. Thus, if the Senate sustains a highly compliable outlook, the government's way in matters of finance is made even that much easier.

The annual budget is voted in the following manner. It is submitted first to the National Assembly by the Minister of Finance, the Assembly

[2] The National Assembly may be asked ten days before the end of the session to pass only those parts of the bill that deal with taxation and expenditure, which then go to the Senate. Or, the government may ask the National Assembly two days before the end of the session to pass special legislation—authorizing the government to collect taxes—which then goes to the Senate.

sends it to its finance committee, and after consideration the latter presents it to the Assembly. The presentation is made by the committee's reporter in a very general fashion; specifics are handled subsequently by the committee's special reporters and followed by discussion by the deputies. They are limited in their ability to discuss to two speeches on each chapter of the budget, unless they are requested by a minister to speak further. Their ability to propose amendments in the form of separate bills is a hollow one inasmuch as they may not introduce such ones as would result in the creation, increase, or decrease of expenditures.

Parliament may delegate its legislative power to the government so as to allow it to rule by decree and authorize it to implement for defined periods such measures as would normally fall within its own jurisdiction. The Third Republic was familiar with this type of legislation. The Fourth Republic prohibited it by stating in its Constitution that the National Assembly alone could vote the laws; but, nevertheless, several of its governments exercised special powers that came very close to enjoying the status of decrees. In general, however, both Third and Fourth Republic Parliaments did guard jealously against frequent delegations of such authority. An example of important decree legislation occurred on February 2–3, 1960, when the Debré government requested and was granted special powers in restricted areas for "the maintenance of law and order, the safeguarding of the State, and the pacification and administration of Algeria." The length of time designated was one year, subject to parliamentary ratification by April 1, 1961, or before the opening of the first ordinary parliamentary session of the same year (this and other such laws are justified on the basis of Article 38 of the Constitution). Article 4 of the law of February 2–3 stated that the law would be null and void in case of the dissolution of the National Assembly. When Premier Debré addressed that body, he stated that "We do not have enough power and we are not asking for too much." In order to soften the criticisms of those who charged that the law amounted to an abdication of parliamentary authority, he assured the deputies that he and his associates had no reason to ask for more power than this and that all reforms of an economic and social nature would be carried through on the basis of normal procedure. He told the deputies, "Your legislative power, your budgetary power, your right of general control over the Government remain. . . . The Government has no ambition . . . to alter in any way whatsoever the foundations of the political system." Despite his assurances, the deputies knew that Debré would make many more demands for decree powers before the end of his premiership. Yet, the legislative habits of yesterday are no longer the habits of today; and now many of the legislators delegate their legislative authority without much heed to possible consequences. Considering the inertness of the mass in which they serve, it is understandable that some give only slight attention to the issue. Of course, the Parliament continues to retain the constitutional right to refuse the government the power to legislate by decree; but it is hardly in the position to refuse. President de Gaulle has warned it that it must remain servile.

The government's unwillingness to submit to legislative harassment is apparent; it is not in the least receptive to the adoption by Parliament of rules of behavior that would interfere with its domination of the chambers. This was reflected in the way in which it clearly restricted the possibilities to which oral and written questions asked of the ministers by the legislators might lead. According to a decision of the Constitutional Council, questions may be put to the Premier and the ministers, with or without debate; but such questions and debate may not lead to a vote unless the government wills and requests it. Such questions take place every Friday afternoon. When asked with debate, the legislator putting the question is allowed after the minister's answer only five minutes in which to comment. The minister may reply to any question or point made by the legislator but other discussion is prohibited. When asked with debate, the questioner is allowed half an hour for his presentation. After the minister's reply, other legislators are allowed—according to the discretion of the President of the Chamber—as long as fifteen minutes each in which to comment. Further reply by the minister is not mandatory. In no instance may such questions be followed by a resolution and its voting, unless it is defined by the rules of the chamber as pertaining to the creation of a special commission, the organization of the National Assembly, or a demand for an individual to be tried by the High Court of Justice. Legislators may also submit written questions to a minister and they should be answered within one month. Some are never answered at all. It is, however, within the power of the President of the chamber to invite the author of an unanswered written question to present it orally.

The Constitution allows the National Assembly the right to force the resignation of a government (this right exists when Article 16 is in effect, too, providing that the Assembly is not in extraordinary session). It denies the Senate this power. Resignation may be forced only by a motion of censure passed by an absolute majority of the members of the National Assembly. The resolution of censure must be initiated by one-tenth of its members, and the vote may not be taken for another forty-eight hours. On May 5, 1960, 122 members of the National Assembly voted for a motion of censure against the government following its refusal to convoke a special parliamentary session after 287 deputies had petitioned it. The 122 deputies described the refusal as a "violation of the Constitution." Those who voted for the motion were Socialists (44), Radical Socialists (17), MRP (9), Independents (18), Communists (10), *Entente démocratique* (13), *Unité de la République* (6), and others (5).

Inasmuch as the motion fell short of the required majority, the position of the government was not endangered. M. Brocas of the Radical Socialist party had difficulty in understanding why only 122 deputies voted for the censure motion when 287 had petitioned previously for a special session of Parliament. This motion of censure was the second successfully repulsed by the Debré government, the first having occurred on November 28, 1959. On that date, 109 votes were cast against the budget. In reality, however, these motions were not calculated by their authors as being capable of seriously endangering the Debré government and as true tests of the regime. They were viewed, rather, as steps in the process of shaping up the opposition and seeking to enlarge it for future use. The "big show" on a motion of censure came on October 26, 1960, when 207 deputies sought to bring down the Debré government on its bill to create a French nuclear force (*force de frappe*). Although the attempt fell short of its required 277 majority, the vote showed that the opposition was growing stronger. Those supporting it were Communists (10), Socialists (44), *Entente démocratique* (13), MRP (21), Independents (62), *Unité de la République* (26), and others (13).[3]

Parliament meets briefly in two annual sessions (the first session opens April 2 and may not last more than ninety days; the second opens October 2 and lasts eighty days). It may not sit for more than five and a half months of each year. It may meet in extraordinary session at the request of the Premier or at the request of a majority of its members—whenever the President of the Republic allows it to do so. Limiting such sessions to presidential discretion constitutes a sharp departure from the practices of the Third and Fourth Republics. The constitutional law of July 2, 1875, obligated the President of the Third Republic to convoke the chambers in extraordinary session whenever the request was made between sessions by an absolute majority of the members of each chamber. The Constitution of the Fourth Republic stated that when the National Assembly was not in session, its bureau could convoke Parliament in extraordinary session. Under both Republics, the convocation of Parliament in extraordinary session at the request of the majority of deputies was automatic insofar as the Presidents of those regimes were concerned. This is not the case with the President of the Fifth Republic. Early in 1960, a majority of the members of the National Assembly (287) petitioned for a special session. The deputies did so after many of their agrarian constituents demanded the convocation in the hope that the government would resort to emergency measures in order to alleviate the agrarian crisis. President de Gaulle declined their request. He told the country that he prevented the

[3] On November 10, 1960, the Senate rejected the *force de frappe* by a vote of 186 to 83. Premier Debré then constituted a mixed committee to find a compromise between the Senate and Assembly.

session in order to prevent partisan minority interests from applying pressure that could be only to the detriment of the general welfare. He said that he would not bow to the demands of a majority of the elected representatives if he felt that they spoke for only a minority of the populace. There was no doubt that he considered himself a more accurate interpreter of the majority will than the deputies themselves. In September, 1961, the Presidents of both legislative chambers requested a special parliamentary session for the purpose of inquiring into the agricultural *malaise*. This time, De Gaulle informed them that he would not block the session as long as he remained convinced that it did not have a "legislative objective."

Finally, the National Assembly may be dissolved by the President of the Republic at any time. Disputes relative to its rules and elections are resolved not by itself but by the Constitutional Council. A truly independent legislative body is capable of formulating its own rules of procedure; it is the master of its own behavior. The Assembly of the Fifth Republic is not. It is a cripple. Its weaknesses and its position in French political life are the consequence of the way in which De Gaulle came to power. Its members voted him extensive powers, and now they enjoy few of their own.

THE COMMITTEES OF PARLIAMENT

The committee system of the Fifth Republic is less well developed than the one that existed under the Fourth Republic. The latter had nineteen standing or permanent committees for each of its chambers of Parliament. The Fifth Republic has six standing committees for each house of Parliament and such temporary, special committees as the government may create from time to time to which bills may go, rather than to permanent committees. Committee members are elected from their respective chambers on the basis of proportional representation, and the committees are staffed so as to reflect the strength of the parties comprising thirty or more members in each chamber. Legislators belonging to groups numbering fewer than thirty can be elected to committees by their chamber to fill such vacancies as may subsequently appear. Staffing takes place at the beginning of each legislative term; members sit for two years. Meetings of the committees are usually closed to the public but open to ministers who may speak in them. Individuals may be brought to the committee hearings to be heard or to hear the proceedings, or both. All committees have a president, two vice-presidents, two secretaries, and a reporter.

The committees are limited, both in terms of their number and competence. They are restricted in their ability to specialize, thereby assuring the government that its members will not be confronted with some of the obstacles evolved by committees of preceding regimes. It is obvious that the strength of a legislature is dependent, in part, on its ability to create committees with real competence capable of making extensive findings and unveiling the results to its members, to members of the legislature, and to the public. If the committees of the Fifth Republic are weak, it is because President de Gaulle wanted a weak legislature. If the committees continue to remain this way, it will be because he is determined to keep the Parliament weak. Those committee members who seek to develop the activities of their committees know that this will not necessarily strengthen the Parliament or give the National Assembly greater control over the government. It matters little if the organism strengthens its fingers, for its arms remain paralyzed.

Fundamental to the work of a legislative committee is the examining of proposed legislation and the keeping of its eyes on those government departments whose activities relate to its own competence. The committees of the Fifth Republic may examine proposed legislation, but they can do less with their findings than can be achieved by most committees in most other legislatures. The tables are now reversed. Fourth Republic legislative committees could amend out of shape important bills referred to the legislature by the government. Fifth Republic committees now have little real influence on important government bills. Now the government first presents its case for a bill instead of listening first to committee criticism and amendment of it. The committees do have the right to conduct investigations and to subpoena witnesses, subject to the permission of the legislature and to certain conditions set by it. However, the days are gone when committees could harass a minister and extract from him information by threatening to bring down his government. Such activities can hardly be part of a regime in which the chief of state decides what is truly important and what should be done about it, while the government approves and the Parliament ratifies.

THE NATIONAL ASSEMBLY AND THE QUEST FOR PARLIAMENTARY PREROGATIVES

Many Frenchmen conclude that the restricted status of the Fifth Republic's "parliamentarism" is in keeping with the "real France" and that it constitutes a realistic adjustment to the exigencies of political life. They contend that parliamentarism is a foreign importation that has infrequently worked well in France. There may be considerable truth in such contention. The record of the Third Republic was marred by bitter competition for superiority between the executive and legislative powers, one that hardly operated to the benefit of the nation. Fourth Republic legislatures proclaimed their dominance over the executive by subjecting it to "government by Assembly." Governments were eventually unable to govern, and they fell without being able to modify the problems with which they were confronted. The result was often near-anarchy. At the end of the regime, it was anarchy. Now the National Assembly of the Fifth Republic enjoys no executive powers and fewer legislative powers than French legislatures are accustomed to having.

Despite the devaluation of the Parliament, practices associated with certain regimes usually outlive them and find their way into subsequent systems. Édouard Herriot once observed that the psychology and the habits of the French deputy are perhaps more important than the rules of procedure. The Republics may come and go, but it is difficult for deputies to be powerless under any of them. They seek always to strengthen their position. Already there is evidence that the dull legislative mass of today wishes to become more of a force tomorrow. Some members of the National Assembly acted as though they had not heard of its weaknesses when they went into special session in January, 1959. They reacted against their minimal status by attempting to adopt in that session rules of procedure that reflected their unwillingness to remain docile. They managed to extract certain concessions from the Debré government; it was agreed that parliamentary committees would remain in operation during parliamentary intermissions and that parliamentary resolutions would be subject to fewer restrictions than was initially forseen. The Debré government even went so far as to request Assembly approval—despite the fact that Fifth Republic governments need not do so (Fourth Republic governments did). This was followed by debate of Premier Debré's policy, which was—in reality—debate of President de Gaulle's policy, despite the constitutional limitation that the President's messages may not be debated by the National Assembly. However, when an attempt was made to have oral questions followed by debate and the voting of resolutions, it was brushed aside by Debré on the grounds of unconstitutionality and his fear that it might revive the system of interpellations characteristic of the Third and Fourth Republics. The same controversy was reopened almost immediately when the National Assembly opened its official session in April, 1959; but the deputies soon discovered that the government firmly retained the right to fix the "order of the day," or the parliamentary agenda. With the government fixing unilaterally the order of the day, the deputies found themselves excluded from important questions. They discovered that the government could not prevent them from asking written and oral questions but that only a motion of censure deposited by one-tenth of their number could oblige it to undertake discussion of a problem that it wishes to evade. With the right of interpellation narrowly limited and its usage restricted to the exclusive object of a fall of the government, the deputies found that they had few ways in which they could disagree with the Government without being obliged to defeat it by a motion of censure. In the session of June 28, 1961, the deputies resorted to blockage, refusing to examine the business included by the government in the order of the day. Recognition of legislative criticism has commendable things to be said in its behalf; nevertheless, the machinery of the Fifth Republic is so constructed as to allow the government to ignore it when it wishes to do so. (Yet, in the Assembly of today, there are types of criticism that Premier Debré finds psychologically impossible to ignore—particularly those that are addressed to him. During his government's first year of life, he went out of the way to equate these with tendencies that are "anti-French," a term that he did not hesitate to apply to many of his critics, not Communists, either.)

There are diverse factors that presently discourage some deputies from seeking a stronger brand of parliamentarism. First, seated in the National Assembly are some Left elements who feel that by strengthening the Assembly, they will strengthen its Gaullist component; and this option they seek to avoid. They regard De Gaulle as being less of a "Gaullist" than many of the deputies who speak in his name. They acknowledge that he is a wielder of personal power, but they also view as implausible the present reconstruction of French democracy. They regard the General as the one man capable of making peace in Algeria. Observers have compared this situation to the one that existed under the Charter of 1814, when in the Chamber moderates supported a moderate monarch as a means of defense against an immoderate majority. Left members of Parliament know, too, that the alternative to De Gaulle could be the military and not the UNR; and so they acknowledge that there are times when it pays to look in the direction of an excessive presidentialism.[4] At the same time, the temptation is great for the Socialist parliamentary group to want to gravitate in the direction of a stronger brand of parliamentarism; and future allies far to its Right may be not too hard for it to find. The Independents, not greatly pleased by the financial policy of the new regime, could become potential recruits. Second, the results of the municipal elections of April, 1959, served as a warning to the "new men" of the new legislature. They witnessed a comeback by many of the "old men" of the Fourth Republic and a popular reaction against many of the men associated with the movement of May 13. A similar trend was evidenced in the subsequent Senate elections. Even if a number of Gaullists in the Assembly should become disenchanted with De Gaulle, a display

[4] For the concern of some deputies for acquisition of stronger parliamentary prerogatives, see Lowell G. Noonan, "Some Political Aspects of the French Fifth Republic," *Western Political Quarterly*, June, 1960, pp. 473–75.

of opposition by them will not result in strengthening the Assembly to the extent where it acquires stronger controls over the government—undoubtedly it would result instead in a dissolution of the Assembly, new elections, and the passage of many UNR seats to other forces. Recent prefectural reports to the Ministry of the Interior suggest that the UNR would not triumph in many of the districts in which it won in 1958, and that in some regions the traditional parties have regained already some of the strength that they enjoyed prior to the elections of that year. For example, the Independents have strengthened themselves in the west, north, and in the Paris region. The Socialists and Radical Socialists are stronger now in the Midi, and the MRP has refound some of its former strength in the west. Although many UNR voters are now opposed to the financial and economic measures initiated by the Debré government, the UNR has not attempted to exert pressure on the government in order to get it to soften its policies. Certain elements in the country most favorably inclined toward the party in 1958 have since been hit the hardest by the new regime—particularly farmers, war veterans, and merchants—and it is not likely that they would give strong support again to the UNR. In other words, many of the men who captured seats as a result of the elections of 1958 appear to be the very ones who would not be favored again with a political environment so readily conducive to another "free ride" to Parliament. If they cannot face another election, it is probable that they will not seek situations that would result in Parliament's dissolution. Third, legislative salaries of $1,050 per month—a very large income in France—have a way of encouraging some deputies to ride quietly along with the trend of the times and discouraging them from contributing to the creation of situations that might undermine their condition of existence.

THE SENATE AND ITS "POWERS"

It has been said that the Senate has most of the powers of the Senate of the Third Republic, that its personnel is of the Fourth Republic, and that it exists under the Fifth Republic. Its powers are almost the same as the legislative powers of the National Assembly of the Fifth Republic, and it votes the law the way that it is voted by the Assembly. Unlike the National Assembly, it may not, however, reverse the government and thereby bring about its downfall. It may not be dissolved by the President of the Republic. If there is a disagreement between it and the National Assembly, the Premier can resolve the conflict by calling a meeting of a mixed committee composed of an equal number of senators and deputies. If the committee finds it impossible to reach an agreement, or if the agreement at which it arrives is not approved by both legislative chambers, the government can ask the National Assembly to rule definitively on the issue. Thus, the Senate can act as an obstructive force insofar as the government is concerned; and yet the latter may clear the way by seeking the aid of the National Assembly. On the other hand, real conflict between the Senate and the Assembly is possible, but it can hardly be significant. The Senate may act as an instrument of prevention when the government allows it or encourages it to act in such a way, but what the Senate is capable of doing rests ultimately on the will of the government. If the Senate wishes to restrain legislation, the government has at its disposal means to remove such restraints—except, however, in the area of constitutional reform where the laws must be voted by each of the two chambers.

THE CONSTITUTIONAL COUNCIL

The Constitutional Council is one of the important legal organs of the Fifth Republic—that is, it is when it is allowed to be and when it actually exercises the powers vested legally in it. The Council consists of the former Presidents of the Republic, who serve ex officio for life, and nine other members. The President of the Republic, the President of the National Assembly, and the President of the Senate each appoint three members to the Council for nine-year terms; they may not be reappointed. One-third of the total seats on the Council fall vacant every three years (made possible by the fact that three of the first appointees were appointed for three-year terms, three for six-year terms, and three for full nine-year terms). The members of the Council are not allowed to serve simultaneously in the government, National Assembly, Senate, or the Economic and Social Council. They may retain their positions in the civil service during their tenure as councilors, but during this period they may not be appointed to any new positions in the public employ.

The Constitution states that it is the responsibility of the Council to see that the legislature and the executive do not exceed their legal authority, that legislation remains within constitutional bounds, and that the regularity of elections is assured. It states also that the President of the Republic is obligated to consult the Council as to the legality of measures that he may possibly seek in time of emergency under Article 16 of the Constitution (it does not say that he must accept its advice). The Constitution also states that if the government wishes to alter any laws by decree, only the Council may declare that they are capable of being modified, and that whenever Parliament seeks the passage of organic laws the Council must verify their constitutionality. All Council opinions relative to the constitutionality of proposed laws are supposed to be delivered in advance. Proposals of law may be submitted to it only by the President of the Republic, the Premier, or the Presidents of the National Assembly and the Senate. The Council guards the regularity of the election of President of the Republic and receives such complaints as may be presented concerning it. It releases the results of the presidential vote, it determines presidential disability, it insures the regularity of referenda, and it resolves disputes relative to the election of senators and deputies. Decisions and opinions of the Council may be taken in the presence of only seven or more of its members, and these decisions and opinions may not be subject to appeal inasmuch as the Council is supposed to be the final interpreter of constitutionality in the Republic. It does not have, however, the power to see that its decisions are respected.

The members of the Constitutional Council are former Presidents Auriol and Coty (life), Léon Noël (6 years), Maurice Patin (3), Georges Pompidou (9), Victor Chatenay (3), Pasteur Vallery-Radot (6), Jean Michard-Pelissier (9), Maurice Delepine (3), Charles Le Coq de Kerland (6), and Jean Gilbert-Jules (9). Their average age at the time of appointment was sixty-four years, five of the eleven being over seventy. Although seven of the eleven had law degrees, their experience was confined by no means exclusively to that area. One was a prominent physician, another was an engineer, and five served at different times as deputies or senators.

What the Council is supposed to do and what it is doing are two very different things. Vincent Auriol, former President of the Fourth Republic, departed from it in July, 1960, on the grounds that it cannot discharge its constitutional duties because of President de Gaulle's wielding of "personal and arbitrary power." Auriol charged that the Council was unable to act on even the most obviously unconstitutional measures because of the unwillingness of De Gaulle to submit such measures to it. He criticized De Gaulle's "free and easy manner toward the national sovereignty and our basic charter," and he charged that the General is pushing the nation into a regime that "is in opposition to the rules and essential principles of democracy." He said in his letter to Léon Noël, head of the Council, that he did not wish "to remain either helpless or silent in the presence of attacks on the national sovereignty." This was not the first time that Auriol had criticized De Gaulle's contempt for established constitutional procedure. In 1958 in open letters in newspapers, he expressed his reservations concerning De Gaulle's methods and the means he employed to come to power.

THE ECONOMIC AND SOCIAL COUNCIL

The Economic and Social Council is a holdover from the Fourth Republic. It comprises 205 members who serve for five-year terms. Membership in it is the result of selection by professional associations or by the government.[5] The Council performs in a capacity that is primarily technical and that is in keeping, incidently, with the nature of the present regime. Its advice may be solicited by the government, or it may offer it whenever it has definite views relative to the economic and social development of the Community or the Republic. It meets in private instead of in public, as it did under the Fourth Republic.

AMENDMENT OF THE CONSTITUTION

The Constitution states that the initiative for constitutional amendment "shall belong both to the President of the Republic on the proposal of the Premier and to the members of Parliament," that all government or parliamentary bills for amendment must be passed by identical motions by a majority of the total membership of the National Assembly and Senate, and that they shall become law after popular approval in a referendum. The latter need not be resorted to, however, if the President of the Republic decides to submit the bill to Parliament convened in a Congress, in which case it becomes law if it secures a three-fifths majority of all the votes cast by the Congress. The republican form of government may not be amended, a constitutional provision, by the way, that is now very ambiguous. The Fourth Republic included the same provision in its Constitution.

SELECTED READING

BROMHEAD, P. "Some Notes on the Standing Committees of the French National Assembly," *Political Studies,* No. 5 (1957), 140–57.

GOOCH, R. K. *Parliamentary Government in France: Revolutionary Origins, 1789–1791.* Ithaca, N.Y.: Cornell University Press, 1960.

———. *The French Parliamentary Committee System.* New York: Appleton-Century-Crofts, Inc., 1935.

HOWARD, J. E. *Parliament and Foreign Policy in France.* London: Cresset Press, Ltd., 1948.

LIDDERDALE, D. W. S. *The Parliament of France.* New York: Frederick A. Praeger, Inc., 1952.

MAVRINAC, A. *Organization and Procedure of the National Assembly of the Fifth French Republic.* London: Hansard Society, 1960.

[5] Forty-five representatives of manual and professional workers; forty-one representatives of business and the nationalized and private industries; forty representatives of agriculture; twenty representatives of Algeria and the Sahara; fifteen representatives of diverse social, economic, and cultural interests at home; fifteen representatives of social activities; ten representatives of the Overseas Departments; ten representatives of diverse interests overseas; seven representatives of diverse special interests; and two representatives of the middle class.

16

The Executive

THE PRESIDENCY UNDER THE THIRD AND FOURTH REPUBLICS

The Constitution of the Third Republic called for a strong President who could withhold his signature from Cabinet decrees, designate the Premier, seek the Senate's permission to dissolve the Chamber of Deputies, and order new elections for the country. These provisions became obsolete in 1877 when the republicans prevented the dictatorial President MacMahon from dissolving the Chamber of Deputies. In subsequent years, the republicans subjected the presidential office to legislative domination. They elected to it men who were unlikely to engage in autocratic exercises of power, which converted it into a refuge for recluses from the political wars. These men became parliamentary servants; whenever they threatened to "get out of line," they risked involvement in situations in which their only alternative was to resign. This was the case in 1924 when the Chamber of Deputies favored Herriot for the premiership and President Millerand supported Francois-Marsal. Herriot became Premier and Millerand announced his resignation.

The Constitution of the Fourth Republic called for a weak President. Its fathers were influenced by the history of the office under the Third Republic and the shadow that General de Gaulle cast on the scene. They proceeded on the assumption that the vitality of representative institutions depended on limiting presidential power. They created a constitution that was based on the concept of "government by assembly." Elected by Parliament, the President was little more than the delegate of the deputies. His term of office was seven years and he could be re-elected but once. He held the title of commander-in-chief of the armed forces, but real control was entrusted to the Premier. The President was prohibited from assuming its active direction in time of war. He ratified international agreements, but there was no constitutional allowance for his ability to initiate or negotiate treaties. He was powerless before the acts passed by the National Assembly. He could not dissolve Parliament; that right was reserved to the Premier, with the agreement of the President of the National Assembly, if two ministerial crises occurred within an eighteen-month period. He did name the Premier, but the act was nominal—his selection having been determined previously by the forces that composed the National Assembly. Endowed with few powers and little leeway for constitutional activity, he was intended by law as a kind of Hamlet. President Auriol sought to strengthen the office, but his efforts were unsuccessful. President Coty's interventionary activities during the last days of the Fourth Republic hastened its abolition. In May, 1959, after extensive discussions with De Gaulle, Coty informed the country that he would resign if the National Assembly did not invest the General as Premier.[1]

THE CABINET UNDER THE THIRD AND FOURTH REPUBLICS

Cabinets of the Third Republic were dominated by the Senate and the Chamber of Deputies. Because the President was weak and unable to dissolve the Chamber of Deputies in order to resolve conflicts between it and the Cabinet, the latter was left without a weapon that it could utilize in its own defense. It became the creature of the Chamber and hardly more than a parliamentary committee whose functions consisted primarily of supervising the bureaucracy. Its ministers were subjected constantly to irresponsible use of the interpellation; they knew that their Cabinets could be brought down even if the opposition was unable to find a replacement. Bringing them down became a game as opposition deputies looked forward to their own future ministerial careers. Although the interpellation was intended to allow deputies to prevent ministers from abusing their authority, the deputies used it opportunistically to serve ends other than those for which it was created.

Because the Cabinet of the Third Republic had to satisfy both the Chamber of Deputies and the Senate, either house was capable of bringing it down by a vote of non-confidence. Thus, its problems went beyond those of a Cabinet that need face only one house. This unhealthy situation might have been modified had not the Senate enjoyed coequal powers with the Chamber. In competing with the Chamber, the Senate was always conscious of pulling out in front of it whenever it could. Therefore, its activities ranged from the subtle to the brazen; and it did not hesitate to pull down Cabinets on various occasions.

[1] See *Le Monde*, January 8, 9, 1959, pp. 3, 2 for Coty's reflections and how he helped to "save" the society from civil war; *New York Herald Tribune* (Paris), May 30, 1958. Coty stated, "If thus I passed beyond the traditional limits established by my predecessors, I believed myself authorized to do so."

Under the Third Republic, Cabinet instability was intensified by the political parties' inability to implement discipline. Undisciplined deputies from the center and more conservative of the Left parties often united with independent deputies for the singular purpose of voting against a Cabinet. The undisciplined deputies generally had little to fear; they knew that their parties could do little about their activities because they were strong in their own electoral districts.

In the Chamber of Deputies many parties of almost equal strength viewed a strong Cabinet as dangerous to themselves, and so they purposely kept it in a weakened condition. Some of these parties contended that the emergence of their own unified and homogeneous majorities constituted the precondition of a strong Cabinet. That phenomenon never materialized. The Third Republic fell; it was succeeded by the Fourth Republic, and from the time of its inception its Cabinets were also dominated by the National Assembly. One defect of the Third Republic was corrected when the Fourth Republic's Cabinets were not made constitutionally dependent on the Council of the Republic, the second of the two legislative chambers. Nevertheless, in the National Assembly, the deputies continued to view them as meddling in their own activities. Cabinets continued to pursue shifting majorities, and their position became weaker as the years went on. They evaded the problems, or they faced them and fell before they were able to modify them.

Many proposals for increasing Cabinet stability were presented in the National Assembly during the last years of the Fourth Republic. Those that attempted to make the Cabinet other than a weak servant of the Assembly were put to death by the deputies. In 1957, Premier Felix Gaillard sought to allow for the defeat of a Cabinet by a motion of censure on a legislative measure only when passed by an absolute majority of the total membership of the Assembly, and not by a majority of its members voting. He also wanted a Premier to be able to dissolve the Assembly at any time, instead of being held to the constitutional restriction that two Cabinets had to be defeated within an eighteen-month period before the power could be exercised. He argued that the adoption of these proposals would prevent different parliamentary groups from coalescing for the singular purpose of bringing down governments and that it would lead to the formation of a genuine opposition united on an authentic program of censure. His recommendations were brushed aside by the deputies. Ex-Premier Paul Reynaud argued that they would convert the Assembly into the "vassal of the government" and result eventually in the suspension of the parliamentary system. He was supported by Henri Queuille, another ex-Premier, who insisted that the power of dissolution should never become a permanent "threat" in the hands of the Cabinet. The great debate continued, parliamentary paralysis increased, and the political environment came to border on anarchy. The deputies refused to reduce the prerogatives of the National Assembly, even after witnessing the lengthy constitutional crisis that followed the collapse of the Bourgès-Maunoury government in October, 1957, when sixty-seven days elapsed before the Assembly was able to produce another government. They knew that it was preferable to modify parliamentary forms in order to prevent the country from going so long without a government, and yet they refused to tend to the need. Like the ministers of Louis XIV, they conveyed the impression that the political system would last forever. While they argued, the army acquired the habit of making major policy decisions of its own, ones that an impotent Cabinet could not block. The army made its most important decision in May, 1958, when it took matters into its own hands and asserted its control over the political system. By this time, it was unimportant that the Pflimlin government was sponsoring a constitutional reform bill similar to the one proposed by the late Gaillard government. Pflimlin announced his proposals on May 24, eleven days after the beginning of the army revolt in Algeria, when his government had only six days more to live.

THE PRESIDENT AND THE CABINET UNDER THE FIFTH REPUBLIC

The Constitution defines the President of the Fifth Republic as an arbiter between government and Parliament. The President appoints the Premier and receives his resignation after he has been defeated by the National Assembly on a motion of censure. The President may dissolve the Assembly and order new elections for the country. He has exceptional powers to which he may have recourse in time of national emergency, after "consultation" with the Constitutional Council—powers that are described in Article 16 of the Constitution. He may submit referenda directly to the voting public for their approval or disapproval. He has the power to request of the National Assembly a second reading on a bill. He negotiates treaties and appoints high civil and military authorities. He is commander in chief of the armed forces of the Republic. As President of the Republic, he is also President of the French Community. In his address at the Place de la République on September 4, 1958, General de Gaulle explained the President's role as a "national arbiter—far removed from political bickering, elected by the citizens who hold a public mandate, charged with the task of ensuring the normal functioning of the institutions, possessing the right to resort to the judgment of the sovereign people, accountable in the case of extreme danger, for the independence, the honor and integrity of France and for the safety of the Republic."

Article 16 allows the President of the Republic to take the necessary measures to deal with threats to the Republic, its institutions, and territorial integrity "whenever the regular functioning of the constitutional public authorities has been interrupted" after consulting with the Premier, the Presidents of the National Assembly and Senate, and the Constitutional Council. President de Gaulle had much to do with the drafting of this article. On August 14, 1958, he told the Consultative Constitutional Committee that "The exercise of these powers is tied to a situation entirely abnormal, characterized essentially by the inability of the public powers to function properly." On August 27, 1958, Michel Debré told the *Conseil d'État* that Article 16 is an "exceptional responsibility of the head of state in a tragic period." Thus, misfunctioning of the public powers and existence of a "tragic period" appear to be the preconditions of its invocation. Article 16 allows the Minister of the Interior and the prefects to prohibit mobility and political meetings, make night arrests, create zones of "special protection," and intern those involved in subversion or those suspected of encouraging it (all of which they generally do without Article 16). Invocation of Article 16 modifies Article 30 of the penal code, which states that a person must undergo judicial inquiry forty-eight hours after detention; a person may be held for fifteen days before being transferred to a judicial court (some have been held longer without Article 16 being in effect). Invocation of this article also means that persons and property can be requisitioned by the state (in keeping, anyway, with the laws of July 6, 1877 and January 7, 1959). The President of the Republic cannot use Article 16 to suspend or dissolve Parliament, and it is believed that he cannot use it to amend the Constitution. Originally, Article 16 was foreseen as capable of being invoked for twelve days maximum duration. Resorted to for the first time during the general's revolt of April 21, 1961, De Gaulle told the nation on April 23 that it would be enforced until the termination of the war in Algeria. It was withdrawn September 30, 1961, after strong opposition to it by most of the political parties.

The Constitution of the Fifth Republic was created for one man; so were its organs of government. Despite the Constitution's separation of powers and its description of a President who acts as an "arbiter" between the Cabinet and the National Assembly, the real source of political authority in contemporary France is President Charles de Gaulle. There is no true political demarcation between the President of the Republic and the Premier. Article 21 of the Constitution states that the Premier directs the action of the government, and Article 20 charges the government with determining and conducting the policy of the nation. Yet it is common knowledge that President de Gaulle is determining and conducting national policy, that the government is subordinate to him, and that the National Assembly and Senate are tagging along weakly behind both. Traditional Cabinet government died with the creation of his regime. The

Cabinet is limited now to the performance of functions that are primarily advisory and subexecutory. Its "power" is the result of De Gaulle giving it his authority. It does not perform as did Cabinets of the Third and Fourth Republics. The President decides and the ministers approve. They belong to him, not to anybody else. After the Debré government's creation, De Gaulle sent a letter to Chaban-Delmas, President of the National Assembly, telling him exactly what it can and cannot do.

There is no evidence of a bicephalic executive; the temptation to allude to its possible existence derives from De Gaulle's tendency to single out specific areas for presidential consideration, leaving certain ministerial departments with what appears to be almost autonomous status in decision making. He is preoccupied with the areas of defence, diplomacy, Algeria, and the French Community and has entrusted each to the supervision of civil servants placed there by him. He makes delegations of power in other areas, but they do not amount to an abandonment of authority. He always reserves the right to intervene whenever he thinks that he should and if he feels that the issue involved will lead to possible conflict between the government and Parliament. There was a time when the Ministers of Finance and Information appeared to be relatively free from his control; that was, however, but a matter of appearance. When he decided to get rid of Finance Minister Antoine Pinay and Information Minister Jacques Soustelle, they left at his insistence; it made little difference whether Premier Debré approved or that Article 8 of the Constitution states that the President of the Republic shall appoint the members of the government and terminate their functions only at the proposal of the Premier. Pinay's views on foreign policy had differed from De Gaulle's. Soustelle's view had been repugnant to De Gaulle, and even during his last months as Minister of Information he was casting about for other employment. The President of the Republic has no difficulty in consuming ministers whenever he feels that the occasion demands it.

De Gaulle is not a traditional President; neither is Michel Debré a traditional Premier. Debré and his ministers were chosen because of their loyalty to the President. Their portfolios were distributed according to his discretion. And whenever Debré's government is reconstituted, generally the President is the one who does it. The cabinet shake-up that occurred in August, 1961, appears to have constituted an exception to this trend; at least this appears to have been so with reference to the dismissal of Edmond Michelet from the Ministry of Justice. It is said that Debré wanted to get rid of Michelet and that De Gaulle wanted to retain him in the post. At any rate, Michelet was immediately reassigned by De Gaulle to "other functions" in the government.

When De Gaulle wants ministers from an area other than the National

Assembly he does not hesitate to bring them in from outside. As of January, 1960, twelve of the twenty-one ministers had previously served in Parliament; only nine had seats when they were called to the Cabinet.

De Gaulle has not yet seen fit to discard the constitutional provision that precludes members of the Cabinet from serving simultaneously as members of Parliament; it is likely that he will not want to do so as long as conditions remain as they are, for this restriction helps to sever the bond between the ministers and the parties, allowing them to gravitate around the President himself.

Cabinet meetings are now infrequent; the Cabinet performs more as a committee than anything else—one to which the President of the Republic can give his guidance and over which he can maintain personal control. This "government committee" is broken down into various sub-committees that deal with important areas of state. Though the President of the Republic is inclined sometimes to delegate questions to the Cabinet, allowing it to deliberate and even decide, most delegated questions bear the imprint of his close supervision; and, most solutions lie ultimately in his hands. Moreover, his appointees to the Cabinet often are technicians rather than politicians, ones who would have been found normally in the bureaucracies of preceding regimes. This is calulated to bring his powers and bureaucratic policy into a position where the former consistently dominates the latter. In other words, De Gaulle has altered the "traditional picture" in which Cabinets "presided" and the bureaucracy "governed."

Seldom does the President of the Republic allow the Cabinet to deal with a crisis on its own; and considering the nature and competence of its members, they probably would be helpless without him. They were picked by the President more for their loyalty than for their ability (Debré is described periodically as that "martyr of fidelity.") De Gaulle permitted the Cabinet to face the Algerian mutiny of January, 1960, for five full days before he intervened to command the army to hold fast to the regime. When it was time to demand emergency powers for the Cabinet, De Gaulle "commanded" them and Debré and his associates received them. If the Cabinet enjoys very little power, it must be remembered that it commands little.

With President de Gaulle's backing, the Cabinet enforces to the letter of the law those constitutional provisions that regulate its relationship with Parliament. Article 34 outlines the limits of Parliament's legislative domain. The Cabinet does not let the National Assembly forget that although it votes the laws it does not have the competence to determine the means by which they shall be implemented. By holding the Assembly to strict constitutional adherence to Article 34, and by determining itself those means by which laws are effected, the Cabinet overshadows the Assembly.

Article 38 allows the Cabinet to be authorized by Parliament to expedite ordinances that fall normally within the latter's jurisdiction. It has little difficulty securing such permission because of the Parliament's tottering and insignificant status. On February 2, 1960, when Parliament voted the Cabinet special powers of one year's duration, which allowed it to deal directly with threats to the state, law and order, and "pacification and administration of Algeria," these ordinances, although they were "decided on" in the Cabinet, really originated in the presidential office. Debré sought to assure the Parliament that suspicions should not be attached to the motives of his government and that it would retain its legislative, budgetary, and censure powers, as well as "its right of control over the government." De Gaulle decided, the Cabinet demanded, and the Parliament gave—what else could it do? Under existing circumstances, Article 38 is really a "little article 16."

If De Gaulle treats Debré as a faithful servant, the latter treats Parliament as a delinquent child. During the first year of his premiership, he viewed it with contempt; and on occasion his behavior was little short of scandalous. He subjected the opposition in the Assembly to indignities characteristic more of a Peronista than a French chamber. "The angry one" (as he is known) dismissed the opposition as illigitimate and referred to it periodically as the "anti-France." He created the impression that he considers it impossible to be anti-De Gaulle and anti-Debré without being unpatriotic. He complained frequently about the absence of a constructive legislative opposition, and yet before the National Assembly he was perfectly willing to employ tactics that encouraged it to become increasingly destructive. Perhaps he forgot that the majority must also be responsible, that it must attempt to set an example for the opposition, and that it is to a Premier's disadvantage to employ the shabbiest kind of political behavior. He is a constant irritant to the Assembly, and many of its members look forward to the time when circumstances will permit him to "retire" from the presidency of the Council of Ministers.

In summary, the strength of the President of the Republic derives from his personal power and status, not from the Constitution. The office would not be strong if it were staffed with a person less than De Gaulle, or is it likely to be as powerful when he passes from the scene. He is not the overseer of the government—as was intended by the Constitution—but the government itself. He does not arbitrate between the government and the National Assembly, as is prescribed by the Constitution—he constantly rebuffs the Assembly in the name of the government. In the final analysis, this is more in his own name than in that of anything else. Now, the President governs, the Cabinet advises and endorses, and the Parliament ratifies. Now, the latter is nothing; perhaps this is because once it was "everything."

PRESIDENT DE GAULLE AND THE NATIONAL ASSEMBLY

President de Gaulle is less of a believer in indirect representation (as implemented by the representatives of the parties in the National Assembly) and more of a believer in the Rousseauian tradition of a direct representative link between himself and the body politic.

De Gaulle was not nominated by a party for the presidency. He does not have a definite party or a program that is based on party. He came to power chanting the inadequacies of the "regime of parties." He views himself as standing above parties and, in the final analysis, as being quite independent of them.

De Gaulle has never exhibited very much respect for the institution of Parliament. It is said that a relative once told him that he should pay more attention to it, and that De Gaulle told him that the deputies made him want "to vomit." He frequently refers to the referendum of September 28, 1958, as having conferred on him an imperative mandate from the people, and that his power has its origin in them. Yet even if this is so, he has at his disposal few institutional devices that would enable him to discover when this mandate no longer continues to exist. One that he does retain is the referendum. Nevertheless, between September 28, 1958, and September, 1961, the referendum was more of a word than a reality. It was used twice in three years.

Although conscious of public opinion, De Gaulle is relatively unheedful of it when it expresses itself through the deputies. In March, 1960, he informed the deputies that he was willing to ignore their majority's request that Parliament meet in the special session after 287 deputies had petitioned it. He told the President of the National Assembly that under Article 5 of the Constitution he alone is responsible for the proper functioning of French institutions and for their respect and that this took precedence over Article 29, which allows the Parliament to meet in special session whenever it is proposed by the Premier or by the majority in the National Assembly. He contended that their demand for a special session was the result of pressure exerted on them by the Farmer's Association—in other words, by a minority segment of public opinion, one that fell far short of a majority. He proclaimed that the deputies did not really want the special session! His behavior made it clear that he considers himself a more accurate interpreter of the majority will than the deputies themselves. Of course, he also gave additional reasons for not holding the special session. He said that after two special sessions since the close of the last ordinary session, another one was clearly unnecessary and that, moreover, no assembly could in but twelve days properly address itself to the task of preparing adequate legislation!

Whatever De Gaulle's ability to interpret the majority will is, the fact remains that the National Assembly represents the only national expression of universal suffrage. In downgrading the Assembly, he is subjecting national opinion to a position that is little short of contemptible. The result is that the opposition outside the Assembly is the sole vehicle for interpreting those currents of national opinion that are actually in conflict with the opinions articulated by the President. As M. Barrachin said in the 1960 Congress of the Independent party, "When the opposition is not in the parliament, it is in the streets."

In effect, the President has removed himself from public opinion and those devices that may enable him to actually know what it is. He is the government, he is the President, he is everything. Parliament is insignificant. Everything rides and rests with one man, for better or for worse—or both. The most important institutions have been subordinated to his personal manipulation. If there is consolation in the fact that he is a man who, despite his arrogance and his overbearing conviction that he "is France," does understand the French and have their real welfare deep within his heart, it must also be conceded that he is less than a god and that all the faith that exists will not make him into one, or see to it that his most important decisions are free from error.

The devaluation of Parliament and the concentration of authority in one man has encouraged French society, according to André Philip, to adopt a collective attitude of "leave everything to big Charlie."[2] What will happen, however, after *le grande* Charles dies? Who will then go on doing the things that the majority wishes to entrust to a source of authority other than itself. Will it take back that authority, or will it wish to retrieve it and find out that it is too late for it to do so, and will it then find itself confronted with the spectacle of authority vested in a man who rules in such a manner that his own ends come before all else? Abdications of authority are always dangerous in a state that professes to be democratic, for ultimately the recall of such authority can become well-nigh impossible. The attitude of "let Charlie do it" can be disastrous to a democratic society because the tendencies that it encourages among the members of the body politic are hardly compatible with democracy itself. It sets the stage for its destruction by decreasing public participation in the business of politics. It tells all to trust their welfare and their fate to one omnipotent father, as was the case in Argentina with Peron, in Germany with Hitler, in Portugal with Salazar, in Italy with Mussolini, and in the Dominican Republic with Trujillo. De Gaulle is no Hitler, or even a Salazar—nevertheless, the most decent of men can prepare the way for the worst of things. The danger is not De Gaulle but in the tendencies that he encourages. Félix Gaillard, former President of the Council

[2] André Philip in an interview with the author, November 24, 1959.

of Ministers, told the Interregional Congress of the Radical Socialist party in May, 1960, that De Gaulle, in the light of French history, heads precisely the type of regime that will not enhance French democracy. Said Gaillard, "We are not a monarchy, we are not a dictatorship, we do not have a parliamentary regime, we are in a new regime, personal, brilliant in appearance, paternalistic, amiable but without a tomorrow."

It is likely that the deputies will be forced to continue their insignificant status within a devaluated Parliament as long as De Gaulle remains in the presidency. Roger Priouret states that there is a "law" of French politics by which the legislators tend to devour all power that does not proceed from themselves, that they always seek to enlarge theirs by installing a "government of deputies," and that they "are just now building up their appetites."[3] Despite their anticipation, it appears, nonetheless, that they will go hungry for some time to come.

General de Gaulle in his speech that was delivered in Bayeux in 1946 said that the public powers should be "clearly separated and strongly balanced." After 1958 and the coup of that year, his spokesmen stated that they were formulating a constitution in which the powers would be separate so that they could "avoid the arbitrary" and "combine at the same time liberty and authority." When Michel Debré unfurled the Constitution, he described it as giving "equal importance in the conduct of State" to both the executive and legislative organs. Nevertheless, things have not evolved this way in the few years that have elapsed since 1958. The Parliament was soon told that it was not within the meaning of its business to pry into the affairs of the executive. At the same time, the executive did not exhibit any qualms about prying into business that might be construed as being within the competence of the legislature. With the passage of each day, the powers of the executive grew stronger and those of the Parliament weaker. Yet, the recipient of this executive power has not been the Cabinet—as was foreseen by the Constitution—but its dominator, the President himself. As a result, the presidential and Cabinet organs are blending into each other.

PRESIDENTIALISM OR PARLIAMENTARISM?

The Constitution of the Fifth Republic contains the essential ingredients of parliamentary government—the principle of ministerial responsibility. It allows for a Cabinet to be brought down by a vote of censure passed by an absolute majority of the members of the National Assembly. This right is legally present, but the political and social conditions for its implementation are not. The deputies are hesitant to go all the way in attempting to compel true governmental responsibility. Many deputies

[3] Roger Priouret, *La République des Députés* (Paris: Grasset, 1959.)

feel that if they bring down the Debré government, they might prepare the stage for the subsequent destruction of the few rights that they presently enjoy. In other words, rules for the exercise of parliamentarism exist in the Constitution but not in the present political environment. Therefore, there are great discrepancies between what the Constitution prescribes and the way in which the political game is being played. Nobody is more aware of this than De Gaulle himself, and frequently there are reports that he is giving serious consideration to a new Constitution that would bridge the gap between constitutional theory and actual practice and provide legally for a presidential regime.

Is the present regime presidential or parliamentary, or is it something other than these two? First, the regime's political system seeks to combine parliamentarism with a separation of powers; it is dominated by the President, not by Parliament—the ministers belong to the President, and ministerial responsibility is a legal fact and political fiction. This type of regime is "presidential," not in the North American but in the Latin American tradition where the legislature is a "rubber stamp" in the hands of the President. Some French observers go beyond this criticism; they claim that the present system exhibits most of the characteristics of a non-dynastic monarchy. Others say that it is poised not somewhere between presidentialism and parliamentarism, but between an extreme presidentialism and Caesarism.[4]

It would be misleading to compare American presidentialism with the "presidentialism" operating today in France. American presidentialism is based on the existence of two large parties in competition with each other. It has nothing to do with a system of "arbitration" such as the one referred to by De Gaulle, and which is essentially more monarchical than presidential. The American President may compromise with Congress, he may oppose it, he may seek to ignore it, or he may dominate it. Under no circumstances may he reduce it to nothing. Some Americans may be tempted to say that President Franklin D. Roosevelt did just that. However, although he ruled both with Congress and without it whenever he could, Congress always remained in a position where it could recall its delegations of legislative authority to him. That prerogative was never endangered. Moreover, the highest court in the land remained capable of upholding successfully that provision of the Constitution that states that "All legislative power herein granted shall be vested in a Congress of the United States," and it did inform President Roosevelt that the National Recovery Act (NRA)—which formed the heart of his early New Deal program—was unconstitutional and therefore inapplicable. In De Gaulle's

[4] See essays by Georges Vedel, "Une equivoque: le Regime présidentiel," *Le Monde*, January 20, 1960, p. 1; and Maurice Duverger, "Un Regime présidentiel," *Le Monde*, January 22, 1960, p. 6.

Republic, however, the Constitutional Council seems to be committed to reaffirmation of the decisions taken by De Gaulle, whether they are constitutional or not. In some instances, it is not even entrusted with issues on which it should rule. It, too, is shriveling in the bright light of the presidential office.

De Gaulle's regime has already known crises that would have brought down governments of the Fourth Republic, perhaps even that Republic itself. It has survived them because it is farther removed from public control than was the Fourth Republic and its governments. As a result, there has evolved what might pass for a certain amount of stability. However, unlike those governments of the Fourth Republic who were confronted with problems and who fell before they were able to modify them, certain of the problems of the Fifth Republic remain unmodified; and yet De Gaulle continues in the presidency. The Fourth Republic failed to solve the Algerian problem, and so it collapsed. De Gaulle has not solved it, and yet the Fifth Republic lives on. Algeria constitutes the present crisis of the existing regime, and it cannot be hidden behind the façade of stability acquired by the Republic since its creation in 1958.

Thus, the present regime is characterized by the progressive devaluation of a Parliament elected by universal suffrage, a government that has become more and more like a consultative council, and a President who is inclined to dominate more than he arbitrates. The problem with this arrangement of public powers is that the rupture between the policy-making organs of government and public opinion induces the leader of the regime to believe that its problems are fewer than they actually are. He prides himself on his realism; but because he is far removed from public opinion, he also is removed from existing realities. He prides himself on his direct link with the populace, but he has few means at his disposal with which he can actually discover what its thoughts happen to be. He gives practically all his attention to the grand problems of diplomacy, and he is apt to wake some morning surrounded by deterioration on the domestic scene. He concentrates on his duties as sovereign head of state in the international sphere and pays less attention to internal responsibilities. He conveys the impression that he believes that any state that he heads cannot exhibit internal tendencies that are other than truly cohesive. He says much about public opinion, and yet he has little to do with it. He regards himself as France herself, and he has even said so on many occasions. He sees himself as the symbol of all that the French really want. He knows history well, and yet he is inclined to overlook some of its most obvious lessons—namely, one which is usually realized too late in the game by leaders who are inclined to take public opinion too lightly. Monarchy belongs to the past, not to the world of the present. He has demonstrated that a "poor man's" version of it can exist in this century;

the only question is, how long can it survive? The greatest French actor is not to be found at the Odéon but in the Élysée Palace.

DE GAULLE: THE RISE, THE "RETIREMENT," THE RESURRECTION

General de Gaulle served as an officer in World War I and as head of the Free France Movement in World War II. After the Liberation, he was President of the provisional government until his resignation from the post on January 20, 1946. Then he "retired" from political life to Colombey-les-deux-Églises, where he remained until his return to the premiership of a dying Fourth Republic in June of 1959.

Born in 1890, as the son of a militarist, he was groomed to follow his father's profession. He relates in his memoirs that he was twelve years of age when he received the "call" and realized that someday the destiny of France would be placed in his hands.[5] In 1911, he was commissioned a lieutenant in the army. In 1922, he became a member of the staff of the War College where his writings and lectures on the use of mechanized warfare attracted favorable attention from the Germans and noticeable opposition from the French. After his defense of Laon in 1940, he was promoted to the rank of Brigadier General and later that year served under Premier Reynaud as Secretary of War and National Defense. He fled to London shortly before the French government concluded an armistice with Germany. In 1941, with British aid he established in London the French National Committee and in 1943 the French Committee of National Liberation, which he moved to Algiers after the Allied reconquest of North Africa. He returned to France after the liberation of Paris, on August 25, 1944, and became the leader of the newly established provisional government. Irritated with the Constitution passed by the Constituent Assembly, which was designed to serve as the basic law of the new Fourth Republic, and dismayed by the activities of "the politicians," he resigned his post without warning and returned on January 20, 1946, to his hometown of Colombey-les-deux-Églises. Between 1946 and 1948, he had a great deal to say about practically all aspects of politics—particularly political leadership—a subject that he had previously explored in some of his earlier writings. In June, 1946, he delivered his famous speech in Bayeaux in which he condemned the Fourth Republic and the way in which its Constitution reduced presidential power. He asked for the adoption of a Constitution in which the powers were separated and a President who could choose and dismiss his ministers even though they were responsible to the National Assembly and who could dissolve the Assembly and submit to popular referenda government-sponsored bills defeated by that

[5] Charles de Gaulle, *War Memoirs; the Call to Honour* (New York: The Viking Press, Inc., 1955), p. 3.

body. The contents of this speech subsequently served as the basis for the Constitution of the Fifth Republic.

In 1947, a Gaullist party that called itself the Rally of the French People (RPF) was formed. It asked the French to turn their backs on the "regime of parties" and forget their differences in a new kind of national unity. Within a short time, it verged sharply to the Right and soon included a number of Fascists. In 1953, De Gaulle made it clear that he wanted nothing to do with the party.

The RPF was strong in parts of France that were traditionally of conservative orientation; at the same time, it was not weak in industrial areas historically of Left disposition and inclined to deliver up a substantial rightist vote during economic crises. Electorally, it won a great victory in the municipal elections of 1947 when it cut into Radical Socialist, MRP, and Independent support and accounted for approximately 39 per cent of the total vote cast. At first, this appeared to resemble a great ground swell for De Gaulle. However, soon it was obvious that the victory had more to do with the enthusiasm of many candidates for electoral victory than with their attraction to De Gaulle, the RPF, or "its doctrine." Practically all the Radical Socialist and conservative councilors ran in the large cities on RPF tickets. Many were not Gaullists before they were elected and they did not become ones after they were installed in their new posts. Gaullism was then a symbol of anticommunism, and many of these men had been searching for a "sure ticket."

By 1954, it appeared that De Gaulle was far removed from the political scene and that he had settled down in his hometown to the life of a recluse. He maintained an office in Paris that he visited each Wednesday afternoon where he conducted discussions with visitors and associates. Whenever periodic crises occurred, some calls went up for his return to power but they were not taken too seriously. He managed to maintain the impression that he had settled for retirement. However, on June 1, 1958, just eighteen days after the beginning of the crisis of May 13, he was invested as the last Premier of the Fourth Republic. He came to power on the shoulders of a revolutionary movement that had been able to take advantage of a Republic already close to collapse. He entered office for the express purpose of abolishing that Republic and erecting in its stead one modeled along the lines of his own legal and political preferences. It was then obvious that the "recluse of Colombey" had not been greatly "inactive" in the years between 1946 and 1958.

DE GAULLE AND FRANCE

President de Gaulle believes that he is destined to enable France to recover her lost greatness. He has said: "Instinctively I have the feeling that providence has created her [France] either for complete successes or for exemplary misfortunes . . . France is not really herself unless in the front rank . . . our country must aim high and hold itself straight, on pain of mortal danger. In short, to my mind, France cannot be France without greatness."[6] Like all French nationalists, De Gaulle is convinced that the history of Europe is really the history of France and that the future of Europe rests with the future of his own country. The idea that the future of the world lies in an area other than Europe repels him, even betrays him into excluding as legitimate the idea that Europe has had its day and that it is doomed to the status of a lesser force in world diplomacy. As President, he sets high goals in the international sphere and is inclined to dismiss the idea that France lacks the means to carry them out. His strong sense of history sometimes makes him the captive of that quality, and frequently he attributes to France an international role that is in keeping more with what she once was than with what she now is. He is inclined to take nationalism for granted and to see in it more than it actually contains. Convinced that her "only salvation lies in greatness," he is blind to certain facts about the nature of France's condition. He is apt to overlook the fact that a nation's effectiveness in the international order is limited greatly if it suffers from grave internal divisions.

With all of his inadequacies, De Gaulle has been able to realize some of his objectives; and in the international sphere, he has brought France to more of an independent bargaining position. He goes about this in a fashion that is suggestive of the diplomacy of the nineteenth century. He seeks what is to France's interest, and then he sets out to secure it. He is not bound to any one given policy but rather to alternative ones calculated to keep the nation abreast of changing world conditions, and he assumes that each will work at some given time under certain given circumstances. He shifts his policies constantly and conducts diplomacy like a professional boxer—dodging, feinting, slipping blows and inflicting them, threatening and changing his style whenever the match demands that he adjust to new situations. He seeks to strengthen his position by taking advantage of all of the means that he has at his disposal, even by taking ones that he does not actually possess—as, for example, his efforts to change world nuclear policy by building and exploding in the Sahara an atomic bomb whose force was greatly inferior to the one that was dropped on Hiroshima.

De Gaulle views the international arena as one in which each nation-state seeks to extend its position at the expense of the other nation-states. The existence of a balance of power is the thing that prevents war from taking place. There is one at this time, but he is convinced it is not the right type of balance. It is divided between the United States and Russia

[6] *Ibid.*

—the kind of balance from which France cannot benefit. He subscribes, therefore, to different tactical alternatives designed to alter this balance and to substitute for it one that would give France a more influential role in shaping the course of world events. One alternative has been the attempt to create a western European power block under French leadership. Another has consisted of proposed agreements with the British to induce them to bring pressure on the United States in order to achieve a greater voice for France in the Western bloc.[7]

De Gaulle views the United Nations as something to be avoided—at least for the present—because it is dominated by the United States-U.S.S.R. balance of power. He feels that NATO also imposes limitations on French foreign policy by attempting to confine it within its own periphery. He resents France's inability to share equally in NATO with the United States and Great Britain decision making, atomic secrets, and world strategy. He proposes that all three nations determine in NATO all aspects of Atlantic strategy. When the United States refused his demands, he retaliated by disengaging French naval forces in the Mediterranean from NATO in time of war, by withholding the French Air Corps from it, and by denying the United States access to missile bases and atomic stockpiling on French soil.

De Gaulle has at his disposal strong bargaining weapons. France constitutes the heart of the anti-Soviet defense line in western Europe, and so it is to the advantage of the United States to make concessions to him in order to get him to accept full cooperation in NATO. NATO is not to the advantage of the Soviet Union, and so it is to the latter's interest to enter into agreements with France in order to induce her to stay out of it. France is a member of the Common Market; before Britain joined, it was to her advantage to secure agreements with France for the purpose of altering the undeclared economic war that then existed between the two, one by which Britain suffered greatly. In turn, it was to France's advantage to get the British to agree to support various French political demands. It is to Germany's advantage to remain France's "good friend" and ally, in order to count on her unqualified support relative to the Berlin question. All of these weapons are calculated by De Gaulle to allow France to more advantageously resist any "outside" interference that might threaten French power and result in the territorial alienation of French possessions overseas.

Finally, De Gaulle approaches the Common Market with a point of view that is more political than economic. Although originally he looked coldly on this institution, after he came to power in 1958, he agreed to sustain French participation in it because the commitment to do so was

[7] Throughout De Gaulle's writings runs a conception of diplomacy that consists of negotiating necessary alliances without accepting any type of dependence.

already fixed. Now, he professes to be receptive to economic integration of the Common Market variety; but he continues to resist all arrangements that might possibly lead to European political integration. He contends that France's relations with the Soviet Union, as well as the latter's relations with the rest of the world, would be endangered by it. At the same time, he is not in the least opposed to the strengthening of political ties among the participants of the Common Market for this might hasten the formation of a European bloc that other European nations might then be induced to join. Economic integration is viewed not as a step toward political integration, but as a mechanism that might give rise to the birth of a "Third Force" between the East and the West, one that would be under French leadership.[8]

In conclusion, it should be apparent that De Gaulle's diplomacy has succeeded to some extent, that he has strong bargaining weapons, and that Paris has been restored as one of the great diplomatic centers of the world. Nevertheless, his conviction that the world situation can be furthered by reliance on national efforts belongs more to the nineteenth than the twentieth century. It remains to be seen as to how much farther he can carry this type of diplomacy. His entire policy is historically dated and outmoded. It belongs to a diplomacy of the past and not to the future. The hope for the West is in integrated alliances, not in loose ones in which national sovereignty overrides all else. The West can present very little defense if its policy rests on the national plan. Statements by De Gaulle's Premier, Michel Debré, that suggest that the free world rests on the national idea are hard to defend.

SELECTED READING

BRUUN, G. *Clemenceau.* Cambridge, Mass.: Harvard University Press, 1943.

FISHER, H. A. L. *Bonapartism.* Fair Lawn, N.J.: Oxford University Press, 1908.

LIDDERDALE, D. W. S. *The Parliament of France.* New York: Frederick A. Praeger, Inc., 1952.

MALRAUX, A., and BURNHAM, J. *The Case for de Gaulle.* New York: Random House, Inc., 1948.

WILLIAMS, P. *Politics in Post-War France; Parties and the Constitution in the Fourth Republic.* New York: Longmans, Green & Co., Inc., 1958.

WRIGHT, G. *Raymond Poincaré and the French Presidency.* Stanford, Calif.: Stanford University Press, 1942.

[8] Prior to 1956, most French industrialists were opposed to the idea of economic integration; now they are more favorable to the idea, with the understanding that the Common Market is about as far as they can be expected to go in this direction. For some, the Common Market offers protection against socialism, even though they know that it presupposes that they adhere to rules which seek to inhibit discrimination in a part of the world in which trusts have been "the thing" for so very long. Thus far, agreement has been easy to obtain on relatively simple issues. Agreement has been much more difficult in such complicated areas as transport, agriculture, and the framing of antitrust legislation.

17

Local Government and Administration

The administrative structure of the French state is highly centralized and reaches from its seat in Paris down through the smallest communes. It is this way because of reasons that go far back in the nation's history. First, an exposed geographical position and constant threats of invasion necessitated this type of apparatus. Second, the absolutist prerevolutionary regimes concentrated on keeping the administration under the tight control of Paris. During the Napoleonic era the administration was centralized further. Lines of authority radiated everywhere from Paris—through the prefects and down to the officials of the lowest organs of local government. Subsequent regimes introduced few changes in administration. The Emperor was gone, and yet it was almost as though he continued to rule from his tomb on the Left Bank. The administration remained absolutist in structure, and its outlook went ill with the spirit of a republic. Even today, it exhibits a detached haughtiness and convictions of grandeur more in keeping with a monarchical than a democratic regime.

THE MINISTRIES

Each Cabinet is composed of ministries, or executive departments; the ministries constitute the highest level of administrative authority in those areas in which the state maintains activities. The number of ministries varies from Cabinet to Cabinet. The Debré Cabinet includes the Ministries of Finance and Economic Affairs, Justice, Interior, Armed Forces, National Education, Public Works and Transport, Industry and Commerce, Agriculture, Cooperation, Labor, Public Health and Population, Construction, Posts and Communications, War Veterans, Information, Algerian

Affairs, Sahara and Overseas Departments and Territories, and Culture. Each ministry is headed by a minister, who is also a member of the Cabinet. Each ministry is divided into sections; it is the minister's job to coordinate their activities. The sections are staffed with permanent civil servants.

Ministers are constantly in contact with the high echelons of the civil service; and so they must know as much as they can about administrative procedure, policies, and "maneuvering." At the same time, they can hardly be expected to master the technical information with which some administrators are endowed. This is furnished by their own personal cabinet, or secretariat, staffed with political appointees and former civil servants, or ones on leave from the administration. They act as assistants by advising the minister and acting as intermediaries between him and the administrators.

For the most part, the minister's job is not an enviable one. He and his secretariat are subject to all kinds of pressures. Some come from other ministers of the same Cabinet in which he serves. Others come from high civil servants, deputies, and interest groups within the country who are always concerned with the acquisition of certain favors.

Some ministries have undergone a striking transformation since the advent of the Fifth Republic. The trend toward top-level administrators and fewer politicians is part of De Gaulle's "technocratization" and "depoliticization" of government. Moreover, meetings of the *Conseil des Ministres* (ones attended by the ministers and presided over by the President of the Republic) are frequent; while meetings of the *Conseil de Cabinet* (ones attended by the government) are infrequent. Finally, certain ministries have been reorganized and interministerial committees have found increasing favor. The Ordinance of January 7, 1959, completely reorganized the system of national defense with considerable effect on certain ministries. It empowered the Committee on Defense to make decisions on the administration of defense and the Committee on Military Defense to make decisions on military strategy. Both committees are chaired by the President of the Republic. The Committee on Defense includes the Premier; the Ministers of Foreign Affairs, Interior, Armed Forces, Finance, and Economic Affairs; and any other minister called to it by the President. Each minister is responsible for those defense measures that involve his department. To the Minister of the Interior is entrusted civil defense; to the Minister of Foreign Affairs, responsibility for negotiations relative to defense; and to the Minister of Finance and Economic Affairs, responsibility for directing the action of the different ministers concerned with the requisition and allocation of war materials, and production and industrial mobilization.

THE DEPARTMENT

The largest territorial administrative unit in France is the department. The metropole is divided into ninety such areas. Each department has a council that is elected by universal suffrage on a majority basis. Each *arrondissement* within each department is entitled to one seat on the council. The council is presided over by the prefect; he is the civil servant who represents the central government in the department. During the council's two annual sessions, it determines the few departmental services with which it deals. Its president and his committee may air out certain matters, but their views are seldom held to be of great importance.

The Constitution of the Fifth Republic states in a very general way that the prefect is responsible for the national interest, administration, and respect for the laws. He is nominated by the Ministry of the Interior, although his formal appointment comes from the President of the Republic through the Council of Ministers. In performing his work, he must be aware of all phases of activity and trends of opinion within the department. In his monthly report, he supplies the Minister of the Interior with a great deal of helpful material. Because of the wide range of his activities, the government sees that he is not maintained in one department for too long a time—lest he be tempted to "personalize" the post to the point where this would interfere with the performance of his duties.

The prefect is a civil servant who resembles no other. He not only supervises local administration, but often controls it. In his own department, he is "the government"—with the exception of the department of the Seine where he is overshadowed by the more important figures in the capital. He appoints various individuals to the public services of the state performed within his department, subject to the limitations imposed on appointments by existing civil service requirements. These restrictions place a few obstacles in front of his power to make appointments that are purely political.

Inasmuch as he is directly responsible to the Minister of the Interior, the prefect controls the municipal police in his department—with the exception of those larger cities that have a separate prefect of police. He does not control the Republican Guard, the military force that is under the jurisdiction of the Ministry of Defense and which is used to maintain civil order throughout the nation. (This organization poses a definite problem because of its antirepublican political tendencies and frequent violation of established civil liberties. Guardsmen moving across the squares of the Republic, Concorde, or Nation to quell civil disturbances often go out of their way to apply their clubs, or "asparagus sticks," to the heads of rioters and bystanders alike.)

The relationship between the central and local governments is dominated by the former; consequently, the latter's functions have more to do with administering than with governing. The chain of command is generally uninterrupted and operates from the Ministry of the Interior through the departmental prefects and down into the communes.[1] The commune is the smallest territory unit of administration; there are approximately 38,0000 in all. Only 3,000 have populations in excess of 2,000 people. Each commune has a mayor and a municipal council.[2] The mayor is elected by the council, and he is charged with executive implementation of its decisions. He also performs such functions as inquiring into violations of the law; exercising police power in order to apprehend lawbreakers; and registering marriages, births, and deaths.

The members of the municipal councils are elected by universal suffrage for terms of six years each. Under the Fourth Republic, all communes with populations in excess of 9,000 people employed proportional representation as the method of election. Those with fewer than 9,000 used list voting on a majority basis. In 1958, the Fifth Republic passed a series of measures designed to reform certain aspects of municipal elections. Municipal councilors are elected now by list voting on a majority basis in communes whose populations do not exceed 120,000 people and by proportional representation in those that comprise more than that number.

The municipal councils meet approximately three months each year. Each votes its local budget and provides for such necessary services as fire and health protection and others not specifically prohibited by law. Each council is under the direct supervision of the central administration; by law it may be dissolved by the government in the event of conflict between the mayor and its majority, or if in the judgment of the government it is negligent in its pursuance of communal interests. Over the council's decisions hang the possibility of prefectural annulment—that is, if they are illegal or in excess of the powers enjoyed by the council. Removal of a councilor may be effected by a prefect if in the opinion of the latter the councilor falls short of performing those functions demanded of him by law, if he lacks eligibility for his post, or if he is excessively absent from meetings of the council.

[1] For detailed description, see Brian Chapman, *Introduction to French Local Government* (London: George Allen & Unwin, Ltd., 1953). Departments are divided into relatively unimportant administrative areas called *arrondissements.* Communes are grouped around cantons, another relatively unimportant administrative area which centralizes certain administrative activities which otherwise would be performed by the communes on an independent basis.

[2] Paris is organized on a somewhat different basis. It has two prefects (one departmental, one police) and twenty *arrondissements.* The *arrondissements* elect a municipal council of ninety members (for electoral purposes, each *arrondissement* is divided into *quartiers*). Each *arrondissement* is headed by a subprefect. Paris does not have a mayor.

After the liberation, various movements called for greater political decentralization. The Constitution of the Fourth Republic recognized the need, but Parliament failed to give it support. In 1958, the Fifth Republic passed measures that were assigned to further the independence of municipalities and bring about greater local responsibility in administration. The central government acknowledges that it is interested in retreating from "dictation to supervision." It seeks for local government greater budgetary independence, more flexibility in securing loans, fewer restrictions on corporations and concessions run by local government, and local tax reforms relative to property and professional licenses. Responsibility for municipal road construction has been transferred from the general councils of the departments to the municipal councils. Intermunicipal relations have been liberalized with a view toward making it easier for communes to join each other in order to undertake mutually beneficial services. An example of this is the integration on an intercommunal basis of some fire-protection facilities in the Paris suburbs.

In Paris and its suburbs, reforms have been undertaken in transportation and the central markets (*Les halles*). The Regional Office of Parisian Transportation, formerly under the Ministry of Public Works, has been replaced by an agency that seeks to reflect the views of the local communities as well as the state. It has the competence to determine the future organization of transportation. The central food markets of Paris will eventually be transferred elsewhere. By law, the government may regulate them and transfer elsewhere any transaction related to any of the many products handled there. Whether this reform will be carried through to the extent that it aids other municipalities remains to be seen. If it is, it will constitute a long step in the direction of establishing a modern system of food distribution and break the archaic stranglehold that now exists. Moreover, at least from a hygienic point of view, such a transformation will bring some relief to some residents of the Right Bank. If *Les halles* is presently the "belly of Paris," it is also its shame and a threat to public health.

Finally, the Fifth Republic has grouped together the departments on a regional basis, with the programs in each department under the supervision of its prefect to whom the minister may delegate his authority. The central idea here is to plan for the future not only on a national basis, but on a regional one as well. Attempts are being made to connect the different regions with each other and to make regional administrations available.

The regime admits that excessive centralization is a thing of the past and that decentralization must be achieved. In point of implementation, however, the regime has still far to go. Thus far, most of its reforms have been of a minor nature and few great ones are foreseen for the near future. It continues to generalize about the advantages of decentralization, but its aspirations still are far ahead of its achievements.

THE CIVIL SERVICE

Under the Third Republic, the principle of merit operated only within the various ministries and bureaus. There was no commission charged with the general supervision of the civil service with respect to recruitment, promotions, salary, etc. No general statute detailed the rights and obligations of civil servants. As a result, the bureaucracy exhibited favoritism, internal diversity, and periodic intervention in it by Parliament for private rather than public ends. Reforms were initiated in 1937, but they failed to secure the support of the Chamber of Deputies. Pressure for their adoption came from those within the service. They emphasized the need for new methods of recruitment, restriction of the ability of the ministries and bureaus to prescribe diverse standards and practices, and the adoption of a general statute that would apply in the same way to all members of the service.

Some civil service reforms were undertaken immediately after the liberation by the provisional government of General de Gaulle. They were twofold, aimed at both the service and the educational system. The service was put under the supervision of the new office known as the Direction of the Public Service. This office in turn was placed under the office of the Premier. Efforts were made to ameliorate some of the most prevalent abuses. The service was reorganized, and all civil servants were divided into two general classes and four categories. A distinction was made among those engaged in policy making (the civil administrators), those involved in carrying out policies (the secretaries of administration), and those who performed lesser functions (the administrative assistants and clerical aides). Codes detailing rights and privileges were introduced, along with new wage scales more in keeping with existing conditions. The Law of October 19, 1946, "Concerning the General Status of Civil Servants." granted certain assurances to civil servants.[3] Qualified ones were guaranteed facilities for further training and entrance into higher categories in the service. The right to form unions was recognized, and such unions as were established were allowed to plead before all jurisdictions. They could appeal to the administration against regulations relative to the status of personnel and individual decisions that might affect "the collective interest of civil servants." Established also was a Superior Council of the Civil Service, presided over by the Premier or his delegate and

[3] Reproduced in Lionel Laing, Manfred Vernon, and Samuel Eldersveld, *Source Book in European Governments* (New York: William Sloane Associates, Inc., 1950), pp. 137–41.

comprising twenty-four members appointed by decree in the Council of Ministers—of whom twelve were appointed on the proposal of civil service unions. The Council was empowered to perform advisory functions and had a considerable role in determining standards for the calculation of minimum existence for civil servants and the creation of commissions for the purpose of improving methods of recruitment, ratings, efficiency, promotions, etc. Thus, the Fourth Republic did succeed in bringing about certain long overdue changes in the civil service.

The civil servant is generally capable, conscientious, and poorly paid (although not as badly as agricultural and manual, non-salaried workers). During the last three years, he has witnessed his purchasing power decrease at least 4 per cent. Legally, he has certain rights and obligations, most of which were made available to him by the Fourth Republic. He does not exercise responsibility for those of his official acts that may give rise to litigation; such responsibility is the Republic's, not his. He is responsible, however, for those acts of his that are personal and that are carried on outside or beyond the realm of his duty. He generally is precluded from assuming other paying positions while a member of the service. He may participate directly in politics and may take public office, although only after he has secured leave from the service—something that is granted as a matter of routine. He may go on strike (although not the police and the public prosecutors), but only for reasons that would not affect other public services and that do not have political connotations. In practice, however, such restrictions as the latter tend to break down.

Top-echelon "civil administrators" are recruited from the National School of Administration, a creation of the Fourth Republic, which allows for their greater training and further coordination of their activities with those of the government. The course is three years; it includes practically every phase of administration (academic and field), and one receives pay while enrolled in it. It is open to qualified public officials who pass competitive examinations after at least five years in the service. "The school" may also be entered by students who pass competitive examinations and who are graduates of one of the Institutes of Political Studies (political and administrative training schools in which there is intensive emphasis on the social sciences, stringent examinations, and a three-year course of study). Those students who go from the Institutes to the National School of Administration are placed on the payroll, and they commit themselves to at least twelve years' service; the penalty for not fulfilling this obligation is repayment of the salaries they have received during their three years of training. In the National School, the training is intensive, the examinations are stiff, and periodic weeding is carried out among a student body that is highly selective. Finally, the Center for Advanced Studies, another creation of the Fourth Republic, makes specialized training available to twenty-five or so qualified, younger administrators for three months of each year.

The top-level career officials in the civil service belong to what is known as the *Grand Corps* of the state. They have been the most influential insofar as the shaping of policy is concerned. They are found in the principal ministries and agencies, concentrated primarily in those areas that form the *Grand Corps*—diplomacy, finance, the Council of State, and the Court of Accounts. Because of their social backgrounds and the nature of the educational system in which they have been trained, their outlook is generally suspicious of broad change. If their tasks are supposed to be administrative, it is difficult to know where administration ends and politics begin. In fact, it seldom does. In view of the fact that a minister's knowledge of his area is less than that of the most highly qualified technician in his department, he is really dependent on the advice of a technocrat who is in an excellent position to impose his views on the minister, although certainly there are times when the personality and forcefulness of a minister prevent this. The point, however, is that the top echelon of the administration has always influenced the making of regulations that it is intended to administer; and, therefore, its role is also political.

ADMINISTRATIVE COURTS

Administrative courts were created originally to guard against interference in the administration by ordinary courts. Now they offer a way of settling disputes between individuals and the government. They receive, for example, cases that are the result of damage inflicted on private property as a consequence of state policy, acts by a state officer that exceed the power of his office and constitute a "personal fault," etc. Their jurisdiction and personnel are different from those of ordinary courts.[4]

There are approximately fifty administrative jurisdictions. Some have permanent courts; others create or revive inactive ones, according to need. At the bottom of the administrative hierarchy are courts that may receive only certain kinds of cases, and from which appeal may be made to the Council of State, the top of the administrative hierarchy. The National Education Council (*Conseil supérieur de l'education nationale*), which supervises the schools, acts also as a court and receives appeals that have to do with decisions in education. Councils for administrative litigation (*conseils du contentieux administratifs*) receive cases from the French Community overseas. The Court of Budgetary Discipline (*Cour de discipline*

[4] See Gerald L. Kock, "The Machinery of Law Administration in France," *University of Pennsylvania Law Review*, CVIII (1960), 366–86, which brings up to date the classical article of Francis Déak and Max Rheinstein, "The Machinery of Law Administration in France and Germany," *University of Pennsylvania Law Review*, Vol. LXXXIV, 1936.

budgetaire) restricts public personnel to the budgetary limitations imposed on them. The Court of Accounts (*Cour des comptes*) supervises the accounts of public personnel. The Councils of Revision (*conseils de revision*) decide disputes falling within the compulsory military act.

At the next level of the administrative judiciary are thirty-one courts (*tribuneaux administratifs*) of general jurisdiction but limited with respect to parties. One party must be a member of the administration (any level), and his rights and obligations must be at issue. These courts are composed of a president and several councilors; three members must sit in order for the court to convene. Appeal is to the Council of State.

At the top of the administrative judiciary is the Council of State, which receives appeals from lower administrative levels and acts in an advisory capacity to the government (the Constitution states that legislative texts that the government seeks to modify by decree must first be the object of consultations between it and the Council of State and that government bills must also be discussed with the Council before being filed with the Secretariat of the National Assembly or Senate). The Council of State traces its origins to 1799, when it was introduced by Napoleon for advisory purposes and the drafting of legal codes. Today, it comprises 168 members. Its judges come primarily from the National School of Administration. Its 58 auditors, who do much of the preparatory work for its higher members, come to it by competitive examination from "the school." Three-fourths of its 51 masters of requests come from the auditors. Two-thirds of its 51 councilors of state come from among the masters of requests. The government reserves the right to appoint to it qualified members (with the exception of the lowest level).

Jurisdictional disputes between the ordinary and administrative judiciaries are resolved by the Conflicts Court, which determines the system to which a case is assigned (see Chapter 19).

SELECTED READING

Barker, E. *The Development of Public Services in Western Europe, 1660–1930.* Fair Lawn, N.J.: Oxford University Press, 1944.

Chapman, B. *Introduction to French Local Government.* London: George Allen & Unwin, Ltd., 1953.

———. *The Prefects and Provincial France.* London: George Allen & Unwin, Ltd., 1955.

Robson, W. A. "Nationalized Industries of Britain and France," *American Political Science Review,* XLIV, No. 2 (June, 1950), 299–322.

———. *The Civil Service in Britain and France.* London: Hogarth Press, Ltd., 1956.

Schwartz, B. *French Administrative Law and the Common Law World.* New York: New York University Press, 1954.

18

The French Community

In 1946, the Fourth Republic changed the name of its overseas structure from Empire to Union—it altered very little else.[1] The Union consisted of the Republic (Metropolitan France and the Overseas Departments of Guadeloupe, Guiana, Martinique, and Réunion); the Associated Territories (The Cameroons and Togoland); the Associated States (Cambodia, Laos, Morocco, Tunisia, and Vietnam); and the Overseas Territories in Africa (Dahomey, Ivory Coast, Mauritania, Niger, Senegal, Sudan, Upper Volta, Chad, Gabon, Middle Congo, Ubangi-Shari, etc.), Madagascar, Antarctic, and the Pacific. The Union's major organs were the High Council and the Assembly. The former was composed of French representatives and those permitted each Associated State. Its function was to assist the French government in the "general conduct of the affairs of the Union." Soon it became a meaningless institution and stopped meeting. The Assembly was staffed half with members who represented Metropolitan France and half with representatives of the Overseas Departments, Associated States, and Associated Territories. It was able to express its opinions on resolutions submitted to it by its members; but it was not imperative that they be

[1] The Overseas Departments were granted representation in the National Assembly (83) and in the Council of the Republic (71). The Cameroons and Togoland underwent a change in status from trust territories to Associated Territories under the control of a French high commissioner. The term "Associated State" was never precisely defined. It meant generally a state which was tied to France by certain bonds and sovereign in some of its attributes. In the Overseas Territories—or colonies—political and administrative organization was defined by the National Assembly. French laws applied there by provision or decree; special provisions could be enacted by the National Assembly after "consultation" with the Assembly of the Union. In reality, the deputies never gave it much attention. In each territory, a "government council" was under the presidency of the French territorial governor; it acted in an advisory capacity. Four of its seven members were elected by the territorial assembly and three were selected by the governor. Finally, all nationals of Overseas Territories ultimately acquired the status of French citizens.

accepted or brought to the attention of the National Assembly, the High Council, or the French government. It could not compel governmental responsibility.

The Constitution of the Fourth Republic sought to convey the impression that the relationship between France and her possessions was other than colonial. This constitutional picture was the result of conclusions arrived at in Brazzaville in February, 1944, in a conference that concerned itself primarily with evolving methods whereby France could give away a little and retain a lot. The themes discussed there were decentralization of authority, more home rule, and the introduction and implementation of civil rights and liberties. Independence was not one of the conference's objectives, but it did agree that the Republic could encourage good government and some degree of self-government in its possessions abroad. The conference prepared for the subsequent modification of the principle of "assimilation" to that of "association."

The first great change in the nature of the French Union came in 1956 with the passage of Premier Guy Mollet's "framework law." In Equatorial Africa (Chad, Gabon, Middle Congo, and Ubangi-Shari), the federative form was abandoned to allow for the emergence of self-government. Mollet's decrees provided for the creation of government councils, greater powers for the territorial assemblies (basing them on universal suffrage), and greater participation in administration by natives. Also established was a grand council for all of Equatorial Africa. Generally, the same approach was followed in West Africa (Dahomey, Ivory Coast, Mauritania, Niger, Senegal, and Sudan).

Mollet's decrees decentralized administration to the extent that the Equatorial and West African territories acquired definite personalities. The decrees did not go all the way in ameliorating discrepancies between the political objectives and legal positions of these territories, but they did encourage their assemblies to assume further control over some affairs previously entrusted to colonial administration. This had the effect of stimulating local political activity. Mollet believed sincerely in self-government, and yet it is doubtful if he fully comprehended what was happening and that all would end in independence. Voices in the territories now viewed self-government not as an end in itself, but as a step on the road to sovereign existence.

In 1958, the Fifth Republic substituted the term "French Community" for "French Union." It turned almost immediately to the task of attempting to retain its possessions while implementing in them the process of decolonization. It stated that the "principle of self-determination will, from now on, govern all relations between France and the overseas countries which, under the Constitution of 1946, were attached to France by political institutions." During the six-month period following the promulgation of the Constitution, the Republic allowed the Overseas Territories to choose among the following alternatives: (1) to retain their existing status, (2) to become Overseas Departments more closely integrated with the Republic, and (3) to become autonomous states while remaining members of the French Community on the same basis as the Fifth Republic. Twelve territorial assemblies voted to become autonomous member states of the Community. They were Madagascar, Sudan, Senegal, Mauritania, Chad, Gabon, Middle Congo, Ybangi-Shari, Dahomey, Ivory Coast, Upper Volta, and Niger. Five retained their existing status. They were Somaliland, Comoro Island, Saint-Pierre, Miquelon, Polynesia, and New Caledonia. During this same period, France also recognized the right of member states to federate with each other or to become independent and thereby drop their membership in the Community. Title XIII of the Constitution held the door open for return to the Community of former members of it or the French Union and for admission to it by others who might wish to belong to it as member states. Article 88 stated that "The Republic or the Community may make agreements with States that wish to associate themselves with the Community in order to develop their own civilizations."

The Overseas Territories responded favorably to France's offer—with the exception of Guinea, who asserted her independence and cut every tie with France. Rumor first had it that her secession was "prearranged" and that she would subsequently re-enter the Community and provide a "great lesson" as to its advantages. That possibility—if it ever existed—became highly improbable after French political influence was terminated in Guinea and French private investments withdrew from it.

CHANGES IN THE FRENCH COMMUNITY

The Constitution of 1958 set up the machinery for the Community in a very general way; soon most of this machinery was obsolete because various constitutional provisions had been amended, ignored, or deliberately bypassed. What the Constitution originally prescribed and what subsequently happened are impossible to reconcile.

Originally, the President of the Republic, as President of the Community, presided over its Executive Council, which comprised also the Premier of the Republic, the heads of government of the member states, and ministers of the government of the Fifth Republic entrusted with the affairs of the Community. These ministers were appointed to the Executive Council by the President of the Republic and were free from supervision by the Republic's National Assembly and Senate. The Executive Council's competence extended to general Community policies, jurisdictions in which the member states were not sovereign, and the Community's administrative and common policy budget. Its agenda and meetings were secret, and its secretary-general and the personnel of its services were appointed by the President and responsible to him. It was not responsible to the Senate of the Community. By 1961, the obsolescence of the Executive Council became obvious, as a result of the total transfer of "jurisdictions" from the Fifth Republic to the new African states.

Originally, the Senate of the Community was constituted on the basis of one seat for every 300,000 inhabitants, with a minimum of three seats per state. It had 284 members when it was first established. One hundred and eighty-six members came from Metropolitan France, Algeria, and the Overseas Departments and Territories. Ninety-eight came from the states of the Community. Madagascar had the largest representation of all the African states with seventeen seats; the Gabon and the Congo, with populations of 400,000 and 700,000, received three seats each. The Senate examined acts, treaties, or international agreements relative to the Community. It was capable of being asked by the President of the Republic for its opinions on common economic and financial policies voted by the Fifth Republic's Parliament or the legislative assemblies of the member states. It was capable of making binding decisions in areas in which it received powers delegated from the legislative assemblies of the member states. It was empowered to hold two ordinary sessions per year, limited to one month's duration each. After it was created, it met only twice—in July, 1959 and June, 1960. By 1961, it was obvious that the Senate of the Community was obsolete; in fact, it had ceased to exist, as some African leaders pointed out to De Gaulle in letters that they sent to him. The Senate of the Community was officially abolished on March 16, 1961, when Premier Debré informed Gaston Monnerville (President of the Senate of the Republic) by letter that the life of that body had been terminated.

Originally, the Court of Arbitration of the Community had jurisdiction over disputes among the member states relative to interpretations of the Constitution, its organic laws, and Community agreements and conventions among the member states. Its personnel consisted of seven members (five were French) appointed by the President of the Republic; they were to serve six-year terms and were not subject to dismissal. Cases were to come before the Court by "petitions presented either by a state of the Community, or in the name of the Community," and its decisions were binding upon the entire Community. Thus far, the Court of Arbitration has not been eliminated by the Republic; at the same time, it cannot be said that its role is of real importance. In fact, it can be said that it has never succeeded in "getting off the ground." Even during the Mali crisis, no appeal was made to it.

Originally, the Constitution reserved to each member state local government administration. Member states were to share in common with the

Fifth Republic jurisdiction of foreign policy, defense, currency, economic and financial policies, and policy on strategic raw materials. The sovereignty of the member states was viewed as capable of being limited by supervision of the courts, higher education, telecommunications, external transportation, and transport within the Community. Exclusive of these areas, the member states were to be sovereign and could through special agreements create other common jurisdictions or transfer them from the Community to one or more of its members. This picture changed drastically, too, with the passage to true independence of the former French African possessions.

Originally, the entire juridical structure of the Community was built around a President who presided over its Executive Council and formulated and communicated its decisions and headed its administration. The Senate met at his bidding and he was responsible for its agenda; consequently, it had virtually no power at all. To the Community's Court of Arbitration, the President could give questions relative to Community agreements, organic laws, elections, and the Constitution. He named its judges. Finally, he was not responsible to anybody. By 1961, the juridical structure of the Community was very different from its original form.

As a result of the profound changes that had occurred in the structure of the Community, by 1961 the Fifth Republic was compelled to handle political relations with the African states and Madagascar through its Ministry of Foreign Affairs. In May of that year, the Republic instituted by decree a Council of African and Madagascar Affairs. It is empowered to deliberate on decisions relative to relations between the Republic and the new African states and Madagascar. The members of the Council are the Premier of the Republic, the Minister of Foreign Affairs, the Minister of Cooperation (a new post, its functions are strictly non-political, being limited to technical assistance), the Secretary of State for Foreign Affairs (another new post), the Secretary-General for the Presidency of the Republic for African and Madagascar Affairs (new post), the Secretary-General of the Government, ambassadors, high representatives of the Republic, and high-ranking French envoys to the African states of French expression. At this time, it is too early to determine whether this arrangement will produce one policy relative to Africa and Madagascar or different conflicting policies that have their origin in the presidential office, the government, the Ministry of Foreign Affairs, and the Ministry of Cooperation.

WHAT THE CONSTITUTION DID NOT FORESEE

Senator Édouard Bonnefous states, "The French Empire created by the Third Republic lasted half a century; the French Union, a work of the Fourth, lasted fourteen years. The Community, daughter of the Fifth Republic, terminated its brief existence at the end of a year and a half." The generalization is almost entirely correct; there is still a Community, but it is not much of a one. It is, moreover, far from what the Constitution foresaw. It took many years to progress from Empire to Union, very little time to go from Commonwealth to *Communauté rénovée,* and practically no time to go to hardly any Community at all. An indication of what was to come occurred on February 4, 1959, when President de Gaulle opened the first session of the Executive Council of the Community. The organ resembled the High Council of the French Union, so De Gaulle went out of his way to convince people that it owed its origin to a more liberal conception. At the same time, he did not hesitate to suggest that he was not the least bit interested in seeing it evolve into an institution analogous to the Conference of Ministers of the British Commonwealth. The first sessions of the Executive revolved around what appeared as the federalist and antifederalist positions of the African leaders; yet there was no doubt that the word "federalism" was employed as a synonym for independence. The "federalists" grouped around M. Dia of Senegal, and the "anti-federalists" united around M. Houphouet-Boigny of the Ivory Coast. Within hours, the federalists circulated a petition demanding that no decision relative to the Community be taken outside of its Executive (e.g., nomination of the judges of the Court of Arbitration) and that executive decisions of the Community should be left to the diligence of each member state. The independence movement was gathering momentum. Now it was apparent why many African leaders had gone along with the Constitution in the referendum of November, 1958. They had hesitated to cut themselves off from future French financial aid. By playing the game a certain way, they could win both financial aid and their independence. Now, they did not hesitate to articulate a conception of the future completely different from the one expressed by the President of the Fifth Republic. They won real independence within a matter of months.

Independence was achieved by orderly constitutional procedures. France recognized the inevitable and consequently she went along with these broad changes. Prior to May, 1960, relations between Metropolitan France and the Community were governed by Article 86 of the Constitution:

> A change of status of a member State of the Community may be requested, either by the Republic, or by a resolution of the legislative assembly of the State concerned confirmed by a local referendum, the organization and supervision of which shall be ensured by the institutions of the Community. The procedures governing this change shall be determined by an agreement approved by the Parliament of the Republic and the legislative assembly concerned. Under the same conditions, a member State of the Community may become independent. It shall thereby cease to belong to the Community.

Article 86 was amended in May, 1960, in order to allow member states of the Community to become independent without ceasing to belong to the Community. The amendment also auhorized independent states to join the Community without losing their independence. Article 85 was amended in order to allow for alterations in the status of the Community's member states simply by agreements concluded among themselves. Both amendments were voted by the Fifth Republic's National Assembly (280 to 174) and Senate (146 to 127). Premier Debré resorted to an expeditive procedure in order to assure the rejection of amendments unacceptable to the government by applying Article 44 of the Constitution, "If the government so requests, the assembly concerned shall decide, by a single vote, on all or part of the text under discussion, retaining only the amendments proposed or accepted by the government."

Following are examples of the way in which some of these states progressed to total independence; once the transformation had been accomplished, some announced that they no longer belonged to the Community. The former territory of Madagascar secured its independence in 1960; its sovereignty was voted by the French Parliament who transferred to it the jurisdictions formerly vested in the Community. The Parliament did this, however, only after Madagascar agreed to conclude in advance certain treaties with the Republic. The following agreements were signed. France will supply Madagascar with certain types of aid (finance, educaion, etc.). It will have its own army (instructed and equipped by France), but with the Republic it will resort to common defense in foreign policy. French investors in Madagascar are guaranteed that they will be secure in their investments and holdings, and that expropriations will not be resorted to without just compensation. All litigation between Madagascar and the Republic will go to the Court of Arbitration of the Community, and acceptance of its decisions is obligatory. The former territories of Senegal and Sudan had joined on January 17, 1959, to form the Federation of Mali (the head of its federal government was Sudanese Modibo Keita, its Assembly was headed by Senegalese Léopold Sédar Senghor, it comprised six and a half million people and was three times the size of France). Soon, the Fifth Republic was confronted with Mali's demand for total transfer to her of jurisdictions reserved till then to the Community, or real independence. It was granted on June 20, 1960. A short time later Senegal seceded and Mali consisted solely of Sudan. The former associated territories of Cameroon and Togoland received their independence in the same year, as did the members of the Council of the Entente (Ivory Coast, Dahomey, Niger, and Upper Volta) by transfer of jurisdictions from the Community. That transition was accomplished by treaties approved by the French National Assembly and Senate, and the parliaments of the respective states. The member states of the Council of the Entente made it clear that their independence had to be granted prior to the signing of agreements of future cooperation with France and that they intended to enter the United Nations. Houphouet-Boigny—their spokesman and head of the government of the Ivory Coast—told France in 1961 that they no longer belonged to the Community. His conversion is said to have caused President de Gaulle surprise and concern. Houphouet was his former minister who had once fought the proposals of Senghor, Lamine Guyeye, and Sekou Touré for a confederation of sovereign African republics. He had argued against African independence—even prior to 1951 when he was a member of the French Communist party—and had exerted pressure on Dahomey and the Upper Volta in 1959 to induce them to withdraw from the Mali Federation to which they had originally given their approval. No longer does he argue this way; now, he knows that no African leader can afford to swim against the rising nationalist tide. Once he spoke exclusively of an Africa inseparable from France; now, he states simply that "Africans are sure of finding in the French spirit that sense of humanity, liberty, and fraternity that has always been the essence of their aspirations." In March, 1961, the Council of the Entente signed economic and cooperative agreements with the Fifth Republic and agreed to remain within the *franc* zone and associate with the states of the Community. At the same time, it refused all institutional ties with France, it declined to receive any French military bases on its territory, and it made clear that it would not have with France any part of a system based on the concept of common defense.

What the future holds for these new, independent African states is difficult to say, primarily because the whole of the African Continent is in a state of flux. These states may or may not blend into three or four great federations that will cover west and central Africa. In November, 1958, Guinea foresaw the emergence of a United States of Africa, following a series of discussions with Ghana. In June, 1960, Senegal and Sudan spoke of becoming the heart of a West African federation based on French culture. That union lasted only a few months. In December, 1960, Sudan (now Mali) joined the Guinea-Ghana Union. These and other efforts must be considered forerunners of new larger ones. Competing for west and central African leadership are Sekou Touré, Senghor, Houphouet, and Nkrumah. Their conflict will be confined not within the artificial nineteenth-century territorial divisions created by the West, but to the whole of western and central Africa. It goes without saying that not all of these men can triumph.

The extent to which the west and central African states federate will have more than a little to do with their needs. Some want it, others regard it with suspicion, few can afford to resist it. For example, the African and Madagascar Union was created on March 28, 1961. It includes thirteen states, and all of its decisions must secure the approval of all of its members. Its structure and orientation reflect the influence of Houphouet. Six members of the Union are members of the Community (Senegal, Gabon, Chad, Central African Republic, Congo, and the Malagasy Republic), five have signed various types of agreements with France (Council of the Entente and the Islamic Republic of Mauritania), and two have never been affiliated with the Community (the Cameroons and the ex-Belgian Congo). Within the Union exists some amount of uneasiness. Mauritania is poor and can profit by associating with a prosperous partner; nevertheless, she is also Islamic and will tolerate no infringements on her religion. The rich Ivory Coast may not be as enthusiastic as it seems to be about federation when it must associate with poor partners. Niger has rich resources, and Senegal would relish the opportunity to take advantage of them.

What will be the new states' attitude toward France? This also is difficult to ascertain. It will be shaped to some extent by France's ability to terminate the Algerian War. The new states are receptive to Algeria's independence. They are now members of the United Nations, and their foreign policies are likely to differ sharply with that of the Fifth Republic. Some may turn their backs on France; others may go so far as to sever all relations with her.

Nobody knows what the new states will become; everybody knows that they will be very different from what they were before the beginning of the Fifth Republic (when they were colonies) and that they will be African, not French, for the latter have had their day in west and central Africa.

SELECTED READING

DECRAENE, P. "The French Community of Nations," *British Survey*, February, 1960, pp. 1–23.

DELAVIGNETTE, R. *Freedom and Authority in French West Africa*. Fair Lawn, N.J.: Oxford University Press, 1950.

HAMMER, E. *The Struggle for Indo-China*. Stanford, Calif.: Stanford University Press, 1954.

PRIESTLEY, H. I. *France Overseas: A Study of Modern Imperialism*. New York: Appleton-Century-Crofts, Inc., 1938.

QUIGLEY, C. "The French Community and Western Security," *Current History*, August, 1960, pp. 101–7.

19

The Judicial System

Monarchical ordinances accreted prior to the Revolution to form a great repository of national law. The Revolution and the era of Napoleon represented the consolidation of this process. The legal codes of 1804, 1806, 1807, 1808, and 1810 constitute the base from which most of the laws of modern France derive. They are altered from time to time by statutes passed by Parliament. Legal cases are resolved by judicial reference to existing codes and statutes.

THE ORDINARY COURT SYSTEM

The French judiciary is divided among ordinary and administrative courts.[1] At the top of the ordinary courts is the Court of Cassation (*Cour de cassation*) (Figure 19–1); at the top of the administrative courts is the Council of State (*Conseil d'État*). Both court systems enter into occasional jurisdictional disputes. The Conflicts Court determines the court system to which jurisdictionally contested cases are assigned.

At the bottom of the ordinary court system are courts that are restricted jurisdictionally to certain types of disputes. Labor Courts (*conseils des prud-hommes*) judge labor-management conflicts and perform both arbitral and conciliatory functions in industrial and commercial disputes. Their members are elected by interest groups—at least two by management, two by labor—and do not form part of the judiciary. Decisions are by majority; when a tie occurs, the judge of the local Court of First Instance sits as its president and casts the tie-breaking vote. Appeal is to the local Court of Appeal, subject to the condition that the sum of money involved is greater than that over which the local Court of First Instance has

[1] See Gerald L. Kock, "The Machinery of Law Administration in France," *University of Pennsylvania Law Review*, Vol. CVIII, June, 1960.

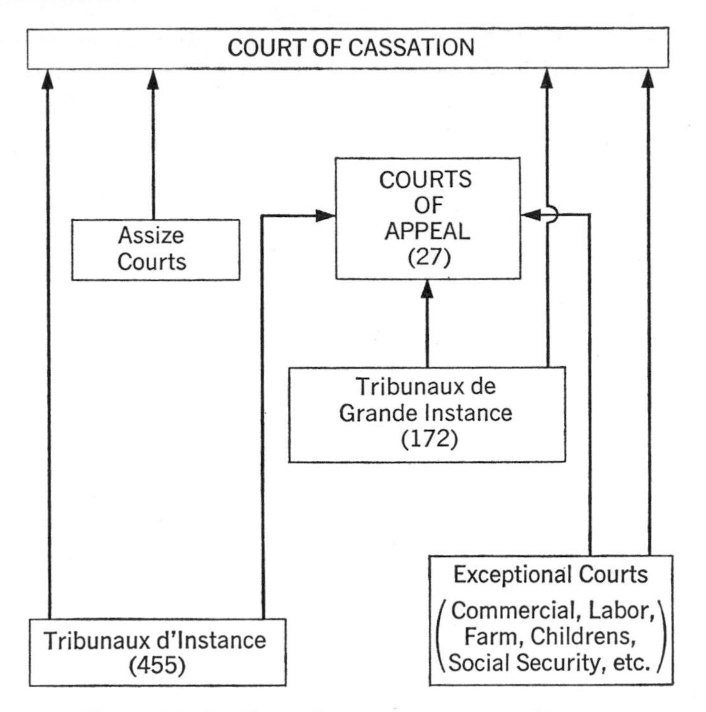

Figure 19–1. The ordinary court system of France.

jurisdiction. Petition for review of a decision is to the Court of Cassation, but solely on the grounds that the Industrial Court has exceeded its powers. Commercial Courts (*tribunaux de commerce*) in the *arrondissements* exercise jurisdiction over certain commercial disputes. Their members are businessmen elected for two-year terms and at least three judges who serve for three-year terms and who have had previous experience as alternate judges for three-year periods. All decisions are final if the sum involved does not exceed 150,000 francs,[2] although the parties to the dispute may agree to accept the decision as final even if the sum exceeds that amount. Courts of Rural Equalization (*tribunaux paritaires de baux ruraux*) supervise rents in rural areas. They are staffed with landlords, renters, and a judge from the Court of First Instance.

Next in the judicial hierarchy are 455 local Courts of First Instance (*tribunaux de première instance*), situated in the capitals of the different *arrondissements* and exercising both civil and criminal jurisdiction. They try minor cases. Civil litigation may not exceed 300,000 francs per person and 500,000 francs for a joint claim. Civil case decisions that do not exceed 100,000 francs per person, or 150,000 francs for a joint claim, and crimi-

[2] Throughout this chapter, monetary units are expressed in "old" francs.

nal case decisions that do not exceed five days' imprisonment or 6,000 francs, or both, are final—although subject to possible review by the Court of Cassation. These courts are staffed with several judges who are not on circuit and who reside in the area. Their decisions are delivered by single judges. The Fifth Republic hopes that they will become the keystone of its judicial system. They replace the Fourth Republic's numerous justices of the peace who performed in the cantons functions that were judicial, administrative, and to a lesser degree conciliatory. Justices of the peace were trained lawyers with jurisdiction over civil suits and were vested with the power to rule with finality in cases not in excess of certain monetary limits. Their competence extended also to certain misdemeanors and minor violations, and they had the right to imprison.

At the next level of the ordinary court ladder are the major Courts of First Instance (*tribunaux de grande instance*). They exercise jurisdiction within each of the departments in which they are situated. One hundred and seventy-two such courts replace the Fourth Republic's 359 civil courts whose competence did not extend beyond the administrative division known as the *arrondissement*. Major Courts of First Instance are presided over by three judges. The Judiciary Act of 1958 prescribes that the number must be uneven and that their decisions must be rendered on a majority basis. Provision is made for creation of more than one of these courts in those departments that are heavily populated and in which there is greater activity. This court's civil chamber has original competence if litigation has not been limited already to a special court or restricted to an administrative tribunal. Its criminal chamber has appellate jurisdiction and hears appeals from Courts of First Instance, Commercial Courts, and Labor Courts. Because this court handles both civil and criminal cases, it is possible for an individual to submit in a criminal prosecution a civil claim for damages inflicted as a consequence of a criminal act.

Next in the ordinary court hierarchy are the Assize Courts (*cours d'assises*). One exists in each department. Its membership consists of three judges. Its president comes from the Court of Appeal; the two other judges come from the same kind of court if one exists where the Assize Court is convened. If the Assize Court is convened where a Court of Appeal is unavailable, the two judges come from the court having primary jurisdiction in the area in which the case is tried. Assize Courts try felony cases, which they receive from the indicting chamber of the local Court of Appeal or from the Court of Cassation. Once they accept a case, they are obligated to decide it. This condition is binding even if the court discovers that the legal violation is other than a felony. There is no appeal, although its decisions may be reviewed by the Court of Cassation. Assize Courts use jury procedure. Nine jurors and three judges convict by a two-thirds majority and prescribe sentences by a simple majority.

Close to the top of the judicial hierarchy are the Courts of Appeal, staffed with five or more judges, which exist within the twenty-seven judicial districts of France. Their jurisdiction ranges over from one to seven departments. They receive appeals from lower courts within their jurisdiction, rehear them in their entirety, and allow for their final disposition. They also rule in cases sent to them by the Court of Cassation, when the latter has rejected the decision of another Court of Appeal.

At the top of the judicial hierarchy is the Court of Cassation, the highest Court of Appeal in France. It sits in Paris. It is divided into one criminal chamber and four civil chambers. Its membership comprises a Chief Justice, five chamber presidents, and sixty-three councilors. Criminal councilors confine their activities to fixed tasks within its criminal chamber; civil councilors circulate from section to section within its civil chambers, and their duties oblige them to deal with a wide variety of cases. The Court of Cassation sees that French law is interpreted correctly by inferior courts and that its uniformity is secured. It has the right to accept or reject a petition for review, and consequently it tries decisions rather than cases. If it decides that a lower court's ruling is correct, it rejects the petition and the ruling is finalized. If it accepts it, it assigns the case to a lower court at the level at which it originated, but not to the court that heard it originally. Should the lower court adhere to the original ruling and refuse to accept the ruling of the Court of Cassation, the latter may then convene at least thirty-three of its sixty-three councilors and again assign the case to a lower court. The lower court is then obliged to rule according to the opinion of the Court of Cassation.

CRIMINAL PROCEEDINGS

Criminal cases are investigated and prosecuted by state lawyers affiliated with the Ministry of Justice. They are "standing" instead of "sitting" judges who form part of the *parquet*, or the office of the public prosecutor. They are attached to all courts except minor ones.

French criminal law allows for three kinds of offenses: petty, misdemeanors, and felonies. Three kinds of penalties are prescribed: petty, correctional, and criminal. A petty offense may not result in a fine in excess of 200,000 francs and two months' imprisonment. A misdemeanor may not result in a fine in excess of 200,000 francs and five years' imprisonment. A felony may result in death, deportation, or imprisonment. Three kinds of courts handle criminal cases—Police, Correctional, and Assize.

A criminal case may begin with a complaint, accompanied or unaccompanied by a claim for civil damages. If a claim is filed, the judge may begin his investigation. If a claim is not filed, the local prosecutor will decide whether to recommend to the judge that he should investigate. If the judge decides to investigate, he calls before him the suspect and those witnesses he may wish to summon. He acts as an examining magistrate (*juge d'instruction*) in order to determine whether the case should be continued. The suspect is allowed right of counsel, and the inquiry is conducted in private. The judge decides whether a formal charge is to be made. If he decides not to prefer charges, the prosecutor or any private party who feels that his interests have been prejudiced can appeal to the local Court of Appeal.

The preliminary investigation determines the facts in the case and whether there are sufficient grounds on which to prefer charges; if there is a case, this investigation serves to route it to a trial court of proper jurisdiction. If the offense is a petty one, it is assigned to a Police Court; if it is a misdemeanor, it will go to a court of first jurisdiction; if it is a felony, it will go to the indicting chamber of the local Court of Appeal. The indicting chamber may order the felony to be tried, in which case it is sent to an Assize Court and the trial takes place within ten days, or the indicting chamber may decide that the case requires further investigation. After subsequent investigation, it may decide that the case should be dropped or that it falls short of qualifying as a felony, in which case the indicting chamber may transfer it to a Police or Correctional court.

When a Police Court tries a petty offense case, parties may appear before it voluntarily or by petition of the accuser or the prosecutor. The bailiff of the court serves the appearance citation, and the accused must comply within twenty-four hours. Misdemeanor trials are conducted in much the same way. Most are handled by the criminal chamber of the tribunal of *grande instance.* Proceedings are open unless the court decides that they should be held in private. Arguments are made by both the prosecution and the defense. The court then decides whether it has jurisdiction. If it decides that it is a felony, the case is sent to an examining judge at the proper judicial level in order to proceed with prosecution. If it decides that it falls within the jurisdiction of a Police Court, it may simply decide itself instead of sending it to a Police Court. If it is within its own jurisdiction, that is, clearly a misdemeanor, the judge decides the case—on both criminal and civil grounds, if both have been charged. If appeal is made, it is sent to the local Court of Appeal. Felonies are tried by Assize Courts after they receive the case from the indicting chamber of the local Court of Appeal. The accused may engage his own counsel or have one appointed for him by the court. Trial is by jury, and the proceedings are held in public unless the court decides that they are to be held in private. Arguments are presented by both the defense and prosecution. Questions are put to the defendant by the president of the court, judges, and jurors (with the president's authorization). The defendant is presumed innocent until his guilt is demonstrated, although the procedure and atmosphere sometimes make it appear otherwise. Particularly is this so when "in search of the truth" examination is pressed by the presiding judge, and sometimes certain personal factors are given credence and admissibility beyond the extent that they are received in Anglo-American law. (An excellent illustration appears in Albert Camus' novel, *The Stranger,* the story of an individual convicted as much for his moral orientation as for murder. An important part of his trial consists of determining if he has been a "good Christian," if he was negligent in caring for his aged mother, and why he had a mistress.[3]) After the arguments, the president, judges, and jurors determine by secret ballot the guilt or innocence of the accused. Conviction results if eight of the twelve members of the court vote it. The court also votes the penalty by secret ballot. If a civil charge has accompanied the criminal charge, it is decided by the three judges. The defendant may be held liable for civil charges even if previously he has been cleared of criminal guilt. There is no right of appeal from an Assize Court, although a petition for review may be forwarded to the Court of Cassation.

PREVENTIVE DETENTION AND PROVISIONAL RELEASE

French penal procedure provides for preventive detention, a condition to which an individual may be subjected while awaiting a final criminal decision, and for provisional release, a condition under which the individual is allowed to remain at liberty, or to regain it, until the completion of criminal proceedings. The Code of Penal Procedure of 1957–1958 defines preventive detention as "an exceptional measure" that is "justified by the frequent exigencies of public policies or of the quest for the truth." It is possible only if the defendant is liable to imprisonment for a misdemeanor or felony. When resorted to, it is frequently deducted from the final sentence, providing that such is authorized by the court.[4]

Provisional release is obtainable under the following conditions. Article 138 of the Code of Penal Procedure states that, "in a correctional case, when the maximum penalty prescribed by law is less than two years' imprisonment, an *inculpé* domiciled in France cannot be detained longer than five days after his first appearance before an examining judge, unless he has been previously convicted of a crime or sentenced to imprison-

[3] Albert Camus, *The Stranger* (New York: Vintage Books, Inc., 1958), particularly p. 125.

[4] For a precise account of provisional release and detention, see Robert Vouin, "Provisional Release in French Penal Law," *University of Pennsylvania Law Review,* CVIII, 1960, pp. 355–65. This article fails, however, to give attention to violations of provisional detention which have become scandalous under the Fifth Republic (and were equally so under the Fourth). Under the Fourth Republic, there was one case of an individual being detained nine years.

ment for an unsuspended term exceeding three months for an offense under the general law." This is known as mandatory release, a part of French penal procedure since 1856. The Penal Code also states that, "in every case where it cannot be claimed as of right, provisional release may be ordered by the examining judge of his own motion . . ." Finally, provisional release may be applied for by the defendant.

The Penal Code states that "Preventive detention can only be ordered if there are both very serious indications of guilt and reasons to fear that the *inculpé* may misuse his provisional release," and that "as soon as one of these two conditions ceases to be fulfilled, the preventive detention must come to an end." It also prescribes provisional release as "a matter of right" when "there are no substantial grounds for the belief that the *inculpé* may flee, exert pressure on witnesses, destroy evidence, commit new offenses or disturb public order . . ."

Although preventive detention is limited to a period of two months, there is no limit to the number of times that it can be renewed. In recent years—primarily because of the Algerian War—there have been many cases of lengthy individual detentions. Provisional release may be interrupted at any time if in the opinion of the court termination is warranted by the defendant's behavior. He must maintain residence in the judicial area in which he is being examined or tried, and he may be subjected to compulsory residence if he is a foreigner. Finally, he may be compelled to post security as a guaranty of his reappearance; forfeiture results in it being used for the costs and damages of those against whom his act was directed, as well as for those of the State.

JUDICIAL SUPERVISION: THE HIGH COUNCIL OF THE JUDICIARY

Supervising the judicial system is the High Council of the Judiciary, an institution created in 1946 by the Fourth Republic to decrease the political influence of the Ministry of Justice over the judiciary and to further the latter's independence. The Council seeks to see that judicial promotions and assignments are respected; it guards against manipulation of judges by the Ministry of Justice, although its success in restricting the Ministry's political influence has been more theoretical than real. The Council meets at the call of the President of the Republic. He is its president, and the Minister of Justice is its vice-president. Both are ex-officio members. The Council also includes three members of the Court of Cassation (one must be an advocate-general), three judges from the Courts of Appeal or lower courts, one councilor of state, and two non-judges who are not public officials or practicing lawyers. Their terms of office are four years. The Council nominates judges for openings on the High Court of Justice, the Court of Cassation, and for such first-presidencies of the Courts of Appeal that may become vacant. The power of appointment rests firmly in the hands of the Council's president (who is also President of the Republic). The Council may advise the Minister of Justice regarding his nominations for judgeships. It watches over violations committed by members of the judiciary and sits as a disciplinary court whenever necessary. When it is constituted for this purpose, the President of the Court of Cassation presides, and its political members are excluded from it.

RESOLVING JURISDICTIONAL DISPUTES: THE CONFLICTS COURT

The Conflicts Court (*tribunal des conflits*) resolves jurisdictional case disputes between ordinary and administrative courts by assigning them to the proper judicial system. This is the reason for the court's existence, and it may not interpret the law. Its membership comprises three councilors from the Court of Cassation, three from the Council of State, and two other councilors from either or both of these courts. The Conflicts Court is chaired by the Minister of Justice. Jurisdictional disputes may arise in the following ways. First, a prefect may petition a civil court to release a case on the grounds that it falls within the competence of an administrative court. There can be no dispute if the civil court complies with the demand. If it refuses, the prefect may by decree order the case to the Conflicts Court and thereby prevent the civil court from ruling on it. The Conflicts Court must determine the case's jurisdiction within three months —if after four months it fails to inform the civil court of its decision, then the latter may decide the case. Second, if individuals file identical claims against each other and both suits are rejected by both ordinary and administrative courts, one party may petition the Conflicts Court to nullify the decision refusing jurisdiction and thereby compel one kind of court to try the case. Finally, a parliamentary statute can result in the Conflicts Court receiving a case and deciding it on its own merits after both kinds of courts have refused jurisdiction over it.

THE JUDGES

Candidates for the judiciary must have attained twenty-three years of age, a legal degree, and at least two years' experience in certain aspects of the law. Entrance into the judiciary is by competitive examination for such openings as are available. The declaration of vacancies is made by the Ministry of the Interior. Membership in the judiciary carries with it membership in the civil service. First assignments are usually in the Ministry of Justice or the lowest courts. Salaries are low, although they are higher now than under the Fourth Republic.

The Statute of the Judiciary of 1958 foresees the creation of a new Center of Judicial Studies to which candidates will be admitted by competitive examination. The course of study will be four years, and it will provide members of the judiciary with training as intensive as that which is now available to qualified administrators in the civil service. The Statute allows for higher judicial salaries, and the regime hopes that this will attract qualified people to the service. Finally, the Statute stipulates that a judge must no longer move to a new court in order to receive a promotion; and the regime hopes that this change will supply judges with greater incentive and the opportunity for greater judicial specialization.

French judges find the law in provisions of the legal codes. In the absence of statutory dictate, they may or may not rule by reference to precedent. Because code reference is bound to be somewhat rigid, decisions tend to take on something of a fixed character. Parliament must give constant attention to the upkeep of these codes, lest they be neglected to the point where they have little to do with the needs of society.

THE HIGH COURT OF JUSTICE

The High Court of Justice has the competence to try the President of the Republic for treason; ministers of the Republic for felonies, misdemeanors, and treason; and accomplices who aided them in plotting against the security of the state. The one way in which the High Court can receive such cases is by an identical motion passed by an absolute majority of the members of both houses of Parliament (not by the National Assembly exclusively, as was the case under the Fourth Republic). The total membership of the High Court is twenty-four; the National Assembly and the Senate each name to it twelve of their members. This is accomplished after each general election, in the case of the National Assembly, and after each partial renewal, in the case of the Senate.

SELECTED READING

AMOS, M. S., and WALTON, F. P. *Introduction to French Law.* Fair Lawn, N.J.: Oxford University Press, 1935.

ENSOR, R. C. K. *Courts and Judges in France, Germany and England.* Fair Lawn, N.J.: Oxford University Press, 1933.

KOCK, G. L. "Criminal Proceedings in France," *The American Journal of Comparative Law,* IX (1960), 253–62.

———. "The Machinery of Law Administration in France," *University of Pennsylvania Law Review,* CVIII (June, 1960), 366–86.

VOUIN, R. "Provisional Release in French Penal Law," *University of Pennsylvania Law Review,* CVIII (June, 1960), 355–65.

III

POLITICS AND GOVERNMENT OF ITALY

ITALY
Showing cities of more than 100,000 population
Scale of Miles
0 25 50 100
SWITZERLAND
AUSTRIA
FRANCE
YUGOSLAVIA
TUNISIA
CORSICA
(France)
VALLE D'AOSTA
AOSTA
PIEDMONT
TURIN
Turin
VERCELLI
NOVARA
ASTI
ALESSANDRIA
CUNEO
LOMBARDY
VARESE
COMO
SONDRIO
BERGAMO
Bergamo
Milan
Brescia
BRESCIA
PAVIA
MILAN
CREMONA
MANTOVA
TRENTINO-ALTO ADIGE
BOLZANO
TRENTO
BELLUNO
FRIULI-VENEZIA GIULIA
UDINE
GORIZIA
TRIESTE
Trieste
VENETO
VICENZA
TREVISO
Verona
VERONA
Padua
PADUA
VENICE
Venice
ROVIGO
EMILIA-ROMAGNA
PIACENZA
Parma
PARMA
Reggio
REGGIO NELL'EMILIA
Modena
MODENA
Ferrara
FERRARA
Bologna
BOLOGNA
RAVENNA
FORLI
LIGURIA
SAVONA
GENOA
Genoa
IMPERIA
LA SPEZIA
Le Spezia
MASSA-CARRARA
TUSCANY
LUCCA
PISTOIA
FLORENCE
Florence
Leghorn
PISA
AREZZO
LEGHORN
SIENA
GROSSETO
SAN MARINO
MARCHES
PESARO E URBINO
ANCONA
MACERATA
ASCOLI PICENO
UMBRIA
PERUGIA
TERNI
LATIUM
VITERBO
RIETI
Rome
ROME
FROSINONE
LATINA
ABRUZZI AND MOLISE
TERAMO
PESCARA
L'AQUILA
CHIETI
CAMPOBASSO
CAMPANIA
CASERTA
BENEVENTO
Naples
NAPLES
AVELLINO
SALERNO
APULIA
FOGGIA
Bari
BARI
TARANTO
Taranto
BRINDISI
LECCE
BASILICATA
MATERA
POTENZA
CALABRIA
COSENZA
CATANZARO
REGGIO DI CALABRIA
Reggio Calabria
SICILY
Palermo
Messina
TRAPANI
PALERMO
MESSINA
AGRIGENTO
CALTANISSETTA
ENNA
CATANIA
Catania
RAGUSA
SIRACUSA
PANTELLERIA
SARDINIA
SASSARI
NUORO
CAGLIARI
Cagliari
Adriatic Sea
Tyrrhenian Sea
MEDITERRANEAN SEA
Ionian Sea

20

Foundations of Italian Politics

HISTORICAL ANTECEDENTS

Despite their millennial history and ancient civilization, the modern Italians are a relatively young nation in terms of constitutional heritage and political institutions. The present Italian state was formed just a century ago (1861) as the Kingdom of Italy. A patchwork of small states, most of them autocratically governed protectorates of the Habsburg Empire, was unified by means of war and revolution under the authority of the House of Savoy into a constitutional monarchy. The man who engineered the unification of the Italians was Cavour. His skillful diplomacy isolated the Austrians and won French intervention in a venture that drove the Habsburgs from most of Italy. His political skill united republicans and monarchists into a single national liberation movement (the *Risorgimento*) and made possible the fusion of north and south into a representative upper-middle-class constitutional monarchy. The Italians fought three successful wars against their historic enemy, the Habsburgs, in a period of nearly sixty years in order to liberate their conationals and raise Italy to the status of a major power in Europe.

The democratic experiment in Italy (1861–1922) failed for many reasons. The propertied and middle classes became frightened lest democracy pave the way to a Socialist majority in Parliament. They were generally hostile to the social and economic demands of organized labor and sought relief from strikes, sit-in seizures, collective bargaining, rising wage demands, and the extension of cooperative enterprises by the labor movement. They were angered by the electoral triumphs of the Socialists in the cities and provinces of north-central Italy and by the progressive fiscal reforms and social services that the local Socialist administrations had inaugurated. Middle-class Italians were infuriated by the relative loss of economic and social status that they had suffered as the result of price controls and inflations; much of their savings had been invested in state bonds during the war, and inflation had nearly wiped them out. The middle class resented the rise of working-class income and living standards and the inevitable blurring of class distinctions, which resulted from this equalization of wealth. The middle class felt that it had been beguiled and defrauded by the government's patriotic appeals during the war. It had responded faithfully to the call to arms and money; while the workers had opposed the war policy, improved their bargaining status and wages, and shifted the burden of taxation to the middle class. The middle class felt itself the victim of the pacifists, slackers, and profiteers. It blamed the lost peace on the pusillanimity of democracy and longed for the return of stability, order, and the status symbols of class security that were being swept away by an uncontained tide of social revolution. These goals could be re-established only by means of a counterrevolution and a conservative dictatorship.

The Catholics and Socialists also contributed to the collapse of parliamentary institutions in Italy as a result of their political immaturity and irresponsibility. Together they might have formed a powerful coalition and commanded a majority in Parliament, or they might have supported liberal administrations that were (initially at least) dedicated to the defense of Parliament and the maintenance of law and order. Instead, they opposed and obstructed the operation of parliamentary government and incited the Fascists to overthrow the constitutional order.

Major responsibility for the success of the Fascist counterrevolution rests with the men who held supreme positions of leadership in the government: the King, the Premiers (particularly Giolitti, Bonomi, and Facta), the ministers who were responsible for the maintenance of public law and order, the military elite, and the bureaucratic apparatus of prefects and police chiefs. The Italian government was itself disillusioned with the operation of democracy and proved incapable of governing the country in a climate of freedom. It blamed the Socialists and the Catholics for the breakdown of parliamentary institutions and decided to crush these popular movements with the hired gangs of hoodlums and thugs who masqueraded as nationalists. The blackshirted squads of Fascists were enlisted by the government as well as by the industrialists and landowners to crush the Socialists and intimidate the Catholics. The parliamentary elections of May, 1921, were accompanied by organized violence, inspired and abetted by the authorities. Democracy was foiled and the liberal constitutional order was irreparably damaged. The final decision to turn the state over to the Fascists was made by the King in October, 1922. Vittorio Emanuele III had overturned parliamentary rule in 1915 when he decreed Italy's intervention in the war and used violence to compel the members of Parliament to acquiesce. He laid democracy and the constitution he had inherited from his ancestors to final rest in 1922 when he imposed Mussolini upon the nation and supported the megalomanic dictator through twenty years of criminal violence.

Fascism won substantial consensus from the propertied and middle classes, including the intellectual elite of the country for a few years. Many of its economic policies were favorable to property owners and employers. The lower middle class was pleased with the financial stability and the economic benefits that it received from the regime in the form of jobs in the elephantine bureaucracies of the state, party, and corporate economy. Landowners and farm operators were satisfied by the policies of price supports, subsidies and bounties, and the cheap labor supply that the regime imposed through new forms of serfdom. Industrialists were given protection by autarchic economic policies and lucrative military contracts to fatten their profits. The masses were given some satisfaction in the form of greater job opportunities and security, and from the social services that the regime provided through the *Dopolavoro.* For this they gave the regime a certain amount of deference. Conformity and obedience to the will of *il Duce* and his party were demanded of all in return for the benefits of social peace and economic security that the regime provided.

Mussolini made peace with the Catholic church in 1929 on most generous terms. The church was compensated for its property seizures by the state; granted a public subsidy; allowed to operate its own schools; permitted to indoctrinate students in the public schools; authorized to maintain its own youth and lay organizations; protected from all criticism and competition by rival churches; and allowed to invest its wealth in land, real estate, corporate securities, as well as government bonds. The religious orders were given legal status and church properties were exempted from taxes. Defrocked priests and other clerical expellees were legally excluded from all but the most menial forms of employment. Antireligious expression was made a criminal offense, and the laws regulating marriage and divorce were amended to conform to clerical policy. The church was made a partner with the Fascist party and the monarchy in the new trinity that upheld the state.

The long heralded promises of national glory and empire that were used to justify the increasing privations and regimentation that set in after 1935 were cause for slight satisfaction once the euphory of the Ethiopian conquest subsided. Budgetary deficits got so far out of hand that more and more paper currency was issued, which set in motion the dread spiral of inflation, devaluation, and rising living costs. The call for austerity and sacrifice brought forth increasing opposition to the regime among Italians of all social classes. The interests of the nation and those of the regime became increasingly divergent. Passive resistance was met by the regime with more regimentation and repression until it resulted in the cementing of a united opposition front extending from the monarchy to the Communists. The disastrous foreign policy of imperalism and alliance with Nazi Germany culminating in the folly of intervention in the war was too much for the fragile Italian economy to bear. The air bombings of Italian cities and the Allied invasion of Sicily finally split the Fascist party itself. The armed forces proved incapable of defending the country against the vengeful Germans, and the state disintegrated under the impact of foreign invasion and occupation. The entire nation was humbled in befitting penitence for its supine subservience to the dictator's megalomania.

A scramble for power began even before the regime had collapsed between the monarchy, the Fascist conspirators led by Mussolini's son-in-law Ciano, and the clandestinely formed opposition parties. The monarchy won the first round because it had the backing of the army, but the opposition parties soon gained the upper hand when the army disintegrated and the partisan brigades became the backbone of the Italian resistance. Mussolini and his remnant band of diehards degenerated into a frightened, cruel, and spiteful corps of mercenaries in the pay of the Nazis. The eighteen months of civil war between Fascists and anti-Fascists rekindled the hatreds of the early twenties and led to a bloodbath. A battered and hungry nation was politically aroused, particularly in the northern half of the country, against the entire legacy of the previous twenty-five years. The presence of the Allied armies of occupation alone prevented the creation in 1945 of a popular front regime by the resistance movement. A democratic compromise was worked out between the resistance movement, now split between the advocates of a popular front and the supporters of a conservative restoration, the monarchy and the Catholic church. The fruit of this compromise was the decision to hold a popular referendum on the future of the monarchy and to allow the people to elect a representative constituent assembly to frame a new constitution. From the results of the June 1946 referendum-elections, the monarchy was succeeded by the republic; and a shaky coalition was formed by Catholics, Socialists, and Communists, who emerged as the three most powerful parties with over three-fourths of the popular vote among them.

The mantle of leadership fell to the Catholics, whose dual role of popular party and defender of the church and its interests gave them voters' appeal and the financial backing of the big business and landed oligarchies. The timely split within the Socialist party broke the power of the Left and made it possible for the Catholics to establish their hegemony over the government. This hegemony was legitimated by the coalition of Center-Left parties (Social Democratics and Republicans) and Center-Right party (Liberals), which was formed by the Catholics to provide a parliamentary majority for their rule. Since 1948, when the coalition won a resounding 64 per cent of the popular vote, a gradual displacement of votes to the Left has occurred. Catholic political hegemony has been imperiled since 1953, when the Christian Democrats lost their parliamentary majority. The Catholics have been unable to agree among themselves on the choice of new allies. If they should go to the extreme Right to prop their parliamentary majority, a popular front would most likely be formed to combat them; such a division of interests would imperil social peace and democracy as well as Catholic influence in Italy. One attempt was made in this direction in 1960, only to be quietly scuttled when it threatened to split the Christian Democratic party and produce a popular front. All attempts to seduce the Socialists to collaborate as mere camp followers have proved unsuccessful; the Socialists have insisted upon a partnership alliance, drastic economic and social reforms, and completion of the process of political democratization as prescribed by the Constitution. The strain of having to choose between clerical loyalty and democracy may eventually pull the Christian Democrats apart. In that case, democracy and social peace might be endangered. The church holds the key to Italy's immediate political future. If it should again, as in the early twenties, undermine the progressive leadership of the Christian Democratic party, a dangerous division of the country into clerico-Fascists and popular front might easily result. The consequence could be a dictatorship and civil war.

CAUSES FOR POLITICAL DISUNITY

Italy must still forge a social value system that responds to the needs and aspirations of her masses. The absence of a viable national value system has impeded the growth of political consensus in the democratic Constitution. It makes democratic collaboration among the parties difficult and casts discredit upon parliamentary democracy and constitutional legitimacy. By national value system is meant the acceptance of common ideals, goals, and principles of action, and cooperation to make the Constitution the basis for a way of life rather than a temporary truce between dictatorially oriented political movements. Until the present ideological estrangement is healed by a compromise between the major political movements on basic social, economic, and political values, government will lack moral legitimacy in the minds of half or more of the electorate. What are the causes for ideological estrangement, and how can a bridge be constructed to unite the antagonistic sociopolitical movements so that the goal of politics will not be dictatorship but democratic accommodation? These are questions that interest students of politics as well as practitioners.

Diverse factors influence the political thinking and shape the voting response of the Italian people. The most significant among these are perhaps education and temperament, social status and economic interests, religious and ethical values, and regional and sectional traditions. Thought patterns and loyalties have been crystallized into ideologies; and the individual has become imprisoned within a complex social movement through his emotional and rational identification with that movement, its ideology, leaders, organizations, and membership. Understanding Italian political behavior requires some knowledge of individual and group identifications with the ideologically defined social movements of which the political parties are but action committees.

Despite their cynicism and individualism, Italians are prone to idealistic thinking and to hero worship. Italian youth has had a tradition for over a century of self-sacrifice for ideals. The French Revolution stirred the idealism of Italian intellectuals and students after centuries of languid conformism. The *Carbonari* societies and the Young Italy society that Mazzini led in the nineteenth century were dedicated to the ideals of liberty and social justice as developed by the French utopian Socialists. The youth who followed Garibaldi to fight for freedom from foreign oppression and autocracy were certainly idealists. The anti-Fascists who enrolled in the republican forces to fight against European fascism in Spain during the 1930's included thousands of Italians. And during World War II, upwards of 300,000 Italians braved extreme hardship and immense personal peril to enroll in the partisan fighting formations in order to strike a blow against fascism and help bring about the better world that their ideals told them existed.

Ideals are the product of education and culture. The ignorant are incapable of idealism, although superstition can make fanatics of them. Idealism has been propagated within the Italian schools and universities through a classical curriculum that has emphasized heroic deeds and noble ideals. The pre-Fascist public schools, like those of the Fascist and post-Fascist period, as well as the Catholic schools, have all contributed to the exaltation of heroic qualities in the individual. The forms of heroism have differed, as have the moral examples used to bolster a particular creed, but all have emphasized as virtuous individual dedication to a cause.

The rational tradition in Italian culture is also strong, both in the Catholic and secular traditions of thought. Catholic doctrine has deduced a complete moral philosophy; and from this it has derived an idealogy with social, economic, political, and legal content. Secular thinking has been equally systematic, although not nearly so unified in its basic assumptions or value content. The emphasis on history and philosophy has been about as strong as that on literature in Italian schools; so that Italian students, in the classical curriculum particularly, have been prepared intellectually to embrace a *Weltanschauung* system of thought. The rational and systematic approach to knowledge tends toward dogmatism and absolute beliefs and leaves little place for philosophic compromise. Intellectual dogmatism and philosophic absolutism are noticeable in all Italian social movements and particularly in their ideological belief patterns. The fact that an unusually large number of Italian politicians are intellectuals trained in the classical curriculum has meant that dogmatic doctrines and systematic ideologies have been transplanted to the sphere of political action.

The intellectual hold on Italian sociopolitical movements has contributed to make these into absolute belief systems. This has fostered considerable unity within the movement, given the leaders greater authority, and provided them with a sense of mission and a certain amount of fervor and zeal. By giving themselves the stamp of idealism in the service of a cause, the political leaders have found it easier to win adherents and a mass following. Ideology has helped politicians to disarm the natural cynicism of the Italians and to politicize them. It has helped to promote mass participation in political life. But, by preaching ideal goals to its followers and making political power appear to be the artifact of absolute justice, ideology has revolutionized the political contest and endangered social peace.

Although Italian sociopolitical movements are conceived as ideologies, they must strike a positive response among the electorate by promising to achieve tangible goals by means of governmental authority once power or a share of it has been won. Specific policies must be proposed and developed as part of the political program of action. This task is performed on behalf of the movement by the party. The specific appeals of the parties are intended to capture as broad a mass following among the electorate as possible. All Italian political parties of national character, as distinct from those of purely regional scope that act as defenders of specific minorities, pose as ideal representatives of the entire nation. However, all of them lean toward a particular social class of the population: the propertied class, the middle class, the industrial workers, or the peasantry. This is explained by the nature of Italian parties; they are action committees of sociopolitical movements that are anchored in the social classes and economic interest groups.

THE CLASS STRUCTURE AND POLITICS

With the exception of the numerically small regional parties that represent minority interests, Italian parties are essentially class oriented, particularly in their policies. Although the Christian Democracy has some interclass appeal, it has become increasingly a middle-class and propertied-class spokesman. The class orientation of Italian parties is the consequence of widespread personal attachment and identification by the voters to social-class ideals and traditions. Most Italians are status conscious and think in terms of social class because of the rigid social stratification that has persisted for thousands of years in their culture. The sense of being a member of a social class because of birth, education, occupation, and wealth forms part of Italian mores. The social structure has had greater permanence than most other social institutions in Italy. Despite the many revolutions and wars that have occurred in their millennial history, the Italians are still divided into social classes, each of which has its own particular customs and ideals, habits, and modes of thinking. The static social structure, in which the incidence of upward occupational mobility is only 8 per cent, perpetuates intraclass values and strengthens conformism to class ideals. Italians who are socially integrated within a well-defined social class form strong attachments to their class mores. To get ahead economically and socially, the average Italian must support his class organizations and their leaders; by promoting the collective interests of the class, the Italian has greater hope of improving his status. Limitations on individual opportunity have strengthened class solidarity and encouraged class organization and action. In a society where class status has an almost permanent stamp, the major social tensions have developed along the line of interclass relations. Such social tensions magnify individual reliance upon the peer class and strengthen class interpretations of social justice. In this manner, the individual tends to accept the class ideology as a *Weltanschauung* or absolute conception of justice.

Restricted opportunity for upward social movement accounts for widespread fatalism and apathetic drive among lower-class Italians. Feeling impotent to better their social status through individual action, they hope for a miracle to lift them from the dead end of social despair. The popularity of the lottery and other games of chance is indicative of the widespread hope in economic miracles. Belief in quick solutions to individual poverty and social inferiority also finds expression in political utopianism. Demagogic promises of easy solutions to mass poverty are popular among the uneducated classes. Like the lottery, revolutionary politics provides perpetual hope for the attainment of social utopia.

Glaring contrasts in consumption patterns between the well-to-do and the masses add more fuel to social unrest and political extremism. The lower classes might accept their occupational status more readily if their incomes were improved or if the upper class lived more frugally, so that extreme differences in living standards were not so evident. The sheer inadequacy of wages, salaries, and farm income, particularly when contrasted with the conspicuous consumption of the propertied and professional classes, is a principal cause for social grievance among lower-class Italians.

So long as the lower classes submitted to poverty, inequities, and social debasement as though these were in accordance with God's will and natural to mankind, interclass relations did not reflect tensions. The stratified social structure and its glaring contrasts once may have seemed legitimate to the masses. However, since the war and the democratization of Italy, equalitarian ideals have been propagated by labor organizers and aspiring politicians in even the most remote villages. The once lethargic masses of humble and poor folk have become socially and politically aroused. Strikes, occupations of untilled land and factories, public gatherings and demonstrations have been spurred as a means to exacerbate social tensions and channel social discontent into mass support of labor organizations and extremist politicians. The numerous poor and lowly born Italians have become increasingly uphappy and frustrated over their economic and social lot, despite actual improvements in their living standards, simply because they have been led to expect revolutionary improvements and total equality. Their value aspirations have grown much too fast for existing social and economic realities.

ECONOMIC CAUSES FOR POLITICAL DISSENT

In the rural areas of Italy, the shortage of land and its inordinately high sale and rental value, together with the limited opportunities for urban employment or for emigration, have resulted in overpopulation and intense competition for the right to cultivate the land by farm laborers and sharecroppers as well as tenants. Agricultural income for laborers and sharecroppers is only $500 per family, while that of sharetenants may rise to a maximum of $800. If the size of the average peasant family is considered, especially in the south, the per capita income of the peasantry is below $100 per annum. These poor peasants were once resigned to their poverty and humility, since they saw no hope of ameliorating their condition except by emigration. Now that they have become the object of political education (some would say miseducation) by competing political parties, the peasants have used their suffrage rights to protest against the injustice of the status quo. They have been voting increasingly for the candidates of the Communist party.

Urban workers are somewhat better remunerated, provided they enjoy permanent employment. Unskilled and semiskilled workers are able to earn $500 or more annually; so that with the earnings of their wives and children, provided these can find employment, the working-class family may dispose of more income than the average peasant family. But the social needs and aspirations of the working-class family are correspondingly greater. The result is that the workers are an intensely dissatisfied social group who have responded to the appeals of the extreme Left.

Skilled workers are able to earn from $1,000 to as much as $1,500 per year in the north when fully employed the year around. Their consumption standards are comparable to those of white collar workers; and their children enjoy the opportunities to acquire secondary and even higher education, so as to elevate themselves socially into the middle class. Skilled workers and their rural counterpart, the sharetenants, are economically more secure and enjoy more prestige socially, so that they are politically more moderate in their choice of party loyalties. While most of these support the Socialists, a substantial number incline toward the Democratic Socialists and Christian Democrats. In some instances, however, social rejection by the middle class, strained interpersonal relations with members of the upper of middle classes, or simply family traditions cause these groups to vote for extremist parties.

The white collar employees are an expanding class numerically; but since mobility into this class exceeds the supply of new employment opportunities, there is considerable unemployment and job competition, with consequent depression of salaries. The plight of the school teacher is typical. Salaries average about $120 per month, so that the income status of the white collar employee is about the same as that of the skilled workers. Since the educational status of most white collar employees is considerably higher than that of skilled workers and a higher social status is attributed to white collar employees, most of these persons are economically dissatisfied. They desire a higher income status that will conform to their educational status. When they compare their income with those of the middle class as a whole, they become frustrated and turn to political extremism, usually of the Right-wing variety. Under the Mussolini regime, their economic treatment was considerably better, nearly approaching that of a coddled group. That they are nostalgic for the past should cause little wonder.

Middle-class Italians attempt to pattern their way of life and values on those of the upper class insofar as their limited income permits. The poorer and more insecure they feel, the greater is their need to accentuate their status as members of a class that is superior to the peasanty and workers. This feeling of superiority comes from sharing certain common values with the upper class, such as the emphasis on education and culture, despise of physical labor, accentuation of patriotism or religious conformism as a manifestation of idealism, neatness in dress, and maintenance of a certain level of decorum in speech and manners. In their desire to accentuate their superiority over the lower classes, middle-class Italians are conservatively oriented socially and politically. The principal exception comes from those upwardly mobile elements within the middle class who have not been socially integrated because of their lower-class birth origins. Many of these upwardly mobile persons cling to kinship ties and preserve much of the social outlook and political orientation of their birth status.

The upper class, composed of the traditional aristocracy and bourgeoisie, benefits most from the stratified social structure and its relative immobility, since these phenomena permit its members to enjoy conspicuous consumption patterns in a poor country, to dominate the economy, the higher bureaucracy, the conservative and moderate parties, and, through these, to monopolize the policy-formulating positions in the government. The upper stratum forms the elite class in Italy because of the preponderant role that its members enjoy in the management of the economy, the cultural media, the church, the bureaucracy, and in the parliamentary and Cabinet elites. Through these socially dominant positions over the institutions of the country, the upper stratum has forced its socioeconomic and political-legal values on Italian society. Its political influence is also predominant at the level of policy determination in the government, despite its having to recognize certain demands of other social classes as the price for the continued exercise of social, economic, and political leadership.

Most members of the upper class in Italy have an articulate sense of status as a dominant social elite and wish to preserve that position. They are conservatives with few exceptions. Aberrant upper-status persons are generally intellectuals who have a strong guilt complex that causes them to reject their class values. Some have interpersonal grievances and frustrations or an unfulfilled power drive. Individual alienations are minimal, however.

The declassed groups of Italian society do not constitute a well-defined social stratum whose behavior is conditioned by essentially class mores. They lack internal group cohesion, a unitary morality, and an integrated value system. The only common characteristics that they display consist of hostilities against the established social order. The declassed groups are inclined to identify their personal aspirations with an idealized, romantic abstraction of the nation because they lack combative group organizations to effectively espouse their interests within a democratic competitive order. They pose as super patriots and seek in the name of patriotism to discredit and destroy the group and class interests of the more integrated and politically organized social classes. Some declassed persons find status within the working-class elite and become political radicals. Most of them follow the Right-wing parties due to a confused sense of middle-class superiority.

CAUSES FOR SOCIAL IMMOBILITY

Three important factors have perpetuated the static condition of the Italian social structure. These are the undemocratic educational system, the regressive tax structure, and the low ratio of capital accumulation and investment to population. Educational opportunity is almost non-existent for peasant and working-class offspring. Inaccessibility to secondary and higher education by the lower classes is due to their poverty. Lower-class children must work to increment low family incomes. The costs of education are beyond their means, and even those who do manage to acquire formal training have difficulty in finding employment for lack of social connections. The overwhelming preponderance of those persons who enter the professions, management positions, the bureaucracy, and even teaching are from the upper middle class. Together with the upper class, the upper middle class has monopolized the prestige and good income jobs, so that there is slight occupational mobility either upwards or downwards.

The Italian tax structure lacks progressive features and facilitates the concentration of wealth among the upper and upper middle classes. Almost 80 per cent of tax revenues come from indirect levies that weigh heavily upon the low-income groups. Passage of the income tax law in 1951 was possible only because severe penalties were not attached to evasion. As a result, few Italians pay income taxes; and those who do, pay minimal amounts. It is administered as a voluntary system and its results have been discouraging.

Taxes on property—particularly land—are regressive, in that the rates are higher on small holdings than on larger holdings. Estate and inheritance taxes are very modest and leave properties more or less intact from one generation to the next. These oligarchical features of the tax system stabilize the class structure and prevent downward mobility among the wealthy. They also leave insufficient consumer power among the lower income groups by which to expand market demand for goods and services.

The low ratio of capital accumulation and investment in primary and secondary industries, such as agriculture, fishing, mining, and manufacturing, has kept productivity down and necessitated the overemployment of workers at low wages. Unit costs and prices have remained high while wages and salaries have remained depressed, both of which have kept consumption levels down. The demand for middle-class forms of employment has in turn been limited.

The shortage of capital resources, which are required to revolutionize production methods, stimulate consumption by enlarging the market, and create new and higher forms of employment, is a defect that afflicts all underdeveloped countries. Italy is relatively underdeveloped, since over 40 per cent of her population is supported by primary pursuits, such as agriculture, fishing, and mining. About 35 per cent is supported by manufacturing, 20 per cent by services, and the remainder by the state bureaucracy and church.

The present pace of capital growth and investment is not sufficient to create optimism among the present adult population in intrageneration improvement of its living standard. The rate of productivity growth is little more than 5 per cent per annum; whereas it should, to stimulate morale, be twice that rate. The volume of capital accumulation and investment should be increased beyond current levels of 20 to 23 per cent of national income. Without accelerated capital growth, the high birth rate and limited emigration will increase demographic pressures on the already strained economic resources and cause living standards to remain static.

With gross national income at around thirty billion dollars and with fifty million people to support, any expansion of capital growth would require the depression of living standards of the upper and middle classes, or that of the lower classes. The latter solution was tried by fascism and would require a police state, even if it avoided a civil war. The working class and peasantry are more highly organized and far more combative than in 1921, and their leaders have threatened to unleash civil resistance to protect democracy. For the government to enforce austerity upon the upper and middle classes would require a cohesive popular front to provide it with authority. Such a government would have to place serious curbs on private enterprise and centralize economic planning. Although the groups that might support such a policy constitute a majority, they are presently much too divided ideologically and politically to be able to collaborate successfully.

RELIGION AND POLITICS

Religion is a powerful and important influence in Italian politics because of the vast power and wealth of the Catholic church and its psychological hold on the minds of a substantial segment of the electorate. The Catholic church is the most powerful organized force in Italian politics. It disposes of an intricate labyrinth of clerical and lay organizations whose members number in the millions. Every conceivable social group comes under the influence of the church, which makes a methodical effort to draw Italians of all ages into its social and religious functions. The church operates schools, colleges and universities, orphanages, hospitals, and clinics; it is active in the labor movement, cooperatives, children and youth groups, and women's clubs; it provides recreational and entertainment facilities; it publishes a vast assortment of educational and propaganda material, including books, periodicals, and newspapers. The public schools include religious instruction in the Catholic faith as part of the compulsory curriculum in the elementary and secondary grades.

The Catholic church owns a tremendous amount of property in the form of land, real estate, banks, holding companies, and investment securities. It receives contributions from its foreign affiliates throughout the world. From the Italian government, the Catholic church receives a generous subsidy to finance its parishes and dioceses as well as many of its schools, colleges, and universities. Its properties are exempted from the payment of taxes to the state and Vatican citizens are exempt from personal taxes in Italy. The immense revenue of the Catholic church in Italy enables its organizations to permeate the country and establish close and direct contact with the people. The church performs many valuable social services for the population, second only in scope and importance to the state.

Through its vast economic power, the church exerts pressure and influence over a numerous clientele to which it dispenses favors of many kinds: jobs, leases, contracts, etc. It may expect political favors in return. The economic power of the church and that of its clientele is enlisted to finance and staff its many organizations whose main purposes are political and ideological.

While its economic power is in itself a source of great political influence, the church uses its spiritual influence as a major source of ideological and hence political suasion among the voters. The spiritual power of the church over Italian Catholics is difficult to assess. The estimates of the number of practicing Catholics range from 20 to 80 per cent of the population. Perhaps not more than half the Italians attend church services regularly and receive communion periodically. Many more attend church infrequently, observe the marriage rites in church, and request baptism for their offspring. There are relatively few Protestants, Jews, or admitted freethinkers; but many nominal Catholics are indifferent to the injunctions of the church. A very high percentage of Italians are anticlerical, possibly a majority of the adult population. Many anticlericals are devout and practicing Catholics in strictly spiritual matters. Their anticlericalism may stem from antipathy against the clergy, many of whom are regarded as unholy parasites; vulgar and scurrilous remarks about clerics are quite common. Others may be considered anticlerical because they oppose the church in politics and resent clerical dictation in secular matters. The church has never been able to persuade a majority of the Italians that they have a blind duty as Catholics to obey the clergy in secular matters. Despite the injunctions of the church against certain parties, Italians have, in a majority of cases, ignored clerical threats and supported these parties. Yet the influence of the church is strong enough to guarantee from 35 to 42 per cent of the vote to the Christian Democratic party. How much of this political suasion is the result of the ideological power of the church and how much must be attributed to its economic influence is impossible to estimate. There is a strong presumption that a substantial number of Italian voters obey the political directives of the clergy from ideological loyalty to the church; perhaps as high as one-third of the electorate believes it has a spiritual obligation to support the church's views in politics. Because of this strong presumption, the Christian Democrats have never dared to defy the church whenever the latter issued a strongly worded injunction, for fear that the church would disown them and sponsor another party. Thanks to the influence, money, and organizations of the church and its lay movement, the Christian Democrats dominate the central government and most of the regional, provincial, and communal administrations. The Christian Democratic leadership has judiciously prevented total clericalization of the state by exercising power more or less constitutionally and more or less democratically. This has prevented the formation of an anticlerical political coalition and resulted in a slow but gradual consolidation of Catholic influence and authority.

SELECTED READING

BANFIELD, EDWARD C. *The Moral Basis of a Backward Society.* Chicago: The Free Press of Glencoe, 1958.

CANTRIL, HADLEY. *The Politics of Despair.* New York: Basic Books, Inc., 1958.

CARLYLE, MARGARET. *Modern Italy.* London: Hutchinson University Library, 1957.

DICKINSON, ROBERT E. *The Population Problem of Southern Italy.* Syracuse, N.Y.: Syracuse University Press, 1955.

GRINDROD, MURIEL. *The Rebuilding of Italy: Politics and Economics, 1945–1955.* London: Royal Institute of International Affairs, 1955.

21

Political Ideologies

THE ROLE OF IDEOLOGY

To be taken seriously by the voters, candidates for public office in Italy must be sponsored by organizations having a recognized and accepted social and political doctrine or ideology. Independent candidates who do not represent an ideology have little or no chance of being elected. The *Weltanschauung* mentality of the educated class has permeated the thinking of most Italians to the point where the voters seek ideal solutions in politics. Italian politics have an ethical basis, not a pragmatic one as in the United States. Italians wish to believe that they are voting for an ethical end and not for a mere individual. By idealizing the drive for power of political parties, ideologies contribute the moral cause that legitimates the parties and ennobles their pursuit of power. Thus, a nation of individualists with a propensity toward anarchy can be politicized and inspired to support party rule.

OPERATIVE IDEOLOGIES

There are five operative ideologies in Italy: liberalism, socialism, Catholicism, authoritarian nationalism, and communism. Catholicism and communism enjoy institutional status through the Vatican and Catholic church and through the Soviet Union and Communist world movement. Catholicism and communism are monolithic ideologies based upon dogmatic beliefs; the former is based upon natural law philosophy, while the latter stems from dialectical and historical materialism. Their doctrinary character is impressive to Italians, since it lends to each the quality of dogmatic certainty. Catholicism and communism also have the advantage that their leaders evoke charismatic responses. Confidence in liberalism, socialism, and authoritarian nationalism is substantially weaker because these ideologies are not institutionalized, their elites are divided into discordant parties, and they are judged to be historically superceded doctrines. Much of their content (particularly of liberalism and socialism) has been absorbed into Catholicism and communism. Finally, the popularity of Catholicism and communism derives in great measure from the bandwagon effect of their sudden success since the end of World War II.

Liberalism

Italian liberalism developed historically during the middle of the nineteenth century as an ideology in opposition to feudal vestiges, autocracy, clericalism, and foreign (Austrian) domination. Its purpose was to politicize and motivate the bourgeoisie and middle classes into supporting national independence, unity, and constitutional government for all of Italy, which was then no more than a geographical expression. Liberalism equated nationalism and constitutional government with the social, economic, and political aspirations of the bourgeois and middle classes, which consisted at that time of social, political, and legal equality; economic opportunity; and personal freedom. Its outstanding intellectual representatives were Cavour and Mazzini.

Philosophically, Italian liberalism was derived from utilitarianism and positivism. It idealized the individual and conceived of the state as the instrument of the self-assertive individuals of society. It exalted individual self-interest and ambition to the status of a moral principle and defined the duty of the state as that of protecting individual freedom, security, and competition. Liberalism aimed to remold society in the image of the successful bourgeois who had carved out his own economic and social place of importance in the community by means of sustained competition in the pursuit of wealth. Politically, liberalism wished to reward the economically successful with the status of governing class within society through its advocacy of jurisdictional controls over the bureaucracy, subordination of the executive to the legislature, and bourgeois control of the legislature through limited suffrage.

Economic laissez faire satisfied the desires of the Italian bourgeois and middle classes for freedom to invest capital, hire labor for wages, trade within the national and international markets; and for security or freedom from governmental interference in business, excessive taxes on property, income, inheritance, or the distribution of goods. The main function of the government by liberal standards was to protect bourgeois and middle-class life and property from all forms of violence. The political counterpart of economic laissez faire consisted of constitutionalism and limited democracy, by means of which liberalism guaranteed to the bourgeois and middle classes security and freedom to pursue their economic and social interests.

As the interests of the bourgeoisie and middle classes diverged following the unification of Italy, liberalism was split between the old conceptions and a more radical and democratic emphasis. The Radicals never departed from the liberal ideology but merely modified its political content to the point of forcing the extension of the suffrage to the lower middle class. Henceforward, the exercise of power and leadership over the government was shared by the elites of the bourgeoisie and middle classes. The balance of power between the two classes was preserved by gradual and periodic extensions of the suffrage to the working class and eventually to the peasantry. Another motive for the gradual extension of suffrage rights to the masses was liberal and radical desire to legitimate the political action of the lower classes instead of revolutionizing it. The exclusion of the lower class elites from Parliament threatened the security of the internal status quo and menaced the international status of Italy as a European power. The extension of democracy in the form of universal suffrage by the Liberals and Radicals during the second decade of the twentieth century domesticated the elites of the working class and peasantry to some degree.

Extension of the suffrage forced liberalism to revise much of its doctrinal content, which permitted it to absorb many tenets of the Radicals and reform Socialists. Rapid industrialization had stimulated the growth of monopolistic enterprises, trusts, and cartels. Instead of being absorbed into the middle class, the workers and peasants were being impoverished by competition for wages and land leases by the growing scarcity of jobs and land. Economic laissez faire led to the gradual formation of a socially conscious proletariat in the rural as well as in the urban regions of Italy. The threat to existing institutions that resulted from the spread of socialism, and later of communism, caused the twentieth-century spokesman for Italian liberalism, Benedetto Croce, to cut out economic laissez faire from the body of liberal doctrines and to adopt an eclectic attitude toward the problem of the ideal organization of the economy. A liberal economy could no longer be gauged in terms of freedom for the monopolistic producer to gouge the unorganized consumer. The interest of the many (consumers) established a liberal preference to defend the freedom of the consumer to buy competitively; and if this were impossible or unfeasible, to regulate prices.

Twentieth-century Italian liberalism was forced to revise its concept of freedom in the face of worker-employer relations. In order to redress the balance between employers and workers, the latter had to be permitted the liberty to organize and bargain collectively, to strike and boycott, and to engage in other forms of economic warfare that did not include physical violence. The duty of the state was to remain impartial in the struggles between organized labor and employers, so long as their competition did not degenerate into personal violence or destruction of property. The consequences of such economic warfare might lead to hardship for the consumers and to the weakening of the national economy. The liberal must draw a line between the abuse of freedom by the few, resulting in the loss of freedom by the many, and the legitimate exercise of freedom, which does not conflict with the interest of the many or with the survival of the basic institutions of the state. This recognition of the ultimate supremacy of the collective interest over the myriad individual interests in conflict led liberal doctrine to accept some degree of state intervention as being necessary and, therefore, good.

Italian liberalism has gone so far as to accept in principle the concept of the welfare state as the outgrowth of the individual's desire in a complex industrial society to enjoy certain services and forms of security that cannot be purchased individually. The rationalization of industry and commerce and the formation of specialized categories of productive workers would condemn the many to slavery unless the state acted to correct the deformities that have resulted from the transformation of capitalism from competitive to monopolistic. Croce condemned economic laissez faire for being hopelessly archaic in industrial societies and defended vigorous state intervention to restore to the individual the freedom and initiative to change his economic and social station in life and to obtain the material and cultural standard of living to which he might rationally aspire. Socialism, provided it did not destroy economic incentive and the creative spirit or drive of the individual, might be reconcilable with liberalism, just as laissez faire had once formed the economic content of the liberal creed. To be compatible with liberalism, the economic order of society must allow the individual the necessary mobility and freedom to attain the rewards and status that will make him contribute to the progress of society. A socially and economically static society is the antithesis of a liberal order, whether its structure be capitalistic or socialistic, feudalistic or equalitarian.

The political content of liberal doctrine is shaped by concern over individual freedom and security. Although the liberal accepts the state as socially necessary to establish and maintain order and peace, and to protect individual freedom in the social, cultural, and economic spheres, he fears the consequences of such omnipotence and seeks to erect effective safeguards against the misuse of power by the governing elite. He also seeks to legitimate all political activity that is compatible with the constitutional order and laws, even though the aims of such activity be initially incompatible with the status quo. The state must be impartial and tolerant toward all political movements so long as these conform in their practices to the norms of society. Political competition under conditions of freedom and legal impartiality develops a sense of responsibility and realism among rival political elites; in time, these tend to succumb to tradition and to accept the constitutional order as legitimate insofar as they succeed in utilizing this order as a means to obtain status within the governing elite.

The political goal of liberalism is constitutional democracy—majority rule derived from a socially representative suffrage system and constitutionally ordered so as to contain arbitrary action against individual freedom. Italian liberalism has always favored parliamentary democracy, since political conditions in Italy encourage party multiplicity and require political alliances, which form a built-in system of checks and balances within the citadel of power itself—the Cabinet and Parliament. The parliamentary system preserves social peace and legality through the operation of a political balance of power, with its ever shifting alliances. The elaborate system of jurisdictional controls that Italian Liberals fashioned during the late nineteenth and early twentieth centuries, and to which they have returned after the Fascist interregnum, were designed to protect individuals, groups, and parties against arbitrary coercion by officials of the administration. Thus, while parliamentary democracy checked the growth of despotism from the pinnacle of authority through the balancing of forces, bureaucratic respect for individuality and personal and group freedom was obtained by means of institutionalized jurisdictional controls. The impartial head of state, the civil and administrative courts, and more recently a constitutional court have all been utilized as effective checks against irresponsibility by administrators.

Liberalism also believed in the ideal of decentralized government; but in the postrisorgimental period, Minghetti's regional self-government plan had to be abandoned in favor of centralized administrative rule in order to build a nation and level the feudal heritage of seigneurial-clerical absolutism. Consistent Liberals in Italy supported the majority within the Constituent Assembly, which implemented the regional autonomy scheme, and proposed local self-government for provinces and communes in the republican Constitution. Through decentralization, or devolution of power, liberalism hopes to limit the scope of state (centralized) activity and leave to the people direct control of their public affairs, thus realizing the ideal of democracy in its ancient vintage.

The social goal of government that emerges from the liberal creed in Italy might be said to be the creation of a middle-class society in which there would be slight class differences in educational, cultural, and socioeconomic status. Unless the politically dominant middle class is to suffer extinction as the governing class through the transformation of its bourgeois elements into an oligarchy, it must elevate the mass of workers and peasants to middle-class status by legal reforms of the economy, the educational system, and the tax structure of society. A mobile social structure is essential for the operation of democracy and the attainment of individual freedom. Italian liberalism thus advocates legal injunctions against the restratification of society. The main difference between liberalism and socialism lies in the eclectic approach of liberalism to the needs of the individual and in its emphasis on freedom of choice for the individual. Socialism is more doctrinaire and bureaucratic in its approach to individual needs and thinks first of bread-and-butter security and then of the moral status of the individual. The political program of Italian liberalism is not dissimilar from that of welfare liberalism in the most advanced countries of the West: progressive taxation on income and inheritance; nationalization of monopolies; redistribution of agricultural land to cultivators; extension of low-interest loans and free technical assistance to farmers, small entrepreneurs, and merchants; recognition of maximum freedom to workers to defend their economic interests; social insurance at state expense; public works to absorb unemployment; liberalization of trade; and promotion of competitive market conditions in the interest of consumers.

Socialism

The Socialist ideology in Italy stems from nineteenth-century positivism and revisionist Marxism. Its most erudite contributors were Antonio Labriola and Filippo Turati. Despite its frequent aberrations and flirtations with ideas imported from anarchism, syndicalism, and communism, the Socialist movement in Italy has developed an ideology of social democracy that is not substantially different from British Fabianism. To the Italian voter, socialism represents a form of society in which the value of social equality is paramount and where the major functions of the state are to provide social services, raise living standards, insure employment and income to the masses, wipe out privilege and inequalities, and elevate the cultural life of the people. Socialism equates justice with social equality and seeks to eliminate class distinctions and privileges through economic and social reforms enacted by the state. There can be no real freedom for individuals in a society that is divided into rich and poor, educated and ignorant, powerful and weak. Substantial equality is required for individual freedom to flourish socially.

Italian socialism holds that as capitalistic society evolves into a complex and interdependent industrialism in which the individual producer is separated from any proprietary interest in the means of production (capital) that he operates, the state must socialize capital. The state will be forced to socialize capital if the productive system is to operate efficiently (without recurrent cycles) and the consumers are to be supplied with goods and services. Since capitalism cannot insure either operational efficiency of the productive system or satisfaction of the consumers' requirements, any society made up of dependent workers and consumers whose income is derived from wages and salaries will eventually force the state to end economic anarchy and establish economic order through socialization of the economy.

The ideal type of economic structure envisaged by Italian socialism consists of a mixture of public enterprise, cooperative enterprises, and private enterprise, coordinated by state-planning agencies to fulfill the objectives of social policy as formulated by the government. The public sector would be limited to such basic enterprises as service industries (banking, transportation, communications, power, etc.), heavy industries supplying the primary materials for manufacturing, industries requiring large sums of capital for rational production, and foreign trade. This policy is justified by Socialists on grounds of social interest and economic efficiency; removal of the profit motive from the monopolistic sector would lower prices and stimulate maximum production, consumption, and employment. It would also give the state the means to implement its planning more effectively, since it would have complete control over fixing the output of basic goods and services and over determination of the price structure. Competitive production would be encouraged through both cooperative and private enterprises in most of the consumer industries, in agriculture, and in the distribution of these goods.

Italian socialism favors the imposition of direct workers' participation within every enterprise as an instrument of social control over the management, whether it be public, cooperative, or private. The purpose of worker's councils is not only to protect the interests of the labor force, but to give the worker a joint responsibility with the managerial staff in plant management so that maximum efficiency and minimum costs might be secured.

In the agricultural sector, Italian Socialists propose the total abolition of capitalistic relations between landowner and cultivator through the expropriation of land owned by non-cultivators. The land would either be leased by the state to cooperatives to be operated along industrial lines or distributed to peasant families for private operation. The social interest of the cultivator and the economic needs of society would be reconciled by the elimination of all middlemen between agricultural producers and consumers and through the assumption by state agencies of all the services required by agricultural producers.

In the field of distribution, Socialists would encourage the formation of consumer cooperatives and the gradual elimination of the mass of middlemen who add to the cost of goods without performing adequate social functions to justify their status or their appropriation of income. The mass of small merchants and property owners and rentiers would be absorbed into the labor force to serve the needs of society more effectively and to eliminate social tensions.

Socialism differs from communism rather substantially in economic concepts in that the former would keep economic enterprises as decentralized as possible, limit bureaucratic authority, provide active participation in plant management to the labor force, preserve a measure of competitive private enterprise, and foster cooperative enterprise in preference to public enterprise wherever possible. The Communists adhere instead to the Soviet conceptions of statism and bureaucratism.

The social goals of Italian socialism include the elimination of class conflicts through the absorption of all persons into the labor force in one form or another; the facilitation of job mobility through the extension of educational opportunities; the equalization of income status and living standards through a progressive tax structure and the extension of social services; and the wiping out of poverty, ignorance, poor health, and other social ills of stratified societies. There is not too much dissimilarity in professed aims between socialism and communism in social policy; Communists make such goals an ultimate objective, while Socialists are more determined to equalize social conditions from the outset. Communists are more emphatic on the need to preserve highly differentiated levels of income status throughout the period of transition from capitalism to communism, which in Soviet Russia continues after forty years without abatement.

The political concepts of Italian socialism contrast even more with those of communism. The democratic state and its existing Constitution are accepted by Socialists as the definitive form of the legal order in Italy. The state under the democratic Constitution that prevails today in Italy cannot be considered as the exclusive instrument of the bourgeoisie but as a legal political structure of organs that share certain responsibilities and that are influenced to varying degrees by different parties in relation to their relative power and influence within society, in Parliament, and the majority coalition. If the bourgeoisie dominates the state under the democratic Constitution, it is due to the consummate skill of this class and its elite groups in the exploitation of popular symbols on behalf of its ideology. The democratic state is open to the political influence of the working class and peasantry and middle class through elites that are more resistant to bourgeois influences than the Christian Democratic party, for example. The problem for socialism in becoming the dominant ideology of Italy is one of competing more effectively for the consensus and loyalty of the worker, peasant, and middle-class electorates. The democratic state provides a vehicle through which socialism can influence both directly and indirectly the content of the law, the structure of society, the relationships of individuals and groups, and the way of life of the nation.

The democratic Constitution contains *in nuce* the rudiments of the Socialist ideology, upon which a Socialist society could easily be constructed within the normative provisions of the legal order as presently constituted.

From the legal standpoint, socialism has won its objective of democratizing the foundations of the state. That much of the programatic content of the Constitution remains a legal non-reality is the consequence of the political ineffectiveness of the Socialist movement and the failure of its ideology to penetrate the electorate. Socialism must not only increase its ideological appeal at the expense of other competitive ideologies; but it must be prepared to collaborate and compromise with other movements on the practical plane of politics, if not on the ideological plane of principles. The Socialist complaint that the democratic state has not allowed adequate participation in the formulation of policy to the elite groups of the working class is due in great measure to the ideological inflexibility of socialism, its fear of being misunderstood by the masses that support it, and the poor bargaining power of the Socialist elite groups. Realization that Socialist reforms can be instituted in part and in piecemeal fashion with the support of middle-class elite groups or bourgeois interest groups without deforming the ideology or committing political heresy (transformism), while simultaneously respecting the terms of the compromise and the legitimate interests of other movements and elites, has finally taken root within the Socialist movement. Acceptance of compromise solutions is not only practical and progressive, but it reconciles middle-class and bourgeois elites to the prospect of continuous change and reform in small doses and strengthens democracy and the Constitution against the threat of fascism or conservative reaction. The democratic state cannot survive the combined criticism and opposition of the Left and Right unless the left-of-center parties form a strong bond of unity and gradually widen their consensus. Socialists must also gain experience in democratic leadership through intimate contact within a coalition before they will be prepared to assume full responsibility to direct the central government and administration of Italy, as did the Labor party in Britain from 1945 to 1951.

Italian Socialists have learned from bitter experience with fascism that they must legitimate their political status in the eyes of the bourgeoisie and the middle class if they are to assert a realistic claim as an alternate governing elite of a constitutional democracy. They must insert themselves into the legal and moral praxis of the democratic order as a nationally responsive governing elite that can command at least the passive consensus of the bourgeoisie and middle class if social peace is to be assured in Italy. Their failure to present a sincere and convincing faith in constitutional democracy has justified the persistent refusal of the bourgeois and middle-class parties to admit them to any share of governmental responsibility within the governing coalition as the spokesmen of the legitimate interests of the working class. By clinging to the integral or maximalist dogmas of nineteenth-century Marxism, Italian socialism has revealed its political immaturity and has condemned itself to a role of sterile oppositionism against the bourgeois and middle-class parties that have monopolized power in Italy since 1947. Since 1956 (Khrushchev's speech condemning Stalinism and the suppression of the Hungarian workers' rebellion), the maximalist orientation of Italian socialism has become discredited and abandoned by the majority of Socialists. Democratic reformism has been embraced by both parties of Italian socialism.

Catholicism

Catholicism as a political ideology was developed in Italy in consequence of the liberal revolution (*Risorgimento*) of the nineteenth century, the growth of political democracy and secular culture, and the spread of Socialist economic and political doctrines. The liberal state was the avowed enemy of the Papacy for decades after 1871, not only because the former had stripped the latter of all temporal power and seized church properties, but also because of the government's penchant for secularism. The state had replaced the church as the guardian of public morality and was undermining its spiritual role in Italian society. For decades, the church refused to recognize the legitimacy of the liberal state in Italy. It used its moral influence to ban all collaboration by Catholics with the government in hopes that the latter would disintegrate in the face of hostile internal and external pressures. The political goal of the church was to establish a regime that would restore clerical hegemony over the state and society in Italy.

By the end of the first decade of the twentieth century, it became obvious to the church authorities in Italy that the growing crisis of liberalism might easily be resolved in favor of socialism and that a Socialist succession to public power would doom the church to total extinction in Italy. Both liberalism and socialism had widely diffused secular values of materialism and democratic concepts of authority among the middle and working classes. The democratic reforms of the liberal state, which were designed to legitimate and accommodate working-class aspirations within an expanding middle-class capitalistic society at the expense of the peasantry, had paved the way for the eventual conquest of public power through the ballot box by the Socialists.

The social and political doctrines of contemporary Catholicism are derived authoritatively from the papal encyclicals and messages of the past seventy years, when the problem of how to meet the growing alienation of the working class from the church was first faced. In his encyclical *Rerum Novarum,* Pope Leo XIII pointed out with considerable feeling the evils of capitalism, which, by uprooting the worker from the means of production and transforming him into a mere commodity (labor), had reduced a once proud social class to the status of pariah. Unbridled exploitation of the workers had resulted in their mass impoverishment and despair and in their moral alienation from Christianity, so that a once humble folk was now becoming a mass of heretics aiming at the overthrow of the state and the destruction of the social order. The trust of the workers must be won back to the teachings of the church, so that they might respect the social order and the political institutions of the state. What Pope Leo XIII sought to accomplish was to restore social unity in capitalistic society by reforming those glaring injustices and inequities that had caused the alienation of the working class and that threatened to spread atheism among the peasantry. He wished to head off the headlong flight of the masses toward the heresy of socialism by limited reforms that might satisfy the needs and wishes of the poor.

Rerum Novarum was both a warning to the bourgeoisie, who formed the ruling class in Italy, to return to the traditional values of the natural law before the revolutionary impetus of the masses became a tidal wave and an exhortation to Catholics to use their political influence to reform the policies of the government. Legislative reforms were necessary to permit the workers to form associations to protect their interests against rapacious employers by means of collective bargaining. Social legislation to limit the workday and guarantee minimum wages for work was also recommended, so that workers might earn sufficient income to raise their families and educate their children to respect Christian values. The honest workingmen must be permitted to save enough to acquire the necessary property from which to derive security, status, and pride. Unless the lower classes were given a stake in the defense of private property, they could not be expected to support that institution or respect the social classes that abused it by monopolizing all wealth.

Subsequent papal messages, such as *Quadragesimo Anno, Divini Redemptoris, La Solennità della Pentecoste,* the Christmas message of 1944, and Pope John's 1961 encyclical *Mater et Magistra* have added little to *Rerum Novarum.* Their importance lies in the continued reminder by the church of the duties of Catholics toward the workers and peasants. To the worker must be restored the dignity of a Christian through protective laws and associational freedom. To the peasant must be restored the natural right of property, so that he might perform his backbreaking toil with love. The propertied classes and the state are exhorted to employ their wealth to provide remunerative work and increase the yield of labor through productive investments.

Here and there in the papal doctrines are reminders of the earlier doctrines of Augustinian inspiration; toil and suffering were decreed by God as the lot of mankind on earth for the expiation of original sin, and it is not the will of God that man should obtain heaven on earth. That some should toil physically while others cultivate the arts and that inequality should prevail among men are justified in the papal messages by the old Aristotelian argument that such practices are part of the natural law, without which civil society could not function, the means to worship God could not be provided, and the transcendental purpose of man (redemption from sin) could not be accomplished.

But on the whole, the tone of the papal social doctrine is pragmatic. Because the masses are dissatisfied with their social and economic conditions, particularly when they contrast their lot with the life of the upper and middle classes, and, since they are prepared to renounce the faith and embrace the heresy of socialism to obtain social and economic betterment, which would pose a grave threat to existing institutions, the church had best accept reality and pose as the defender of the poor. What is condemned as immoral when advocated by Liberals and Socialists (the pursuit of material wealth and happiness) becomes fully moral when supported by the church, simply because the church regards material betterment, not as an end in itself, but as a means to a spiritual end—the return of the masses to the fold of the church and the re-establishment of the authority of the state.

Catholic doctrine and policy propose to restore the solidarity of interests between workers and employers, peasants and landlords, and between the people and the bureaucrats by introducing such reforms as profit sharing by workers in industry, management-labor committees, compulsory arbitration of industrial-labor disputes, land expropriation and redistribution to cultivators, the expansion of cooperative enterprises, the decentralization of authority from the state to the localities, and functional representation of interest groups.

The aim of the church is to break down the social-class approach to political and economic problems and develop instead a group approach that cuts across social-class alignments. It is essentially the corporatist approach of grouping together persons within an industry, profession, or service, whether they be owners, managers, technicians, skilled workers, or common laborers. The social consequences of the Catholic program of dismantling traditional capitalism in favor of associational capitalism or solidarism would be the elimination of the dichotomies of proletariat and bourgeoisie, peasantry and landlords, and the creation of a middle-class society in which all persons would perform some form of labor and all would earn some degree of dividends from the enterprise.

Catholic reformism is gradual and seeks the cooperation of all vested interests in the formulation of just procedures of economic and social transformation. The bourgeoisie must accept the necessity of submitting to the gradual process of social reintegration into the middle class and seek for its offspring other forms of status based on education and leadership instead of accumulated wealth or face the dangers of total social annihilation inherent in the Marxist program.

Next to the problem of re-establishing social justice in society, the church is interested in the organization of the state, particularly in a Catholic nation, where the church must rely upon the faithful to defend Catholicism as the official state religion and its rights over marriage law and education, through which it asserts its moral authority. Although the Lateran pacts of 1929 provided the church with certain legal guaranties of its status and competences, the Mussolini regime was not too scrupulous in its respect for these agreements. Mussolini would brook no interference from the church in his determination to infuse the Fascist spirit of chauvinism among the Italian youth. The church was in no position to call upon the faithful to defend its status and rights against the arbitrary persecutions of the government. For this reason, the church seems determined to entrust to a democratic state the future of its status and functions in Catholic countries. A Christian-inspired electorate provides the church with the best possible defense of its status and role in Italian society.

Also fundamental to the natural law doctrines of Catholicism is the insistence by the church that the state limit the competence of government through the imposition of constitutional restraints on its legislative power. Only through respect by the government for the "higher law" can the freedom and dignity of the Christian be safeguarded and the church permitted to perform its spiritual functions in society. This is the theme of the encyclical *Immortale Dei* (1885) of Leo XIII and of Pius XII's Christmas message of 1942. To insure governmental respect for the higher law, Catholic doctrine accepts such institutional devices as bicameralism; judicial review; popular initiative and referendum; and legislative decentralization to regional, provincial, and communal councils. Although the church is confident that under liberty and democracy it can succeed in the ideological conversion of the majority of the Italian electorate, it nevertheless distrusts the concentration of power in the hands of a centralized political elite. It hopes to avoid the recurrence of the millennial church-state rivalry by establishing among the people a preference for constitutional and moral restraints upon their political elite.

Authoritarian Nationalism

One of the oldest political traditions in Italy is the authoritarian, which stems from the imperial tradition of Rome, the Ghibelline movement of the Middle Ages, and the theories of monarchical absolutism expressed in such famous tracts as Machiavelli's *The Prince*. Authoritarian rule was fastened upon most of Italy during the sixteenth century and lasted until the promulgation of the *Statuto* by King Charles Albert of Sardinia-Piedmont in 1848. The unification of Italy by the liberals and radicals served to discredit authoritarianism, and the progress toward democracy by 1900 was so marked that an article of Sidney Sonnino caused consternation.

Authoritarian concepts re-emerged during the decade before World War I as the result of the romanticism of such writers as D'Annunzio, the nationalist sentiment aroused by the conquest of Libya, and the growing middle- and upper-class fears and resentments over the progress of socialism and the labor movement. Most of the early twentieth-century authoritarians were grouped within the loosely organized nationalist movement. Some were to be found within the conservative wing of the Liberal party, among the Right wing of Catholicism, in the Left wing of the Socialist party, and among the syndicalists.

What the authoritarian nationalists had in common was contempt for democracy; representative parliamentary institutions; responsible government; and the concept of government under law, or constitutionalism. They did not believe that justice could be obtained by means of political compromises and the give-and-take procedures of Parliament or that the quantitative interests represented in Parliament should have the right to override the qualitative interests that might be represented there or not, simply because of the majority principle. The authoritarians believed in absolute principles of justice, virtue, and truth and refused to accept any compromise set of values simply because they might be pragmatic. They asserted that the state must hold to absolute principles in fashioning its laws and policies, instead of kowtowing to the voters, their elected representatives, the Constitution, the higher law, or tradition. Their ideal government would consist of virile conquerors and supermen who knew how to wrest power by force and establish and maintain their authority by domination. They idealized militarism and all of its trappings because these symbolized power, domination, and order. The authoritarians made a fetish of the state simply because the state was the supreme symbol of the power that they hoped to exercise—an unlimited power to carry out whatever policy they might select, both internally and externally. They ridiculed the concept of a higher law, be it natural law, divine law, custom and tradition, the Constitution and its usages, or the body of international law and comity. Laws are made by the strong to be broken by the stronger was the essence of the authoritarian mentality.

The social basis for the sprouting of authoritarian nationalism in Italy was the growing insecurity of the middle classes, which stemmed from their frustrated social and economic aspirations and from the threat from below to their status, which had resulted from the rapid emancipation of the working class and which democracy and socialism promised to level. The most rebellious group within the middle class, who formed the political vanguard of the nationalist movement, consisted of intellectuals and pseudointellectuals whose personal aspirations seemed to be blocked by existing conventions and institutions. They aspired to higher social and economic status but found an impenetrable barrier in upper-class exclusivism. Their aim was to arouse the middle classes politically, enlist them as a force with which to win recognition and status as a ruling elite, and achieve integration into the upper class.

The authoritarian nationalists had to fashion an ideology that would motivate the middle class politically against democracy and provide the power with which to capture the leadership of the government. The middle class had to be morally inspired and given a mission to perform. What was needed was a moral crusade for some noble and romantic cause. This cause was the redemption of Italians who were suffering oppression under foreign rule and the expansion of Italian civilization and culture into the Mediterranean Basin. The Italians must assert their nationality in the world in competition with other nations by rebuilding the empire that was once Rome. Only through empire could the middle class find opportunity for economic, social, and political advancement.

Conquest of an empire was to be the means to attain individual and collective greatness. Everything must be subordinated to the goal of empire, and everyone must accept the duties and sacrifices imposed by the wars that must be waged for the conquest of an empire. Although middle-class resentment was originally directed against the upper and working classes, it was now displaced against the national enemies who blocked Italy from realization of her imperial mission. In this way, both the upper and working classes could be enlisted in the cause. The upper class was eager for profits, while the working class needed employment, both of which would be provided by war production.

An imperialist policy meant regimentation of the nation and the expansion of the military forces. Positions as officers would be opened to the sons of the middle class. Those who distinguished themselves as heroes would rise quickly to prominence and power and soon be in a position to assume direction of the government. A new elite to govern the nation would be formed in the heat of battle against the enemy. Who could deny the right of the national heroes to govern the nation? In the interest of national survival and expansion, the military-political elite would have to abolish decadent institutions such as political parties, Parliament, the Constitution, and such practices as elections and democratic liberties, since these weakened the power of the nation before its enemies. A new Caesarism would be established to bring order and glory to the nation.

Nationalism was anti-Christian because the religious values of universal brotherhood, pacifism, and equality were incompatible with its goals.

It was antidemocratic since democracy worshipped utilitarian, pacifist, and equalitarian values. Christianity, democracy, and socialism, which was the outgrowth of democracy, made the individual the purpose and object of society and the state; whereas nationalism reduced the individual to the role of servant of the nation-state and its elite class.

Nationalism justified the subordination of the individual to the service of the nation-state and its elite class because the individual exists only thanks to the security that the state and its elite provide. Through the security that comes from the creation of order, the individual may obtain those satisfactions that he seeks. The elite class and its leader must exercise absolute power if order, justice, security, and prosperity are to be established and maintained. There must be no interference by the subjects with the authority of the elite and its leader, since these are selected for leadership by display of their natural virtues, especially the will to fight and the ability to conquer. Nationalism represented a reversion to the pagan worship of the warrior-hero, the man of courage and stamina whom nature has selected through contest in battle to lead other men. The physically strong and morally courageous are the naturally fit to rule.

The nationalist creed of action struck a responsive chord among the middle class, whose humdrum existence required the spiritual uplift of an adventure saga and whose social frustrations and threatened status required moral justification against the equalitarian values of democracy and socialism. Participation in the national crusade gave the bourgeois a feeling of exaltation, a sense of self-importance, and the moral fiber to reassert his social superiority and defend his economic status against the claims for equality by the workingman and peasant. The bourgeois hoped to be sheltered by the authoritarian state against the leveling influences of monopolistic capital and socializing labor unions.

Fascism, through its marriage with nationalism, absorbed the nationalist ideology integrally and became the ideal authoritarian political order of the frightened and disoriented middle class. It re-established order, security, and status for the middle class and, through the internal life of the party, gave the bourgeois a feeling of importance and power. As a party member, he was part of the ruling elite, the backbone of the community, and the object of fear and respect by the lower classes. Through the authoritarian state, the oligarchical structure of society was institutionalized and idealized, even though it required a totalitarian police apparatus to enforce conformity. The masses learned to know their place in society through beatings and imprisonment and to give up the equalitarian aspirations they had been taught by the democrats and Socialists. They were taught to work, believe, obey, and fight at the command of their leaders and to find happiness in serving the state, for their only purpose in life was to contribute to the glorification of the state. The state, personified by the leader, became the new god whose will was law, violation of which brought swift retribution.

The authoritarian tradition remains popular with large numbers of Italians of middle-class status or of declassed status. It also has the support of many persons of the upper class. It is particularly noticeable among students who are in need of a hero and a cause as well as a scapegoat on whom to vent their aggressions. Its irrational appeal attracts the emotionally insecure, those who are unable to fend for themselves in the competitive world and lack the group and class organizations necessary to provide them with proper defense of their interests. It attracts mostly those persons who have a power drive that has been frustrated. The present-day authoritarians are nostalgic for the return of the military tradition and the strong leader—a king or a duce. The authoritarian tradition is presently represented by the Monarchist and neo-Fascist movements.

The social content of present-day Italian authoritarianism is reactionary, since it would annul the legal rights of labor to improve the status of the workers and peasants and render the social structure even more static and immobile. It would magnify the social and economic distinctions between the masses and the middle class, so as to re-establish political unity between upper and middle classes and insure the status of the upper class. Economically, the authoritarians are divided between the restoration of decision-making power to the state, as under fascism, or the accentuation of capitalistic institutions. They appear to be more united in their opposition to the land-reform policies of the postwar governments.

The most significant feature of the authoritarian program lies in the constitutional-political order. It would like to overthrow the democratic parliamentary system; outlaw the democratic parties and those seeking social reform; reduce the courts to instruments of the executive; centralize all authority under the executive-administrative organs, with a chain of command from the dictator to the police; and annul all legal restraints on the power of the executive. The major differences among the votaries of authoritarianism are over the ideal form of the state and the locus of authority. Monarchists favor the restoration of royalty and the oligarchical rule of the aristocracy and bourgeoisie via a bureaucratic state. The neo-Fascists prefer a dictatorial republic, governed by a single-party elite recruited from the upper and middle classes, with a dual bureaucracy—that of the state administration and that of the party, with the latter exercising predominance.

Communism

Italian communism is based doctrinally on the ideas of Marx and Lenin. Inspiration came from the Bolshevik Revolution, and current doctrines are derived from the experiences of the international Communist movement. The ideals and goals of Italian communism are identical to those of Soviet communism: the establishment of socialism and the development of a classless society of workers, a state-directed economy to create economic abundance, and the gradual withering away of the state and inauguration of communism. Italian communism regards the form of government as no more than a means to the end of social and economic goals. If socialism can be attained through parliamentary democracy and established constitutional forms, Italian communism is willing to accept these political institutions. Should these institutions be impenetrable to Communist influences, they would be rejected; and communism would have no choice but to work for their overthrow by revolution and seek to establish in their place a dictatorial regime. The immediate goal of Italian communism is to transform the economic system from capitalism to socialism and eliminate social classes. How this is done (democratically or dictatorially) is unimportant. Who directs such a social and economic transformation of Italian society is also unimportant to communism, so long as the results are the liquidation of capitalism and social classes.

Italian communism accepts democracy and constitutional forms as a means to the ends of first socialism and then communism. It places no intrinsic value in such political institutions, and it will not compromise on its social and economic goals. It regards democracy and constitutionalism as institutions that have utility only during an historic epoch—the rise of capitalism and its transition to socialism. Recent doctrinal interpretations by Italy's number one Communist, Palmiro Togliatti, support the retention of democracy and constitutionalism through the historic epoch of socialism, provided these institutions do not serve counterrevolutionary purposes, such as the restoration of capitalism. The Italian Communist leader has gone further than other Communists in the endorsement of evolutionary reforms as stepping stones to socialism. His most recent doctrinal statements, made in a report to the ninth congress of the Italian Communist party in 1960, sound very much like the evolutionary socialism of Turati. The democratic republic and its Constitution make it possible for the Communists to intensify the class struggle legally and to motivate the majority of the electorate toward acceptance of and insistence upon adoption of social and economic reforms of such magnitude that capitalism and the class system based upon it can be superseded by socialism. Togliatti is convinced that the majority in Italy will elect the Communists to power in due time, once it learns of the superiority of socialism and the even vaster social benefits of communism, as these evolve into reality in the Soviet Union. His Marxist training has convinced him that capitalism has reached its final and ultimate form of development in Italy and that further progress toward higher social and economic standards cannot be made without the leap into socialism. The transition from capitalism to socialism can be peaceful so long as the democratic Constitution is not truncated or subverted. The struggle for socialism is taking the form of popular defense of democracy and electoral pressure on the parties to enact the whole of the Constitution into law and policy.

Togliatti has not dwelt on the subject of whether a Communist majority would allow itself to be criticized freely once in power or whether it would consent to free elections and removal from power by a non-Communist majority should the electorate become disillusioned with Communist leadership. The presumption is that, based on experiences in other countries and the endorsement by Togliatti of the suppression in Hungary in 1956 of the popular uprising, the Italian Communist party would impose a dictatorship in order to retain public power should it meet with an electoral defeat. Once the Communists take power, any attempt to remove them would be interpreted as counterrevolutionary, whether this was done democratically and in accordance with the Constitution or not. Italian Communists would never vacate public power as the British Labor party did in 1951 on the strength of a parliamentary defeat. All the efforts by Italian Communists to legitimate their party and doctrine by virtue of their contributions to Italian democracy in the struggle against fascism cannot erase the fact that they do not accept the responsibilities that go with the democratic exercise of power. Communism seeks to exploit the privileges that flow from democracy and constitutionalism while it plays the role of critic of the elite in power. It is not willing to confer equal rights upon its opponents once it becomes the power elite. Wherever the Communists have taken power, they have ignored the restraints of Constitutions and democratic fair play. This latent authoritarianism of Italian communism has made it suspect and feared by the democratic parties.

The party program and its electoral promises are also concrete. There is not much difference between the concrete proposals of the Communists and those of the left-of-center parties. On the practical level of politics, communism is indistinguishable from social reformism. This bread-and-butter approach to existing social problems is designed to win popular consensus and votes and pave the way to power via democracy. The Communists seek to become identified with the majority, and their election campaigns and parliamentary record indicate how broad their social appeal has become. It is their contention that the masses prefer socialism to democracy and security to freedom.

The tremendous appeal of communism among Italians is due to various factors and circumstances. The criticism of existing society made by Communists is largely a valid one. The concrete proposals that have been made by the Communists are essentially sound. The democratic parties have played footsie with the conservatives and have discredited themselves as serious and dedicated popular elites. The Communists are a dedicated elite who are seriously bent on the goals that they preach. The Communists are known to be ruthless to their class enemies, and this gives many Italians hope that real changes will be made only through a Communist elite. Impoverished Italians and those who smart under other forms of social oppression because of their humble station and nonconformism to middle class standards would gladly exchange the freedom of elections and democratic constitutionalism for the tangible rewards of socialism: permanent employment; three meals a day; meat, sugar, and milk in the diet; decent housing; educational opportunity; entertainment; vacations and excursions; etc. To the growing millions who want higher living standards, security, and social equality, communism is attractive.

SELECTED READING

Croce, Benedetto. *My Philosophy and other Essays on the Moral Problems of Our Time.* London: George Allen & Unwin, Ltd., 1949.

Del Bo, Dino. *Italian Catholics in Crisis.* Milwaukee: Marquette University Press, 1957.

Freemantle, Anne (ed.). *The Papal Encyclicals in Their Historical Context.* New York: S. P. Putnam's Sons, Inc., 1956.

Mussolini, Benito. *The Doctrine of Fascism.* Florence: Vallecchi, 1936.

Partito Comunista Italiano. *Problems and Perspectives Before the Italian Working Class: Writings and Documents of the Italian Communist Party.* Rome: P.C.I., 1958.

22

Political Organizations

Political activity is conducted in Italy through three types of interrelated organizations: interest groups, parties, and mass organizations. The interest groups formulate social and economic demands in terms of specific legislation and policies and employ the parties to promote these. The parties attempt to secure election of their nominees to public office (legislative), while the mass organizations mobilize political consciousness among voters and potential voters on behalf of the parties and their interest groups. The interest groups, parties, and mass organizations are united by common ideologies and interlocking elites, so that they form unitary political movements. The ultimate objective of each political movement is to monopolize the power of government or, failing this, to share with other political movements in its exercise.

INTEREST GROUPS

The most important interest groups in Italy are either institutional, like the Catholic church, or economic, such as the numerous associations of landowners, farm operators, professional men, industrialists, investors, merchants, proprietors, pensioners, public employees, artisans, industrial workers, and farm laborers. Interest groups cannot operate effectively through independent lobbies directly upon individual legislators in Italy because legislative initiative is exercised collectively by the parliamentary parties, which in turn are directed and controlled by the external party elites who formulate party policies. The individual legislator is not an independent politician, responsible only to his constituents. He is the agent of his party, which nominates him, secures his election, and keeps him under constant and severe discipline. Because of this monopolization of political representation by centralized parties, the interest groups must press for their demands through the parties. By supplying the parties with financial resources and other services of incalculable benefit, the interest groups have obtained inclusion of their own agents within the party apparatus and a voice in party policies and selection of party nominees for public office.

The Italian interest groups make direct contributions to the parties and finance many of the public opinion media through which the voters are influenced. Most of the newspapers, magazines, books, pamphlets, leaflets, posters, etc., are printed at the expense of the interest groups, particularly among the center and Right-wing movements. Some interest groups, like the church, also finance and direct numerous mass organizations, through which large groups of people are mobilized for ideological and political indoctrination and molded into loyal party supporters.

The most potent and active single interest group in Italy is the Catholic church, which conducts political action directly through its clerical apparatus of archdioceses, dioceses, parishes, parochial schools, colleges, and universities; its numerous religious orders; and indirectly through its secular organ, Catholic Action. Catholic Action consists of laymen who work under the supervision of the Vatican Holy Office. Catholic Action operates through a number of subsidiaries, the politically most important of which is perhaps the National Civic Committee and its thousands of zonal and local civic committees, which carry on intense electioneering activities. Other subsidiaries of Catholic Action are the Christian Associations of Italian Workers; the Professional Unions of artists, teachers, jurists, physicians, etc.; the Christian Women's Associations; and the Italian Catholic Youth groups.

The ostensible purpose of these organizations is to promote Christian values among Italians and guide them morally away from sin, so that they will be able to receive holy salvation. The real purpose is to impart political indoctrination and guidance, so that the voters will cast their ballots only for candidates who enjoy the confidence of the church. Catholics who vote for the candidates of parties that are banned by the Vatican Holy Office commit mortal sin and are automatically excommunicated, while those who do not exercise their right and duty of suffrage are also acting sinfully. The clergy is instructed to deny all sacraments to Italians who do not vote for the sponsored party, which is presently the Christian Democracy.

The most influential employers' organization in Italy is the General Confederation of Italian Industry (Confindustria). It is a union of industrial producers' associations, which are industry-wide groupings of all major industries gathered together in a voluntary organization. Confindustria acts as national bargaining agent for its member associations and performs many other useful services for them and their individual members, such as public relations and information, and representation of general political interests. Confindustria subsidizes many media of public opinion and contributes funds to various parties, notably the Liberal, which acts as its spokesman in Parliament.

The Italian General Confederation of Commerce (Confcommercio) represents the numerous commercial associations nationally. Like Confindustria, it is politically oriented toward the Right. The agricultural producers are represented by such powerful interest groups as the General Confederation of Italian Agriculture (Confagricoltura), which is a union of agricultural associations representing the larger operators; the Confederation of Direct Cultivators, or small holders engaged in commercial farming; and the Federconsorzi, a semipublic group of marketing associations having public subsidies to finance the operations of its members, and now largely controlled by the direct cultivators' organization. While Confagricoltura is politically oriented toward the Right, the Confederation of Direct Cultivators is closely tied to the Christian Democracy, through which it wields tremendous influence over the government's agricultural policy.

Trade-Unions

Organized labor in Italy is badly split ideologically and organizationally into four major confederations and hundreds of independent company unions. The experiment with a unitary trade-union organization lasted only a few years after the war (until 1948), when the reconstructed General Confederation of Italian Labor was split by the defection of the Catholic, Democratic Socialist, and Republican trade-unionists. The division of the large confederation was the result of the political breakup of the anti-Fascist coalition in 1947 and the increasing bitterness between the newly established center coalition and the extreme Left, which resulted from the 1948 parliamentary elections and the attempted assassination of the Communist party leader Togliatti. The Catholic trade-unionists formed the Free General Confederation of Italian Workers (LCGIL), while the other two groups formed the Italian Federation of Labor (FIL). In 1950, these two labor organizations fused into the Italian Confederation of Workers' Unions (CISL), but immediately thereafter a dissident group of Republican and Democratic Socialist trade-unionists formed the Italian Union of Labor (UIL). The fourth national labor organization is the Italian Confederation of National Workers' Unions (CISNAL), which is affiliated with the neo-Fascist Italian Social Movement. Statistics on the membership of these confederations are not reliable; but the CGIL retains about 3,500,000 followers, CISL about 2,000,000, UIL some 300,000, and CISNAL less than 100,000.

The confederations consist of industry-wide federations, each of which has a national organization and provincial branches. Locally, several of the confederations unite unions of different categories into chambers of labor. The labor confederations perform many services for the parties. They conduct political indoctrination of their members and instruct them to vote for the party's candidates. They publish newspapers, magazines, pamphlets, books, and leaflets that follow the party line. They encourage their members to become active members of the party that they support and to spread their ideology among their families, relatives, and friends. In return, the labor unions expect the parties to promote their interests, some of them not only through political action in the legislature and Cabinet, but also through party pressures and influences upon employers. CISL leaders are able to use the influence of the Christian Democratic party and Catholic Action to obtain special contractual concessions from employers sometimes, while CGIL must fight for whatever concessions it receives from the employers. On the other hand, CISL is often prevented by party and interest-group pressures from engaging in strikes against certain employers. Italian workers do not remain affiliated with CGIL unions unless they are ideologically in support of the Communist and Socialist parties, since employers offer inducements for them to join company unions, or the more pliant unions.

MASS ORGANIZATIONS

Innumerable mass organizations have been fostered by the interest groups and parties to serve them as instruments for ideological penetration and indoctrination of voters and as a training ground and recruitment center for party membership. They try to develop an intense political awareness and sense of political responsibility among their members so that these persons will take an active part in party affairs. Persons who may be reluctant to join a party may join a mass organization. Some Catholic mass organizations are subsidiaries of Catholic Action, while others are affiliated with the Christian Democratic party. The Communist and Socialist parties maintain their own mass organizations under direction of the party elites. There are mass organizations for women, youth, students, sporting clubs, professional and vocational groups, veterans, former partisans, etc.

POLITICAL PARTIES

Several Italian political parties have developed mass memberships as a means to collect dues and contributions for party finances, to secure an army of volunteer party workers to campaign for the party, and to develop intense political interest and loyalties among the voters. Party members develop a strong sense of mission in the service of the party and use their personal influence to attract members of the family, relatives and friends, and associates to support the party candidates.

The mass party was originated by the Socialists as a means to awaken the workers and peasants from a condition of anarchic cynicism and lethargic fatalism and make them active supporters of the Socialist movement in its drive to gain control, through elections, of local, provincial, and national public offices. As a radical reform party that sought to carry out a social revolution through the assumption of governmental power, the Socialist party had to organize and coordinate the activities of party groups in the cities, towns, and villages. Mass membership of the common people in the party gave these a personal stake in the success of the party, a sense of responsibility and a feeling of idealism. It also produced a multitude of popular leaders for the Socialist party, which, until its organization spread out, was a sectarian party of essentially bourgeois and middle-class nonconformists.

The success of the Socialists was quickly registered in election results, particularly after the extension of the suffrage in 1912; and by 1919, the Socialists held one-third of the seats in the lower house of Parliament. When the Catholics formed the Italian Popular party in 1919, they copied the mass membership and centralized organizational structure of the Socialists. The Communists have perfected this to where, in 1960, they had some 1,800,000 members.

The bourgeois parties remain essentially cadre-type organizations of loosely associated political groups and coteries clustered about influential sponsors. They have improved their internal discipline somewhat; but they have no mass membership to perform political services and make contributions, and, so, must rely upon the services of the interest groups that back them. Without concentrated financial backing and support from public opinion media, these cadre parties would wither away. As things stand, they are unable to penetrate the minds of the mass of voters without the day-by-day efforts of thousands of party activists in constant contact with voters to interpret the party's ideology and program in the light of daily occurrences.

The Communist Party

The Italian Communist party (PCI) was founded in January 1921 by dissident Socialists who wished to affiliate with the Third International and adopt the Leninist methods for the total conquest of power and the creation of a workers' state (Figure 22–1). The party did not have the necessary freedom during the 1920's to spread its influence much beyond its original centers in northern Italy's industrial areas and in Naples. Small nuclei of party cells survived underground and managed to penetrate many Fascist labor syndicates, through which they were able to foment strikes against the regime during the war years, 1941–1943. Communists were influential in forming committees of national liberation (anti-Fascist

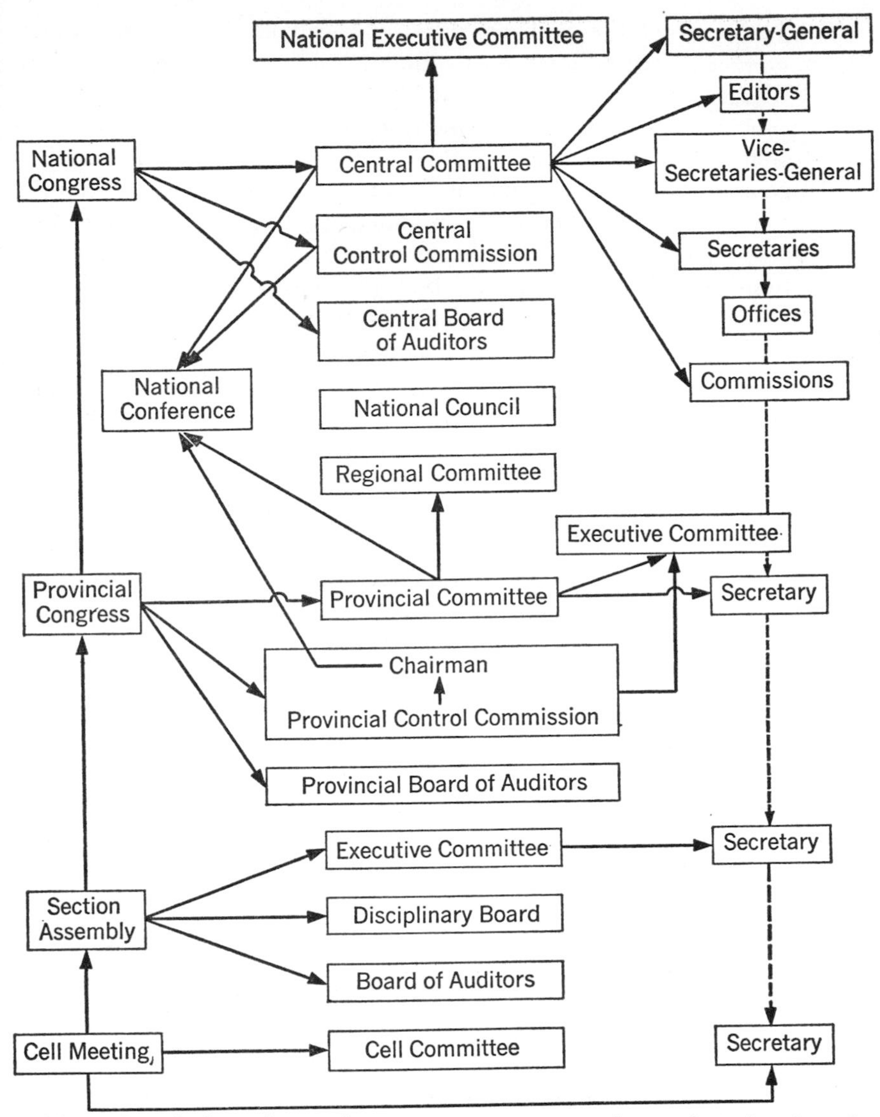

NOTE: Straight lines denote election or appointment and control. Broken lines denote direction and control only.

Figure 22–1. Organization of the Communist party.

coalitions) with the representatives of other parties, in securing official recognition of these committees as governmental organs in the occupied zones, and in receiving material assistance from the Allies to form the Volunteer Freedom Corps (CVL) under the direction of the northern (Milan) Committee of National Liberation.

The hard core of the CVL consisted of Garibaldini, who were Communist-oriented partisans, poised to establish a "people's democracy" in May 1945. The "northern wind," which promised a social revolution for Italy, was quickly dissipated when the Communists accepted Allied directives to demobilize the partisan bands, since they were not prepared to challenge the Allied forces in Italy as their Greek comrades had attempted without success in 1944. The Allied military occupation forced the Communists to abandon the revolutionary course of action in favor of a policy of democratic collaboration with the bourgeois parties designed to restore constitutional government and democracy to Italy.

The Italian Communist party pursued simultaneously the policies of the "united front from above" and the "united front from below." Through the former, it hoped to form an electoral bloc or union with the other working class and democratic middle-class parties, which would be able to win the elections and monopolize the power of government. The Communists intended to act as the political vanguard of this coalition, indicate the policies that it should follow, and have responsible administrative powers entrusted to members of their party. Through the policies of defascistization, confiscation of illicit profits, special taxes on capital assets, monetary reform, nationalizations, and expropriations of private property, which were adopted by the anti-Fascist government, the Communists sought to restaff the public administration, impoverish the bourgeoisie and strip it of its economic power, and place their own labor organizers in direct control, through the workers' councils in the factories, of the major industries. Once the economic and political power of the bourgeoisie had been broken, the Communists hoped to use their own organized mass power to force socialism upon the country through the gradual elimination of the private sectors of production and distribution.

To insure the political collaboration of the other anti-Fascist parties with the policies of "democratic reconstruction," the Communists pursued the "united front from below," which was essentially the unification of workers, peasants, and employees into a single labor confederation, and the diffusion of Marxian values among the masses through this and other mass organizations. Once these unitary mass organizations became identified with the interests of the masses, the collaborationist parties would be unable to split the coalition and isolate the Communists without losing the backing of the mass organizations. Unitary organization of the workers, peasants, and employees would constitute the source of power of the Communist party and would be used as a revolutionary instrument to keep the party in office without the cooperation of the other anti-Fascist parties, should these attempt to break their coalition at the top. By forcing the other anti-Fascist parties to cooperate with them, the Communists hoped to impress their will upon the coalition and gradually establish their hegemony within the government. This is the procedure that the Communists pursued successfully in eastern Europe.

The first setback for the Communists came in June 1946 with the election of the Constituent Assembly, where a bourgeois majority was returned, which gave the Catholics the balance of power and the right to assume the major positions of power in the government. The Christian Democrats took over the central bureaucracy and staffed it with conservative administrators and a depoliticized police corps. With the protection of the Allied powers, who were still technically in occupation until the ratification of the peace treaty in November, 1947, the Christian Democrats expelled the Communists and Socialists from the central government in May, 1947, and established single-party administration with the majority parliamentary backing of the bourgeois parties.

The parliamentary election of April, 1948, represented the second major defeat of the Communists, since this returned a Catholic majority and undermined the united front between Communists and Socialists. The fusion policy of the two working-class parties was disavowed by the Socialists, who began a slow process of self-reaffirmation as an independent working-class party. The Khrushchev revelations of early 1956 on the tyranny of Stalin, and the Soviet military intervention against the Hungarian workers later that year, split the Socialists politically from the Communists in Italy and isolated the Communist party, which was forced to defend the Soviet intervention. A number of influential Communist intellectuals and members of the party elite defected to the Socialists, which resulted in the loss of popular votes for the Communist candidates in the parliamentary elections of 1958 to the advantage of the Socialists.

Should the divided Socialist movement reunite, it might displace the Communists as the chief representative of the Italian working class; for the center of Communist popular strength is gradually passing from the working class to the poor peasantry. Italian Communist leaders have been cautious not to alienate the Socialists any further, since the Socialists might then form a bloc with the Catholics and compose a coalition working-class–middle-class government to democratize and socialize, under freedom, the social and economic structure of Italy.

The Socialist Parties

The Italian Socialists were split into two parties in January 1947: the Italian Socialist party (PSI), headed by Nenni, and the Italian Workers' Socialist party (PSLI), headed by Saragat. A subsequent merger (1950) between the PSLI and a splinter group from the PSI resulted in the formation of the Italian Democratic Socialist party (PSDI) (Figure 22–2).

The immediate cause for the division of the Socialists was ideological and political disagreement over the recently adopted (October, 1946)

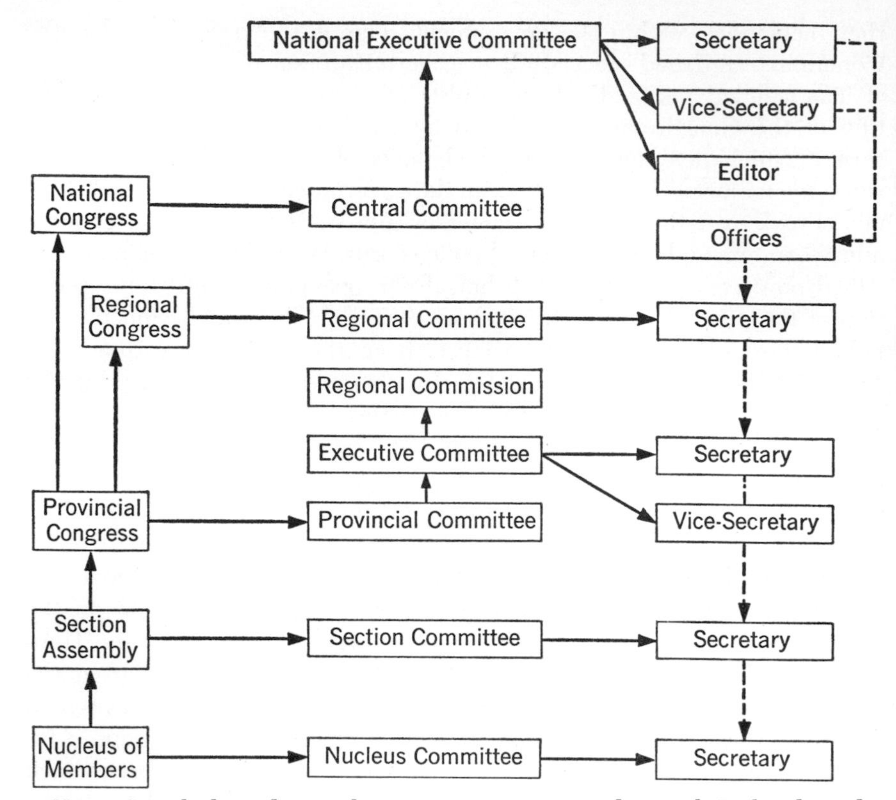

NOTE: Straight lines denote election or appointment and control. Broken lines denote direction and control only.

Figure 22–2. Organization of the Socialist party.

united action policy by the Italian Socialist party with the Communists and its proclaimed aim of fusion into a united workers' party. To the Democratic Socialists, a policy of fusion between Socialists and Communists would have resulted in the extinction of the Socialist movement and in the polarization of political influence between Communists and Catholics. If the Communists had proved to be successful in attracting the votes of the workers, poor peasants, and impoverished lower middle class to the symbol of a united working-class party, the result would have been dictatorship and the conversion of Italy into a Russian satellite. Should the Communists have failed, Italy would likely have fallen under a clerical dictatorship. In either case, there would have been no socialism and no democracy.

By forming a separate party, the Democratic Socialists hoped to instill among the Italian workers their faith in the primacy of democracy as a political value and build a "third force" that might hold the balance of power between the parties of the extreme Left and the center-Right parties. They believed that if such a "third force" could be fashioned, a progressive coalition of Democratic Socialists, Republicans, social-minded Liberals (Radicals), and Christian Democrats might gain and maintain democratic control over the government and adopt positive reform legislation that could mitigate, and eventually resolve, the problems of poverty, unemployment, and inequality.

Late in 1947, the Democratic Socialists joined with these other democratically oriented parties to form the quadripartite coalition in order to consolidate the democratic republic and initiate reforms that, it was hoped, would win back the consensus of the poor to the democratic experiment. Had they refused to join this coalition, it is possible that the Christian Democrats would have formed a conservative coalition, and that a democratic Constitution might never have been approved and promulgated.

The Italian Socialist party languished in the shadow of the Communists from 1947 until 1956, when it too, threw off the ideological yoke that had chained it to the futile and sterile role of junior partner to the Communist party. Khrushchev's startling revelations of the Stalinist dictatorship and the suppression of the workers' insurrection in Budapest in 1956 so shocked Nenni that he returned the Stalin peace prize that he had been awarded in 1952. The Italian Socialist party repudiated political dictatorship and praised Western parliamentary democracy and liberty under law in its 1957 and 1958 congresses. It invited the Democratic Socialists to join it in forming a new united Socialist party in order to put pressure on the Christian Democrats to form a coalition government pledged to implement the progressive social and economic provisions of the Constitution. It has refused steadfastly, however, to withdraw its trade-unionists from the CGIL, which is predominately Communist since the walkout in 1948 of the Catholics, Republicans, and Democratic Socialists. The Socialists believe that all workers should be united into one confederation in defense of their interests against the united power of the employers' confederation. Just as employers conduct their politics through several parties, the working class should have different parties to promote its general interests.

The Democratic Socialists were split by a walkout of several of their most important leaders in January 1959, which precipitated the resignation of the Fanfani government and the withdrawal of the PSDI from its entente with the Christian Democracy. The walkout was motivated by the conviction, which is widespread among Democratic Socialists, that the interests of the working class and the goal of socialism can be promoted best through a merger of the two Socialist parties. Continued opposition by Saragat to Socialist unity could result in the internal disintegration of the PSDI. The main obstacle to Socialist unity is centered about trade-union policy: can a united Socialist party support the trade-union activities of the CGIL, which remains Communist dominated, as well as those of UIL, which has Democratic Socialist and Republican sympathies?

A united Socialist party could possibly salvage the political initiative for the working class, which was lost in 1947, by offering its collaboration to the Christian Democrats on a program of accelerated social reforms and economic planning to heal Italy's structural deficiencies, chronic unemployment and underemployment, low consumption among the masses, and social unrest. Refusal by the Christian Democrats to collaborate with a united Socialist party could endanger the unity of the Christian Democracy or alienate much of its working-class following. The specter of Communist dictatorship could no longer be exploited by the church to divide the working class and exclude its political representatives from governmental power. Socialist unity would offer the lower classes of Italian society the first real opportunity to have their interests represented effectively at the policy-making level of the government since 1947.

The Christian Democracy

The Christian Democratic party (DC) was formed by the leaders of the old Popular party and persons active in Catholic Action during 1943 (Figure 22–3). De Gasperi was the acknowledged leader from the outset; and the old program of the Popular party was integrated with such new demands as land reform, nationalization of public services and sick industries, and promotion of cooperative institutions in industry and agriculture and commerce. The Christian Democrats supported the unity of the anti-Fascist coalition until they were able to secure approval of the Lateran agreements as constitutional norms with the votes in the Constituent Assembly of the Communists. Then, with assurances from the conservative parties in the Constituent Assembly that they would be supported, the Christian Democrats formed a single-party regime in June, 1947. This apparent collusion between the church and the reactionary interest groups forced the Democratic Socialists and Republicans to flank the Christian Democracy and the Liberals in a democratic coalition to implement a moderate program of limited reforms and promulgate the Constitution.

The Christian Democrats ended three years of collaboration with the leftists because they were fearful of the economic and political consequences of continued cooperation. The financial and economic policies of the tripartite coalition of Christian Democrats, Communists, and Socialists were precipitating an exodus of private capital from the country and hampering economic recovery. The capitalists had no confidence in the future, and the middle class was disquieted over the apparent conversion of the Christian Democracy to Marxian policies. The United States be-

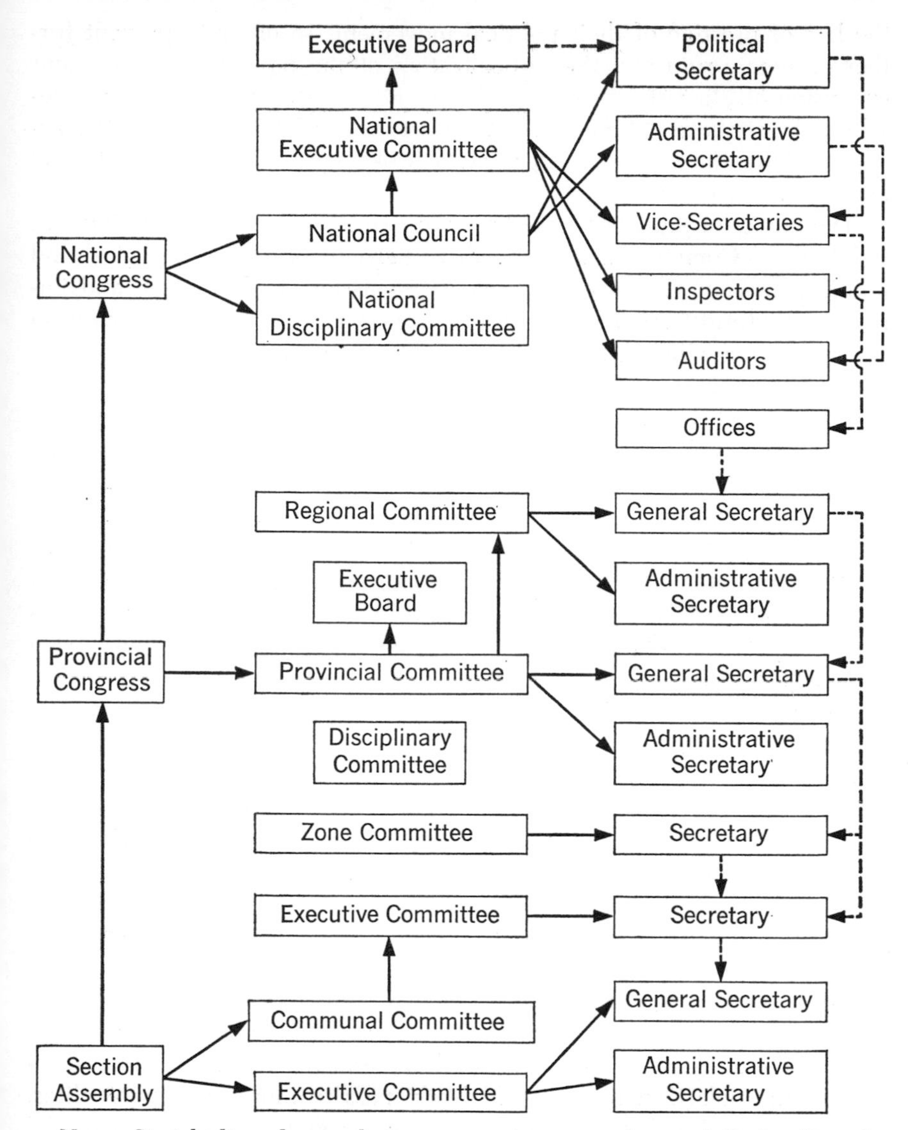

NOTE: Straight lines denote election or appointment and control. Broken lines denote direction and control only.

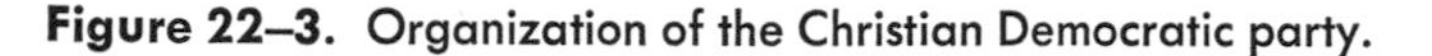

Figure 22–3. Organization of the Christian Democratic party.

came insistent, at this time, that the Marxists be removed from the government if Italy was to receive further economic assistance. In local elections, held late in 1946, the Christian Democrats had lost heavily to the Common Man movement; and the clerical authorities were disturbed at the loss of prestige of their political movement. In order to prevent further economic ruin and the radicalization of the poor, with consequent expansion of Marxist influence in the country, and to prevent the wholesale flight of the middle and upper classes toward the parties of the extreme Right, the Christian Democrats broke with the Communists and Socialists.

The tactics of the Christian Democracy since 1947 have been aimed at isolating the Communists and Socialists, perpetuating the ideological and political division of the workers and peasants and middle class, and impeding the formation of unitary social-class parties and their polarization into rival blocs. Christian Democratic power comes from the ability of the church to hold together disparate social and economic group interests and the flexibility that this provides the Christian Democracy in concluding alliances with other parties having common interest-group support. The Christian Democrats shift to the Left or to the Right to round out their parliamentary deficit and secure the necessary majority to perpetuate their hold over the government. By straddling the center of the political spectrum in substantial strength, the Christian Democrats have been able to block the formation of hostile combinations and dictate the terms of collaboration with their coalition partners. They have, in short, been able to monopolize the political initiative without a parliamentary majority by offering personal inducements to the leaders of the other parties in the form of ministerial appointments, a generous share of the patronage, the use of slush funds from government sources, and the inclusion of minor demands from these parties in the governmental program. Maintenance of this balance of forces has permitted the Christian Democracy to establish an enduring hegemony over the government of Italy.

The major problem that the Christian Democrats face in retaining democratic power in Italy is the maintenance of unity among their own competing factions and interest groups. Should either the trade-union group or the propertied interests that support the Christian Democracy defect, the party would lose its pivotal position. A realignment of parties on the basis of social-class interests would follow, and the initiative and leadership of the polarized blocs would likely pass to more aggressive elites. The Catholic church would doubtless be forced to take sides with the conservative bloc, as it did in 1923. Prospects for continued democracy and constitutional government would become dim.

Both the Right- and Left-wing parties in Italy are anticipating the disintegration of Christian Democratic unity and hoping that it will presage their rise to power. The church, however, is determined to keep the party together by using ideological pressures and religious sanctions on the voters to support the Christian Democrats in elections, since Catholic hegemony constitutes the only secure defense of Vatican interests in Italy.

Liberals, Republicans, and Radicals

The Liberal party was reconstituted around the venerable figure of the respected scholar Benedetto Croce in 1943 in order to participate in the anti-Fascist coalition, through which the Allies decided to govern occupied Italy in 1944 (Figure 22–4). Since the other parties of the coalition

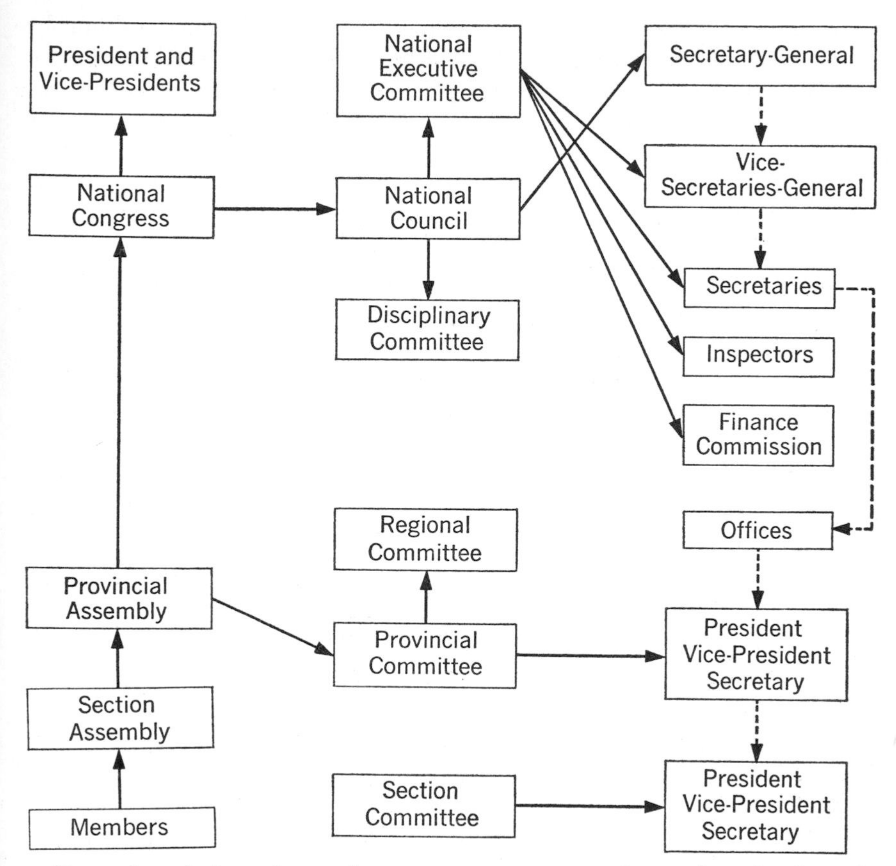

NOTE: Straight lines denote election or appointment and control. Broken lines denote direction and control only.

Figure 22–4. Organization of the Liberal party.

were considerably to the Left of the Liberals in their social and economic, as well as political, ideas, the Liberal party became the object of upper-class attention. It was the only effective vehicle by which the conservative economic interest groups could defend themselves from the reforming zeal of the anti-Fascist majority.

The Liberals operated within the coalition from 1944 to 1946 as a conservative brake, impeding the adoption of reform legislation by the Committee of National Liberation Government and delaying the election of a Constituent Assembly. Their only program was to preserve as much as possible of the status quo, such as the monarchy, the unitary state structure, the centralized system of administration, the sanctity of private property, the free enterprise system, etc. The Liberal party was oblivious to the aspirations of the masses for economic security and clung stubbornly to the most outmoded form of Manchesterian laissez faire. The younger Liberals, who had regarded Croce as the beacon of freedom during the two decades of Fascist rule, failed to induce a change in the conservative orientation of the party and walked out in 1946. Some entered the Republican party, which was more compatible with the liberal ideology; but after finding opportunism within its ranks, most of these eventually entered the Radical party in 1955.

Ever since the first postwar elections of June 1946, the Liberals have sought to rebuild their tarnished prestige among the middle class without any degree of success. Liberalism is a historically dead political movement in Italy, and efforts to breathe life back into it have failed miserably. The Liberal party remains the political spokesman of the Confindustria and other conservative interest groups; and, despite the enormous expenditures that these groups of Italian capitalism have made to popularize the party, it is hastening toward political oblivion. The values of liberalism have become the common possession of the Socialists and Catholics, as well as of the parties that continue the direct tradition of nineteenth-century liberalism. The Socialists and Catholics have succeeded in blending political liberalism with a certain amount of social and economic collectivism, which makes their ideologies and movements far more attractive to the common people.

The Liberal party has been willing to collaborate politically with the Christian Democrats since 1947, but its price for collaboration has been the limitation and postponement of much of the Catholic social reform program. The two parties are actually not too far distant in their economic thinking and seem to agree readily on matters of foreign policy. Tactically, the Liberals are adamantly opposed to the widening of the majority in Parliament to include the Socialists and have threatened to form a united front with the extreme Right to prevent any accentuation of social reformism by the Christian Democracy.

Efforts by the Republicans and Radicals to reconstruct a liberal political philosophy along more progressive lines, by emphasizing the need of the middle class for protection of its social and economic interests through the assumption by the state of more social services; the expansion of democratic self-government regionally, provincially, and locally; and the protection of the consumer by means of a vigorous policy of antimonopolism by the government, have not produced many votes for their own candidates in elections. The Republicans and Radicals have found it impossible to compete with the Social Democrats and Christian Democrats, or with the Socialists, for the lower middle-class vote. They have met with substantially the same limitations that destroyed the Action party in 1948: an overemphasis of anticlericalism and of intellectualism, and the absence of a clearly expounded mass ideology, so that neither the interest groups nor the electorate have confidence in them.

The Monarchists

A group of Monarchists formed the Italian Democratic party in 1943, which was excluded from the Committee of National Liberation. In 1946, it merged with other Monarchist groups to form the National Monarchist party but split in 1953 when the Popular Monarchist party was formed. Having recomposed their differences by 1959, they fused into the Italian Democratic party. After losing considerable representation in Parliament by defections, the party is faced once again with a rival in the form of the new Italian Monarchist party, which was formed in May 1960.

The Monarchists have no program beyond the restoration of the monarchy, the unitary state and the centralized administration, the proscription of the Communist party, regimentation of labor, and the substitution of landlord and employer's paternalism for the combative rights the lower classes enjoy from the democratic Constitution. The Monarchists are opposed to democracy and would like the government to derive its authority from an absolute monarch or dictator instead of from a majority of political representatives elected by universal suffrage. They would proscribe political parties, especially those that have popular support.

The tactical objective of the Monarchists has been to undermine the prestige of the Christian Democratic party among the middle class and, with the Liberals and neo-Fascists, to form a national block that would force the church to choose between joining a united front with the conservatives or with the Marxist parties as coalition partners. The Monarchists are confident that if they can succeed in undermining the middle-class voting base of the Christian Democracy and splitting the conservative interest groups away from it, the church will disown the Christian Democrats. The Monarchists have sought to discredit the Christian Democrats by propaganda against their reformism, which has been attacked as socialistic. They hope to break the centrist coalition, estrange the Christian Democrats from the parties of democratic reform, and hasten the polarization of Italian parties so that an authoritarian regime of the Right might be formed.

The Italian Social Movement

The Italian Social Movement (MSI) was formed by a small band of ex-Fascists in Rome in December, 1946 (Figure 22–5). The organization was extended throughout Italy and attracted sufficient votes to displace the Common Man movement as the party of the extreme Right in the 1948

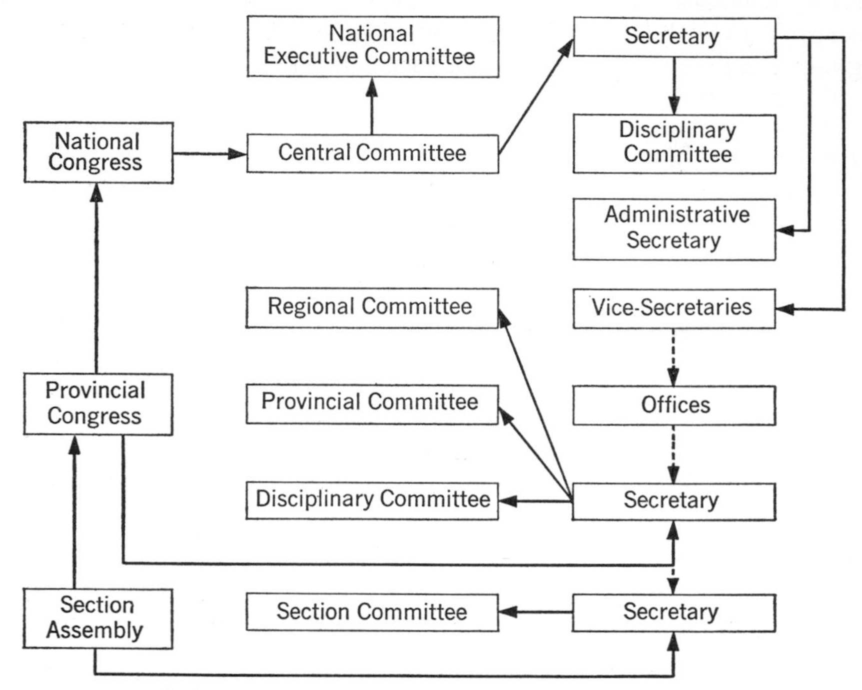

NOTE: Straight lines denote election or appointment and control. Broken lines denote direction and control only.

Figure 22–5. Organization of the Italian Social Movement.

elections. The ideology of the MSI is largely rhetorical nationalism and abominates democracy, freedom, and constitutional government as symptoms of anarchy. It would like to restore the centralized bureaucracy of the dictatorship, regiment the working class and peasantry, militarize the youth and children, restore the absolute power of employers and landlords, and pursue an imperialistic foreign policy. The first act of the MSI, should it come into power, would be to proscribe other parties and punish the Communists, Socialists, and former partisans for treason. Like the Monarchists, the MSI hopes to ride to power within a national bloc of reactionaries and conservatives to abolish the Constitution and liquidate democracy.

PARTY ORGANIZATION

Membership in most Italian parties is open to citizens of eighteen years of age. The Republicans limit membership to legal adults, while the MSI admits youths of fourteen. Requests for membership must generally be in writing, supported by one or two party members, and have the approval of the section or provincial committee. Members must pay dues, make contributions as fixed by the party, respect the party program, conform to internal discipline, and serve actively in party work.

Communist and Socialist members are grouped into cells and nuclei, respectively. These may be formed at the place of work or in the neighborhood of residence. Through these groups, the parties keep the members in close contact within vital centers of production, distribution, and public service, where they can spread propaganda among fellow employees, assume leadership of the shop committees, and direct strikes and seizures. They try to politicize and draw into the party, its mass organizations, or the CGIL those with whom they have personal contacts. The work of cell and nucleus members goes far beyond occasional electioneering.

The other parties group their members more casually into membership meetings called "section assemblies" by commune. Communist and Socialist section assemblies consist of delegates of the cells and nuclei. Meetings of the section assembly are held once a year in most Italian parties, although the Republicans and Democratic Socialists have four annual meetings and the Socialists meet monthly. To compensate for the absence of cells, the Christian Democrats require their members to work together by precinct under a precinct leader who is designated by the section committee. This activity is solely electioneering.

The work of the party section is performed by a committee, which is elected in most parties by the assembly, and by a secretary, who is generally elected by the committee, and in some parties by the assembly. The section organization is responsible for handling party propaganda and publicity locally, recruiting new members, proposing nominees for election to the communal council, controlling the actions of party representatives in the communal council and of the local administration in case the mayor is a party representative, and of directing the local units of affiliated mass organizations.

The section organization comes under the control and supervision of the provincial organization, which can depose the section officers, take over direction of the section through an agent or fiduciary, and convene the assembly for new elections of officers after providing for discipline of individual members, through suspension or expulsion. Centralized authority from above prevents any deviation of local sections from the policies of the party elite. If it becomes too coercive, the local sections may wither from lack of members. Should section membership prosper, the provincial organization may establish multiple sections within a commune. In this case, most parties require the formation of a coordinating committee by the section officers.

The provincial organizations, also known as federations, consist of a congress of delegates elected by the section assemblies; a committee elected usually by the congress; an executive committee or board; a disciplinary committee; and one or more secretaries, who are generally salaried officers, since their work is usually full time. Provincial congresses meet annually, biannually, or triannually to hear the reports of the provincial secretary and to elect new officers as well as delegates to the national congress. Occasionally, a spirited debate may take place at the provincial congresses in the process of electing delegates and instructing them. Delegates are elected by lists. In most parties, a form of proportional representation is employed; while a few use the majority system, which deprives the minority factions of representation in the national congress and on the provincial committees. A number of parties provide representation on the provincial committee to affiliated mass organizations and ex-officio membership to party officers and dignitaries holding public office as representatives of the party. The MSI follows the leadership principle by having the committees appointed by the secretary, who is omnipotent so long as he enjoys the confidence of the national secretary. Provincial committees, or their executive committees, nominate party candidates for election to provincial, regional, and national offices, although the consent of the central organization is usually required for the lists of nominees for parliamentary elections. The work of provincial committees is coordinated through a regional committee, which consists usually of the provincial secretaries meeting *ad hoc*. The secretary of the provincial organization is the link between the central apparatus of the party and the local sections and carries out higher directives, keeps the central apparatus informed of opinion at the base of the party, and maintains morale and discipline. He is the chief party officer below the central leadership, and his importance to the party is attested to by the prohibition in most parties against his holding any other responsibilities.

The central or national organization of Italian parties vests supreme authority in the national congress of delegates, most of whom are elected by the provincial congresses. In several parties, the representatives of affiliated organizations and party officers and public representatives or dignitaries enjoys status as delegates. The national congress meets annually, biannually, or quadrennially. The congress must approve the report of the party secretary, which is a defense of his policies and administration; vote changes in the party statutes and program; adopt directives on policy to bind the party leadership; and elect one or more of the central organs of the party. The delegates vote on motions, which are debated, sometimes acrimoniously. Decisions are generally reached by plurality; while election of officers is usually by lists, with some form of proportionality employed to give limited representation to minority lists. Some parties use the plurality list system, in which case the minority factions receive no representation in the national party organs.

All Italian parties have a central committee or national council that is elected entirely or in part by the national congress. This organ will meet normally once every two or three months to adopt general policy decisions to guide the executive committee and party secretary. It elects all or most of the members of the executive committee, and in several parties elects the party secretary. It has the power to censure and remove the party leadership, so that the central committee or national council is the supreme organ of the party. Most of the parties include on this organ numerous party officers and representatives in public office as well as national representatives of affiliated organizations, so that it has a tendency to become oligarchical. Where, as in the Communist party, the central committee is exclusively elective, oligarchical control is achieved by use of a single list compiled by the election committee of the national congress, and by co-option of new members to fill vacancies during the four-year intervals of the national congress.

The policy-making organ of Italian parties is the executive committee of the central committee or national council, although the Christian Democrats and Monarchists have a smaller executive board, consisting of the most influential members of the executive committee and the party secretary, which exercises this power. The executive committee or board issues directives to the parliamentary groups on important political decisions that arise in Parliament, such as confidence and censure motions, legislation, participation in coalitions, etc. The party executive may suspend or expel from the party any of its members in Parliament and bar him from further participation within the parliamentary party group. This deprives the member of Parliament of status on legislative commissions and the right to participate in debate on matters reserved to party groups. The party executive may order its representatives in the Cabinet to resign, on penalty of expulsion should they refuse, thus depriving ministers of all discretion in political questions.

The authoritative leader of most Italian parties is the secretary of the national executive committee. He directs the party secretariat and the commissions of the central committee. The secretariat is divided into numerous offices headed by a vice-secretary. Such matters as organization and administration, political studies, propaganda and information, finances, elections, international problems, trade-union and cooperative relations, welfare, and local government are administered through the offices of the secretariat. The editor of the official party newspaper and magazine generally enjoys such high status that he is responsible directly to the national executive committee or board, of which he is invariably a member ex officio.

SELECTED READING

EINAUDI, MARIO, *et al. Communism in Western Europe.* Notre Dame, Ind.: University of Notre Dame Press, 1951.

———. *Christian Democracy in France and Italy.* Notre Dame, Ind.: University of Notre Dame Press, 1952.

GRINDROD, MURIEL. *The Rebuilding of Italy: Politics and Economics, 1945–1955.* London: Royal Institute of International Affairs, 1955.

LA PALOMBARA, JOSEPH. *The Italian Labor Movement: Problems and Prospects.* Ithaca, N.Y.: Cornell University Press, 1957.

WEBSTER, RICHARD A. *The Cross and the Fasces: Christian Democracy and Fascism in Italy.* Stanford, Calif.: Stanford University Press, 1960.

23

Elections

VOTERS

The suffrage is regulated in Italy by constitutional and statutory law. Citizens over twenty-one may vote unless they have been legally disqualified for reasons of insanity, bankruptcy, police interdict (*ammonizione*), preventive detention, imprisonment, or deprivation of electoral rights by sentence of a penal court. Political disabilities that were once attached to former officers of the Fascist party and affected some 250,000 persons, barring them from voting or being candidates, were lifted in December, 1947, to permit these persons to participate in the April 1948 parliamentary elections. The sole exception to the universal application of the right to vote at age twenty-one is the constitutional requirement that twenty-five be the legal age for voters in elections of the Senate.

VOTING PROCEDURE

Permanent lists of voters are compiled by the communal authorities from the civil register once a year. The compilation is made by the electoral commission of the communal council, on which all political groups are represented proportionally. The lists are authenticated by an elections board that is appointed by the president of the Court of Appeal; its members include a magistrate, a civil servant, and three registered voters. The mayor prints the electoral roll and issues election certificates to the voters of the commune once a year. Persons whose names are omitted must petition the Court of Appeal to correct the election roll. Voters who change their legal domicile are registered in another commune.

All registered voters are assigned to a polling section, which includes from 100 to 800 voters. Special polling sections may be formed in hospitals; and military personnel, officials, and merchant seamen may vote outside their assigned section. Voters are allowed reductions of 70 per cent in railroad fares to return to their domicile to vote, and returning emigrants from foreign countries travel free on the state railways. Failure to vote must be explained to the mayor, who must note the omission in the civil register and on the citizen's certificate of conduct, unless the omission is legitimately excusable.

Polling sections are administered by an election committee consisting of a chairman, who is appointed by the president of the Court of Appeal; five members who are selected by the electoral commission of the communal council; and a secretary whom the chairman selects from the local staff of court or administrative clerks.

Ballots are printed by the Interior Ministry and distributed by the prefect to the electoral commission and thence to the election committees. Separate Australian short ballots are used for the election of each representative body. The names of the candidates are printed under the party symbol in the order in which they were filed. In districts having plurinominal representation, straight voting is done by marking the circle over the party list. In that case, the voter accepts the order of preference of the list, which is determined by the party. Voters may prefer to write the names of one or more preferential candidates or place preferential numbers after the names of favored candidates. In elections of the Chamber of Deputies, preferential voting is allowed only from one party list. Cross-list voting is permitted only for the election of communal councils in towns with less than 10,000 inhabitants.

Voting takes place from 6 A.M. to 10 P.M. on Sunday, the date being decreed by the President of the Republic for parliamentary elections, and by the prefect for provincial and communal elections. Each party having candidates may depute two poll watchers at each polling section and election office. The polling section makes a preliminary count; reports to the prefecture; and sends the ballots to the district election office, which consists of three judges (from the Tribunal or Court of Appeal). This office verifies the totals and assigns the seats to the successful candidates. Regional election offices formed of five appellate judges assign the plurinominal seats for the senatorial elections. The Court of Cassation acts as the national election office to assign the residual seats for the Chamber of Deputies.

CANDIDATES

Qualifications for elective offices vary. All candidates must be registered voters. For communal and provincial elections, the legal age for candidates is twenty-one. For the Chamber of Deputies, it is twenty-five; and for the Senate, forty. Candidates for election to the Chamber of Deputies may file in several constituencies; but senatorial candidates must reside in the region, although they are permitted to file in three uninominal districts of the region. There are many disqualifications. Candidates for election to Parliament must not hold the following positions: magistrate, regional representative, chairman of the provincial deputation, mayor of communes having over 20,000 inhabitants, public security officer, prefect and vice-prefect, general officer of the armed services within his command area, and administrative assistant of a minister. Such persons who resign 180 days before scheduled elections, or within 7 days following the proclamation of anticipated elections (in the event of early dissolution), are eligible.

FILING PROCEDURE

Candidates for election to the Chamber of Deputies file by party list through an agent of the party's national secretary before the district election office. Each list includes from three names to the number of seats in the plurinominal district. It must be sponsored by 500 voters from the district and is presented between the fifty-fifth and the forty-fifth days prior to the election. The prefect orders the printing of the lists after authentication by the district election office.

Candidates for the Senate file individually before the clerk of the Tribunal in one, two, or three separate uninominal districts of a region and indicate the names of other candidates in different districts of the same region with whom they wish to form a combination, which may include candidates of different parties. They require 300 signatures of registered voters from each election district. The applications are authenticated by the regional election office, and the prefect orders the names to be printed and posted.

ALLOCATION OF SEATS

In elections of the Chamber of Deputies, the district election office totals the votes of each list as well as the over-all total. The latter is then divided by the number of seats assigned by law to the district plus two, which produces the modified quotient. The modified quotient is then divided into the total of each party list; this is the number of seats the list receives. The residual votes as well as all unassigned seats are transferred to the national pool. The district election office computes the preferential votes on each list and assigns the seats won by the list to the candidates having the largest number of preferences. Parties that win at least one seat in a district and accumulate nationally a total of 300,000 votes are permitted to participate in the division of the unassigned seats in the national pool. This is done by totaling the residual votes of all eligible parties and dividing this by the number of unassigned seats to obtain the national quotient, then dividing the national residue of each party list by the national quotient. The candidates to whom these residual seats are assigned are those having the next preferential status on the District lists that have the highest percentage of residual votes. Should a deputy vacate his seat because of death, resignation, or expulsion, the vacated seat goes to the candidate from the same list and constituency with the next highest number of preferences.

In senatorial elections, the election office in the uninominal districts counts the ballots and proclaims the election of those candidates who receive over 65 per cent of the votes cast. Very few senators are elected from the uninominal districts, since it is rare for a party to have such a compact and overwhelming majority. Should there be no winning candidate (which is customary), the ballots are forwarded to the regional election office (Court of Appeal), where the computation of the regional totals of the combinations of candidates is made. Seats are assigned to the combinations having the highest average quotient (the d'Hondt system), after which the individual votes of the candidates are totaled by individual district, multiplied by 100, and this figure is divided by the number of registered voters in the district. The candidates who form successful combinations are then listed in order of the highest percentile vote and assigned the seats on the basis of preference. Thus, it is the candidate who wins the largest percentage of votes in one uninominal district, and not the greatest number of votes in one or several districts of the region, who receives the first seat that has been allotted to the combinations. The regional election office posts the names of the elected senators and notifies the secretary-general of the Senate.

LEGAL REGULATIONS AND PENALTIES

Election propaganda of a printed nature for public display may be posted only in such places as the commune has designated. Each party or candidate must be allowed equal space. Illuminated forms of propaganda may be used only by parties having candidates in the election. Political gatherings in public or in places open to the public must take place only after the campaign has been officially decreed by the competent authority (President or prefect). No political gatherings are permitted on the day prior to the election. No election propaganda may be displayed or speeches made, and groups may not form within 200 meters of any polling section on election day. Alcoholic beverages are not sold on election day. No gifts (food, clothing, money, etc.) may be offered to a voter so as to influence his vote during the seven days preceding an election. Efforts to bribe or intimidate a voter in any way for election purposes are punishable by imprisonment of from three to five years. Similar punishments are inflicted upon those who disturb an authorized election rally, deface election posters or announcements, or threaten or commit acts of violence within any polling section. Fraud and falsification of ballots are punishable by stiff penalties, as are double voting or voting by a legally disqualified person. Even negligence on the part of election officials is punishable by jail sentences of up to six months.

ELECTION CAMPAIGNING

The election campaign may not commence until after the date for the election has been decreed and the public rallies (*comizi*) have been authorized. Seventy days must transpire between the proclamation and the actual election date, which provides a reasonable campaign period. The party newspapers and other publications print the party manifestos, platforms, and speeches of the principal leaders; and the candidates tour their constituencies in order to speak directly to the voters, since brilliant oratory is a cherished political tradition in Italy. The radio and television, being a state monopoly, are not permitted to broadcast political propaganda or the speeches of the candidates, although in the news summaries the content of such speeches may be reviewed.

Party members are expected to work on behalf of the candidates in their constituencies under the direction of the local party section committee and secretary. Vehicles with loudspeakers are not allowed to tour about blaring propaganda; and posters may be displayed free of charge only on designated walls, provided they conform to specifications. No free postage is allowed for mailing newspapers or leaflets, and no gasoline or paper allowance is made as in other countries. No cash deposit is required of the candidates; and there is no legal limitation on the amount of money that may be contributed to or spent by political organizations, although a proposal of the late Senator Sturzo is before the Senate to impose such legal restrictions and regulations. Most campaign propaganda is negative criticism of other parties (mudslinging), yet it has the merit of arousing the voters to a certain pitch of enthusiasm. A few parties provide car service for the ill and infirm and hope that these people will support their ticket. The most effective campaigning is the public rally led by a topflight party leader and the less heralded personal canvassing of voters by volunteer party workers and the auxiliary groups and organizations.

PROPORTIONAL REPRESENTATION

The proportional system of representation is presently supported by all the Italian parties. It enables the minor parties to survive and condition the power of the dominant Christian Democratic party. Splinter parties that would have been swept away under a plurality system of voting hold the balance of power in Parliament. The Christian Democracy supports the system, despite the fact that a plurality form of voting would give it absolute control over both houses of Parliament, because it wishes to avoid the polarization of parliamentary representation around the two major parties: the Christian Democratic and Communist. The Christian Democrats prefer to govern in association with the splinter parties, so they cannot be accused of having dictatorial ambitions. The Communists favor proportional representation because it provides them with greater tactical mobility and enables them to survive as a legal party. Neither the Christian Democrats nor the Communists wish to face each other alone in a political struggle that could terminate only in the elimination of one or the other. The splinter parties make it possible for the Christian Democrats to govern democratically and for the Communists to operate as a democratic opposition. The result of proportional representation has been to perpetuate a multiparty political structure, within which the minor parties hold the balance of power, and enable the two major parties to respect the Constitution and the rules of democratic fair play.

A majority system of election for the Chamber of Deputies was voted into law in March, 1953, by the coalition of Christian Democrats, Social Democrats, Liberals, and Republicans, which, had it been successful, would have given the plurality party (the Christian Democracy) an absolute majority of seats. Under that law, the coalition that succeeded in accumulating a simple majority of popular votes nationally would have received two-thirds of all the seats, which, divided proportionally among the members of the coalition, would have given the Christian Democracy an absolute majority of the seats. The reaction of the electorate was negative; the coalition failed to win a popular majority and suffered a severe loss of popular votes, which forced it to revise the election law in the interest of democracy. The electorate showed far greater political wisdom than the parliamentary majority. Proportionalism was thereupon accentuated under the 1956 revision of the law on the election of the Chamber of Deputies.

A two-party system would be disastrous to the Constitution and to the operation of political democracy in Italy today, because the two major parties would not be able to operate the system democratically. Proportional representation provides a realistic defense of constitutional democracy through the constructive role that the minor parties perform as collaborators and as opponents of the Christian Democracy.

VOTING PATTERNS

The Italian electorate numbers about 33 million and increases annually at the rate of 400,000. Because of the compulsory and automatic character of voters' registration, which is performed by the commune once a year, very few qualified Italians are omitted from the electoral rolls. The ratio of active voters to the electorate is in excess of 90 per cent, which makes the Italians among the most highly politicized nations in the world. Mass voting is due largely to the obligatory suffrage law, but also to the activity of the parties, mass organizations, interest groups (particularly the church), etc., to "get out the vote" for their candidates.

Voting habits tend to become static in those areas that are not undergoing rapid economic development and social change, provided the electorate has reached a certain level of ideological preparation. The north has shown far more stability and consistency than the south in the pattern of voting. Since 1946, there have been a number of visible trends; the most significant of which has been the growing uniformity of voters' response between the north and the south. This indicates the increasing rate of political maturity among the southern electorate. The Communist vote has gradually spread out from the north to the south; from a limited working-class electorate, it has become the expression of an aroused peasant consciousness. The Christian Democracy has also affirmed its character as a national party by spreading its influence into the south. The traditional parties of conservatism, which once drew their power from the servile southern electorate, have been nearly eliminated from the rural areas and small towns of the south. A third trend has been the gradual resurgence of popular support for the Socialists, particularly in the north, which indicates a growing desire of the Italian electorate to develop a democratic two-party system.

The Christian Democracy is the plurality party in all but three of Italy's twenty regions. However, the backbone of Catholic electoral power lies in the rich agricultural belt of the north among the numerous small but independent farm operators. Christian Democratic majorities of over 70 per cent are common in many northern districts. Catholic strength is weakest in central Italy—above all in the regions of Emilia-Romagna and Toscana. In certain districts of this area, the Christian Democrats poll less than 25 per cent of the votes. A strong anticlerical tradition and the existence of a sizeable agricultural proletariat account for the weakness of Catholicism and the strength of communism in central Italy.

While the Communists are the second most important party nationally, they hold the position of primacy in the regions of Emilia-Romagna and Toscana, with an average plurality here of about 35 per cent. In some districts, they reach majorities of 60 per cent. They are being pressed strongly by the Socialists and Social Democrats in the industrial centers of northern and central Italy, however. The industrial proletariat is returning to the Socialist fold, particularly in the regions of Piemonte, Lombardia, and Liguria. Outside the industrialized urban centers, there is, as yet, little mass support of the Socialists, because of the absence in the south of a pre-Fascist Socialist tradition. The politically emancipated southern peasantry has entrusted its "protest vote" to the more articulate Communists, whose status of political pariahs corresponds to the socially pariah position of the southern peasantry.

Table 23–1. Results of Italian Elections, 1946–1958

Party	1946 (%)	1948 (%)	1953 (%)	1958 (%)
Christian Democracy	35.5	48.5	40.1	42.4
Communist	19.0	31.0 (Communist and Socialist)	22.7	22.7
Socialist	20.7 (Socialist and Social Democrat)		12.7	14.2
Social Democrat		7.1	4.5	4.5
Monarchist	2.8	2.8	6.9	4.8
Liberal	6.8	3.8	3.0	3.5
Neo-Fascist	–	2.0	5.9	4.8
Others	15.2	4.8	4.2	3.1

The conservative and reactionary parties that form the political Right (Liberals, Monarchists, and neo-Fascists) have been reduced to a limited following in the urban centers of the south and a scattered electorate in the northern cities. Their combined electorate is less than that of the Socialist party nationally, but in the south they total nearly 25 per cent of the popular vote. Of the three Right-wing groups, the neo-Fascists display the greatest consistency; while the Liberals and Monarchists have lost heavily to the Christian Democrats. The fact that the Right-wing parties find democratic competition politically unrewarding has soured their taste for democracy (Tables 23–1 and 23–2).

Table 23–2. Results of Parliamentary Elections, 1958

	Chamber of Deputies			Senate		
Party	Votes	Per Cent	Seats	Votes	Per Cent	Seats
Christian Democracy	12,521,000	42.4	273	10,781,000	41.2	123
Communist	6,705,000	22.7	140	5,701,000	21.8	59
Socialist	4,207,000	14.2	84	3,696,000	14.1	35
Social Democrat	1,345,000	4.5	22	1,164,000	4.4	5
Monarchist	1,437,000	4.8	25	1,285,000	5.0	7
Liberal	1,047,000	3.5	17	1,009,000	3.9	4
Neo-Fascist	1,408,000	4.8	24	1,150,000	4.4	8
Others	892,000	3.1	11	1,465,000	5.2	5

The minor parties exist because of regional and local peculiarities or as the expression of a diffused intellectual orientation. The Republicans retain small pockets of strength in central Italy only because of the century-old tradition that the followers of Mazzini enjoy in this region. Their electorate is passing to the Socialists, however. The regional parties of German and French-speaking Italians exhibit an indomitable will to survive as spokesmen of the principal ethnic minorities. In the Val d'Aosta, the autonomists represent the anticlerical majority; while in the Alto-Adige, the Sudtirol Volkspartei has split the Catholic vote over the issue of autonomy for the German language minority. The Radicals have a sprinkling of adherents in the urban centers formed of anticlerical intellectuals who are too nonconformist to vote for the ideology-bound Marxists and too progressive to support the Liberals. They have not been successful in the parliamentary elections, even in alliance with the Republicans. It is unlikely that the tiny Comunità party will survive the death of its founder Adriano Olivetti.

SELECTED READING

ADAMS, JOHN CLARKE, and BARILE, PAOLO. *The Government of Republican Italy*. Boston: Houghton Mifflin Co., 1961. Pp. 163–77.

EDELMAN, MAURY. "Causes for Fluctuations in Popular Support for the Italian Communist Party Since 1946," *Journal of Politics*, XX (August, 1958), 535–52.

MANGONE, GERARD. "Italy." In *European Political Systems*, Part IV, Taylor Cole (ed.). New York: Alfred A. Knopf (a division of Random House, Inc.), 1959.

PRYCE, ROY. *The Italian Local Elections of 1956*. New York: St. Martin's Press, Inc., 1958.

———. "The Italian General Election, 1958," *Parliamentary Affairs*, XI (Summer, 1958), 318–27.

24

Parliament

COMPOSITION

The Italian Parliament consists of the Chamber of Deputies (lower house) and the Senate (upper house). The number of deputies is fixed constitutionally in the ratio of 1 per each 80,000 inhabitants and final fraction over 40,000 inhabitants within the thirty constituencies other than the Val d'Aosta, which is entitled to one seat. Prior to each election, the Government decrees the number of seats that are to be assigned to each constituency on the basis of the latest population count. The number of deputies for the third legislature (elected in 1958) was 596.

The number of senators is also fixed constitutionally but combines elective, appointive, and ex officio methods of designation. By far the largest number of senators is elective (presently 246 out of 250). These elective senators represent the regions in the ratio of 1 per 200,000 inhabitants and final fraction over 100,000 inhabitants. However, no region may be assigned less than 6 senators, other than the Val d'Aosta, which is limited to 1 senator. There are 5 appointive senators, whose selection is made by the President of the Republic from persons who have made outstanding contributions to the nation in social, artistic, literary, and scientific work. These appointive senators hold permanent seats, which are refilled only when they resign, die, or disqualify themselves for continuation in office through some legal incompatibility. The ex-officio senators are former Presidents of Italy who accept designation and do not disqualify themselves. During the first legislative term (1948–1953), there were some 97 one-term senators who were appointed by right in accordance with transitional norm III of the Constitution, which sought to reward anti-Fascist legislators. Since 1953, the Senate has demanded a constitutional amendment to increase its membership so that its members will not be required to serve on more than one legislative commission and in order to increase the size of these commissions from the present figure of 22 or 23 to at least 27 or 28. Another motive behind senatorial insistence that the membership of the upper house be increased seems to be a desire to improve the ratio of senators to deputies in joint meetings of Parliament.

A Government bill, which was presented to the Senate on November 24, 1958, as a proposed constitutional amendment, would increase the number of elective senators by one-fourth the presently prescribed number based upon population for each election; double the number of appointive senators from 5 to 10; and confer upon ex-presidents of the Constituent Assembly and presidents of the Chamber of Deputies and Senate, who have served continuously for three years or more, the right of permanent membership. The proposal would restrict candidacy for the additional elective senatorial seats to former legislators of the National Consultative Council (1944–1946), the Constituent Assembly (1946–1948), and the houses of Parliament since 1948, and set up a system of preferences based first upon seniority as legislators since 1944; second, upon status, such as (1) presidents of the Council of Ministers, (2) ministers, (3) vice-presidents of the Chamber of Deputies or Senate, and (4) high commissioners, undersecretaries of state, chairmen of parliamentary groups and commissions, quaestors and secretaries of the houses of Parliament; and third, upon the highest number of individual votes (preferences) in the last elections. These candidates would be elected by national lists, whose votes would be computed from the totals of corresponding regional lists. Each national list would be assigned seats in proportion to the total regional vote of each—presumably the d'Hondt system, which is used regionally for senatorial elections.

MEMBERSHIP

Members of Parliament enjoy the rights of legislative office from the moment they are proclaimed elected by the appropriate election offices, while the rights of office of their predecessors terminate at the moment of proclamation of the newly elected members. This right of the individual member must be confirmed by the house to which he has been elected following its convocation by the President of the Republic, the election of its officers, and the appointment of a board of elections by the president of each house. The board of elections reviews the electoral reports of the electoral office in order to verify the eligibility, the filing procedure, and the counting of the ballots of candidates who are proclaimed elected to the house. It also receives complaints that are sent to the house by opponents or voters charging irregularities in the conduct of the newly elected members or of persons acting in their interest. The board of elections investigates the complaints, holds hearings, and permits the presentation of witnesses and documentary evidence. The plenary house debates its reports and votes confirmation of election or annulment. Once members have been confirmed, they are subject to expulsion only for legal incompatibility arising from personal disqualification as prescribed by law, such as the sentence of a penal court, which involves automatic alienation of voting rights, or acceptance of a position that is incompatible with legislative office. Expulsion is never a sanction for poor attendance or for parliamentary misconduct.

Members of Parliament cannot be forced to resign for political motives by their party. The custom among Italian parties of requiring candidates to sign undated letters of resignation that the party secretary may later date and address to the house is not binding upon the houses of Parliament. The board of elections conducts hearings in cases of "resignation" to ascertain the true motives of the member and will not be bound by any contractual agreement between a party member elected to Parliament and his party.

Members of Parliament receive a monthly stipend plus a daily allowance for attending sittings of the houses and their commissions. The per diem allowance is greater for members who do not have a permanent residence in Rome. Both payments are exempt from direct taxation. Members may ride the state railways free of charge, and they receive a number of free tickets for members of their families. There are no allowances for assistants and secretaries or franking privilege. Members of both houses may use the title of "honorable" even after they cease to hold legislative office.

IMMUNITIES

Members of Parliament are legally immune from liability for all opinions that they may express in either house and for the way they may vote. They enjoy immunity from arrest (except in cases of *flagrante delicto*) and from trial on criminal charges as well as from police search, seizure or confinement until the house of which they are members votes explicit authorization in favor of the police, and authorizes judicial proceedings against them. Parliamentary immunity does not extend to civil judgments or injunctions (*interdizioni*), although there is some controversy among Italian jurists over this point. Requests to proceed against a member of Parliament are sent by the Minister of Justice to the president of the house, who refers these to the board of examination (Chamber of Deputies) or the Justice Commission (Senate), where an inquiry is conducted, a report compiled for the house, and the matter debated and voted upon by a plenary setting. Parliamentary immunity is designed to protect members of the legislature from undue interference by the executive and is deemed essential to enforce the primacy of Parliament.

LEGISLATIVE TERMS

The Chamber of Deputies is elected for a term of five years, which may be shortened by anticipated dissolution decreed by the President at any time except the last six months of his term of office. The Senate is elected for a term of six years; but in 1953 and again in 1958, the Senate was dissolved simultaneously with the lower house after only five years. One of the proposals in the Government bill to reform the Senate includes a provision to reduce the normal length of the legislative term of the Senate to five years. The major argument behind this proposal is that all bills die in both houses whenever the legislative term expires in one house, so that staggered elections would interfere with the legislative process. Whether the constitutional amendment is adopted or not, there is a precedent to make the terms of both houses coincide by holding elections of both simultaneously.

The legislative term of the houses of Parliament is not broken by sessions but is continuous from initial convocation by the President of the Republic within twenty days following elections until dissolution by presidential decree. The term must end normally at the latest five years from the date of the preceding elections, since the parliamentary mandate of the members expires legally five years from proclamation of their election. However, the Constitution authorizes Parliament to extend the legislative term by law in time of war. The legislative term is interrupted by periodic adjournments for holidays and summer vacation, although the legislative commissions generally continue to function nevertheless during the periods of recess of the plenary sittings of the houses. The houses generally fix the date of reconvocation following recess in the motion of adjournment. The Constitution requires automatic convocation of the houses the first non-holiday of February and October. The houses may be convoked by decree of the President of the Republic at any time following deliberation of the Council of Ministers in order to permit the Government to introduce urgent bills to empower it to deal with a crisis. One-third of the members of either house may demand that the President of their house convoke the house; this demand may not be refused except when regular convocation is imminent. When the president of one house convokes its members, the other president is required to follow suit, since the two houses must assemble simultaneously and adjourn together.

ORGANIZATION OF PARLIAMENT

Officers

The two houses of Parliament are nearly identical in organization. The principal officers include a president, four vice-presidents, three quaestors, and four secretaries. At the initial meeting of the houses following an election, the provisional president of the Senate is the oldest senator, while the provisional president of the Chamber of Deputies is the ranking vice-president of the previous legislature; or should none of these be present, the oldest deputy presides. The six youngest senators act as provisional secretaries, while in the Chamber the six ranking secretaries from the previous legislature perform this function; or should these be absent, the youngest members assume the role.

The permanent president in both houses is elected by absolute majority on the first ballot, which must be secret. Should this be inconclusive, the second ballot, also secret, requires a vote between the top two candidates, with the plurality candidate being elected. Four vice-presidents, three quaesters and eight secretaries are elected by limited vote. Each member votes (by secret ballot) for two vice-presidents, two quaestors, and four secretaries; and the persons receiving the highest number of votes are elected to the positions in order of highest vote. Should the president be absent from a plenary sitting or from a meeting of the office of the presidency, the first vice-president takes the chair, and so on. The use of the limited vote permits members of the opposition to hold several vice-presidencies, quaestorates, and secretaryships.

These elected officers of each house of Parliament form the so-called offices of the presidency, which are the internal executive for the Chamber of Deputies and Senate, respectively. Each office of the presidency is directed by the president of the house; it supervises the work of the secretariat of each house. The office of the presidency approves the budget and the audit of accounts prepared by the quaestors for the internal administration of each house and submits these to the appropriate legislative commissions and to the plenary body of the house for authentication. It adopts the regulations respecting the status of personnel of the secretariat as well as the organization, powers, and functions of the secretariat. Once a week during sittings of the houses, each office of the presidency meets with the chairmen of the legislative commissions and the chairmen of the parliamentary groups to prepare the order of business (agenda) for the coming week. Members of the office of the presidency who accept appointment to the Government (i.e., ministerial appointment) forfeit their status as officers of the Chamber of Deputies or Senate.

The presidents of the Chamber and Senate recognize the right of members of the legislature to speak; they direct all discussion, maintain parliamentary order and enforce the rules of procedure, apply the disciplinary sanctions for infractions of the rules, put all motions to a vote, proclaim the results of a vote, and adjourn the sitting. They may call a member to order (admonition) for improper behavior; and if this is not heeded, the president of either house may order the member excluded from the remainder of the sitting. For more serious violations of parliamentary discipline, the president must have house confirmation of his ruling to exclude the member from the deliberations or from the premises of the house for periods of two to fifteen and two to eight days, respectively. Such exclusions result in the curtailment of the per diem allowance. In the event of a tumult, the president may suspend the sitting simply by rising from his chair. Should it continue, he may adjourn the sitting and order the house police to clear the hall. Should the house police be unable to cope with the situation, the president may call upon the national police to intervene to quell the disturbance. Unruly spectators may be expelled by the president; should they commit an outrage against the dignity of the house or its officers, members, or staff, they may be arrested by the house police and turned over to the judicial authorities for criminal indictment and trial by order of the president of the house.

The president of each house of Parliament appoints the secretary-general and his staff in accordance with the personnel regulations of the house. He appoints the members of the board of elections, the board on procedural rules, and the Library Commission. In the Chamber of Deputies, the president also appoints the members of the board of examination, which considers waivers of parliamentary immunities on requests of the Justice Ministry. The president of the Senate is acting President of the Republic whenever the incumbent is impeded from performing his duties. The president of the Chamber of Deputies convokes the two houses of Parliament in joint meeting for the normal and extraordinary election of the President of the Republic. Both legislative presidents are consulted by the President of the Republic before their respective houses are ordered dissolved. They represent their respective houses at state ceremonials.

The three quaestors of each house of Parliament manage the finances of the house (formulating the budget, keeping the accounts, and authorizing payment for services), provide for all the services of internal maintenance, direct the house police, and discharge all ceremonial functions within the house. They work under the direction of the president of the house. The secretaries are in charge of the records; they are responsible for recording the minutes of the plenary meetings and the deliberations of the office of the presidency; and they supervise the editing and publication of the stenographic reports, summaries, and other publications of the houses of Parliament. They compile the list of members who are scheduled to speak on bills, motions, interrogations, and interpellations; provide for the printing and distribution of these measures; read the *procès verbale,* the text of bills and motions and documents; call the roll on roll-call voting; and record the voting results and other deliberations. They too work under the direction of the president.

Parliamentary Boards and Commissions

The board of rules in both houses consists of ten members appointed by the president of the house, with the latter presiding. Its function is to propose amendments to the rules of procedure to the house, which may adopt them after debate by absolute majority. The boards of elections consist of twenty-one senators (Senate) and of thirty deputies (Chamber), respectively—the members being appointed by the presidents of the houses. (Their functions have already been described.) The Library Commission for the Senate is appointed by the president of that body and consists of three senators, while the corresponding Chamber of Deputies Commission consists of three deputies and two quaestors named by the president. The board of examination on requests for authorization to proceed judicially against a deputy consists of twenty-one members of the Chamber and is appointed by the president. Although there is no rule that the membership on these boards and commissions be proportional to the representation of the party groups, they generally include persons from various party groups. Members who are lax in the performance of their assignments may be dismissed by the president.

Parliamentary Groups

Members of Parliament form separate party groups in each house, provided they number no less than twenty in the lower house and ten or more in the upper house. Members of splinter party groups may be included in a larger party group with the consent of the latter, or they become included in the mixed group. A member may change his group affiliation but must notify the secretary-general. Four days after the initial meeting of the Chamber for the new legislative term (ten days in the Senate), the party groups are convoked by the president into separate organizational meetings to elect a chairman and one or more vice-chairmen and secretaries. The parliamentary party groups then designate their components to serve on the legislative commissions in the ratio of one for each commission per twenty component members and final fraction over ten in the Chamber of Deputies, and one for each commission per eleven component members in the Senate. The office of the presidency in each house assigns the residual members of each parliamentary group to a legislative commission. Deputies may belong to only one legislative commission. In the Senate, parliamentary groups that have only ten members must assign one to each of the eleven legislative commissions, so that an exception to the general rule of limiting membership to one legislative commission may be necessary. A member of Parliament who changes his parliamentary group affiliation will not be reassigned to another legislative commission until the revision of membership is made; in the Chamber of Deputies this is done annually after July 1, while in the Senate this is done biannually. This could leave the smaller parliamentary groups without any representation on one or more legislative commissions temporarily. Only assigned members of the legislative commissions have the right to vote in commission. The office of the presidency may allow a parliamentary group to designate a substitute to a legislative commission for a particular bill.

The chairmen of the parliamentary groups meet (generally once a week) with the office of the presidency and the chairmen of the legislative commissions (in the Senate this meeting is called "the council of the presidency") to arrange the order of business for the house. Parliamentary group chairmen are consulted by the President of the Republic following the resignation of the ministers in order to express their views on the appointment of a new President of the Council of Ministers. Ceremonial deputations from the houses of Parliament will include the chairmen of the parliamentary groups.

Beyond the requirement of the house rules of organization that each parliamentary group elect its chairman, two or more vice-chairmen, and secretaries, each parliamentary group is free to adopt its own internal rules of organization and procedure. The standard organization of the parliamentary group includes a general assembly of the members, which meets when summoned by the chairman or at the request of a certain number of the members. This body elects the executive committee and the chairman, vice-chairman, and secretaries, and determines the general policy of the group, such as support of or opposition to the Government on motions of confidence and censure, voting on bills and other important motions, designation of members to serve on legislative commissions and in the Government as ministers or undersecretaries or high commissioners, and initiation of legislation; it confirms the disciplinary measures applied by the executive committee. The executive committee acts as the group steering committee. It directs all participation by members of the group in debate within the house; it instructs them on how to vote on motions and bills and when they may submit an interrogation or interpellation, an amendment to a motion or bill, or introduce a motion. The individual member can do little without permission from the executive committee of his group in plenary meetings. His attendance in the house and in commission meetings is carefully recorded by the executive committee, since non-attendance is punishable by suspension from the group. Infraction of discipline is punishable by suspension; and if the external party executive organs concur, by expulsion. Members of the parliamentary group who are assigned to legislative commissions form separate study groups that prepare reports on the work of their commissions for the executive committee and general assembly. The executive committee appoints one of these to act as rapporteur of the study group. The party groups with large memberships have a disciplinary or control committee to supervise the conduct of the members and recommend disciplinary sanctions against them to the executive committee. The political secretary (or vice-secretary of the party acting in his stead) is a member ex officio of the executive committee of the parliamentary group, provided he is a member of the house. Coordination between the parliamentary groups of the two houses is accomplished by joint meetings of the executive committees or of the chairmen with the political secretary.

Legislative Commissions

Both houses of Parliament have eleven legislative commissions of almost identical competence and function. The membership of each commission is revised annually each July in the lower house and biannually in the Senate. Each commission elects a chairman, two vice-chairmen, and two secretaries; and for each bill that is referred to it for report or deliberation, it elects a majority rapporteur and one or more minority rapporteurs. It may also select a committee to participate in the debate before the house on the bill, which consists of nine in the Chamber and seven in the Senate, including the chairman and rapporteurs. The committee of discussants must represent the minority groups on the legislative commission. The commission may appoint subcommissions to deal with particular aspects of a complicated bill; these, too, must be proportional in representation of the party groups. Legislative commissions are convoked by their chairmen (the secretary-general notifies the members of their meetings) during periods of house adjournment as well as during plenary sessions. The quorum for senatorial legislative commissions is normally one-third of their membership, and only one-fourth in the Chamber. When these are authorized to act definitely in place of the plenary house on a bill by the president of the house, and without manifest opposition from a parliamentary group, one-fifth of the members of the commission or one-tenth of the members of the house, the quorum is an absolute majority. Meetings of the legislative commissions are never public. Ministers and other officers of the Government may be invited to meetings of the commissions. However, whenever these commissions act with deliberative powers, the presence of the affected minister or his representative is mandatory. Commissions may request the presentation of information, documents, and other data of any ministry or agency of the administration affecting their competence. A deputy who initiates a bill (private-member bill) has the right to attend the meetings of the commission (other than his own) that is considering it and may be designated to act as rapporteur by the commission. All bills that contain provisions that require appropriations or that propose an increase in taxes are referred to the Finance and Treasury Commission as well as to the commission having material competence over the matter. The former commission will inform the latter of its opinion concerning the financial provisions of the bill; the views of the Finance and Treasury Commission must be included in the report of the competent commission on the bill to the house. The budget estimates of each ministry are referred to the parliamentary legislative commissions having general competence over the affairs of the ministry in question as well as to the Finance and Treasury Commission. The latter acting through its chairman appoints nine of its members to sit together with the members of each of the other legislative commissions in the Chamber of Deputies when considering these budgetary estimates. Vice versa, each legislative commission having competence over a ministry may appoint (in the Chamber of Deputies) a committee of nine members to meet with the corresponding subcommission of the Finance and Treasury Commission in that commission's consideration of the general budgetary estimates of the Government. Differences between the Finance and Treasury Commission and the other legislative commissions over bills that are of common concern to both should be ironed out through such joint meetings between their components; but failing this, each house settles controversies between its commissions in plenary meeting. Legislative commissions normally are required to report on all bills that the legislative president refers to them within a period of two months (exclusive of holidays and recess adjournments). If a motion of urgency is adopted by the house following first reading (presentation) of the bill, the commission must make its report within one month. The president of the house may normally grant an extension of two additional months to a legislative commission in cases of complicated bills.

Commissions of Inquiry

Adoption by one or both houses of Parliament of a motion to investigate any problem results in the appointment of an *ad hoc* inquiry commission by the president of the house (or houses, in case a joint investigation is approved) on designation by the parliamentary groups in the same proportion as with legislative commissions. The inquiry commission has the same powers of investigation as the judicial authorities; it may summon witnesses, sequester evidence of any kind, require testimony under oath, and dispose of the police forces of the state. Officials are required to cooperate fully with parliamentary investigations. The purpose of such inquiries is to assist the houses in formulating legislation, to control the Government, and to determine whether impeachments of the President of the Republic and the ministers of the Government are warranted.

PARLIAMENTARY PROCEDURES

The order of business of each house is arranged by the office of the presidency with the chairmen of the parliamentary groups and legislative commissions (in the Senate this body is called the council of the presidency) on a weekly basis and announced to the house by its president. A motion to adopt must be presented and approved; if the Government disapproves of the agenda, it may attempt to have it amended before it is voted upon, using its parliamentary majority to obtain this. Once the order of business is adopted, a three-fourths majority of the members present is necessary to change it. After the order of business has been announced, members of the house may sign up to speak once for the allotted time (fifteen minutes) on any scheduled item before discussion begins on that item of business. Members who sign the debate roll are called upon alternately pro and contra in order of signature. Ministers, chairmen of legislative commissions, and rapporteurs who are directly involved in the matter under debate have the right to speak at any time and without limit as to the number of times on a single item.

The legal number (quorum) in either house for the consideration of the order of business or any item on it is an absolute majority. The legal number is presumed to exist by the president unless ten or more members request a count. Those members of the house who have been excused in advance for absence or who are carrying out an assignment are not counted as part of the total membership in determining the quorum. Seats that have been vacated by death, resignation, or expulsion and have yet to be filled by authentication and convalidation are also deducted from the total in calculating the legal number.

Voting may be conducted in four different ways. The simplest and most used method of voting is by having the affirmative rise and the negative remain seated. The least used method is the division, which must be requested by ten members and is performed by having the affirmative line up on one side of the room and the negative on the other. The roll-call vote must be requested by fifteen members, and the secret ballot requires the insistence of twenty members. Certain items of business must be voted upon in secret, such as all bills on final approval and the amendment of existing or adoption of new rules of procedure. Before any vote is taken, the president orders that a legal count be made of the number of members present. Those who wish to abstain are not included in the count. An affirmative vote requires one over half the members present and voting. The secret ballot is conducted by issuing two small balls (white and black) to each member who intends to vote and having these dropped into the corresponding urns (white and black). This provides a double count and prevents eavesdropping. Prior to the commencement of the voting, any member may request the right to declare his intention to vote for or against a bill. The Government may not couple a confidence motion to any final vote on a bill, since bills are approved always in secret; while confidence motions require a roll-call vote as do censure motions. In the event of a tie vote on any item of business, the status quo is retained. No proxy voting is allowed.

BILLS PROCEDURES

Bills may be initiated by the Government, any member of Parliament, a regional assembly or council, other organs of the state vested with this power (such as the National Economic and Labor Council), and by 50,-000 or more registered voters. Government bills are deliberated by the Council of Ministers and decreed by the President of the Republic with the countersignature of the minister who proposed the bill before they may be presented to the authorized house of Parliament. It is the responsibility of the Government to initiate bills to implement prescriptive norms of the Constitution, to fulfill treaty obligations, and to amend legislation that has been annuled in part by the Constitutional Court. The budgets of all central ministries and agencies of the state are presented by the Government as are the appropriation measures to cover these expenditures. Private-member bills that require any expenditures must indicate the means of financing these. Any bill having similar content to another bill that has been rejected by the house may not be initiated until at least six months after the rejection. Bills having the same general purpose of a measure that has been approved by the other house may not be initiated. If a similar bill is already before the other house, initiation is suspended for three months.

All bills are deposited with the president of the house. After printing and distribution to the members, the bill is placed on the order of the day by the office of the presidency and announced by number and title. The person initiating the bill may request permission to explain the purposes of the bill at a subsequent sitting. Normally, the bill is referred by the president to the appropriate legislative commission, unless the bill provides for public expenditures, in which case a date is set for initial consideration (first reading). The initiator of a bill may, upon announcement of its presentation, request that the legislative commission be instructed to report the bill urgently, which means that instead of the normal two-month period for commission study (exclusive of vacations), only one month will be allowed. All requests for urgent reports must be approved by the house (simple majority). A motion to omit reference of the bill to legislative commission and proceed to its immediate consideration may be presented following announcement; approval of such a motion requires a two-thirds majority.

Once the bill reaches the legislative commission there are four possible procedures by which it may be considered. The ordinary procedure, which is required for certain types of bills (constitutional measures, elections, authorizations to ratify treaties, delegations of legislative power, and budgetary and appropriation measures) and is used most commonly for other bills, is for the commission to designate a majority repporteur and one or more minority rapporteurs to prepare a report on the bill. The discussion is conducted more or less as it would be in plenary sittings; and after the presentation of the reports, the bill is read bit by bit and amendments are considered. Once the bill has been approved, the majority rapporteur revises his report so that it will provide a true interpretation of the views of the majority of the commission and illustrate the meaning of the bill as this has been adopted by the commission. Bills may be amended, revised, or redrafted entirely by the legislative commission. This commission version is illustrated in the reports of the rapporteurs and the committee of speakers representing the commission before the house plenary body. However, the basis for consideration is not the commission's bill, but the original version, unless the person who initiated it consents to the commission's version of the bill. The reports of the commission must be printed and distributed no less than one day before the bill is scheduled for discussion on the order of the day in the Chamber of Deputies and two days in the Senate. Prior to the opening of general discussion (or even after discussion has commenced), the house will accept an order of the day proposing that the bill be remanded to commission with instructions or postponed for deliberation. Discussion on the bill is postponed to debate the prejudicial or suspensive question (similar to the so-called previous question), which, if adopted, puts an end to further consideration of the bill for the time being. Other orders of the day proposing modifications in the general content of the bill are debated after general discussion has ended if the prejudicial or suspensive question is not previously adopted. In the general discussion of a bill, the rapporteurs read the majority and minority reports after the minister or member in charge of the bill has developed the purpose of the bill. Members who have signed the debate register may then speak in order (pro and contra) for fifteen minutes. Members of the legislative commission who are deputed to speak on the bill may ask for the floor at any time, along with the rapporteurs or person in charge of the bill (the initiator), with the latter having the final word. This constitutes first reading for most bills (other than bills that are first discussed after announcement, and then referred to the legislative commission, or that are discussed in principle—first reading—immediately and then scheduled for second reading without referral to the legislative commission—second reading constituting immediate consideration of the measure article by article). If the bill is approved on first reading, a date is set for consideration of the articles (second reading). Amendments may be proposed by any member at this point. Should an amendment to an article be adopted by the house (simple majority), the bill absorbs this change. This process of detailed consideration of the contents of the bill continues until the articles have been exhausted. Final reading is then scheduled. No amendments may be offered, and discussion is limited to a brief (five-minute) speech on the intention of the member to vote for or against. This is followed by final vote on the bill, which is always by secret ballot. The bill is certified by the president of the house and sent to the other house; or, if already passed by that house, it is sent to the President of the Republic for signature and promulgation.

The second procedure for consideration of bills is the abbreviated method, which is followed whenever the house has voted a motion of urgency in referring the bill to commission, which reduces the time for commission consideration to one month, or whenever the house has voted to omit referral of the bill to commission and to proceed to first reading followed by detailed consideration of the articles (second reading).

The third method is the decentralized procedure, by which bills are referred to legislative commission by the president with instructions to deliberate definitively on the measure without any necessity to report the bill to plenary sitting of the house. In such instances, the commission acts with the same degree of competence as the full house and must follow the same procedure as the house (three readings). After final passage, the bill is certified by the president as having passed the house. Final deliberation by the commission is not permitted should the Government, one-fifth of the members of the commission or one-tenth the members of the house demand that the bill be returned to the plenary house. In such instances, the commission may be required to follow the ordinary procedure, or the bill as completed in second reading will be referred by the commission for third reading before the plenary house.

The mixed method allows the legislative commission to proceed with consideration of the bill through second reading and requires final reading to be made by the plenary house.

The bill must pass the approval of both houses in identical language before it is ready for presidential promulgation. Should the house versions differ, the bill is shuttled back and forth until agreement is reached, without the benefit of conference committees. Such bills on return from the other house are placed upon the order of business and only the differences contained in the bill are debated, not the commonly agreed portions of the bill. If the bill is not approved by the end of the legislative term because of continued disagreements between the houses, it dies; and the entire process must recommence from initiation in the next legislature.

The President of the Republic participates in the legislative process to the extent of returning a bill that has passed the two houses with a motivated message containing his objections to its contents or to the circumstances and procedures under which it was adopted. This must be done within a month after his receipt of the measure, or sooner if stipulated by the houses as an urgent measure. The objections raised by the President are discussed in plenary sitting and voted upon, after which the bill must again be approved, with or without the changes recommended by the President. Upon its return the second time to the President, promulgation is mandatory.

FINANCIAL BILLS PROCEDURE

The two general finance measures that require the approval of Parliament are the budget estimates and the General Report on Expenditures, both of which are prepared by the Finance Minister and presented to the Chamber of Deputies in January or February. The budget estimates consist of the itemized projected financial needs of the central government for the coming financial year (which begins July 1) and the presumed amounts of available revenue, while the General Report on Expenditures is a detailed statement on spending by the central government during the financial year that ended the previous June 31.

Following general discussion of the budget estimates and preliminary approval (first reading), the contents of the estimates are distributed to the various legislative commissions having material competence over the work of the ministries and administrative agencies as well as to the Finance and Treasury Commission; and each ministry budget is considered as a separate appropriations bill. Having approved the estimates in principle, the houses cannot thereafter increase the total amount of funds that the Government has requested; they may reduce the estimates and change only the amount of funds to be earmarked in the various appropriations bills for individual ministries or services within a ministry or agency. There are no earmarked funds, so all financial needs must be appropriated annually, and those which remain unspent revert to the general Treasury fund. Since discussion on the estimates continues well beyond the beginning of the new financial year (July 1), the Government must secure approval by the houses of a provisional appropriations bill, which will authorize the ministries and agencies to draw funds from the Treasury on a monthly basis until the end of October.

Included in the estimates will be proposed increases in tax rates or new taxes altogether to cover the financial requirements of the budget. These will be approved in separate tax bills presented by the Finance Minister. The Government must also secure parliamentary authorization for permission to borrow funds or to increase the circulation of money. In order to assist the houses on the consideration of the budget estimates, the Treasury Minister is required to submit to both houses a detailed Report on the General Economic Conditions of the country no later than March of each year.

The General Report on Expenditures is scrutinized carefully by the Finance and Treasury Commissions of the houses and then discussed in plenary meeting in order to verify the proper expenditure of appropriated funds by the ministries. Expenditures that have been authorized by the Court of Accounts with reservations following insistence by the Council of Ministers must be authenticated by the houses.

CONSTITUTIONAL BILLS PROCEDURE

Changes in the Constitution and passage of fundamental or organic laws prescribed by the Constitution (such as regional charters and the statutes on the Constitutional Court, the Superior Council of the Judiciary, and the National Economic and Labor Council) require a special legislative procedure. Constitutional bills may be initiated by the Government, members of Parliament, regional assemblies or councils, the National Economic and Labor Council, and by 500,000 voters in the same manner as the ordinary legislative initiative. Consideration and passage of such bills must follow the ordinary procedure in both houses (not the abbreviated, the decentralized, or mixed procedures). After final passage by both houses, the bill is not sent to the President for promulgation, but is retained in both houses and, after an interval of no less than three months, placed on the order of business simultaneously in both houses for general reconsideration without the possibility for members to propose new amendments or dilatory motions (such as the prejudicial or suspensive questions). Passage of the bill by the two houses the second time requires an absolute majority. If the final vote (by secret ballot) should carry by two-thirds of the total membership of both houses, the constitutional norms are promulgated by the President—presumably within the thirty-day period required of ordinary legislation but apparently without the right to return the measure to the houses for another deliberation, since the measure has by this time already been deliberated twice. Should the bill on second passage be approved by an absolute majority but not the absolute two-thirds majority, a demand for referendum may be proposed within three months by one-fifth of the members of either house, five regional legislatures, or 500,000 voters. The President is required then to submit the proposed constitutional measure to popular verdict. No quorum of voters is required (as with referenda held on ordinary statutes or decree laws, where an absolute majority of the registered voters must participate and a simple majority must approve). A simple majority suffices to annul the constitutional measure by referendum.

INTERROGATIONS AND INTERPELLATIONS

Interrogations are questions addressed in writing by members of either house of Parliament to a minister seeking information about a matter that is under the minister's administrative competence. They are deposited with the president of the house, who reads them to the house and places them on the order of the day after the interval of the next meeting. Interrogations are considered as the first item of business at each meeting of the house; the Chamber of Deputies allows a maximum of forty minutes and no more than ten questions per meeting, while the Senate permits a full hour. Only interrogations for which a verbal reply is specified will be answered orally by the minister, and these only if the interrogator is present. Other questions are answered by letter. The interrogator is permitted to reply orally to the minister for no more than five minutes to indicate whether he is satisfied or not with the information provided. No supplemental questions are allowed, and a limit of two written questions per meeting for any member is enforced. Questions that are unanswered are dealt with at the next meeting.

Interpellations are questions about the reasons or purposes for any particular action by a ministry or its officials or about the intentions of the Government's policy in a given matter. They seek an explanation of what the Government is doing and why it is going about this in a specific manner. Interpellations are generally embarassing to the ministers, but they increase executive responsibility over the administration and seek to make the actions of the Government coincide with the delegations of power and authorizations of policy granted by Parliament. They constitute a most important instrument of representative control over the bureaucracy.

If the Government makes no announcement within three days of presentation of an interpellation that it wishes to postpone its consideration until a specific future date, the interpellation is placed on the next order of the day for such matters, which is generally Monday. Interpellations concerning similar matters may be lumped together by the house for a single reply by the minister. Each interpellator may reply for five minutes to indicate satisfaction or dissatisfaction with the response of the minister; and, if displeased, he may present a motion for consideration by the house to require specific actions of the minister or Government, or to censure these. This privilege is available to any member. The house must fix a date for discussion of the motion. A motion of censure against the Government (which requires its resignation if approved by either house) must be supported by at least one-tenth of the membership of the house (either Chamber or Senate) and may not be discussed until three days after presentation. Motions that do not propose censure and that do not relate to a reply to an interpellation may be proposed at any time, but they require the support of at least eight senators or ten deputies. Confidence motions are presented by the Government. All motions are discussed in plenary meeting under rules of debate like those used for bills. Confidence and censure motions may not be side-tracked by orders of the day such as a proposal to suspend discussion or remand consideration. Members who wish to participate in the discussion must sign the register, and arguments are heard alternately pro and contra and limited to fifteen minutes each. Passage of all motions is by simple majority, but confidence and censure motions require a roll-call vote.

LEGISLATIVE DELEGATIONS AND AUTHORIZATIONS

Parliament may delegate legislative competence over any matter, subject to statutory regulation, to the Government (Council of Ministers), provided the act of delegation prescribes the purposes and the principles to guide the Government and sets a time limit during which this competence shall be exercised. These legislative decrees have the same legal effect as statutes. Parliament has the power to annul such legislative decrees if they should be contrary to the purposes of the delegation, but the Government is not required to deposit such measures automatically with the houses as in the case of statutory instruments in Great Britain. However, all laws and norms having the force of law (i.e., statutes and decrees) in Italy are subject to judicial control and annulment, while in Great Britain they may not be impugned by the courts. In the event of extraordinary circumstances or crisis (war, rebellion, or other calamity), the Government is empowered by the Constitution to issue provisional decree laws without previous parliamentary delegation; but these must be submitted immediately (the same day if Parliament is assembled) to the houses for conversion into statutory law under prescribed procedures. If Parliament is not assembled, the Government must deliberate the immediate convocation of both houses. In this instance, the houses are required to assemble in five days to review the decree legislation. All decree laws of provisional character lose their validity after sixty days unless they are converted into statutes.

In the event of war (a condition that is deliberated and voted upon by Parliament), the houses may delegate to the Government rather far-reaching legislative powers with the necessity of making minute regulations of the conditions under which this legislative decree power may be exercised. The war-making power is contained in a separate article (Article 78) of the Constitution and implies the right of Parliament to confer "full powers" upon the Government to legislate with complete discretion independently of Parliament, so long as the delegation is not revoked or the legislative decrees adopted are not annuled by the Constitutional Court.

Several executive acts require prior legislative authorization under the Italian Constitution, such as the signature (by the plenipotentiary) and ratification (by the President) of international agreements of political content (alliances or membership in international collective security organizations), which provide for arbitration or adjudication of international disputes, which effect diminutions or additions to the national territory, which impose financial obligations upon the state, or which result in changes of internal law either through self-executing provisions or through the legal obligation to enact internal legislative changes; and the granting by the President of the Republic of amnesties and collective commutations (*indulto*). These authorizations are adopted in identical fashion as bills, even though they are not laws, but merely a means of legislative control over the exercise by the executive of constitutionally conferred powers.

PARLIAMENTARY FUNCTIONS AND POWERS

Parliament's functions consist of constitutive, legislative, control, investigative, judicial, and electoral powers that are explicitly enumerated in the Constitution or implied from the enumerated powers.

The constitutive power is carefully described by the Constitution in its scope and in the procedures that are to be followed by Parliament in its exercise. Any portion of the Constitution is subject to amendment except the republican form of the state. The amending power to change the text of the Constitution and the prescriptive power to implement the Constitution through the adoption of constitutional legislation are vested in the houses of Parliament.

Parliament's legislative powers are not enumerated in the material sense, as in the case of certain federal constitutions like the American, for example. The legislative power (*plenitudo potestas*) is simply vested in the houses of Parliament and has no material limitation except where the Constitution expressly establishes a right or freedom for individuals and a law-making capacity for other organs of state, such as the regional legislatures acting within their constitutionally delegated autonomous legislative competence. Parliament is permitted to delegate partial exercise of this legislative power to other organs of the state within such limits as it may by statute prescribe. There is no need, therefore, for the Italian Parliament to search for an inherent or even an implied power to legislate on any given matter, since the material scope of its legislative competence is total and absolute so long as it does not violate any constitutional norms (those creating substantive rights and legal competences, or those prescribing the content of future legislation, and those establishing principles of guidance). To insure parliamentary respect for those constitutional norms that impose material restraints upon Parliament's legislative power is the duty primarily of the Constitutional Court, and secondarily of the President of the Republic acting through his suspensive veto. Ultimate assurance is provided by the Constitution through the referendum power, by which the electorate is empowered to annul ordinary laws (except taxes and appropriations, and parliamentary authorizations to the executive organs to sign and ratify treaties and to grant amnesties and collective commutations) or delegated norms having the force of law.

The referendum may be invoked by 500,000 voters through the signature of a referendum petition or by five regional legislatures through the passage of an identical resolution proposing popular annulment of an existing law. A majority of the registered voters (nationally) must participate in the referendum, which must be approved by a majority of the valid votes cast. Until action to annul parliamentary legislation of doubtful constitutionality can be concluded, it is the right and duty of the regular courts (civil and criminal) to refuse to enforce the provisions of any law or act having the effect of law that the judge (or judges) may regard as unconstitutional.

Parliament's control powers consist of the authority of either house to refuse confidence to the Council of Ministers or to censure it, thus forcing its immediate resignation; the power to adopt motions ordering a minister or the Council of Ministers to correct an abuse or to perform an action that the house may order, which is required by law; the requirement that all expenditures made by the executive and its administration from the public treasury be both preauthorized and postauthenticated by both houses; and the requirement that all discretionary acts of the executive not authorized by law be subjected to prior authorization by Parliament before these acquire validity.

The investigative power of Parliament is exercised individually by the houses and consists of the right of either house or of its commissions (legislative or special) to summon witnesses on penalty of arrest if necessary, to demand testimony, to search any premise, and sequester any evidence that may be relevant to the purposes of the investigation. No matter is beyond the investigative power of the houses; but the methods employed must be sanctioned by the laws and be compatible with the constitutional guarantees, which means that parliamentary investigations cannot employ coercive measures that are denied to the courts. Another aspect of the investigative power of the houses is the practice of interrogation and interpellation, by which information and the motives behind executive policy and administrative actions are forced from the Government, given publicity, and corrected by means of the control powers of Parliament.

Parliament's judicial power consists of its capacity to vote charges of indictment, in joint sitting of the houses, against the President of the Republic for acts of high treason and conspiracy against the Constitution and against the President of the Council of Ministers and the ministers for any crime that they might have committed while exercising their powers or performing their functions. The indictment results in automatic suspension from office and in the preventive detention of the individual or individuals by the judicial police until trial is held before the Constitutional Court with the participation of sixteen laymen elected jointly by the houses from among citizens having eligibility to be candidates for senatorial election.

The electoral powers of Parliament are numerous. The President of the Republic is elected in joint sitting of the houses of Parliament with the participation of three delegates (proportionally elected) from the regional legislatures (except for the Val d'Aosta, which deputes only one). The President of the Council of Ministers and the ministers, undersecretaries of state, and high commissioners who form the Government require confirmation (which is granted by a vote of confidence) from both houses following their appointment by the President of the Republic. One-third of the judges of the Constitutional Court are elected by the houses of Parliament in joint sitting as are one-third of the members of the Superior Council of the Judiciary.

SELECTED READING

ADAMS, JOHN CLARKE, and BARILE, PAOLO. *The Government of Republican Italy.* Boston: Houghton Mifflin Co., 1961. Pp. 59–73.

———. "The Implementation of the Italian Constitution," *American Political Science Review,* XLVII (March, 1953), 61–83.

MANGONE, GERARD. "Italy." In *European Political Systems,* Part IV, Taylor Cole (ed.). New York: Alfred A. Knopf (a division of Random House, Inc.), 1959.

PRYCE, ROY. "Parliamentary Government in Italy Today," *Parliamentary Affairs,* VIII (Spring, 1955), 183–91.

25

The Executive

THE PRESIDENT OF THE REPUBLIC

Election and Term

The qualifications for election to the Presidency of the Republic are constitutionally prescribed. Any Italian citizen aged fifty or more and having full civic and political rights (including women) is eligible. The newly elected President automatically forfeits any public office or position and must resign any privately held position upon taking the oath of office in the presence of the members of the houses of Parliament meeting together.

Election of the President is held normally on the thirtieth day prior to the end of the incumbent's term, which commences on the day he takes the oath of office and terminates seven years later. It is the duty of the president of the Chamber of Deputies to convoke the Electoral College, consisting of the members of the houses of Parliament and three delegates from each regional council (except for the Val d'Aosta, which sends one delegate) elected proportionally by those bodies, on the constitutionally prescribed day. However, should the term of the incumbent terminate prior to the normal date of expiration because of death, resignation, removal from office on conviction of high treason or conspiracy to overthrow the Constitution, or declaration of his permanent incapacitation to hold office by either the Government or the houses of Parliament, it is the duty of the president of the Chamber of Deputies to convoke the Electoral College within fifteen days after the incumbent has vacated the office. Should either house of Parliament be dissolved and awaiting elections or lack three months or less from normal expiration of its term, the president of the Chamber of Deputies is to convoke the Electoral College within the first fifteen days following parliamentary elections. In such an instance, the term of office of the incumbent President is automatically extended until his successor takes the oath of office. Should the president of the Senate be acting President of the Republic under such circumstances, he would merely continue as such until after election and administering of the oath of office to the newly elected President.

The president of the Chamber of Deputies presides over the Electoral College. No nominations are made and no discussion concerning candidates is allowed. The members of the Electoral College cast a single secret ballot on which they write the name of a qualified person. A majority of two-thirds the membership of the Electoral College is required for election on the first three ballots, after which an absolute majority suffices. There is no limit to the number of terms, each of seven years, that the President may be re-elected to serve.

Immunities and Privileges

There is considerable controversy as to whether the President enjoys personal immunities from the jurisdiction of the ordinary courts for civil and penal liability. The Constitution omits any reference to presidential liability for personal acts that are unconnected with the functions of his office. The presumption is, from strict logic, that the President remains personally liable to arrest, prosecution, and civil suit under the Penal and Civil Codes, even though this may be highly embarrassing politically. No parliamentary authorization is necessary for judicial arrest, indictment, prosecution, and sentencing of the President for crimes that he may commit in his personal behavior.

The President is immune from civil and penal responsibility for all official acts (i.e., acts that are countersigned by a minister), unless these acts should result in such constitutionally proscribed crimes as high treason or attempted overthrow of the Constitution. Charges against the President for high treason and attempted overthrow of the Constitution are made by an absolute majority of the members of Parliament in joint meeting; and trial is before the Constitutional Court, with the participation of the sixteen supplemental judges of parliamentary designation in addition to the regular bench of fifteen judges. With these two exceptions, the President is legally irresponsible for his official acts. Responsibility is assumed by the President of the Council of Ministers or by a minister, or both, who are required to countersign all official acts of the President before these become legally valid.

The President is also politically irresponsible for his official acts because of the constitutional requirement for ministerial countersignature of presidential acts. Not only do the ministers countersign presidential acts whose content is deliberated by the Council of Ministers or proposed by them individually; but they also are required to sign acts of presidential discretion, such as appointment of judges to the Constitutional Court, granting of pardons and commutations to individuals, return of bills to Parliament for reconsideration, appointment of the President of the Council of Ministers following resignation of the incumbent, dissolution of the houses of Parliament, and appointment of senators. In the latter instance, ministerial countersignature serves as an attestation of the legality and propriety of the presidential action. In the former instance (where the President merely signs measures deliberated by the Council of Ministers or proposed by a minister), the ministerial countersignature indicates who has exercised discretion in the matter; while the President's signature serves as legal attestation of the legality and propriety of the measure. Not only the Constitution (Articles 89, 90, 95), but also the Penal Code (Article 279) divests the President of political responsibility for acts of the Government; the latter provision makes it a delict punishable by as much as a year in prison and 80,000 lire fine to impute political responsibility for Governmental acts to the President or criticize him publicly for the policies of the Government. The President enjoys special protection under the Penal Code, which provides severe penalties for those who threaten, assault, injure, offend, insult, restrain, or interfere in any way with the President.

Despite these apparent immunities from political responsibility, the President is politically subject to Parliament, which can vote charges of permanent impediment or disability against him (by absolute majority in joint meeting) for moral and political misconduct unbefitting his office. The members of Parliament, who form the overwhelming majority of the Electoral College, can also refuse to re-elect the incumbent President as a sign of displeasure against his political conduct.

Emoluments

The President of the Republic receives a tax-free salary and an allowance, both of which are fixed by statute. He has an official residence (the Quirinale) and other state-owned properties at his personal disposal, as well as unlimited use of all state services (post, telegraph, railroad, military, and naval conveyances) for official purposes. He may appoint a personal staff of advisers, assistants, aides, and employees to enable him to perform his duties and to administer his affairs. The staff is headed by a secretary general and is referred to as the presidential secretariat. The President may draw upon the public administration (civil, diplomatic, military) for his staff appointments or from the state universities, but not from the ranks of members of Parliament, unless these resign their representative status.

Functions and Powers

As chief of state, the President of the Republic coordinates the functions of the principal organs of government in Italy and insures the proper and effective exercise of authority and discharge of competence by these organs. He enjoys some measure of control over Parliament; the Government; the regular courts; the administration; and the regional, provincial, and communal organs of government. He may return bills to the houses with a message to reconsider, in which he may make legislative recommendations. He may order the dissolution of the houses of Parliament whenever these no longer appear to be politically responsible to the electorate and order elections to be held whenever he feels these would be most opportune (except during the last six months of his term of office), subject to ministerial countersignature.

He has considerable discretion during a ministerial crisis resulting from the forced resignation of the Government on parliamentary passage of a censure motion or defeat of a confidence motion. He may appoint as President of the Council of Ministers a person who will countersign his decree of dissolution and his decree convoking the electorate. He may thus be able to break the unfair advantage of an incumbent party during the election campaign and insure an impartial consultation of the voters. The President may, in the wake of a ministerial resignation, exercise considerable discretion in the appointment of a Council of Ministers, particularly in a situation where no single party enjoys a parliamentary majority or where there are several strong factional heads and poor internal discipline among the parliamentary party group that enjoys a majority or preponderant plurality, such as the Christian Democracy has enjoyed since 1946.

The President may retaliate against a Government which refuses to countersign decrees, whose issuance the Constitution has made a matter of presidential discretion, by himself refusing to sign measures deliberated by the Council of Ministers or proposed by a minister in pursuance of such deliberation. Such presidential refusal to authorize ministerial action on a host of measures, ranging from the initiation of bills before the houses of Parliament to the issuance of decrees, without whose authorization no Government could function in Italy, might easily result in the voting of parliamentary sanctions against the President (i.e., suspension from office on charges of attempting the overthrow of the Constitution or declaration of his permanent disability and consequent removal by an absolute majority). A President who incurs the wrath of the Government that has strong parliamentary backing is bound to emerge the loser in any contest of strength. He cannot refuse requests by the ministers, backed up by deliberations of the Council of Ministers and the solid confidence of the majority in the houses of Parliament, to act positively on their proposals any more than he can insist upon ministerial countersignature of his discretionary decrees, where these are politically inexpedient or unfavorable to the party or coalition in command of the Government. The President, in such a situation of political strength enjoyed by the Government party or coalition, can function as little more than a rubber stamp of the ministers and the President of the Council of Ministers.

The relationship of the President toward the regular courts is limited to his function of decreeing personal pardons and commutations on his own discretion, but with the countersignature of the Minister of Justice required, and to his role as chairman of the Superior Council of the Judiciary, in which he merely presides over the deliberations of the organ that has competence over the intial appointment, promotion, transfer, and disciplinary measures relating to judges of the regular courts (penal and civil). Authorizations by Parliament for the issuance of decrees of amnesty and collective commutation (*indulto*) by the President do not vest the latter with any discretionary authority, but merely permit the Council of Ministers to deliberate and the Minister of Justice to propose presidential compliance with the parliamentary authorization.

Presidential influence over the public administration is formal and not discretionary, since the President must act on the advice of either the Council of Ministers, a minister, or the Council of State in the performance of all his administrative functions. Appointments of ministers; undersecretaries of state; high commissioners; commissioners; and high-ranking civil, diplomatic, and military officers (such as prefects, ambassadors, generals, and admirals) are made by the President on nominations submitted by the President of the Council of Ministers on the latter's discretion or after deliberation by the Council. The only appointments that the President makes on his own discretion are to his personal staff (headed by the presidential secretary-general), none of which has any administrative competence. Subordinate functionaries are appointed by the ministers in accordance with legal provisions (statutes) regulating the recruitment of public officials and public employees.

The President is required to sign all regulations having the force of law (enforceable by the courts), which are deliberated by the Council of Ministers either in pursuance of decree-making authority delegated to it by parliamentary acts or in application of executive discretion to formulate such rules as may be necessary and proper to effectively enforce the law—the so-called independent rule-making power as against the delegated rule-making power. Both types of regulations are in effect executive ordinances, which may stipulate penalties for violation of their norms. Although the courts must enforce these norms by issuing sentences of punishment against their violators, and may therefore refuse to do so on grounds of illegality (incompatibility with statutes or the Constitution), the President may refuse *ab initio* to sign such executive ordinances as deliberated by the Council of Ministers on grounds of doubtful legality, constitutionality, or compatibility with the intentions of Parliament. This presidential power is one of the most effective forms of legal control over the executive, since it constitutes a preventive check against executive abuse of its discretionary and delegated authority. The President must be cautious in the exercise of this power; since in any contest with the Council of Ministers (Government), the latter can secure parliamentary backing, if necessary, in the form of additional legislation.

The President exercises similar control over coercive acts of the executive that may be directed against locally constituted authorities, such as regional councils and their executives, provincial councils and deputations, and communal councils and mayors. These local government bodies may be dissolved only by presidential decree deliberated by the Council of Ministers, and agents of the Government are appointed to exercise temporary governing authority locally by similar decree. Such power of interference by the central executive in the local affairs of autonomous regions, provinces, and communes would be incompatible with the Constitution's strong orientation toward local self-government if it were carried to such excess as to prevent opposition parties to the Government party from forming any local administration. The President's obligation to sign such decrees of the Government is a constitutional check on the power of the Council of Ministers and the dominant party that controls that vital executive organ.

The remaining functions and powers of the President are largely ceremonial. He confers honors upon those singled out by the Government, presides over the Supreme Defense Council and exercises formal command over the armed forces in accordance with the deliberations of the Council of Ministers; accredits diplomatic representatives and receives the letters of credence of foreign emissaries on deliberation of the Council of Ministers; declares war and ratifies treaties on the deliberation of Parliament; decrees elections on deliberation of the Council of Ministers; and decrees referenda on demand of the required number of voters, regional councils, or members of Parliament with the countersignature of the President of the Council of Ministers.

Functionally speaking, the Italian President is poorly equipped with either independent status or discretionary legal powers to perform the role of arbiter between the Government (conceived of especially as the majority party or coalition in Parliament) and the opposition, or minority parties. He can scarcely be called the guardian of the Constitution, as is true of the British monarch, since this function in Italy is legally vested in the Constitutional Court. The President's legal powers are sufficient only to permit him to recommend caution to the parliamentary majority and its elite, which directs the executive and administrative organs of the state. The President can address himself to the nation in order to warn the electorate of dangers to the Constitution arriving from a condition of political malaise.

THE GOVERNMENT

The Government in Italy is constitutionally defined as "the President of the Council and the Ministers, who together constitute the Council of Ministers" (Article 92, paragraph 2). This has been interpreted to mean that the Government has three constituent parts: the President of the Council, the ministers, and the Council, which is the President of the Council and the Ministers acting as a collegiate organ. Each of the constituent parts of the Government discharges specific powers and functions that have been constitutionally defined. Coordination of the acts of the three constituent parts of the Government is achieved within the Council, through the interministerial committees and through the leadership of the President of the Council.

The President of the Council

The President of the Council is appointed by presidential decree following the resignation of the incumbent, which is made to the President of the Republic. The newly appointed President of the Council countersigns his own appointment and takes his oath of office before the President. He then proposes the names of the ministers to the President, who signs the decree of appointment, which is, in turn, countersigned by the President of the Council. The latter must, no later than ten days following the appointment of the ministers, appear before each house of Parliament and announce the composition of the new Government and state the general policy that it intends to pursue. The newly appointed President of the Council, together with the ministers, must secure the vote of confidence of both houses, failing which he must resign collectively for the Government. The President of the Council has no fixed term of office, but enjoys tenure only as long as the Government retains the confidence of the houses of Parliament. Censure or rejection of a request for confidence entail mandatory resignation by the Government and dutiful acceptance by the President. The latter may not retain in office a Government that has lost or failed to secure the confidence of either or both of the houses of Parliament, which means that a decree of dissolution may not be issued following the Government's loss of confidence or prior to its confirmation by a vote of confidence in the case of a newly appointed Government. Such Governments have only "caretaker" functions and may not deliberate any matter of substance or countersign significant presidential decrees.

The President of the Council enjoys only such immunities and privileges from arrest and prosecution, or civil suit, for non-official actions that he may commit in violation of the law as he may possess as a deputy or senator. He is therefore subject at all times to civil suit, and the house of which he is a member has the authority to authorize his arrest and arraignment on charges before a criminal court. However, for crimes that he may commit while acting in an official capacity, even if this means a misuse of official power for personal gain, the President of the Council may be charged only by the two houses of Parliament in joint meeting, voting by simple majority. The only court that is competent to hear charges formulated by Parliament against the President of the Council is the Constitutional Court, whose regular judges are incremented by the sixteen special judges of parliamentary designation for such criminal trials. The President of the Council bears legal responsibility for all presidential decrees that have his countersignature, whether these measures have been "proposed" by him, deliberated by the Council of Ministers, or initiated by the President. He is also responsible for the acts of his subordinates that require his authorization. Arrest and arraignment for crimes committed in a non-official capacity as well as parliamentary indictment for crimes committed in an official capacity result in automatic disqualification of the President of the Council from office and require the President to accept his resignation whether proferred or not.

The President of the Council is specifically empowered by the Constitution to direct the general policy of the Government, for which he must assume political and legal responsibility; to maintain the political and administrative unity of acts of the constituent parts of the Government; and to coordinate the actions of the ministers. The power of direction of the general policy of the Government is interpreted to mean that the President of the Council may formulate the general policy of the Government before the Council and seek its approval, that he may recommend changes in the general policy, and that he may insist upon approval of this policy on threat of submitting the collective resignation of the Government or of recomposing the Government with ministers who will agree to his proposals. While it is true that this policy must be deliberated and adopted by the Council, it is also true that the Council cannot force its will upon the President of the Council, who has the power to resign (with collective effect for all the members of the Government), to demand the resignations of the ministers who oppose him or refuse to affix his countersignature to the Council's deliberations. Once the Council has deliberated and adopted the general policy or agreed to changes of this policy, it is also the right of the President of the Council to interpret this policy with considerable finality and to impose this interpretation upon the ministers or demand that they resign.

The President of the Council maintains political and administrative unity between the acts of the ministers and coordinates these with the general policy of the Government by requiring the ministers to notify him in advance of every decision or action they or their subordinates have in mind that might affect the general policy of the Government, and by suspending any ministerial action or decision that he regards as being at variance with the general policy of the Government, at least until this can be discussed by the Council. All important outgoing diplomatic communications are referred to the President of the Council before they may be dispatched, and other ministries must submit all information requested from his office immediately and heed his advice on matters affecting general policy or that of another department. He has administrative control over the so-called "auxiliary organs" of the state (the Council of State, Court of Accounts and Advocate General's Office), through which he can control all the actions of the other ministries. The President of the Council presides over a number of interministerial committees, some of which are political (consisting of the various coalition leaders of parties collaborating to form the Government) and in the nature of inner cabinets, others of which are technical, such as the Interministerial Committee on Reconstruction; the Interministerial Committee on Prices; and others on credit, savings, and the Fund for Southern Development. These bodies plan and coordinate the activities of various ministries as subcommittees of the Council of Ministers. The President of the Council may appoint one or more ministers without portfolio to assist him in exercising direction and supervision over the ministries and interministerial committees, so that effective coordination may be achieved.

The President of the Council prepares the agenda, convokes and presides over all meetings of the Council. He may invite whom he wishes to attend its deliberations in a purely consultative role. He keeps the minutes of Council proceedings and notifies both the President and Parliament of its deliberations. Council deliberations requiring presidential decrees must be approved by the President of the Council, whose countersignature is mandatory on such decrees. He also countersigns all presidential decrees having legislative effect even though these have been "proposed" and countersigned by a competent minister. He alone may move consideration of a confidence motion before either house of Parliament. He presents the addresses to the houses of Parliament on the general policy of the Government. He alone decides when the Government will submit its "voluntary" resignation (as distinct from the mandatory resignation, which either house of Parliament imposes) to the President. He must consent to the initiation of all legislative bills by members of the Government. He must authorize speeches by members of the Government on matters affecting the general policy of the Govrnment, whether these are made in Parliament or outside.

The Ministers

The ministers are selected by the President of the Council largely if not exclusively from the ranks of members of Parliament. The primary consideration in guiding the choice of ministers is political—the necessity to obtain the consensus of both houses of Parliament. Senators as well as deputies must be well represented in the Government, and the primary factions within a large party (like the Christian Democracy) as well as smaller party groups whose votes are necessary to provide the Government with a parliamentary majority are generally represented in the Government. Bargaining power often determines also the choice of specific ministerial posts (i.e., who will receive the coveted posts of foreign affairs, internal affairs, defense, finance, etc.). The number of ministers to be included in the Government is not fixed by law and may be increased by the President of the Council by simple inclusion of ministers without portfolio, since the number of ministries is legally determined.

The tenure in office of the minister depends upon the confidence that he retains both with the President of the Council and the houses of Parliament, since he may be forced to resign by invitation of the President of the Council or by personal censure of either house. Should he be unable to agree in good faith with the general policy of the Government and to accept the role that Council deliberations may require of him in carrying out this policy, he should resign. The legal privileges and immunities of ministers are identical to those of the President of the Council insofar as they are members of Parliament. Ministers too are charged for criminal violations committed in the exercise of their official functions by the houses of Parliament and tried by the Constitutional Court. They must resign upon arrest for non-official crimes or upon being charged for official crimes.

Ministers perform two distinct functions in the Government: they participate as deliberating members of the Council of Ministers to discuss and adopt the general policy of the Government and the many other measures for which collective deliberation is required and they direct the policy and the officials of an important branch of the central administration, for which they assume political and legal responsibility. Although the minister is interested primarily in promoting the requirements and interests of his own department of administration within the general policy of the Government, he must accept the necessity of coordinating his department's functions with those of the other departments. He acts as a judge within the Council on the merits and propriety of his fellow ministers' proposals and is in turn judged on the measures that he sponsors on behalf of his department. Once he wins Council approval of his proposals and is authorized to initiate a legislative bill, the minister must direct the bill through the houses of Parliament to insure approval of the bill without substantial revision of its content. He must know when to accede to constructive amendments and when to mobilize party pressures against the opposition in Parliament. He must present and defend his department's budget requirements before the Council of Ministers against the pressures for reduction of the Finance Minister; then he must repeat the operation again twice before the houses of Parliament. If his department is refused authorization by the Court of Accounts to spend public funds, the minister must secure authorization from the Council of Ministers. He must answer for his actions and those of his subordinates before the houses of Parliament under interrogations, interpellations, and motions that threaten his authority and reputation, and possibly his career. The minister must secure presidential signature of decrees to empower him and his subordinates to perform their functions, for which he assumes responsibility by countersignature. The minister appoints, assigns, disciplines, and removes public officials under his authority and has a limited patronage power in staffing his personal cabinet of advisers. Ministers receive a salary as fixed by law, have free use of state-owned and -operated public facilities. They are protected by special provisions of the Penal Code (Article 341), which makes it a criminal offense to offend the honor of prestige of a public official because of his exercise of official functions or to threaten or commit violence against him. Ministers may use the title Excellency even after they cease to hold office.

The Council of Ministers

The Council of Ministers is the deliberative organ of the Government. Only ministers and the President of the Council have the right to participate in its deliberations with equal vote. Others may be invited to attend the meetings of the Council by its President, such as undersecretaries of state, high commissioners, and regional presidents, whenever matters concerning their competences are under discussion, but without the right to vote. The Council is convoked by its President at his discretion—generally once a week. Its agenda is prepared by the Office of the President of the Council under the latter's direction; one of the two undersecretaries of state attached to this office performs this task as well as that of secretary of the Council, transcribing the minutes and compiling the texts of its deliberations for initialing by the President of the Council. Ministers who wish to present matters for discussion before the Council must have these items included in the agenda. The discussion is conducted rather informally by the President of the Council, who may either request a vote or formulate the consensus of the Council on the basis of the opinions expressed. The deliberations are all confidential, and only the President of the Council may release information concerning these to the press. Ministers who cannot agree with resolutions of the Council are expected to resign. Should the President of the Council be opposed by a majority of the members of the Council, he must either submit to their will or resign collectively for all the members of the Council. In this sense, the President of the Council has an absolute veto over his colleagues, since he can frustrate Council action by resignation.

Functions and Powers of the Council of Ministers. The specific functions of the Council of Ministers are indicated in the Constitution (Articles 71, 76, 77, 78, 81); in statutes of Parliament that are compatible with the Constitution; and in certain decrees of the chief of state (royal decrees and presidential decrees) authorized by statute, compatible with presently valid statutory law and the Constitution. Article 71 of the Constitution vests the power to initiate legislative bills before the houses of Parliament in the Government, while Article 81 requires the Government to present to Parliament the general and individual department budgets and the report on expenditures (audit) annually. Under Article 76, Parliament is permitted to delegate its legislative power to the Government for limited periods of time and within clearly defined principles and purposes. Such decrees are to be considered as having the force of law only insofar as the courts judge them to be compatible with the statute delegating the power, and with other statutes not specifically amended, and, of course, with the norms of the Constitution and laws of constitutional character. This power is often used to codify statutory law on a specific subject matter or to carry out in detail complex legislation for which Parliament has little time. It is not required by Parliament that the Government submit such decrees to its inspection; the President of the Republic exercises preliminary supervision to insure compatibility between the decrees and the delegating statute. Ultimate control is vested with the courts, and particularly the Constitutional Court. Article 77 (paragraph 1) expressly prohibits the Government (without specific delegation by Parliament under Article 76) from issuing decrees having the same character as statutory law (i.e., legislative decrees), such as was possible under the monarchy and the provisional regime that preceded the constitutional order of the Republic. Legislative decrees once had the same character as statutory laws. These legislative decrees were issued by the chief of state (King, Lieutenant-General, Provisional President) after approval by the Council of Ministers and the (non-binding) advice of the Council of State. Since they had equal status with statutes, legislative decrees could annul or revise the statutory law and take its place. During the period of Fascist rule, Parliament ceased to exercise the legislative power except occasionally when the Government wished to mollify the feelings of the parliamentarians. Most legislation was adopted as legislative decrees and decrees by deliberation of the Council of Ministers. During the period of the provisional regime following the overthrow of Mussolini and the Fascist regime, there was no parliamentary organ to legislate; so the Government or Council of Ministers and the chief of state legislated by means of legislative decrees, under the authority of the Allies for some years, and then under the political (though not legal) aegis of the Constituent Assembly. However, in the event of extraordinary cases of necessity and urgency, the Government may, under paragraph 2 of Article 77, "adopt provisional measures having the force of law," provided these provisional decree laws are submitted the same day to both houses of Parliament for conversion into statutes, failing which after sixty days the provisional decree laws become null and void *ab initio*. If the houses are not convoked, they must be summoned to meet within five days; even if the houses have been dissolved, a summons must be issued to deliberate on the provisional decree laws. Article 78 authorizes the houses of Parliament to "confer upon the Government the necessary powers" to wage war following parliamentary deliberation of such a condition. While this delegation might include the competence to revise statutory law by means of decree for the duration of the war, it is not sufficiently broad a power to permit the suspension of the constitutional norms, except where these expressly allow, as in the extension of the parliamentary term so as to obviate the necessity for wartime elections. This article does not apparently question the validity of the legislative decree of July 8, 1938, *n.* 1415, which is the so-called "law of war" that permits the Commander-in-Chief of the armed forces or any military commander on his delegation to proclaim martial law over all or part of the national territory, as well as occupied territory, in the event of a threat of military invasion of the national territory, or extension of hostilities. In the event of war or its imminence and the possibility of hostilities extending to the national territory, the legislative power of the state passes into the hands of the supreme military commander and, on his delegation, to general command officers in the field. The scope of martial law is unlimited and would include the suspension of constitutional norms in the endangered territory as well as the substitution of military government for civilian authorities. The validity of certain provisions of the norms on public order and police security and the norms of public sanitation (Single Text, June 18, 1931, *n.* 773 with subsequent modifications of the laws on public security; Single Text, July 27, 1934, *n.* 422 of the laws on public sanitation) have been questioned with reference to Article 77 of the Constitution, since these norms permit the Minister of Internal Affairs and, on his delegation, the prefect to decree a "state of public danger" and a "state of civil war" for part or all of the country and the Minister of Public Sanitation to issue ordinances in time of epidemic. Such ordinances constitute legal norms, and there are few limits on their scope except from higher administrative organs of the state, i.e., the Council of Ministers.

Acts of Parliament determine when deliberation by the Council of Ministers shall be required for the appointment by the President of high civil, diplomatic, and military officers. Acts of Parliament also determine when presidential measures shall require the countersignature of the President of the Council as well as that of a minister. Acts of Parliament are now required for the authorization of changes in the organization, functions, and powers of both the Presidency of the Council Office and the ministries, and in the number of ministries; whereas this was once the prerogative of the Government and chief of state. Even the organization of the public administration is under the competence of Parliament, although the Council of Ministers may be delegated such functions.

The specific functions of the Council of Ministers are listed under a royal decree of November 14, 1901 (*n.* 466), which continues to have validity within the scope of the new Constitution and legislation adopted under its provisions. By this decree, the Council of Ministers deliberates on the following matters: (1) all questions of public order and high administration; (2) presentation and withdrawal of bills before the houses of Parliament; (3) proposals for treaty commitments and interpretation of existing treaties; (4) Government decrees to implement delegations of legislative power, formulate administrative regulations for the execution of laws, and to set aside administrative acts against the decision of the Council of State; (5) disputes over competence between ministries; and (6) registration "with reservations" of demands for funds of ministries by the Court of Accounts. Other matters requiring Council deliberation are (1) dissolution of regional, provincial, and communal councils; (2) suspension of regional statutes and referral to the Constitutional Court for legitimacy; (3) relations with Parliament, such as requests for confidence, dissolution of the houses, elections, and extraordinary convocation; (4) other matters that may be indicated by statutes, or which the President of the Council may refer because of their political importance; (5) the appointment of high functionaries and officials of the central administration, diplomatic corps, and military forces: undersecretaries of state, councilors of state, councilors of the Court of Accounts, ambassadors, and envoys extraordinary or ministers plenipotentiary, the secretary-general of the Foreign Ministry, the directors-general of the ministries, high commissioners, prefects, and the directors-general of the Banks of Italy, Naples, and Sicily, the chief advocates general (civil, military, and revenue), provisional administrative boards of regions; (6) requests for extradition; and (7) all matters of international importance.

The deliberations of the Council of Ministers do not themselves assume the character of legal norms but constitute mere "recommendations" to the President of the Republic to adopt the substance of the deliberation in the form of a particular decree. The countersignatures of the President of the Council as well as the minister (in some cases) are legally required for all presidential acts taken upon the deliberation of the Council as legal evidence of compatibility between the President's decree and the Council's deliberation. The President of the Republic may refuse to act upon Council deliberations, thus opposing their content through a veto, whenever he feels that the measures "recommended" are incompatible with the

Constitution or statutory laws or are politically improper. He has legal control over the legitimacy as well as control in merit of Council deliberations. Presidential veto of Council recommendations might be criticized in Parliament through interrogations and interpellations or through a motion requesting confidence by the Government. Should the Government receive parliamentary backing in disputes with the President, the latter would be forced to concede or be exposed to parliamentary sanctions—declaration of permanent impediment for reasons of "mental incapacity" or indictment for violation of the Constitution on grounds of impeding the exercise of functions by the Government.

Since the Council of Ministers is a constitutional organ of the state and not an administrative organ of the Government, it is permitted to regulate its own internal organization and adopt its own rules of procedure, formulate its own operating budget, and designate its own staff by simple deliberation and decrees issued by the President of the Council. It may create interministerial committees to function as subcommittees of the Council for purposes of study and report or to coordinate actions between several ministries. The Council does not maintain a separate secretariat headed by a secretary-general as do the houses of Parliament and the President of the Republic. Instead, it draws upon the permanent staff of the Office of the President of the Council; and one of the undersecretaries of state to the President of the Council functions as its executive secretary. The functions of this staff do not include the legal drafting of Council measures or bills, which is done by the advisory section of the Council of State, but are limited to the preparation of the Council's agenda, distribution of this and the minutes of the meetings to the ministers, recording of the deliberations, communication of these to the appropriate organs to which they are directed (such as the President, the presidents of the houses of Parliament, the ministers, regional presidents, high commissioners, the Council of State, the Court of Accounts, and the Constitutional Court, and release of a press statement.

SELECTED READING

ADAMS, JOHN CLARKE, and BARILE, PAOLO. *The Government of Republican Italy.* Boston: Houghton Mifflin Co., 1961. Pp. 75–89.

———. "The Implementation of the Italian Constitution," *American Political Science Review,* XLVII (March, 1953), 61–83.

MANGONE, GERARD. "Italy." In *European Political Systems,* Part IV, Taylor Cole (ed.). New York: Alfred A. Knopf (a division of Random House, Inc.), 1959.

PRYCE, ROY. "Parliamentary Government in Italy Today," *Parliamentary Affairs,* VIII (Spring, 1955), 183–91.

26

Administration

Public policies in Italy are directed and executed by a complex array of administrative organizations of four basic types: the centralized state administration; the autonomous public service enterprises of the state (*aziende autonome dello stato*); the autonomous publicly constituted corporations (*enti di diritto pubblico*) performing delegated functions for the state; and local government administrations of the regions, provinces, and communes.

The most important areas of public policy from a political standpoint are administered directly by the state through its central administration, which consists of the ministries, a few commissariats, the services under the Presidency of the Council of Ministers, together with numerous field services and field offices operating under the direction of these national departments of administration. The many and varied technical and social services of the state have been entrusted to more specialized business-like administrations in the interest of sound management, which operate efficiency and budgetary planning. Among the services that are administered by the *aziende autonome* are the railroads, the post office, telegraph and interurban telephone, the state highways, the public forests, state monopolies, public debt management, the deposits and loan fund, and the religious fund. A far greater number of social services as well as technical services have been delegated to a host of public corporations, some of which include social insurance and welfare, insurance, housing, land improvement, credit and banking, tourism, sports, public entertainment, cultural activities, public education, mineral exploration, industrial development, promotion of commerce and handicraft industries, radio and television broadcasting, public transportation services, etc. These publicly constituted corporations have separate legal personality from the state and operate very much the same as private corporations, except for the fact that they do not distribute any dividends. Their capitalization and part of their operating funds are supplied by the state in return for the services that they provide the government.

Supreme authority over the various branches of the public administration is vested in the Council of Ministers, which is the highest policy-making organ of the state and the principal organ of coordination between the different branches of the public administration. A number of interministerial committees, created by statute and by decree, assist the Council of Ministers in the determination of administrative policy in such matters as prices, reconstruction, credit, extraordinary works of public interest, winter assistance to the needy, southern economic development, and state participation in the private economy. These interministerial committees exercise powers on delegation from the Council of Ministers.

THE STATE ADMINISTRATION

The direct or bureaucratic administrative services of the state in Italy are presently organized into nineteen national departments or ministries: foreign affairs, interior, justice, budget, finance, treasury, defense, public instruction, public works, agriculture and forests, transportation, posts and telecommunications, industry and commerce, foreign commerce, labor and social security, merchant marine, state participations, public health and tourism and public entertainment. The ministries are created by act of Parliament, which must also determine their organizational structure, powers, and functions. The administrative procedures of the ministries are established by decree of the President in the form of general administrative regulations deliberated by the Council of Ministers. The Presidency of the Council of Ministers administers only a few minor services, such as public information and copyrights, since the transfer of the public entertainment sector to the new Ministry of Tourism and Public Entertainment. The former High Commissariat of Health and that of Tourism, which operated under the Presidency of the Council of Ministers, were abolished when their functions were transferred to the new ministries. Slightly lower in rank than the high commissariats are the ordinary commissariats, which operate autonomously within a ministry; the proposed Commissariat of Civil Aviation would function autonomously within the Ministry of Interior.

Each ministry is organized under separate legislation to meet its particular requirements. Some ministries entrust most of their services to autonomous public services (*aziende autonome*), such as the Ministry of Posts and Telecommunications. Others prefer to delegate specific functions to various *enti di diritto pubblico* along with financial grants, whereas the more traditional ministries assign their administrative tasks to the state bureaucracy. For purposes of consultation and advice, the ministries utilize the services of ministerial councils, committees, and commissions, which are made up of civil servants from the ministries and their field offices, personnel from other public agencies, technical experts, and professional consultants, as well as representatives of the professional, business, labor, and other organized associations.

The relationship between the minister and the administrative services that fall under his general authority varies considerably. As the bureaucratic head of the ministry's non-technical services, the minister has absolute authority over his subordinates, who act only within the scope of such decision-making powers as the minister delegates. Their decisions are subject to annulment by the minister, who assumes legal responsibility before the courts and political responsibility before the Council of Ministers and Parliament for the acts of his subordinates. Instead, acts of the autonomous public services (*aziende autonome*) are the legal responsibility of the director-general; while the minister is politically responsible for the general policy that the latter pursues. The minister merely represents the autonomous agency before the Council of Ministers and the houses of Parliament in his capacity of chairman of the agency's council of administration and coordinator of the latter's policies with those of the ministry.

The Ministries

Every minister is assisted by a small personal staff of his own choosing, consisting of one or two administrative assistants (*capo* and *vice capo di gabinetto*), a personal secretary, and a secretariat. The administrative assistants are drawn from the higher levels of the civil service of the ministry or from any other branch of the public administration. As senior civil servants holding permanent positions of director-general, divisional director, prefect, or councilor of state, they are administrative experts of considerable experience and ability. They handle all the communication of an official character between the minister and the directions-general of the ministry, and between the minister and other ministries. They advise the minister on all matters of an official character relating to his administrative duties. The personal secretary, instead, is generally not a civil servant, but a confidant of the minister who handles the latter's unofficial affairs, such as political correspondence, and arranges his personal calendar of appointments, visits, etc. As an intimate collaborator of the minister, the personal secretary will generally follow the minister from one post to another until he is rewarded by some lucrative patronage appointment or nomination to an important party position. It is not uncommon for future ministers to begin their careers as personal secretaries to some minister. The secretariat is recruited from various levels of the ministerial staff.

Members of the minister's personal staff serve at his pleasure and revert back to their former positions upon termination of their services. Although the administrative assistants are authorized to demand information from the permanent officials of the ministry at any time, they are not permitted to issue directives.

Each ministry has one or more undersecretaries of state appointed by the President on nomination by the Council of Ministers. Undersecretaries of state are members of Parliament who serve as junior ministers or assistant ministers. They have broader functions than British parliamentary undersecretaries, since they direct one or more sectors of the ministry on delegation of authority from the minister; they are comparable to the British ministers of state in that they relieve the minister of much of the burden of active direction over specific administrative sectors. The Italian undersecretary of state acts as an independent administrator and not as a subordinate of the minister over those sectors that have been delegated to him. However, he may be relieved of his authority by the minister at any time; and he is subject to dismissal by the President on deliberation of the Council of Ministers or mere request of the President of the Council of Ministers. Undersecretaries of state may appoint a small personal staff, consisting of a chief secretary, a personal secretary, and a limited secretariat.

With the exception of the Ministry of Foreign Affairs and the Ministry of Defense, which centralize administrative direction under a secretary-general, who corresponds more or less to the British permanent undersecretary, Italian ministries divide administrative direction among a number of directors-general. Each director-general heads a direction-general and has direct access to either the minister or the undersecretary of state. The directions-general are subdivided into divisions and offices, each one having a divisional director in charge who is responsible to the director-general; there are certain offices, such as public relations, legislation, studies, and documentation, that operate directly under the minister or the undersecretary of state. Each ministry has an autonomous office, the accounting office (*ragioneria centrale*), that reports directly to the General Accounting Bureau of the State (*Ragioneria Generale dello Stato*), of which it is a detached office. The lowest level of organization within a ministry is the section, which is headed by a section director and subordinated to a division.

In addition to their operational divisions and offices, most Italian ministries have a number of advisory bodies, known as councils, committees, or commissions, many of which are divided into sections, subcommittees, and subcommissions. These technical and consultative bodies of experts, consultants, and representatives of various ministries, agencies, professional associations, and other socioeconomic organizations examine and report on the technical aspects of administration to the minister. The minister is required by law or administrative regulations to seek the opinion of these advisory bodies on determined problems, but the minister is free to accept or reject such advice.

Every ministry has a council of administration consisting of the directors-general and the secretary-general, two divisional or office directors, and either the minister or undersecretary as chairman. This council meets every month to evaluate the reports of the directors-general and to assist the minister to prepare his annual report to Parliament, to discuss the ministry's budgetary needs, to make recommendations regarding promotions of ministry personnel, to approve the competitive examinations for the recruitment and promotion of personnel, and to select the examining commission. Its deliberations are advisory.

The disciplinary commission in each ministry functions as a personnel court to hear charges filed by the personnel director of the ministry against ministerial functionaires and employees below the rank of director-general. Its decisions are recommendations to the minister, who must decree all penalties that go beyond mere censure. These penalties range from temporary salary reductions to removal and disqualification from public service and deprivation of pension rights. The disciplinary judges include a director-general and two officials with the rank of either divisional director or inspector-general, appointed by the minister.

The Field Offices. Every ministry maintains its own administrative field offices in convenient centers within the country and, in the case of the Ministry of Foreign Affairs and the Ministry of Foreign Commerce, in foreign cities as well. Most of the field offices are found in the provincial centers, which correspond to American county seats. The field force of each ministry operates from one or more directions-general, to which it is directly responsible. Coordination among the field services of a ministry is achieved through a common field superior, such as the *prefetto* or the *intendente di finanza,* who head the provincial offices of the Ministry of Interior and Ministry of Finance, respectively.

The most important ministerial field office is the prefecture or *prefettura,* because of the variety of administrative functions that it performs and due to the exceptional police powers that it exercises—also because of its coordinating function among the other ministerial field offices. There is a prefecture in each provincial center; and recently a number of subprefectures have been created as prefectural branches in a number of provinces, in line with the government's policy of administrative decentralization. The subprefectures exercise only limited powers, however, and are subject to control from the prefecture. The principal functions of the prefecture concern police administration, fire control and prevention, religious affairs, elections, public health, and public assistance. It also administers such matters as vital statistics, state archives, public lands and monuments, citizenship, refugees, protection and assistance of minors, motor vehicles, expropriations, publication of laws and decrees, control of local government authorities, contracts involving the state, issuance of commercial licenses, hunting and fishing permits, approval of public works' projects and municipal planning, care of homeless, and control of public housing.

The prefecture is headed by the prefect or *prefetto*, who is assisted by a vice-prefect. The latter acts in the place of the prefect during the latter's absence and directs part of the prefectural administration on delegation of authority by the prefect. Besides directing the provincial administration of the Ministry of Interior, the prefect coordinates the administrative services of all central field offices in the province. He resolves administrative disputes between different offices after direct consultation with the appropriate ministries, with which he may communicate to obtain ministerial authorization to compel the heads of field offices to conform to his decisions. The prefect has broad decree authority to enforce all laws by such means as he feels are both necessary and proper; this is particularly true of laws to protect persons and property from violence. In the event of the threat or outbreak of violence that might imperil the public peace (riots, demonstrations, public meetings, etc.), the prefect may prohibit public gatherings, impose martial law, and suspend ordinary liberties over part or all of the province. He disposes of all the police and military forces in the area of the province for such purposes and may request reinforcements from the Ministry of Interior. The prefect may act similarly to protect public health in the event of an epidemic or such calamities as earthquake, flood, eruption, and fire. Whenever the public interest requires that private property be expropriated, the decree of expropriation is issued by the prefect.

Control of local government authorities takes up a large portion of the prefect's time. He must supervise the work of the provincial council and its executive committee to see that these elective bodies fulfill their legal duties and provide the mandatory services that are required by law, and to prevent these from assuming financial obligations or from extending the optional services beyond the financial resources of the province. All deliberations of the provincial council and its executive committee must be communicated within eight days to the prefect, who has the authority to annul such measures within a period of twenty days for reasons of illegitimacy—viz., violation of the law, incompetence, excess of power. The prefect is no longer permitted, as before, to annul acts and decisions of the provincial authorities merely because he thinks they are improper or ill-advised. Certain contracts stipulated by the provincial authorities require the authorization of the prefect, who furthermore must countersign all provincial contracts involving sums in excess of 2,500,000 lire ($4,000). In the event the provincial authorities should fail to provide the public services required of them by law, the prefect may decree that such services be provided together with the necessary budgetary and appropriation revisions. To insure proper administration of all legally required public services by the provincial services, the prefect may even suspend the authority of the elected provincial executive committee or of its individual assessors and transfer their powers to a prefectural agent acting as a commissioner. Should the provincial council fail to replace the provincial assessors, the prefect may request the Minister of Interior to advise the President to dissolve the provincial council. In such instances, the province is placed under the administration of a prefectural commission for a period of from three months to one year, after which elections must be ordered by the prefect. The prefect has similar powers of compulsion over the communal authorities.

Prefectural control over the provincial and communal authorities is administered through a corps of inspectors, headed by a vice-prefect. These inspectors are authorized to examine any matter connected with the local administrations and report to the prefect. Should the inspection reports indicate administrative irregularities, incompetence, or malfeasance of local officials, the prefect may order an investigation. The inspection corps is woefully undermanned, however, and is able to make only random checks.

In the administration of the prefecture, the prefect relies upon a cabinet of advisors consisting of the various councilors of prefecture and vice-prefects; these officials advise him on policy decisions and direct one or more divisions of the prefecture. Each division is divided into sections, which are headed by a secretary of prefecture. All of the personnel of the prefecture serves under the Ministry of Interior's direction-general for civil administration. The police, instead, form a field service under the Interior Ministry's direction-general of public security and are headed in each province by the *questore*. This official is subject to the directives of the prefect, however, since the latter, as chief civil administrator for the Ministry of Interior in the province, disposes of the police ordinance power. An accounting office that reports to the General Accounting Bureau of the State in the Treasury also operates as an autonomous office within the prefecture to verify the accounts of the prefecture and those of the local government agencies.

The prefect presides over the prefectural council (*Consiglio di Prefettura*), which functions both as a consultative organ and as a jurisdictional body. The advice of the prefectural council is required before the prefect is legally competent to make certain decisions, such as the issuance of expropriation decrees and orders to carry out public works. In this capacity, it consists of the prefect and two councilors of prefecture. As a jurisdictional organ, the prefectural council audits all financial expenditures made by the provincial and communal authorities to insure conformity with the budgets approved by the appropriate local councils; its audits are countersigned by the prefect. The prefectural accounting office refers reports on financial irregularities to the prefect, who presents these to the council of prefecture, which may impose administrative penalties upon the local officials for violation of the accounting regulations. Such decisions are subject to appeal before the Court of Accounts. As a jurisdictional organ, the prefectural council includes, in addition to the prefect and two councilors of prefecture, the chief accountant of prefecture and the director of the accounting office of the *intendenza di finanza,* or provincial revenue office.

Each province includes a *giunta provinciale amministrativa,* or provincial administrative board, which performs various important functions for the prefecture. It exercises control over the propriety of decisions of local government bodies and officials (so-called merit control). It is an organ of consultation to the prefect, who is bound by law to act on its advice in designated matters such as the municipalization of public services or the redistricting of local election districts. Its prior consent is required before local government bodies are permitted to exercise certain powers, such as appropriation of public funds, borrowing of funds, sale of public property, lease of public property, and signature of certain contracts. The provincial administrative board has the authority to annul the acts of local administrators on grounds of violation of the law, incompetence or excess of power, and impropriety. Examples of the type of administrative acts that the provincial administrative board may annul for impropriety are ordinances of the mayor in matters of public health and sanitation, enforcement of the building code and the public security code, public works projects, dismissal or retirement of local employees by the communal and provincial authorities, and improper election of communal and provincial councilors. Persons in the employ of the communes or province may appeal to the provincial administrative board for review of disciplinary measures taken against them.

As a consultative body, the provincial administrative board consists of the prefect (chairman) or vice-prefect acting for him; the *intendente di finanza,* or revenue officer; the provincial inspector; the chief accountant of the prefecture; two councilors of prefecture designated by the prefect; and four qualified private persons elected by the provincial council. Any five members together with the chairman constitute a quorum. As a jurisdictional organ to review administrative decisions of local government bodies and their officers, the provincial administrative board is formed by the prefect or vice-prefect (chairman), two councilors of prefecture, and the two oldest members elected by the provincial council.

The prefect presides over a number of advisory bodies, such as the provincial sanitation council, the provincial committee of public assistance and charity, the provincial commission of police injunction, the provincial commission on the licensing of pharmacies, the provincial commission on the sale of alcoholic beverages, and the provincial committee on prices. The sixteen-member sanitation council advises the prefect on all matters concerning the problems and measures to be taken in the protection and promotion of public health; its advice is binding on the prefect in the revision or extension of general regulations on public health and sanitation. The public assistance and charities committee exercises control over all charitable organizations in the province and advises the prefect on all matters concerning their operation. The provincial commission on police injunction and confinement is an administrative tribunal that reviews police charges against persons who are considered socially pernicious or dangerous and formulates the administrative penalty, which may consist of various injunctions, confinement to the locality of domicile, confinement to an isolated locality under police surveillance, etc. Its sentences must be approved by the President of the Tribunal (i.e., Court of First Instance of the district) before they may be executed.

The prefect and those who act on his instructions are immune from all civil and criminal liability for measures that they take against persons and private property in the exercise of their discretionary powers of administration before the ordinary courts, except for violation of the election laws, and in other cases, only after issuance of a presidential decree on the advice of the Council of State and with the approval of the Council of Ministers. This legal irresponsibility, except through a political waiver of immunity by the Government, of the prefect and his staff has been justified as necessary to maintain central authority within the provinces; but it has also been criticized as being incompatible with the Constitution and democratic tenets of administration.

The prefect may intervene with the judicial authorities through the procurator-general of the Court of Appeal to have a lawsuit, which is pending before any regular court in the province, suspended if he feels that the legal questions involved concern administrative law, whose interpretation is reserved for the jurisdiction of the administrative courts. The prefect's intervention suspends the trial action before the regular court until the Court of Cassation has adjudicated the conflict of jurisdiction. All administrative offices in the province (prefectural offices, autonomous public corporations of local government bodies as well as the offices of the local governments) that are affected by judicial invasion of their authority must rely upon the prefect to suspend court proceedings and apply to the Court of Cassation for determination of the question of jurisdictional competence.

The prefect's authority to discipline officials and employees of the prefecture is limited to simple censure. More severe disciplinary penalties must be imposed by the disciplinary commission of the Ministry of Interior. The sanitation officer, however, may be dismissed outright by the prefect, since he is not a state functionary, but a provincial officer. Employees of the provincial administration are subject to suspension by order of the prefect on report of incompetence or malfeasance by the provincial inspector. Disciplinary penalties against these locally responsible public servants must be recommended by the provincial disciplinary commission and approved by the provincial council or its executive committee. Should the recommended penalties not be approved by one of the latter local bodies, the prefect may decree their execution, subject to appeal and review before the provincial administrative board.

Present legislation provides for the appointment of no more than 100 prefects, of whom only 15 may be kept on disposition by the Ministry of Interior. Prefects form a special corps of officers and are not recruited or protected by ordinary civil service regulations. They are appointed by the President on nominations made by the Minister of Interior and approved by the Council of Ministers. They serve at the discretion of the Minister of Interior. The law requires that three-fifths of the prefectoral corps consist of functionaries of the state having group A status in the directive or administrative class of the personnel of the Ministry of Interior. The others require no particular qualifications and are commonly referred to as "political prefects," since they are patronage appointees. Prefects may be moved from one post to another or placed on the unassigned or inactive lists by the minister. They enjoy great prestige and hold exalted rank within the public service and are provided with a generous allowance and comfortable quarters and services. Prefects who have served for five or more years are entitled to a cash indemnity if they are dropped by the minister from the corps; those who have served for over ten years receive a pension.

ADMINISTRATIVE COORDINATION

The vast number of administrative offices having specific grants of public authority (competence) results in disputes over competences whenever the same matter is subjected to different regulations by two or more administrative offices. Disputes between administrative offices of the same ministry or of agencies subject to the general policy directives of the minister are resolved by the latter. Disputes that involve different ministries or autonomous agencies located in different ministries are resolved by the

Council of Ministers. Disputes between an administrative office and a jurisdictional organ, such as a regular court, or in some cases even an administrative court, over questions of competence are resolved by the Court of Cassation in united sections. Disputes between organs having constitutionally defined powers over matters of competence derived from such powers are decided by the Constitutional Court. The most common type of dispute over competence in the area of administration involves the public administration and the regular courts—the former generally taking exception with the latter's exercise of jurisdiction over its acts.

General coordination at the ministry level is performed by the Council of Ministers, by interministerial committees, by the President of the Council of Ministers, by the Minister of the Budget on the allocation of funds, and by the Treasury on matters of budgetary accountability. Locally, the task of administrative coordination is performed by the prefect with the assistance of the prefectural council and the provincial administrative board, which assume locally the same general functions as the Court of Accounts and Council of State, respectively. As head of the prefectural administration and chief agent of the central government to the province, the prefect has general authority to resolve conflicts among administrative offices operating within the province. Prefects are subject to the authority of multiple ministries, each operating within its own sphere of competence through its own officials in the province but relying upon the prefect to coordinate the actions of its field agents with the general policy of the Council of Ministers. As a rule, the President of the Council of Ministers acts as Minister of Interior in order to exercise direct control through the prefect over the civil and military administration of the province.

Consultative and Advisory Organs

In addition to the numerous consultative councils, committees, and commissions that serve the ministries, there are three consultative organs that function independently of the ministries to provide expert advice directly to the Council of Ministers. These are the National Economic and Labor Council, the Council of State, and the Advocate-General's Office. The National Economic and Labor Council is a constitutional organ whose organization is provided by statute. It may discuss any measure or policy suitable for legislative enactment proposed by the Council of Ministers or by its own membership on matters affecting the economy or the status of labor, outside the purely budgetary problems. It also may exercise legislative initiative with the consent of the President of the Council of Ministers. Sixty of its eighty members represent economic and social interest groups: organized labor, industry, commerce, cooperatives, agriculture, public service enterprises, welfare agencies, and professional orders. The other twenty members are experts on social and economic problems. All the members are appointed by the President on the advice of the Council of Ministers.

The Council of State is a constitutional organ organized by statute and vested with consultative functions as well as jurisdictional competence over acts of the public administration. The first three sections of the Council of State specialize in consultative matters, such as drafting legislative bills that have been approved in principle and general content by the Council of Ministers; drawing up legislative decrees and decree laws for the Council of Ministers on precise instructions from either the President of the Council of Ministers or a minister; and writing up administrative regulations, rules, orders, and important contracts for the ministries. The consultative work of the Council of State is divided among the three sections in accordance with criteria of specialization. On occasion, a consultative commission is formed of members of different consultative sections by the President of the Council of State, who may also assign councilors temporarily to different sections. A general assembly of the Council of State is formed, upon specific request by the Council of Ministers or a minister, of the full membership to provide advice on important matters, such as general administrative regulations, delegated legislation, legislative bills, appeals to the President of the Republic for annulment of an administrative decision, and important contracts. The general assembly is convoked, as a rule, only after an advisory section has studied the matter first. The Council of Ministers is seldom bound by the advice of the Council of State, but such departures from competent advice must be noted in the government's act of promulgation. The only decree that requires the consent of the Council of State concerns the restoration of Italian citizenship.

The Council of State consists of a president, twelve section presidents, sixty councilors, seven first referendars, and seven ordinary referendars. It is assisted by a secretariat drawn from the public administration. Appointments of ordinary referendars are made on the basis of competitive examinations from the ranks of directive personnel having a law degree in the public administration. Those who distinguish themselves during their first two or more years of service are eligible to promotion as first referendars. Every second (i.e., first, third, fifth, etc.) vacancy that occurs in the ranks of the councilors must be filled by appointment of a first referendar. The other vacancies are filled by promotion of administrators who have attained the rank of director-general, prefect, or inspector-general. Section presidents are normally appointed from among the senior councilors, and the president of the Council of State is usually a senior section president. Appointments of the councilors as well as the section presidents and president of the Council of State are made by the President of the Republic on deliberation by the Council of Ministers. These members all enjoy permanent tenure on good behavior and may be suspended or removed only after an absolute majority of the general assembly of the Council of State and the Council of Ministers have consented to a proposal made by the President of the Council of Ministers. The referendars are, instead, subject to disciplinary measures ordered by the president and section presidents acting as a council of presidents. The latter forms the personnel or administration council for the referendars and the members of the secretariat of the Council of State.

The Office of Advocate-General of the State acts as legal consultant to the ministries and state agencies and represents them in court. It gives legal advice to the administration on the interpretation of all laws and on the scope of administrative authority, on the drafting of legislation, administrative regulations, and rules; it also draws up legal contracts for administrative offices and advises these on the filing of legal suits before the civil courts.

The office is formed of the advocate-general, who is nominated by the President of the Council of Ministers, and six vice-advocates-general, who are proposed by the advocate-general; all are appointed by decree of the President of the Republic and are subject to removal in the same manner as appointment. A host of subordinate personnel is employed by the Office of the Advocate-General of the State and consists of assistant advocates-general, vice-advocates and assistant advocates; chief procurators, procurators, assistant procurators, and adjunct procurators. The procurators are legal technicians who assist the advocates in the preparation of legal documents, but they are not permitted to appear before the major courts. The assistant advocates and adjunct and assistant procurators are recruited by competitive examinations. Promotions fill the vacancies in the various ranks of the subordinate advocates and the procurators. The personnel commission of the Office of the Advocate-General of the State is formed by the advocate-general and the six vice-advocates-general, who also function as a disciplinary commission for all subordinate personnel.

THE SCOPE OF ADMINISTRATIVE AUTHORITY

Administrative authority in Italy includes the power to issue general rules, such as regulations, rates, and ordinances, and a host of orders, such as prohibitions, injunctions, compliance and performance, dispensations, authorizations, licenses, concessions, recognitions, and revocations. The general rule-making authority of Italian administrators is derived by delegation from statutes, decree laws, legislative decrees, general regulations, and other executive decrees. Under existing legislation, it is considerable. The penalties for violation of administrative rules must be fixed by statutory law and sentenced by a regular court. The authority to issue ordinances is derived from the police power and is exercised by a number of ministers, certain directors-general, prefects, regional presidents, police quaestors and commissioners, mayors, university rectors, military commanders, and commanders of merchant vessels and airplanes. The law indicates when ordinances may be promulgated, and the Penal Code prescribes the penalties that the courts may inflict in the enforcement of their provisions. Ordinances must be compatible with the law from which the authority for their issuance is derived, and the law must not violate the Constitution. It is the responsibility of the courts, and of the Constitutional Court in particular, to protect the rights of citizens from unconstitutional invasions by public administrators.

Most administrative acts take the form of specific orders and decisions that are addressed to individuals. The administrator may order a person to make payment of an assessment or to demolish a building in the interest of public health and safety. He may order the expropriation of private property for public interest purposes, revoke a license or concession, restrict personal freedom, rescind a passport, etc. He may refuse to grant a license, concession, passport; dispensation from military service or payment of a tax; permission to legitimize or adopt a child; etc. An example of the authority of Italian administrators is the power of the police quaestor to issue injunctions or *diffida* to persons whom he regards as socially or morally offensive. Failure to obey the police injunction permits the quaestor to issue an order of prohibition or *ammonizione,* which places the individual under restricted liberty, such as a duty to report daily to the police, observe a curfew, avoid certain places and the company of certain persons, and refrain from certain specified activities or from carrying dangerous objects. The regular courts have no control over these police orders; and review lies exclusively with the superior administrative authorities, such as the minister or the administrative tribunals; the latter examine only the legitimacy and not the propriety of such orders. Violation of an order of police prohibition or *ammonizione* is punishable by a year of imprisonment on sentence of a summary court. The police quaestor may order a person to return to his birthplace through issuance of a *foglio di via obbligatoria,* or repatriation order. Such an order now requires the signature of the president of the Tribunal or Court of First Instance for the province. Similar police orders may provide for deportation and confinement to a work camp without the procedural guaranties of a judicial trial.

ADMINISTRATIVE CONTROLS

Administrative acts are subject to a variety of financial, legal, and jurisdictional controls, some of which take place prior to promulgation of the administrative decision and all of which are subject to subsequent controls. These controls are applied by the Court of Accounts; the accounting offices maintained by the Treasury in the various ministries; the General Accounting Bureau of the Treasury; the so-called administrative courts, consisting of the provincial administrative boards and the Council of State; and to a limited extent by the regular courts. The civil courts have the competence to issue declaratory judgments against acts of an administrator that require the payment of damages for injuries resulting from breaches of the legal rights of persons and corporations. In the event the civil court is challenged on the question of its jurisdiction, the highest civil court (Court of Cassation) is competent to decide whether the lower court may hear the case. Criminal courts may refuse to inflict penal sanctions on behalf of administrative measures that they regard as illegal, in which case the administration is powerless to enforce its decisions. But neither the regular courts nor the Constitutional Court have the competence to annul an administrative act, even though it should be declared to be in violation of the law and of the Constitution, since this prerogative is reserved by law to the administrative courts.

Fiscal Controls

Control over expenditures of public funds by administrators takes the form of authorizations to spend and verification of the actual expenditures. These functions are performed by the Court of Accounts and, to a more limited extent, by the General Accounting Bureau (*Ragioneria Generale dello Stato*) of the Ministry of Treasury. The latter compiles an annual report from the data supplied by its detached offices in the ministries on behalf of the Treasury, which must then submit its general financial report, together with the report of the Court of Accounts, to the houses of Parliament. Final accounting of public expenditures as contained in the *Rendiconto Generale,* or general financial report, requires as many as twenty years, as in the case of the reports for the years 1941–1942 to 1946–1947, which are now (1960) before Parliament. By the time parliamentary approval has been voted, such irregularities as may have been discovered are beyond repair. The Court of Accounts must place its seal on all ministry requests for expenditures and register these before the Treasury is permitted to authorize the withdrawal of public funds from the government's account. Unless the expenditure has been authorized by Parliament, the Court of Accounts must remand such requests to the minister. However, the minister may secure an order of the Council of Ministers requiring the Court of Accounts to affix its seal to the authorization. In such instances, the Court of Accounts affixes its seal "with reservations" and promptly notifies the presidents of the houses of Parliament. The Court of Accounts also audits the financial report of the Ministry of

Treasury and refers its report to the President of the Council of Ministers for presentation to the houses of Parliament.

Legal Controls

The Court of Accounts is legally charged with the duty of registering most presidential decrees, ministerial decrees concerning public personnel, and contracts negotiated by ministries and state agencies. The Court of Accounts checks the legality of such decrees and contracts to determine whether these have been authorized by law and whether they have met all the conditions specified by the law. Should it discover any legal irregularities, the measures are remanded to the minister or President of the Council of Ministers for correction. The Council of Ministers may, however, order the Court of Accounts to affix its seal and register these administrative measures, albeit with reservations. These formal controls aid Parliament in maintaining a check on the public administration.

The Court of Accounts was created in 1862 by statute. It is now considered a constitutional organ, since its continued existence is required by Article 100 of the Constitution. The Court of Accounts consists of a president, 6 section presidents, 27 councilors, a procurator-general, 2 vice-procurators-general, 114 referendars and assistant procurators-general, and 262 vice-referendars. All are appointed by decree of the President of the Republic. However, the selections below the rank of procurator-general are made by the president of the Court of Accounts instead of by the President of the Council of Ministers. Like the members of the Council of State, its higher membership enjoys permanent tenure on good behavior, subject to removal only by a joint parliamentary commission consisting of the presidents and vice-presidents of both houses of Parliament. The subordinate membership is subject, instead, to disciplinary measures proposed by the president of the Court of Accounts and agreed to by the President of the Council of Ministers. The exercise of legal control over administrative conduct is performed by the control section, which consists of seven or more councilors and a section president, or by the general assembly, which consists of eleven or more councilors and the president of the Court of Accounts. The procurator-general and his subordinates are attached to the jurisdictional sections and have the task of representing the interests of the state in all litigation before the Court of Accounts.

Jurisdictional Controls

Complaints against the public administration are normally filed before the administrative courts instead of before the regular courts in Italy, unless the case involves a claim for the award of damages. Administrative courts do not have the competence of civil courts to award the payment of damages to an individual for the tortious acts of public officials. Their function is to annul administrative decisions that are in violation of a law or administrative rule or that invade the legal rights of the individual to the detriment of a private interest. They are empowered to issue administrative orders that public administrators have refused to do in order to defend a legitimate personal interest. They may also order the payment of damages awarded by a civil court in favor of a private litigant against a public administrator. They may override administrative decisions and substitute their own rulings. Should the administrators refuse to execute the rulings of the administrative courts, the persons who are thereby injured have legal grounds for tort action against the individual administrators who are remiss in performing their legal obligations. Such private persons may also file a complaint with the Public Ministry, or prosecuting magistrates of the criminal courts, for penal proceedings against the omissive officials.

Administrative courts are empowered to judge whether administrative acts or omissions are necessary and proper (so-called merit judgment), as well as whether these are compatible with the law (so-called legitimacy judgment). The legality of an administrative act may be impugned before an administrative court for various reasons: if the administrative act violates a law, if the administrator acted without sufficient legal authority (incompetence), or if the administrator abused his authority (excess of power). An administrator may exceed his authority in a number of ways: by employing his public authority for purposes that were not intended by the law (misuse of power), by misinterpreting the facts in making a ruling, by applying illogic or poor judgment, by ignoring administrative precedents of higher administrators and of administrative tribunals, or by acting outside the instructions contained in ministerial directives. In merit judgments, the administrative court may enter into the motives of the administrator to determine whether his action coincides with the public interest; it may conceive of the public interest in a different way and so overrule the administrator.

The primary purpose of the administrative courts is to protect those private interests that are grounded in legal rights and that serve the public interest from inopportune administrative rulings. The administrative courts have the power to interpret public policy rather broadly and to mitigate the harshness of administrative enactments. An example would be the annulment of an administrative order requiring the demolition of a building for purposes of public safety or public health, unless the latter were really threatened. The administrative courts also have the competence to review the personnel decisions of public authorities and the disciplinary measures taken by these against public employees of the civil and military as well as the central and local administrations.

The Court of Accounts has three jurisdictional sections to hear administrative suits involving financial and civil (tort) responsibility of public employees, together with the determination of the fine or amount of damage to charge against these, and to consider cases involving pension rights of retired public employees. The individual sections are staffed by at least four councilors and a section president. The Court of Accounts may form what is known as combined sections, or a full panel of the jurisdictional sections, to hear complaints of its own personnel; combined sections must include ten councilors and the president of the Court of Accounts or a section president. Combined sections also hear appeals from a section of the Court of Accounts. In suits involving the personal liability of public officials handling public funds (mismanagement of public funds), the procurator-general of the Court of Accounts prosecutes before the second section; appeal is permitted to combined sections. The second section also reviews appeals from the prefectural councils. The Court of Accounts may form itself into what is known as plenary assembly to review certain decisions of the individual jurisdictional sections. A plenary assembly consists of eighteen councilors (six from each jurisdictional section) and is presided over by the president of the Court of Accounts. Decisions of the plenary assembly are subject to appeal before the Court of Cassation on grounds of excess of power or incompetence. Within the scope of its jurisdiction, the Court of Accounts has the authority to annul ministerial decisions of administrative character and to issue administrative orders that an administrator has refused to do.

The Council of State acts as an administrative court through its three jurisdictional sections, through *ad hoc* jurisdictional commissions formed of members of two or more jurisdictional sections, and through the plenary assembly, which consists of four councilors from each of the three jurisdictional sections, presided over by the president of the Council of State. It has original jurisdicion over suits against a ministry or other administrative agencies of the state and appellate jurisdiction over cases heard by the *giunte provinciale amministrative,* or provincial administrative boards, that operate at the provincial level to review the decisions of the provincial and communal authorities.

There are certain conditions under which recourse to the administrative courts, and especially the Council of State, is barred. Before the Council of State may assume jurisdiction over a complaint, the administrative decision must be definitive; in other words, it must be the conclusive act of the administrative authority in question, which means that the decision is not subject to further administrative review by a superior administrator. The decision of the administrator must not be a "political act" (like British acts of state) involving a matter over which the minister or his agent have complete discretion. The statutory time limits regulating administrative litigation must also be observed, and the administrative office in question as well as interested private parties in the matter must be informed of the complaint. Finally, a copy of the administrative decision, or a certificate attesting to its nature, together with all the particulars of the complaint, including relevant documents, must be presented to the registrar of the Council of State, or in local suits to the provincial administrative board. If the plaintiff has applied for administrative review to the President of the Republic, he is precluded from seeking jurisdictional remedies, since the application for presidential review of administrative acts involves consultation of the Council of State in its consultative capacity (through its advisory sections), and the Council will not permit its jurisdictional sections to review decisions made by its advisory sections.

THE CIVIL SERVICE

The Italian public administration is divided into four basic careers: directive, technical, clerical, and manual. Each of these careers is subdivided into numerous ranks. Administrative directors range from the position of director-general, inspector-general, divisional director, section director, to first, second, and third councilor of administration. The councilors do not exercise responsibility but merely assist one of the directors. Most councilors are young university graduates; occasionally, persons from the technical career succeed in advancing upward into the directive career. Admission to the directive career is by competitive examination, consisting of written and oral questions involving largely theoretical, but some practical, knowledge. Each ministry may fix the maximum age limit for applicants below the normal statutory limit of thirty-two years. Certain categories of persons, such as public employees of another ministry, war invalids, and veterans, are given legal dispensation from these age restrictions. The examinations are held periodically in Rome. They are conducted by an examining committee appointed by the administration council of the ministry and consisting of consultants of the ministry (generally university professors) and high officials of the ministry. The number of vacancies are filled by appointment of the examinees having the highest cumulative score. Persons who have failed twice are not permitted to repeat the examination. Those who are appointed serve as apprentices for six months; if this period is insufficient, the apprenticeship may be extended for another six months.

The administration council must recommend all permanent appointments to the minister. Its decisions are based on the reports of the section directors who have supervised the apprentices and upon the grades received in the courses of instruction conducted by the ministry. Advancement within the career is one rank at a time. Qualifications for promotion include seniority, written and oral examinations, publications, and a good service record. In-service training is compulsory, and inefficiency in such course work may result in disciplinary sanctions. The directive career is employed in the higher positions of the regional and provincial offices of the central administration as well as in the ministries at Rome. Such persons as prefects, vice-prefects, quaestors, and divisional heads of the prefecture are of the directive career. The only example of officials of the directive career who are not appointed by the ministry are mayors, who are elected by the communal council. Yet mayors are considered also as public officials of the state insofar as they perform duties required of them by law for the central administration. They are subject to removal from office by presidential decree on the advice of the Minister of Interior.

The directive career of the Foreign Ministry is organized under a separate presidential decree (January 11, 1956, *n.* 18) that sets up five major categories: diplomatic and consular, emigration, commercial, oriental, and press. Within each category, there are as many as nine ranks. The administration council of the Foreign Ministry consists of the minister, the secretary-general, the chief of diplomatic ceremonial, the officials in charge of the directorates-general, and offices under the direct authority of the minister. No person may transfer from other branches of the public service or the professions into the Foreign Ministry, and the normal age (maximum) limit is thirty.

The technical career is divided into the following ranks: chief secretary, principal secretary, first secretary, adjunct secretary, and vice-secretary. Secretaries may be employed in minor administrative tasks, in technical functions, or in bookkeeping and accounting activities. They must have a diploma from a higher secondary school in order to apply for the ministry's competitive examinations, unless they are already public employees in the highest rank of the clerical career and have a certain number of years of seniority as well as the recommendation of the administration council. The Ministry of Interior employs many secretaries for administrative tasks, such as communal secretaries or chief clerks, who act as agents of the prefecture to insure the legality of the mayor's acts.

The clerical career has five separate ranks ranging from chief archivist to adjunct operator. It consists of typists, office machine operators, file clerks, registration clerks, archivists, etc. The minimum qualification required for application to take the competitive examinations is a diploma from a lower secondary school (equivalent to eighth grade).

The lowest career of public employees is formed of manual workers who are engaged in various aspects of maintenance operations: custodians, janitors, gardeners, watchmen, errand runners, drivers, etc. Those who take the basic literacy test and have the diploma of the elementary school (fifth grade) form the so-called auxiliary personnel of the public service and are divided into five basic ranks from chief helper to servant. These employees are salaried on a monthly basis. There are other manual employees who are paid daily wages and form the lowest group in public employment.

Public employees are not permitted to hold any other position of emolument, public or private, without specific authorization, on penalty of immediate discharge. They are subject to immediate suspension should they file candidacy for most public offices filled by election, with the exception of university professors, who are allowed to teach while holding parliamentary seats or even ministerial portfolios. Public employees are not permitted to engage in any strikes or sympathy walkouts on penalty of fine, imprisonment, and immediate discharge with loss of pension rights. They are not allowed to bargain collectively. Public employees who belong to the police forces, the military forces, or to the diplomatic and consular corps are not allowed to be members of any political party or to engage in any sort of political activity other than voting.

SELECTED READING

Adams, John Clarke, and Barile, Paolo. *The Government of Republican Italy.* Boston: Houghton Mifflin Co., 1961. Pp. 91–107.

Galeotti, Serio. *The Judicial Control of Public Authorities in England and Italy: A Comparative Study.* London: Stevens & Sons, Ltd., 1954.

Miele, Giovanni, et al. "Italian Administrative Law," *International and Comparative Law Quarterly,* III (July, 1954), 421–53.

Treves, Giuseppino. *The Control of Public Enterprise in Italy.* Rome and Geneva: International Political Science Association, 1958.

———. "Judicial Review in Italian Administration," *University of Chicago Law Review,* XXVI (Winter, 1959), 419–35.

27

Local Government and Administration

Legislative and administrative powers and functions are decentralized in Italy territorially among the regions, provinces, and municipalities. To each of these subdivisions of the state are accorded certain spheres of legislative and administrative competence, within which locally constituted legislatures, executives, and administrative organs are permitted limited discretion in designated matters of government.

THE REGIONS

Regional self-government represents an innovation in Italy from the traditions of centralism that were imposed in 1861 by the Liberal monarchy in the interest of developing national unity. It is still an embryonic experiment, which was adopted to promote democratic institutions within the new Republic. The majority of delegates to the Constituent Assembly were convinced that the success of fascism had been facilitated by the centralized bureaucratic state and that democracy at the center could be made secure against dictatorial revivals only by decentralizing political and administrative powers and functions territorially.

The Italian Constitution creates two types of region: the special regions having a more pronounced degree of autonomy because of their peculiar cultural and linguistic individuality (Sicily, Sardinia, Val d'Aosta, Trentino-Alto Adige, and Friuli-Venezia Giulia) and the ordinary regions. The special regions have charters that enjoy the status of constitutional law, while the charters of the ordinary regions are mere regional laws. Ironically, the special regions, although they do enjoy certain exceptional prerogatives, do not have the competence to alter their own charters; this remains a function of Parliament as regulated by Article 138 (constitutional revision). The ordinary regions, instead, may draft their own charters and alter them, subject to the consent of Parliament.

Ordinary Regions

Ordinary regional charters must await parliamentary enactment of certain basic legislation, such as a general law on regional elections (all election laws are adopted by Parliament), a general law providing the regions with their own sources of revenue or share of national revenues, laws defining the fundamental principles to which the regions must adhere in enacting their own legislation, and laws to regulate the transfer of administrative functions and personnel from the central administration to the region. Adequate control machinery has already been provided for by the Law of February 10, 1953. Once the basic enabling legislation has been passed by Parliament, the President of the Republic may, on the advice of the Government, decree the election of the regional councils and permit these to deliberate their own charters.

The content of ordinary regional charters is minutely predetermined by the Constitution and the Law of February 10, 1953, so that the regional councils, once elected, have little discretion in adopting their own charters. Every region will have a unicameral legislature (regional council), elected directly by the voters in accordance with central election regulations. The regional council elects a regional president and an executive committee from its own membership. Both the regional president and assessors may be removed by the regional council either singly or collectively. The regional president may not decree the dissolution of the regional council, a prerogative that is reserved for the President of the Republic acting on the advice of the Government and a joint parliamentary commission. The dissolution power of the central authorities (President, Government, and Parliament) is constitutionally conditioned (Article 126) and is not entirely discretionary, so that abuse of this power could be appealed by the regional authorities to the Constitutional Court.

The legislative powers that the Constitution reserves for the ordinary regions concern only local technical matters. Even these rather paltry functions are circumscribed by the constitutional requirement that central legislation fix the fundamental principles within which such powers might be exercised. The central authorities determine how the regions shall exercise their own legislative powers. Until such "instructions" are issued by Parliament, the regions are not permitted to exercise any original legislative powers except as permitted by Article 9 of the Law of February 10, 1953. Should these instructions be altered by Parliament, all regional laws adopted in pursuance of their predecessors would become null and void insofar as they conflicted with the new principles issued by

Parliament. The regional councils are required to make changes in regional legislation to conform with the changing standards set for them by Parliament within ninety days.

Special Regions

The special regions have an "exclusive" sphere of legislative competence limited only by constitutional norms; basic social and economic reforms (particularly land reform and industrialization) that Parliament might adopt nationally; and, in the case of Sardinia, Val d'Aosta, and Trentino-Alto Adige, by national interests. The exclusive powers are somewhat broader in the case of Sicily, which has the right to organize local government, elementary schools, industry and commerce; expropriate for public uses; carry out land improvements and public works as well as regulate agriculture and forestry, mining, hunting, fishing, public charity, tourism, urban planning, etc. However, court decisions have reduced the scope of this regional legislative power by allowing Parliament to legislate in matters of "exclusive" regional competence insofar as the regions have not exercised such functions; in the event of differences between national and regional legislation in such exclusively regional matters, court decisions have sided at times with the regions and at other times with Parliament. The special High Court for Sicily, which was established in 1946 to resolve controversies between the regional government and the central Government, proved to be an effective safeguard of regional rights by correcting decisions of the ordinary courts that limited the scope of regional autonomy. Its functions have been assumed by the Constitutional Court since that organ came into existence in 1956.

Central Control Over the Regions

To insure compliance by the regional councils with the legislative directives of Parliament, all regional legislation (statutes and regulations) must be submitted within five days of passage by the regional council to the Government commissioner in the region, who has thirty days to refer the matter to the Government for instructions on whether to certify or return it to the regional council with the reasons for the Government's objections. Should the regional council approve the bill by absolute majority, the Government has fifteen days during which to impugn the measure before the Constitutional Court (for reasons of legal incompatibility) or before the houses of Parliament (for reasons of merit or conflict of interest between the Government and the region). The region can appeal to the Constitutional Court against the act of Parliament that annuls such regional measures under Article 134 of the Constitution (conflict of powers between the state and a region.)

The executive committee deliberates all administrative policy within the scope of regional legislation and normally issues merely instructions, circulars, and orders to its administrative heads, since the regional council usually issues the administrative regulations to implement legislative norms. In cases of urgency, the executive committee may decree administrative regulations, which must be ratified by the regional council at its subsequent convocation. The executive committee concludes contracts on behalf of the region, formulates all plans for public works (which must be approved by the regional council), draws up the budget (whose enactment is by the regional council), and presents the audited report on expenditures to the regional council. It may order the transfer of funds from one to another item within the same authorized budget chapter, subject to approval by the regional council.

Control over the acts of the executive committee is vested in a special control commission appointed by the President of the Republic at the suggestion of the President of the Council of Ministers in agreement with the Minister of Interior. This regional control commission must be reappointed whenever the regional council is re-elected. The actual composition of this commission is predetermined to a large extent by the Law of February 10, 1953.

The regional control commission may annul all administrative acts of the regional council or its executive committee that conflict with higher law. Such annulments must be decreed within twenty days and must be supported by reasons; they are definitive decrees not subject to appeal to higher administrative tribunals such as the Council of State but are presumably subject to review by the Court of Cassation and by the Constitutional Court. The regional control commission also exercises merit control over certain acts of the regional organs, such as the budget and item changes in it, any commitment to spend money for more than five years, contracts imposing financial obligations, alienations of regional property, the purchase of stocks and bonds not guaranteed by the state, and extensions of public services by the region. However, the control commission has no authority to annul regional administrative measures because of disagreement over their propriety; it may simply require the regional council to reconsider the questions raised and vote the matters by absolute majority the second time.

Since the regions are recipients of financial assistance from Parliament, they are placed under the fiscal control of the Court of Accounts, in conformity with Article 100 of the Constitution, so that regional expenditures will require preliminary authorization of the Court of Accounts as well as subsequent auditing and report to Parliament.

Regional Administration

To prevent unnecessary duplication of administrative offices, the Constitution and the statute on regional organization require the regions to delegate administrative tasks to the existing provincial and communal offices wherever this is possible, instead of creating special regional field offices. Should the provincial and communal offices prove to be ineffective administrators, the regional executive committee may reassume its powers and establish its own administration or complain to the prefect, so that this official of the Government might dissolve the negligent or incompetent provincial and communal councils, dismiss the mayor, and insure local administrative efficiency via commissioner rule.

The ordinary regions are not likely to be allowed direction of the police forces of the state, as has been allowed to some of the special regions, or the exercise of the police ordinance power of the prefects. Of the special regions, Sicily enjoys the greatest degree of police power, since its charter (Article 31) vests the police ordinance power and the command of police forces in the regional president, although the Government may place its own commissioner or police chiefs (quaestors) in charge of public security in "exceptional cases." The Government may delegate limited or full police powers to the regional presidents of Sardinia and the Val d'Aosta, who must exercise these powers under the direction of the Government commissioner on instructions from the Interior Ministry or Council of Ministers. The Government may remove the police ordinance and command powers entrusted to these regional officials at any time and place them in the hands of the commissioner or the quaestors (provincial police chiefs appointed by the Interior Ministry). In the region of Trentino-Alto Adige, the police powers are divided between the Government commissioner, who retains the most important police authority once exercised by the prefects in this area, and the presidents of the provincial executive committees (of which there are just two, in the German-speaking province of Bolzano and the Italian-speaking province of Trento), who have limited police ordinance powers under the regional charter. The ordinary regions will not receive, apparently, any autonomous authority over matters of public safety, which are to remain in the hands of the provincial prefects as under the existing laws of public security. The committee of the parliamentary commission that reported the bill on the ordinary regions concluded (majority opinion) that the prefect should be retained to coordinate the action of all officials within the province who administer affairs for the central ministries and to direct the maintenance of public safety within the area of provinces, including the communes.

THE PROVINCES

The regional charters of both Sicily and Val d'Aosta have eliminated the province as a self-governing territory, while that of Sardinia permits the regional council to modify the extent (territory) and functions of the three provinces at the request of the majority of the people (referendum) in each province. In the Trentino-Alto Adige, the two provinces have been accorded vast new powers and functions that correspond to those of the region itself. In the ordinary regions, the provinces will be preserved much as they are at present, as areas of limited self-government within the scope of national and regional laws. The province has also served as an administrative district for the Government and ministries, as a judicial district for the regular civil and criminal courts, as a jurisdictional district for primary administrative tribunals, and as an electoral constituency for parliamentary elections.

As a self-governing territory, the province functions through a popularly elected council consisting of as few as twenty-four members (in provinces with less than 300,000 inhabitants) to forty-five members in the larger provinces (over 1,400,000 inhabitants); an executive committee consisting of from four to eight assessors, elected by the provincial council from its own membership; and a president of the provincial council and executive committee, elected by the council. The members of all three provincial organs hold office for four years.

The provincial council must be convened at least once a year by its president, and may be convened additional times if necessary, to deliberate matters that cannot be delegated to the executive committee. The latter functions permanently; and, in cases of urgency, may exercise the deliberative powers of the council, subject to subsequent ratification by the council. It has limited powers of decision: it formulates the provincial budget, makes all decisions concerning provincial employees (excepting those of directive rank), stipulates contracts of limited value (up to 2,500,000 lire), authorizes payment for all mandatory expenditures required by law of the province, deliberates court suits for matters of limited value, prepares reports for consideration by the council, and gives an account of its actions to the council and to the prefect—the Government's representative in the province. The provincial president represents the province in all lawsuits, directs the administration of all decisions of the council and its executive committee, and may stipulate the terms of contracts whose general content has already been deliberated by the council or the executive committee. The bureaucratic officials and employees who staff the provincial offices are headed by the secretary-general (who is an official of the Interior Ministry) and form the provincial secretariat, which is the administrative staff of the province.

The provincial authorities have certain mandatory functions to perform as required by the law and other optional functions that they are permitted to carry out. Among the obligatory functions are provision of proper facilities for the use of the central administration (prefectural building and residence for the prefect, police barracks, and offices, etc.);

provisions of public health and sanitation services (control of certain diseases, such as smallpox, malaria, tuberculosis, rabies, pellagra, etc., and maintenance of health centers); maintenance of provincial roads and bridges; provision of physical facilities and maintenance personnel for the secondary schools; contribution of funds to schools and universities; operation or subsidization of institutions for the mentally ill, the mentally retarded, orphans, abandoned children, blind and deaf-mute persons, expectant mothers, and infants; and financial aid to such services as pest and insect control, census, land registry, and the provincial administrative board. Among the optional functions that the province may assume are direct management and operation of services such as public utilities (gas, electricity, water supply, etc.), transportation (buses and street-cars and local trains), telephone, greenhouses, and plant nurseries.

The provincial authorities have a limited power to draw up legal regulations over such matters as rice cultivation, animal health inspection, and ocean fishing. The provinces have limited taxing authority over land, buildings, income, profits, and animal-drawn vehicles; and they share certain revenues that the central administration collects (such as automobile taxes and land income). The provinces also derive income from services that they provide and may be authorized to borrow funds.

THE COMMUNES

All populated areas of Italy are grouped into communes, which is the legal term applied to all urban and rural communities. The Constitution defines the communes (Articles 128 and 129) as both self-governing bodies and administrative subdivisions of the regions and state. Communes are essentially public corporations consisting of a resident population inhabiting a fixed territory and endowed with legal personality in order to promote the well-being of the population and serve the interests of the state. Statutory laws and delegated legislation (presidential decrees) define the qualifications, composition, organization, powers, functions, and duties of communes. Italian communities are not permitted to formulate their own charters; they are, however, permitted limited authority to regulate their internal organization within existing legal confines. The Constitution (Article 133) confers upon the regions authority to establish, modify, and abolish communes; but outside the special regions whose charters permit such functions, the communes must rely upon statutes of Parliament and presidential decrees to recognize their status, define their boundaries, and permit them to expand or merge or to be divided. Communes must be able to provide those essential services required by law in order to continue their separate existence or they may be attached to another commune. It is relatively easy for districts to secede from a commune and form separate communes or join a different one.

All communes have a popularly elected council, an executive committee elected by the council from its own councilors, and a mayor similarly elected. The size of the council varies in accordance to population of the commune: cities with over 500,000 inhabitants elect eighty councilors, those with over 250,000 elect sixty, those with over 100,000 elect fifty, and those with over 30,000 elect forty; towns with more than 10,000 inhabitants elect thirty, while those having over 3,000 elect twenty, and all smaller communities elect a council of fifteen members. The size of the council's executive committee (*giunta*) varies from eight assessors and three alternates for the two largest categories of commune to six, four, and two assessors and two alternates. The mayor presides over the executive committee as well as over the council.

The mayor and assessors are elected at the first meeting of the newly convened council. A quorum for elections is two-thirds the councilors. Election is by a majority of votes cast. If because of multiple candidates there is no majority after two ballots have been taken for the mayor, a runoff is held between the top two candidates of the second ballot. A similar runoff ballot is required for the assessors; the number of candidates on the runoff ballot is limited to twice the number of vacancies, and these are selected from those who had the highest number of votes on the second ballot. Councilors cast one vote for each vacancy to be filled.

The normal term for the council, the assessors, and the mayor is four years. This may be shortened for a number of reasons: should the number of councilors fall below the quorum (majority) because of death, resignation, or removal for incompatibility; should the population of the commune be increased or decreased by more than one-fourth due to modification of its boundaries; or should the council be dissolved by presidential decree. The mayor is subject to removal by the council or may be dismissed by presidential decree at any time; in such instances, the council must elect a new mayor. Assessors may also be removed by the council; they may disqualify themselves (as may the mayor) by being sentenced to more than one month of jail or by being placed under police interdictions. Assessors who absent themselves without valid reason from meetings of the executive committee three consecutive times and councilors who fail to attend an entire session are to be removed by the council. While new assessors may be elected at any time by the council, no by-elections of councilors are permitted; when the legal number is no longer available, new elections must be decreed for the entire council. The prefect may instruct the council to remove the mayor or one or more assessors for reasons prescribed by law (disqualification) and decree their immediate suspension; should the council remain negligent for more than a month, the removal is decreed by the President.

The council meets normally for two sessions annually (March to May and September to November) and in extraordinary session called by the mayor, the prefect, the executive committee, or one-third of the councilors. The mayor must summon the councilors and inform the prefect of all sessions. Normally, the quorum is a majority; in some instances, as few as four councilors constitute a quorum; while deliberations are always by a majority of those present and voting, except where extraordinary majorities are specified. Deliberations of the council must be communicated to the prefect within eight days and posted for fifteen days before they are enforceable. The prefect has twenty days in which to annul the deliberation for reasons of illegitimacy. Contracts deliberated by the council require the subsequent authorization (*visto*) of the prefect before they may be executed. Certain deliberations of the council, as specified by law, require the authorization of the provincial administrative board; while others require central authorization by the Minister of Interior or the Minister of Public Sanitation. Once the regional organs are established, the commune will be subject to control committees of the region established in each provincial center to exercise power of annulment of acts of the communes that are in any way illegal—a power that is presently vested in the prefect.

The communal council is the deliberative organ of the commune that formulates all basic policies and exercises the limited legislative authority of the commune within the limits of the law, subject to the controls of the central administration.

The executive committee is a permanent organ of the commune that acts on behalf of the council between the latter's sessions. It may exercise any power of the council on delegation of authority and, during emergencies, may act in place of the council, subject to the latter's subsequent ratification of its actions. It exercises full authority over minor personnel employed by the commune; may authorize changes in the budget; and regulates such fees for local cabs, boats, baggage porters, and parking that may be charged for services. It has limited power to stipulate the terms of contracts and initiate lawsuits on certain matters; and it compiles tax tables and communal obligations, the preliminary budget, draft ordinances and bylaws, and other matters for council consideration. It supervises the commune's departments and offices; an assessor is placed in charge of one or more departments for this purpose. It executes the decisions of the council where this is required. The committee acts by majority vote of its members present, and a quorum is a majority of the entire membership. Assessors who have a personal interest (or family interests) in any matter requiring deliberation are not permitted to participate in its discussion.

The mayor is head of the commune's administration, chairman of its council and executive committee, and also agent of the central administration. The mayor directs the deliberations of the council and its executive committee and signs these, taking such measures as are required to implement them. He communicates all deliberations to the prefect, directs the local departments to carry out all policies and enforce all regulations and bylaws and ordinances, suspends local employees, stipulates certain contracts, supervises all local administration, represents the commune in all lawsuits, and attends auctions of municipal property. As an agent of the central administration, the mayor must report all matters affecting public order and safety to the *questura*, take such measures as are necessary to preserve public order and safety within the scope of his police ordinance power, direct the local police authorities to carry out his orders, and order the arrest of persons for violations of law. He must order such measures as are necessary to enforce the sanitation and health laws and regulations, the building codes, etc. He is required to keep the civil register (record of births, marriages, deaths, etc.) and the population register (record of residents and changes of domicile); to compile the electoral list, the military list, and the census; to issue certificates and identity cards; and perform civil marriages. He may requisition private housing during emergencies and order the demolition or evacuation of dangerous premises as well as expropriations of private property for purposes of public utility. He must publish all laws, decrees, and regulations of the central authorities and prefecture and perform the duties of recruiting the manpower for the armed forces on behalf of the Ministry of Defense.

SELECTED READING

ADAMS, JOHN CLARKE, and BARILE, PAOLO. *The Government of Republican Italy.* Boston: Houghton Mifflin Co., 1961. Pp. 107–23.

CHIARELLI, GIUSEPPE. "Rome." In *Great Cities of the World: Their Government, Politics and Planning,* pp. 517–48, William A. Robeson (ed.). London: George Allen & Unwin, Ltd., 1957.

ZINC, HAROLD, *et al. Rural Local Government in Sweden, Italy and India: A Comparative Study.* London: Stevens & Sons, Ltd., 1957.

28

The Judicial System

Societies that are to be governed under law require a powerful judicial arm with competence to judge the constitutionality of legislation and the legality of administrative acts. Courts protect the legal rights and legitimate interests of subjects from the arbitrary rule of political elites and their administrators. They constitute the first line of defense of the value system of society as prescribed by its Constitution and laws.

The Italian courts have a great responsibility in upholding the Constitution and the laws enacted by the legislature in pursuance of it because of the lengthy list of personal rights that are constitutionally guaranteed. Such rights would be meaningless unless the legislature can be compelled to respect and implement them, and the administration is forced to abide by the restraints that they impose.

THE CONSTITUTIONAL COURT'S POWERS AND FUNCTIONS

The Constitutional Court may decree the unconstitutionality of any law or act having the force of law because of substantive incompatibility or due to formal irregularities accompanying the enactment of such measures. This applies to statutes of Parliament, the regional assemblies and the assemblies of the autonomous provinces of Bolzano and Trento, and to legislative decrees emanating from the executive. The Constitutional Court has authority to review the legality of constitutional legislation on formal or procedural grounds, but most authorities deny its power to judge the substantive content of such enactments. In addition to this function of reviewing the constitutionality of laws and acts having the force of law, the Constitutional Court judges conflicts of authority that arise between the Government and the regions or between the regions;

it also hears conflicts involving the autonomous powers of the provinces of Bolzano and Trento. The Constitutional Court also functions as a criminal court whenever Parliament accuses the President of the Republic or members of the Council of Ministers under Article 90 and 96 of the Constitution.

The jurisdiction of the Constitutional Court may be invoked directly by Parliament, to judge criminal charges against the President or ministers; by the Government (i.e., Council of Ministers), to resolve conflicts of authority with the regions; and by the president of the regional executive, to resolve conflicts with the Government or with another region.

On controversies concerning the constitutionality of laws or acts having the force of law, the jurisdiction of the Constitutional Court is invoked indirectly by application of a court for a ruling that affects the outcome of a lawsuit under trial. Private subjects are not permitted to apply to the Constitutional Court for a ruling on the constitutionality of any law or act having the force of law. This must be done by the court during the course of a trial, whenever the constitutionality of a law or act having the force of law is in doubt; and the outcome of the trial depends upon the validity of that measure. Parties to a lawsuit that is being tried in court (in criminal, civil, or administrative tribunals) may raise the question of constitutionality, at any time to the presiding judge, of a law or act having the force of law that has a direct bearing on the rights or duties of the litigants and that affects the decision of the court in the case. It is for the court to decide whether there is in fact a question of constitutionality involved and whether this is relevant to the case under consideration. If the trial court accepts the proposal to refer the question of constitutionality of a law or act having the force of law to the Constitutional Court, the presiding judge suspends the trial and applies for a ruling. Notification of the application to the Constitutional Court must be made to the litigants, the Public Ministry, the President of the Council of Ministers, and the presidents of both houses of Parliament (if the law in question was approved by Parliament), or to the regional president and assembly president if a regional law is involved. The president of the Constitutional Court orders publication of the application in the *Official Gazette* or *Regional Bulletin,* and the parties who have been notified may file written depositions within twenty days before the Constitutional Court.

Upon expiration of the twenty-day period, the president of the Constitutional Court designates one of the judges to prepare the preliminary report for discussion. Copies of this report, together with the depositions, are circulated among the judges of the Court not less than ten days before the hearing. The interested parties who have filed depositions are notified twenty days before the hearing is scheduled so that they may present additional memorials and be prepared for the oral presentations, which are delivered by legal counsel; the Government is represented by the advocate-general.

Eleven or more judges must be in attendance at every session of the hearings, and only those who have attended all of these are permitted to vote on the decision. The judges deliberate in chambers, with the judge of instruction voting first, followed by the other judges in order from youngest to eldest and ending with the vote of the president of the Court. The president of the Court appoints a judge to write the definitive decision as approved by the majority, and all the judges who have deliberated must sign the sentence. Copies of the sentence are sent within two days to the Minister of Justice and the houses of Parliament, if the law in question was enacted by the latter, or to the regional president and assembly if the sentence affects a regional law. Legislative measures that have been pronounced as unconstitutional cease to be enforceable the day after publication of the sentence.

Criminal charges against the President of the Republic or ministers are formulated by a joint commission of Parliament consisting of ten deputies and ten senators who are elected by the houses for the legislative term. The houses in joint meeting must adopt the charges by simple majority vote and elect one or more members to act as prosecuting commissioners before the Constitutional Court. Parliamentary adoption of criminal charges results in automatic suspension of the President and the ministers. The president of the Constitutional Court designates a judge to compile a report on the charges raised by Parliament against the ministers; the president of the Court must compile the report when the President of the Republic is the defendant. The judge of instruction may order such security measures to be taken to prevent the evasion of the defendant while he is compiling the report. The judge of instruction is not competent to acquit the defendant even if the charges lack sufficient evidence to establish probable guilt. His report is read in court during the trial, which is conducted like any criminal trial. The defendant is represented by personal counsel and has the right to speak in his own defense. The parliamentary commissioner supports the charges and requests the punishment, which is not indicated in cases involving the President of the Republic and must therefore be left to the discretion of the Court. Ministers are punished in accordance with the provisions of the Penal Code, with added severity permitted at the discretion of the Court. The sentence of the Constitutional Court in criminal trials is not appealable or open to review; it may be revised by the Constitutional Court at some future date if new evidence to support the innocence of the defendant can be established. Sentences that establish the guilt and punishment of the defendant result in automatic removal from office, as well as such penalties as may be voted by the Court.

COMPOSITION OF THE CONSTITUTIONAL COURT

The Constitutional Court consists of fifteen regular judges and sixteen adjunct judges. The adjunct judges participate with the regular judges only in trials of the President of the Republic or ministers of the Government.

Regular judges of the Constitutional Court are selected in equal proportion (i.e., five) by the two houses of Parliament in joint meeting, by the President of the Republic, and by the three higher courts (i.e., the Court of Cassation, which elects three; the Council of State and the Court of Accounts, which elect one each). The five constitutional judges elected by Parliament must each receive a three-fifths majority. If after two ballots the effort has failed to obtain the requisite majority, a relative three-fifths majority of those members present and voting suffices. The nominees of the President are selected by the chief of state from the same categories prescribed by the Constitution for all regular constitutional judges: (1) retired or incumbent judges of the higher tribunals, (2) professors of law, and (3) lawyers with twenty or more years of advocacy before the courts. All magistrates of the Court of Cassation (procurators-general and advocates-general as well as councilors and presidents) and of the Court of Accounts and Council of State participate by majority vote in the election of their quota of constitutional judges. Constitutional judges serve a twelve-year term, which is not immediately renewable. Vacancies on the Court are to be filled within a month, and the newly elected judge serves a full term. Constitutional judges who incur legal disqualification by assuming appointive or elective public office, private employment, the exercise of a profession, responsible positions in a political party or pressure group, or engage actively in politics are removed from the Court by two-thirds of their colleagues. Constitutional judges who are charged with criminal offenses enjoy immunity from arrest and prosecution until the Court votes by majority to waive the privilege. This results in automatic suspension, while conviction of a crime is cause for removal. Constitutional judges are therefore free from political intimidation or persecution. The regular judges elect the president of the Court for a four-year term, and he in turn may appoint an acting president.

The sixteen adjunct judges are elected by a three-fifths majority of the two houses of Parliament in joint meeting whenever criminal charges have been approved against the President of the Republic or the ministers. The adjunct judges must have the legal qualifications for election to the Senate but must not be members of Parliament. A list of eligible persons is compiled every twelve years by Parliament from which the sixteen are to be selected when the occasion arises.

THE SUPERIOR JUDICIARY COUNCIL
(CONSIGLIO SUPERIORE DELLA MAGISTRATURA)

The regular civil and criminal courts (i.e., those exclusive of the administrative and military tribunals) constitute a self-governing arm of the state under the Constitution and the statutory law. They have been separated from the administrative control of the executive and are directed administratively by the Superior Judiciary Council.

The principal functions of the Superior Judiciary Council are to (1) compile and conduct all competitive examinations for appointment and promotion in the magistracy, (2) appoint magistrates to posts on the bench and to the procuracy or Public Ministry, (3) assign the magistrates to judicial districts and courts within them, (4) transfer and promote magistrates, (5) impose disciplinary penalties on magistrates, (6) increase the number of court sections, (7) assign magistrates to specific sections and functions, and (8) determine its own procedural rules within the norms of the law.

The Minister of Justice is not a member of the Superior Judiciary Council; but he controls the exercise by the Council of most of its powers, since the Council is not authorized to deliberate and make decisions of any importance except on matters specifically requested by the Minister. The Minister of Justice initiates action before the Council on all important matters through recommendations, but the Council is not bound to accept these. He retains the personnel files of all magistrates, which he supplies to the Council at its request. He reports cases of individual negligence and incompetence of magistrates to the Council and recommends disciplinary measures. He sits with the Council's personnel committee and recommends the appointment of presiding judges to all collegial benches. The budgetary requirements of the judiciary are determined by the Minister of Justice, who is responsible for securing parliamentary approval of judiciary appropriations. The Council may request the Minister to initiate bills before Parliament concerning the needs of the judiciary but is not permitted to propose legislation directly to the houses of Parliament. The Minister may by order delay the departure of a magistrate to his new post or he may order the magistrate to proceed in advance to his reassignment.

The Superior Judiciary Council consists of twenty-one elective members (fourteen by the magistrates and seven by Parliament) and three members ex officio (the President of the Republic, the president of the Court of Cassation, and the procurator-general of Cassation). The magistrates elect fourteen members to the Council from their own ranks by a curiously discriminatory method that favors the magistrates of the Court of Cassation and the Courts of Appeal. The magistrates of Cassation form an electoral college in which each magistrate casts a vote for six of his colleagues; those who receive a majority are elected in order of largest totals. The magistrates of the Courts of Appeal and of the lower courts form separate electoral colleges in each of four geographic areas, and each electoral college elects one representative from its own ranks to membership on the Council. The remaining seven members of the Superior Judiciary Council are elected by Parliament in joint meeting by a three-fifths majority vote, as in the case of constitutional judges. Eligibility for these members is prescribed constitutionally; they must be law professors or lawyers with fifteen years or more of practice before the courts. They may not hold seats in Parliament or in a regional assembly or exercise a profession after they have been elected. Persons from the magistracy who are elected to the Council are placed on inactive status during the four-year term of membership on the Council. Members are not eligible for immediate re-election. The four-year term may be curtailed by presidential decree of dissolution at any time should the Council fail to discharge its functions efficiently.

The presidium of the Superior Judiciary Council arranges the latter's agenda, manages its expenditures, and insures proper enforcement of its decisions and those of its committees. It is the Council's executive body. The presidium consists of the vice-president of the Council (chairman) and the president and procurator-general of the Court of Cassation.

The most important committee of the Superior Judiciary Council is the so-called disciplinary section, which imposes disciplinary measures against all magistrates on behalf of the Council. It must investigate denunciations of magistrates that are reported by the Minister of Justice or by the district judiciary councils. The disciplinary section is composed of ten members and four alternates but deliberates with only seven members. Four of the seven members of the disciplinary section serve by right on all of its hearings, while the remaining three are picked by lot from their respective categories. In the event the President of the Republic is required to preside, the vice-president of the Council does not participate. The procurator-general of Cassation prosecutes all cases of disciplinary trial against magistrates. Magistrates who have been sentenced to disciplinary penalties by the bench of the disciplinary section of the Superior Judiciary Council have the right of appeal to the united sections or full bench of the Court of Cassation.

All decisions of the Superior Judiciary Council that require enforcement are issued in the form of presidential decrees and are countersigned by the Minister of Justice. Since these decrees are considered to be administrative acts, they must be registered with the Court of Accounts, which has authority to review their legality on purely formal grounds (legitimacy). Non-disciplinary decrees of the Council that affect the career status of magistrates (such as decisions on promotions and assignments) are subject to jurisdictional review by the Council of State on petition by the aggrieved magistrate. The Council of State has authority to annul such decisions on grounds of merit as well as for formal violation of the law.

JUDICIAL PERSONNEL

The personnel that serve the regular courts consist of magistrates, auxiliary court functionaries (such as clerks, secretaries, and bailiffs), and judicial police. Only magistrates are administratively under the Superior Judiciary Council. The auxiliary personnel and the judicial police are employees of the Ministries of Justice, Interior, and Defense. There are two types of magistrate: regular and honorary. Honorary magistrates are either unpaid or granted a per diem honorarium for their services as conciliators, vice-conciliators, vice-praetors, non-legal experts on the juvenile courts, and people's judges on the Assize and Assize Appeal Courts. Regular magistrates are separated by reason of function and tenure into judges, procurators, and judicial auditors.

The Constitution requires (Article 106) that regular magistrates (with the exception of councilors of Cassation) be appointed by merit on the basis of individual performance in competitive examinations. Examinations for entrance into the magistracy are open to male citizens who have no criminal record, who possess full civil and political rights, and who hold a degree from a law faculty of an Italian university. Applicants must be between the ages of twenty-one and thirty. Annual quotas for appointment to the rank of judicial auditor are very limited and must be filled from the list of those who have qualified on the examinations in order from the highest score. Career magistrates enjoy great social prestige despite the fact that the salaries of most magistrates are not high, and magistrates are precluded from exercising a private profession.

Judicial auditors serve from two to three years as apprentice magistrates in the offices of the procurators of the Republic or in the lower courts (*Pretura* and Tribunal), where they receive practical training and perform minor duties as vice-praetors. They must pass a practical examination before the end of their third year. Those who are successful are promoted to the rank of judicial adjunct and are assigned to the office of the procurator of the Republic as an assistant procurator or to one of the lower courts as a judge (praetor or judge of Tribunal). The unsuccessful ones are dismissed from the magistracy.

Further advancement in the magistracy is by meritorious service, which is evaluated by competitive examinations and appraisals of the quality of sample judicial sentences and other publications written by magistrates. Promotions are made one step at a time, so that advancement to the Court of Cassation is slow for even the most capable magistrates. The average magistrate can expect to rise to the position of procurator of the Republic or president of Tribunal, which is comparable to that of assistant procurator-general or councilor of Appeal, if he is reasonably diligent. Magistrates below the rank of councilor of Appeal and assistant procurator-general of Appeal must be retired upon completion of forty years of service, provided they have reached age sixty-five. They may not serve beyond age seventy in any case. The higher magistrates are retired at age seventy. Once a magistrate has completed his probationary service, he is irremovable unless he is found guilty of acts that cause automatic disqualification under the law by the disciplinary section of the Superior Judiciary Council.

THE COURTS

Italian courts are divided by jurisdiction into a number of separate and distinct judicial branches. These are the administrative tribunals (discussed in Chapter 27), the regular civil and criminal courts, the military tribunals, and such special courts as port captaincies. Only the regular civil and criminal courts are discussed in this chapter (Figure 28–1).

The Conciliator

The lowest court in Italy is the Conciliatory Court, which adjudicates civil claims of less than 10,000 lire ($16) that are not assigned by law to other courts. The conciliator may apply equity to claims involving less than 2,000 lire ($3.25). Appeal from the conciliator's decisions is to the praetor. Conciliators are honorary magistrates who are appointed by the first president of the Court of Appeal on nomination by the procurator-general of the Court of Appeal district.

The Praetor *(Pretore)*

The praetor exercises civil and criminal jurisdiction of limited scope. Civil suits involving claims of less than 100,000 lire ($160) as well as eviction cases and civil injunctions may be heard by the praetor. His criminal jurisdiction is somewhat broader. He hears criminal charges that are punishable by fine alone or by a maximum penalty of three years of imprisonment. The praetor dispenses summary justice, since he performs the functions of the Public Ministry, and then judges those whom he has charged with criminal offenses. He may investigate crimes and order the arrest and summary interrogation of suspects and witnesses; those who make a plea of guilty are tried by him immediately. Those who wish to defend themselves must be given at least five days of preparation before trial is held. The praetor must notify the procurator of the Republic in the province of his sentences and decrees in all criminal judgments so that the latter may file an appeal against them. The praetor is also required to turn over all the evidence he has concerning crimes that exceed his jurisdiction to the procurator of the Republic. Decisions of the praetor may be appealed to the Tribunal.

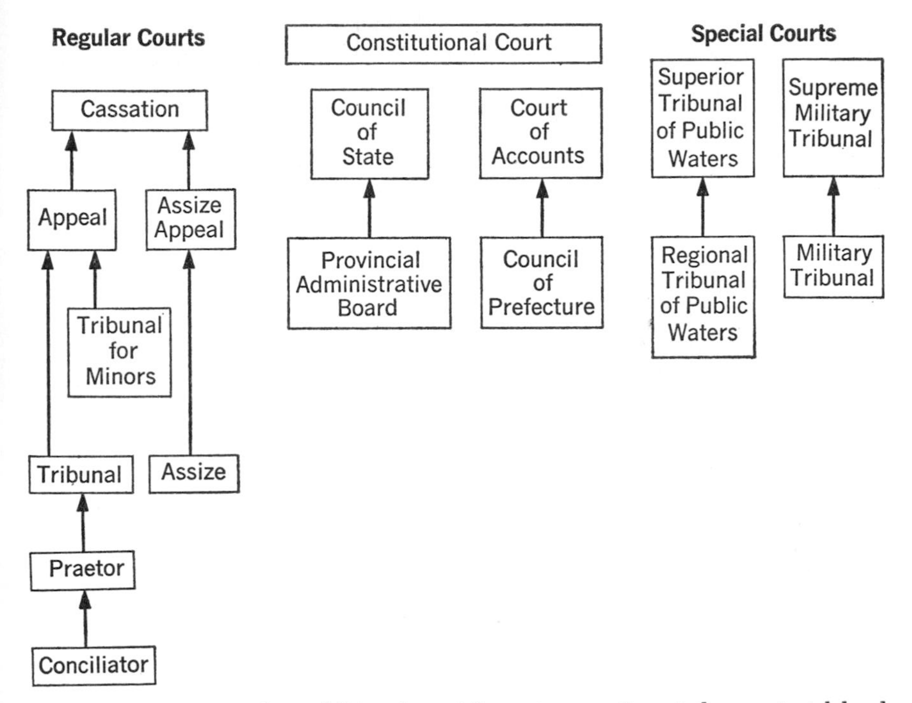

NOTE: There are a few additional special courts operating at the provincial level such as financial tribunals, port captains, and local tribunals of public waters. The latter operate as special sections of the regular Tribunal. Consular courts operate overseas. The lines and arrows indicate the direction of appeals. The Constitutional Court receives petitions from courts of every level to determine the constitutionality of a law or act having the force of law.

Figure 28–1. The Italian court system.

The Tribunal

In addition to its appellate jurisdiction, the Tribunal exercises broad original jurisdiction over civil and criminal offenses. All civil lawsuits that are not reserved by law for the conciliator and praetor are heard by the Tribunal, which is the court of unlimited original civil jurisdiction. The Tribunal judges all criminal offenses that are not reserved by law for trial by the praetor and the Assize Court, which covers a wide range of crimes, i.e., those punishable by more than three years of imprisonment to less than the maximum penalties. Offenses that were committed under aggravating circumstances are often removed from the praetor's jurisdiction and assigned to the Tribunal by the procurator of the Republic so that more severe penalties may be imposed upon the offender. Conversely, the procurator of the Republic may remove a criminal case from the Tribunal to the praetor's docket when attenuating circumstances are present in the commission of the crime. The Tribunal does not normally try juvenile offenders under eighteen, unless these are involved in a crime in which adults are also involved.

The Tribunal dispenses justice through a collegiate bench of three judges in all cases—civil, criminal, and appeals. Separate sections or even multiple sections may be constituted within the Tribunal, to which the president of the Tribunal assigns the cases. The bench decides all matters such as liability, guilt, and punishment by majority vote, which is taken in chambers secretly. No dissenting opinions are recorded, and all the judges sign the decree or sentence.

The Tribunal has duties that are entrusted to a single judge, such as the formal investigation of evidence and the charging of a suspect of a crime for trial, which is performed by the judge of instruction, and the imposition of measures of personal security on persons who are denounced as social delinquents by the police chief of the province, which is done by the judge of surveillance. The assignment of judges to the instruction or surveillance sections of the Tribunal is made annually.

There is a Tribunal in each province. It is generally located only at the provincial seat, but sections may be established in other provincial localities. In the event there is a controversy between different Tribunals over jurisdiction, the locus of the trial must be determined by the Court of Cassation.

The Tribunal for Minors *(Tribunale per i Minorenni)*

The Tribunal for Minors has unlimited jurisdiction in criminal matters where juvenile offenders are involved. There is only one such court in each judicial district of the Courts of Appeal; it therefore handles juvenile cases for a number of provinces. The Tribunal for Minors is presided over by a councilor of the Court of Appeal, and its other judges include a regularly assigned judge of Tribunal and an expert layman who has accepted appointment as an honorary magistrate of this specialized court. This Tribunal uses no jury. It has its own instruction section and a special procurator having the rank of assistant procurator-general of the Court of Appeal to formulate the charges and prosecute before it. This Tribunal may suspend sentences conditionally if the punishment is less than three years of detention. Minors who are sentenced to more than three years of detention are eligible for pardon when they are twenty-one and twenty-five (depending on the nature of the sentence and the age of the juvenile offender at the time of sentencing), provided they have exhibited to the Tribunal proof of moral and social rehabilitation while in custody. The Tribunal for Minors is competent also to order the confinement of juveniles in a reformatory until the age of twenty-one on denunciation by the police, the Public Ministry, the parents, or the legal guardian for conduct, which is morally and socially reprehensible but not criminal. Court orders to confine a juvenile for educative purposes are not appealable.

The Assize Court

Serious crimes such as homicide, kidnapping, aggravated robbery and extortion, sale or maintenance of slaves, and endangering of public health through such acts as water pollution are tired before the Assize Court. It is the only regular criminal trial court (i.e., non-military) that can impose the maximum penalty, which is life imprisonment at hard labor. The Assize Court functions in the judicial district of the Court of Appeal, but it is convened in the provincial center where the crime was committed by order of the president of the Court of Appeal at the request of the procurator-general of Appeal whenever a person has been charged with a serious crime. The Assize Court draws its professional judges from the Court of Appeal, which supplies a councilor to preside, and from the Tribunal, which furnishes a judge. The remainder of the Assize bench consists of six laymen or people's judges, who must be citizens of good moral character who enjoy full civil and political rights, possess a diploma from a lower secondary school, and are between the ages of thirty and sixty-five. The people's judges are selected from a list of eligible citizens that is prepared by a local committee of the communal council and certified by the praetor's committee, formed by the town mayors and the praetor in the latter's district. The list of people's judges is further authenticated by the president of the Tribunal having appellate jurisdiction over the praetors and the president of the Tribunal located in the provincial seat. Either the president of the Court of Appeal or of the Tribunal, depending on where the Assize Court is constituted, must draw ten names of eligible persons to serve as people's judges during the session and ten supplementary names. On the opening day of the session, the president of the Assize Court appoints the people's judges in order of extraction. People's judges sit with the regular judges behind the bench and participate as equals with them in determining guilt or innocence and in fixing the sentence. Appeals from sentences of the Assize Courts are heard by the Courts of Assize Appeal.

The Court of Assize Appeal

There is only one Court of Assize Appeal in each judicial district of the Court of Appeal. It is composed of two councilors of the Court of Appeal, one of whom presides as directed by the president of the Court of Appeal, and six people's judges. The Court of Assize Appeal considers only appeals from the decisions and sentences of the Assize Court on application by the defendant or the Public Ministry.

The Court of Appeal

The Court of Appeal functions principally as a court of appellate jurisdiction for civil and criminal appeals arising from sentences of the Tribunal and the Tribunal for Minors. Its other function is to conduct pretrial investigations at the request of the procurator-general of Appeal whenever the latter has lifted the investigation from either the judge of instruction, a magistrate of the Public Ministry, or the praetor. The Court of Appeal functions through four specialized sections: civil appeals, criminal appeals, juvenile appeals, and instruction. The appellate sections operate with five judges; however, the juvenile section employs four professional judges and one non-legal judge, who must be a professor of biology, pedagogy, psychiatry, or criminology. The instruction section consists of three judges. Decisions by any section of the Court of Appeal are by majority.

The Court of Appeal does not hear the case *de novo* but will rule on the merit of the decision and sentence of the trial court as well as on violations by the court of the procedural rules. It may order a retrial by the original trial court with instructions; or it may annul the sentence completely, thus reversing it; or it may amend the sentence in part.

The judges of the Court of Appeal hold the rank of councilor of Appeal and are attached to the twenty-four courts, each of which is directed by a president and has a number of section presidents. The court districts correspond to the region or to territorial subdivisions of the region, in which are grouped two or more provinces. Each court has a variable number of judges.

Attached to each Court of Appeal is a regional Tribunal of Public Waters having a special jurisdiction to protect the public interest and individual rights to the use of water resources. It is a court of original jurisdiction that has civil and criminal competence. The regional Tribunal of Public Waters operates with a bench of three judges, two of whom are councilors of Appeal and the other judge is a civil engineer employed by the public corps of engineers. The president of the Superior Council of Public Works recommends the civil engineers who serve on these specialized Tribunals following formal appointment. Appeals from this Tribunal may be made by the parties to the case before the Superior Tribunal of Public Waters.

The Court of Cassation

The Court of Cassation is not an appellate court in the usual sense, since it normally may not inquire into the merit of the decisions or sentences of the inferior courts. Since the sentences of original trial courts are appealable only once, and the sentences of the appellate courts are considered definitive and unappealable, the Court of Cassation is permitted to quash or annul the sentences of inferior courts normally only when an inferior court has been charged by the petitioner with having committed a violation of substantive or procedural law contained in the legal codes. The Court of Cassation may quash the orders, decrees, and sentences of any magistrate or court in part or completely. It may remand the case to the trial court with instructions to retry the case; or by quashing the original sentence completely, it may thereby reverse the judgment. Although Article 111 of the Constitution establishes a personal right to petition the Court of Cassation to review the legality of all judicial sentences that deprive the individual of personal freedom, the right may be exercised only when it is permitted by law or on leave granted by the Court of Cassation.

Defendants who have been sentenced to imprisonment for violation of the criminal law may apply for revision of their sentence at any time by supplying new and relevant evidence. The Court of Cassation may grant leave for a hearing if the new evidence is sufficient to decree total annulment of the previous sentence. Should this be the case, the Court of Cassation may itself decree the acquittal, or it may instruct the original trial court to issue an order of acquittal in consequence of the annulment of its earlier sentence. The Court of Cassation may order financial reparation in favor of an applicant for revision or review if he has suffered hardship and loss because of detention while awaiting justice from the courts.

The Court of Cassation consists of a president, a procurator-general, an advocate-general, a number of section presidents and assistant procurators-general, and numerous councilors—a total of 350 magistrates who form the apex of the regular judiciary and maintain the uniformity of law over the inferior courts. The president assigns the cases to the appropriate section; supervises the section presidents; and himself presides over the united sections, to which he may refer any case that he regards as important. When a lower court has refused to obey instructions issued by a section of the Court of Cassation, the subsequent application for review must be referred to the united sections. The president of the Court of Cassation also presides over the Superior Tribunal of Public Waters, which is a mixed tribunal of four councilors of Cassation, four councilors of State, and three members of the Superior Council of Public Works.

THE PUBLIC MINISTRY

The Public Ministry forms a specialized corps of prosecuting magistrates whose presence and influence in the administration of justice is ubiquitous even though they are excluded from the actual determination of court decisions. The Public Ministry is the principal arm of the state in the enforcement of the criminal law and has the right to intervene in civil cases to protect the public interest.

The Public Ministry directs the judicial police, ascertains the existence of crimes, conducts searches and seizures for evidence, questions witnesses and suspects, orders arrests and conducts the preliminary as well as all summary investigations of suspects, arraigns suspects before the proper court for formal instruction (more complete investigation by the judge of instruction) or for trial, participates in the formal instruction, takes an active part in the trial proceedings in support of the charges against the defendant, controls the legality of trial proceedings by impugning improper or irregular court actions before the appellate courts and the Court of Cassation, and is responsible for the enforcement of court actions.

There can be no judicial action in the enforcement of criminal laws without the initiative of the Public Ministry, which arraigns all criminal suspects before the proper court and authenticates the evidence necessary to support the charges in a formal instruction and public trial. Should the nature of the crime require summary instruction by the Public Ministry, the latter requests the competent court to issue the decree of indictment should the evidence establish probable guilt. For crimes that require formal instruction by a judge of instruction (crimes that come under the jurisdiction of the Tribunal or Assize Court), the Public Ministry must turn over all the evidence that it has collected during the preliminary investigation to the judge of instruction and allow the latter to decide whether the evidence warrants an indictment of the suspect and the ordering of a trial. The Public Ministry may appeal the instruction judge's refusal to indict before the indictment section of the Court of Appeal.

The Public Ministry is represented at all criminal trials in order to support the evidence against the defendant and obtain conviction. The procurator sums up the case for the prosecution and recommends a specific punishment to the court. He makes observations to the court during the trial proceedings and is barred from chambers only when the court is deliberating the decision and sentence. The procurator may appeal the decision and sentence of the trial court on charges of improper presentation of evidence, incorrect interpretation of the law, or procedural violations.

The procurator of the Republic heads the Public Ministry in each province, which includes a number of assistant procurators and a secretariat. This office investigates and prosecutes all crimes that are subject to the jurisdiction of the Tribunal. The procurator-general of Appeal and his assistants handle all criminal investigations and prosecutions before the Assize Court and the Court of Assize Appeal. They may also appeal decisions of the lower courts or impugn their sentences to the Court of Cassation should the procurator of the Republic fail to act. Besides his numerous assistant procurators-general of Appeal, the procurator-general of Appeal is aided by one or more advocates-general of Appeal, who are in charge of a subdivision of the judicial district and are midway in rank between the procurator-general and the assistant procurators-general of Appeal. The procurator-general's office handles all appeals for the public from the Assize Court to the Court of Assize Appeal and has sole competence on behalf of the public to impugn the latter court's decisions before the Court of Cassation.

The procurator-general of Cassation, who is comparable to the solicitor-general of the United States, intervenes directly or through the advocate-general or assistant procurators-general of Cassation in all cases (civil and criminal) that are heard by the Court of Cassation. His opinions are required in the deliberations of the Court on applications for criminal and civil review and judicial revision of definitive sentences. He participates without vote in the deliberations of that Court in all civil hearings.

The Public Ministry at all levels is responsible for ordering the execution of judicial orders, decrees, and sentences to the proper police and custodial authorities. It compiles letters rogatory and requests these when necessary in the performance of international comity.

The magistrates of the Public Ministry are recruited, promoted, and assigned in the same way as bench magistrates. It is customary for magistrates to be shifted between the bench and the Public Ministry.

INDIVIDUAL RIGHTS

The individual's right to enjoy freedom and dignity in Italy are safeguarded against arbitrary acts of the police and the judiciary by the Constitution and the Penal Procedural Code, in theory if not always in practice. Arrests may be made by the police without a magistrate's order only when offenders are apprehended *in flagrante delicto;* otherwise, arrests must be ordered by the Public Ministry, the praetor, the judge of instruction, or the instruction section of the Court of Appeal. The police may search persons and premises and seize incriminating evidence under conditions of urgency without an express order of the magistrate; normally, the latter's written order is required. Evidence that is discovered by the police may be seized and used against persons in court even if it is totally unrelated to the crime under investigation. The individual has no real safeguard in court against unlawfully secured evidence. Arrests made by the police must be reported promptly to the praetor or to the office of the Public Ministry (within twenty-four hours under the Penal Procedure Code).

Preliminary interrogation to establish probable guilt and to justify the issuance of an order of detention by the magistrate must be commenced within three days following notification to the magistrate of the arrest. The length of time a person may be held in detention varies. For lesser offenses punishable by the praetor, the maximum duration of detentive arrest is thirty days. For crimes that are being investigated by the Public Ministry under summary procedures of instruction, the maximum duration of detentive arrest is forty days. Persons who are being investigated by the judge of instruction may be held under detentive arrest for three months if the maximum punishment for the crime is less than four years of imprisonment and for six months if the law provides for more than four years of imprisonment. Persons who are suspected of serious crimes may be held under detentive custody for as much as two years if the maximum punishment under the law exceeds twenty years of imprisonment.

Provisional freedom may be granted to criminal suspects at the discretion of the judicial authorities only if the crime under investigation is not a serious one. Within these limitations, the magistrate who is conducting the instruction may grant the suspect provisional freedom on deposit of a bond (whose amount is fixed by the magistrate) only if the suspect is of high moral reputation. Once the suspect has been indicted and is remanded for trial, provisional freedom may be granted only by the trial court. The defendant in a criminal trial who has been sentenced, but who has appealed or applied for judicial review, may seek provisional freedom only from the court from whose sentence he is appealing. Such requests are seldom granted.

The investigation of crimes is conducted in secrecy. The suspect is not informed of the charges or the evidence to support these until he has been indicted for trial. The defense counsel is then allowed to study the charges and supporting evidence up to the day of the trial, which is fixed by the presiding judge of the trial court. The length of time that the defense counsel is allowed between the dates when trial is announced and when it commences varies. In trials held before the praetor, the defense has at least five days; in Tribunal, it is given at least eight days, and no less than fifteen days in Assize. If the accused has not appeared for trial he may be tried *in contumacia,* since his presence is not essential for proper trial to occur. Defendants may not be forced to appear in court for trial, in which case the trial is conducted *in absentia.*

There is no requirement that the defendant must be confronted by the witnesses in open court. Their testimony is valid if presented in the form of sworn depositions. The defense counsel has no chance to interrogate or cross-examine witnesses, since these answer only the questions put to them by the presiding judge. The defense counsel, like the prosecution, may make observations to the court and participates in the summation; the defense is reserved the right of final summation. The court retires to chambers to debate the decision and sentence, both of which are made by majority vote. In the event of a tie vote (the Assize Court has a total of eight judges), the verdict favors the defendant.

SELECTED READING

ADAMS, JOHN CLARKE, and BARILE, PAOLO. *The Government of Republican Italy.* Boston: Houghton Mifflin Co., 1961. Pp. 125–46.

———. "The Italian Constitutional Court in Its First Two Years of Activity," *Buffalo Law Review,* VII (Winter, 1958), 250–85.

CALAMANDREI, PIERO. *Procedure and Democracy.* New York: New York University Press, 1956.

CASSANDRO, GIOVANNI. "The Constitutional Court of Italy," *American Journal of Comparative Law,* VIII (Winter, 1959), 1–14.

TREVES, GIUSEPPINO. "Judicial Review of Legislation in Italy," *Journal of Public Law,* VII (Fall, 1958), 345–61.

IV

POLITICS AND GOVERNMENT OF GERMANY

GERMANY
Showing cities of more than 100,000 population
Scale of Miles
0 25 50 100
North Sea
Baltic Sea
DENMARK
Kiel
SCHLESWIG-HOLSTEIN
Lübeck
HAMBURG
Harburg
Hamburg
Altona
Wilhelmshaven
Bremerhaven
BREMEN
Bremen
Oldenburg
Elbe R.
LOWER SAXONY
NETHERLANDS
Hanover
Brunswick
Osnabrück
Münster
Bielefeld
Weser R.
NORTH RHINE-WESTPHALIA
Gelsenkirchen
Bottrop
Recklinghausen
Herne
Oberhausen
Dortmund
Duisburg
Bochum
Krefeld
Essen
Hagen
München-Gladbach
Mülheim
Wuppertal
Düsseldorf
Solingen
Remscheid
Cologne
Aachen
Bonn
Kassel
WEST GERMANY
HESSE
BELGIUM
Rhine R.
Wiesbaden
Frankfurt
Mainz
Darmstadt
RHINELAND-PALATINATE
LUX.
SAAR
Saarbrücken
Ludwigshafen
Mannheim
Heidelberg
Fürth
Nuremberg
BAVARIA
Regensburg
Danube R.
Karlsruhe
Stuttgart
BADEN-WÜRTTEMBERG
FRANCE
Augsburg
Munich
Freiburg
SWITZERLAND
AUSTRIA
CZECHOSLOVAKIA
EAST GERMANY
(SOVIET ZONE)
Elbe R.
WEST BERLIN
EAST BERLIN
POLAND

29

Nature of German Society

THE SOCIAL FOUNDATIONS

The social fabric, which is created and developed by accepted social values, mores, and traditions, is dependent on the history and experience of the society; these social factors, however, mould political institutions and actions and are responsible for revolutionary changes, wars, victories, and defeat. The people, therefore, are not only the creatures, but also the makers of history.

There is probably no nation on earth that places more emphasis on the idea of the *Volk*, the people, and its almost mystical spirit as the Germans; it was less than one hundred years ago, in 1871, that the German people were able to achieve a unified German Reich. This Reich was partially responsible for two world wars; and German unity, which arrived so late, came to an end in 1945. In 1871, under the leadership of Prussia, the German Empire finally emerged; thirty-odd separate German states were incorporated in it. The differences between them, culturally and geographically as well as economically, were deep and varied; but one combining element existed among all of them and was nourished by their idealistic nineteenth-century philosophers, such as Fichte, Hegel, and Schelling, and such romantic poets as the brothers Schlegel and Eichendorf. This was deep seated love for anything that could be referred to as German. The German forest, the German song, the German poet, German efficiency, and German faithfulness—even more the German soldier—all these were good and beautiful because they were German, and for this specific reason they were superior to all others. Such a mentality must be considered as a cornerstone for a prevailing set of social values.

The Germans call themselves in the field of art and science "*das Volk der Dichter und Denker*," the people of the poets and thinkers. As a military people, they are braver and more efficient than any other nation.

The German historian and philosopher, Oswald Spengler, whose book *The Decline of the West,* one of the most provocative that appeared at the beginning of this century, reflects this attitude when he says that the Prussian-German people have had three great moments in their recent history (1813, 1870, and 1914); and this is more than others have had.[1] From time to time, this set of values was successfully transferred from society as a whole to the individual, thus creating the individual values of the *homo teutonicus,* the teutonic man. The national anthem "*Deutschland, Deutschland ueber Alles*" (Germany, Germany above everything) and the famous dictum of the iron chancellor, Prince Bismarck, "we Germans are afraid of God and nothing else in the world," shows this spirit very clearly. In addition to this basic nationalistic tendency that pervaded the whole of German society, there are two other closely interrelated factors that have influenced the German national character and help to explain the nature of Germany's past and present political and social institutions. Strict discipline and obedience to authority is one factor; reducing individual and collective responsibility to comply with orders given from above, to accept them dutifully without hesitation or even criticism, is the other. This situation existed in the structure of the German family where the authority of the father was beyond challenge until not very long ago. A similar relationship exists between teacher and student, between superior and inferior in every possible combination. Individual freedom, political or otherwise, did not have much opportunity in such a social climate.

There are several historical explanations for this phenomenon, and the geographic location of Germany in the center of Europe also has its strong influence. France in the west, the Scandinavians in the north, the Slavs in the east, all were continuously actual or potential enemies. There was, therefore, a legitimate need for strong defense and an equally strong temptation for aggression. From this point of view, it is not surprising that Germany has been a militaristic nation with all its implications. Prussia under the Hohenzollern kings made itself the spokesman and representative of German militarism. In its long struggle with the Austrian Habsburgs over hegemony in Germany, it was finally triumphant. Friedrich II (the Great) during his long reign (1740–1786) made Prussia the leading and most powerful state in Germany. In spite of the fact that German unification was achieved under Prussian leadership, and its King proclaimed himself Wilhelm I, as German Emperor in 1871, there was specifically in the southern parts of Germany a permanent resentment against the Prussian influence, which even Adolf Hitler was unable to eliminate. Even now, under the West German Federal Republic, there

[1] Oswald Spengler, *The Decline of the West* (New York: Alfred A. Knopf, a division of Random House, Inc., 1932), p. 36.

exists a separatistic movement in Catholic Bavaria, which, though not too influential, is nevertheless existent.

In a militaristic atmosphere, authority, discipline, and compliance with orders are very highly valuated; and the person whose function it is to issue and execute orders, the officer, commands the highest prestige in this society.

The emphasis on obedience is also found in the ideas of the Protestant Reformation in Germany. Martin Luther gave the Germans a doctrine of utter subservience to authority. He allied himself completely with the princes against the exploited population, specifically the peasants, whose revolt was crushed at the beginning of the sixteenth century (1524–1525) with the utmost cruelty and violence. He justified these actions with such utterances as: "There are no better works than to obey and serve all those who are set over us as superiors. For this reason also disobedience is a greater sin than murder, unchastity, theft and dishonesty and all that these may include." Or "The princes of this world (representing authority) are Gods, the common people are Satan," or his comparison of the rebel who defies authority, any authority, even the most oppressing one, with a mad dog that must be killed. Theodor Heuss, the first President of the Federal German Republic, a representative of German democratic thought in the best sense, in a very able and scholarly attempt to explain but not to excuse the German people, made the point that one can find counterparts of such authoritarian mentalities in the Anglo-Saxon and Latin orbits like Hobbes and Machiavelli.[2] But, whereas a direct line can be traced in Germany from Luther to Hitler, Anglo-American social spirit rejected the Hobbesian authoritarian emphasis on obedience and developed its social values and political institutions in the line of Locke, Montesquieu, and Jefferson. It should not be overlooked that the Germans had at least an equal share of defending individual liberty and human dignity; Lessing, Goethe, Schiller, Kant, Heine, Mann, to name only a few, were outstanding liberals. However, it was not their ideas but the romantic mystical nationalism of Richard Wagner that transformed itself into political and social reality. One must be very careful not to consider individuals as necessarily representing national character, but an existing set of social values reflects itself upon the individual, and it is no exaggeration to state that until after World War II a perverted nationalism and a perverted respect for authority and love of discipline were basic in the German national character and basic to its social values.

If these two factors are kept in mind, an astute analyst might trace the close relationship between the German society that created a certain type of leadership and the leadership that influenced and shaped this society.

[2] Theodor Heuss, "German Character and History," *The Atlantic,* March, 1957, pp. 103 ff.

It was of necessity that an extremely nationalistic leadership emerged in Germany over and over again. This leadership provided for and took advantage of the national aspirations and frustrations; it led and directed the Germans without any difficulty into aggressive wars internationally and into human oppression and bestiality domestically. From this point of view, German society is just as responsible for Adolf Hitler, the scourge of the century, as Hitler was responsible for the crimes he caused this society to commit. They were not done in the name of Hitler, but in the name of Germany. Hitler and his henchmen conceived them; German society carried them out.

Realistically, there is hardly a nation in which the moral qualities of the leadership were more important than in Germany. Since discipline and compliance with law and order, any law and order, was for centuries considered a supreme virtue, the humanitarian character of law and order became of greater significance than law and order itself. One should realize, therefore, that the phrase "government of law and not of men" has different meanings in Germany and in Anglo-American society. Many Germans, prosecuted after the end of World War II by the new democratic government for acts committed during the Nazi regime, were unable to understand that they had done anything wrong, even when they were guilty of murdering children or denouncing their closest relatives. As long as they were covered by law or by orders from a higher authority, no guilt existed for them and no guilt feeling could be detected. Such attitudes make a society highly organizable and manageable, and this statement can be made without reservations in connection with the Germans. It also makes the task of the organizer and manager, in other words, of the political elite, not only much more important, but also much easier, as soon as its elite status is established and generally accepted.

THE HISTORICAL CLASS STRUCTURE

The landowers of the agrarian northeast, the Prussian Junkers, represented for generations the elite class and furnished the leadership personnel for the agencies of the Prussian state and of the German Empire, military as well as civil. The origin of this landed gentry goes back to the Order of the Teutonic Knights, which, in the late twelfth century, was the first instrument to Christianize and Germanize the Slav territories in the east. The Prussian princes, who were able administrators, started the development of a strongly centralized bureaucracy. As early as the seventeenth century, they used the Junkers to staff the higher administrative positions; they also held the leading positions in the army. The notorious General Staff, which dates back to the seventeenth century, was always dominated by the titled Junker class. This group provided to a very large degree the leadership in Prussia and in Germany after the unification. Its influence could not be subdued during the Weimar Republic, and the Junkers had their part in bringing Hitler to power. With a very few exceptions, they were extremely reactionary. Their devotion and loyalty to monarchical principles can easily be understood. They were indebted to the Kings for the leading postions in the army and the civil service. As soon as they were entrenched in these positions, the Kings were also dependent upon them. Also during the twentieth century, the title "von" indicated adherence to monarchical principles. The Junkers were by definition extremely nationalistic. They were the bulwark against the East; they hated and feared their Slav neighbors. For a long time, they held a virtual monopoly on the government, civil and military, and were the great leaders whose political actions led to the unified Reich.

A nobility does not necessarily have to be undemocratic and opposed to liberty in its political activities, as the example in Great Britain shows. It may be opposed to liberty but, like the French aristocracy, highly aware of cultural and intellectual values. The Junkers, however, had nothing that made them politically, economically, or socially liberal. As a class, they were anti-intellectual. Hindenburg was proud of the fact that the only literature he read was army regulations, and music was banned from his estate. Rudeness, rigor, and brutality were at a premium; whereas humanity and grace were considered weaknesses. "One lies in German when one is polite," said Goethe.

The Junkers, by controlling the influential positions in the army and in the bureaucracy, were an extremely powerful political force. But this was not enough, when the impact of the industrial revolution made industry the basic necessity for Germany's greatness. For these functions, the Junkers were not suited.

The industrialists and business leaders emerged from the middle class. But this did not work in the direction of liberalizing German society; on the contrary, the successful leaders of commerce and industry achieved an elite status themselves, although it did not reach the heights of the Junkers and the officers. When the German Empire under Wilhelm II became more and more imperialistic, the big industrialists, the barons of the Ruhr factories, such as the Krupps and the Thyssens, commanded at times a more powerful influence than the Junkers.

It is not surprising that the leaders of German industry and business were also nationalistic and favored military expansion. A strong Germany assured them an extended market for their products, so German industry and finance were closely linked with German militarism. The big corporations and corporative combines, the cartels, were strongly assisted by the government, which wanted them strong for the production of war materials. The coalition between the landed gentry, the bureaucracy, and the military on one side and big business on the other side was mutually beneficial; they needed each other. The rise of the industrial barons did not lead to democratization of German society or greater social flexibility.

As far as social prestige was concerned, the officers' caste stood on the top of the social hierarchy. For the more prosperous members of the middle class, the military commission was the highest social distinction. The greatest achievement was to become a "Lieutenant of the Reserve." With this exaggerated prestige attributed to military rank and military values came an almost childish love for uniforms, badges, and distinctions. When the Nazis organized their party groups, they took advantage of this deep-seated love for distinctions and established an elaborate hierarchical system of ranks and uniforms.

We have seen how a political elite group developed and how influential it became in German society. The question has to be asked, where was the middle class, which became so influential during the nineteenth century in England as well as in France and which formed the foundation of political liberalism? There emerged a middle class in Germany during the nineteenth century, and it attempted to become a political force. Burghers, merchants, artisans, intellectuals, professors, and students staged a revolution in the year 1848; and their slogan was liberty and unity. While attempting to achieve political liberty, they made demands for civil rights, freedom of speech, freedom of press, freedom of assembly, equality before the law, a freely elected representative government, etc. However, the nationalistic tendencies of the German middle class were more important than liberal reforms. Power and national honor became more significant than liberty and democracy.

The middle class was successful in convening a constitutional convention, which assembled at St. Paul's Cathedral in Frankfurt in March, 1848; and a German national assembly was elected in which the middle class was by far the predominant influence. But the Revolution failed and the Parliament failed. Neither unity nor democracy was achieved in 1848. Although the liberal and national tendencies of the middle class expressed themselves in the writings of the liberal professors and the speeches of the liberal deputies, these forces were politically too inexperienced and too weak to force the Prussian king and the other German princes to accept a change in political power. After a very short interlude, political power relapsed into the hands of the existing ruling class. The Revolution of the middle class in Germany came too late.

The industrialization of Germany had already begun and a new class, the laborers, emerged. They participated in the 1848 Revolution. Marx and Engels had already published their *Communist Manifesto*. One of the greatest weaknesses, and under the circumstances of the mid-nineteenth century an understandable one of the crucial middle class, was the fear of the radical "proletarians," what we would call now the fear of the red danger. The middle class, caught between the reactionary forces of the state authority and the revolutionary radicalism of the extremely inexperienced laborers, had to make a choice. For the intellectuals, the property owners, large and small, the authority of the state, representing itself in uniform and guaranteeing law and order, was more acceptable than the egalitarian and often anarchical demands and tendencies of the "Left." When it became apparent that property rights were in danger, the middle class buried its desire for political leadership; the blessing of political freedom ceased to be important. Liberty was forfeited for security. The state and the authority of the state achieved an even greater status and respect.

The state and the political leadership, especially under Bismarck, made it easy for the middle class to accept this situation. The middle class was forced to accept the political rule of the Junkers and the reactionaries, but it was given the opportunity to control the economy. In this respect, the middle class was fully supported by the government—protective tariffs, expanded markets, and protection against the proletarian threat. Protected by a strong state, the middle class felt secure in its own sphere, the accumulation of wealth. At the end of the nineteenth century, the nobility still had a privileged position in the state and society. This position was strengthened by the military victory in 1870 over France under the leadership of the generals, all of them recruited from the nobility. Again, the long struggle for unification was achieved under the traditional elite as represented by Bismarck.

The middle class became a strong supporter of the existing order; its German nationalism was of no lesser degree than that of the aristocracy. Politically and socially, the middle class remained inferior; and the inferiority complex resulting from this situation was compensated by an irrational feeling of superiority to everything non-German. This class specifically developed the arrogant attitude that made Germany so unpopular in the world. One should never forget that the German middle class was economically very prosperous until the defeat in 1918. This position changed after World War I, and it changed under a democratic form of government.

In the period 1918–1923, a catastrophic inflation occurred. The middle class suffered most and its main asset, economic security, was wiped out. Its savings were lost; pensions and interest payments lost their value. The democratic Weimar Republic was blamed for it. As a result, social traditions were shattered and the moral fiber of the middle class was destroyed. The lower middle class, the little fellow, the butcher, baker, and the like, became a marginal group, afraid to fall from their own, although very limited, social status in a strongly inflexible society to the status of the worker. To this dissatisfied, unbalanced, and insecure group, Hitler had the greatest appeal; and it became the backbone of the Nazi movement. This development was not detected at once.

In November, 1923, the German Finance Minister, Karl Helferich, finally ended the inflation. He established the temporary rentenmark as a kind of goldmark, backed by the productivity of industry, commerce, and agriculture. This rentenmark was later changed to the reichsmark, with the rentenmark equivalent to one reichsmark. From 1924 to 1929, primarily because of the financial genius of Hjalmar Schacht, there was prosperity in Germany. The middle class, including the little fellow, recovered to some extent while new fortunes were made. But then, the world depression hit Germany; and everything that had been achieved was in danger again. Less than a decade before, the middle class had lost its savings; and now, it was afraid the depression would destroy it again. The opportunity came for the radicalization of this traditionally docile class. From the lower middle class, the small shopkeepers, the artisans, the school teachers and the like, came the support for the Nazis; and these people made the movement a mass movement. In the Reichstag election of September, 1930, the Nazi party succeeded in rising from 12 to 107 seats, with a popular vote of more than six million. The middle class provided these votes. It became finally a revolutionary movement, but not in the direction of liberty and democracy—on the contrary, against it. During the first half of the twentieth century, the leading group of the nineteenth century, the Junkers and the officers, retained to quite a large extent their political leadership, remaining reactionary and nationalistic as ever. The middle class, for different reasons, after the defeat in 1848, became equally reactionary and nationalistic.

THE LABORING CLASS

The industrialization, which took place in the nineteenth century, created a new class, the urban proletariat. Cities such as Essen and Dortmund in the Ruhr area became industrial centers, while the population of Berlin doubled between 1816 and 1846. The increase of the industrial population did not mean that the new developing labor masses lived under satisfactory conditions. Wages were extremely low and working hours extremely long. The exploitation, specifically of child labor, was most cruel. At this time, the working class was not yet able to fight for better economic conditions, and even less for political freedom. Occasionally, out of sheer desperation, they revolted—for instance, the weavers in Silesia in 1844 and the workers in Berlin in 1847, in the so-called "potatoes insurrection." The working class participated in the 1848 Revolution, giving it a proletarian turn, which was partly responsible for its failure. Karl Marx and Friedrich Engels made themselves spokesmen for this emerging class. Both came from West Germany, where industry developed at an early time; and they studied the situation of the working classes in England for their attack against the capitalistic system. In spite of this, it is of great importance to understand the special contribution of Marxism to the working-class movement in Germany.

The rigid class structure, which existed in Germany, especially in Prussia, made social mobility among the different classes extremely difficult. The worker was at the bottom of the social hierarchy; but, according to Marxian doctrine, his destiny was to overturn this structure. The aristocracy and the bourgeoisie were doomed to fail, while the future would belong to the worker. In the rigid class stratification that existed in Germany, this doctrine had a strong emotional appeal; the working class became proud and independent, also inflexible, a class conscious proletariat, the only group that fostered social and economic progress, the advance guard for democracy. It took many years for the working class to become a force in Germany.

The prevalent economic philosophy during the ninteenth century became purely capitalistic. Whereas in England economic capitalism could be identified loosely with political liberalism, in Germany only the economic features of liberalism were accepted. Economic freedom and *Gewerbefreiheit* (freedom of trade) opened the door for the free interplay of economic forces and competitive capitalism, whereby, according to the interpretation of classical economic liberalism, the economic well-being of the German nation was secured. In this specific instance, however, the proletariat was not included in the nation. The well-being of the masses was entirely neglected. Ferdinand Lassalle, a middle-class, highly educated lawyer, became the spokesman for the German working class. He did not believe that its position could be changed within the existing economic order; the "iron law of wages" would always keep the worker at the subsistence minimum. To his efforts can be attributed the fact that the workers began to organize their own interest representations as a distinct economic and social group. He proposed, in March 1863, the foundation of a workers political party; the first organization of the German workers was the *Allgemeine Deutsche Arbeiterverein.* It should be noted that this first organization was not strictly Marxian, but democratic in nature. Here, among the workers, we find the first demand for democratic institutions, a demand for universal suffrage, against which the so-called German "liberals" were opposed. Since Lassalle's first demand was universal suffrage, his way was not revolutionary in the Marxian sense, but parliamentary democracy. From this time on, it was mainly the German working class who represented democratic ideas in Germany. In spite of the fact that a group under August Bebel and Wilhelm Liebknecht seceded from Lasalle's organization in 1869, founding the German Social Democratic party at Eisenach, and in spite of the fact that the German labor movement became strongly Marxian after the two organizations joined in 1875 under the Gotha program, the democratic character of the German working class was always dominant. In the many elections held under the Weimar Republic, the Communists were never able to surpass the Social Democrats. The fight for democracy, and whatever progress had been achieved in this fight, can be attributed in Germany to the organized working class under the banner of socialism. They were the first to stand for a democratically organized state protecting the basic political and civil rights of everyone, including the worker.

In discussing the German working class, another factor must be mentioned that distinguishes it from the other social groups. The Marxian slogan "proletarians of all countries unite" gave the German Social Democratic party an international flavor. The extreme nationalism that prevailed in Germany was not as strong among the workers as among the Junkers and the middle class. This made the workers a target for attack; it insinuated that the fatherland did not mean as much to them as could be demanded and expected from good Germans. In this respect, the social values of the whole society have to be considered. In Germany, loyalty to the fatherland was a supreme moral value, which was also true for the German worker. In 1914, when war came, Emperor Wilhelm II stated, "I don't know parties anymore, I know only Germans." The German workers, enthusiastically, or at least dutifully, went to war. Nonetheless, the German working class, organized in the Social Democratic party, was the most, if not the only, democratic group and at the same time the least nationalistic. No wonder Bismarck hated the Socialists and had the anti-Socialist laws passed in 1878, with the support of the liberals, who gave the government the power to suppress labor organizations, Socialist meetings, and the Socialist press. The laws were on the books for twelve years until the dismissal of Bismarck.

In November, 1918, the democratic Socialists under their leaders Fritz Ebert and Philipp Scheidemann (the latter was the man who had proclaimed the Republic) took over the government of a defeated Germany. Unfortunately at the same time, a split occurred in the German working class that lasted the whole Weimar period and was a major factor that enabled Hitler to come to power. The extreme Left organized the Spartacist (later Communist) party under Karl Liebknecht and Rosa Luxemburg. It is extremely significant to note that at this time the German tradition of law and order was still so strong that the majority of the working class, represented by the Socialists, preferred to crush a leftist revolution with the help of the old reactionaries to making an all-out effort to eliminate the influence of the Junkers, the big industrialists, and the officer corps. In the tradition of Luther, Fritz Ebert declared, "I hate revolution like sin." The formal framework of a democracy was created with the Weimar Constitution. The greatest failure of the working class, a failure that can be explained from the then existing set of social values, lay in its inability to create a living democracy by leaving the power of the undemocratic forces intact. As far as the social fabric was concerned, there was only the smallest shift toward democracy.

THE RELIGIOUS FACTOR

There is another factor that must be mentioned in order to get a more complete picture of German society. Germany is divided by religious lines on a territorial basis. Neither the Protestant Reformation nor the Counter Reformation were able, after the destruction of the universal church by Luther, to control the whole of Germany. In 1555, the treaty of Augsburg divided Germany on the principle *cuius regio eius religio,* the religion of the prince was the religion of his country. So, historically, the religious partition between Protestantism and Catholicism followed strictly dynastic divisions. Broadly speaking, the north and northeast were Protestant; the south and southwest, Catholic. Hohenzollern Prussia was the spokesman for the first; Habsburg Austria for the other. The tension between the Protestant majority and the Catholic minority that coincided with the struggle between Prussia and Austria also influenced German society, but more for political than for religious reasons. Between 1870 and 1887, the Catholics in the so-called *Kulturkampf* were strongly attacked by Bismarck (the situation arose in connection with those Catholic priests and teachers who refused the dogma of infallibility of the Pope that was declared on July 18, 1870, by Pope Pius IX). Bismarck finally made a compromise with the Catholics. As a consequence of the *Kulturkampf*, the Catholic minority, organized in the Center party, became an important political factor and influential in the second Empire as well as in the coalition governments of the Weimar Republic. In general, however, nationalism as a kind of secularized religion had a stronger appeal than religious beliefs. Hitler's paganism persecuted Protestants and Catholics alike. The ardent Nazi was supposed to give up his religious affiliations; he had to turn away from Christianity in all forms in order to become *gottglaeubig*, a believer in God, believing also in the God-given leader. The record of the German Catholics in the fight against bestiality and for human values is much better than that of the Protestants. The figure of Cardinal Faulhaber, the Archbishop of Munich during the Hitler period, outshines, from the viewpoint of Christian morality, even the famous Pastor Niemoeller, who incidentally was a Nazi himself until the conflict between Hitlerism and Christianity became unsurpassable. Religious division is not a major problem to be faced in Germany. In West Germany, the Catholics made up, for some time, a majority of the population. This fact should not be misinterpreted to mean that the West German Catholics are less in favor of unification than the Protestants. The nationalistic tradition, stimulated in the given situation by the ideological struggle between East and West, absorbs all religious dividing lines.

THE POSTWAR SOCIAL PROBLEMS

Between the two world wars, as was already mentioned, an actual change in the social structure was brought about by the great 1919–1923 inflation. It left the old feudal class and a part of the peasant class intact; also, the upper middle class (including the industrial class grouped around the heavy industries of the Rhineland and Westphalia and the big chemical industries) emerged from it not only without losses, but with increased power. On the other hand, the lower middle class was most severely hit economically, almost to extinction; it was by no means willing to join the ranks of the old proletariate, either socially, spiritually, or politically. This class became the backbone of the Nazi movement. If the Nazi regime is to be held responsible for World War II, the consequence of this war had far greater effect on the social body of the German nation than anything before, which can be explained only partly by the material destruction during the war, chiefly by allied bombing.

There is the problem of the refugees and expellees from the East now living in West Germany. This is the most pressing social problem faced in Germany now, not only by reason of their staggering number (more than twelve million people), but also due to the suddenness of the influx and the unsettling effect they have had on the German public in general. It is very doubtful whether these refugees could have been assimilated if the social structure had been intact, but this was not the case. At the end of the war, the German middle classes, who had supported the Nazis because they had expected that it would break the process of proletarization to which they already felt themselves subjected, were uprooted, spiritually no less than physically. The group of expellees and refugees is by its sheer numbers (close to one-fourth of West Germany's population) of extreme importance, and its incorporation and absorption as full-fledged members of society is a precondition of a peaceful social development. The refugees and expellees represent, in spite of their regional, social, and occupational differences, a new, if not unique, social stratum—a group of declassees, placed in the new society on a much lower level than they were before and, therefore, definitely subject to political radicalization.[3] The amazing

[3] Siegmund Neumann, in Hans J. Morgenthau, *Germany and the Future of Europe* (Chicago: University of Chicago Press, 1951), pp. 25–39.

economic recovery of West Germany during the last decade has meant that this problem of the refugees and expellees is to some extent less burning than it would have been otherwise; nonetheless it still exists. There are now communities and districts in Germany that contain up to 40 per cent new citizens from territories long settled by Germans in the east and southeast. In many cases, economic integration was possible with regard to their professions; but in spite of their specific emphasis on their *Deutschtum,* their being Germans for which they have now to suffer, their social acceptance was not easy and discontents and hostilities arise because traditions are being upset.

In 1948, the prohibition of organizing the refugees in groups was lifted; and since then, many organizations have been founded, so-called *Landsmannschaften,* to foster and maintain their regional cultural heritage. It is perhaps not entirely correct to call these people a special and separate social group, since they represent a community of fate; but they have nevertheless a terrific impact on the social structure of present Germany. They at least will seek to return to the places they were forced to leave and will strongly support, if not lead, a German policy directed to this end. This group represents one of the sore spots underlying German society now; although, as has been pointed out, it cannot be submitted under the headings of traditional class differentiations.

Another group is in a similar position; although it surely cannot command the sympathies that, at least from a humanitarian point of view, can be granted to the refugees. This is the leadership group that ruled Germany during the period of the Third Reich, which led Germany to disaster and had to pay a rather limited penalty for this. Again, this is not a cohesive group; it was recruited from different social backgrounds—the working class was perhaps the least involved, the lower middle class the most. The political influence and the social status of this lower middle class was very limited until Hitler came to power. These people enjoyed for twelve years all the advantages of unlimited power, which they abused to an extent unprecedented perhaps in recorded history. For this half-educated, cruel, antireligious, and anti-intellectual elite group, 1933 to 1945 was a period of glory never experienced before. Then came the collapse, which meant that they lost their position of leadership and, in addition to this, were individually and collectively held responsible for the crimes committed by the regime. This is another frustrated group that is a problem for German society. After an overemphasis on denazification, it was possible to incorporate them again into the economic life. It is very doubtful whether their social prestige ever suffered. As a matter of fact, there are many examples of men who were very high in the Nazi hierarchy who can be found now in important and responsible positions, inside the government as well as outside. One should not consider them a social group. Politically, they have been amazingly unsuccessful; although many have found their way into the existing political parties that were only too eager to include them in their ranks with the slogan "everything is forgiven and forgotten." However, their common experience of power and glory, followed by an experience of common persecution, has made them a unique group; they must be considered when the social problems of postwar Germany are discussed.

The Americans especially were concerned with the problem of denazification and democratic re-education, and many of their edicts and instructions in an atmosphere of wartime passions were foolish in practice and had to be scrapped step by step. The same is true for the laws enacted by the Germans themselves to punish the Nazis. The stringency of these decrees and laws inflicted painful wounds upon individuals, and nasty personal scars still remain. The fact that persecutors became persecuted, even if the new persecution took place within the framework of due process of law, was and is detrimental to the cohesion of German society. In this respect, we are faced with a social and moral problem of the highest significance, the extent of which can only be explained by the inhuman nature of the Nazi regime. The atrocities committed during this period called for revenge. There were so many denunciations that after the collapse the denunciations were reversed. The fellow who denounced his competitor or his office colleague was now held responsible for this act. So, denunciations went on; very often they were actual, but sometimes the acts were imaginary. It happened frequently during the period 1945–1950 that an entirely or almost innocent person was punished and had to suffer needlessly.

What were the social consequences of this? Some injustices committed by the victorious powers (not only by the Russians) and by "democratic" Germany can be used to justify all the injustices and inhuman crimes of the Nazis. Hatred and mutual mistrust can thus be perpetuated and can be found among small communities, even within a family unit, as well as throughout the whole nation. Therefore, in addition to all the political and economic tensions every nation has to face, Germany is haunted by the problem of the refugees and the deep-grained animosities that arose from the impact of the Nazi crimes on the whole society. Many foreign observers who are concerned with the question of whether or not there is a feeling of guilt among the Germans for all the crimes and cruelties committed in their name are rather skeptical that such a feeling exists. They maintain that the Germans are extremely sorry for themselves, rather than penitent; so many pretend that they had known nothing of the cruelties of the Nazi regime that one cannot possibly believe them.

Guilt, like life itself, is an individual experience and can only be applied with great reservations to a collective body. The die-hard Nazi surely has no feeling of guilt; the many fellow travelers used and trained to obedience can easily erase any guilt feeling under these premises; and there are also many, most likely those who never committed any indecent act, who feel guilty for what has been done in the name of Germany (among the last group, Germany's most famous psychiatrist Karl Jaspers is included; he maintained that in a metaphysical sense, all Germans, even the anti-Nazi like himself, were guilty because they survived the mass murders of civilians). It is also noteworthy that in present Germany a kind of new appreciation, a very acute, sometimes hysterical, awareness of this complex question of guilt has appeared, for which to some extent the dramatization of *Anne Frank's Diary* has been given credit.[4] Nonetheless, one would never be able to find a genuine collective guilt feeling penetrating through all phases of German society. Such an idea of collective guilt has, from the viewpoint of Western democratic thought, to be rejected under all circumstances, for to accept it would amount to perpetuating the Nazi horror of laying a curse on a whole people or a whole group.

It is still too early to formulate a correct picture of the new German social life as it has developed during the last fifteen years. The old social structure was destroyed, and no new leading class has emerged since. The highest national values in Germany society, nationalism, militarism, discipline, and authoritarianism, led Germany twice during this century to defeat and disaster. The destruction and the hunger and sufferings that followed created a skeptical approach to these values. Militarism has perhaps for the first time been discredited. The creation of a German Army, even within the framework of the Western alliance, is opposed by large segments of the population and is nowhere accepted with enthusiasm. This does not mean, of course, that the departure from the traditional militarism is permanent; but it is quite indicative, in this respect, that the West German Ministry of Defense found it necessary to stimulate the lack of military spirit among the young soldiers by emphasizing the glorious past of the German Army. This example shows that the old social values, which have been attacked and temporarily destroyed, have not yet been replaced by new values; so it may be necessary in some instances to come back to them. In this area, lies a potential danger.

One has to realize that, after 1945, the leadership fell back to the older men who very unsuccessfully led the Weimar Republic and had survived the terror regime; former President Heuss and Chancellor Adenauer are the outstanding examples. The age group that should provide leadership now and for the next decade is made up of men who, due to their experiences of the war and the immediate postwar period, are extremely skeptical. Specifically, there developed a mistrust of political ideas and

[4] Alfred Werner, "Germany's New Flagellants," *The American Scholar*, Spring, 1958, pp. 169–78.

beliefs within this age group of present businessmen, teachers, and parents; it represents a definite antipolitical, if not totally antisocial, attitude. The old social values, which required from the individual a great amount of idealism and readiness for sacrifices for the sake of the whole nation, have lost their appeal; they left a vacuum. If a social attitude can be traced in present German society, it is a deep-rooted skepticism of politics and ideologies, an egotistical materialism evaluating soberly the economic possibilities of the individual, the community, and the nation. Economic prosperity and material progress have become the most important factor in the political and social behavior during the postwar years. From this point of view, the amazing, almost miraculous, economic recovery of West Germany can be partly explained, also the failure of extreme political ideologies to gain any substantial success. At present, this attitude can be illustrated by collectively applying the famous words of Goethe's Faust to the larger part of German society, "I hear the message well, but I lack the belief." This materialistic sobriety can hardly be considered a positive social value. It contains the old danger that it may be directed into authoritarian rather than democratic lines. Exalted, hysterical ideas and leaders, as were found so frequently during the second empire and the Weimar Republic, have been discredited so much by the Nazi regime that no such messages would be received today by the sober Germans. The more dangerous totalitarianism from the Left, which already controls East Germany and behind which stands the power of the U.S.S.R., has no appeal as long as economic prosperity and temporary security can be achieved more easily with less personal sacrifices within the political-economic framework of a Western democratic type. Nonetheless, it would be premature to believe that the message of democracy, the idea of equality and human dignity, humanity as a basic social concept rather than an individual characteristic, has been genuinely and permanently accepted by the German people; but, perhaps for the first time in German history, these concepts stand a good chance to be incorporated into the scheme of social values and permanently replace the old extreme militaristic and authoritarian values. Such a change would require two prerequisites. First, the deep, intense universal aspirations for German unity must be achieved in a peaceful manner, eliminating the possibility of a long lasting frustrated nationalism that only too easily may become arrogant, aggressive, and violent again. Second, the economic growth and prosperity must continue for an extended period without such disturbances as a large amount of unemployment so that as many Germans as possible may enjoy a high standard of living and security. If national unification and economic prosperity should be achieved by a democratic government, upholding and defending personal freedom and dedicated to the principle of equality of nations and people, a remarkable change may take place within the German national character.

SELECTED READING

KOHN, HANS. *The Mind of Germany: The Education of a Nation.* New York: Charles Scribner's Sons, 1960.

LOEWENSTEIN, PRINCE HUBERTUS. *The Germany in History.* New York: Columbia University Press, 1945.

NEUMANN, SIGMUND. "The New Crisis Strata in German Society." In *Germany and the Future of Europe,* Hans J. Morgenthau (ed.). Chicago: University of Chicago Press, 1951.

POLLOCK, JAMES K., and HOMER, THOMAS. *Germany in Power and Eclipse.* Princeton, N. J.: D. Van Nostrand Co., Inc., 1952.

STERN, FRITZ. "The Fragmented People that is Germany," *Commentary,* Vol. XXI, No. 2, February, 1955.

VALENTIN, VEIT. *The German People.* New York: Alfred A. Knopf (a division of Random House, Inc.), 1946.

30

Political Ideologies

CONSERVATISM AND NATIONALISM

The famous nineteenth-century German historian Heinrich von Treitschke wrote in his *Die Politik,* "It is of the essence of the state that it should be able to enforce its will by physical force." German political theory has emphasized the authority of instruments that express the will of the state. The writings of the great German philosophers of the eighteenth and nineteenth centuries provide the origins of this authoritarian tradition in the realm of political ideology. Although they oriented German political thought toward some degree of constitutionalism, their theories exalted state authority so highly that they had no difficulty in accommodating despotism. Immanuel Kant, the famous philosopher from Koenigsberg, whose categoric imperative is perhaps one of the greatest expressions of an ethical idea in the area of moral philosophy, was an authoritarian political theorist. Accepting the doctrine that all authority is instituted by God, not as a historical fact, but as a principle of practical reason, he concluded that one should obey the existing power, whatever its origin. To attack this power is to place oneself outside the law; yet, if a revolution proves successful, the newly arisen power is as absolute and as potentially eternal as its unfortunate predecessor. Johann Gottlieb Fichte, the first of the great followers of Kant, began as an extreme individualist who built his theory on the concept of the absolute ego and turned later to the state as bearer and champion of the highest spiritual and cultural good of the nation. His famous *Addresses to the German Nation* (1808) strongly influenced the German uprising against Napoleon. He was the first German thinker to link German nationalism to the concept of the state, and he called upon the hero (the leader or *Zwingherr*) to build the German nation-state upon the basis of freedom and reason. While Kant only accepted state authority in an abstract sense, Fichte's ideas went beyond his and represented a fusion of state and legal authority and the emotional force of nationalism. This unhealthy combination became a dominant factor in German political ideology.

In Georg Friedrich Hegel (1770–1831) exists the strongest philosophical and spiritual background for the authoritarian tradition in Germany. As a professor of philosophy in Berlin, he became the official philosopher of the Prussian state and to a great degree the philosophical dictator of the whole of Germany. He invented a new methodology, the dialectic. His philosophy is both a philosophy of the absolute and a philosophy of perpetual change. The absolute is the "idea" (reason in the widest sense) that realizes itself finally in world history: "All that is rational is real and all that is real is rational." The expression of highest rationality and therefore of highest reality is the idea of the state, "the march of God in the world." Thus, the state is "the actual God," and "men must venerate the state as a secular deity." It is in all of its actions supreme, the objectivation of the absolute idea of the rational. The state expresses its absolute supremacy by the freedom to act in whatever way it chooses. He concluded that "the state is the realized ethical idea—this substantive unity is its own motive and end," prescribing that "this end has the highest right over the individual, whose highest duty is in turn to be a member of the state."[1] Thus, the essence of the Hegelian idea is glorification of the state and projection of its authority into an autocratic and powerful government. Hegel's concept of the state as "the true, absolute, final end" led also to his philosophical justification of German militarism. He regarded war as enabling the supreme power of the state to express itself in such a way as to emphasize the individuality of the state and the submission of its subjects; in doing so, he set the stage for its glorification. More than a century later, Erich von Ludendorff spoke of World War I as "the blessing of the last bath of steel," expressing his pity for the young German generation who had been deprived of this experience. Hegel's philosophy provided the philosophical background for authoritarianism, nationalism, and militarism; and at least one type of German conservatism subsequently incorporated all three of these phenomena.

Hegel believed in the existence of the unbroken historical chain that linked the present to the past and the future to both past and present. So also did English conservative thought at the time of Burke, but it rejected the idea of an exalted nationalism and subsequently evolved in the direction of democracy and protection of individual rights. German conservatism became in turn chauvinistic and reactionary, despite attempts by

[1] T. M. Knox (trans.), Georg F. W. Hegel's *Philosophy of Right* (London: The Clarenden Press, 1942). Para. 257–58.

conservatives like Friedrich Julius Stahl to guide German political life in the direction of constitutionalism. Stahl attempted to build a conservative theory that repudiated to some degree Hegel's monistic state. Individual personality and an "ethical Reich" were for him the two roots of law and state. The famous German concept of the *Rechtsstaat* can be traced to him. He defined it as follows: "What the state should be is a *Rechtsstaat*. . . . It has to define in the terms of law the paths and limitations of its activity and the spheres of freedom of its citizens, and to guarantee the inviolability of these limitations and spheres. . . . This is the concept of the *Rechtsstaat*."[2] This definition incorporates explicitly the idea of limited or constitutional government, as opposed to the unlimited power vested in the police state. The *Rechtsstaat* is, therefore, of conservative origin. However, the concept of the Rechtsstaat was so twisted by German theorists during the nineteenth and twentieth centuries that its main element, the "spheres of freedom" of the citizens in relation to the state, lost practically all its meaning. Stahl maintained also that a constitutional separation of powers was necessary in order to protect the individual personality from the arbitrariness of both the ruler and the sovereign people; at the same time, he also sought to maintain the legitimacy of the monarchical principle. Although his thought is closer to the conservatism of Burke than of Hegel, his fear of revolution induced him to accept practices more reactionary than his thoughts. As a true conservative, he viewed religion as the most important component of monarchical government. Divine right was the heart of his system. He argued that God instituted the state and civil authority for the realization of the divine moral order, or Christianity, and that the state's function is to protect and foster it and the Christian church.

The outstanding representative of German political conservatism during the second half of the nineteenth century was Otto von Bismarck. To him, the constitutional side of theoretical conservatism did not mean anything; he was specifically opposed to the idea of a free parliamentary system. In a speech made in 1862 he stated, "The great questions of the time will be decided, not by speeches and resolutions of majorities (that was the mistake of 1848 and 1849), but by blood and iron."

By the time of the collapse of the monarchy and during the Weimar Republic, the Christian aspect of German conservative thought was virtually abandoned. Under these circumstances, it was possible for the leader of the German National party, Alfred Hugenberg, to cooperate with the anti-Christian national socialism for the destruction of the Weimar Republic.

[2] Friedrich Julius Stahl, "Die Philosophie des Rechts," quoted in *State and Sovereignty in Modern Germany* by Rupert Emerson (New Haven, Conn.: Yale University Press, 1928.) P. 35.

LIBERALISM AND NATIONALISM

During the nineteenth century, the disunited condition of the German states precluded the emergence of a politically strong liberal movement. The idea of freedom developed not in the political sphere, but rather in the realms of literature and philosophy. Lessing, in his *Nathan the Wise,* spoke out as early as the middle of the eighteenth century for religious tolerance. Friedrich von Schiller, in *Don Carlos,* beseeched an absolute monarch to "grant us freedom of thought"; and, in philosophy, Kant defended individual rights against governmental arbitrariness.

In the western states of the Rhine Federation, French occupation forces in the early nineteenth century conveyed the liberal ideas of the French Revolution. That era also marked the first application of liberal ideas to German political and economic life. In Prussia, Stein, Hardenberg, Humboldt, and others expounded principles that reflected the economic influence of Adam Smith and the ethical ideas of Immanuel Kant. Both Stein and Hardenberg were great Prussian statesmen who influenced German reform at the beginning of the nineteenth century, yet they concentrated on specific reforms in particular fields and not on the development of liberal ideology.

From the very beginning of the German liberal movement, a patriotic demand for unification was closest to the hearts of its representatives. In the case of Stein, the connection between liberal reform and strong German nationalism is perhaps clearer than with any other German of his day. He spoke and acted always as a German patriot. "I have but one fatherland, which is called Germany," he wrote. "To me in this moment of transition, the dynasties are completely insufficient; they are mere instruments; my wish is that Germany should become great and strong. . . . My confession of faith is [German] unity."

Wilhelm von Humboldt (1767–1835) is perhaps the first German who theoretically separated liberal political theory from the practical application of governmental reform. The title of his principle work is *Thoughts Concerning an Attempt to Determine the Limits of the Activity of the State.* His individualism, like that of Mill and Spencer in England in later decades, assumed that the exclusive purpose of the state was the protection of the population from external attack and internal disorder. This was the task that the state was to perform, and it had no further claim upon individual freedom.

How was his liberal theory applied? In 1809, Humboldt became chief of the Section of Education and Religion in the Prussian Ministry of the Interior and in this capacity reorganized the Prussian educational system. His reforms had a permanent influence. They help explain the character of German liberalism and also the general German attitude toward education. Academic freedom was recognized and strongly emphasized, and general elementary education was instituted for all social classes. Humboldt maintained that the intellectual's ultimate goal is free inquiry into the truth and that its prerequisite is academic freedom. A premium was placed on the accumulation of knowledge so as to enable the individual more effectively to find the truth. Thus, in the true liberal sense, everyone can and should become as clever and wise as he can, but always within the framework of the existing social order and with the final purpose of fostering the interests of the state. Humboldt and many of his successors also sought to separate intellectual from political liberalism. State educational policy should train subjects for good citizenship and yet foster the ideal of free inquiry into truth. It is obvious that these two goals were often antagonistic; and a theoretical reconciliation was found only in nationalism, the historical ally of German liberalism. Academic freedom would establish the superiority of German scholarship over other nations, and in doing so it would strengthen the political power of the state. It would also increase the prestige of Prussia within Germany as the instrument of unification. For all this, a good citizenry is necessary; hence, it is the duty of the state to gear education in this direction. Thus, intellectual freedom was emphasized but its basis was strongly nationalistic. This explains how nationalistic influences were frequently able to dominate or eliminate such liberal concepts as the protection of civil liberties. As a result, there were few, if any, liberal ideas left in the German universities in the twentieth century.

A similar discrepancy between theory and practice at the beginning of German liberal thought can be found in Humboldt's attitude toward civil liberties such as freedom of speech and press. Although in his writings he declared that unlimited freedom from censorship was the only right principle, he was also opposed to the application of such a principle. In his official capacity, it was his duty to supervise all Prussian censorship and to endorse and apply its restrictive provisions. Governmental censorship in Prussia, Austria, and in others of the German states was extremely oppressive. The poet Heinrich Heine, the most brilliant advocate of freedom in the nineteenth century, described this situation in his *Travel Pictures*, in which he parodied existing censorship. His twelfth chapter consists only of the following:

> The German censors of the press . . . .
> . . . .
> . . . .
> . . . . blockheads . . . .
> . . . . !

Nonetheless, at the beginning of the nineteenth century, some far-reaching liberal reforms had been established. The liberation of the serfs, the dissolution of the rigid guild system and municipal autonomy, and the abolition of interstate tariffs among German states are illustrative of these achievements. These first breakthroughs in the early nineteenth century were interpreted and defended as patriotic deeds in Prussia during the reactionary period subsequent to the Congress of Vienna in 1815. However, the people were not successful in their demand for political and civil liberties, and as a result liberalism was forced more and more in the direction of radicalism. Much to its disadvantage, this split the German liberal movement into a democratic cosmopolitan wing and a more moderate constitutional wing. The liberal groups were divided when they met in 1848 in the constitutional convention in Frankfurt and founded, in line with these divisions, separate liberal political parties.

The radical wing of the liberal movement up to 1848 was composed entirely of intellectuals. It included the brothers Bauer, Feuerbach, Karl Marx (for a time), and many others. They attempted to liberalize the Hegelian philosophic system. The Young German Movement, whose most outstanding representatives, Ludwig Boerne and Heinrich Heine, were forced to emigrate to Paris, was more a literary than a political movement. However, this radical wing was aware that it had to create a wider basis among the population in order to combat successfully the regional princes and other reactionary forces. As a consequence, it became increasingly concerned with socioeconomic problems and exhibited a sympathy for many types of Socialist ideas. The upper middle class soon withdrew support from ideas that appealed largely to the lower middle class and skilled laborers.

After 1848, it was much more in the economic than in the ideological area that German liberalism became active. In 1857, Victor Boehmert issued an appeal for the foundation of a German economic association; and the Congress of German Economists was founded with a program of free enterprise; tariff reform; and freer movement in transportation, banking operations, and currency. In 1859, the founding of the *Nationalverein* (National Association) made possible for a limited period cooperation between the radical and moderate elements of German liberalism. It attempted to organize the German bourgeoisie on a national scale, and it used the idea of national unity to achieve this end. This led to the creation of the German Progressive party in 1861, the first of the German liberal parties. In 1848, however, the German middle class had failed in its attempt to synthesize political liberalism with democracy, as nationalism proved stronger than true liberalism. This conflict is best illustrated by a statement of Boehmert to the National Association: "The times are serious enough so that a choice between unity and freedom is necessary . . . we must strengthen this [Prussian] power, however hard it may strike even temporarily anti-liberal tendencies. . . . Prussia's representatives have at the moment greater duties toward the future of their state than to tend to mere liberalism." Others, too, believed that German unification could only be achieved under Prussian leadership and liberal ideas had to be postponed, if not sacrificed, for this goal.

In 1867, the moderate Right wing of the liberal movement separated from the Progressive party and founded the National Liberal party. This development conformed with the tendency of the upper middle class to relinquish liberal aspirations in return for economic protection by the government. This group became Bismarckian after the unification and no longer did it resist the coalition of large agrarian interests and heavy industry that dominated German policy until World War I. It settled instead for the material benefits derived from governmental orders, especially military contracts. In 1909, as a defense against the reactionary tendencies of the large agrarians (Junkers), the Hansa Federation for Trade, Commerce and Industry was established for the specific purpose of reactivating in a truly liberal sense the political life of the middle class. The outbreak of World War I with its war economy worked against the theoretical basis and the practical activities of the Hansa Federation. However, during the whole Weimar period, it maintained a continuous fight against state socialism and Left-wing totalitarianism, attempting to collect the liberal middle class as a strong political center. It also opposed national socialism without compromise until 1933.

After World War I, several attempts were made to unify the liberal movement. They were unsuccessful because of the timidity born of the historically frustrating experiences of the German middle class and their reluctance to accept the principles of a free market economy. These principles, incidentally, now have been implemented by the West German Republic.

DEMOCRATIC SOCIALISM AND COMMUNISM

The beginning of a Socialist movement in Germany goes back to the 1830's, under the influence of Frenchmen like St. Simon, Fourier, and Proudhon. Wilhelm Weitling, a tailor, and Moses Hess, who published a few short-lived newspapers with Communist tendencies, were the first German representatives. However, systematic Socialist doctrine was developed only after the 1848 February Revolution by Karl Marx and Friedrich Engels. It was laid down in the *Communist Manifesto,* which appeared in the same year and contained the basic elements of the Marxist doctrine so important to the later development of socialism in Germany.

Karl Marx was born in 1818 in Trier, the son of a Jewish lawyer who became a Christian in 1824. He studied in Bonn and afterwards in Berlin, where he came under the influence of the New Hegelians. He became chief editor of a newspaper, but he subsequently was forced to resign because of his radical writings. He emigrated to Paris and from there to Brussels. Becoming very friendly with Engels, the son of a rich textile manufacturer, Marx finally went to England, where Engels supported him from 1850 to his death in 1883, giving him the opportunity to conduct extensive studies for his classical work *Das Kapital.*

Marx's point of departure is the philosophy and dialectical method of Hegel. But whereas Hegel was a philosophical idealist, Marx was a materialist, asserting that he turned Hegel upside down and placed him on his feet. He writes in *Das Kapital:* "For Hegel the process of thought, which under the name of the idea, he even transforms into an independent subject, is the demiurge of the real world, while the real world is only its external appearance. With me, on the contrary, the ideal is nothing other than the material after it has been transposed and translated inside the human head." He concluded that society itself is determined by the economic relations of each individual to the means of production (land, raw material, machines, etc.). The consequence is that ideas, such as religion and the state and the law, are all parts of the superstructure of society, based upon the material conditions that constitute the economic substructure. On these concepts, historical materialism and economic determinism are built, from which important consequences derive for a political program. The proletariat can only take over the instruments of production in a revolutionary situation. Such a revolution is therefore desirable and should be the essential political goal of a labor party. In this revolution, the industrial labor class acts in the name of the whole working population to attain political power, which is exercised by a "dictatorship of the proletariat." Marx saw no contradiction between democracy and the dictatorship of the proletariat. On the contrary, in his terminology, democracy can only be represented by the proletariat. Only when this democracy has defeated its enemies with armed force can it start to disband the existing institutions of the state. Only then will the state wither away because the classless society will have no further need for it. It is easy to understand why aspects of the Marxian thesis were in direct conflict with traditional German political, social, and ethical values. Marx's advocacy of violent revolution was alien to a nation where for centuries the mere idea of revolution was considered a sacrilege. He actually visualized an end to the institution of the state, which in Germany had been so highly glorified.

The parties that had been founded on Marxian doctrines developed in various directions. With the formation of the Social Democratic party at Gotha in 1875, a compromise was temporarily achieved. Nevertheless, the party congress that met in Erfurt in 1891 adopted a new program that was authored by Karl Kautsky, which was strongly attacked by Lenin, who became the leader of the Russian Revolution. The Erfurt Program was theoretically Marxian in the emphasis on the economic doctrines of Marx and Engels, but it did not include his belief in the necessity of revolution. It stated that, "the struggle of the working class against capitalistic exploitation is of necessity a political struggle. . . . it cannot bring about the transfer of the instruments of production to social ownership without having first come into possession of the political power." The Social Democratic party saw the way to political power as a democratic one within the framework of the capitalistic state. Its first goal, therefore, was the establishment of political democracy in Germany and ultimately of socialism. Within the ranks of the Socialists were found the most active if not the only sincere fighters for political democracy in Germany. After the adoption of the Erfurt Program, the German Social Democratic party was not Marxian in a political sense, although it made partial use of Marxian doctrine.

The labor movement in Germany ceased by 1900 to be exclusively theoretical. After the abolition of the anti-Socialist laws in 1890, its radical Left wing, represented by Liebknecht and Bebel, was entirely opposed to any cooperation within the existing state and it lost some of its influence. Under the same theoretical premises that accepted political democracy there developed a climate favorable to parliamentarism. In addition, the practical organizational work in trade-unions and consumer cooperatives showed that it was possible within the existing social order for the position of the labor class to be improved. Even the Erfurt Program included quite a number of practical demands for improvements. When comparing the Program in its final form with the *Communist Manifesto,* there can be detected a significant difference on the issue of political participation. The sociopolitical measures of the government were recognized, and the active participation of the Social Democratic party in such decisions was required. In view of this development, it is not too significant that the theoretical part of the Program, drafted by Kautsky, drew strongly from Marx and Engels. With the theorists, the influence of the Marxian school was still growing. The practical politicians, however, took only some useful propaganda slogans from the teaching of the master and never made the essential Marxian program the basis for their work. As early as 1891, leader of the Bavarian Social Democrats Vollmar recommended the concentration of efforts in the direction of specific reforms. As an example, he demanded a change of the agrarian policy of the party to protect the small and medium-sized independent farmer. This, of course, was in contradiction to Marxian theory.

In 1900, another important leader of German socialism, Eduard Bernstein, returned from England where he had spent many years in exile. Influenced by the Fabian Socialists, he declared that Marx was wrong in his thesis that the capitalistic order must necessarily collapse and held that socialism could be achieved by transferring the instruments of production to social ownership in a gradual process of social reform, for which political power was not necessarily a precondition. This "revisionism" (the term given to Bernstein's ideas) therefore rejected social revolution and substituted for it democracy achieved by legal parliamentary methods. Theoretically, this basic emphasis on reform work was strongly opposed, especially by Kautsky, who emphasized the theoretical part of the Erfurt Program ("Marxian orthodoxy") against the more flexible teachings of Lassalle. Nonetheless, the "revisionist" movement was finally successful, mostly through practical political work. This development was helped by the fact that the trade-unions, unhampered by political ideology, were forced to adhere to practical methods that could show quite significant successes. One can see, therefore, the deep-rooted ideological difference that existed in the German Socialist movement.

As far as the original Social Democratic party was concerned, it turned more and more to the achievement of practical political aims and accepted also the political methods common to intensive parliamentary work. During the twentieth century, and specifically under the Weimar Republic, parliamentarism became a cornerstone of the political philosophy of the Social Democrats. However, this situation eventually brought about a split in the German Socialist movement. It started at the beginning of World War I when the Left wing of the party, under the leadership of Karl Liebknecht and Rosa Luxemburg, took the position that it was the duty of the party to prevent the war by the use of any means, even the general strike. In 1916, the opposition group began the publication of an illegal newspaper, which appeared under the name of *Spartacus,* most of it written by Rosa Luxemburg. From this time on, the group became known as the Spartacists and kept this name until it officially changed it in January 1919 to that of the Communist party of Germany.

During the war, the ideological emphasis of this group had been on the international principle. The proletarian had no fatherland. The patriotic talk of the duty to defend the "fatherland," accepted by the Social Democratic party, was not really socialistic. The main task for the present time was an international class struggle against the war in order to force peace through the will of the masses. The Spartacists were in close relationship with the radical Socialists of all countries. Most of them were at this time in exile in Switzerland and under the spiritual leadership of Trotsky, Lenin, and Radek. After the Russian Revolution in 1917, the Spartacist league accepted Russian bolshevism entirely, including the Leninist interpretation of the dictatorship of the proletariat. Besides this radical opposition against the official policy of the party, there existed also a more moderate one. At the beginning, it was under the leadership of

Hugo Haase, the chairman of the party, and was theoretically defended by Karl Kautsky in the periodical *Die Neue Zeit.* This moderate opposition was composed of people who fluctuated between Marxist theory and political expediency. It finally separated from the party and constituted itself as the Independent Social Democratic party. The constituent meeting took place in April, 1917, in Gotha, the same place where in 1875 the Marxians and Lassalleans met to constitute the unified Social Democratic party of Germany. In contrast to the Spartacists, who were operating unofficially, the position of the Independents was one of a recognized political party. Thus, after 1917, there were two workers' parties comprising different wings of the Socialist movement in addition to the Spartacist league. All of them claimed to be the sole rightful guardian of the Erfurt Program. Only the Spartacists and, to a lesser degree, the Independents were in favor of a revolution in 1918.

The majority Socialists were the most democratic party during the Weimar Republic and participated in several coalition governments. In Prussia, they headed democratic coalitions until 1932. The Independent Socialists rejoined the majority in November, 1922; this, however, did not mean that the German working class was ideologically and politically unified. The breach between socialism represented by the German Social Democratic party and the totalitarian bolshevism represented by the Communist party became deeper and deeper during the twenties and thirties. Ideologically as well as politically, these two groups, although their doctrines were founded on Marxism, became bitter enemies as they appealed to the same group of voters and competed for its support. This feud only helped the rise of Hitler.

Whatever the faults of the German Social Democrats, they represented the most democratic element in German political life. They were not free from nationalistic and even chauvinistic tendencies, but they adhered to the principles of constitutionalism and civil liberties against the totalitarian Left and Right, though in a manner that was truly suicidal. To this extent, they share responsibility for the downfall of the Weimar Republic. Their attitude was perhaps best expressed by Otto Braun, the Social Democratic prime minister of Prussia, who later said while in exile in Switzerland, "politicians of various countries ask me: how was it that the Hitler dictatorship could arise in Germany? I can only answer again and again: Versailles and Moscow."

FASCISM

German fascism holds a unique position among all forms of totalitarian dictatorships. It developed as a movement against the revolution of 1918 and the establishment of parliamentary democracy in Germany. It included, however, a certain number of traditional German tendencies that, under the impact of the unexpected German defeat of 1918, gained an unforeseen political dynamism. National socialism turned to several militant ideological theories, which, often misunderstood and misrepresented, became the background of the Nazi *Weltanschauung* (world view). Behind this ideology was an aggressive nationalism that was based on the tradition of the superior character of the German people and the ideas of a great German unified Reich. It demanded practical struggle against the restrictions of the Versailles Treaty and the extension of the frontiers of the German state to include all *Volksdeutsche* (the Germans living in separate German-speaking states like Austria, or in non-German states like the Sudetenland in Czechoslovakia). The mad claims of German leadership manifested themselves in the imperialistic drive for an enlarged German *Lebensraum* (living space).

The Nazis contended that the specific nature of the German community and the German national state contradicted the "Westernized and Christianized" decadence of parliamentary democracy. The emphasis was on collective unity, subordination under a leader who was not elected from below but imposed from above. Considering the authoritarian tradition of German society, this leader ideology had a strong appeal in the vacuum of a state deprived of a monarch. The political and civil rights of the individual and their protection in the Western liberal tradition were attacked as an expression of "Jewish decadence." The weakness of the new democracy called for a strong man, a Fuehrer. The increasing postwar tensions attracted the masses of Germans who longed for order and unity and mystical faith to the militant Nazi movement. For the sober and often frustrating attempts of the democratic parties for compromise and cooperation, German fascism substituted the irrational faith in the infallibility of the leader. His promises to solve all social and political problems justified an "escape from freedom." Connected with these promises was the strong psychological need for authority of a population that had been ruled for centuries from above. To all this was added an appeal to the military tradition of the population. Emphasis was placed upon the heroic war experiences of World War I and the vicious but widely believed lie that the defeat in 1918 had been caused only by unfortunate circumstances, treason, and the stabbing in the back of the "glorious German Armies."

This "betrayal" had to have a scapegoat, and so a tangible group was declared the absolute enemy and the incarnation of all that is evil. This group was composed of Jews, who represented a small minority of the German population, not much in excess of 1 per cent. National Socialism practiced an extremely aggressive and brutal anti-Semitism. By the end of Hitler's "1,000-year Reich" (which lasted twelve years), six million European Jews, mostly from east European states, were annihilated in gas chambers and concentration camps. This myth of the race enemy was derived from a widely propagandized power philosophy that considered the essence of all politics the unlimited power of the strong over the weak. The misused and falsified ideas of Friedrich Nietzsche of the "superman" and the "blond beast" were coupled with the pseudoscientific nineteenth-century race theories of the Frenchman Count de Gobineau and the Englishman H. S. Chamberlain. The result was a horrible racism.

The fight against international socialism and communism was another major Nazi doctrine. The slogan of "National Socialism" was originally created to denote a democratic social reconciliation of the nation by the liberal politician Friedrich Naumann, who died in 1919. It became after the end of World War I the essence of a counterideology against international socialism.

It has been indicated that an explanation for the advent to power of Nazism can be found in the external and internal difficulties of the Weimar Republic. This Republic emerged out of a revolution that was not wanted by a substantial part of the German population. Penalized by a hard peace treaty and social catastrophies such as inflation and subsequent mass unemployment, it became demoralized and discredited. The political goals of National Socialism appeared before World War I in small splinter groups in Austria and Bohemia. It became important, however, only in the postwar atmosphere when it found an unchallenged leader in the person of Adolf Hitler.

Hitler was born in Austria in 1889 and served in the German Army during World War I. In 1919, he worked as an informer for the army and met in this capacity the six members of a newly founded group that soon became the National Socialist German Workers party (NSDAP). After the Proclamation of the Twenty-Five Points Party Program in 1920, Hitler became the sole leader of the movement. His first attempt in Munich in 1923 to seize power was unsuccessful; and he was interned in the fortress Landsberg, where he wrote his book *Mein Kampf* (*My Struggle*). Rudolf Hess, the later deputy leader, whose flight to England in 1941 became one of the most famous episodes of World War II, acted on this occasion as his secretary. After 1925, the party was reorganized; and Hitler's book and Alfred Rosenberg's *Myth of the 20th Century* laid down the ideological background. By 1930, the party had become a mass movement; and in the election of July, 1932, it was the strongest party in the Reichstag (37 per cent of the seats). After von Hindenburg's death on August 2, 1934, Hitler as "leader and Reichschancellor" became omnipotent; and the NSDAP under his leadership was declared the "sole bearer of the political will of the German people." This totalitarian claim extended to all phases of the economic, legal, cultural, and religious life of the nation. Hitler proclaimed also the doctrine of submergence of the individual to the collective will of the party and its submission to the authoritarian command of its leader. The organizational machine of the party reached almost every group, including school children (Hitler Youth), the military organizations (SA and SS), and the numerous professional organizations.

The bestiality with which the National Socialist ideas were carried out distinguished nazism from other totalitarian regimes, especially Italian fascism. In this connection, special reference must be made to the elite corps of the SS under the leadership of Heinrich Himmler (who committed suicide in 1945). The SS became a state within the state. The administrative techniques of the SS, in establishing a "new order" in Europe under National Socialistic hegemony, surpassed in organized cruelty anything ever experienced in recorded history. It developed concentration camps, exterminated hundreds of thousands in gas chambers, and systematically persecuted and annihilated millions who belonged to politically or racially undesirable groups.

This system of terror was assisted by the fact that nazism was not bound to a rational philosophic system. Both the Twenty-Five Points and *Mein Kampf* contained only negative doctrines: against capitalism and Marxism; against liberalism and religion; against all political systems (except fascism); against individualism and Christianity; and, most of all, against Jews and Judaistic ethics. The result was an aggressive and expansive imperialism in external affairs and an internal barbarism that has not been surpassed. Hitler finally blamed the generals and to some extent his own master race, the German people, for the catastrophe that he himself escaped by committing suicide on April 4, 1945. In his political testament, he considered the murder of six million Jews his most important historical deed. Future historians will have a different opinion, but at the present there is still no satisfactory answer to the question: How was it possible?

SELECTED READING

COPER, R. *Failure of a Revolution, Germany in 1918–1919*. New York: Cambridge University Press, 1955.

EMERSON, RUPERT. *State and Sovereignty in Modern Germany*. New Haven, Conn.: Yale University Press, 1928.

HALLOWELL, JOHN H. *The Decline of Liberalism as an Ideology with Particular Reference to German Political Legal Thought*. Berkeley, Calif.: University of California Press, 1943.

KLEMPERER, KLEMENS VON. *Germany's New Conservatism: Its History and Dilemmas in the Twentieth Century*. Princeton, N.J.: Princeton University Press, 1957.

KOGON, EUGEN. *The Theory and Practice of Hell*. New York: Farrar, Straus & Cudahy, Inc., 1950.

SCHLESINGER, RUDOLPH. *Marx: His Time and Ours*. London: Routledge & Kegan Paul, Ltd., 1950.

31

Political Organizations

HISTORICAL DEVELOPMENT

Analogous to Germany's slow constitutional development, the formation of political parties started later in Germany than in western Europe. However, even before 1848, there existed a liberal and a conservative dichotomy; during the 1848 Revolution, the first universal German parties were created. The failure of the Revolution, which was basically a liberal movement, revealed the weaknesses of the liberal parties. In addition to the loss of prestige and the frustrations that a political movement was bound to suffer when it took the extreme step to revolt and then became afraid of its own courage, which was exactly the situation with the liberal middle class, there occurred a split in the organized political liberal movement in 1860 between the Progressive party and the National Liberal party, the latter representing the Right wing. The Catholic Center party was formed in 1870 and allied itself from this time on either with the rightist bloc (Conservatives and National Liberals) or the Left (Progressives and Social Democrats).

There were two significant factors that distinguished the development of German political parties from the parties in other countries that had a tragic influence after 1918. Under the Kaiser, parties were excluded from the exercise of direct political power and responsibility. Being more the expression of political philosophies than the executors of the political will of the people, the parties remained ideologically inflexible and unable to develop the art of parliamentary compromise. Consequently, the programs of the parties were not mainly documents for political goals and methods, but were primarily philosophical statements, expressing and justifying a specific *Weltanschauung*. The other factor peculiar to the character of the German political parties was their organization around the representation of economic, regional, ethnic, and religious groups and classes. From this point of view, the German parties during the second empire were to a great extent interest groups, representing separate sections of the population. These characteristics continued during the Weimar Republic.

Before the outbreak of World War I, there were a relatively large number of organized political parties participating in the elections for the *Reichstag*. Among them were several representing national minorities like the Polish party, the Danish party, a party representing Alsace-Lorraine, and several minor splinter groups. An interesting forecast for future developments was the existence of a specifically anti-Semitic party since 1890 that was organized openly under the name of *Antisemitische Partei,* which was able to win sixteen seats to the 1912 Reichstag in the last pre-World War I election.

During the second empire, the Conservatives were the important party of the Right. Basically, they represented the Junker class, the large agrarian land owners. In the 1870's, there developed several factions within the Conservative ranks, including one group that strongly attacked Bismarck, calling him a stockmarket speculator. Out of this situation came the foundation in 1876 of the *Deutsche Konservative Partei.* Most of its strength came from the agrarian movement and the military circles close to Wilhelm II after the fall of Bismarck in 1890.

In 1893, the Federation of Farmers was founded. Its expressed purpose was to organize all farmers to influence legislation, specifically with regard to protective tariff, tax exemptions, and supervision of the produce market. This group supported the Right-wing parties; opposed liberalism; and was friendly to the Anti-Semites, whose principles were indirectly accepted in their program. For the Conservatives, this federation was very important, because it gave them the organization that attracted certain population groups as electoral masses. The Conservatives received, therefore, a certain mass foundation without which an important party cannot exist. The party also was supported by the military circles that surrounded the Kaiser. An interesting point in the ideological development of the Conservatives is the fact that in 1892 they accepted into their party program the main principles of the Anti-Semites that were later laid down in the so-called Tivoli Program. This was done because they feared that the support of the Anti-Semites among the middle class would be lost, and this also indicated that anti-Semitic tendencies had a strong appeal to certain German groups long before Hitler used it as his most important propaganda weapon.[1]

[1] That anti-Semitism is by no means dead in present Germany was shown in an incident in 1959 when a high school teacher in a small town was convicted by a German court for violent anti-Semitic utterances. In this case, the community was entirely behind him; and he finally escaped with the toleration of the local authorities to Egypt.

It was already indicated that the liberal movement was not represented by a strong unified party during the second empire. Nonetheless, about the time of the foundation of the Reich, from 1867 to 1878, the National Liberals were the dominant political party. They were organized by Rudolf von Benningsen, who supported Bismarck's expansionist foreign policy without reservations. With regard to parliamentary reforms, the party was compromising. This situation led to the split of the liberal movement, the Progressive party representing the Left wing. The National Liberals represented the economic interests of heavy industry, incorporating free trade in their program; but they were generally considered as a Right-wing party, voting in many instances during the shifting parliamentary coalitions with the Conservatives. It is not surprising, therefore, that the Left wing of the liberal movement attempted to achieve a working agreement with the Social Democrats. Under the leadership of Friedrich Naumann and under the influence of the eminent German sociologist Max Weber, this group disengaged itself from the classical concept of free play of economic forces and approached the Social Democrats in the hope that the contradiction between the bourgeois parties and the Labor party could be solved. In local elections, quite frequently coalitions with the Social Democrats occurred.

An extremely important position among the parties was held by the Center party, a situation that carried over into the Weimar Republic. Originally founded in 1852 to defend Catholic interests, it was reorganized in 1870 on a Catholic basis and occupied a middle position between the Right and the Left. Without the Center, major parliamentary programs could not be carried out successfully; this fact alone imposed upon it a large degree of responsibility. After the end of the *Kulturkampf*, which ended with a compromise, the Center learned to make a moderate use of its key position and was also frequently able to compromise on basic principles. Working together with the National Liberals, it can take the credit for the passing of the unified Civil Law Code for the whole Germany in 1900. In the area of family law, the civil marriage was maintained, although strongly opposed by the Center, which of course supported religious marriage. It threatened in the negotiations to vote against the whole code but could not do so for practical political reasons; through compromise it was able to get some detailed formulations according to its wishes. This tactic was carried out by the Center in many important instances and reflected the shrewd position of a party that was unable to get a majority of its own. It supported the colonial policy of Bismarck in the 1880's and the naval policy and military budgets of Wilhelm II in the beginning of the century. In these activities, it stepped out of the limitations of a mere religious party but remained active in defending the power and the liberty of the church; it was also able to maintain in the end its religious basis. Its position as a middle party was also assisted by the fact that its followers were composed of people from the different regions and representatives of the various classes and economic interests. The party was consequently forced to find compromises within itself and was, therefore, less in the position to represent politically a special interest group. It stressed general social problems and supported perhaps more agricultural demands than those of commercial and industrial interests. In spite of its key position, the Center party was never a leading party in the sense that it could have taken the initiative in the solution of a political problem. Even in the area of social policy, it was rather slow to support necessary reforms; on the other hand, it was not willing to glorify the past to the extent of ignoring many currently rising problems. During the Weimar Republic, the party headed several coalition governments. Actually, the last government that could be called democratic and that fell in May, 1932, was under the leadership of Chancellor Heinrich Bruening, a leader of the Center party.

Several references have already been made to the Social Democratic party and the tensions and frictions that developed during and immediately after World War I in the interpretation of the Erfurt Program of 1891. It is noteworthy that at the election of 1912 to the Reichstag, the Social Democratic party, in spite of many handicaps, became the strongest party, holding 110 seats of the 397 seats in the Reichstag and getting approximately one-third of the popular vote. However, until the outbreak of the war in 1914, the domestic policy of the Kaiser was based on a sharp separation between the bourgeois parties and the state on one side and the Social Democrats on the other. In the summer of 1914, an immediate change of policy became necessary because the cooperation of the Social Democrats was needed for the war effort of a unified people against the enemy. It is interesting to note that it was specifically the reactionary Foreign Office that influenced Wilhelm II to modify his attitude toward the Social Democrats; as a result, by the end of August, 1914, the military prohibition against the Social Democratic literature was lifted, and the employment of organized Social Democrats in the state-owned railroads was permitted. It took a war to give the Social Democratic laborer citizenship status with equal rights. In spite of the opposition of Karl Kautsky, the Social Democratic representation in the Reichstag voted unanimously for the war credits asked for by the government, as well as for the other war measures.

In view of the fact that the Social Democrats in Germany, as elsewhere, were principally pacifistic, this position was definitely contradictory. The reasons for this are various. In a formal sense, the party justified its position that the war was of a defensive nature and it was always believed that in the case of a war of defense the party would unconditionally support the war effort. It takes an active imagination to interpret as defensive Germany's involvement in World War I, but it shows that the nationalistic and military trend was also existent among the Social Democrats. From an ideological point of view, the position was facilitated by the involvement of Tsarist Russia in the war; because in accordance with the views of Marx, the party had always looked on Russia as the bulwark of reaction and the deadly enemy of socialism. In addition to this came, in spite of all pacifistic theory and the general opposition to the imperial government, the feeling of each individual for national solidarity, which the Social Democrats were neither willing nor able to ignore.

The position of the party at the beginning of the war enabled the government to establish something like a domestic armistice. There is nothing peculiar about this situation; the same happened in other belligerent nations. France, for instance, had the "Union Sacree." Nevertheless, the relationship of the Social Democrats to the war was different from that of the other parties. The bourgeois parties had an almost blind confidence in the supreme command that was even strengthened because of the victories over the Russians by Hindenburg and Ludendorff. These military leaders were expansionist and in favor of territorial annexations, and in the sphere of domestic policies were absolutistic and authoritarian. Actually, there developed very soon, in spite of the political armistice, many tensions, which during the first years of the war did not come into the open, but eventually became more acute. Three main problems were involved: in the area of foreign policy, the question of the war aims, namely annexations; in the area of military policy, the question of the unrestricted U-boat war; and in the area of domestic policy, the question of the development of parliamentarism. Germany really went to war in 1914 without political aims; this was true of the government as well as of the parties and public opinion. In this respect, only the Social Democratic party had something like a program. From their basic attitude that only defensive wars are permissible, the only deduction was that territorial conquests were not permissible. Even in the declaration that explained the consent to the war credits, this basic position to the war aims was already expressed.

From the end of 1914, Scheidemann, the Social Democratic leader and the man who proclaimed the Republic and became its first Chancellor, agitated openly for a compromise peace to end the war. The policy of the Social Democrats was definitely opposed to annexations and of course also against the unrestricted U-boat warfare. However, the first front-line successes of the German Army had a strong illusionary effect on public opinion (the same happened at the beginning of World War II) and led the government to establish a far-reaching expansionist policy, which, of course, became known to the Social Democratic circles who were strongly opposed to it. This opposition was even stronger due to the fact that the spokesmen for annexations were at the same time the enemies in the area of domestic policy of a development toward democratic parliamentarism. The position of the Social Democratic party during World War I demonstrated again that it was the only important politically organized group in Germany that stood for democratic ideals and to some degree against militarism. This does not mean that there were no different tendencies within the German Socialist movement itself; these finally led to the split of the party in 1917.

THE PARTIES OF THE WEIMAR REPUBLIC

The inherent weakness of the German political parties, namely, their exclusion from governmental responsibility, their incapacity for political compromise, and their inflexible adherence to a *Weltanschauung,* became specifically tragic after 1918, when the parties had to take over, under the most difficult conditions, full responsibility of the parliamentary democratic government established by the Weimar Constitution. The heir to the Conservatives, the *Deutschnationale Volkspartei* (German National People's party), became a nationalistic, reactionary monarchistic mass party representing the Junkers and substantial parts of the upper middle class. It fought the Republic with all possible means. In 1920, it endorsed the notorious Kapp Revolution, which attempted to overthrow the new democratic government and to revert to the former structure of the Prussian German state. In 1931, this party and its military organization, the *Stahlhelm* (steel helmet), allied itself with the Nazis in the so-called "Harzburger Front." Its leader, Hugenberg, who came from the National Liberals, was intensely antidemocratic and had his share of responsibility for bringing Hitler to power. He became Minister of Economics in Hitler's first Cabinet.

The National Liberal party split into two parts. Its Right wing founded the German People's Party; its Left wing united itself with the Progressives and founded the German Democratic party. The main difference between these two parties was in their attitude to the new republican form of government. The German Democratic party supported the Republic fully but very soon lost its middle-class support. The German People's party became the spokesman of heavy industry and left the question of the form of government open. In reality, the majority of its followers favored the restoration of a monarchy, combined with a parliamentary system. In spite of its lukewarm acceptance of the Weimar Republic, the party participated in all coalition governments. Its leader, Dr. Gustav Stresemann, headed two Cabinets in 1923 and remained as Foreign Minister in all Cabinets until his death in 1926. In general, the German

People's party tended more toward cooperation with the German Nationals than with the Social Democrats. An exception was support by the party of the Locarno Treaty of 1925, which was negotiated from the German side by Stresemann and provided for the admission of Germany to the League of Nations. The German Nationals were opposed to this treaty. The People's party withdrew from the Cabinet in 1931 when the attempt of a customs union with Austria, proposed by Foreign Minister Curtius, a member of this party, did not succeed due to the opposition of the Western powers. From this time on, the party lost its importance.

A key position was held by the Center party, which unconditionally accepted the Weimar Constitution and headed several coalition Cabinets under Wilhelm Marx in 1924 and under Bruening from 1930–1932. Even Franz von Papen, who followed Bruening as Chancellor in May, 1932, was a member of the Center party in the Prussian style; although he belonged to an extremely small reactionary minority. Some difficulties of the Center party were due to its position as a real middle-of-the-road party. Its electorate was composed of men from all segments of the population and included also monarchistic groups. There was always the danger of losing them if the cooperation with the Social Democrats was too close. There was the additional danger that such a cooperation might drive some labor groups, which for religious reasons voted for the Center party, permanently to the Social Democrats. However, when in the spring of 1925, due to the sudden death of Ebert, presidential elections became necessary, the Center party together with the Social Democrats supported Marx against Hindenburg unsuccessfully. By 1930, the party under Bruening had changed to a policy of collaboration with the Right-wing parties. The general opinion is that General Schleicher, who was the last Chancellor before Hitler's appointment and was killed in June, 1934, by the Nazis, recommended the appointment of Bruening as Chancellor to Hindenburg. Bruening, who had strong authoritarian leanings and definitely belonged to the Right wing of the Center party, headed the government at a most difficult time. The impact of the world economic crisis was desperately felt in Germany.

The elections held under the chancellorship of Bruening brought the Nazis for the first time into the limelight; with 107 parliamentary mandates and over six million votes, they became the second largest party. Also, the Communist numbers increased and became an important factor with 77 mandates. The composition of the Reichstag from this time until Hitler took over was such that the government, due to the opposition of the extreme Right and Left, and in spite of the toleration of the Social Democrats who considered the Bruening government as a lesser evil, did not control a working majority. Bruening was forced to resort, with the backing of Hindenburg, to the rule of emergency decrees bypassing the legislature in order to stay in office. The constitutional basis for this was the notorious Article 48 of the Weimar Constitution granting emergency power to the Reichspresident. It is interesting to note that, due to the political and economic situation, a government headed by the Center party that stood firmly on the basis of a parliamentary democracy had to resort to undemocratic means.

The Bavarian wing of the Center party had already deserted it in 1920, founding the Bavarian People's party, which had a definite monarchical and clerical tendency.

The Social Democrats were consistently the strongest party in the Reichstag until the advent of the Nazis. Their followers were the skilled and semiskilled workers. They assumed governmental responsibilities four times, the last time under Chancellor Mueller from 1928 to 1930; but they always had to cooperate with the bourgeois parties. The Social Democratic party was honestly democratic and the only stout defender of the Weimar Constitution and of the Weimar Republic. Its fate became a really tragic one; for in order to defend the Republic, the party forfeited its ideological goal of the realization of socialistic ideas, while the Republic became more and more conservative and reactionary. Even when the democratic features of the Republic became almost fictitious, the Social Democrats always remained faithful to the Constitution, defending its framework against the extreme Right and the extreme Left. In the struggle, the party found itself again and again in the situation of having to ally itself with the Right and even with the reactionary groups against the extreme Left. For this very reason, many disappointed Socialists defected to the Communists, who became consequently a mass party.

The *Kommunistische Partei Deutschlands* (German Communist party), under the influence of the Russian executive committee of the Internationale, directed its principal fight against the Social Democrats, whom it attacked as preparing the way for fascism. This position of the Communists led to a split in the labor movement, the only truly democratic force in Germany. A deciding role in this stand was the Russian interpretation that the cooperation of the Social Democrats with the bourgeois parties on foreign policy was directed against the Soviet Union. In the early thirties, the party also accepted the theory that the destruction of democracy led to fascism, which represented the last stand of capitalism; at this point, the dictatorship of the proletariat would take over. In practice, this amounted to a catastrophical policy. In 1931, when the Harzburger Front representing the extreme Right introduced a plebiscite to dissolve the Prussian Diet, the Communists voted for it. During the last years of the Republic, they constantly formed a negative coalition with the Nazis, voting against the government. At the same time, violent street fighting went on between the military organizations of the extreme Right and Left.

The Nazi party developed as a party of the uprooted and declassed. Hitler himself belonged to this group, as did the people who surrounded him. His first followers were men who had failed in their careers, such as former professional soldiers. Added to these were the victims of the inflation, a large part of the middle class, including the bureaucracy. The world economic crisis accelerated the trend toward the Nazis, and from 1932 they were the strongest party in Germany. The development of the Nazi party was not without drawbacks even after it became the strongest group. In the presidential elections of 1932, Hitler ran against Hindenburg and was beaten by the old field marshal, who had the support of the Social Democrats. This is another example of the tragic position of this party, which had to accept such reactionary personalities as Hindenburg as a lesser evil. There were two Reichstag elections in 1932; in the first one, the Nazis had over thirteen million votes and 230 mandates. In the second one in November, 1932, they lost two million votes and 34 seats, which showed that they could be defeated. Some observers thought that the Nazi party would disappear just as fast as it had risen.

The appointment of Hitler as Chancellor by Hindenburg on January 29, 1933, was followed by several actions against the other parties. On June 22, 1933, the Social Democratic party was outlawed by a special ordinance. On July 14, 1933, the law prohibiting the formation of new political parties made the continuation of parties other than the Nazi party a criminal offense. With this law, the life of political parties in Germany was made legally impossible.

THE PRESENT PARTY STRUCTURE IN WEST GERMANY

The party structure of the West German Republic is to some degree similar to that of the Weimar Republic and the empire. Among the parties authorized by the victorious powers, the Communist and Social Democratic parties were the legal successors of the old parties of the same name. New parties were the Christian Democratic Union (CDU) and the Christian Social Union in Bavaria (CSU), a combination of former politicians and voters of the Center party that included Protestant Christian forces and anti-Socialist middle-class people and farmers. Several liberal and national groups combined as a Free Democratic party (FDP). Later the German party (DP) developed as a conservative and national party, and several neo-Nazi parties were formed, such as the Socialist Reichs party (SRP) (outlawed in 1952 by the Federal Constitutional Court) and the still active German Reichspartei (DRP). The BHE (Federation of the Expellees) represents the interests of the refugees and expelled people from the east. The Social Democratic party has, with approximately 600,000 members and over 7,200 local groups, the strongest organization. The

CDU has 245,000 members and 4,400 local groups. The FDP has about 80,000 and the DP about 45,000 members. The BHE had in 1952 approximately 20,000 members. The Social Democrats organized their party on June 17, 1945, in a large meeting of functionaries in Berlin. For some time, the activities of the party suffered from ideological differences among the leading personalities.

At the beginning of the occupation period, many leaders, who were probably influenced by the memories of the last two years of the Weimar Republic, thought that the creation of a Unified Labor party based on a unified German labor union was the correct thing to do. The Communists refused, and for some months relations with them were strained. This situation was clarified when Dr. Kurt Schumacher, who became active immediately after his liberation from a concentration camp, called a conference that took place in October, 1945, in Wenningen. There it was decided that party policy in all occupation zones should be conducted according to the same directives, to refuse any merger with other parties, but to accept cooperation with other democratic parties. At this conference, the Social Democratic program for postwar Germany was laid down in broad outline. The concept of the collective guilt of all Germans was sharply repudiated, as was the plan to reduce Germany to a purely agrarian state. Later, the party protested against the taking of machines and other capital equipment from Germany and imposed as a duty on all party functionaries and party members open defense of the interests of the German population against the occupation forces. In the debates of the Constitution for the West German Republic, the Social Democrats took a position in favor of a more centralized state than that desired by the CDU. In the area of economic policy, they favored a planned economy, socialization of the basic industries, and governmental control of banks and other financial institutions. It is interesting to note that the party is opposed now to outright nationalization but proposes instead a system of socialized property in which the *Laender*, local communities, and consumer organizations should participate. In comparison with its history before 1945, the Social Democratic party has changed in several respects. The former hostile attitude to the churches has been modified, partly under the influence of the active opposition of the churches against the Nazis, partly under the influence of religious Socialists. It is hard to say yet what will be the consequence of this change on the relationship to the electorate, although the observation can already be made that the party has developed a followership that goes beyond the laborers. The number of followers from other groups has increased substantially, especially from the so-called intellectuals and from lower middle-class and small-farm groups.

Since the first elections to the Bundestag (August, 1949), when it became, with almost seven million votes and 131 mandates, the second largest party, it has been the leading opposition party in West Germany. At this time, the party made it known—and this is different from the era of the Weimar Republic—that it was not ready to participate in a coalition government, mostly in view of the existing differences over economic policies. The area of economic policy is the main point of the Social Democratic opposition, not only in principle, where it is opposed to the liberal economic policy of the Minister of Economics, Professor Erhard, but also over numerous individual policies. The party was frequently in opposition to the government over tax problems, over the question of assistance to industry, and similar matters. It was possible, however, to achieve compromises between the party and the government on questions of social policy because in this area also the CDU had to take the interests of its employee followership into consideration. Some discrepancies existed between the government and the opposition on foreign policy. This was already true under the leadership of Dr. Schumacher and remained the same under Erich Ollenauer, who succeeded Schumacher as party leader. Chancellor Adenauer took the initiative for a policy of very close cooperation with the Western powers. In the eyes of the opposition, he accepted this cooperation unconditionally. The Social Democrats demanded generally that any cooperation should be based on full German equality, including military matters. The Chancellor believed that this equality would come about as a consequence of collaboration. Different positions were taken on the question of German rearmament and also on the basic problem of German reunification.

During the Nazi regime, both the Catholics and the Protestants had to fight the same struggle against the totalitarian state. Under these conditions, they became closer, reduced their differences, and assisted each other against the common enemy. The unbelievable cruelties committed by the Nazis influenced many Germans who had a passive attitude toward religion to return to the ethical values of Christianity. Even outspoken opponents of the churches were impressed by the courage of many clerical leaders like Catholic Cardinal Faulhaber and Bishop Count Galen and later Protestant Pastor Niemoeller. Out of this grew the new idea in the middle forties, after the collapse of the Hitler regime, to cooperate politically on the basis of Christian principles. This is the ideological background of the Christian Democratic Union. Conferences to organize a party started very early (May, 1945) at different places, the most important taking place in Cologne, a stronghold of the Center party during the Weimar Republic. (Chancellor Adenauer, then a member of the Center party, was Lord Mayor of Cologne before Hitler.) The CDU is to a certain extent the successor of the Center party, but it was agreed in the early discussions that the former Catholic religious basis was too narrow. One reason for this position was that such a limited party could easily be overcome by the Social Democrats and the Communists, especially because the possibility existed that these two parties might unite. The decision was therefore made not to renew the old Center, but to found with the Protestants a Christian party. A formal unification on a nationwide basis was only achieved, however, at the first party convention in October, 1950, at Goslar. Even there, most of the Bavarian Catholics organizationally remained outside. The Bavarian Christian Social Union belongs to the fraction of the CDU in the Bundestag but considers itself as an independent group and has its own organization and discussions.

The CDU is similar to the former Center in that it is in every respect a middle-of-the-road party, not only in relation to the other parties, but also within itself. It includes the most diverse groups of the population, because their appeal to the electorate is basically not political but religious; therefore, the party must try, in order to keep all groups, to compromise the various conflicting economic interests within itself. Generally, it can be said that the emphasis of the CDU in comparison to the former Center party is a little more to the Right, because the support from the Protestant side is composed to some extent of the followers of the former Right-wing parties. In addition to this, its economic policy was from the very beginning influenced and guided by Professor Erhard, who favors a free economy. The party rejects economic planning and regulations, even with regard to basic industries. In this respect, it has the support of the German party and of the Free Democratic party. This policy was continued by the party in the Bundestag since 1949, especially after Erhard took over the Ministry of Economics. The CDU maintains also the tactical freedom to conclude political alliances with the Right as well as with the Left. In the Bundestag, the coalition was extended to the Right; but this policy was not extended to the Laender, where frequently coalitions were made with the Social Democrats. In the first Bundestag in 1949, the CDU took over the formation of the government as the strongest party under Adenauer; and it has kept this position to the present time, although it received a serious setback in the last elections in September, 1961. In the various local elections of the Laender, the CDU and the SPD frequently change positions as the strongest and second strongest party. The position of the party in the area of foreign policy has been continuously, under the leadership of Adenauer, directed to the West. Until now, the party has been able to keep its internal cohesion in spite of substantial losses in the last elections. This is probably due to its extremely able leadership (Adenauer, Erhard, Schaefer, and others), and even more to the remarkable progress made under its economic program.

The reorganization of the Liberal party was difficult because the liberal parties of the Weimar Republic were already very weak before Hitler came to power. Dr. Theodor Heuss, the former Federal President, was very active in the formation of such a party. In November, 1948, the Free Democratic party was founded, holding its first party convention in June, 1949, in Bremen. The party represents the old liberal ideas against the religious emphasis of the CDU. In the area of cultural policies it usually works with the Social Democrats; in economic policy it represents economical liberalism, so it has had no difficulty in supporting the Erhard program. The party has more centralistic than federalistic tendencies and favors executive rather than legislative dominance. As far as the general attitude of the party is concerned, it is significant that its deputies took their seats in the Bundestag to the Right of the CDU. The Free Democratic party has a different structure than the other parties, as its voters have no religious, professional, or territorial cohesion, and is therefore a party of individualism. It participated in the first coalition government under Adenauer. Under the leadership of Dr. Erich Mende, the party was remarkably successful in the elections of 1961, gaining almost two million votes.

Further to the Right we find the *Deutsche Partei* (German party), which is federalistic in its views. In the sphere of economic policy, it advocates a strictly private economy and rejects a planned economy as well as any interference with private property, especially with regard to land. The party is strongly antisocialistic, to such an extent that its representatives to the parliamentary council that drafted the Bonn Basic Law rejected it because it gave too much power to the central government and too few guaranties against possible interference by the government with the economy. The party was from the very beginning opposed to denazification and showed a keen interest in the former members of the German armed forces. The party admitted to membership a certain number of former Nazis but has been, at least until now, very careful not to identify itself with extreme Right-wing radicals. (It even expelled one of its deputies to the Bundestag who made extreme statements.) It has also participated in the coalition government. If one observes the development and the general tendencies of the German party since 1945, he sees that it represents the root of a strongly conservative party. It is not yet possible to see whether the party will become outright reactionary. Utterances of several leading members of the party indicate that the party would welcome the restoration of the monarchy. Of course, at the present time, there does not exist any practical possibility of this. The party merged with the All-German Bloc in 1961 under the name *Gesamt Deutsche Partei* (GDP) but was only able to get 2.8 per cent of the vote in the 1961 elections. It is not represented in the fourth Bundestag.

Another party of the Right is the Bavarian party, whose aim is the independence of Bavaria. It advocates as the solution of the problem of German unification a confederation of independent and equal member states. The Bonn Republic is not recognized by the party legally, but only *de facto,* because the basic law was adopted in the Bavarian Diet only by a simple majority, whereas according to the Bavarian Constitution a two-thirds majority was required. The party is in membership a middle-class party, representing the interests of the old established families in Bavaria, rural as well as urban, against the newcomers from the east.

All the parties mentioned thus far had the advantage that they were able to begin their work soon after the collapse of the Nazi regime. The occupation forces did not allow for some time the political organization of the refugees and expellees from the east and southeast, whose number ran into millions. It was only in 1950 that a separate party, at first in the Laender, representing specifically the interests of these people was founded under the name of *Block der Heimatvertriebenen und Entrechteten* (BHE; the name means "bloc of those expelled and deprived of their rights"). In the election to the first Diet of Schleswig-Holstein in 1950, the new party had great success and became the second largest party. In 1951, the party constituted itself on a national basis. The political program of the party is not limited to special demands concerning the refugees. With regard to foreign policy, the party refuses to give up the claim for the eastern German territories, that is, the territories east of the Oder-Neisse line. It demands the return of these territories to Germany. It is in favor of European cooperation, with Germany as an equal partner. The party is neither on the Right nor on the Left with regard to domestic policy. Its program is not very clear in many respects. The same is true of its relationship to the other parties. On the national level, it has supported the Adenauer government; whereas in some of the Laender, it has allied itself with the Social Democrats. At the party convention in 1952, the party changed its name to All-German Bloc; and a new party program was adopted that was expressly in favor of private property and against socialism and state capitalism. In 1961 it merged, unsuccessfully, with the German party.

It can easily be understood that the occupation forces were very suspicious of the political organization of the extreme Right. Several organizations were founded on a local basis. On October 2, 1949, the socialistic Reichspartei was founded by Dr. Dorls and General Remer.[2] The party won followers among former Nazi party members and army personnel. In some local elections in those areas that in the years previous to 1933 had been strongly for Hitler, the party had 10 to 11 per cent of the votes. It has been proven that the party leaders were without exception former members of the Nazi party. The program of the party had strong similarities to the Nazi program. It accepted the leader principle and was definitely antidemocratic. The party did not include in its official program

[2] The latter saved Hitler after the unsuccessful attempt on his life on July 20, 1944.

Hitler's race theory or the demand for German hegemony, although these points were part of its ideology. This was proven by the evidence brought before the Federal Constitutional Court, which outlawed the party as undemocratic in 1952[3] (the same happened to the Communist party of West Germany in 1956). It is interesting to note that the court considered the attacks by the Reichs party against Presidents Roosevelt and Truman and especially against leading Jewish American personalities like Morgenthau, Lehman, Baruch, and Frankfurter (who were called criminals against humanity by this party in 1950 and 1951) as significant proof of the undemocratic character and methods of this party. There are a few more splinter parties in West Germany now with little or no importance.

The party system of the Federal Republic is, however, still built on the tradition of a multiparty system. It is characteristic of such a system that political parties act also as interest groups. For this reason, the political parties in Germany express to a larger degree special interests than the parties in the United States. The problem is not so much the pressure of interest groups on the legislative and administrative agencies of the government directly from the outside, but their influence from the inside on the parties that they support. There exists the danger that the parties may be controlled by various organizations; the representation of the parties in the Bundestag and in the several Laender legislatures are frequently composed of important officers of these organizations. Their influence on legislative decisions is very strong.

The relationship among the parties and the different groups runs along the expected lines. Business and farm organizations are entrenched in the CDU, the German party, and the Free Democratic party. Trade-unions and other employee organizations rely on the Social Democrats.

Industry, business, and trade are organized in various organizations. The regional organs of employers are the Chamber of Industry, Commerce, and Trade. They represent district associations of business people in all branches and are combined in the German Industrial and Trade Convention (*Deutscher Industrie und Handelstag*) with headquarters in Bonn. The interests of industry are represented by the Federal Association of German Industry (*Bundesverband der Deutschen Industrie*), which is concerned with foreign trade, credit, fiscal and monetary policy, etc. There are 90,000 industrial enterprises connected with this organization. The most important representation of employers in the Federal Republic is the Federal Confederation of German Employers Organizations (*Bundesvereinigung der Deutschen Arbeitgeberverbaende*), which was founded in 1949 and has its headquarters in Cologne. This organization stated its policy principles in 1953 in a publication *Thoughts on the Social Order,* which strongly supports the social market economy of Professor

[3] Decision of the Federal Constitutional Court of October 23, 1952, 1BVB 1/51.

Erhard but also recognizes the trade-unions as equal and independent economic partners.

The farm interests are represented in the German Peasant Union of more than one million members and the German *Raiffeisenverband,* which embraces 23,500 rural cooperatives with a total membership of 3.3 million. Both organizations are closely connected with the CDU-CSU.

German trade-unionism with its long and distinguished tradition came to an end in 1933 when Hitler disbanded all trade-unions, confiscated their property, and prohibited all union activities. In October, 1949, the German Federation of Trade Unions (*Deutscher Gewerkschaftsbund*) was re-established. Its chief organ is the Trade Union Congress that meets every three years. The Congress elects an executive committee of nine men, supplemented by the chairmen of the sixteen unions that make up the Federation; it now has close to 6.5 million members. The inclusion of office and white collar workers into the Federation of Trade Unions could not be achieved, in spite of serious attempts in this direction. These employees are now organized in the German Employee's Organization (*Deutsche Angestellten Gewerkschaft*) with some 450,000 members. The civil servants are organized in the German Civil Servants Union (*Deutscher Beamtenbund*) with some 550,000 members.

The relationship between the political parties and these interest groups consists mainly in the financial assistance given by the interest groups to the parties, the guidance of the interest groups with regard to the voting behavior of their members, and their supply of experts needed by the parties.

SELECTED READING

HEIDENHEIMER, ARNOLD J. "Federalism and the Party System: The Case of West Germany," *American Political Science Review,* LII (September, 1958), 809–28.

MEYER, E. W. *Political Parties in Western Germany.* Washington, D.C.: Library of Congress, 1951.

NEUMANN, S. "German Political Parties," *Encyclopaedia of the Social Sciences,* XI (1933), 615–19.

SALIN, E. "Social Forces in Germany Tody," *Foreign Affairs,* XXVIII (1950), 265–77.

SCAMMON, RICHARD M. "Political Parties." In *Governing Postwar Germany,* Edward H. Litchfield (ed.). Ithaca, N.Y.: Cornell University Press, 1953.

SCHNEIDER, CARL. "Political Parties and the German Basic Law of 1949," *Western Political Quarterly,* X (1957), 527–40.

32

Elections

THE SUFFRAGE DURING THE EMPIRE

Considering the ultraconservative nature of the German Empire under Bismarck and under Wilhelm II, it is perhaps surprising that the method of election to the lower house of the national legislature, the Reichstag, was democratic; German suffrage was at this time more democratic than in England and in the United States. The Imperial Constitution vested legislative functions in an upper and a lower house, the latter based upon so-called *Wahlkreise* (electoral districts) into which the whole territory was divided. There were 397 of these single-member districts; consequently, the Reichstag was composed of 397 members. The term of office, until 1885, was for three years; it was later increased to five. Suffrage was given to all registered male citizens over the age of twenty-five and was unrestricted by qualifications. The elections for the Reichstag were direct, by secret ballot, and with no possibility of plural voting.

Although the suffrage was liberal, popular elections did not succeed in democratizing German government or society. The electoral system provided for election by an absolute majority. If necessary, the absolute majority was to be achieved by a second ballot (held two weeks after the first) between the two most successful candidates. In such runoff elections, the Right and the Center parties frequently combined in coalition, so that the more conservative or reactionary candidate was mostly favored. Moreover, the democratic features of the suffrage were strongly curtailed by the unequal distribution of the 397 districts, which were based on census figures dating back to 1869. Reapportionment of seats did not take place during the existence of the empire, despite the large population changes that occurred during its time. However, the main reasons a democratic election system failed to influence the prevailing authoritarian conservatism stemmed from the relatively insignificant position of the Reichstag during the Bismarck and Wilhelmian eras.

The *Bundesrat* (Federal Council) was a much more important body, but its members were not selected by the same system as the representatives to the Reichstag. As a matter of fact, it was not an elective body. The Council did not represent the people but rather the Laender, and it amounted to a permanent congress of delegates appointed by the princes of the Laender. The political parties had therefore only a very limited influence on the composition of the Council.

Each *Land* (state) was represented in the Council by a fixed number allotted in the Constitution, the total membership being at first fifty-eight and later sixty-one when three seats were given to Alsace-Lorraine. Of these sixty-one, Prussia had seventeen and thus enjoyed from the beginning a dominant position in the Council.[1] Another conspicuous feature of the Council was that the votes cast by the delegates had to be cast as a unit. The Council was presided over by the Imperial Chancellor, who was usually also Prime Minister of Prussia.

For all practical purposes, the Federal Council was used largely as an instrument to keep Prussian hegemony over the German federation. The Council, and not the popularly elected Reichstag, was one of the most powerful organs of the empire. Even Bismarck treated it with much consideration. As Prime Minister of Prussia, he had the large Prussian delegation under his control. Under these circumstances, the electoral system that prevailed in Prussia during the empire was of much greater importance than the system used for the election of the representatives to the Reichstag.

PROPORTIONAL REPRESENTATION DURING THE WEIMAR REPUBLIC

The Social Democrats introduced the system of proportional representation in Germany when they took over the government during the 1918 Revolution. It was later incorporated as a principle of the Weimar Constitution. In view of the strong criticism frequently made against this system (it is sometimes blamed for the collapse of the Weimar Republic), it is appropriate to discuss briefly its main features. In this system, parliamentary seats were apportioned to the different parties in the same proportion as votes were received by them. The number of votes necessary to receive a seat was fixed by law and called the election quotient. This

[1] The other seats were distributed as follows: Bavaria, six; Saxony and Wuertemberg, four; Baden and Hessen, three; Mecklenburg and Brunswick, two; and the other seventeen *Laender*, one each—making a total of fifty-eight plus the three seats of Alsace-Lorraine.

number under the Weimar Republic was 60,000. In other words, for each 60,000 votes, a seat was allotted in the Reichstag.

This system has different effects according to the size of the electoral districts, whether they are small, medium, or large. In Germany, the constituencies were quite large, for there were only thirty-five of them, each district having at the beginning a population of about 1,700,000. As neither the Constitution nor the electoral laws established the size of the Reichstag, the number of deputies was flexible because the election quotient of 60,000 remained fixed. The size of the Reichstag under the Weimar Republic increased from 459 in 1919 to 661 in 1933, the increase of population reflecting itself automatically in a larger number of parliamentary seats. A reapportionment of seats was therefore not necessary. As a result, there was no opportunity for gerrymandering of districts.

A criticism of this system was that the voters could only cast their vote for a given party list and that they were not allowed to change the order of the candidates as they appeared on the party list. In Germany, the system was adopted in its extreme form. Party lists, prepared for each of the thirty-five constituencies, in most instances included as many candidates as there were seats on the basis of the election quotient. In addition to this, a national list was prepared by the parties to take care of surpluses remaining from the districts. If a party received 80,000 votes in one district and 100,000 in another, the surpluses of 20,000 and 40,000 would be totaled, giving the party three seats. The argument in favor of this system was that it was in one sense the most representative. In the system of single-member districts, as used in the United States and Britain, all votes cast for a losing candidate are not reflected in the representation of the legislature; for all practical purposes, they are lost. Proportional representation is surely the most effective device to safeguard each individual vote, and a legislature elected on the basis of this system represents a true quantitative picture of the existing social and political divisions of the electorate.[2]

In spite of its justice, this system had many shortcomings. It encouraged the formation and growth of many small splinter parties and led to a multiparty system which required the formation of coalitions in order to establish a government. It led also to the formation of negative coalitions between parties with antithetical programs, which combined in Parliament against the government, thus making the parliamentary process unworkable. Such negative coalitions against the government were

[2] It can be added to this that the plurality single-member district system favors the large parties in the legislature, whereas the chances of smaller parties are greatly curtailed. The constant failure of third parties in the United States and the present underrepresentation of the Liberal party in Britain in comparison with its still substantial popular vote could be used as an argument in favor of proportional representation.

continually formed by the Nazis and the Communists. The opponents of proportional representation have pointed out that the main function of a Parliament is not to represent a mirror of the social forces of the society, but to have the ability to make decisions; to form governments; to support and to control them and, when necessary, to dismiss them. These functions require clear-cut majorities that can be achieved more easily by a plurality single-member district system.

There was another feature of the proportional system that deprived the Weimar Republic to a great degree of its democratic character. The voters did not vote for individual candidates but for party lists. They did not have any influence at all in the selection of the candidates, who were chosen by the parties themselves. The ballot contained a list of the parties running in the election and also the names of the first four candidates on each party list, but the voters had to vote for one of the party lists on a straight ticket. For all practical purposes, they did not vote for individual candidates but for a party list.

There was already significant opposition to the system of proportional representation in the Weimar Constituent Assembly. One of the most important opponents was Friedrich Naumann, who told the constitutional committee of the Assembly that the adoption of proportional representation would render impossible the formation of a parliamentary government. The Social Democrats, however, clinging to the Erfurt Program, did not compromise in this respect. Competent observers maintain that proportional representation prevented the Social Democrats from obtaining an over-all majority in the first elections to the Reichstag in 1919. The majority Social Democrats obtained at this election around 38 per cent of the total vote, getting 165 of the 420 seats. There was a strong possibility that the Social Democrats together with the Independent Socialists would have received a majority under a single-member district system with run-off elections.

THE PRESENT SYSTEM OF ELECTIONS

During the Nazi regime, elections lost all real meaning. Elections were held infrequently, and close to 100 per cent of the electorate turned out to these irregular occasions. Nevertheless, only the Nazi party put up candidates for the Reichstag (other parties were outlawed), which was never formally abolished but was without importance. Its main function really was to act as a captive audience when Hitler found it necessary to make important speeches for domestic and foreign consumption. It was also used to confer a mandate upon people who were placed on the public payroll and given unimportant offices for which no qualifications whatever were required. The Reichstag was surely of the lowest possible quality.

The extreme application of proportional representation during the Weimar Republic was one of the reasons for its failure. Even the Social Democrats, during the closing years of the Weimar Republic and during the Third Reich, were in favor of a majority system, notwithstanding the Erfurt Program. The exiled executive committee of the party issued in 1934 the so-called Prague Manifesto that called for a future system of "popular representation elected according to a universal, equal, direct, and secret franchise, in single member constituencies."

After the collapse of Hitler, the party changed its position again, mostly under the influence of Dr. Kurt Schumacher, its leader, and came out again in favor of proportional representation. In this connection, it is important to note that the Russians, obviously understanding the disadvantage of proportional representation for a future German democracy, also favored it for the German federal Parliament and for the parliaments of the Laender (states). In spite of this and in spite of the American tradition of a simple plurality system, the postwar elections held in the American zone on a state-wide scale were organized along the lines of the system existing during the Weimar Republic. It was British and not American influence that brought modifications to this system, first in the British zone and eventually on the federal and state levels.

During the debate on the drafting of the new West German Constitution by the so-called Parliamentary Council, the question of the electoral system was intensively discussed; arguments in favor of a plurality system were not accepted by the representatives of the smaller parties. The Parliamentary Council decided finally on a plan that was approved by the military governors and became the election law that served as the basis for the first Bundestag election in 1949. It represented a synthesis of proportional representation and election by plurality vote in single-member districts. A Land was divided into a certain number of districts, within which a candidate with a plurality of the votes was declared elected. Sixty per cent (the number was later reduced to 50 per cent) of the members of the Bundestag were to be elected in such single-member districts. There was additionally a reserve list, which incorporated elements of proportional representation; on this list, the remaining 40 per cent was made available to the different parties. The over-all representation of a party was to be determined on the basis of proportional representation for the Land as a whole. The seats of party candidates elected in single-member constituencies were deducted from the party total. Party lists that failed to secure 5 per cent of the votes in the respective Laender, or did not elect at least one candidate in a single-member constituency, were not entitled to seats from the reserve list.

In the spring of 1953, new parliamentary elections were approaching; and a new electoral law that was similar to the law of 1949 was enacted. The Christian Democratic party under Chancellor Konrad Adenauer proposed a single-member district system, which would have eliminated proportional representation entirely. The Social Democrats favored the re-enactment of the 1949 law. With minor alterations, their draft was passed, with the help of the Free Democratic party, by the Bundestag by a vote of 202 to 175 on June 26, 1953. This law increased the number of seats from 402 to 484, and they were distributed among the several Laender according to population. The whole territory of West Germany was divided into 242 districts (half of the total seats) in which candidates were to be elected by simple majority. The remaining 242 seats were divided among the parties in the Laender according to proportional representation. Seats gained by direct elections were deducted from the total amount of seats due to a party from the Land list under proportional representation. If the situation arose whereby a party received in the individual districts of a Land more seats than it was entitled to under proportional representation, it nevertheless retained those directly elected seats.

The election process thus works in this fashion. A party list of candidates is first put up in each of the Laender, and the 242 members elected by proportional representation gain their seats in the order in which their names appear on the ballot lists. Incidentally, it is possible that the candidates for the individual constituencies may also appear on the party lists, which means that a candidate defeated in the individual district may still become a member of the Bundestag if he ranks high enough on the party list. On the other hand, if a person is dropped from the party list, he may be elected by a simple majority in the individual district.

The chances of splinter parties, ordinarily very much enhanced by a system of proportional representation, were effectively restricted by the so-called *Sperrklausel* (restriction clause). According to this provision, for a party to share in the distribution of the seats from the reserve party lists, distributing 242 seats according to proportional representation, it must have at least 5 per cent of the total vote cast in the whole federation or at least have received one seat in a constituency by direct election. (Since the federal elections of 1957, this number was increased to three.) This provision definitely worked to the disadvantage of splinter and also minor parties in general.

As far as voting procedure is concerned, the new law provides that each voter has two votes, a first vote (*Erststimme*) to be given for a candidate in his own district, and a second vote (*Zweitstimme*) to be given a party list of candidates nominated in his state. Thus, the two principal new features of the 1953 election law were the provision restricting minor parties by the *Sperrklausel* device and the provision for two votes, one for direct election of a candidate in a single-member district and the second for a party list, the seats to be distributed according to proportional representation. This type of election system (the so-called *personalisierte Verhaeltniswahl*—personalized proportional election) has great advantages over the system of proportional representation based on rigid party lists that prevailed during the Weimar period. Not only does the new system discourage the creation of small splinter parties, but with regard to candidates for the individual constituencies, such candidates, in order to be successful, necessarily must have a closer relationship to the voter than under a rigid list system. In the new situation, the candidates presented in the 242 single-member districts must be more than just representatives of one economic interest; they must appeal to the general type of voter upon whom the party in question relies. As a result, the voter is likely to get a broader-minded personality, at least from the single-member districts, to represent him than was true in the Weimar Reichstag. Foreign observers generally agree that the material for political leadership in the Bundestag is better by far than it was in the Reichstag.

The system of personalized proportional representation has drawbacks, however. The German voter still thinks, most likely, in terms of parties rather than of candidates. The influence of party bosses upon candidates remains very strong, because every candidate for an individual district is naturally eager to be included in the party list and high on it as added insurance against defeat. Already in the 1953 elections, the minor parties, beginning with the Free Democratic party, elected practically everybody from the reserve list. In the 1957 elections, only one politician of the FDP and two from the German party, including the then Vice-Chancellor Bluecher, were elected from constituencies; all other candidates were defeated in the direct elections.

In the 1961 elections, 155 candidates of the CDU-CSU and 91 candidates of the SPD were directly elected in their districts. Chancellor Adenauer was re-elected in his traditional district Bonn for the fourth time. Mayor Willy Brandt did not run in a district but led the party list of the SPD in North Rhine-Westphalia. In spite of the success of their party, no candidate of the FDP was directly elected. The party is, therefore, represented in the new Bundestag only via the party lists.

The nomination of candidates for public office is entirely in the hands of the political parties; they have a virtual monopoly in the selection of candidates. In the 1949 elections, three non-partisan representatives were elected to the Bundestag; not a single independent candidate was elected in the 1953, 1957, and 1961 elections. According to paragraph 22 of the Federal Election Law of 1953, the nomination of candidates in an electoral district takes place in a meeting of the party members of this district (or in a meeting of delegates elected by the party members for this purpose) by secret ballot. The National Committee and the Laender committees are allowed to object to the nominations; in this case, a second and final vote has to be taken. A record of the vote has to be submitted to the election officials. The chairman of the meeting or two delegated members must declare under oath that the nomination of the candidates took place by secret ballot. The basis of this provision of the Election Law is Article 21, Section 1 of the Basic Law, which requires that the internal organization of the political parties must conform to democratic principles.

The percentage of party members in relation to the number of voters in the Federal Republic is very small. The SPD has approximately 650,000 members, about 8 per cent of its voters; the CDU has 350,000 members, about 2.5 per cent and the FDP and the German party each have 70,000, about 7 per cent.

Few official regulations exist with regard to campaigns. There are no legal restrictions on expenditures. Article 21, Section 1 of the Basic Law requires, however, that political parties publicly account for the sources of their funds.

Article 38 of the Basic Law guarantees universal, direct, free, equal, and secret elections for every sane German over twenty-one years who resided at least three months in the Federal Republic. High voting participation is facilitated by easy registration requirements. Voters are permanently registered in voting lists kept by the municipalities. There is neither literacy, nor property, or other requirements.

Legal requirements exist for persons who wish to run for office. A candidate must have the right to vote, be over twenty-five years old, and possess German citizenship for at least one year. Refugees and expellees are exempted from the last qualification. Article 48 of the Basic Law contains several provisions to protect and to guarantee the right of every qualified person to run for office. No one may be prevented from accepting or exercising the office of deputy to the Bundestag, or may he be dismissed from employment on this ground. It also contains the quite generous provision that any candidate seeking election to the Bundestag is entitled to a paid leave of absence from his employer for the time necessary for his election campaign.

Four elections have taken place to the Bundestag, the election period being four years. These elections occurred in August, 1949; September 6, 1953; September 15, 1957; and September 17, 1961. The number of seats to the first Bundestag was 402; the electoral law of 1953 increased the number to 484; the number was later increased to 497, 10 of which were given to the Saar territory that was reincorporated into the West German Republic. Added to this number are 22 representatives from West Berlin who have not, however, the right to vote.

There were 31,179,433 eligible voters of which 78.5 per cent participated in the elections of 1949. In the 1953 elections, there were 33,120,940 eligible voters and 86 per cent of the electorate participated. See Table 32–1 for the comparative strength of the different parties and the distribution of the respective seats in the Bundestag after the 1949 and 1953 elections.

Table 32–1. Distribution of Popular Votes and Seats in the Bundestag in 1949 and 1953

Party	1949		1953	
	Seats	Votes	Seats	Votes
CDU-CSU	139	7,359,804	243	12,444,055
Social Democratic party	131	6,934,975	151	7,944,953
Free Democratic party	52	2,829,920	48	2,629,169
Bavarian party	17	986,478	–	465,641
German party	17	939,934	15	896,230
Communist party	15	1,361,708	–	607,761
Economic Reconstruction party	12	681,888	–	–
Center party	10	727,505	3	217,078
German Rightest party	5	429,031	–	295,746
Independents	2	1,406,489	–	–
South Schleswig Voters Ass'n.	1	75,387	–	44,585
Others	1	318,418	–	–
All-German Bloc	–	–	27	1,616,936
Total	402		487	

Comparison of the results of the two elections produces two interesting facts. First, there was the great growth of the Christian Democratic Union (attributed largely to the prestige of its leader, Chancellor Adenauer, and to the amazing economic recovery that took place during the period 1949 to 1953). Second, of greater significance was the decline by approximately 50 per cent of the representation of the minor parties in the Bundestag. Only six parties sent deputies to the Bundestag as a result of the 1953 elections. The minor parties in 1953 received about 30 per cent of the votes but only about 19 per cent of the seats. In the 1949 elections, the minor parties received about 40 per cent of the vote and about 32.5 per cent of the seats. In 1953, a drop of approximately 10 per cent in their vote reduced their seats by more than 20 per cent. With a little more than 50 per cent of the seats and an absolute majority, the CDU-CSU was the strongest party. The Social Democrats held about 31 per cent of the seats.

At the September, 1957, elections, there were 35,196,124 eligible voters, of which 88.24 per cent participated. Figures 32–1 and 32–2 show the over-all results of the 1957 elections in comparison to the elections of 1953.

The All-German Bloc, which was able to get twenty-seven seats in 1953, did not win a seat in 1957. The same was true for the Center party, which previously had three seats.

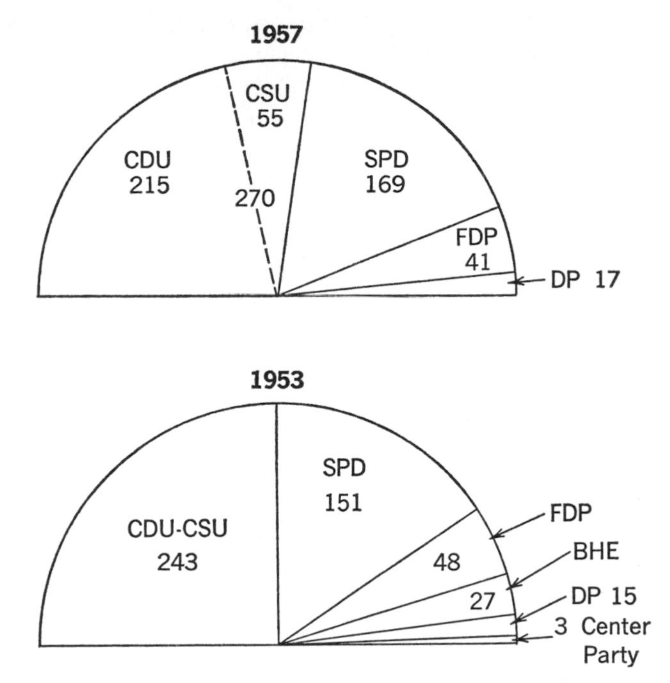

Figure 32–1. Seats in the Bundestag: 1957 and 1953.

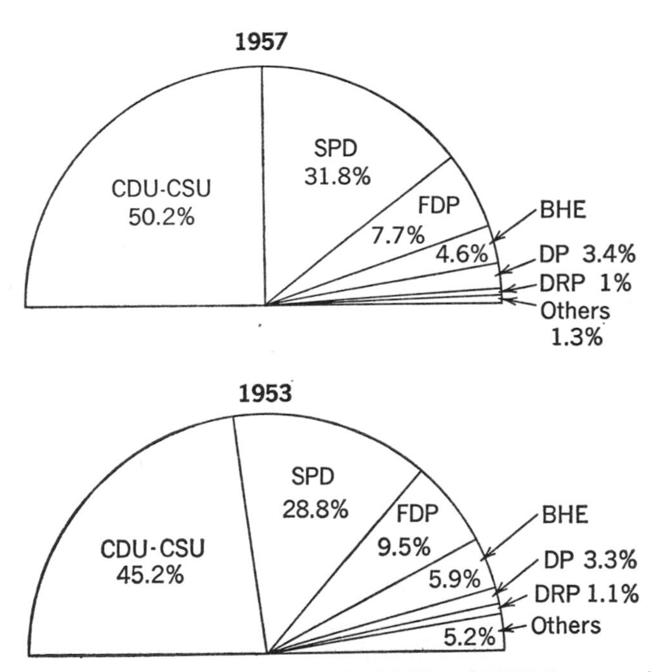

Figure 32–2. Percentage of votes in the 1957 and 1953 German elections.

A comparison of the composition of the Bundestag immediately before and after the 1957 elections is given in Table 32–2. The total vote with regard to parties is broken down in Table 32–3. Table 32–4 gives the individual Laender representation in the 1957 Parliament.

Table 32–2. Composition of Bundestag Before and After 1957 Elections

Party	Seats	
	Before	After
CDU-CSU	255	270
Social Democrats	153	169
Free Democratic party	36	41
German party	33	17
All-German Bloc	19	–
Total	496*	497

* One vacancy.

The results of the elections of September, 1957, deserve additional comment. The party of Chancellor Adenauer (CDU) fared better than it did in the 1953 election. The votes cast for the Union party (CDU-CSU) exceeded their gains in 1953, and in 1957 their parliamentary representation became even stronger. In 1953, the party had about 45 per cent of the total vote cast; the 1957 elections gave it more than 50 per cent. In 1953, the party had a little more than 50 per cent of the Bundestag seats; in 1957, it controlled more than 54 per cent of the seats. These

Table 32–3. Breakdown of Total Vote of 1957 Elections

Party	Votes	Percentage
CDU-CSU	14,998,754	50.18
Social Democrats	9,490,726	31.75
Free Democratic party	2,304,846	7.71
German party	1,006,350	3.36
All-German Bloc	1,373,001	4.59
German Rightest party	307,310	1.02
Others	400,000*	2.00*

* Approximate.

results are unprecedented in German parliamentary history. Even Hitler, in the elections of March, 1933, which for all practical purposes were other than free elections, was unable to get an absolute majority or more than 44 per cent of the vote for the Nazi party.

After a bitter campaign, intensified by the Berlin crisis, the German voters went to the polls on September 17, 1961, to elect the fourth Bundestag. There were 37,412,354 eligible voters of which 87.5 per cent participated. The most important result of this election was the loss of the absolute majority of the CDU-CSU. The Adenauer party still remains by far the strongest but depends on a coalition for the formation of a government. Only the CDU-CSU, the SPD, and the FDP are represented in the

Table 32–4. The 1957 Parliament

Laender	Total	CDU-CSU	Social Democrats	FDP	DP
Schleswig Holstein	23	14	7	1	1
Hamburg	19	7	9	2	1
Lower Saxonia	61	27	22	4	8
Bremen	6	2	3	–	1
North Rhine-Westphalia	154	87	54	11	2
Hessen	46	20	19	4	3
Rhineland-Pfalz	31	18	10	3	–
Baden Wuertemberg	67	37	18	11	1
Bavaria	82	53	25	4	–
Saar Territory	8	5	2	1	–
Total	497	270	169	41	17

new Bundestag. Five additional parties had set up candidates, but each received less than 3 per cent of the votes. Under the 5 per cent clause they are not eligible for representation in the Bundestag. Among these parties is the German party, which was represented in the last Bundestag with seventeen seats. In spite of a merger with the All-German Bloc in the spring of 1961 under the name *Gesamtdeutsche Partei* (all-German party), it was only able to receive 2.8 per cent of the vote.

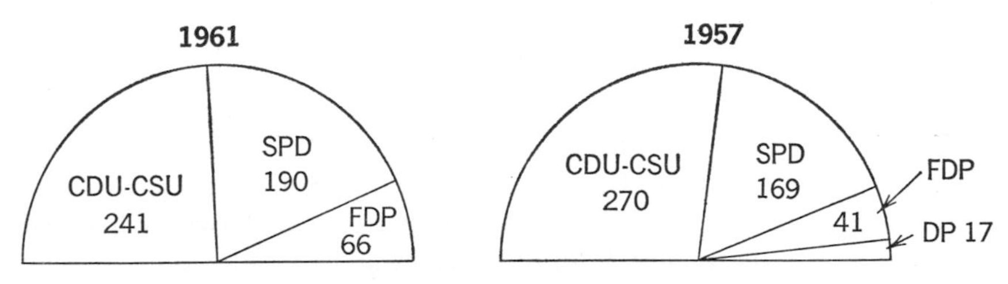

Figure 32–3. Seats in the Bundestag: 1961 and 1957.

The CDU-CSU lost twenty-eight seats, the SPD gained twenty-one, and the FDP gained twenty-five. The CDU-CSU received 45.3 per cent of the total vote; the SPD, 36.3 per cent; and the FDP, 12.7 per cent. The composition of the new Bundestag in comparison to the last one is given in Figure 32–3. The breakdown of the 1961 election and the representation in the new Parliament are given in Tables 32–5 and 32–6.

Table 32–5. Breakdown of Total Vote of the 1961 Election

Party	Votes	Percentage
CDU-CSU	14,239,894	45.3
Social Democrats	11,406,253	36.3
Free Democratic party	4,009,988	12.7
All-German party	871,208	2.8
Others, approximately	900,000	3.0

The result of the elections, although not unexpected, represented a definite setback for Dr. Adenauer, whose party, after leading the country for twelve years, lost the absolute majority it had enjoyed for eight years. This happened in spite of the unprecedented prosperity over this period. A negative reaction against a man who was in power for so many years and is in addition high in his eighties is not surprising, but it surpassed expectations because the party lost about 10 per cent of their votes and parliamentary seats. Also, the major opposition party, the Social Democrats under Mayor Brandt, did not do as well as they had hoped.

Table 32–6. The Individual Laender Representation in the 1961 Parliament

Laender	Total	CDU-CSU	Social Democrats	FDP
Schleswig Holstein	24	13	8	3
Hamburg	18	6	9	3
Lower Saxonia	60	26	26	8
Bremen	5	1	3	1
North Rhine-Westphalia	155	76	60	19
Hessen	45	17	21	7
Rhineland-Pfalz	29	15	10	4
Baden Wuertemberg	66	32	22	12
Bavaria	86	50	28	8
Saar Territory	9	5	3	1
Total	497	241	190	66

The real winner of this election was the Free Democratic party under the leadership of Dr. Erich Mende. The party gained twenty-five parliamentary seats and almost 1.8 million votes and is, under these circumstances, in an excellent bargaining position to enter a coalition government.

Besides the loss of the absolute majority by the CDU-CSU, the most important observation to be made of the elections of 1961 was a further step away from the multiparty system that harassed the Weimar Republic. In 1957, there were still four parties represented in the Bundestag; now there are only three. The similarity to the British House of Commons becomes even more pronounced. This means, on the domestic scene, a rejection of the extremists on the Right and on the Left; the West German voters decisively rejected the appeals of splinter parties. The three parties that were returned to the Bundestag have repeatedly put their allegiance to democracy on record, and there are until now only few indications that they are not genuinely attached to democratic principles.

SELECTED READING

HERMENS, FERDINAND. *Europe Between Democracy and Anarchy.* Notre Dame, Ind.: University of Notre Dame Press, 1951.

KITZINGER, V. W. *German Electoral Politics: A Study of the 1957 Campaign.* Fair Lawn, N. J.: Oxford University Press, 1960.

NEUMANN, SIEGMUND. (ed.). "Germany, Changing Patterns and Lasting Problems." In *Modern Political Parties.* Chicago: University of Chicago Press, 1956.

NEUNREITHER, K. H. "Politics and Bureaucracy in the West German Bundesrat," *American Political Science Review,* September, 1959, pp. 713–32.

POLLOCK, JAMES K. "The West German Electoral Law of 1953," *American Political Science Review,* March, 1955, pp. 107–30.

———. (ed.). *German Democracy at Work.* Ann Arbor: University of Michigan Press, 1955.

SCAMMON, RICHARD M. "Elections." In *Governing Postwar Germany,* Edward H. Litchfield. (ed.). Ithaca, N. Y.: Cornell University Press, 1953.

33

The Legislature

THE BUNDESTAG, DEPUTIES, AND FRACTIONS

The West German Parliament has a bicameral structure. Article 20 of the Basic Law provides that all state authority emanates from the people. The only federal organ that exercises this authority by a direct mandate of the people is the lower house of Parliament, the Bundestag. The people elect the Bundestag for a period of four years. The second chamber of Parliament, the Bundesrat (Federal Council), is not elected directly by the people but is composed of members of the Laender governments. The popularly elected house of the legislature, the Bundestag, alone elects the Federal Chancellor and can recall him under certain conditions. The Bundestag, together with an equal number of delegates elected by the legislatures of the Laender, forms the *Bundesversammlung* (Federal Convention). This Convention elects the Federal President for a period of five years. The Federal President nominates and dismisses upon the recommendation of the Federal Chancellor the federal ministers. The two houses of Parliament elect the members of the Federal Constitutional Court, which is empowered to declare acts of the legislature unconstitutional and also decides in case of impeachment of the Federal President. It can be seen that the Basic Law establishes a certain amount of checks and balances among the highest federal authorities. This was done with the definite purpose of avoiding the possibility of a repetition of the executive predominance of the Reich President under the Weimar Constitution.

The Bundestag is the representative body of the people. The legislative term normally lasts four years, provided no dissolutions are made by the Federal President. A new election has to take place in the last quarter of the fourth year of the legislative term, or in the case of dissolution, within sixty days. Any decision of the Bundestag made after the expiration of the election period or after its dissolution is invalid.

Article 38 of the Basic Law specifically provides that the members of the Bundestag are representatives of the whole people and are not bound by orders and instructions from any other source, subject only to their conscience. They are, therefore, legally not the representatives of a specific district, a specific interest group, or a specific party. The individual representative is not obliged to support the parliamentary fraction of his party. The fraction is a free association of the deputies of a party in the Bundestag. The majority of a fraction can attempt to force a legislator to cast his vote in accordance with the majority's decision; it can also decide that the whole fraction, including the dissenting minority, shall vote in accordance with the majority's decision. This pressure, called *Fraktionszwang,* is, at least legally, not binding upon the individual representative. In practice, however, it is extremely difficult for a dissenting deputy to vote against the majority of his fraction. The fraction is entitled to expel an obstinate member. He will, of course, remain a member of the Bundestag but may encounter many political difficulties; and his chances for re-election are very much diminished. Due to the existence of strong party discipline, it is a rare occasion that a deputy does not vote in line with his fraction. This party discipline is strongest in the SPD and weakest in the FDP (Free Democratic party). The CDU requires members who disagree with a majority decision to present their objections to the fraction meeting.

The fractions (*Fraktionen*) are organizations of members of the Bundestag who belong to the same party. The party and the fraction are formally separate organizations, but in practice they are closely interrelated. The leader of the party (*Parteivorsitzende*) and the leader of the fraction (*Fraktionsvorsitzende*) are usually the same person.

Each fraction elects a presidium with a chairman. The latter is assisted by a secretary, usually a senior deputy, whose duties are of an organizational and liaison nature and who functions as a party whip. This, of course, is a very influential and important position. The fractions of the two large parties in the Bundestag are organized in a similar manner. The SPD has a presidium composed of four members; on the next level is an inner circle of forty-five deputies, the rest of the deputies making up the outer circle. The CDU-CSU, which now provides most of the ministers, has a four-level organization: the Cabinet members, an inner circle of the presidium composed of five persons, the whole presidium composed of twenty-four persons, and the rest of the fraction.

Article 46 of the Basic Law provides for the customary legislative immunity. A representative cannot, except in the case of defamatory insults, be subjected to civil suit on account of his vote or because of utterances made in the Bundestag or one of its committees. He can, however, be arrested and prosecuted for criminal offences with the permission of the Bundestag. In the latter instance, the public prosecutor applies for suspension of the legislative immunity of the Bundestag member. A committee of the Bundestag then examines the accusation and submits a recommendation to the full body of the Bundestag for a final decision. Representatives are also entitled to refuse to give evidence before the courts with regard to information obtained from confidential informants.

The members of the legislative body are entitled to a remuneration adequate to insure their independence and are provided free transportation on all state-owned transport. The legislators receive a monthly salary of 1,100 German marks ($262) tax exempt. To this is added a monthly sum of 600 German marks ($143) for office expenses, and 500 German marks ($119) for other expenses.

COMMITTEES AND LEGISLATIVE PROCEDURE

A legislative body of almost 500 members obviously cannot take all the preparatory steps necessary for legislative acts; it has to make use of committees. The West German Bundestag has at present twenty-six standing committees, composed of 15, 21, 27, or 31 members. The representation of a party in the various committees is calculated on the basis of its proportionate strength in the Bundestag. A party fraction in order to be assigned committee seats must have at least 15 deputies. Each party fraction nominates its committee members. The chairman of the committee is chosen by a Council of Elders in accordance with the strength of the parties. In case a party does not receive representation in a committee by this calculation, it still may send a member to the committee; however, such a member has no voting rights. The meetings of the Bundestag committees are not public, because it is believed that this would handicap the intensity of the consultations and would also be detrimental to the preparatory functions of the committee's activities. The results of the meetings are not secret; committee members are allowed to give information relating to the debates, including information to the press. In addition, Bundestag rules permit any member of the Bundestag to attend committee meetings and also allow all federal ministers, senior members of executive departments who are involved in the discussions of the committees, and members of the Bundesrat the same privilege. The sessions of the standing committees for foreign affairs, all-German and Berlin problems, and constitutional questions, however, are restricted to the voting members of these committees.

The twenty-six standing committees of the Bundestag deal with the following matters:

1. Election immunities and rules
2. Petitions
3. Foreign affairs
4. Defense
5. Interior
6. Cultural policy
7. Local communities and public assistance
8. Health
9. Family and youth problems
10. Law
11. Budget
12. Finance
13. Equalization
14. Economics
15. Special problems of the middle class
16. Foreign trade
17. Food, agriculture, and forests
18. Traffic, post, telephone, and telegraph
19. Atomic and water energy
20. Labor
21. Social policy
22. Disabled veterans
23. Restitution
24. Expellees and refugees
25. Reconstruction and housing
26. All-German and Berlin problem

The committee on foreign affairs and the committee on defense were established by a constitutional amendment on March 19, 1956, and are therefore entrenched in the constitution. At the same time, another constitutional amendment was adopted that created the office of a Defense Commissioner (*Wehrbeauftragter*) to be appointed by the Bundestag to safeguard basic rights and to assist the Bundestag in exercising parliamentary control. This person is responsible to the Bundestag and has to be a civilian. This provision is intended to safeguard civilian control over the military.

The German Constitution provides for four special committees. Article 44 of the Basic Law makes provision for an investigating committee, which is established by the Bundestag upon the demand of a fourth of the members. It serves to protect the interests of the legislature against the government as well as to insure the protection of the rights of a parliamentary minority against a parliamentary majority. The investigating committee represents a type of parliamentary tribunal; it is, however, limited to ascertaining facts and cannot hand down decisions. Its main task is to investigate public grievances, as, for example, errors and mistakes of the government or of individual ministers or their departments, misconstructions of laws or institutions, and also violations by members of the Bundestag. The investigating committee reports its findings to the Bundestag. The committee is selected in the same manner as all other committees, namely, according to the proportional strength of the parties in the Bundestag. This fact, of course, insures predominance by the majority and is not necessarily helpful for the determination of objective facts. The minority of the investigating committee has the right to present a minority report to the full body of the Bundestag.

Article 45 of the Basic Law provides for a permanent committee appointed by the Bundestag. This body has the function of safeguarding the rights of the Bundestag in relation to the federal government during the interim period before new elections. These rights do not include the power to legislate, to elect the Federal Chancellor, or to impeach the Federal President. The permanent committee has also the powers of an investigating committee.

The Basic Law requires the establishment of a legislative committee for the selection of judges. This committee selects half of the judges of the higher federal courts and of the Federal Constitutional Court.

The Basic Law provides for the appointment of a negotiating committee composed of eleven members of the Bundestag and the Bundesrat, respectively. This committee is an innovation of the Basic Law and was introduced under the influence of the American practice of conference committees. Its purpose is to find a compromise in case of differences between the two houses with regard to legislative decisions.

The first session of a newly elected Bundestag is presided over by the oldest member, the Alterspraesident. The main function of this person, who may belong to any party, is to direct the election of the presiding officer of the Bundestag, his deputies, and the secretaries. The presiding officer or President is in charge of the Bundestag and exercises the police power in the Bundestag building; without his permission, no searches or seizures may take place on its premises. He recognizes members of the floor and appoints and dismisses the staff of the Bundestag. The President of the Bundestag is normally elected from the strongest party, his deputy from the second strongest.

The Bundestag also has a Council of Elders (*Aeltestenrat*). This Council is composed of the President of the Bundestag, his deputy, and fifteen members appointed by the fractions according to their strength; though each party must have at least one representative on the Council. The Council assists the President in running the business of the Bundestag; it is also influential in the selection of committee chairmanships. It is, however, only an advisory body and is not entitled to make any binding decisions.

Important decisions of the Bundestag (e.g., the election or dismissal of the Federal Chancellor or the enacting of federal legislation) can only be made by the full body of the Bundestag. Its sessions are open to the public; but upon demand of one-tenth of the members or on the demand of the federal government, the public may be excluded if the decision is supported by a two-thirds majority of the body.

The President of the Bundestag determines the order of speakers. Members of the Bundesrat (Federal Council) and the federal ministers are permitted to attend all meetings of the Bundestag and must be heard upon their request. On the other hand, the Basic Law provides that a majority of the Bundestag or a committee can demand the presence of any member of the federal government.

The Council of Elders determines the period of time devoted to debate on a certain subject matter. It also divides the speaking time allotted to the parliamentary fractions (not to individual members).

The President of the Bundestag is authorized in case of a violation of orderly conduct to expel a member from the session and in very grave cases may exclude a member for thirty days.[1]

The necessary quorum for decisions of the Bundestag is one more than half of the members; the presence of a quorum is assumed as long as it is not challenged. This can be done by at least five members.

A vote in the Bundestag can be taken in three different forms: (1) the usual method by the standing vote, (2) the so-called Hammelsprung (mutton jump), or (3) by roll call. The Hammelsprung means that upon request of the President, the members leave the chamber. All in favor of the measure re-enter the chamber through one door, all opposed through another, all abstaining through a third one. Roll call takes place only upon demand of fifty members and serves principally the purpose to determine in important cases the personal responsibility of a member. The vote of each member is included in the records by name.

The decisions of the Bundestag require a simple majority unless the rules of procedure provide otherwise. In a number of instances, as for example the election of the Federal Chancellor, his dismissal, or the passing of legislation against the veto of the Bundesrat, an absolute majority is required. A constitutional amendment requires a two-thirds majority. The rules of procedure of the Bundestag provide that in case the house is equally divided on a specific measure, the measure is considered to be defeated. The only exception to this rule occurs in the case where two persons receive an equal number of votes for the office of the President of the Bundestag. In such a situation, the decision is made by lot.

TYPES OF LEGISLATION

Three types of legislation can be considered by the legislative body: constitutional amendments, federative law, and simple legislation. Constitutional amendments require a two-thirds majority of the members of the Bundestag and the Bundesrat. Federative laws (also called *Zustimmungsgesetze*—consent laws) require the consent of the Bundestag as well as of the Bundesrat.

Simple laws can be passed by the Bundestag alone but can be vetoed by the Bundesrat. The Bundestag can overrule such a veto with a qualified majority. Consent legislation outnumbers simple laws; it consists of laws pertaining to the powers of the Laender. According to the Basic

[1] This happened once to the late leader of the Social Democratic party, Dr. Kurt Schumacher, who interrupted a speech of Chancellor Adenauer calling him "the Chancellor of the Allies."

Law, the Laender determine the establishment of administrative authority and administrative procedures in their states and are permitted to execute federal laws, unless otherwise provided. If the Bundestag makes an exception to the normal rule of Laender execution of federal law, the consent of the Bundesrat is required. It follows, therefore, that almost all federal laws that are executed by the Laender require the consent of the Bundesrat.

In regard to the division of legislative competence between the federation and the Laender, one can distinguish between two types of legislative powers: exclusive and concurrent powers. The exclusive federal powers prohibit the Laender from legislating in certain areas unless they are specifically authorized to do so by federal law. The division of legislative power is laid down in Articles 70 to 75 of the Basic Law, which basically recognizes the power of the Laender to legislate, insofar as the Basic Law does not vest legislative power in the federation. However, the national legislature has exclusive power with regard to all important matters. Article 73 enumerates eleven areas of exclusive federal legislation including foreign affairs, citizenship, currency and coinage, customs, railroads, air traffic, and postal services. The list of concurrent legislation is more extensive. Article 74 mentions twenty-three different fields, of which civil law, criminal law, and the structure and procedures of the courts are some of the more significant. This would indicate that a large area of legislative freedom is left to the Laender. Article 72 provides that in the field of concurrent legislation, the Laender have the power to legislate only insofar as the federation makes no use of its legislative power. In reality, only municipal police, schools, and cultural matters are left to the legislatures of the Laender.

Bills can only be introduced in the Bundestag. The legislative initiative lies with the federal government and the Bundesrat as collegiate bodies or with individual members of the Bundestag. The rules of procedure provide that the right to initiate legislation can be taken away from a single member and given to a group of members. Bills introduced by the federal government (through the office of the Chancellor) have to be submitted first to the Bundesrat (Federal Council), which is entitled to give its opinion on the bill within three weeks. Bills introduced by the Bundesrat are submitted to the Bundestag by the federal government. The federal government has to state its own opinion on the bill. Each bill requires the customary three readings.

FINANCIAL LEGISLATION

The budget is prepared by the federal government and submitted to Parliament. The Basic Law requires the budget to be balanced. It is the responsibility of the Finance Minister to insure this balance. This provision, which prevents in principle the possibility of a federal deficit, is directed against legislative irresponsibility. It obviously also affects the government in the preparation of the budget. The practice of the government during the years 1920–1923 in the attempt to cover the deficit through the issuance of new banknotes led to a catastrophic inflation. The provision of the Basic Law for a balanced budget has the purpose of preventing the repetition of such a development. In addition, as a further protection of a balanced executive budget, the Basic Law provides that decisions of the legislature increasing the expenditures proposed by the government or including or implying new expenditures for the future require the consent of the federal government. The Federal President can refuse to sign an unbalanced, and therefore unconstitutional, budget; he may also refuse to sign any other act of the legislature calling for additional expenditures. The federal government possesses an absolute veto of financial legislation; its refusal of consent cannot be overruled by the legislature.

In accordance with the rules of procedure for the federal government, the Finance Minister possesses a limited veto on all questions of financial significance. A decision of the federal government taken without the Finance Minister or opposed by him has to be debated and a new vote must be taken. The opposition of the Finance Minister against a decision of the Cabinet can only be overruled by a majority of the federal ministers, provided the Federal Chancellor votes with the majority. The Federal Chancellor and the Finance Minister thus have an absolute veto power with regard to increases of expenditures.

It should be noted that the veto power of the federal government is limited to actual increases of total expenditures. If the legislature appropriates an amount larger than requested for one specific item in the budget, but cuts an equivalent sum for another budgetary item, the federal government is legally unable to refuse its consent, even though it does not agree with the change.

The fiscal year begins April 1 and ends March 31. The budget has to be presented to the Bundestag by January 5. According to the Basic Law, all government bills go immediately to the Bundesrat, which is entitled to give its opinion within three weeks. This rule applies also to the budget.

The financial committee in the Bundesrat, which includes the finance ministers of the Laender, examines the budget first. From there, the bill is sent to the Bundestag. The most significant deliberations take place in the budget committee; ministers and department heads participate in the deliberations of the committee. From the committee, the budget, like any other bill, is referred to the plenum of the Bundestag. The Bundestag may or may not consider changes proposed by the Bundesrat. It may also alter the budget on its own initiative, except that any increase of total expenditures requires the consent of the government. After the Bundestag has passed the budget, the appropriation bill is again submitted to the Bundesrat in accordance with the normal legislative procedure.

The execution of the budget is subjected to a two-fold control. After the end of the budget year, the Finance Minister submits a report of the actual revenues and expenditures as well as assets and liabilities to the legislature. In addition, a special agency, the *Rechnungshof* (Federal Court of Audit), examines all individual expenditures with regard to their legality and economy. It has also the duty to bring irregularities to the attention of the government. The comments of the Court of Audit have to be submitted to the legislature together with a general report. Upon the request of the government, the legislature has to decide on a discharge for the federal government.

The Rechnungshof is an extremely important agency, independent of the federal government and serving as guardian over the expenditures of all federal agencies. Its members enjoy the same independence as judges; they are not allowed to belong to the Bundestag or the Bundesrat.

The budget therefore passes through four different stages: (1) preparation by the federal government, (2) consideration and enactment by the legislature, (3) execution by the federal government, (4) examination by the Rechnungshof and discharge by the legislature.

The annual budget is widely publicized; copies are available in all important libraries. The printing costs alone amount to almost half a million German marks yearly. This is quite a contrast to the practice of the Nazis, who failed to publish the budget after 1934. The Nazis were obviously reluctant to mention certain expenditures connected with the extravagancies of the leading figures or the erection and maintenance of concentration camps and gas chambers.

ELECTORAL FUNCTIONS

The Bundestag alone, without the Bundesrat, elects the holder of the most important office of the Federal Republic, the Federal Chancellor. It also participates in the election of the Federal President and elects half of the members of the federal courts. The Basic Law provides for a complicated system for the election of the Federal Chancellor. It strives first for the election of the chief of the government by a large majority; on the other hand, it attempts to make an election possible in the case of a lack of a majority. For this reason, the Basic Law provides for three subsequent possibilities, one after another in case the previous is unsuccessful.

The procedure for electing the Chancellor is as follows: (1) The Federal President proposes a candidate. If the candidate receives a majority in the Bundestag, he is elected. (2) If the person proposed by the Federal President is not elected, the Bundestag may vote within a period of fourteen days for a second time. It can nominate a candidate on its own, not being bound to the proposal of the Federal President. A candidate receiving a majority vote in the Bundestag has to be appointed by the Federal President within seven days. (3) If a candidate does not receive a majority on the second ballot, a third ballot takes place without delay, in which the person with the greatest number of votes is elected. However, the decision of this plurality is not automatically valid. The Federal President can either appoint the elected person within a period of seven days or, if he does not appoint him, he must dissolve the Bundestag. The newly elected Bundestag elects the Federal Chancellor according to the same procedure.

The reason for this complicated system is to be found in the traditional multiparty composition of the German legislature, where a single party very rarely controlled a majority of the parliamentary seats. Under these conditions, it was necessary to achieve a coalition of several parties to form a government.[2] The new plan for electing the Chancellor attempts to prevent a negative majority from controlling the office of the chief executive. For this reason, the third ballot requires only a plurality. However, this vote is cast with the risk of dissolution of the Bundestag. New elections are expensive, and the parties will seriously consider during the second ballot if it is worthwhile to take the risk of a new election. On the other hand, the dissolution of the Bundestag represents also some risk for the Federal President. It is possible for the parties whose candidate was rejected by the Federal President to be successful in the new election and elect this person when the new Bundestag convenes. The participation of the Federal President in the first and third ballot limits the powers of the parties without making him a predominant figure in the election of the Federal Chancellor.

The Chancellor is elected for the duration of a legislative period (four years). Each newly elected Bundestag has therefore to elect a Chancellor; the incumbent can be re-elected. The Bundestag is entitled to dismiss the Chancellor prior to the end of the legislative period only under the condition that it is possible to select a successor by absolute majority. This system of dismissal by replacement has been called the constructive vote of non-confidence. The simple non-confidence vote, whereby a simple majority can force the resignation of the Chancellor, or the whole government, or each individual minister, was responsible for many extended governmental crises during the Weimar period. Governments composed of the moderate middle parties were repeatedly overthrown by a negative

[2] In the elections of 1953 and 1957, the party of Chancellor Adenauer received an absolute majority in the Bundestag. This meant his election on the first ballot.

majority of the extreme Right and the extreme Left. This negative coalition, composed mostly of Nazis and Communists, was of course never in the position to form a government. The non-confidence vote as used during the Weimar period became very destructive and detrimental to the prestige of the legislature as well as the government. For this reason, to avoid the experiences of the Weimar period, the Basic Law of the Federal Republic provides for a combination of the dismissal and replacement of the Federal Chancellor.

A vote of non-confidence has to be proposed by one-fourth of the members of the Bundestag. In order to avoid the immediate excitement inherent in such a situation, the Basic Law provides for a cooling-off period; there must be an interval of forty-eight hours between the motion and the election of another Chancellor. Several candidates can be nominated. There is only one ballot. The Federal President has to appoint the candidate who receives an absolute majority. If no candidate receives an absolute majority, the non-confidence vote is defeated. This provision of the positive non-confidence vote means that a majority wishing to overthrow the Chancellor has also to prove that it is in the position to form a new government. The result of this provision is that a change of government during a legislative period is made very difficult. It can only happen in the case of a split in the major party of the coalition forming the government or in the case of the defection of one of the minor coalition parties.

The Bundestag is not entitled to dismiss an individual minister. It can only ask the Chancellor to propose the dismissal of a certain minister to the Federal President; the Chancellor is legally not obliged to comply. In the case of the election of a new Chancellor by the Bundestag, the whole government resigns together with the Chancellor.

The Bundestag also participates in the election of the Federal President, representing half of the membership of the Bundesversammlung (Federal Convention), and is indirectly involved in the election of half of the members of the Federal Constitutional Court and of the judges of the higher federal courts.

The rules of procedure of the Bundestag provide for three types of parliamentary questions and interpellations; the large interpellation, the small interpellation, and the question by a member. The large interpellation has to be signed by thirty members; the small interpellation by ten members; the Council of Elders provides at least once a month for a question hour for oral questions. Each member can submit questions to the minister involved, and these are answered by the minister during this period. The subject of the oral question must be submitted to the minister three days in advance.

In contrast to the Weimar Constitution, the Bonn Basic Law does not provide for impeachment of the Federal Chancellor and ministers by the

Bundestag. It retained the power to impeach the Federal President and added this power also with regard to federal judges. A two-thirds majority of the Bundestag can impeach the Federal President for willful violation of the Basic Law or any other federal law. The impeachment trial is held in the Federal Constitutional Court. If this Court convicts the President, he is removed from office. The Bundestag, by a simple majority, can also impeach a federal judge. Thus far, no impeachment proceedings have been instituted against federal officials.

THE BUNDESRAT (FEDERAL COUNCIL)

Article 50 of the Basic Law allows the Laender to participate in federal legislation and administration through the Bundesrat. Each Land has at least three votes in the Bundesrat. Laender with more than two million inhabitants have four votes, and those with more than six million inhabitants have five votes. Each Land can send as many members to the Bundesrat as it has votes. The members and their substitutes are appointed by the governments of the Laender; they have to belong to the Land government; in other words, they have to be ministers of their respective Laender. The Bundesrat is now composed of forty-one members or votes.[3] The votes of each Land may be given only as a bloc vote. It is therefore impossible for a Land to pass a bill with three votes and reject it with two. The members of the Bundesrat must vote according to the decisions and instructions of their respective governments.

The Bundesrat is actually more a permanent congress of ministers of the Laender than a genuine second chamber. It is distinguished from the Senate of the United States and all other second chambers in federal states by the fact that its members are not free in exercising their votes, but have to cast them in accordance with the instructions received from their governments.

The Bundesrat elects one of its members to serve as President for a period of one year. The rules of procedure do not provide for a specific succession, so a tradition has developed that this office is assigned to the Laender according to their size. In the first year of the Bonn government, the Prime Minister of the largest state, Rhineland-Westphalia, became President of the Bundesrat; in the second year, the Prime Minister of Bavaria, the second largest Land. The office of the President of the Bundesrat may become very significant in the case of the disability of the Federal President or if a vacancy should occur. In such an event, the authority of the Federal President is exercised by the President of the Bundesrat.

The Bundesrat makes decisions by an absolute majority vote. Only the impeachment of the Federal President and constitutional amendments re-

[3] Berlin is represented by four non-voting delegates.

quire a two-thirds majority. A quorum requires the presence of more than half of the votes, which at the present time is twenty-two members.

The Bundesrat is empowered to initiate legislation. It has to submit all proposals first to the Cabinet, which must send the matter to the Bundestag. The legislative initiative of the Bundesrat lags far behind the Bundestag, but it has increased considerably in comparison with its predecessor of the Weimar period, the Reichsrat. The Bundesrat is entitled to express an opinion within three weeks on legislative proposals of the government, then it must submit such measures to the Bundestag. Due to the fact that most bills are introduced by the government, the introduction by way of the Bundesrat is the most frequent procedure.

Every bill passed by the Bundestag, whether it originated in this body, with the federal government, or in the Bundesrat, has to be returned immediately to the Bundesrat. If the Bundesrat does not agree, it can demand within a period of two weeks that the bill be brought before a conference committee.

The conference committee, composed of eleven members of the Bundesrat (each Land is represented) and eleven members of the Bundestag, can propose changes, additions, or the complete rejection of the bill. In the case of consent legislation, the Bundestag as well as the federal government are also entitled to bring the bill before the conference committee. After the deliberations of the conference committee, the bill has to be voted upon again by both the Bundestag and the Bundesrat. If the proposed bill pertains to consent legislation and one of the two houses rejects the draft of the conference committee, the bill is defeated. In the case of simple legislation, which does not require the consent of the Bundesrat, objections by the Bundesrat can be overruled by the Bundestag.[4] The Bundestag also participates in the election of the members of the Federal Constitutional Court, half of whom it elects with a two-thirds majority.

LEGISLATIVE EMERGENCY

In contrast to the Weimar Constitution, the emergency powers of the Federal President and the federal government have been very much restricted. In view of the experiences with emergency powers during the second term of President Hindenburg, the framers of the Bonn Basic Law were afraid to grant to the government or to the President extraordinary powers in case of an emergency. The Weimar Constitution included the

[4] Since the Bundesrat deliberates by absolute majority and its objections to a bill referred by the Bundestag may be overridden only by a corresponding majority, the Bundestag may pass the bill a second time only by absolute majority vote. If the Bundesrat opposes the measure by a two-thirds majority of its voting membership, the Bundestag may secure second passage only with a two-thirds relative majority, provided this constitutes an absolute majority as well.

possibility of presidential predominance, not only in relationship to the Chancellor and the Cabinet, but also in relationship to the legislature.

The provision of Article 48 of the Weimar Constitution, frequently called the dictatorship article, gave the President emergency powers to such a degree that it provided a constitutionally entrenched dictatorial power. It empowered the President to replace temporarily the normal parliamentary process with emergency ordinances and, if necessary, to enforce the execution of national policy in the Laender by military action. It must be added that this dictatorial power was constitutionally restricted. The Reichstag was entitled to demand by simple majority the abolition of emergency ordinances and other emergency measures. Article 48 also specifically provided that a national law should be passed to define the general provisions of the Article in a more precise manner; in other words, it was up to the legislature to spell out in detail under what circumstances the emergency powers of the President could be used. However, such a law to define the general provisions of Article 48 was never enacted by the legislature. In addition, the control of Parliament with regard to emergency actions of the President was actually eliminated by the constitutional right of the President to dissolve the Reichstag and so deprive it of any possibility of control. From 1930 on, the presidential emergency power of Hindenburg, based on Article 48, was the foundation of practically all important governmental actions of the Reich. The establishment of the Hitler regime was greatly assisted by the dictatorial power of the Reich President and the emergency ordinances based on these powers.[5]

The Bonn Basic Law also contains in Article 81 certain provisions relating to emergency legislative powers that may be invoked by the executive and exercised with the consent of the upper house or Bundesrat. Should the Bundestag refuse to approve a bill initiated by the federal government and considered urgent by the government the Chancellor may demand a vote of confidence. If the Bundestag should defeat the motion for confidence, the Chancellor may either ask the President to dissolve the Bundestag and order general elections to be held or may advise the President to declare a state of legislative emergency; this requires the consent of the upper house. Once a state of legislative emergency has been proclaimed, all federal government bills become law with the sole consent of the Bundesrat irrespective of whether they are rejected by the Bundestag. The period of legislative emergency may persist for a maximum period of six months. If the Bundestag is still hostile but unable to replace the Chancellor at the end of the period of legislative emergency, the Chancellor would have to request the President to order the dissolution of the Bundestag or be forced in effect to resign. The legislative emergency provisions of the Basic Law allow the executive to govern the country with

[5] Emergency Ordinance of February 28, 1932.

the consent of the upper house temporarily in the event there is no constructive majority in the Bundestag. A legislative emergency may not be proclaimed more than once during the term of office of the Chancellor; an election would have to intervene. The Basic Law limits the scope of the emergency legislative powers that may be exercised by the executive and the Bundesrat to non-constitutional legislation; i.e., the Basic Law could not be amended by this emergency procedure. During the period of legislative emergency, federal government bills continue to be submitted for approval to the Bundestag. Should the latter reject such bills outright, approve them in a modified version that is unacceptable to the Chancellor, or delay passage of the measures for more than four weeks, the measures become law upon approval by the Bundesrat.

No state of legislative emergency has yet been proclaimed under the Basic Law. It presupposes a condition of serious political instability in which there is no working majority in the Bundestag to support a positive program; i.e., a situation such as existed from 1930 to 1933, when the Communists and the Nazis could obstruct parliamentary government.

The federal executive has also a potent ordinance power under the Basic Law, which authorizes the federal government to issue general administrative rules with the sole consent of the Bundesrat. These general administrative rules (Rechtsverordnungen) have the force of law and are just as binding on the regular courts as statutes are. General administrative rules are supposed to implement statutory law or make existing law executory; they must never override or supplant statutes. This ordinance power is no substitute for legislation; but where legislation does not specify any particular method of enforcement, the executive may do so by issuing general administrative rules. The regular courts could refuse to enforce Rechtsverordnungen on grounds of incompatibility with statutory law. The requirement of Bundesrat consent provides a further check on any possible abuse by the federal executive of this power.

SELECTED READING

DORR, HAROLD M. "Legislation." In *Governing Postwar Germany, Edward H. Litchfield* (ed.). Ithaca, N. Y.: Cornell University Press, 1953.

GOLAY, JOHN F. *Founding of the Federal Republic of Germany.* Chicago: University of Chicago Press, 1958.

HISCOCKS, RICHARD. *Democracy in Western Germany.* Fair Lawn, N. J.: Oxford University Press, 1957.

PRITTIE, T. "The Federal German Parliament," *Parliamentary Affairs,* VIII (1955), 235–39.

ULLMAN, R. K., and HALL, S. KING. *German Parliaments: A Study of the Development of Representative Institutions in Germany.* New York: Frederick A. Praeger, Inc., 1955.

U. S. HIGH COMMISSION IN GERMANY. *Germany's Parliament in Action.* February, 1950.

WALDENBERG, HANS. *Report on Democratic Institutions in Germany.* New York: American Council on Germany, 1956.

34

The Executive

THE TRADITION OF EXECUTIVE PREDOMINANCE

Several reasons, among which the authoritarian background is perhaps the most significant, can be given for the phenomenon that governmental authority in Germany emanates mostly from the executive and is guided by it to a greater extent than is customary in the Anglo-American tradition. Since the establishment of the empire, and even before unification, it was always the executive power that led the German nation to triumph and defeat and made German history. The outstanding events of German history provide ample proof for this. It was under the leadership of Bismarck, the iron Chancellor, that German unification was finally achieved; Emperor Wilhelm II was more responsible than anyone else for the catastrophe of World War I; Hindenburg, the Reich President, had his share in the decline and final collapse of the Weimar Republic. Hitler, the Fuehrer and Reich Chancellor must be given special consideration, for he reversed Germany morally and culturally to a degree that is even now beyond comprehension; World War II was only the most significant part of the general degradation of a nation for which no parallel can be found in recorded history. However, Adenauer, the Federal Chancellor of the last decade, has made Germany respectable again and reinstated her, at least economically, as the foremost power of western Europe. All these episodes were dominated by the executive power, and it does not make any difference whether it was exercised in the name of the Emperor, President, Leader, or Chancellor. It would be misleading to assume that this executive predominance was exercised only by means of a despotic dictatorship. With the exception of twelve years of the Nazi regime, the preponderance of the executive over a frequently impotent legislature and a formally independent but actually servile judiciary, expressed itself within the constitutional framework, largely representing the cornerstone of what can be loosely referred to as the "living Constitution." The German executive is not necessarily antidemocratic in character, although it has operated almost without exception along authoritarian lines. This can easily be understood for the period of the empire; but unfortunately it happened also during the Weimar period, when the attempt was made to establish a genuine democracy. Professor Carl Schmitt, who later became the outstanding legal theoretician of the Nazis, stated as early as 1929 that he saw in the Reich President the guardian of the Weimar Constitution, pointing to specific articles of this document, especially Article 48, to prove his point. As the events have shown, Reich President Paul von Hindenburg was the gravedigger rather than the guardian of this Constitution. The executive guardianship theory could be conceived as a bulwark of democracy if one remembers that a thoroughly democratic system should be guarded by the chief executive. The Weimar Constitution provided that the President was to be elected directly by the people. This would appear to be a strong democratic feature, but it did not work this way. The main reason is not to be found in any inherent antithesis between executive leadership and democracy, but in the unbalanced social and political situation that surrounded the Weimar experiment. In this case, the antirepublican and antiparliamentary forces were so strong that they were able to use the presidential election as a demonstration against democracy. They saw in the presidential election an opportunity to put a reactionary antirepublican personality into office, thereby steering the Weimar Constitution in an autocratic direction. The two elections of Hindenburg have shown that the forces of reaction were stronger than the democratic forces. The Reich President, the supposed guardian of the democratic Weimar Constitution, thus became a substitute emperor and a potential dictator.

As executive predominance could not be kept under control within the strongly democratic framework of the Weimar Constitution, it was strengthened to an extreme under the leader principle of the Nazi regime. Any adherence to the separation-of-powers principle was abolished. The textbooks of this period reveal this trend, for in them it was made clear that national unity demanded that all political power be united in the hand of a leader. The supreme will of the leader became law. The whole political life of the people was decided by the uniform and all-embracing will of the leader. Professor Schmitt pointed out in his writings that no sphere of public life was excepted from the leader principle, for the command of the leader was the law. Schmitt did wish to keep a limited degree of independence for the judges; but during the Nazi era, even this basic feature of the rule of law lost its practical meaning. It is not surprising, then, that Hitler, in July of 1934, could order executions without a court trial.[1]

Naturally, the experiences of the Weimar period and the Hitler regime caused the framers of the Bonn Basic Law to show an understandable fear of the executive. The powers of the Federal President were consequently restricted. But the tradition of executive predominance continued under the Basic Law, for the Federal Chancellor has become by far the strongest figure of the new Republic. Whether this is due to the personality of Dr. Adenauer or to the inherent possibilities of the office, no one can say. But it does seem that the executive power, in one form or other, will always predominate in Germany.

THE FEDERAL PRESIDENT

The Federal President, in distinction to the President of the Weimar Republic, is not elected directly by the people, but is elected by a specific instrumentality convened only for this purpose. This body, the Bundesversammlung (Federal Convention), consists of the members of the Bundestag and an equal number of members elected by the legislatures of the Laender according to the principle of proportional representation. The person receiving the votes of the majority of the members of the Federal Convention is elected President. If no candidate gets this majority in two ballots, a third ballot is taken, and the candidate receiving the most votes is elected. As the Bundestag is now composed of 497 members, a federal convention is 994 strong. The number of representatives of the individual Laender in the Federal Convention is decided by the federal government with the consent of the Bundesrat on the basis of the last official census.

The term of office of the Federal President is five years and re-election is possible only once. Thus, the presidential term is one year longer than the legislative term of the Bundestag. This provision insures that the election of the Federal President and the Federal Chancellor (elected by the Bundestag) do not take place at the same time.

The first election of a Federal President took place in 1949. Dr. Theodor Heuss was elected on the second ballot. Out of the 800 votes in the Federal Convention, he received 416; while his principal opponent, Dr. Kurt Schumacher of the Social Democratic party, received 312. Professor Heuss was re-elected in the summer of 1954 on the first ballot with 871 out of 987 votes cast. The third election in 1959 was preceded by a political struggle within the Christian Democratic Union between Chancellor Ade-

[1] An insurrection against Hitler occurred at this time under the leadership of Ernst Roehm, Chief of Staff of the SA (Brownshirts). He and an unknown number of people, likely several thousands, were killed without trial.

nauer and the Minister of Economics Professor Erhard. Adenauer's initial announcement that he would step down as Chancellor and become a candidate for the presidency appeared to prepare the way for Erhard as his successor. But Adenauer soon changed his mind and decided to remain Chancellor. In spite of some strong criticism inside and outside Germany, Dr. Adenauer did not have much difficulty in imposing his viewpoint upon his party. The Christian Democratic Union nominated as a compromise candidate Heinrich Luebke, Federal Minister for Food, Agriculture and Forestry. He was elected Federal President on the second ballot against the candidate of the Social Democratic party, Professor Carlo Schmidt.

Professor Theodor Heuss, who held the office of Federal President from 1949 to 1959, had lived a distinguished career as a scholar, liberal politician, and journalist before he was called to serve as President. He was closely associated with Friedrich Naumann, one of the outstanding liberal politicians under Wilhelm II. Heuss taught from 1920 to 1933 at the famous *Hochschule fuer Politik* (University for Politics) at Berlin. During the Hitler period, he was able to work for some time as a journalist. After World War II, he was Minister of Culture of Wuertemberg-Baden and Professor of History and Political Science at the Technical University of Stuttgart. He became a cofounder of the Free Democratic party in 1946. In 1949, he was one of the most influential members of the Parliamentary Council which drafted the Basic Law. Professor Heuss is a representative of the best of Germany. As President, he filled the office with dignity and respect, placed it above the struggle for power, and respected in an exemplary way the limits of the office.

His successor, Heinrich Luebke, was a compromise choice and prior to his election was entirely unknown outside Germany. Before 1933, he was managing director of the German Farmers League and from 1931 to 1933 was a member of the Prussian Parliament. During the Nazi regime, he was imprisoned several times, once for a period of twenty months. A member of the Christian Democratic Union, he became in 1947 Minister of Food and Agriculture of North Rhine-Westphalia, where he was able to improve the agricultural capacity of this badly damaged and densely populated Land. In 1953, he became Federal Minister of Food, Agriculture and Forestry. He took the oath of office as Federal President on September 15, 1959. In his inaugural address, President Luebke spelled out his conception of the office of the Federal President. To him, the office is a neutral one raised above the range of ordinary government business and devoted to the preservation of a limited number of functions.

The Parliamentary Council in drafting the Basic Law thoroughly discussed the limits of the office of the President. There was general agreement that the powers of the President must be more restricted than during the period of the Weimar Republic. Nonetheless, the Basic Law assigns several important functions to the Federal President.

First of all, the Federal President is the representative of the German Federal Republic in matters concerning international affairs. He concludes treaties with foreign states on behalf of the federation and accredits and receives ambassadors. These provisions mean that the President is the representative of the Federal Republic in relation to foreign nations; therefore, the German Federal Republic is only bound to a treaty with a foreign nation if this treaty has been signed by the Federal President. Even so, the representation in international affairs by the President has certain conditions attached to it. According to Article 58 of the Basic Law, orders and decrees of the Federal President, including those related to international affairs, require for their validity the countersignature of the Federal Chancellor or the competent federal minister. There are only three exceptions to this requirement provided for by the Basic Law: first, the appointment and dismissal of the Federal Chancellor; second, the dissolution of the Bundestag in a case where a Federal Chancellor was elected on the third ballot with a mere plurality; and third, the request of the President that the Federal Chancellor, after a resignation or electoral defeat, continue to stay in office and transact business until the appointment of a successor. Without countersignature, all other actions of the Federal President are invalid.

The Federal President appoints the federal judges, the federal civil service, and the officers and non-commissioned officers. All these documents and commissions require the countersignature of the Chancellor or the competent minister. The Federal President has consequently the opportunity to participate to a large degree in the staff policy of the federal government. He is able, by refusing his signature, to prevent an appointment or dismissal. On the other hand, he is not able to force the appointment or dismissal of a civil servant. Therefore, his power over personnel policy is more of a veto than anything else. The Federal President can delegate his appointment power, except in cases of the higher civil service, to the federal minister most concerned.

The Federal President, on the recommendation of the Federal Chancellor, also appoints and dismisses the federal ministers. He also participates in the complicated procedure that the Basic Law provides for the election of the Federal Chancellor. As explained in Chapter 33, he recommends the candidate for the first election ballot of the Bundestag. In the eventuality of a candidate's election with only a plurality on the third ballot, the Federal President has the choice between the appointment of the elected candidate or dissolution of the Bundestag. Furthermore, on the proposal of the Federal Chancellor, he may dissolve the Bundestag if a vote of non-confidence is cast against the government and the Bundestag is unable to elect another Chancellor. This dissolution must be made within twenty-one days. Connected with these provisions is the possibility of the declaration of a state of legislative emergency by the Federal President. This action by the Federal President can only be taken upon the proposal of the federal government and with the consent of the Bundesrat.

The Federal President also engrosses the federal bills passed by the legislature, signs them, and promulgates them in the *Federal Gazette*. Only after the promulgation of the legislative act with the signature of the Federal President and the countersignature of a member of the government does it become law. The Federal President may refuse to sign a bill that he believes was formulated without regard for the procedures provided in the Basic Law or that, in his opinion, contradicts the provisions of the Basic Law. Clearly, therefore, a limited amount of the guardianship theory is still maintained. It should be noted, however, that the final decision with regard to the constitutionality of a law lies with the Federal Constitutional Court.

The Federal President exercises the right of pardon on behalf of the federation. But this power extends to individual cases, a general amnesty being granted only by legislative act and not by presidential decree.

Finally, the Federal President announces the decision of the Bundestag when it proclaims a state of national military emergency. If the Bundestag is unable to convene because of insurmountable obstacles, the President can make this decision and issue the proclamation with the countersignature of the Chancellor. In such a case, the presiding officers of the Bundestag and Bundesrat should be consulted if possible.

The Federal President has at his disposal a special agency, the Office of the Federal President (*Bundespraesidialamt*) under a Deputy Minister (*Staatssekretaer*). This person regularly attends the Cabinet meetings in order to keep the Federal President informed.

THE FEDERAL CHANCELLOR

The federal Cabinet consists of the Federal Chancellor and the federal ministers. It is a collegiate body whose chairman or presiding officer is the Federal Chancellor. He presides over the meetings and has the deciding vote in the case of a tie. He directs, with the assistance of a Staatssekretaer in the Federal Chancellery, the whole business of the government.

According to the Basic Law, the Federal Chancellor has the responsibility for the direction of general policy. A similar provision existed in the Weimar Constitution and was there referred to as the Chancellor principle (*Kanzlerprinzip*). Under this principle, neither the Federal President, the Bundestag, nor the federal government is competent to determine the direction of general policy. This authority is placed with the Federal Chancellor, who consequently is the most powerful and important figure in the governmental structure of the German Federal Republic. The Basic Law does not define precisely what are the limits of the words "determination of general policy." In case of doubt, the Chancellor himself decides what is to be included in the category of determination or direction of general policy. For example, the Foreign Minister is not allowed to announce an objective of German foreign policy without the approval of the Federal Chancellor. The Minister of Finance is not allowed to announce a tax reduction without prior approval of the Chancellor. Individual ministers are entitled to challenge the direction of the general policy in the Cabinet meetings, but the final power of decision is in the hands of the Chancellor. However, he does have the obligation to submit all matters of significance for the information and consultation of the federal government.

Since the Federal Chancellor is not limited by the Cabinet in general policy decisions, he is also empowered to overrule a majority of the Cabinet on other questions. If, for example, he considers a bill to be contradictory to general policy, though supported by the majority of the government, he can prevent its introduction.

The provisions of the Basic Law assign in some instances the decision to the Chancellor alone, in others to the government as a collegiate body. The Chancellor alone can ask for a vote of confidence or propose the dissolution of the Bundestag. The federal government as a collegiate body is entitled to introduce a bill. Only the federal government with the consent of the Bundesrat, and not the Chancellor alone, can take the necessary measures against a Land to enforce the Basic Law or any federal legislation by means of federal compulsion (Bundeszwang); the same applies to the request for a declaration of a state of legislative emergency by the Federal President. This request has to come from the federal government, with the approval of the Bundesrat, and not from the Federal Chancellor alone. The Chancellor is unable to introduce a bill against the will of the government; he has, however, the power to prevent the introduction of a bill.

Under all circumstances, the Federal Chancellor is responsible for the direction of general policy, no matter whether he accepts a majority decision of the Cabinet or rejects it. Dr. Adenauer was known for the strong leadership he exercised over the Cabinet, for his personal decisions are in most instances unchallenged by the government. This situation is not to be explained by the personality of Adenauer alone. The fact that the Federal Chancellor carries the burden of responsibility is the justification for his power of final decision.

Under the leadership of Chancellor Adenauer, Germany developed a new type of representative democracy bearing some similarity to the British Cabinet system. The name *Kanzlerdemokratie* (chancellor democracy) has been given to this development. The Basic Law makes the specific statement that all state power emanates from the people. Although basic for any democratic form of government, this concept lost all meaning during the Weimar Republic despite frequent elections. The role of the people under the Bonn Basic Law has developed for the first time to the point that though the people still do not directly elect the Chancellor, they can decide who he shall be. This development was not and could not be foreseen by the drafters of the Basic Law. In the Bundestag elections of 1953 and 1957, the people not only elected the representatives and the parties in Parliament, but at the same time also elected the government. This was made possible by the development of a kind of two-party system during the first decade of the Bonn Republic. This development gave the German people an alternative similar to that enjoyed by the British people in their parliamentary elections, which presents a great contrast to the entanglement and confusion of competing and struggling coalition candidates. In this manner, the power to elect the Chancellor, given originally by the Basic Law exclusively to the Bundestag, was transferred in practice, though not formally, to the voting people, just as the British elect the leader of one of the two major parties as Prime Minister.

There has been almost from the very beginning a certain amount of criticism of this chancellor democracy, in the sense that it does not represent a genuine parliamentary democracy. During the 1950's one often heard the word *Demokratur*. As *Diktatur* is the German word for dictatorship, the inference is clear. As early as November, 1950, in an important debate in the Bundestag, a lady representative of the Center party pointed out that under the constructive non-confidence vote and the powerful position given to the Chancellor, the German Federal Republic ceased to have a representative democracy. She asserted that what really existed was an authoritarian leadership of the state determined by the Chancellor. This complaint, which has since been repeated over and over again by parliamentarians, politicians, and observers, does not derive from Article 67 of the Basic Law, which provides for the constructive non-confidence vote, or any other provision of the Basic Law. The situation can more realistically be attributed to the historic fact of a strong and stable majority government since 1949, which was missing throughout the Weimar period.

The most important reason for the development of the chancellor democracy is with all probability to be found in the character and personality of Konrad Adenauer. There was surely a tendency to authoritarian leadership during the years of the Adenauer regime, although this was not dictatorship but evidence of the old Chancellor's will to carry governmental responsibility within a democratic parliamentary framework. This phenomenon is new to German parliamentary history, especially when one recalls the fate of parliamentary institutions and the shifting and changing coalitions during the Weimar period. In the strict constitutional or legal sense, there is little difference between the Reich Chancellor of Weimar and the Federal Chancellor of Bonn, for both were entitled to determine the direction of general policy. The change under Adenauer consisted in his really doing it. This may be a kind of modified leader principle poorly suited to the preservation of healthy democratic institutions, but it is not yet possible to distinguish between the authoritarian and democratic parts of this chancellor democracy.

Dr. Konrad Adenauer was born January 5, 1876, in Cologne. Being a lawyer, he was active in municipal affairs. Elected Lord Mayor of Cologne in 1917, he kept his post until 1933 when he was dismissed by the Nazis. During all this time, he was a leading member of the Catholic Center party and, as a devout Catholic, a strong and outspoken opponent of the Nazis. After the end of the war, he was reinstated in his position as Lord Mayor of Cologne by the British military government but was dismissed after a very short time on the charge of inefficiency. Adenauer was cofounder of the Christian Democratic Union of North Rhine-Westphalia and became its chairman in the British occupation zone; after 1949, he became the leader of this party. He was presiding officer of the Parliamentary Council that drafted the Bonn Basic Law in 1949 and was elected Federal Chancellor by the first Bundestag in that year. Until 1955, he also held the position of Federal Minister for Foreign Affairs.

The Federal Chancellor communicates to the Federal President the names of persons he wishes appointed federal ministers. The Chancellor is responsible for the appointments, and the commissions installing the ministers carry his signature. From the group of ministers appointed by the Federal President on the proposal of the Chancellor, the latter may select a Vice-Chancellor. This selection does not require the participation of the Federal President.

The federal ministers are dismissed by the Federal President on the proposal of the Chancellor. The Bundestag is not empowered to dismiss by a vote of non-confidence an individual minister; it can only ask the Chancellor to dismiss a certain minister, but the Chancellor does not have to yield to this demand. Naturally, the opposition against such a minister may lead to the expression of a vote of non-confidence against the Federal Chancellor. On the other hand, the dismissal of an individual minister may be opposed by the Bundestag, but there is nothing it can do except to resort to a vote of non-confidence against the Chancellor. This problem was handled in a different manner in the Weimar Republic. The Reichstag was empowered to dismiss the Reich Chancellor as well as the ministers without providing for successors. The Bonn Basic Law, by restricting the constructive non-confidence vote to the Federal Chancellor alone, places the sole responsibility of the government upon him. Appropriate to this responsibility, he is given the power to select and dismiss the federal ministers.

The most important agency the Chancellor has at his disposal in the exercise of his various functions and duties is the *Bundeskanzleramt* (Office of the Federal Chancellor). This office sees that the directions of general policy laid down by the Chancellor are carried out. It is responsible for the information given to the Federal President, prepares the meetings of the Cabinet and the speeches and policy statements of the Chancellor, and performs other similar duties. The Office of the Federal Chancellor is the main coordinating agency of the federal government. It is also the liaison between the Chancellor and all parliamentary and non-parliamentary organizations. The office shows a similarity to the White House Office in the United States; its functions and duties are, however, more clearly specified in the rules and procedures of the federal government. It is, for example, the duty of the Office of the Federal Chancellor to see that only questions of real significance are submitted to the meetings of the Cabinet. In case of differences of opinion between ministries, an attempt to settle the differences has to be made first before the matter can be brought before the Cabinet; the Office of the Federal Chancellor acts in such instances as arbiter between the individual ministries.

The Office of the Federal Chancellor is headed by a *Staatssekretaer* (Secretary of State), who is assisted by a staff of high-ranking officials. The Secretary of State in the Office of the Federal Chancellor is the chief administrative assistant of the Federal Chancellor.

The Federal Chancellor has under his direct control the federal press and information office, which is independent of the ministries and also of the Office of the Federal Chancellor. Under the Nazi regime, there existed a special ministry of propaganda under Dr. Joseph Goebbels, which was in complete control of all media of communication. All freedom of expression was ruthlessly eliminated. This lamentable situation no longer exists, although the federal press and information office is still to a degree a propaganda agency of the federal government. It informs the German as well as the international press of the actions, intentions, and problems of the government. The office not only transmits the news, but also interprets it in the light of official policy. Regular press conferences are conducted for the German and international press. The federal press and information office is a political agency, and its director is appointed by the Chancellor.

The plenipotentiary of the German Federal Republic in Berlin also works directly under the Federal Chancellor. This office acts as a liaison between the Federal Republic and Berlin. Officially, Berlin is not a part of the Federal Republic; but both the Federal Republic and the city of West Berlin act as if this situation does not exist. The city of West Berlin is represented in the Bundestag as well as in the Bundesrat by twenty-two non-voting deputies in the former and four consultative members in the latter. The actual relationship between the Federal Republic and the city of West Berlin is indicated by the fact that the Mayor of West Berlin, Willy Brandt, was the presiding officer of the Bundesrat in 1959.

THE FEDERAL MINISTERS AND THE CIVIL SERVICE

The federal ministers are part of the federal government. An individual minister participates in the Cabinet in collegiate decisions by his vote. At the same time, he is in charge of his department. In the latter capacity, he is empowered to determine the policy of his department within the framework of the general policy directions laid down by the Federal Chancellor. The rules of procedure for the federal government provide that federal ministers have authority within their field of competence. Thus, no administrative appeal from their decisions is permissible. For example, with regard to the collection of taxes, the decision of the Federal Minister of Finance is final and not subject to challenge by the Cabinet or the Chancellor. Of course, it is possible to bring the matter to the administrative court that has jurisdiction in this area.

According to Article 66 of the Basic Law, a person while holding the position of federal minister may not hold any other salaried office or engage in any trade or profession. Ministers remain members of the Bundestag and are naturally permitted to maintain their leading positions in their parties. The rights and duties of the ministers are laid down in a special law relating to federal ministers. The ministers must take the same oath of office as the Federal President.

In contrast to the situation in England and France, the minister in Germany does not have a member of the Bundestag to assist him as political assistant or alter ego in the form of an undersecretary or Minister of State. The German *Staatssekretaer* is the highest administrative assistant of the minister and at the same time his deputy in the ministry. He may substitute for the minister in the legislature and at committee and Cabinet meetings, but he cannot vote. The Secretaries of State normally are taken from the higher ranks of the civil service.

The number of federal ministries is not fixed by the Basic Law or any other federal law, but left to the discretion of the Federal Chancellor.

The Federal German Republic distinguishes between three types of ministries. First are the classical ministries performing the basic functions of the state; the Foreign Ministry and the Finance Ministry are two of these. A second type are the provision ministries, such as the Ministry for Food and Agriculture or the Ministry for Labor and Social Affairs. There are also special ministries; examples of this type are the Ministry for Expellees and Refugees, the Ministry for All-German Affairs, the Ministry for Family and Youth Affairs, and the Ministry for Atomic and Water Economy (Figure 34–1).

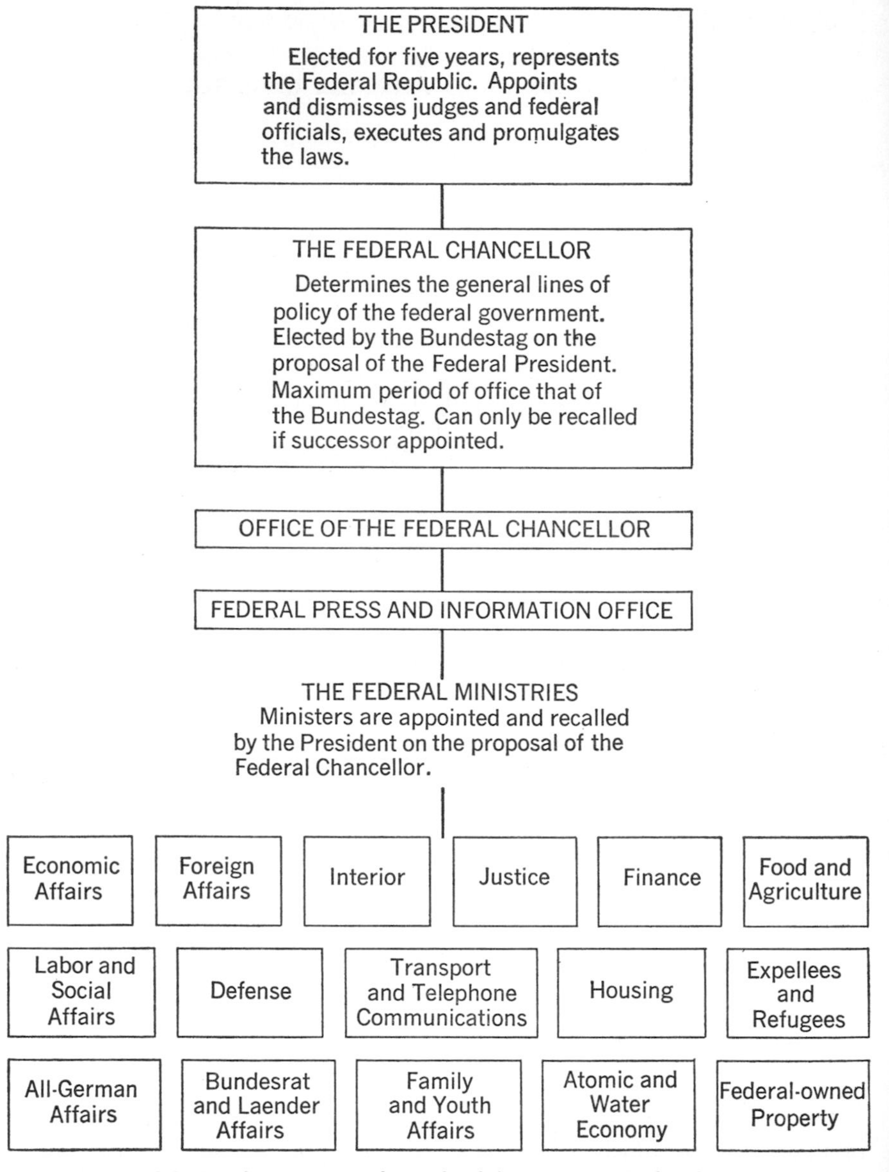

Figure 34–1. The executive branch of the German Federal Republic.

The ministries are divided into several departments. The Ministry of Finance, for example, is divided into six departments: Department I (personnel, organization, and general administration), Department II (general financial policy and public finances), Department III (customs, duties, and consumer taxes), Department IV (property and traffic taxes), Department V (banks and currency), and Department VI (foreign finance, war liquidation, restitution, and legal affairs). Each department is headed by a *Ministerialdirektor* (ministerial director); the departments are subdivided into *Referate* (groups) headed by reporters (*Referenten*). These groups are frequently divided into subgroups. The reporters hold the rank of a *Ministerialrat* (ministerial counsel), *Regierungsdirektor* (government director), or *Regierungsrat* (government counsel).

The bureaucratic tradition of the German civil service is very old, reaching back to King Friedrich Wilhelm of Prussia, the father of Friedrich II. In view of the emphasis on the state and the exalted position given the state in the German set of values, the servants of the state have always commanded high prestige. Civil service positions have been very much sought by young men in spite of the traditionally very modest remunerations.

The carefully defined ranks and titles of the *Staatsbeamte* (civil servants) are scrupulously respected by them. Furthermore, the prestige of this ranking generally extends out beyond the government into the equivalent social and educational strata of society in general. This bureaucratic hierarchy appeals to the Germans. Under this arrangement, the civil service has earned a reputation for efficiency and political neutrality. But loyalty to the state is very strong for the German civil servant, whose attitude is somewhat different from that of his American and English counterparts; the German considers himself a servant of the state—not a servant of the individuals with whom he deals.

The executive and administrative apparatus of the civil service is divided into various departments headed by a single individual. This monocratic principle exists in Germany on all governmental levels. Max Weber, the eminent German social scientist, pointed out that in his country, administration was based upon superiority and subordination instead of equality. The existence of the official hierarchy is thoroughly accepted, and communication is maintained through official channels from lower to higher echelons. This is a fixed and inflexible system of command and subordination whereby the lower levels are supervised by the higher ones. This system permits individual citizens within the framework of the administrative law to appeal a decision of a lower to the next higher authority. Within this hierarchical structure, with its line of command and responsibility, a limited amount of individual authority in dealings with the public is left to each civil servant, even at the lowest level. To a very small degree, even the office attendant in a ministry represents the power of the state. He feels himself important within the limited area of his authority and does not have to worry about problems beyond it, which he automatically refers to his superior. The entire German tradition, attitude, and training is especially suited for this type of administrative organization. The German civil service has achieved a well-earned reputation for efficiency, devotion to duty, honesty, and incorruptibility. But in respect to friendliness, politeness, or what in the United States might be called a democratic attitude, little effort is expended.

The civil service in the Federal Republic is regulated by a federal law of 1953, which provides that an official must serve the whole people, not merely a specific party or group. He must discharge his duties in a neutral and just manner, for in principle the utmost objectivity is demanded from an official. He must perform his functions according to law; and his instructions must be uninfluenced by political parties, interest groups, or his own political preference. This is a great deal to expect, but it is necessary in a pluralistic society in which antagonistic forces are competing. Against the struggle between the various political and economic groups, the bureaucracy is supposed to represent a disciplined and loyal organization, consciously keeping aloof from the disputes of the various rivals in the political contest. Therefore, the bureaucracy is expected to remain intact in its personnel, even during significant changes in the country's political leadership. This is considered to be in the interest of the continuous efficiency of the many activities of the state.

The neutral position of the civil service requires the unconditional loyalty of the official to the state and to the government. In this respect, one has to remember that the German civil service has developed traditions that persisted through the imperial Reich, the Weimar Republic, the Nazi period, and are still existent now. Outstanding among them is the caste feeling of the bureaucracy, its recruitment from the upper classes, its strong authoritarianism, and its tradition of blind obedience. The law of 1953 requires that an official must unreservedly accept the basic constitutional order as established in the Basic Law and that his conduct must be devoted to its preservation. He is obliged to work against all tendencies contradictory to this basic order. It has been pointed out earlier that the German bureaucracy is, in view of its history and recruitment, extremely conservative. The loyalty to the Imperial State and to the Hitler regime was sincere and never questioned. This can be explained not only by the fact that the authoritarian state appealed to the personnel, which was carefully selected by this state, but also by the many privileges that were granted by the state to its servants. For example, a very generous pension system, enacted by the Civil Service Code of 1873, has been of great help in attracting to the civil service the most highly qualified candidates.

The question of loyalty to the democratic governments of the Weimar Republic requires a different answer. The young democracy had to retain the services of the highly professionalized and competent officials of the empire; there were just not enough qualified personnel to replace them. To what extent the democratic process was undermined by these reactionary public servants will probably never be definitely established. The best that can be said is that the attitude of the bureaucracy toward the Weimar Republic was lukewarm. The same problem, to an even greater extent, exists today with regard to former Nazis.

There is one tradition in the German civil service that is still effective; corruption and bribery are very rare. If an official violates his obligations, he can be punished on the basis of disciplinary regulations. Penalties include warnings, reprimands, fines, demotions, and even dismissal. The official involved can bring his case to a federal court of discipline. Specific reference must be made to the fact that, unless otherwise provided, civil servants in Germany are appointed for life. The independence of the official from undue pressure is insured to the extent that he can be dismissed before retirement, which is normally at the age of sixty-five, only by a court decision. This principle of life appointment goes back to the late eighteenth and early nineteenth centuries and was introduced to protect officials from arbitrariness of rulers or immediate superiors. The provisions for life tenure did not protect civil servants under the Nazi regime; many were ruthlessly eliminated if they were not considered faithful Nazis thoroughly permeated with the National Socialist ideology.

The present federal law provides that a candidate's qualifications are the sole basis for appointment to public office. There exists a rigid merit system, with different types of examinations suited to the different positions in the German civil service. There are no other requirements. Even with regard to religious affiliations, the German civil service is almost equally divided between Catholics and Protestants. There is, perhaps, a larger number of Protestants in the higher levels.

The civil service will be one of the major problems of German democracy for some time to come. For this situation, the government of Chancellor Adenauer is only partly responsible. The problem arises from the fact that after the collapse of the Nazi regime, the bureaucracy had to be rebuilt from the existing reservoir of civil servants, which included a large percentage of Nazis or persons who at least had some affiliation with the party or one of its branches. There were still a few qualified persons retired by the Nazis who were available for reactivation.

As the removal of Nazis from governmental positions was a part of the denazification program, the implementation of denazification became an important source of friction between the German authorities and the Allies during the occupation period. It has frequently been pointed out that one of the most serious failures in the attempt to replace authoritarianism with democracy in German public life has been the attempt to reform the civil service. Much of the resistance to reform is due to the need for a competent civil service. Hence, in staffing it, the Germans were inclined to keep a large number of former Nazis in office. The acceptance by these people of real democratic principles must be very seriously doubted. An able observer of the German scene made the point that, due to the special circumstances of the postwar period, the question of democratic reconstruction was soon placed second to the practical urgency in rebuilding German strength, politically, economically, and militarily.[2] Efficient personnel was necessary to achieve this; and the emphasis on efficiency, without asking too many questions about political reliability, opened the doors of the government offices to people who had not been democratic in the past and who showed little promise of becoming so in the future. A further complication of the problem is the traditional resistance of the bureaucracy itself to a democratized public personnel system. The bureaucracy is still unwilling to give up such long-standing class privileges as almost absolute security of office, generous pension rights, military-type ranks and titles, and the discriminatory restrictions on admission to the civil service. With regard to the restrictions mentioned, it is true that the Bismarckian Reich had already established an efficient selection procedure based upon ability; but the range of social groups from which candidates for public office were taken was strictly limited. A prospective career civil servant had to be an officer of the reserve, and in most instances he had to belong to one of the respected university fraternities. Even during the Weimar Republic, membership in the right fraternity was very important to a successful career in the civil service. An *Alter Herr* (old member) of a fraternity would always prefer a young *Bundesbruder* (fraternity brother) to any other candidate. This system of unofficial patronage was self-perpetuating to the extent that certain government offices eventually became the exclusive domain of a particular fraternity. Due to the fact that most of the German fraternities considered dueling a necessary prerequisite to full membership, the majority of the high civil servants had cuts and scars from sabre duels.[3]

Being one of the most reactionary and nationalistic groups during the Weimar Republic, the fraternities became ardent supporters of Hitler. But Hitler opposed their exclusive position as an elite and disbanded them. This antagonized but did not destroy them, for they made their reappearance at the German universities. Their influence, especially in pro-

[2] Kurt P. Tauber, "Over Germany: Shadows of the Past," *The New York Times Magazine,* Section 6, December, 1959.

[3] Dueling is a criminal offence under the German Criminal Code. The police and the public prosecutor are, however, extremely lenient in applying the law against offenders; in many cases, the chief of police and the prosecutor were *Alte Herren* themselves.

viding candidates for the higher career civil service, has not yet been eliminated; and thus among university students, the importance of the fraternities is still recognized.

The infiltration of the civil service by former Nazis or Nazi sympathizers is a well-known fact in Germany. It has attracted some publicity outside Germany in connection with the anti-Semitic incidents that occurred in West Germany in the winter of 1959. In Berlin, there were even demonstrations by democratic youth groups under the slogan "Nazis get out." Several newspaper articles urged that former Nazis be dropped from leading positions within the government, but there has been no significant response from the authorities. Adenauer's view of this problem has been influenced by the need for a competent and efficient civil service and also by his belief that the Nazi past should be forgotten, that the men involved have suffered enough. The outstanding example of a former Nazi in a high position is Dr. Hans Globke, State Secretary in the Office of the Federal Chancellor and one of Adenauer's closest advisers. Globke wrote the official commentaries on the Nueremberg racist laws of 1935. It is quite possible that behind the Bonn government's noticeable tolerance of Nazis is the belief that keeping them in secure governmental positions may more securely attach their loyalties to the existing political structure of West Germany. Whatever the reasons, the fact remains that perhaps half of all senior civil servants in West German ministries were once Nazis. At least eight West German ambassadors were former Nazi party members, and the number of former Nazis in the judiciary is estimated to be in the hundreds. Adenauer once answered criticism on this point by stating that only 66 per cent of the Bonn Foreign Office senior officials had been Nazi party members. He had also frequently made the point that the general majority of Germans, like those in the civil service, served the Nazis only under the hard pressure of dictatorship. This is surely true in some individual cases, but to take this view of the over-all situation is a gross misrepresentation of the real facts. Another formidable aspect of this situation is related to the educational bureaucracy. The teachers of the secondary and grammar schools, themselves tainted by an unholy past, have been extremely reluctant to discuss Hitler with their students. As a consequence, a new German generation is growing up without a proper knowledge of what went on under Hitler. It seems safe to conclude that the present composition of the civil service is still not of a nature to encourage in Germany the growth of a psychological or ideological commitment to the basic principles of democracy.

SELECTED READING

BRECHT, ARNOLD. "Personnel Management." In *Governing Postwar Germany,* Edward H. Litchfield (ed.). Ithaca, N. Y.: Cornell University Press, 1953.

COLE, TAYLOR. "The Democratization of the German Civil Service," *Journal of Politics,* XIV (1952), 3–18.

GLASER, KURT. "Organization and Methods Control." In Litchfield, *loc. cit.*

HERZ, JOHN H. "German Officialdom Revisited, Political Views and Attitudes of the West German Civil Service," *World Politics,* VII (1954), 63–83.

HILLHOUSE, A. M. "Budget Management." In Litchfield, *loc. cit.*

MEIERHOFF, HANS. "Reconstruction of Government and Administration." In *The Struggle for Democracy in Germany,* Gabriel A. Almond (ed.). Chapel Hill, N. C.: University of North Carolina Press, 1949.

MOTT, RODNEY L. "Public Finance." In Litchfield, *loc. cit.*

TAUBER, KURT P. "Over Germany: Shadows of the Past," *The New York Times Magazine,* Section 6, December, 1959.

WEYMAR, PAUL. *Adenauer, His Authorized Biography.* Translated by Peter de Mendelsohn. New York: E. P. Dutton & Co., Inc., 1957.

35

Local Government and Administration

THE LAENDER (STATES)

The Federal Republic of Germany is, as its name indicates, a federal state. The preamble to the Basic Law specifically points out that this Constitution was enacted by the German people in the Laender (States): Baden, Bavaria, Bremen, Hamburg, Hesse, Lower Saxony, North Rhine-Westphalia, Rhineland-Palatinate, Schleswig-Holstein, Wuertemberg-Baden, and Wuertemberg-Hohenzollern. This list is repeated in Article 23 of the Basic Law, which also includes the Land Berlin. Conspicuously absent from this list is the most powerful of the German Laender during most of Germany's history, Prussia.

Since the adoption of the Constitution, several changes in the composition and number of the Laender have been made. In accordance with a special provision laid down in Article 118 of the Basic Law, a plebiscite was held in December, 1951, in Baden, Wuertemberg-Baden, and Wuertemberg-Hohenzollern, which are now combined as the Land Baden-Wuertemberg; and on January 1, 1957, the Saar territory was included in the Federal Republic as a Land. A special situation exists with regard to West Berlin. The three Western Powers do not recognize the sovereignty of the Federal Republic over West Berlin, but the Basic Law applies also to this city wherever it is not in conflict with reservations by the three powers. Consequently, West Berlin is represented in both the Bundestag and the Bundesrat by deputies who do not possess the right to vote.

The Federal Republic consists therefore of ten Laender, not including the city of West Berlin. See Table 35–1 for size and population of the Laender. In comparison, the German Empire was composed of twenty-five states (including the three Hanseatic cities of Hamburg, Bremen, and Luebeck), which were also the constituent Laender of the Weimar Republic. By 1933, this number was reduced to seventeen. Under Hitler, the federal system of the Weimar Republic was abolished and a unitary and highly centralized state was set up. But even during the Nazi regime, fourteen Laender under the name of Reichsgaue survived, at least, as administrative units.

Table 35–1. The Laender of the Federal German Republic, January 1, 1959

Land	Capital	Area (square miles)	Population (thousands)
Schleswig-Holstein	Kiel	6,054	2,276
Hamburg	–	288	1,807
Lower Saxony	Hanover	18,284	6,516
Bremen	–	156	678
North Rhine-Westphalia	Duesseldorf	13,111	15,459
Hesse	Wiesbaden	8,150	4,652
Rhineland-Palatinate	Mainz	7,656	3,355
Baden-Wuertemberg	Stuttgart	13,803	7,433
Bavaria	Munich	27,239	9,278
Saar	Saarbruecken	991	1,040
West Berlin	–	186	2,226
Total		95,918	54,720

SOURCE: Federal Office of Statistics, Wiesbaden, 1960.

The drafters of the Basic Law returned to the federal principle, not only at the request of the occupational powers, but also to accommodate the wishes and intentions of the great majority of the German people. Because of their experiences under the unitary Nazi regime, the return to the federal principle has a deeper meaning to the German people than just legal formality. This federalism is buttressed by Article 28, Section 1 of the Basic Law, which provides that the constitutional order in the Laender must conform to the principles of a republican, democratic, and social Rechtsstaat. A maximum of constitutional homogeneity should exist between the federation and the member states. From this point of view, it is to be understood that the Basic Law stipulates that the federal structure of the German Republic cannot be changed even by a constitutional amendment.

The federal structure of Germany distinguishes between three wide areas of administration: the federation; the Laender; and the local units of government, consisting mostly of communes and municipalities (*Gemeinden*). Since, according to Article 83 of the Basic Law, federal laws are in principle executed by the Laender as matters of their own concern, their position is especially strong as executive agencies. In this situation, which is the normal one, laws are passed by the federal legislature; but the execution and administration are carried out by the Laender or, under the instruction and supervision of the Laender, by the municipalities. As far as federal legislation is concerned, the influence of the Laender can make itself felt only by the Bundesrat. The importance attached to the basic principles of federalism is also indicated by the fact that there is in the federal government a special ministry for Bundesrat and Laender affairs, whose function is twofold: (1) to act as liaison between the federation and the Laender and (2) to transmit their actions and intentions to the Cabinet. It is gratifying to observe that since 1949, there has been cooperation between federation and Laender.

The several Laender of the German Federal Republic adopted permanent constitutions from the years 1946 to 1952. The United States military government took an early lead in this direction. All these constitutions provide for representative parliamentary democracies based upon a broad suffrage and free elections. They all accept the principle of separation of powers. They also contain various provisions for direct democracy through the initiative, referendum, and recall. The constitutions of the Laender are rather lengthy documents due to the inclusion of an extended bill of rights. Most of the constitutions of the Laender of the Weimar Republic did not include such a bill of rights, because the Weimar Constitution with its long list of "fundamental rights and duties" was adopted prior to most of the Laender constitutions of this period. On the other hand, after World War II, the majority of the Laender constitutions were adopted prior to the Basic Law. More conclusively yet, the experiences under the Nazi regime made such detailed safeguards seem absolutely essential.

Before discussing the organizational structure of the Laender, which is very similar to that of the federation, reference should be made to the important problem of the division of financial responsibilities between the federation and the Laender. After the adoption of the Basic Law of May, 1949, the *Bund* (federation) had to take over various burdens that were carried earlier by the Laender in the area of expenditures connected with war damages, social security, and unemployment compensation. The traditional tasks remained with the Laender and the local governmental units (*Gemeinden*). These mainly include internal order and security, education, welfare and public assistance, public health, and road construction. A special place is occupied by the two Hansa cities, Hamburg and Bremen, where the Land and communal budgets are merged to such an extent that they may be regarded as one. The same applies to West Berlin, which was brought into the financial system of the Federal Republic by a law of January 4, 1952. In other Laender too, there are various aspects in the area of welfare and health matters, road construction, and the maintenance of cultural interests that encroach upon both Land and communal interests and may, accordingly, appear as expenditures on various levels of the public administration. Only a very few categories, though financially very important, are borne by the highest level, the Bund, which carries, among others, the burden of defense and the expenses in connection with the NATO Armed Forces stationed in the Federal Republic.

In view of the increased financial responsibilities of the federation, some of the revenues of the Laender were transferred to the federation as a balance for the extended federal burdens. These include customs, the turnover tax, and the tax on consumer goods—excluding the beer tax—together with the non-recurrent levy on capital. With the Laender remained the income and corporation taxes, property taxes, motor vehicle taxes, and several minor taxes. Since the revenues of the Bund did not prove sufficient in view of the constantly increasing expenditures, the Bund has been voted a share of the income and corporation taxes that should have gone to the Laender. Until 1955, the share of the Bund on these taxes was fixed on a yearly basis, which led to severe conflicts between the Laender and the Bund. The Bund wanted to increase its share, especially in view of the increased costs of national defense; the Laender wanted to keep as much as possible. The share of the Bund was 27 per cent in 1951; in the following years, between 37 and 38 per cent.

The distribution of taxes between the federation and Laender was finally settled by a financial reform, introduced by a financial constitutional law of December 23, 1955. This law brought a new formulation to Articles 106 and 107 of the Basic Law. In principle, the existing distribution of taxes between Laender and Bund was maintained; the essence of the reform relates to the percentage of the income and corporation taxes assigned to the federation. According to the new formulation of Article 106 of the Basic Law, the portion allotted to the federation has been 35 per cent since April 1, 1958.

Another aspect of the financial reform does not concern the relationship between federation and Laender, but that among the individual Laender. At the time of the creation of the West German Laender, due consideration had to be given to certain political factors that did not take into account an equal distribution of tax-bearing ability. The wealthier Laender, such as North Rhine-Westphalia and Baden-Wuertemberg, are now balanced against those with little tax-raising power, such as Schleswig-Holstein, Lower Saxony, and Rhineland-Palatinate. To lessen these inconsistencies a horizontal equalization of finances is carried out. In 1958, this affected the following Laender:

To be Paid by:	Million ($)	To be Received by:	Million ($)
North Rhine-Westphalia	84.5	Schleswig-Holstein	65
Baden-Wuertemberg	41	Lower Saxony	49.5
Hesse	11	Rhineland-Palatinate	41
Hamburg	47.5	Bavaria	33
Bremen	4.5		

Another problem exists in relation to the communes. Since they cannot cover their expenditures out of their own revenues, their share of the total receipts from taxes amounts to about 12 per cent only; and in order to insure that they receive their due share of the taxation revenues, they are now receiving a regular percentage of the Land taxes.

The legislative branch of the Laender is called the *Landtag* except in the two city-states, Hamburg and Bremen, where it is called *Buergerschaft.* All the Laender parliaments are unicameral except Bavaria, which has an advisory Senate. They range in size from 90 in Hesse to 215 in North Rhine-Westphalia. The terms of office is in most instances four years. The Senate of Bavaria, which according to the Bavarian Constitution represents the social, economic, cultural, and municipal corporations of the Land, is composed of sixty members. The term of office is six years, one-third of the total membership to be elected every two years. This senate is entitled to initiate legislation and may also object to bills passed by the lower house, the Landtag. These objections, however, may be ignored.

There is hardly a single instance where the political composition of the Laender parliaments and of the governments of the Laender corresponds with that of the federation. While, for example, the Social Democrats in the Bundestag have been in opposition since 1949, they are the majority party in several Laender parliaments, are represented in most of the Laender governments, and provide some of their chiefs. This fact is, naturally, of great importance for the decisions of the Bundesrat, through which the Laender exert their influence on the federal level.

The organization and procedure of the Laender parliaments are very similar to those in the federal legislature. This holds true with regard to matters such as officers of the legislature, standing and special committees, introduction and passage of bills, Councils of Elders, and party groups or *Fraktionen.* Bills may be introduced in the legislature by the cabinet or by one or more members of the Landtag. Similar to the national level, most bills are prepared by the government and introduced by the cabinet.

The chief executive in the Laender is the Minister-President; in the city-states of Hamburg, Bremen, and West Berlin, he is called *Oberbuergermeister* (Lord Mayor). He is elected by the legislature and in turn appoints and heads a cabinet that is responsible to the legislature. An exception is Bavaria. There the Minister-President is elected by the Landtag for four years and cannot be dismissed except by impeachment procedures.

COUNTY AND MUNICIPAL GOVERNMENT

The importance of local government became evident when the higher administrative authorities collapsed in 1945. It was only the local governments that remained to carry on the basic governmental functions. The principal units of local self-government are (1) the *Gemeinde* (municipality) and (2) the *Kreis* (county).

The history of local self-government in Germany is closely connected with its general constitutional development. Local self-government was a significant factor in the medieval towns but was later almost entirely superseded by centralized state administration and a professional staff of state employees. The revival of local self-administration in Germany should be accredited to Baron vom Stein (1757–1831). In his *Nassauische exposee* of June, 1807, he recommended the reconstruction of the Prussian state organization after the Napoleonic Wars on the basis of honorary participation of the citizens in the administration of the local level. He visualized in the *Kommunalselbstverwaltung* (local self-administration) by the citizenry a counterbalance against the monarchical centralized administration by the state. Similar ideas were expressed by Rudolf von Gneist, the *Rechtsstaat* theoretician, who recommended a balance between the monarchical state run by the military and the bureaucracy and a participation of the citizens on an honorary basis in the local and regional administration. In the authoritarian monarchical state, local representation was to be a kind of substitute for self-government of the people.

Baron vom Stein was also responsible for the Prussian City Government Act of 1808, which, although limited by an intense state supervision, became the basis of municipal self-government all over Germany. It remained a permanent institution and was extended to all subunits of the state: provinces, counties, and municipalities.

Local self-administration became more democratic under the Weimar Constitution, which required universal, equal, direct, and secret suffrage for all elections on the basis of proportional representation.

The Nazi dictatorship changed the basis of local self-government; for all practical purposes, it was abolished. This reorganization, on the basis of the *Deutsche Gemeindeordnung* (German Municipal Government Act) of 1935, made the administration of local units uniform all over Germany. Among other things, popularly elected city councils were abolished; the mayor (*Buergermeister*), instead of being directly or indirectly elected, was appointed; the leadership principle was introduced at each local level; and local administration was subject to the most stringent supervision by Reich and party agencies. Under these circumstances, it is not surprising that the allied powers of World War II considered the question of local self-government of utmost importance. The Potsdam Agreement of August 2, 1945, among the United States, Great Britain, and the Soviet Union stated:

> The administration of affairs in Germany should be directed toward the decentralization of the political structure and the development of local responsi-

bility. To this end, local self-government should be restored throughout Germany on democratic principles and particularly through elective councils as rapidly as consistent with military security and the purpose of the occupation.[1]

The reconstruction of local self-government after the collapse of 1945 tended to go back to the pre-1933 precedents.

Since 1945, local administration is regulated by various *Gemeinde* and *Kreisordnungen* (municipal and county government acts) enacted by the several Laender. Contrary to the Weimar Constitution, the Bonn Basic Law leaves, to a large degree, the area of local government to the Laender.

The communes, being organs partly responsible for the execution of laws of both the federation and the Laender, are subject to the supervision of the latter only. When they are called upon to undertake not communal but state duties, they must follow the instructions of the Laender. Except in Schleswig-Holstein, the presidents of the large administrative districts of the Laender (*Regierungspraesidenten*) act on behalf of the Laender governments and exercise legal control over the communes. The self-administration of the communes is laid down by the Basic Law, and in addition is guaranteed by all Laender constitutions. The Basic Law requires the Laender to give the communes the right to regulate all local affairs under their own responsibility and within the framework of the law.

Midway between the Laender and the communes are the *Kreise* (counties). One distinguishes between two types of Kreise: (1) *Stadtkreis* (city-county) and (2) *Landkreis* (rural county). The Stadtkreis evolves from the more populous commune, which initially has the legal title *Stadt;* when the number of inhabitants reaches a certain limit it may become a Stadtkreis. These counties are detached governmentally from the Landkreis in which they are located and are not under the supervision of the county authorities.

The administration of the Landkreis is in part autonomous and in part in the hands of the Land. The *Landrat* (head of the Kreis), or in northwest Germany the *Oberkreisdirektor,* is at the same time in charge of the communal and Land administration. In the case of autonomous administrations, the executive organ is the Kreis council, which is concerned with extra-communal tasks such as road building, hospitals, and welfare. Supervision of the Landkreise and of the administration of the cities, which are themselves Kreise (Stadtkreise), is conducted in the Laender by the Regierungspraesident. The Kreis has not the right to give orders to the communes and does not rank above them.

The several West German Laender constitutions place more emphasis on local self-government than does the Basic Law. They recognize the

[1] "Germany, 1947–1949," in *The Story of Documents* (Washington, D.C.: Department of State, 1950), Publication 3556, p. 49.

two functions assigned to the local units of administration, the communes (*Gemeinden*) and Landkreise. These are units of self-government, entitled to regulate under their own responsibility all the affairs of the local community insofar as they are not assigned to other administrative organs. These so-called *Selbstverwaltungsangelegenheiten* (matters of self-administration) are guaranteed to them by the Basic Law and the Laender constitutions. In addition, the local units of administration are agencies of the Laender for those functions for which no Land offices have been created; in this case, the term *Auftragsverwaltungsangelegenheiten* (matters administered under the mandate of the Land) is used; these are functions of the Land delegated by constitutional provisions or by statute to the local units. In these instances, the units of local government act as agents of the Land and are subject to the orders and supervision of the higher authorities of the Land.

These two areas of activities of the local administrative units are not very easily divided in practice and are a matter of a considerable amount of controversy. In general, it can be said that the ability of the Laender to influence the local units goes further than that of the federation toward the Laender. The Laender can legally issue dictates to the communes in the form of Gemeindeordnungen and Kreisordnungen (municipal and county government acts), order the kind of self-administration that they are to exercise, look into their budgets and finances, alter legally their boundaries, and make the ordinances of the communes dependent on their approval. They have, through the Bundesrat, a decisive voice in the legislation and administration of the federation; whereas the communes have no such authority on the Laender level. On the other hand, since the communes are called upon in frequent instances to administer the laws and must conform to the guidance of the Laender in many of their functions, e.g., the erection of schools, they are demanding and getting a greater share in the apportionment of public income as well as in the preparation of legislation. However, neither the allotment of functions nor the share of charges has yet been finally settled between the Laender and the communes.

The number of self-governing local units at the end of 1958 in the German Federal Republic was 24,526. Of these there are only 3 with a population of over 1 million—West Berlin with 2.2 million, Hamburg with 1.8 million, and Munich with 1 million. Most of the larger cities are located in the Land North Rhine-Westphalia.

Distribution of German Population Living in Communes

24.1% in communes under 2,000 (86.2% of all communes)	12.6 millions
45.4% in small and middle-size cities	23.6 millions
30.6% in large cities	15.9 millions
(Total, excluding West Berlin)	52.1 millions

CULTURAL POLICY AND ADMINISTRATION

It is appropriate to discuss this significant matter in the present chapter because the Basic Law has placed the responsibility for cultural and educational tasks fundamentally in the hands of the Laender. The federation's share in fostering and regulating cultural activities is restricted to only a few spheres of competence, among which are the promotion of scientific research (jointly with the Laender), the protection and preservation of German works of art, and general legislation concerning the press and film. The federal government maintains in the Ministry of the Interior a Department for Cultural Affairs of the Federation that attempts to decide the general direction of cultural policies so far as they fall within the competency of the federation, as well as to decide upon a number of cultural activities lying outside the sphere of the federation. The most important of these federal activities has to do with the promotion of scientific research. During the last few years, twenty to thirty million dollars were made available by the federal Ministry of Interior yearly for research activities.

The actual administration of cultural affairs belongs to the Laender. This includes the important area of education, especially the supervision of the higher scholastic establishments. Each Land has a ministry of culture that acts as the highest authority in the educational field. Because of the need for coordination beyond Laender boundaries, in 1949 a "permanent conference," where the ministers of culture meet regularly, was created. This is a permanent working group that elects a chairman annually and maintains its own secretariat in Bonn. In addition, the Laender approved the so-called Koenigstein Agreement, which jointly financed scientific institutions of more than regional significance. In 1957, the federation participated in maintaining the Koenigstein Agreement with substantial sums to help the Laender build more and larger engineering schools. The permanent conference of the cultural ministers must be credited with several successes in unifying the German educational system. Especially significant is an agreement of the Minister-Presidents of all Laender of February, 1955. Some of its major actions include: (1) the school year all over West Germany starts at the same time (except in Bavaria); (2) uniform regulation of vacations; (3) reciprocity in recognition of matriculating and teaching credential examinations; and (4) steps to standardize the curriculum, with special regard to languages. Earlier, in 1953, a German Committee for Education and Instruction was set up by the Federal Ministry of Education and the President of the Permanent Conference of the Laender Ministers of Culture. It is independent of the educational bureaucracy and gives services in an honorary capacity. Its task has been to work out an over-all conception of German educational and instructional affairs. This Committee, first instituted for a period of five years and in 1958 extended for a similar period, has made a number of positive and valuable recommendations.

In spite of various regional differentiations, there exists in the educational system of the several Laender a considerable amount of uniformity. The Basic Law provides that the entire educational system is under the supervision of the state. The state authority is in this instance represented by the Laender. However, they do not have an educational monopoly. Dr. Heuss recommended to the Parliamentary Council that the right to establish private schools must be guaranteed and should be included in the Basic Law. Hence, private schools have been protected from undue discrimination by the Land. The majority of the schools are public schools administered by the Laender or their subunits. The distribution of the costs is not uniformly regulated in the different Laender; but in general the Laender pay for the costs of the teaching personnel, and the communes for buildings and maintenance.

Germany was the first country to establish a system of popular education. Beginnings of compulsory education go back to the end of the eighteenth century. Now it is applied in all West German Laender for all children. All children have to attend elementary school (*Grundschule*) at the age of six for four years (in Bremen and Berlin for six); from there they pass to either an intermediate school (*Realschule*) or a higher school (*Gymnasium*). In the latter case, there are stiff entrance examinations. In the former case, that of the Realschule, full-time attendance is mandatory for four years, and part-time vocational training for the remainder. That is, the students must remain in school until they are eighteen. The Gymnasium has stiff entrance and final examinations, but the rewards are commensurate; those who graduate are entitled to continue with university education.

During the last five years, the expenditure for general educational purposes (excluding colleges and universities) has been 7 to 8 per cent of the total spent on all governmental levels. In the year 1958, the sum amounted to about one billion dollars; 69 per cent was expended on behalf of elementary, auxiliary, and special schools; and 31 per cent for intermediate schools and *Gymnasien.*

The German colleges and universities serve both research and graduate instruction. Including West Berlin, the Federal Republic has nineteen universities, eight technical universities, and seven smaller colleges consisting of only one specific field. All these universities have identical constitutions (*Rektoratsverfassung*) and the right of self-administration. German universities do not recognize the distinction between faculty and administration. The *Rektor* (president) is elected yearly by the faculty from the available full professors; the same applies for the deans. They continue, when holding these positions, with their lectures and research.

The colleges and universities are state institutions with the right of self-administration. The most important aspects of these are (1) the *Promotion* (the conferment of a doctor's degree); (2) the *Habilitation* (the conveyance of the *venia legendi,* the permission to lecture on the basis of a scientific work); and (3) the self-recruitment of the faculty, the right to propose candidates for positions to the Ministry of Culture of the Land concerned. Under the Basic Law, the organization and maintenance of these establishments is a matter of the Land in which they are located. The Ministry of Culture has the duty of supervising them.

There are different ranks among the faculty in the academic hierarchy, starting out with the *Privatdozent* who has achieved his *Habilitation.* The next major step is the *Extra-Ordinarius* (approximately the associate professor); and the highest rank is the holder of the academic chair, the *Ordinarius* or full professor. At present, there are some 2,600 academic teachers holding a professorial chair.

In 1958, there were 164,472 German and 14,221 foreign students in all German colleges and universities. They were divided as follows:

Major	Total Number
Theology	6,732
Medicine (including dentistry, veterinarians, and pharmacy)	27,527
Law and Economy	43,728
Arts	34,688
Natural Sciences	25,192
Agriculture and Forestry	2,177
Technical studies	32,438

In addition to maintaining the different educational institutions, the Laender and Gemeinden are actively engaged in maintaining or supporting opera houses, theatres, and orchestras. In the territory of the Federal Republic, there are thirty-nine opera houses, more than in any other country of the world. The Federal Republic and West Berlin have a larger number of theatres than any other European country. There is a total of nearly 200 theatres in ninety-seven towns; about 120 of them publicly owned, the rest being private theatres but also subsidized by the units of local government. The large number of opera houses and theatres, having a season of approximately nine to ten months, can be kept going only by subsidy from public funds. This is regarded as normal procedure, since in Germany the theatre is traditionally considered not only entertainment but also an important part of the cultural life of the community. As a result, there is no unwillingness on the part of the public to support these institutions by taxes. The cost for subsidies and maintenance of opera houses and theatres is quite expensive for the Laender and Gemeinden, amounting to approximately thirty million dollars a year.

THE BERLIN PROBLEM

The problem connected with the division of Germany into two parts is best illustrated by the divided city of Berlin, which is one of the most intricate questions in the East-West relationship. Until 1945, Berlin was the capital of the German Reich. In a legal sense, it had a special position during the empire as well as during the Weimar period. Until 1933, it was at the same time a city and Kreis, a governmental district and a province. Under a charter of 1920, Berlin was organized into twenty administrative districts, each with its own local constitution paralleling the one of the central city government. These administrative districts were retained by the Nazis, but the elected central city council and those of the administrative districts were replaced by appointed advisory councilors. At the end of the war, Berlin was occupied by the Red Army, which was in sole control of the city until July, 1945. In accordance with the Yalta Agreement, Berlin was divided into four sectors in July, 1945; of the twenty administrative districts, twelve are under the control of the Western powers, representing West Berlin, and eight under the control of the Russians, representing East Berlin. The four occupation powers established for Berlin a special Allied Control Council under the name *Komandatura.* On October 20, 1946, the first and only elections for Berlin in its entirety took place, in which the Communists (under the name of the Socialist Unity party) suffered a strong defeat; of 130 seats, they received only 26 of the *Stadtverordnetenversammlung* (assembly of city deputies). This body elected in 1947 Ernst Reuter as Lord Mayor (Oberbuergermeister). Reuter, a Social Democrat with an excellent record of opposing nazism as well as communism, was not confirmed as Lord Mayor by the Russians in the interallied Komandatura. The chamber of city deputies, however, refused the election of another person. The Russians, consequently, attempted in 1948 to separate the city of Berlin from the West by closing the approaches by land and water. This action of the Russians forced the Western Allies to institute the airlift providing the Western sectors with necessary supplies by air. The blockade of the Western sectors of Berlin was continued by the Russians until the spring of 1949.

During this period, in November, 1948, the political division of Berlin into two distinctly separated parts took place. The provisional constitution for the whole city, enacted immediately after the war, was to expire in May, 1948; a new draft had been accepted by the Western powers, but not by the Russians. Under these circumstances, the assembly of city deputies, elected in 1946, called for new elections, which were strongly opposed by the Communists, who arbitrarily appointed a new city government composed entirely of Communists, on November 30, 1948. The next day, December 1, the legally elected city legislature moved from the Eastern to the Western sector, with the exception of the deputies of the Socialist Unity party. From this time on, there have been two different Berlins; West Berlin with 2.2 million inhabitants and a size of 186 square miles and East Berlin with a population of 1.2 million and a size of 156 square miles.

A permanent constitution was adopted for West Berlin on August 29, 1950. According to this constitution, Berlin (West) is a Land and city at the same time like Hamburg and Bremen. The government, called the *Senat,* is composed of the governing Lord Mayor (*regierender Buergermeister*), a second mayor, and eleven senators. A chamber of deputies composed of 127 members elects the governing Lord Mayor and upon his recommendations also the members of the Senat. The Lord Mayor from 1949 until his death in September, 1953, was Ernst Reuter; his successor, is Willy Brandt.

The preamble to the Basic Law does not mention Berlin as a Land of the Federal Republic; Article 23, however, enumerates Greater Berlin as one of the Laender. The constitution of Berlin (West) of 1950 calls Berlin one of the Laender of the Federal Republic. This provision has been suspended by the Allies, who did not permit the official incorporation of West Berlin into the Federal Republic in order to avoid a further deterioration of the conflict with the Soviet Union. At the present time the question is settled in such a manner that the representatives of West Berlin are sitting in the Bundestag and the Bundesrat without having the right to vote. These representatives from Berlin are not elected directly by the people, but by the chamber of deputies of West Berlin. On the other hand, a federal law becomes valid in Berlin only after it has been passed by the legislature of the city. Until now, all federal laws have been re-enacted by the chamber of deputies of Berlin. In practice, the Federal Republic and West Berlin act as if Berlin is an integrated part of the Federal Union, although this is not legally true in a formal sense. So, for example, the Federal Constitutional Court cannot examine the statutes of Berlin. On February 6, 1957, however, the Bundestag declared Berlin as capital of the Federal Republic; but the seat of the federal government continues to be Bonn.

The financial situation of West Berlin is mainly characterized by an enormous expenditure of almost 300 million dollars for social purposes. The explanation for this is that about one-third of the population depends wholly or partly on public assistance. As Berlin is included in the financial system of the Federal Republic, it is granted special subsidies to cover the budgetary deficit that arises from its peculiar status. The contributions received by West Berlin from the federation during the year 1958 amounted to almost 400 million dollars.

Berlin represents one of the most difficult problems of the East-West conflict. The Soviet Union demanded on November 27, 1958, that West Berlin should be made a so-called free city without any interference by any foreign power. It is obvious that the populations of West Berlin and of the Federal Republic are strongly opposed to any change in the status of Berlin that would mean a dissolution of the many political, legal, economic, and financial connections of the city with the Federal Republic and the Western world in general. The Berlin problem is not the cause but the consequence of the division of Germany. From a broad point of view, the crisis over Berlin is part of the whole problem of Germany and beyond this a part of the larger struggle of our time between the democratic and the Communist world. Nowhere in the world are the two systems placed so closely together; therefore, nowhere is there so much opportunity for friction, which makes Berlin a constant threat to peace.

SELECTED READING

Clay, Lucius D. *Decision on Germany.* New York: Doubleday & Co., Inc., 1950.

Gillen, J. F. J. *State and Local Government in Western Germany, 1945–1953.* Office of the U.S. High Commission in Germany, 1953.

Lewis, Harold O. *New Constitutions in Occupied Germany.* Washington, D.C.: Foundation for Foreign Affairs, 1948.

Plischke, Elmer. *Berlin: Development of Its Government and Administration.* Office of the U. S. High Commission in Germany, 1952.

Pommerening, H. E. "Local Self-Government in Western Germany," *Quarterly Journal of the Local Self-Government Institute,* XXV (1959), 299–306.

Wells, Roger H. "Local Government." In *Governing Postwar Germany,* Edward H. Litchfield (ed.). Ithaca, N.Y.: Cornell University Press, 1953.

———. "State Government." In Litchfield, *loc. cit.*

36

The Judicial System

NATURE AND HISTORICAL BACKGROUND

Germany is a civil law country. Its legal system makes a definite distinction between private and public law. The term "private law" as used in German jurisprudence signifies all legal provisions regulating the relations between the citizens among themselves and society as private individuals. It includes, therefore, civil and criminal law. (*Zivil* and *Strafrecht.*) Public law refers to that body of legal norms that regulates all official relations and functions of the Bund and the individual Laender and of their agents exercising governmental authority within the framework of existing legal provisions.

In civil law countries like Germany, the judge in principle is not supposed to create law; his duty is only to apply it to given circumstances. The law, any law, public or private, is already in existence.

Germany was made a civil law country by the reception of the system of Roman law in the sixteenth and seventeenth centuries. It has been said that Rome conquered the world three times, first by her armies, second by her religion, and third by her law; and that the third conquest, most pacific of all, was perhaps the most lasting. It definitely affected the legal systems of the different German states, including Austria.

Roman law was received as codified law; this condition persists to the present time. The purpose of the codifications was to bring about uniformity of law, and codifications had been attempted in different parts of Germany even before the French Codes Napoleon. As early as 1495, Emperor Maximilian I organized a Central Imperial Court of Justice, the *Reichskammergericht,* located at Wetzlar. This Reichskammergericht formally declared Roman law to be the common law of the empire.

The first general codification occurred in the field of criminal law. The *Constitutio Criminalis Carolina,* promulgated in 1532 by Emperor Charles

V, exercised a dominant influence on German criminal law for over two centuries. It was superseded in 1769 by a new criminal code, the *Constitutio Criminalis Theresiana.*

Even before this date, a movement was started in Austria to codify the civil law. The first draft of a civil code of 1767 was rejected. Finally, after a trial period of another draft in West Galicia, the Austrian Civil Code for the German provinces was promulgated by Emperor Franz I in 1811. This *Allgemeine Buergerliche Gesetzbuch,* although several times amended and supplemented by special legislation, is still the basis of Austrian civil law.

Friedrich II of Prussia had the project of making a general code of the entire Prussian law, both public and private. However, under his reign, only a code of civil procedure was realized. Eight years after his death the *Allgemeine Landrecht fuer die preussischen Staaten* (general territorial code for the Prussian states) was promulgated. Several German states took over the Codes Napoleon and kept them in force after the downfall of Napoleon. All these were superseded after the unification by the German Civil Code (*Deutsches Buergerliches Gesetzbuch*), which went into effect in 1900 and established a uniform system of codified civil law for the whole of Germany. In addition to this codification of the civil law, there are similar codes relating to criminal law, criminal procedure, civil procedure, commerce, bankruptcy, and other matters.

These broad codifications regulate mostly the area of private and criminal law; but some material that may be considered constitutional law, namely, with regard to civil liberties, is embodied therein. Furthermore, in spite of the extensive body of private, criminal, and also public law laid down in the various law codes, a vast number of special laws have been and are constantly enacted dealing with all kind of subjects superseding or supplementing the provisions of the codes under the Roman law principle *lex specialis derogat legi generali.*

A very important factor and difficult problem in Germany is the selection of the professional judges. In contrast to the situation in the United States, where judges are normally elected or appointed from practicing lawyers, in Germany judges are traditionally considered a species of governmental officials. Organized in a distinctive group, quite separate from the practicing lawyers, the judges are members of a hierarchically organized bureaucracy, the judicial service. Until 1945, the appointment of professional judges was solely in the hands of the ministries of justice. These ministries were the highest segment of the hierarchical system; they supervised administratively the judges, attended to promotions, and acted as a link between the judiciary and the legislature. The ministries of justice, as a matter of fact, prepared the great codifications. The judges, of course, were proclaimed "independent and subject only to the law." However, the control of the judiciary, by a ministry of justice with regard to administration, composition, and promotions placed the judiciary somehow in an inferior position. The extreme dangers of this method of bureaucratizing the judiciary and making it to some degree dependent upon executive authority became increasingly apparent under Hitler, when the servility of the judges to the regime was at least equal, if not greater, than that of the other branches of the civil service. The majority of the Laender still maintain the system of judicial appointments by the ministers of justice. The federation uses now, under the authority of Articles 95, Section 3, and 96, Section 2 of the Basic Law, a system whereby the judges of the high federal courts are appointed jointly by the Federal Minister of Justice and a committee for the selection of judges, consisting of the ministers of justice of the Laender and an equal number of members elected by the Bundestag. In the case of high federal courts in the spheres of administrative, finance, labor, and social jurisdiction, the Federal Minister of Justice and the ministers of justice of the Laender are substituted by the ministers competent in the particular matter. Under the authority of Article 98, Section 4 of the Basic Law, the Laender Hesse, Bremen, and the city of West Berlin now use a system whereby the minister of justice, together with a committee for the selection of judges, decide on the appointment of judges on the Land level.

Because the judges represent a special group among public officials, they are not included in the provisions of the civil service law of 1953. The Basic Law provides that the legal status of the federal judges is to be regulated by a special federal law.

German jurisprudence, after the collapse of the Nazi regime, was faced with the difficult problem of finding a way to a new legal order on a democratic basis. Immediately after 1945, a thorough cleansing process was started to eliminate Nazi influences. At the beginning, the occupation forces suspended a number of statutes and norms that were apparently based on Nazi ideology; but they confirmed the validity of the existing law in general. A general clause of the occupation law restricted the use of existing law only to the extent that it included privileges for Nazis or that it discriminated against persons because of their race, nationality, or religion. German democratic jurists, in spite of their limited number at that time, attempted to make basic changes as soon as possible. First, it was found necessary to go back to the pre-Nazi legal system in order to have the legal order based on the principle of equality before the law and justice for all. It was, however, discovered very soon that the elimination of the Nazi norms and the restoration of the previous legal order required a large amount of new substantive law in order to make legal adjustments. In some instances, the Nazi law had to be retained; in some instances it was impossible to reinstate the previous law; in other instances, new laws had to be created to take care of special problems and circumstances. This situation made the administration of justice for quite some time very difficult; judges and lawyers were frequently not sure what type of law was applicable in certain cases.

It was not possible to start the reconstruction of the legal order on a unified and well-prepared basis before the creation of the various agencies of the federal government in the fall of 1949. The Basic Law, adopted in the meantime, laid down the framework for legislation in this area to a considerable degree. It provided for the erection of the Federal Constitutional Court as the guardian of the constitution and for the creation of high federal courts to look after uniform administration of justice and unity of jurisdiction. The Basic Law also designated the area of civil law, criminal law, and procedural law as concurrent legislation, which gives the federation the power to insure a uniform development in these fields. There were three principal aims in the minds of the German jurists: (1) to restore a unified legal order from the many parts of scattered and dispersed legislation, (2) to complete the elimination of Nazi ideas from the legal order, and (3) to prepare the necessary legislation to implement the requirements of the Basic Law with regard to the judiciary.

These attempts have been very successful in establishing uniformity in the areas of civil law, criminal procedure, organization of the courts, and organization of the bar. The creation of the *Bundesgerichtshof* (Federal High Court) as the highest court of appeals in civil and criminal matters obviously works in the direction of a uniform interpretation of the laws. It has its seat in Karlsruhe. Other federal courts in specialized areas were erected in accordance with Article 96, Section 1 of the Basic Law. These are the Federal Administrative Court and the Federal Court of Discipline in Berlin, the Federal Labor Court and the Federal Welfare Court in Kassel, and the Federal Financial Court in Munich.

In the sphere of civil and mercantile law, the progress of unification of law made much progress; it was possible to return without many difficulties to the *Deutsche Buergerliche Gesetzbuch* (German Civil Code) of 1900 as the basis for handling the legal relations in the sphere of civil law.

More difficulties existed in the area of criminal law. The German Penal Code goes back to 1874, but it was found necessary to pass several amendments (*Strafrechtsaenderungsgesetze*) since 1945. Of special significance in this area is the law of August 30, 1951, dealing with treason, subversive activities, and similar matters. There is still, however, a definite need for reform in this area. A commission for the reform of criminal law was created in 1953 under the chairmanship of Dr. Fritz Neumayer, Federal Minister of Justice from 1953 to 1956. The first draft of the report of this commission has been completed.

Attention should also be drawn to Article 102 of the Basic Law, which abolished capital punishment. This provision does not contain a directive to the legislature to act accordingly, but an actual norm with immediate effect to be obeyed by all West German criminal courts. As a consequence, criminal offences that called for the death penalty are now punished with life imprisonment. Capital punishment could be reintroduced only by a constitutional amendment passed by a two-thirds majority of the Bundestag and the Bundesrat.

THE GERMAN COURT STRUCTURE

The traditional structure of the German judiciary dates back to the *Gerichtsverfassungsgesetz* (a law regulating the constitution and procedure of ordinary courts) of January 22, 1877. The distinction between private and public law is still maintained, and it shows its influence on the organization of the courts. Whereas the United States Constitution provided for the creation of a complete system of federal courts for the adjudication of cases arising under federal law, Article 103 of the Weimar Constitution expressly stated that ordinary jurisdiction is exercised by a *Reichsgericht* and by the courts of the Laender. Article 92 of the Basic Law contains a similar provision; namely, that the judicial authority is exercised by the several federal courts provided for in the Basic Law and by the courts of the Laender. National public law is administered in federal courts only, while national private law is administered in the courts of the Laender. This does not apply to revisional or sometimes appellate jurisdiction; the Reichsgericht under the Weimar Constitution and now the Bundesgerichtshof are Federal Supreme Courts in the area of private law.

The Reichsgericht was established by the law of 1877. The Weimar Constitution preserved the Reichsgericht with basically the same functions exercised under the empire concerning civil and criminal law. It was the highest national court exercising appellate and revisional jurisdiction in civil matters over the decisions of the Supreme Courts of the Laender and in criminal cases over the decisions of the criminal courts of appeal and the jury courts of the Laender.

The task of supreme decisions in civil and criminal law, exercised formerly by the Reichsgericht,[1] now falls to the Bundesgerichtshof (Federal High Court). It was created by a law to restore legal uniformity that went into effect on October 1, 1950. This law also created a hierarchy of ordinary courts for the exercise of civil and criminal jurisdiction. The Bundesgerichtshof is the highest court and the only federal court in this structure of ordinary courts. It has taken the place of the former Reichsgericht. All other ordinary courts are courts of the Laender.

In the area of public law, the Basic Law provided for a Federal Constitutional Court. This is an innovation of utmost importance with regard

[1] The Reichsgericht had its seat in Leipzig, which is located in East Germany.

to its special significance to safeguard constitutionalism. In addition, the Basic Law required the establishment of federal courts with administrative and financial jurisdictions. Some of these administrative tribunals already existed during the empire and the Weimar period, but their number and functions have increased under the authority of the Basic Law. The experiences of the Hitler dictatorship strengthened the view of constitutional lawyers that no legal guaranty has any practical importance if the individual is exposed to the unchecked arbitrary action of governmental agencies. On this account, the principle was accepted that all governmental agencies and all state activity are subject to judicial control. The so-called "General Clause" in administrative law gives every person the right to have any decision of a governmental official tested in an administrative court after the channels within the administrative hierarchy have been exhausted. Demands for such judicial control of administrative procedure were already made in the nineteenth century by Rudolf von Gneist as a condition of the Rechtsstaat principle. This control existed in Germany after 1872, but was eliminated by the Nazis.

The administrative courts of the Laender try claims against administrative agencies on all local levels whose actions are *ultra vires.* On the national level, a *Bundesverwaltungsgericht* (federal administrative court) was created. Disputes arising from acts of federal agencies and conflicts between a Land and the federation not involving a constitutional question are handled by this court.[2] It has also appellate jurisdiction with regard to decisions of the administrative courts of the Laender.

Special finance courts were unknown in Germany prior to 1918. A Reich Finance Court was created in the Weimar period, and a federal law of June 29, 1950, established a *Bundesfinanzhof* (federal high court of finance) on the same lines.

The Basic Law provides also for high federal courts in the area of labor and social jurisdiction. Upon a motion of the Social Democratic party introduced in the summer of 1951, a Federal Labor Court and a Federal Welfare Court were established. The Federal Labor Court is the court of highest jurisdiction with respect to adjudication in labor affairs. Legislation was enacted in 1951 for the establishment of federal disciplinary courts for disciplinary proceedings against federal civil servants. According to the Basic Law, these Courts are permissive but not required. There exists now a High Federal Court of Discipline with its headquarters in Berlin.

The normal administration of justice is in the hands of so-called *ordentliche Gerichte* (ordinary courts), which have "ordinary jurisdiction" in civil and criminal matters. Ordinary jurisdiction not only applies

[2] A case involving a constitutional question would go before the Federal Constitutional Court.

to civil and criminal cases but also to matters not representing a controversy between two parties (civil cases) or to trials of accused persons (criminal cases). *Nichtstreitige* (non-controversial) jurisdiction applies to guardianship of minors, execution of last wills, and similar matters. It is also handled by the ordinary courts.

The structure and organization of the ordinary courts under the Bonn Basic Law is very similar to the one under the Weimar Republic. There remains the combination of a high federal court and a hierarchy of courts on the Land level. There are three levels of courts in the Laender. There is the *Amtsgerichte* (district courts) on the local level, which serve a district generally on the basis of population. A large city, therefore, may have several courts of this type. The second level is represented by the *Landgerichte* (regional courts) located at larger places combining a number of Amtsgerichte in their districts. At the seat of a Landgericht there is always also at least one Amtsgericht, usually in the same court building. The highest courts in a Land are the *Oberlandesgerichte*. Each Land has at least one. There are now nineteen courts of this type in West Germany.

The Amtsgerichte have only original jurisdiction. Cases are brought before these courts on the basis of local competence and subject-matter competence (*oertliche* and *sachliche Zustaendigkeit*). Local jurisdiction is held by an Amtsgericht, in civil cases, if the defendant has his residence within the district of the Amtsgericht or, in criminal cases, if the offence was committed in the district. Subject matter competence depends, in criminal cases, on the nature of the offence. Misdemeanors fall under the competence of the Amtsgerichte. In civil matters, the most important factor deciding this competence is the amount of money involved. Amtsgerichte also handle non-controversial matters. The number of judges at an Amtsgericht is dependent upon the size of the court. It is headed by an *Amtsgerichtsdirektor*. On this level, decisions are handed down by a single judge only.

The Landgerichte have original and appellate jurisdiction. They are headed by a *Landgerichtsdirektor* and are normally divided into two branches: one dealing with criminal, the other with civil matters. In these courts, several judges, usually three, sit together and hand down a collegiate decision. In criminal cases, Landgerichte have original jurisdiction with respect to felony. In many instances lay judges (*Schoeffen*) sit as members of the court. These are chosen from a list submitted by the municipalities. In civil cases, original jurisdiction of the Landgericht is normally dependent upon the amount of money involved and on the nature of the case. Divorce cases, for instance, start at the Landgericht level. They also have appellate jurisdiction on decisions of the Amtsgerichte in criminal and civil matters. The appellate jurisdiction in criminal cases is exercised by various *Strafkammern* (criminal chambers). It is noteworthy that in Germany the jury system as it is used in the United States has not existed since 1924. This system, whereby a jury decides independently on the basis of legal instructions issued by the judge on the question of guilt, has been abolished. When a Landgericht is composed of professional and lay judges, they decide together, on the basis of a majority laid down by law, all questions of fact and law and also of punishment. To each Landgericht, one or more public prosecutors (*Staatsanwalt*) are attached. These officials are not judges; their functions, laid down in the code of criminal procedure, are to initiate criminal proceedings against offenders before the competent court and to represent the case before the court on behalf of the state. No criminal proceedings, except in cases of insult and other minor contentions, can take place without the Staatsanwalt; he is legally obliged to start proceedings if a criminal offence comes to his notice; on the other hand, it is in his power to stop the case at any stage of the proceedings. Public prosecutors are not independent but are subject to instructions by their superiors (*Oberstaatsanwalt*), who in turn are under the Minister of Justice of the Land.

The highest court in a Land is the *Oberlandesgericht* under a *Oberlandesgerichtspraesident.* It decides only by a Senate of several judges and has mostly appellate jurisdiction in civil cases with regard to decisions of the Landgerichte. In many cases, it is the court of last instance. The jurisdiction and competence of the Oberlandesgerichte is laid down in the procedural codes. With regard to administrative matters, these courts act as administrative authorities when they supervise the lower courts located within their area, just as they supervise the clerical and non-judicial staff.

In addition to the three levels of courts in the Laender, the Basic Law provides, in place of the Reichsgericht of the empire and the Weimar period, for a Bundesgerichtshof (Federal High Court) with essentially the same functions as were exercised by the former Reichsgericht. The Bundesgerichtshof, the only federal court in the area of civil and criminal law, exercises revisional jurisdiction over the decisions of the highest Laender courts (Oberlandesgerichte) in civil cases. In criminal cases, it exercises appellate jurisdiction over the decisions of the *Strafkammern* of the Landgerichte. Therefore, in many instances, depending on the case, a civil matter may be decided on appeal by three levels of courts—the Landgericht, Oberlandesgericht, and Federal High Court; in criminal cases, only two levels, a *Strafkammer* of the Landgericht and the Federal High Court, are involved.

The judges of the courts of the Laender are appointed by their respective ministers of justice. The election of the judges of the Bundesgerichtshof is handled in a different way. The ministers of justice of the Laender form, together with an equal number of members of the Bundestag, a committee for the election of the judges of the Bundesgerichtshof. This committee elects, together with the Federal Minister of Justice, these federal judges. The election of a judge requires, therefore, a majority of the committee and the consent of the Federal Minister of Justice. The same method is used for the election of the judges of the other federal courts, only the ministers of justice are replaced by other ministers—so in the case of the Federal Labor Court, the labor ministers; in the case of the Federal Financial Court, the finance ministers; etc. The judges of all federal courts are elected for life. The structure of the German Court is given in Figure 36–1.

THE ADMINISTRATION OF JUSTICE

In view of the unprecedented miscarriages of justice that occurred during the Nazi regime, the Basic Law is extremely concerned with human rights, specifically with the rights of the accused. This basic attitude is reflected in the first article of the Bonn Constitution. The first section states: "The dignity of man is inviolable. To respect and protect it is the duty of all state authority." In line with this emphasis on human dignity, Article 104, Section 1 provides that detained persons may be subjected neither to mental nor physical ill-treatment. It was further elaborated in 1950 by the introduction of a new paragraph into the code of criminal procedure that specifies that the freedom of will or action of an accused is not to be limited by ill-treatment, torture, delusions, hypnosis, or force.[3] In addition, the Penal Code provides that any official who uses force, orders the use of force in any investigation, or who enforces confessions or testimonies will be punished with five years' imprisonment.

Under the Basic Law, the freedom of an individual is under the special protection of the courts. Only a judge can decide on the admissibility or on the extension of a deprivation of liberty; imprisonment in jail or penitentiaries, detention in mental asylums, etc., require a court decision. Even admission to an institution for corrective education can be ordered only by a court. An accused and his lawyer have to be heard in a public trial before a sentence can be handed down. Every accused is entitled to choose his own lawyer. If he is a prisoner of the bar, he can confer with the lawyer of his choice without interference by the police. The *Untersuchungsrichter* (examining judge) who prepares the case for trial may, however, be present at the meetings between the accused and his lawyer, if he finds it necessary.

A prisoner of the bar is not considered guilty; he is only under the suspicion of having committed a criminal offence. A judge, normally the Untersuchungsrichter, is entitled to inflict imprisonment on remand (*Untersuchungshaft*) upon a suspected person, but only on grounds laid down

[3] Code of Criminal Procedure, Paragraph 136a, Sections 1 and 2.

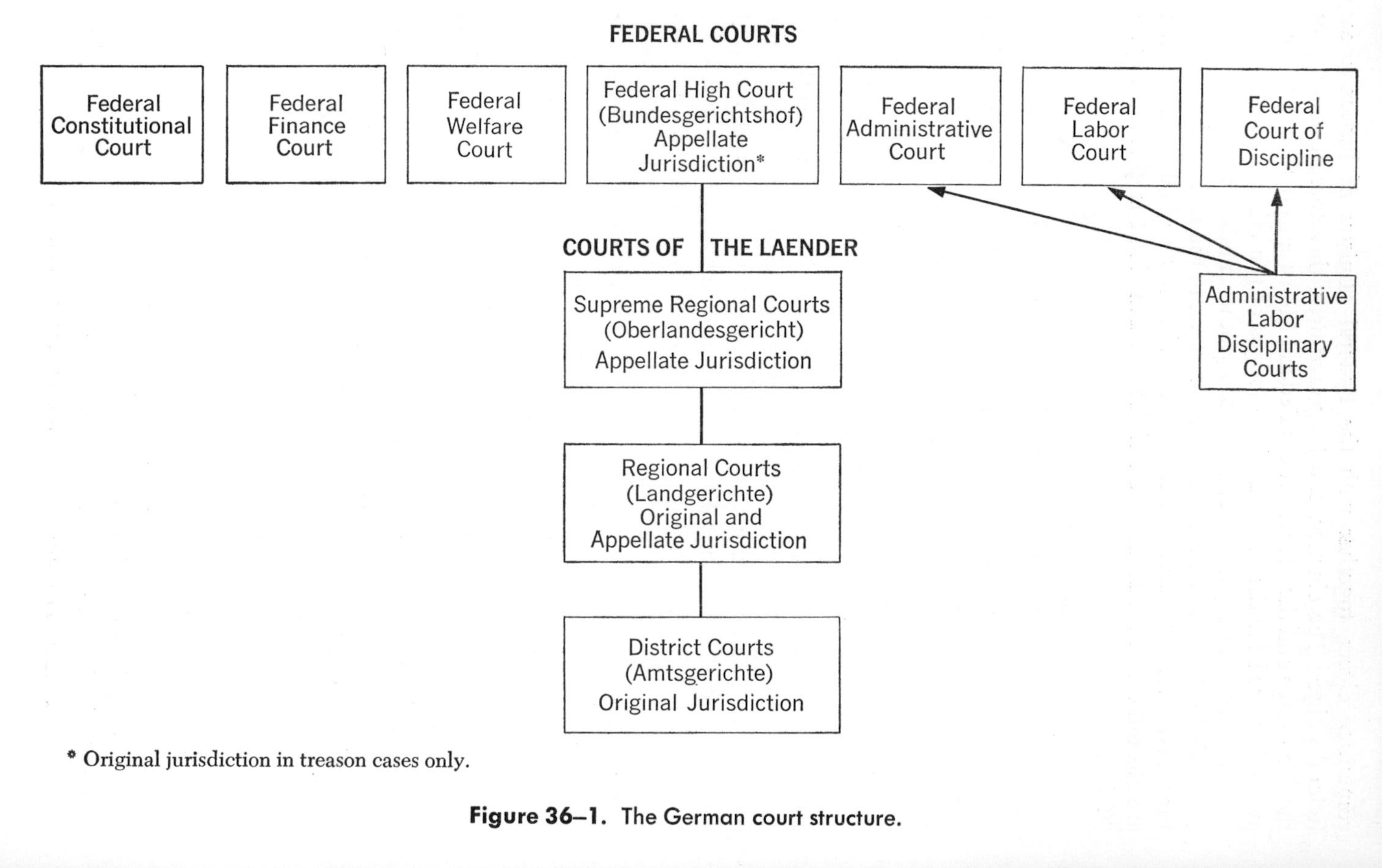

* Original jurisdiction in treason cases only.

Figure 36–1. The German court structure.

by the code of criminal procedure. Certain major crimes make the imposition of imprisonment on remand obligatory; in other cases, the judge is only allowed to impose it if there is a danger of escape, obscuration, or repetition. Only a judge can issue a warrant of arrest, which has to be issued in writing. Against the warrant of arrest, a complaint is possible to a Strafkammer of the Landgericht. In cases where the reasons are gone for the imprisonment on remand, the warrant of arrest has to be annulled and the prisoner is to be set free. The notice of any judicial decision ordering or extending a deprivation of liberty has to be extended immediately to a relative, to his lawyer, or to any person enjoying his confidence. The reason for this provision laid down in the Basic Law can be found in the vicious practice of the Nazis of withholding information about an arrested person's fate from his relatives and friends for months or even years.

The confinement of insane and feeble-minded persons into a mental asylum can also only be ordered by a judge. Any deprivation of liberty not based on the order of a judge has to be authorized without delay by a judicial warrant of arrest. The police may hold no one, on its own authority, in custody beyond the end of the day following the arrest. In addition, the Basic Law provides that any person arrested under suspicion of having committed a criminal offence must be brought before a judge at the latest on the day following the arrest. This judge, almost without exception the Untersuchungsrichter, will inform the suspect of the reasons of the arrest, interrogate him, and give him the opportunity to raise objections. The judge must either immediately issue a warrant of arrest, giving the reasons, or order the release of the detained person. The judge is equally as responsible for the release as he is for the continuation of the arrest. The police are not permitted to rearrest a released or acquitted person. An independent court, of which the Untersuchungsrichter is not supposed to be a member, decides whether a criminal offence has been committed and the extent of the punishment. The public prosecutor has to give information to the court during the whole procedure from the arrest until the sentence or acquittal. The sentence of the trial court has to be handed down in written form giving the reasons for the decision. It can be appealed by the convicted person as well as by the public prosecutor to a higher court, which can change the conviction or the acquittal.

The length of imprisonment on remand, imposed by a judge, is not limited. However, the reasons for the arrest have to be re-examined after one month; and afterwards, every three months.[4]

The courts also can order the compulsory attendance of accused persons, who are not in prison, and of witnesses. The police are permitted to arrest persons caught in the act of committing a criminal offence; they

[4] The prisoner on remand can also appeal to a Strafkammer against his detention.

also may send insane and mentally disturbed persons who endanger the public peace and order to mental institutions. All these police measures have to be brought without delay to the attention of a court and be placed under judicial supervision. The police are empowered to keep drunk persons, vagrants, etc., in custody for forty-eight hours; in such a case, the custody represents a protection of the detained person. After twenty-four hours, however, the matter has to be brought before a judge. Protective custody (*Schutzhaft*) can only take place upon the request of an endangered person. The detention of a person threatened by a mob, for example, not only requires the consent of the detained, but also the confirmation of a judge. The device of Schutzhaft was frequently used at the beginning of the Nazi regime. Demonstrations by a hostile mob were instigated against persons who were not favored for political or other reasons; these persons were detained "for their own protection" and kept imprisoned indefinitely. The inmates of the concentration camps were to a large extent classified as *Schutzhaeftlinge* (protective prisoners).

According to the Basic Law, everyone is entitled to a proper hearing before the courts. Everyone is entitled to state his case and his legal interpretation of the circumstances before the competent court. This applies to civil as well as criminal cases. Nobody can be convicted without having been heard. The Basic Law provides also that an act may be punished only if it was declared a criminal offence by law before it was committed. This provision reflects the principle *nulla poena sine lege* (no punishment without a law) and also represents a protection against ex post facto laws in criminal matters.

In view of the experiences in the administration of justice during the Hitler period, the Basic Law contains a kind of double jeopardy clause, whereby no one may be punished for the same act more than once. It happened frequently that the Gestapo rearrested a released person if, according to their opinion, a too lenient punishment was handed down by the court. Pastor Niemoeller was acquitted by the court in 1938; on leaving the court building he was arrested by the Gestapo and sent to a concentration camp where he remained until the end of the war. Such arrests may occur legally only with the consent of the Strafkammer.

The codes of civil and criminal procedure not only provide for the constitutional guaranty that everyone is entitled to a proper hearing before the courts, but also assure that their legal position is presented professionally. As a consequence, needy persons involved in a civil case are entitled to the *Armenrecht* (right of poor parties), which makes the services of an attorney available to them without costs. In criminal cases, the courts appoint a defending attorney to represent a needy accused person during his trial.

THE FEDERAL CONSTITUTIONAL COURT

One of the most significant changes introduced by the Basic Law as compared with the Weimar Constitution is the creation of a Federal Constitutional Court and the introduction of judicial review. The Weimar Constitution left the question of judicial review of legislation open; Article 93 of the Basic Law gives the power of judicial review to a Federal Constitutional Court.

With regard to the composition and structure of this Constitutional Court, it is remarkable that the Basic Law merely stipulates that the members of this Court shall consist partly of federal judges, partly of others, leaving the details to a special law. The first law determining the organization and procedure of the Federal Constitutional Court was enacted in 1951. It provided for twenty-four members divided into two senates. The original law was amended in 1956; the amendment reduced the number of justices temporarily until August 1959 to ten judges for each senate. Since August 1959, the Court has been composed of two senates of eight judges each. The president of the Federal Constitutional Court presides over one senate, his deputy over the other one. The justices of the two senates cannot substitute for one another. Six justices have to be present before a senate can make a decision. The first senate decides over cases involving the forfeiture of basic rights, the constitutionality of political parties, review of elections in the Bundestag, constitutional complaints, and the constitutionality of legislative acts. The second senate decides in cases of impeachment of the Federal President or the federal judiciary, over disputes among the constitutional organs of the Federal Republic, and over disputes between the federal government and the Laender.

The election of the justices is very complicated. Half of them are elected by the Bundestag and half by the Bundesrat. Six of the present number of sixteen (three for each senate) have to be chosen from the high federal courts; these justices hold office for life. The other ten members are elected for an eight-year term with the possibility of re-election. The members chosen by the Bundestag are elected by an election committee composed of twelve deputies. A two-thirds majority is required in the Bundesrat and in the election committee of the Bundestag.

The justices must be at least forty years of age and be qualified either for a judicial career or for the higher administrative service. They should be distinguished by the possession of special knowledge of public law and by experience in public life. The two houses elect in turn the president and the vice-president of the Federal Constitutional Court. The vice-president is to be elected from the senate to which the president does not belong.

The jurisdiction and competence of the Federal Constitutional Court is laid down in Article 93 of the Basic Law. The most important function of the Court is the so-called *Normenkontrolle* (control of legal norms). The Constitutional Court decides upon the compatibility of federal law and Land law with the Basic Law or on the compatibility of Land law with other federal law. This is done under the principle of a hierarchy of norms; the Basic Law represents the highest norm, followed in turn by federal statutes and ordinances, and the constitutions, statutes, and ordinances of the Laender. The Federal Constitutional Court has to decide whether a lower norm within this hierarchy of norms is in line with the higher norm; for example, a statute passed by the legislature of a Land in an area belonging to the exclusive legislation of the federation must be declared unconstitutional; the same would be true with regard to federal legislation contradicting the provisions of the Basic Law. It is remarkable that the exercise of judicial review by the Federal Constitutional Court can be initiated only in two ways. In the first case, the initiative is given to the federal government, a Land government, and to one-third of the members of the Bundestag. The last situation gives a minority in the legislature the opportunity to appeal to the Constitutional Court with regard to a law that was passed and considered unconstitutional by the minority. This applies, of course, only to enacted legislation and not to mere legislative proposals. Decisions of the Constitutional Court in this area have the force of law and have to be promulgated by the Federal Minister of Justice in the *Federal Gazette*. If the Federal Constitutional Court has declared a federal statute unconstitutional, a similar statute can neither be introduced nor passed by the legislature. The passing of such a law would be possible only by means of a constitutional amendment.

The second possibility of testing the constitutionality of a law is laid down in Article 100 of the Basic Law, giving to the courts the right to initiate procedure before the Federal Constitutional Court. If a court considers a law unconstitutional but feels that its validity is pertinent to its decision, proceedings must be interrupted. In case the violation of a Land constitution is at issue, a decision of the Constitutional Court of the Land shall be obtained. If, however, a violation of the Basic Law is at issue, a decision of the Federal Constitutional Court shall be obtained. This applies also if the violation of the Basic Law by Land law or the incompatibility of a Land law with a federal law is at issue. In this provision, the American principle of judicial review is incorporated in a modified way. All courts may apply only valid law, and they have to examine whether the law to be applied is constitutional or not. The ordinary German courts have only the power to review legislation preliminarily. The law providing for the organization and procedure of the Federal Constitutional Court provides, in accordance with the wording of Article 100 of the Basic Law, that the submission of a legal norm by an ordinary court to the decision of the Federal Constitutional Court is independent from the parties involved in the case. If the courts decide that the law is constitutional, it cannot be brought before the Constitutional Court. Only if the law involved is considered unconstitutional by the ordinary courts can it be submitted to the Federal Constitutional Court. If the Federal Constitutional Court decides that the law is unconstitutional, the court asking for the decision is not permitted to apply the law in the present case or any future one.

The establishment of the Federal Constitutional Court and the recognition of the doctrine of judicial review by the Basic Law initiated speculation in the area of legal philosophy relating to the democratic principle. The Weimar Constitution as well as the Bonn Basic Law pronounced that all state authority emanates from the people. However, the principle of the emanation of state authority from the people lost some of its meaning by the introduction of judicial review, which increased the power of the judiciary. It has been pointed out that the establishment of a Constitutional Court and its relationship to the legislature supersedes the principle that the people are the sole source of state power. Politically, the most important function of the Federal Constitutional Court is to review the constitutionality of legislative acts enacted by the Bundestag, the only federal institution elected directly by the people. In this respect, the judicial power as exercised by the Federal Constitutional Court is superior to the legislative power that emanates from the people. The Constitutional Court cannot issue orders to the legislature and cannot force the Bundestag to pass legislation, but it can annul the work of the legislature; whereas the Bundestag, representing the power of the people as the source of state authority, does not have this power with regard to the decisions of the Federal Constitutional Court. Nonetheless, the drafters of the Basic Law, under the strong influence of the American doctrine of judicial review, considered that the guaranty of the democratic principles laid down in the Basic Law, is best safeguarded by a Constitutional Court.

Among the other functions given to the Federal Constitutional Court, two are of specific interest. They relate to the possibility of a declaration of forfeiture of basic rights and to the possibility of declaring a political party unconstitutional.

One of the main principles of the Bonn Basic Law is to protect the democratic constitutional order from its enemies who would use their constitutional rights for the purpose of attacking the democratic Constitution itself. This position is explainable when one considers the experiences with extremists of both the Right and the Left during the Weimar period. In contrast to most other constitutions, political parties are explicitly recognized by the Basic Law. Article 21, Section 2 of the Basic Law, however, provides that parties that, according to their aims and the conduct of their followers, seek to impair or abolish the basic system of a free and democratic order or to jeopardize the existence of the Federal German Republic, are unconstitutional. It is the function of the Federal Constitutional Court to decide on the question of unconstitutionality of a political party. The proceedings before the Court against a political party start on the request of the federal government, the Bundestag, or the Bundesrat. A Land government can only request to outlaw a political party whose activities and organization are limited to the area of the Land. This constitutional provision is new; it was customary to leave the problem of prohibition of subversive and other dangerous groups to the executive or eventually to the legislature. In a constitutional system like the United States, the constitutionality of such governmental action could be challenged by the parties affected before the courts. In the German Federal Republic, the governmental agencies can only request the prohibition of political parties before the Federal Constitutional Court; it is up to the Federal Constitutional Court to determine what kind of activities represent an attempt to impair, endanger, or destroy the democratic state. If the request of the government or the legislature is justified in the eyes of the Constitutional Court, the political party involved is declared unconstitutional. Connected with this declaration is the dissolution of the party and the prohibition to found a substitute party. Deputies of the party declared unconstitutional lose their seats in the legislature. The Constitutional Court declared the neo-Nazi Sozialistische Reichspartei unconstitutional in 1952. Basic among the reasons given by the Court was the anti-American and anti-Semitic attitude of the leaders of this party. In 1956, the Federal Constitutional Court declared the Communist party unconstitutional.

Similar reasons are behind Article 18 of the Basic Law, which provides that whoever abuses the freedoms guaranteed by the Basic Law with regard to speech, press, etc., in order to attack the free democratic order forfeits these basic rights. The forfeiture of basic rights shall be determined by the Federal Constitutional Court. In these cases, the procedure before the Federal Constitutional Court starts on request of the federal government, the Bundestag, or the government of a Land. The Constitutional Court states in its decision which type of basic right of the defendant is forfeited. The forfeiture can be limited to a certain period, at least to one year. It can be combined with a deprivation of the right to vote or of the right to be elected or appointed to public office. In cases arising under Article 18 of the Basic Law, a re-examination of the decision is permitted. This possibility does not exist with regard to political parties declared unconstitutional under Article 21 of the Basic Law. If the forfeiture of basic rights is unlimited or of a longer duration than one year, the Federal Constitutional Court may abolish the forfeiture of the basic rights partly or fully two years after the original decision.

Among the other functions of the Federal Constitutional Court is the impeachment trial of the Federal President in accordance with Article 61 of the Basic Law and the impeachment trials of federal judges according to Article 98, Section 2 of the Basic Law. The Constitutional Court also hears appeals against decisions of the Bundestag with regard to the loss of the seat of a member.

In addition to the cases that can be referred to it by federal and Laender agencies, by courts, and other organizations, the Federal Constitutional Court also receives petitions for relief, or constitutional complaints (*Verfassungsbeschwerde*), from any individual who feels that his constitutional rights have been violated, either by statute or by administrative or judicial action.

The creation of the Federal Constitutional Court and the introduction of judicial review are one of the most significant innovations of the West German constitutional system. Judicial review, as a means of guarding the Constitution and protecting individual liberties against totalitarian action and undemocratic use of governmental power, was adopted by several European postwar Constitutions. The German Basic Law went especially far in increasing the judicial power as the guardian of the Constitution. The emphasis on civil rights and liberties and the entrustment to the Federal Constitutional Court of their protection is of utmost significance, representing a constitutional change from the traditional predominance of the executive power. In addition, the strong democratic character of the Basic Law, whose protection is the main task of the Federal Constitutional Court, represents an attempt to institutionalize democratic principles by means of judicial control.

The Federal Constitutional Court took over its important functions with vigor and without hesitation. In its first decision, it declared one federal law fully and another partly unconstitutional.[5] It is remarkable that this decision and all that followed were generally accepted all over West Germany. If this tribunal continues in this direction and succeeds in establishing for itself a prestige similar to that which is held by the United States Supreme Court, the outlook for German constitutionalism and democracy should be better than ever before.

SELECTED READING

COLE, TAYLOR. "The West German Federal Constitutional Court, an Evaluation After Six Years." *Journal of Politics,* May, 1958, pp. 278–307.

[5] Decision of the Federal Constitutional Court of October 23, 1951, 2 BVG 1/51.

LEIBHOLZ, GERHARD. "The Federal Constitutional Court in Germany and the South West Case," *American Political Science Review*, XLVI (1952), 723–31.

LOEWENSTEIN, KARL. "Justice." In *Governing Postwar Germany*, Edward H. Litchfield (ed.). Ithaca, N.Y.: Cornell University Press, 1953.

NAGEL, H. "Judicial Review in Germany," *American Journal of Comparative Law*, III (1954), 233–41.

RICH, BENETT M. "Civil Liberties in Germany," *Political Science Quarterly*, LXV (1950), 68–85.

RUPP, HANS G. "Judicial Review in the Federal Republic of Germany," *The American Journal of Comparative Law*, IX (Winter, 1960), 29–47.

37

Germany Today

THE GOVERNMENT OF EAST GERMANY

Germany is a divided country. After World War II, the Soviet Union received as her zone of occupation the territory west of the Oder-Neisse line consisting of the former Prussian provinces of Pommerania and Brandenburg and the Laender Saxony, Thuringia, and Mecklenburg. This territory, the German Democratic Republic or East Germany, has an area of 41,646 square miles, including East Berlin. This is about one-fourth of the former Reich territory. The population is about seventeen million.

In 1945, the Russian occupation authorities permitted four political parties: the Communist party, the Social Democratic party, the Christian Democratic Union and the Liberal Democratic party. The Social Democrats were quickly eliminated as an independent party in the first postwar municipal elections, which took place in September 1946. The party united with the Communist party into the German Socialist Unity party. (*Sozialistische Einheitspartei Deutschlands*—SED). It is interesting to note that at the above-mentioned elections, the SED received only 52.4 per cent of the vote against 40 per cent for the Christian Democratic Union and the Liberal Democratic party; although these two parties were allowed to name candidates in only about 2,000 of the 11,623 municipalities. In the elections for the Laender parliaments held in October 1946, the SED received only 47.6 per cent of the vote.

After these elections, the SED recognized that it was not able to receive a parliamentary majority on the basis of free elections. By means of organizing *Volkskongresse* (People's Congresses), all legal political opposition against the SED was eliminated. The first People's Congress convened in December 1947; the second, which took place in 1948, declared itself a German People's Council and was ordered by the Russians to draft an all-German Constitution. After the West German Basic Law had been adopted, this Council changed itself under instructions of the Russian military authorities to a provincial People's Chamber (*Volkskammer*), which nominated Otto Grotewohl of the SED as Prime Minister and Walter Ulbricht, the general secretary of the party, as Deputy Prime Minister. This Council drafted and a constitutional convention ratified a Constitution for East Germany. Both the Council and convention were controlled by the SED. In spite of this twofold situation, only 66 per cent of the votes were cast for the confirmation of the composition of the convention.

The wording of the Constitution of the German Democratic Republic is similar in many instances to that of the West. Its real importance is, however, not more than that of the Constitution of the U.S.S.R. The real power in East Germany is in the hands of the Politbureau and the Secretariat of the party. They act formally through the institutions of the state as laid down in the Constitution. According to the Constitution, the Volkskammer (People's Chamber) is the supreme authority of the Republic. It is composed of 400 deputies to be elected by the people in universal, equal, and secret elections for a period of four years according to the principle of proportional representation. All citizens over the age of eighteen can vote; all citizens over the age of twenty-one can stand for elections. Insofar as elections occur only on the basis of lists submitted by the SED, the Volkskammer cannot be considered as a real representative legislative body. The proof for this is that its decisions are almost without exception unanimous. Legislation can be enacted either by the Volkskammer or directly by the people by the means of a referendum. According to the Constitution, the Prime Minister is to be appointed by the party with the greatest strength in the People's Chamber. According to the Constitution, all parties having at least forty members are to be represented in the government by ministers or state secretaries in proportion to their strength. Due to the predominant position of the SED, these provisions of the Constitution are meaningless. The government has to be confirmed by the Chamber. The size of the government is subject to constant changes. In 1956, the government was composed of a Prime Minister (Minister Praesident), nine deputies of the Prime Minister, twenty-five ministers, and seven state secretaries. The Prime Minister and his deputies form the Presidium of the Council of Ministers, wherein resides the real leadership of the government. Of course, the Presidium is strongly interlocked with the leadership of the SED. The Constitution also provides for a President, to be elected by the People's Chamber and a so-called Laender Chamber for a term of four years. This Laender Chamber was originally established to represent the Laender. Each Land was to have one representative for every 500,000 inhabitants. A "Democratization Law" of 1952 eliminated the Laender governments and the Laender parliaments because the administration of the Laender was considered a source of possible opposition. To replace them, fourteen administrative districts (fifteen with East Berlin) were created. The People's Chamber can override decisions taken by these districts; East Germany is consequently now a rigidly administered centralized state. The Laender Chamber is still in existence, in spite of the abolishment of the Laender.

The position of the judiciary in the German Democratic Republic is different from the one in the German Federal Republic. The judges are not appointed for life time but only for a period of three years by the Minister of Justice. The justices of the Supreme Court are elected by the People's Chamber for a period of five years. They may be recalled by the Chamber if they violate the Constitution or the law or commit a serious breach of their duties as judges. This means that their judgments have to be in line with the position of the party.

A very important officer in East German government is the *Generalstaatsanwalt* (Prosecutor-General) modeled after the Procurator-General of the U.S.S.R. He is not under the Minister of Justice but directly under the Council of Ministers. He has the authority to appoint and to dismiss the public prosecutors. He is elected by the People's Chamber for a five-year term and has the power of supreme supervision over all ministries and all governmental departments and institutions, as well as over the individual citizens with regard to their strict compliance with the law.

Just like in the U.S.S.R., the real seat of power in East Germany is not to be found in the official structure of the government, but in the party. The Sozialistische Einheitspartei, which is now entirely communistic, is the dominant organization. Its membership, which was reduced over the years, is now around one million. The present statute of the party dates from 1954 and is very similar to the statute of the Communist party of the U.S.S.R. Parts of it are actual translations. The organizational structure of the party is based upon the principle of democratic centralism. The principle means that all organs of the party are elected from below, but that the decisions of the higher organs are binding for the lower echelons. The highest level of the party is the *Parteitag* (party conference), which convenes every four years. It elects the Central Committee, which has to execute the decisions of the Conference and is the highest organ between the party conferences. The Central Committee is now composed of about ninety members and forty-four alternates. It holds a plenary session every four months. In view of its large numbers and the relatively few sessions, it is not very influential; it elects, however, the Politbureau and the Secretariat. The Politbureau is now composed of nine members. First secretary of the Politbureau is Walter Ulbricht, the leading figure of the East German regime. Ulbricht, who has been a member of the German Communist party since its foundation, was in Russia from

1934 to 1945 and since that time has been continuously a member of the Politbureau. He was a Stalinist but even so has been able to hold his leading position during the vicissitudes in the Communist world since Stalin's demise.

The political life of the German Democratic Republic is determined by constantly changing policies of the other states of the Eastern bloc. During the fifties, a basic change in the whole economic structure has taken place, in the course of which the majority of private businesses have been nationalized. It is estimated that by 1956, about 85 per cent of industry and trade had been nationalized. In the course of the agrarian reforms and collectivizations, only a few of the former 83,000 farms of more than 20 hectares are still in existence.

For a long time, the economic conditions in East Germany were incomparably worse than in the Federal Republic. The standard of living is still far behind. A certain improvement has taken place during recent years, as shown by the abolition of the rationing of foods in 1958 and an increase in variety and quantity of consumer goods. The average purchasing power of the population of East Germany is estimated at approximately 30 per cent lower than in West Germany.

The German Democratic Republic is in a unique position as far as its legal international status is concerned. From the point of view of the Soviet Union, East Germany as well as West Germany are both sovereign states; for the Federal Republic and the Western powers, East Germany is neither a state nor part of a foreign state but a part of an undivided Germany, whose population is restrained by a foreign power, namely, the U.S.S.R., from joining the Federal Republic. As can be seen from the preamble to the Basic Law, the German Federal Republic does not claim an immediate unification of the two Germanies, but wants free elections in both areas of a national assembly that could decide over the constitutional, political, and economic structure of a reunified Germany. The West German government is not willing to recognize the East German regime. The East German government, on the other hand, is prepared to recognize the Federal Republic, because either it is ready to maintain the division of Germany or wants to achieve reunification on the basis of a treaty that would institutionally guarantee Communist influence. In spite of the fact that there are no direct official relations between the governments of the German Federal Republic and the German Democratic Republic, it is impossible that the two territories can exist without communications on trade relations. The problem of transportation, railroad connections, and exchange of goods had to be dealt with in some manner. Consequently, there are a number of trade and exchange agreements between the two Germanies. These exchanges amount yearly on both sides to hundreds of millions of dollars.

THE PROBLEM OF REUNIFICATION

The fact that Germany is divided into two politically and economically antagonistic states represents not only the most important German problem, but also a problem of utmost international significance. There is no doubt that there exists a genuine desire of all Germans, no matter whether they are in the East or in the West, for reunification. This basic attitude has to be recognized by all political parties and all political leaders. The West German federal government has attempted, with the backing of the Western powers, to achieve German reunification by means of free elections in all Germany. This position is based upon the justified assumption that such free elections would bring about a crushing defeat for the Soviet supported regime of East Germany. These attempts have hitherto been repudiated by the authorities of the German Democratic Republic under the instructions of the Soviets. Instead, the Soviet Union has proposed direct negotiations between the Bonn and Pankow governments (Pankow in East Berlin is the seat of the East German government). Over and over again, Russia also used the threat of concluding a separate peace treaty with East Germany. At a number of top-level international conferences during the last years, the problem of Germany was the key subject on the agenda; among them were the summit conference at Geneva in 1955 and the Foreign Ministers conference in Geneva in summer 1959. The German problem was also to have top priority at the unfortunate summit conference at Paris in May 1960. At all these conferences and negotiations, there was little chance to find concrete agreement over Germany because of the complexity of the problem and because of its inextricable involvement with the great ideological and power-political controversies between the East and West. The whole problem of German reunification is further complicated by the fact that it is interrelated with the questions of European security, disarmament, and East-West contacts. This is inevitable because the question of the re-establishment of German unity cannot be solved as an isolated problem in itself. This interrelation of so many problems shows that obstacles have to be overcome to find a workable solution. The Ambassador of the German Federal Republic in Washington, Wilhelm Grewe, pointed out that the question, in truth, is not whether and how Germany can be reunited, but rather whether and under what conditions a peaceful settlement between the great power blocs in East and West can be achieved.[1] German reunification is not within the possibility of the will of the German people nor the two German states. For this reason, it is appropriate to indicate in general lines the positions

[1] Wilhelm Grewe, *Germany and Berlin* (Washington, D.C.: German Embassy, Press and Information Office, 1960), pp. 7 ff.

of the Soviet and the Western powers. These positions are backed by the German governments, respectively; the West German government has, without any doubt, a much stronger influence on the West than the East German government on Russia.

The primary feature of the Russian position, as last proposed at the conference of the Foreign Ministers in Geneva in the summer of 1959, is the conclusion of a peace treaty with the two German states and also the creation of a so-called "Free City of West Berlin." The three Western powers, in agreement with the Federal Republic, presented on May 14, 1959, a new proposal for Germany, designated as a peace plan; its main features were reunification of Germany by gradual stages, providing for free elections within a period of two and a half years; early reunification of Berlin as a first step on the way to German unity; a number of general security and disarmament proposals, including a provision of commitments to intervene against aggression; and, assurances by both sides that their armed forces will not advance beyond the former line of demarcation between the two parts of Germany. Until the present time these two positions have been found irreconcilable. The West left no doubt that a peace treaty with two German states is just as unacceptable as the creation of a "Free City of Berlin," which would really change the twofold partition of Germany into a threefold one. The Soviet rejection of the Western proposal was unconditional as far as the West Berlin plan was concerned; but as the Western plan was submitted as an interrelated whole, the Soviet position was equal to complete rejection. Under these circumstances, the reunification of Germany cannot yet be foreseen; the same applies to the conclusion of a peace treaty with a unified Germany. This situation is naturally a constant danger to peace, although it is itself only a result and concretism of the East-West conflict. There is the always existent possibility that the Germans themselves may under certain circumstances undertake the reunification of their country, which under the present power distribution in Europe would indeed be extremely dangerous to peace.

It should be pointed out that pending the signatures of a peace treaty, the territories of the German Reich as it existed before World War II, lying east of a line defined by the rivers Oder and Neisse were placed by the Potsdam Agreement in 1945 under Polish administration, and the northern part of East Prussia was under Russian administration. In 1939, the German population of the eastern territories numbered approximately ten million. This part amounts to almost one-fourth of the total German area according to the boundaries of 1937. The Allies decided at the Yalta Conference to compensate Poland for the territories of East Poland annexed by the Russians by moving the Polish frontiers further to the west and the north. The final boundaries were to be laid down by the peace treaty with Germany; accordingly, the Oder-Neisse line is legally at the present time only a temporary solution. When the Russians occupied these territories at the beginning of 1945, there were only about three and a half million Germans still in residence. Far more than half of the population had fled to the West to avoid the advancing Russian Armies. In the summer of 1945, about one million refugees returned to the eastern territories; the German population of this area at the time of the Potsdam Agreement amounted to about four and a half million. A majority of them were expelled in the years 1945 to 1947. Only about two million of the inhabitants remained. Of these, more than one million were recognized as "autochthonous" on account of Polish sounding names and other factors that made it difficult to decide whether they belong ethnically to Poland or Germany. These "Autochthons" received Polish nationality in 1947. From 1950 to 1957, more than 100,000 people from the Polish administered eastern territories became domiciled in the area of the German Federal Republic on the basis of an agreement to bring separated families together. The exact number of Germans in these territories at present is very difficult to establish; the recognized German minority was officially given by the Polish authorities in 1955 as 150,000 and in 1957, as only 65,000. Since 1945, more than five million Polish settlers have come into this region. The northern part of East Prussia was settled with about 700,000 settlers from western and central Russia. The total population of the territories east of the Oder-Neisse line was at the end of 1958, approximately seven and a half million in comparison with ten million just before the war. As can be seen from these figures, a population movement of major proportion took place in these territories during the last fifteen years; and any attempts to reinstate the status quo ante is quite certain to lead to violent conflicts. The re-expulsion of the millions of Poles from these territories would necessarily also mean an extreme amount of human hardship and misery. A reunified, strong, and militaristic Germany trying by force to regain these territories can only be too easily visualized; this is another, often forgotten, danger point for peace in Europe. There is, of course, no doubt that the historical claim of Germany for this area goes back many centuries.

The position of the two German governments to these territories east of the Oder-Neisse is, naturally, entirely opposing. The Federal Republic maintains the position that the question of the German eastern frontier can be solved only by a peace treaty with a legitimate government of a unified Germany; it also maintains that the territory of Germany at the end of 1937 should be the basis for the German frontiers. The East German government concluded in 1950 an agreement with Poland regarding the inviolable frontier of peace and friendship between Germany and

Poland on the Oder and the Neisse. The Federal Republic considers this agreement as unvalid and argues that the East German regime was and is not entitled to solve questions appertaining to the whole of Germany.

The problem of German reunification is without any doubt the main goal of the foreign policy of the Federal Republic. In view of the political situation emerging from the East-West conflict, the German people by themselves cannot achieve this goal by peaceful means. The restoration of the unity of Germany as one state remains closely connected with the conclusion of a peace treaty that is still as far away as it was fifteen years ago. So far, officially, only the state of war with the German Reich has been ended through unilateral declarations by Germany's former enemies. This political situation is the basis of the close connection between the West German foreign policy and the joint defense policy of the Western powers. It is noteworthy that as a consequence of the division, Germany is not a member of the United Nations Organization. However, the Federal Republic recognized the principles underlying the statute of the United Nations in the Paris treaties of October 23, 1954, which are regarded as a preliminary treaty ending the war between Germany and the three Western powers. The Federal Republic is represented by a permanent observer at the seat of the United Nations in New York and is a member of ten special organizations of the United Nations. Much more significant is the fact that the Federal Republic is a member of the North Atlantic Treaty Organization and of the Western European Union. The Federal Republic became a member of NATO on May 8, 1955. These developments are closely connected with the problem of German rearmament. There was strong opposition to this in Germany. The social democratic opposition voted against German participation in NATO and also against the several military service laws passed afterwards. Nonetheless, the *Bundeswehr* (the name of this new West German Army) soon became a fact. On January 20, 1956, Adenauer greeted the first 1,500 volunteers. In 1959, this new army had approximately 200,000 soldiers and about 50,000 civilian employees. This army, under the leadership of the young and energetic Minister of Defense, Franz Joseph Straus, very soon became a modern and efficient fighting force. At the present time, these armed forces are entirely integrated in the NATO command and are an important part of the Western defense. A German general, Hans Speidel, is the commander of the NATO land forces under the supreme commander, General Lauris Norstad. In the spring of 1960, certain observations could be made that indicated a tendency of Defense Minister Straus to increase German military strength outside the framework of NATO. Negotiations were made with Spain with regard to German military bases in that country. Nothing came out of it; but one should keep in mind that the German military tradition can very easily be revived, and possibly in an aggressive direction. Due to the close connection of the federal government with the West, there does not seem any immediate danger in this direction. Further, the establishment of a German armament industry for heavy equipment has until now not taken place.

As far as the Federal Republic is concerned, it can be expected that the immediate future will not bring a change in its close alliance with the West. The last decade has shown that there exists a possibility that the long lasting hostility between France and Germany can be resolved; the outstanding example in this direction was the amiable solution of the Saar problem. There are more tensions between England and Germany, many of them related to economic problems; but there are no indications that they could not be solved by other than peaceful means. There is also no responsible person in Germany who would consider war with Russia as a means to achieve unification. Even Defense Minister Straus is on record as declaring flatly that war with the Soviet Union would not reunify Germany in freedom. All this means that under the present situation, Germany itself is not a danger to peace; this does not mean that the problem of German reunification and the closely related problem of the city of Berlin may not be the major cause for an armed conflict between East and West. These problems are, for quite some time to come, beyond the control of Germany itself.

THE GERMANS AT THE BEGINNING OF THE SIXTIES

Economically, the German Federal Republic is strong and prosperous. A democratic Constitution provides the legal framework for a stable and peaceful development of German society. Civil rights of the people are guaranteed and protected institutionally as strongly as anywhere else in the Western world. Discounting the unsettled international situation, one can view the future of Germany optimistically. In spite of this, there remains a substantial amount of uneasiness with regard to Germany and the German people, inside Germany as well as outside. One reason for this are the experiences with Germany in the past two generations. Less than two decades have passed since the gas chambers of Auschwitz, Maidanek, and other extermination camps have been put out of operation; and it should be remembered that the operations stopped not voluntarily, but under the pressure of the advancing allied forces and the defeat of Germany. The capture of Adolf Eichmann, the man in charge of the "solution" of the Jewish problem should have brought back to the memory of a fast-forgetting, if not forgiving world, that the German people, only a short time ago, supported a regime whose actions were beyond the imagination of the most cruel and debased individual. It is understandable that many uncommitted Germans do not want to be confronted with the horrible facts that happened in the name of Germany and plead the easy excuse of ignorance, which is not true in most instances. In an outstanding book on the subject of the horrors of the Nazi regime, Dr. Eugen Kogon pointed out that the city of Weimar never showed any sympathy or pity, let alone any active help, for the inmates of the notorious concentration camp Buchenwald, which was only a couple of miles away.[2] This does not support the plea of ignorance.

The major problem of German society at the beginning of the sixties centers around the composition and attitudes of the political, economic, and intellectual elite. It should be emphasized again and again that men in leading positions, representing the age group of forty to sixty, were either brought up and trained during the Nazi regime or participated, with minor exceptions, in the shaping and executing of all phases of social life in Hitler's Germany. This does not mean that all of them have been Nazis, but the shadows of the past are bound to remain with them. For some time to come, their influence has to be strong because they are needed. For this very reason, the denazification program of the Western powers has been a failure. In a complex and pluralistic society such as postwar Western Germany, technical know-how, managerial skill, and scientific training are at a premium; and influence and high position are the reward for qualifications required in the effective functioning of such a society. So, in general, the same elite group guides the social attitude of postwar Germany as before. It is, of course, closely connected with the amazing economic recovery of West Germany, but its adherence to democratic ideas is surely not beyond doubt. Aside from this elite, the average German, enjoying the economic miracle, has become politically indifferent. He is either not aware or not interested in the restoration of conservative, authoritarian, and nationalistic attitudes as long as life is comfortable and pleasant. There are voices inside of Germany aware of the danger in the present social climate. Dr. Max Guede, Prosecutor-General at the Federal High Court, stated that the Germans did not master their past because they did not face it truthfully. Germany has become since 1945, actually a nation without history, through a combination of guilt and destiny. This situation will continue as long as no bridge of consciousness is built over the period of 1933 to 1945, as long as the German people treat this period as if it had not existed, as long as they shy away from the horrible truth, as long as they do not teach the young about it.

There are Germans who cry out from Germany in voices becoming almost desperate. The following passage from a young German writer may sum up the fears of many German democrats: "What we've got is a German democracy. An emergency arrangement bearing no relation to the

[2] Eugen Kogon, *The Theory and Practice of Hell* (New York: Farrar, Straus & Cudahy, Inc., 1950).

convictions of my fellow citizens. Twice they have been forced from the outside to act democratically; and the second time they play the part better."[3]

SELECTED READING

McInnis, Edgar, *et al. The Shaping of Postwar Germany*. New York: Frederick A. Praeger, Inc., 1960.
Speier, Hans. *German Rearmament and Atomic War, The Views of German Military and Political Leaders*. Evanston, Ill.: Row, Peterson & Co., 1957.
Speier, Hans, and Davidson, W. Phillips (eds.). *West German Leadership and Foreign Policy*. Evanston, Ill.: Row, Peterson & Co., 1957.
Strauss, Franz Josef. "Soviet Aims and German Unity," *Foreign Affairs*, XXXVII, No. 3 (April, 1959), 366–77.
Szaz, Zoltan Michael. *Germany's Eastern Frontiers, the Problem of the Oder-Neisse Line*. Chicago: Henry Regnery Co., 1960.
Wiskemann, Elizabeth. *Germany's Eastern Neighbors*. Fair Lawn, N.J.: Oxford University Press, 1956.

[3] Wilfrid Schilling, *The Fearmakers* (New York: Doubleday & Co., Inc., 1960).

V

POLITICS AND GOVERNMENT OF THE U.S.S.R.

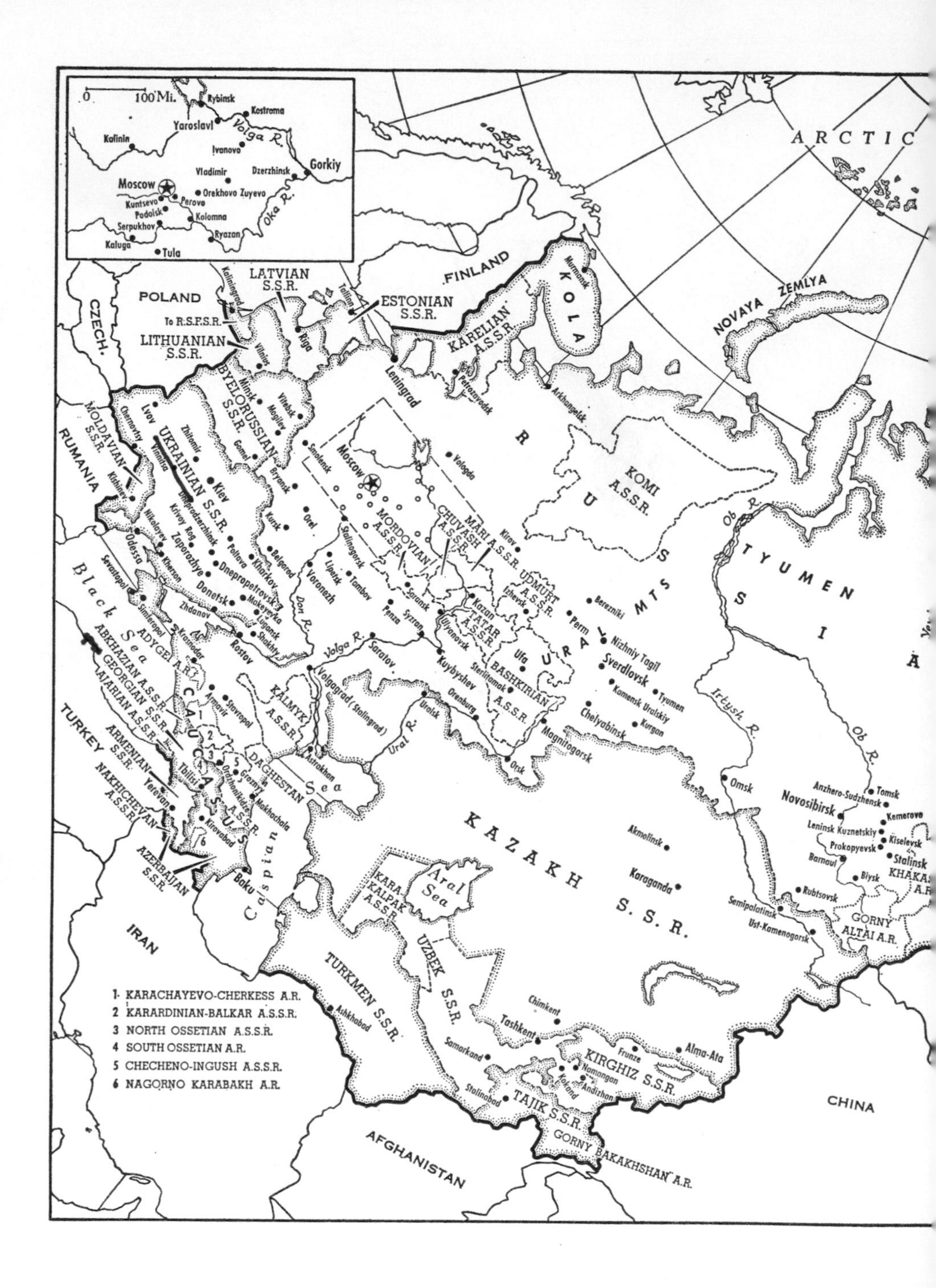

0
100 Mi.
Rybinsk
Kostroma
Yaroslavl
Volga R.
Kalinin
Ivanovo
Gorkiy
Vladimir
Dzerzhinsk
Moscow
Orekhovo Zuyevo
Kuntsevo
Perovo
Podolsk
Oka R.
Kolomna
Serpukhov
Ryazan
Kaluga
Tula
ARCTIC
LATVIAN S.S.R.
FINLAND
POLAND
ESTONIAN S.S.R.
KOLA
CZECH.
To R.S.F.S.R.
LITHUANIAN S.S.R.
NOVAYA ZEMLYA
KARELIAN A.S.S.R.
BYELORUSSIAN S.S.R.
Riga
Leningrad
MOLDAVIAN S.S.R.
UKRAINIAN S.S.R.
RUMANIA
R
U
S
S
I
A
KOMI A.S.S.R.
Kiev
Ob R.
MARI A.S.S.R.
CHUVASH A.S.S.R.
MORDOVIAN A.S.S.R.
TYUMEN
UDMURT A.S.S.R.
Kharkov
Odessa
Black Sea
Dnepropetrovsk
Donetsk
Voronezh
Kazan
TATAR A.S.S.R.
Perm
URAL MTS
Rostov
Volga R.
Saratov
Nizhniy Tagil
Sverdlovsk
ADYGEI A.R.
Ufa
BASHKIRIAN A.S.S.R.
Kuybyshev
Volgograd (Stalingrad)
KALMYK A.S.S.R.
ABKHAZIAN A.S.S.R.
GEORGIAN S.S.R.
AJARIAN A.S.S.R.
CAUCASUS
Chelyabinsk
Irtysh R.
TURKEY
ARMENIAN S.S.R.
Astrakhan
Ural R.
Magnitogorsk
DAGHESTAN
Tbilisi
Yerevan
NAKHICHEVAN A.S.S.R.
Caspian Sea
Omsk
Novosibirsk
Tomsk
KAZAKH S.S.R.
AZERBAIJAN S.S.R.
Baku
Aral Sea
KARA-KALPAK A.S.S.R.
Karaganda
IRAN
UZBEK S.S.R.
TURKMEN S.S.R.
GORNY ALTAI A.R.
1- KARACHAYEVO-CHERKESS A.R.
2 KARARDINIAN-BALKAR A.S.S.R.
3 NORTH OSSETIAN A.S.S.R.
4 SOUTH OSSETIAN A.R.
5 CHECHENO-INGUSH A.S.S.R.
6 NAGORNO KARABAKH A.R.
Tashkent
Alma-Ata
KIRGHIZ S.S.R.
TAJIK S.S.R.
CHINA
GORNY BAKAKHSHAN A.R.
AFGHANISTAN

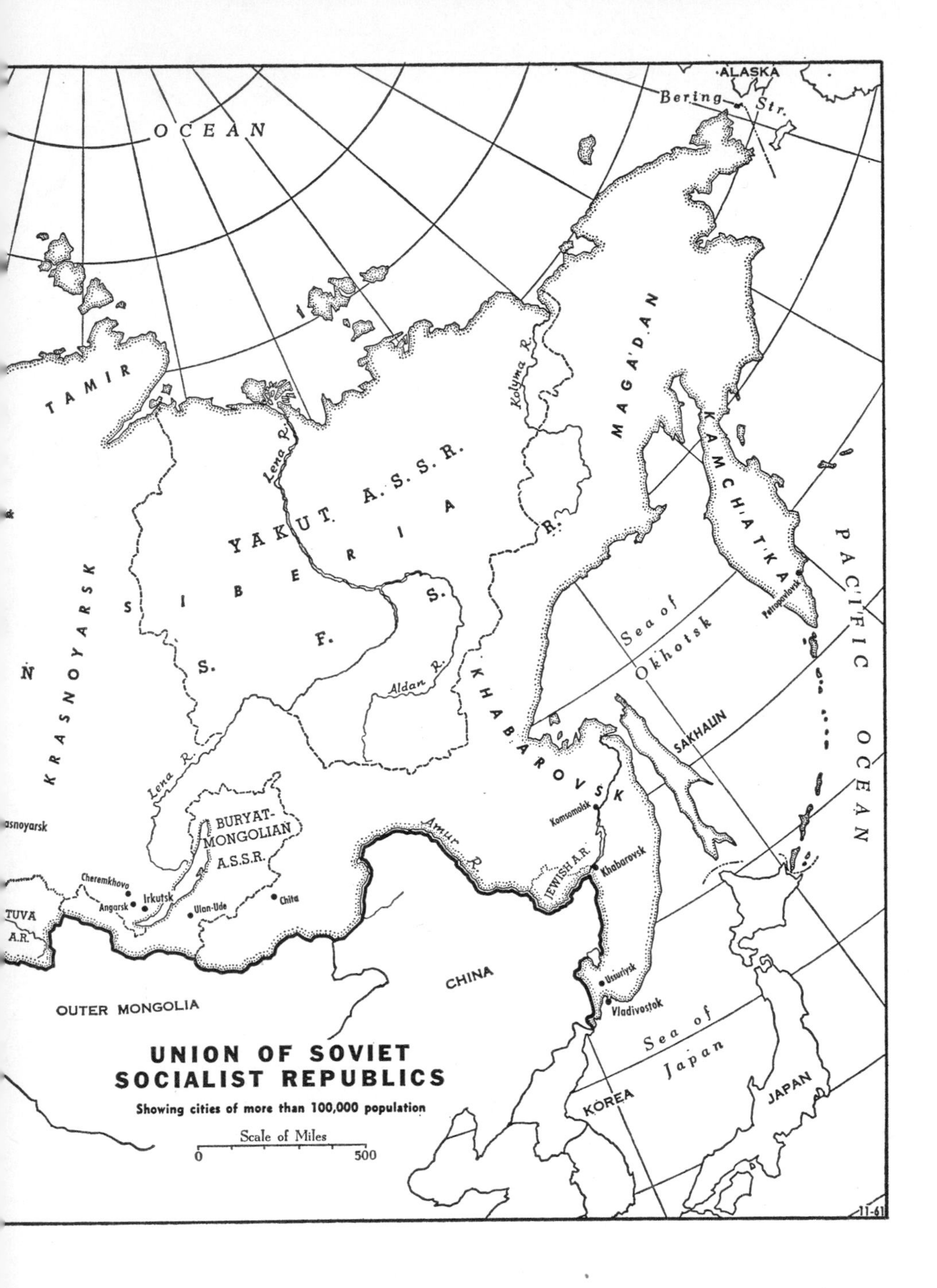

UNION OF SOVIET SOCIALIST REPUBLICS

Showing cities of more than 100,000 population

38

Soviet Social Structure

THE SOCIAL HERITAGE

Soviet society grew out of the social environment of Tsarist Russia and has developed, to a great extent, as a reaction against its rigid social structure. The prerevolutionary society of the Russian Empire had an archaic social structure that was out of harmony with the status and aspirations of its most dynamic classes and groups. An aristocracy of landlords, civil and military bureaucrats and officers, and the higher clergy formed the ruling class. It monopolized political authority and dominated the economy. Tsarist autocracy drew its support from the aristocracy and governed the country through it. The aristocracy formed a highly privileged and largely parasitical social elite. It contributed little or nothing to improve the condition of the masses, whom it regarded as little more than beasts of burden and servants. Public order was enforced by a vast police force supported by the army. The conformist clergy preached blind obedience to the Tsar and his officials. A rigid censorship prevailed, and opposition against the regime was squelched with systematic ruthlessness. The masses were kept in a condition of poverty and ignorance, so that they might know their place in society and accept their lowly status as in keeping with the will of God. Those who got out of line with the law and authorities were sent to Siberian labor camps. The regime provided safe outlets for pent-up frustrations by encouraging alcoholism (which produced revenue for the government) and by permitting *pogroms* against the Jewish ghetto communities.

Between the aristocracy and peasant masses were the members of the middle class: merchants, petty entrepreneurs and artisans, shopkeepers, the lower clergy, and the lowest ranks of the bureaucracy. The economic status of the middle class was fairly comfortable, in sharp contrast to that of the working class and peasants. The growing working class, which was recruited from the peasantry and declassed persons, worked long hours at low wages and enjoyed no legal or organizational safeguards of its elemental interests. The peasantry, which constituted approximately 80 per cent of the entire population, lived in abject poverty. Socially and politically, however, the middle class was accorded little better treatment from the aristocracy or by its bureaucratic minions than what was meted out to the workers. The middle class was expected to exhibit signs of deference to the aristocracy and submit to its arrogance. Mobility upward from the middle class to the aristocracy was rare. A barrier divided the nation into a small privileged social elite and a differentiated grouping of the masses.

The Russian intelligentsia comprised a numerically weak but influentially strong group that was recruited from all social classes. It was neither a distinct professional nor economic group but rather an ideological association that arose out of the most diverse social elements, bound together exclusively by ideas, especially social ones.[1] All were agreed in their negative attitude toward the Tsarist regime with its class differentiation and privileges and about the need for social and political reform. There were differences among them concerning the detailed goals of reform and the methods to effect the reform.

The intelligentsia took the initiative in forming conspiratorial societies, educational and cultural clubs, organizations for economic resistance by the workers and peasants, and finally political organizations, which did not refrain from employing terrorism and assassination against the aristocracy and its regime. The significant role that the intelligentsia enjoys in Soviet society may derive in part from the vanguard tradition that it built for itself during the decades of Tsarist rule prior to the revolution. By organizing and leading the revolutionary movements against the old regime in Russia, the intelligentsia set a pattern of leadership that has carried over into the new Soviet society.

SOCIAL EXPERIMENTATION

The Bolsheviks were the most revolutionary oriented elite group among the movements and parties that opposed the Tsarist regime. Their success in seizing and holding political power in Russia inaugurated the most radical experiment in social and political reconstruction. As revolutionary Marxists, the Bolsheviks were interested in transforming Russia into a Socialist society as rapidly as possible. The subjects of the Russian Empire became the guinea pigs in a gigantic laboratory experimentation program, whose ultimate objective was the creation of a utopia. It might

[1] Cf. Nicholas Berdyaev, *The Origin of Russian Communism* (Ann Arbor: University of Michigan Press, 1955), pp. 19–27.

be argued that the Bolsheviks used the Communist ideology to best their rivals in the game of revolutionary politics or that they have clung to this universal value system in order to undermine competitive national ideologies and establish Russian preponderance and hegemony throughout the world. Such a cynical interpretation of communism would substitute for the religious zeal of contemporary Communists an unquenchable power drive lacking ideological motivation. The ideological consistency of the Bolsheviks and their successors belies the cynical interpretation.

The Bolsheviks were armed with goals that they sought to achieve and with a theory that provided them an indestructible faith in their mission. The actual program and policies were hammered out piecemeal in the face of an interminable series of obstacles. The first and most obvious task that the Bolsheviks had to meet was the consolidation of political power. The small elite group that had seized power had to identify itself with certain social groups and classes in order to utilize their mass power to crush its enemies. It found in the working class and poor peasants the mass forces that were required to protect the regime and that eventually permitted it to carry out the revolutionary transformations of the economy and the social order.

The Bolsheviks divided the society over which they exercised absolute power into workers, peasants, intelligentsia, and exploiters. They set about to liquidate the exploiters and to reindoctrinate the intelligentsia—tasks that were completed officially by the end of 1936. When Stalin's Constitution was promulgated in 1936, the economic transformation of the U.S.S.R. from a capitalistic to a socialistic economy had been completed. Private enterprise was practically non-existent, and all productive wealth was monopolized by the state. The labor force was employed by the state and its subdivisions or collectivized into state and party controlled rural enterprises. The sole vestiges of private enterprise that have survived in the U.S.S.R. have been the individually cultivated "garden plots," a few artisans and tradesmen, very few peasants, and the illicit (black market) commerce in scarce commodities that the regime has tolerated.

By eliminating the capitalists, landlords and *kulaks* or wealthy farmers, and by transforming their properties into social or state property, the Bolsheviks won the friendship and support of the workers and a majority of the landless peasantry. A new managerial class to operate the state-owned economy and the collectivized sector of agriculture was recruited and trained. The workers and peasants supplied the necessary manpower, thereby assuring compatible social relations between the laboring masses and the new leadership class and insuring the regime of the political reliability of the Soviet intelligentsia. The policy of requiring students to perform manual labor in the factories and fields is intended to prevent any social alienation from developing between the laboring classes and the intelligentsia.

Due to the close social ties between members of the intelligentsia and the two basic classes of Soviet society, the Soviet intelligensia is said to constitute a social stratum, not a separate social class. Although direction and management of the Soviet economy are in the hands of an elite corps of party officials, bureaucrats, and technicians, there is no essential contradiction between this fact and the official Communist party view that the workers and peasants operate the Socialist economy. Because the intelligentsia is not officially differentiated from the workers and peasants, the administrative apparatus of society is said to be in the hands of the working people or toilers. Were the intelligentsia to be treated as a distinct class in Soviet society apart from the workers and peasants, the government and the party would obviously cease to be the instruments of the toiling masses, and the intelligentsia would become a governing class.

The first article of the Soviet Constitution stresses the view that the U.S.S.R. is a "socialist state of workers and peasants." The two classes are described as friendly and cooperative, since neither constitutes an exploiting class, and both are striving under the common leadership of the Communist party to build the classless society of communism. It has been the intention of the Communist party to eventually transform the peasants into workers by reorganizing the structure of the farm economy into state farms, which will be factories in the field instead of collective farms. The collective farmer represents a mere transitional status that is designed to prepare the peasant for complete socialization. When the farmers are no longer peasants, but farm workers who respond to the same incentives as urban workers, and when the technological revolution has proceeded to the point where there is no longer a rigid distinction between manual and intellectual labor, the Soviet Union will be on the eve of the long heralded classless society.

Although the Soviet Communists have been pursuing a Leninist policy of social transformation leading to the goals of a classless and equalitarian society, they have been forced by circumstances to make a number of tactical retreats in their social policies. During the initial period of "war communism," the Bolsheviks used slogans of equality to whip up popular enthusiasm for the revolution. Equal remuneration and status won over the workers to the Bolshevik cause and swelled the number of recruits to the Red Army. However, productivity declined in the absence of a system of incentives and rewards to a point where shortages developed, which necessitated a system of preferential rationing. The termination of the civil war and the serious breakdown of the economy caused the Bolsheviks to restore monetary rewards and social distinctions as incentives. The survival of the Soviet state and the creation of socialism in one country demanded the rapid expansion of productivity. The principle of "from each according to his ability, to each according to his work" was enshrined in the Stalin Constitution as the norm of socialism.

SOCIAL STATUS AND MOBILITY

Soviet society is at present one of the most competitive societies in the world. In addition to the differentiated scale of income that divides the common unskilled laborer from the professional class of managers, technicians, artists, writers, and scientists, such added incentives as bonuses and housing priorities are conferred upon outstanding workers of brain and muscle. Citations such as Hero of Socialist Labor confer economic rewards as well as social prestige. The principle of equality is interpreted today as the equal right of all citizens to improve the quality and quantity of their labor output through educational improvement and professional advancement. Unskilled workers are encouraged to learn the necessary skills to become skilled workers or to enroll in evening and correspondence courses for the purpose of studying a profession. The means that the state provides for individual self-improvement are, like the material rewards, used to stimulate greater labor productivity.

Differentiated rewards have produced noticeable variations in consumption patterns and living standards as well as in cultural levels and education. Social gradations or strata are definitely to be observed in the U.S.S.R. The existence of such a hierarchy of social strata resembles class structures in various Western societies. Since there is also a strong desire on the part of the Soviet population to advance socially, the existence of a social hierarchy stimulates individual efforts to improve social status. The only difference between Soviet policy and that of the Western societies is that in the U.S.S.R. there is perhaps greater opportunity for advancement. Because of the rapid pace of economic growth, which creates a permanent demand for qualified personnel, and due to the emphasis that the regime places on education, persons of average or better intelligence are able to improve their professional and social status irrespective of their race, economic status, or sex.

In the Soviet Union, there is no discrimination for reasons of ethnic or nationality status, sex, or social origins. Women occupy the same position as men in practically every field of activity and receive the same rate of compensation. Some 33 per cent of engineers and lawyers are women. The percentages are higher in other fields, such as economists and statisticians, 57 per cent; school teachers, 70 per cent; physicians, 75 per cent. Women constituted 25.7 per cent of the membership of the Soviet of the Union of the Supreme Soviet and 27.5 per cent of the Soviet of Nationalities in 1958. There are outstanding women scientists, university professors, and party leaders. Soviet women have the right to retain their maiden name after marriage and to pursue a career independent of the wishes of the husband. Just as sex is no barrier to professional and social improvement, minority status and peasant origin present no bar to individual advancement within the system of rewards of the U.S.S.R.

The principal vehicle of upward mobility in the Soviet Union is the educational system. Although fees were introduced during the war, since 1956 students in secondary and higher institutions of learning pay no fees, and honor students are awarded substantial grants and scholarships. Factories and farms provide vocational and technical instruction, and there are evening classes that are extremely well attended, while the correspondence course provides additional opportunities for advanced education. Competition is also employed in the educational system, and only the serious and competent pupils and students are rewarded. Enrollment in a university or higher institute is limited to those who pass the difficult entrance examinations and who receive adequate grades. University graduates are immediately placed in positions that provide good incomes and social prestige. The recent educational reform that requires students to do part-time manual labor from the age of fifteen on does not affect the honor students in some fields, who are to be exempted as long as they excel in their studies. These honor students are to be segregated from the other student body in order to accelerate and improve their educational development.

So long as the Soviet economy continues to expand rapidly, thereby creating a permanent demand for highly trained specialists and technicians, the opportunities for upward social mobility will continue to exceed the supply of competent and ambitious persons. Should the need for specialists ever be filled in any field, the supply can be regulated by reducing the material rewards and prestige value of those professions or simply by limiting the flow of students into those areas of study. At the present time, the need for scientists cannot be filled, while the supply of medical students is considered adequate, so that the rewards offered to science majors and graduates are incomparably better than those reserved for medical majors. The same technique has been employed for many years to channel industrial workers into difficult occupations. Coal miners have a shorter work day and receive higher wages than workers in less dangerous occupations; they are also made the object of social prestige.

Despite the policies that have resulted in the development of social strata and favored professions and categories of workers (such as the shock workers of *stakhanovites* of the Stalin era who exceeded their production norms and set an exemplary standard of efficiency for labor), the Soviet regime has sought to prevent the formation of a privileged class or the crystallization of class consciousness or in-group cohesiveness. It has combated the growth of any form of *esprit de corps* among the officer ranks of the armed forces, since this might imperil the elite status of the party, which cannot tolerate the existence of a rival elite. All professional organizations are infiltrated by party members, who must anchor these associations securely to the party.

The members of the professional class do form a social elite group in Soviet society, which gives definite advantages to their offspring. The latter have more opportunity to acquire higher education and to develop their talents than children of mediocre parents. There is not much evidence to support the view that members of high-status families are particularly favored or that there is any excess of nepotism and favoritism in the allocation of professional jobs. The fact that the Communist party conducts frequent campaigns against these practices indicates that some occupational parasitism persists. As is true of Western countries, in the U.S.S.R. the children of high-status parents tend to retain that social status, so long as they do not develop delinquent tendencies or become politically unreliable. Frequently, the children of high-status parents do not receive adequate parental guidance because of the parents' absorption in professional and political work. Such youth often develop delinquent patterns of behavior and become social outcasts. How much downward social mobility exists among the members of the social elite is difficult to gauge. There is a higher rate of nonconformism among the youth of the social elite group, which may compromise their political reliability and impede their professional careers, since the party makes a conscious effort to advance the social conformist and the politically reliable. One of the reasons for the introduction of compulsory labor among students was to arrest what the party regards as parasitism and social degeneracy among the gilded youth.

Party membership is another vehicle of upward social mobility. Tireless and devoted service to the party is often rewarded by appointment to the professional apparatus of the party bureaucracy. Advancement is generally slow until the party functionary has proved his competence as a political worker and established a record for diligence in carrying out his assignments. The party functionary must develop a thorough understanding of Marxism-Leninism and an intuitive skill in interpreting the party line. He must take care to form secure personal ties with leaders who are "in favor" with the leadership core of the party and shift his allegiance before these leaders fall into disgrace. Mistakes and errors in judgment are unpardonable, especially when they cast discredit upon the party or compromise the leadership. The purge is an always present danger, and purged party functionaries seldom are restored to their previous status. They are fortunate if they are allowed to fall into quiet oblivion. A party career offers an insecure future that is replete with risks;

but those who survive its competitive struggle are indeed highly rewarded, for the small (30,000 to 50,000) elite that runs the party constitutes the ruling class of the Soviet Union. Power, prestige, and the comforts necessary for a pleasant existence are the rewards of successful party functionaries. The power elite is socially integrated with the professional class and is officially listed as part of the intelligentsia.

Other factors have contributed to social stratification in the U.S.S.R. besides professional and political careers, differential incomes, bonuses, and consumer priorities. One of these is the right to accumulate and bequeath personal property. Private property may be accumulated in the form of personal possessions: one or two houses for dwelling purposes, automobiles, boats, household furnishings, apparel, etc. Savings may be invested in state securities or deposited in bank accounts. The law permits the heir to inherit the personal possessions and savings of the deceased or to receive these in the form of gifts. The maintenance of limited property rights and inheritance are designed to act as incentives to Soviet citizens to work more productively. Accumulated wealth may permit retired persons to maintain a higher standard of living than those whose income is limited to retirement pensions. It also may permit the offspring of high-status families to retain their accustomed mode of living until they are able to rise professionally to high-income status.

From its inception, the Soviet state has attempted to mold a new social personality in the Soviet citizen. The final stage of communism requires that man's traditional egoism be completely socialized. While stress is constantly being laid upon the Socialist code of ethics, economic policy has been forced to appeal to the basic egoism of the Soviet workers, peasants, and intelligentsia in order to prod them to build the economy of abundance. The incentive system has been utilized to maximize productivity. Vanity has been met by the use of titles, medals, and impressive uniforms as rewards. The desire for prestige has been tapped to promote individual and collective competition to increase work norms and output; the media of information (newspapers, magazines, radio, and TV) single out persons and groups for praise in reporting the outcome of Socialist competitions. Team spirit and national pride are harnessed to the campaign to surpass the United States in productivity and output. Along with these material and emotional rewards for good work, the Soviet regime has fed the people hope in a brighter future—the ideal of a better tomorrow and of eventual bliss in a society blessed with peace and plenty. The gradual rise of living standards and the expanding social services and improved working conditions are proof to the Soviet citizens that tangible progress toward the ideal of communism has been made. By providing the people with an ideal, the Communist party mobilizes yet another emotional response in support of its policies.

SOCIALISM AND THE INDIVIDUAL

The status and condition of the individual in a Socialist society contrasts sharply with those of traditional capitalistic or precapitalistic societies. The Socialist value system is designed to develop different individual and social psychologies. Greater stress is laid upon providing the individual with security and upon integrating him socially than upon developing his individuality. The aim of socialism is to create the person who develops and uses his talents for the good of the entire society rather than for his own personal advancement.

Among the fundamental human rights that the Soviet system seeks to provide the individual are the opportunity to work on a job commensurate with one's talents and abilities, equal pay for equal work, free education and vocational training, free medical care, sick pay and disability payments and benefits, paid vacations and retirement pensions, subsidized housing, and entertainment. The Socialist state guarantees the individual protection against economic want, exploitation, social discrimination, and ignorance. By Socialist standards, social equality and economic security constitute the foundation of personal freedom. To confer political freedom upon individuals in the absence of social equality and economic security is meaningless, since the poor, unemployed, degraded social being will never be capable of exercising any freedom from his exploiters and tormentors. To the Marxist-Leninist, personal freedom is the end product of social harmony.

In contrast to Western societies, where the individual has economic freedom to choose between different employers, enter into private business, or pursue some profession or trade, the Soviet citizen has only a choice between working for the state or in a collective farm enterprise. His chief advantage is the relative ease of finding employment, since the Soviet state assumes direct responsibility for placing persons in jobs commensurate with their abilities and political reliability. However, political demands create strain and tension for Soviet citizens, since errors and shortcomings in any job may be construed by the authorities as evidence of deliberate sabotage or antisocial behavior. Similar faults in Western countries would lead, at most, to a reprimand, demotion, or dismissal; in the U.S.S.R., the negligent worker may be fined, demoted, dismissed, and charged with a political offense against the state or the Socialist order. The price that the Soviet citizen pays for the right to guaranteed employment is the loss of certain freedoms meaningful to most Western-reared citizens.

Under Article 119 of the Soviet Constitution, citizens are guaranteed the right to rest and leisure, reduced working hours for workers who labor under arduous conditions, annual paid vacations, rest and cure centers, and recreation clubs. Although the normal work week is forty-eight hours, in most occupations, the current Seven Year Plan will reduce it to forty-two hours, with corresponding reductions for unwholesome occupations. Some of the facilities for vacations and curative treatments are not as yet available in sufficient quantity, and Soviet workers who belong to the trade-union are given preferential treatment in their use.

Workers may retire on a pension of between 300 and 1,200 rubles per month when they reach age fifty-five and sixty respectively for women and men. Pensions average about 500 rubles.[2] Workers who continue to work after reaching retirement age are entitled to only a portion of the pension. Sick pay and disability payments are relatively good, depending on whether or not the worker belongs to a trade-union, for which he is entitled to double indemnity, and on the length of employment and rate of earnings. They range from 300 rubles to 3,000 rubles per month. Persons who are disabled by their jobs are entitled to receive full wages or salary temporarily; if permanently disabled, they are pensioned. Maternity benefits are allowed for a maximum of 112 days. In the past, social insurance payments penalized workers who moved about frequently from job to job without official authorization. In this way, the government sought to minimize job turnovers. Since January 1, 1961, workers who change jobs have the right to temporary disability benefits regardless of their time on the new job; and they retain their record of "uninterrupted service" if they begin work again in one month.[3] This modification is indicative of greater freedom in Soviet labor relations. Obedience to the law and social conformity are encouraged by the policy of canceling pension as well as social insurance benefits for criminal conviction. The collective farmers are not granted coverage for pensions and social insurance under the state program since they are not employees of state enterprises; collective farms must contribute individually to the social welfare funds for such coverage to be provided.

Other social advantages that Soviet citizens enjoy are free medical attention and dental care as well as hospitalization, inexpensive drugs and medicines, subsidized housing, free care for infants and children of working parents, etc. These social services constitute an important cash value and add greatly to the financial security of citizens. Special subsidies are granted to families with numerous children and to unmarried mothers.

[2] G. A. Prudensky (ed.), *Voprosy truda v SSSR* (*Problems of Labor in the U.S.S.R.*), (Moscow: Gosudarstvennse izdatelstvo politicheskoi literatury 1958), p. 357. In 1960, the monetary system of the U.S.S.R. was revised in such a way that currently the ruble is valued ten times higher than it was previously. Thus, pensions average between 30 and 120 rubles per month. The real value of the pension has not been affected by the monetary revision.

[3] *Current Digest of the Soviet Press,* February 24, 1960, p. 24.

The care that the state provides for the aged, the infirm, orphans, and children is remarkably good and compares very favorably with the social services of advanced Western countries.

RELIGION IN THE U.S.S.R.

Religious worship is tolerated by the Communist party of the Soviet Union for reasons of expediency. Large numbers of the Soviet people are devout, and their good will toward the Soviet regime must not be alienated unnecessarily. So long as the churches respect the state and party and preach submission to their authority, no harm and some good might result from a tolerant policy toward religion. During the German invasion, the Orthodox church preached patriotism and helped to rally national pride in defense of the Soviet state. Foreign peoples and governments who might otherwise be favorably disposed toward the Communist movement or the Soviet regime might be antagonized into a position of hostility by an intolerant religious policy.

The Communist party considers religion to be a relic of mysticism and superstition and therefore totally incompatible with science and with the Marxist-Leninist philosophy. While religious worship is not persecuted any longer and the Constitution recognizes it as a legal right of Soviet citizens, the party and the government do not encourage its diffusion. The educational institutions teach antireligious philosophy, and practically all literature that is printed in the U.S.S.R. is atheistic; religious propaganda is severely circumscribed instead. The party does not permit its members to pay even lip service to any religion, and the youth organizations of the Communist party engage actively in antireligious propaganda. By curtailing the spread of religious sentiment among the younger generations, it is hoped by the Soviet regime that in a few generations religious beliefs will gradually disappear.

PERSONAL FREEDOM

Personal freedom has never been regarded as a fundamental value by the Communist party of the Soviet Union. The Soviet Constitution confers such freedoms as speech, press, assembly, and demonstrations upon citizens as long as these are exercised "in conformity with the interests of the working people and in order to strengthen the socialist system." To abuse any of these liberties for the purpose or with the effect of undermining the prestige or authority of the Communist party, the Soviet state or the Socialist order is a criminal offense. Should any person make a public speech or publish ideas condemning party policy, criticizing socialism, or ridiculing Soviet institutions and leaders, he would be punished severely. Such an exercise of personal freedom is considered antisocial as well as criminal license. There is little opportunity for Soviet citizens to abuse these freedoms in practice, since the press and other media of information and entertainment are carefully controlled by the Agitation and Propaganda Department of the party's Central Committee and by the Chief Administration of Literary and Publishing Affairs (Glavlit), which is a state agency. Not only are all media of information owned and operated by either the party or the state and its agencies, but these also perform rigid censorship. Reporters, editorial writers, and publishers are carefully selected and trained by the party. Khrushchev emphasized the importance of placing the information media "in the hands of the most faithful, most trustworthy, most politically steadfast people devoted to our cause."[4]

The freedom of Soviet citizens to organize is limited to such groups as the party and the state have authorized. These include trade-unions; co-operative societies; youth organizations; sports and defense organizations; and cultural, technical, and scientific societies. The most exalted organization in Soviet society is the Communist party in which "the most active and politically conscious citizens in the ranks of the working class, working peasants, and working intelligentsia voluntarily unite." The Communist party is also constitutionally defined as "the leading core of all organizations of the working people, both public and state." Since all organizations must be licensed by the state, there may not be any "private" organizations; "public" organizations are legally authorized associations open to citizens. No public organizations would be tolerated that could not conform to the wishes of the Communist party. Persons who are not willing or interested in promoting the official ideology by joining the authorized public organizations must refrain from exercising the constitutionally prescribed freedom, since to organize without official sanction would be criminal conspiracy.

There is no place in Soviet society for the exercise of Western-style or bourgeois freedoms. The Soviet citizen is expected to exercise such freedoms as serve the interests of his society, the state, and the Communist party. He who is not willing to conform to the Socialist system of values as prescribed by the Communist party is not considered to be a worthy Soviet citizen.

SELECTED READING

Bauer, Raymond A. *The New Man in Soviet Psychology.* Cambridge, Mass.: Harvard University Press, 1952.

Bauer, Raymond A., Inkeles, Alex, and Kluckhohn, Clyde. *How the Soviet System Works: Cultural, Psychological and Social Themes.* Cambridge, Mass.: Harvard University Press, 1956.

[4] N. S. Khrushchev, *Pravda,* August 28, 1957.

COUNTS, GEORGE S. *The Challenge of Soviet Education.* New York: McGraw-Hill Book Co., Inc., 1957.

INKELES, ALEX. *Public Opinion in Soviet Russia.* Cambridge, Mass.: Harvard University Press, 1950.

INKELES, ALEX, and BAUER, RAYMOND A. *The Soviet Citizen: Daily Life in a Totalitarian Society.* Cambridge, Mass.: Harvard University Press, 1959.

KAMMARI, M. D. *Socialism and the Individual.* Moscow: Foreign Languages Publishing House, 1950.

KLINE, GEORGE L. (ed.). *Soviet Education.* New York: Columbia University Press, 1957.

KULSKI, W. W. *The Soviet Regime: Communism in Practice.* Syracuse, N.Y.: Syracuse University Press, 1954.

39

Political Ideology

THE PREREVOLUTIONARY HERITAGE OF RUSSIAN MARXISM

At the beginning of the twentieth century, Russia was ruled by an autocratic monarch who commanded absolute power over the state and church. According to the official political doctrine of the Tsarist state, authority to govern the Russian masses and subjugated minorities of the empire was vested in the Tsar by the hand of Divine Power. His will was the source of all justice, morality, and truth since he was divinely inspired. The law was the emanation of his command, to which he was not bound. The Tsar's power, like God's omnipotence, could not be restricted. As God's representative, the Tsar was sacrosanct; obedience to his rule was a mandate from Heaven for all who lived within the empire. This doctrine was an anachronism in the nineteenth century, and yet it persisted well into the twentieth century because the Tsar was too conceited and politically blind to compromise with the principles of democracy. The doctrine received its most complete form and elaboration in the writings of Konstantine Petrovich Pobedonostsev (1827–1907), who defended the institution of autocracy and derided constitutionalism, government by people's representatives, checks and balances, and other democratic structures of authority. In order to sustain this archaic institutionalization of power in Russia against the widespread opposition of the Russian intelligentsia, the Tsarist state suppressed all forms of political expression that were at variance with the autocratic doctrines on which it based its authority.

The history of the growth of conspiratorial groups and societies and of the spread of revolutionary doctrines in Russia from 1825 to 1905 is rich and varied.[1] In the absence of a climate of political freedom, all po-

[1] Cf. Franco Venturi, *Roots of Revolution: A History of the Populist and Socialist Movements in Nineteenth Century Russia* (London: George Weidenfeld & Nicolson, Ltd., 1960).

litical activity that was critical of the regime and aimed at constitutional change, social progress, and economic reform had to be conducted clandestinely. The myriad of literary circles that became vogue during this period served often as a front for political discussions, since literary works were treated with considerable leniency by the Tsarist authorities and literary discussion was not considered politically dangerous. Even Karl Marx's *Das Kapital* was published in Russian and sold freely because it was considered to refer to a non-realizable utopian dream. The principal groups in opposition to the regime were loosely organized intellectual movements, not political parties, until 1897. Nearly all of these groups were offshoots of the Populist movement, which constituted the parent trunk from which emerged the anarchists, nihilists, liberals, and Socialists of various types. After the assassination of Tsar Alexander II in 1881 by a fanatical anarchist who belonged to a terroristic group, Narodnaya Volya (People's Will), the government unloosed a campaign of police persecution against all Populists and radicals in an effort to stamp out the political conspiracies. By driving many of the conspirators into exile in western Europe, the Tsarist government brought them into direct contact with the Marxist movement, from which the Russians gained valuable experience.

One year after the formation of the Socialist Revolutionary Party in 1897 by the principal groups of the Populist movement, the Russian Marxists, led by Plekhanov and Lenin, formed the Russian Social Democratic Labor Party, which became an affiliate of the Socialist International. Unlike the Populists and their Socialist Revolutionary Party, who were oriented toward a peasant program of agrarian socialism, the Russian Marxists directed their revolutionary appeal to the industrial workers, who were relatively few in number but were conveniently massed in the large cities. They perceived that the policy of rapid industrialization of Russia would draw an increasing stream of proletarians into the urban centers and that the spread of factories and labor regimentation would weld the workers into a class-conscious proletariat that could supply the mass base for a revolution against capitalism and the Tsarist state. Not all the Russian Marxists were in agreement on the tactics of the working-class movement, however. The so-called "legal Marxists" (Struve, Bulgakov, Berdyaev, and Tugan-Baranovsky), whose articles appeared in respectable journals that were licensed by the authorities, argued that there should be no overt political action by the workers against the state and that they should cooperate with the bourgeoisie in the development of industries and in the spread of capitalism in Russia. Another group, dubbed "Economists" by Lenin, favored the organization of trade-unions and the goal of practical labor reforms by the working-class movement. They believed that the workers would respond more to an economic struggle against the employers than they would to a policy of revolution against the state. The "Economists" were not in sympathy with any form of political revolution and preferred to leave political activity to the middle-class liberals, since they shared the latter's goal of a constitutional and representative government. They were influenced by the "revisionism" of Eduard Bernstein and leaned heavily toward gradual amelioration of working conditions within the institution of capitalism; they were simply reformists. These groups were soon cast out of the leadership of the Russian Social Democratic Labor Party, which came under the control of such revolutionaries as Plekhanov, Akselrod, Zasulich, Potresov, Martov, and Lenin. The task of the party was defined in 1902 by Lenin in a pamphlet entitled *What Is to Be Done?*

According to Lenin, the party had to propagate militant class consciousness among the Russian workers and fill them with burning hatred against the state as well as against their employers. The main purpose of strikes and workers' demonstrations was to train the workers to fight as a compact force against their class enemies and the state, which protected these enemies. The object of improving working conditions was to be more of a stimulus to agitation and struggle than a goal of the labor movement. The labor movement was to supply the party with an army of proletarian fighters who would respond to the party when it issued the call for revolution. Each limited success by the labor movement was to inspire it to increase its demands and enlist broader adherence among the working class. From each engagement with the class enemies and the state, the workers must develop greater combativeness. The party must enlist in its membership only dedicated fighters who placed the interest of the party above personal safety and convenience. Party members must be professional revolutionaries, not mere sympathizers, prepared to carry out the most daring and hazardous assignments upon a moment's notice by the party's order. The revolution was to be "engineered" and directed by the party, which was to form the officer corps or vanguard of an aroused and combative proletariat. To make sure that the party acted with a single determined will, Lenin insisted that all powers of decision be vested in the top elite of the party (Central Committee). Centralism also meant that strict obedience by subordinate units of the party and all members were required by the Central Committee. To make centralism more acceptable to the party membership, Lenin agreed that party deliberations be by majority vote and that the central leadership be periodically renewed by election from below. He refused to allow factionalism within the party organization; the minority must submit to the will of the majority at the Central Committee level, and subordinates must obey the party leadership unswervingly.

Lenin's approach to the art of revolution and his conception of the party were heavily influenced by such non-Marxist precursors as the Russian Populists Tkachev and Chernyshevsky, whose ideas had been criticized by Marx and Engels as sectarian. Conditions in Russia were not propitious for the development of legal tactics, and Lenin was not interested in tying the working class to the interests of the middle-class liberals. As early as 1902, he had formed the idea of transforming every revolutionary situation that might occur in Russia into a bid for total power by the party in the name of the proletariat. He could see no sense in working with the bourgeoisie for the establishment of democracy if the working class could be led to seize power for itself from the 130,000 nobles who constituted the ruling class of the Tsarist autocracy. In order to arouse the peasantry into revolutionary action along with the proletariat, Lenin agreed that the party should openly support the desire of the peasants to seize the land from the gentry as well as the nobility, although he refused to support a pledge to give the peasants title to the land. Lenin also rejected the idea of sharing power with the peasantry once the revolution was successful; all power was to be monopolized by the proletarian party in the name of the workers and peasants. Thus, while most Russian Marxists harbored the belief that the revolutionary government would be a democratic coalition, Lenin, as early as 1902, had claimed for the proletarian party exclusive leadership over the workers' state. The dictatorship of the proletariat was to be a single party rule.[2]

Lenin was not altogether consistent in the expression of his views; at times he reverted to the formalistic interpretation of Marxism adhered to by the Mensheviks that the revolution would come in two stages: first, a bourgeois democratic revolution, which would establish a democratic state and extend capitalism, and a second proletarian revolution, which would establish a dictatorship of the proletariat and socialism. In the heat of the revolutionary struggle of 1917, however, Lenin took the radical course of action in leading the Bolsheviks to seize power before the bourgeoisie had time to consolidate the power of the democratic republic. He justified this and the total exclusion of bourgeois parties from the government on the grounds that the Russian bourgeoisie was not to be trusted. Even though the Bolsheviks represented a small fraction of the people of the Russian Empire in 1917 and the chances of success in retaining power against the host of internal and external enemies were low, Lenin did not hesitate to plunge his followers forward toward total and exclusive power. To succeed, a counterrevolution would require foreign intervention; and under the conditions of general warfare, this was un-

[2] Cf. Leonard Schapiro, *The Communist Party of the Soviet Union* (New York: Random House, Inc., 1960), pp. 38, 45–46, 205–7.

likely. Before the end of the war in 1918, Lenin raised the banner of world revolution in the hope that the workers in other countries would rise against their governments, thus freeing his regime from the threat of foreign intervention. Beset at home with civil war and fighting for their very lives against a powerful array of hostile forces, the Bolsheviks used the ideological appeal of the proletarian revolution and socialism to set in motion the proletariat of the advanced countries of Europe on a similar course of action. When it became apparent that the Western powers entertained no serious intention to intervene in force to restore bourgeois rule in Russia and that in anticipation of the collapse of the Bolshevik regime they would prevent the dismemberment of Russia, the need for and likelihood of international proletarian support of the revolution subsided, and with it, Lenin's interest in the newly formed Communist International. As part of the "new economic policy" to restore economic vitality to the country by fostering a retreat to capitalism, the Bolshevik regime was in need of trade, capital equipment, loans, and technical assistance from the Western powers. Normalization of relations with the bourgeois states made it mandatory to abandon the policy of world revolution. This did not signify that the tactic of world revolution might not be resurrected in the future should the likelihood of its success occur.

While not entirely consistent, there is nevertheless an amazing thread of unity to Leninist thought from 1902 through the successful revolution terminating in the establishment of the first Communist state. Throughout Lenin's doctrinal development, the goal of proletarian revolution was never subordinated to economic determinism or to ethicopolitical values. The revolution was conceived and directed by a dedicated and willful elite whose choice of tactics was never restrained by ethicopolitical limitations. Utility or expediency and positive interpretation of objective conditions became the dominant guides to Leninist theory and action. The drive to achieve absolute power for the party as the vanguard of the masses and to create the force to realize the historically determined mission of Marxism to destroy capitalism and create a Socialist society in Russia became a collective obsession of Lenin and his associates.

Marxist theory provided Lenin and the Bolsheviks with an understanding of the significant characteristics of capitalism: its internal laws of development and operation, its inherent weaknesses, its international scope and conflicts. It helped them to plan their revolutionary tactics insofar as it made it possible for them to predict general trends. It also provided them with a faith in the "historical righteousness" of their ideals and gave them a sense of "mission" in hastening a process that was "historically predestined" to evolve. Since the revolution, doctrine has played an equally important role in guiding the Communist elite of the Soviet Union. What is the essential content of this doctrine; and how significant is it as an expression of political faith, guide to action, and instrument of domination to the leaders and party who profess it as an ideology?

MARXISM-LENINISM AS SCIENCE AND FAITH

The ideology of the Soviet Union is Marxism-Leninism as interpreted and applied by the Communist party. Besides the main body of doctrine as elaborated by Marx, Engels, and Lenin, the interpretations of Stalin and of Khrushchev constitute official dogma. Marxism-Leninism is more than a value system; it constitutes a theory of knowledge or ontological guide in the study of social, economic, and political change. It is in this sense considered the "science of revolution." Ontology and values are inextricably interwoven into Marxism-Leninism. Thus, belief in revolution as an instrument of social change or progress is combined with faith in revolution. Society not only tends toward revolutionary development because of the laws of dialectical progression that are to be observed in the application of historical materialism to social development (economic determinism), revolution is promoted consciously by the Marxist-Leninist or Communist as an article of faith. The Communist must not be content merely to observe the revolutionary process of social development or to find inspiration from the belief that revolution must occur within capitalistic society. He must plunge himself into the political fray to hasten and guide the forces of revolution because of the moral compulsions that stem from his faith in the revolutionary process.

THE SOCIALIST REVOLUTION

According to Marxism-Leninism, capitalistic society is doomed to perish like its predecessors, feudalism and slavery, because it is founded upon the principle of exploitation of man by man. Social exploitation produces contradictions within the structure of social relations. Among these contradictions is the creation of social classes and the gradual polarization of these classes into the exploiters and the exploited. When the exploited become imbued with conscious indignation over their status, they take steps to seize control of the instruments of production and to overthrow the political superstructure of society, or state, through which the exploiters imposed and maintained their social domination.

It is the duty of the Communists to guide and direct the revolutionary overthrow of the capitalistic order so that the foundations of a new society of perfect justice may be established in which the principle of exploitation may be superseded by the value of equality. The initial stage of the new society that emerges from the revolutionary overthrow of capitalism is termed "socialism." While the perfect justice of the second and final stage, or communism, is not possible under socialism, socialism nevertheless establishes a more equitable order of social relations than capitalism. Under the society of socialism, classes are abolished; and the division of society into exploiters and exploited is ended by the socialization of property. The instruments of production (land and capital) are collectivized, and surplus value (which is the difference between the value of labor and the wages paid for labor power) is socialized. The rent, interest, and profit that the capitalists retained in order to lead parasitical lives are distributed to the labor force in the form of higher wages and salaries after society has deducted the necessary costs to refurbish the means of production and the expenses for the maintenance of essential social services.

Socialist society does more than to establish more equitable social relations. It organizes the instruments of production efficiently so as to end economic cycles and provide regular employment and steady consumption of goods and services. It plans the production of goods and services so as to eliminate waste, thus eliminating capitalistic anarchy from the productive cycle. It mobilizes fully the productive power of labor and expands the quantity and quality of the instruments of production to the point where the "economy of abundance" is finally attained. At this point, society enters the threshold of communism, the society of perfect justice where the workers are rewarded on the basis of their needs instead of on the basis of their work output. The economic foundations of social harmony no longer necessitate a money economy by which goods and services are rationed. Greed and envy over wealth will disappear, and with this disappearance will perish the lust for violence and power. The political superstructure of socialism, or workers' state, that is needed during the years of transition from capitalism to communism in order to build the economy of abundance will no longer be required. The process of dismantling or withering away of the state will then begin, provided the Communist society is not imperiled by external foes. In the Communist utopia, no special apparatus of compulsion (state) will be required to enforce social morality. The norms of behavior will be enforced by means of internalized sanctions, by social pressures such as ostracism, and by spontaneous social enforcement of society's norms.

This is the picture that emerges from the speculative doctrines of Marx and Engels found in their numerous literary works, principally *The Communist Manifesto, Das Kapital,* and *Anti-Dühring.* The revolutionary transition from capitalism to socialism would be led by the Communist party, the vanguard of the proletariat or workers, when the latter were able to seize control of the instruments of production and operate the economy without further need of the capitalists. A political seizure of power would be necessitated only if the capitalists resisted the economic sequestration of the instruments of production by the proletariat. Once economic power was firmly in the hands of the proletariat, a workers' state would be created under the guidance of the Communist party—the dictatorship of the proletariat. This revolutionary state would dispossess the capitalists of their ill-gotten wealth and thus wipe out the entire class of exploiters. Marx and Engels presumed that there would be resistance by the class of exploiters, so that a certain amount of violence might accompany the seizure of economic and political leadership by the proletariat and its vanguard. The revolution would be sustained by the vastly superior numbers of proletarians who, under the guidance of the Communist vanguard, would govern themselves democratically while excluding the capitalists from all participation in the exercise of power. The dictatorship of the proletariat would constitute a social and political dictatorship of the most numerous class against the small class of former exploiters. The proletarians themselves would form a workers' democracy to govern society during the era of socialism. Marx and Engels never contemplated a dictatorship by the Communist leaders and the total suppression of political rights among the workers. They both presumed that the revolution would take place in an advanced industrial society where the proletariat constituted the vast majority of the population. A class-conscious proletarian majority would require only limited guidance from the Communist vanguard, not tutelage and total dictation.

LENINISM

Lenin adapted Marxism to the peculiar environment of Tsarist Russia. He used the Marxist "science of revolution" to orient his thought as a revolutionary leader in a society that was barely at the threshold of capitalism. The class of proletarians was a tiny minority of the Russian masses, who were predominantly peasants just liberated from serfdom. To await the multiplication of the Russian proletariat under the evolutionary process of capitalistic development would have required a century to attain the advanced condition described by Marx and Engels as necessary to form the prelude of the revolution. Lenin was a dedicated revolutionary as well as a scholar; he could not bear the thought of leaving to the future generations the joy of witnessing the revolutionary overthrow of the Tsarist state. He sought a shortcut to the revolution. In his study of imperialism (*Imperialism: the Highest Stage of Capitalism*), Lenin found the clue to the accelerated revolution in Russia. Capitalism breaks the confines of the nation-state to erupt into underdeveloped countries in the form of imperialism. In order to keep down wages at home, capitalists must export increasing sums of capital for investment in backward countries. The plethora of capital must be siphoned off, and the industrial reserve army of unemployed workers must be safeguarded at home if surplus value is to be gleaned by the capitalists. If the rate of profit declines too much, capitalists seek foreign outlets for investment. Industrially backward countries with plenty of labor and resources could be developed more profitably. This transnational development of capitalism also permitted the capitalists to intensify their exploitation of colonial labor far beyond that of home labor, since there was no impelling reason for capitalists to make any social accommodations for colonial workers. Workers in the capitalist country could not be alienated from the state by undue exploitation without depriving the state of a source of fighting men in the event of war. Since capitalists from different countries clashed over foreign interests, intercapitalist rivalries presaged conflict and war for the fruits of imperialism.

Lenin welcomed intercapitalist rivalries for the redivision of the world's markets, resources, and labor force, since he felt that these would sharpen class tensions and awaken the proletariat to the need for revolution. He called upon the proletarian conscripts to transform the intercapitalist war into a civil war by turning their arms against their officers and leaders. The mass slaughter on the battlefields and the dislocation of the civilian economy would, he believed, turn the masses against the war. With proper guidance and leadership, the war-weary masses could be induced to rise against their leaders to halt the carnage and suffering. This would provide the Communists with an opportunity to lead the revolutionary movement against capitalism.

Lenin's diagnosis bore fruit in Russia, where defeatism among the soldiers and economic hardship among the civilian population produced a sudden collapse of state authority in 1917. The revolutionary organs (soviets) that sprang up became the nucleus of the proletarian dictatorship, since they could be easily infiltrated by Communists, and because they permitted the formation of a broad popular front within which the Communists could unite the disparate opponents of the state under their leadership. This example was to be repeated during World War II in France and Italy, where Committees of National Liberation were created with a revolutionary purpose; these committees did not succeed in their aim of substituting their authority for that of the legitimate organs of the state because foreign military occupation forces opposed revolution. In Russia, the provisional government in 1917 was not supported by adequate military power, so that the revolutionary organs (soviets), led by a resolute party (the Bolsheviks), were successful in transforming themselves into a viable government.

Communist doctrine still holds to the Leninist view that capitalism in the monopoly stage breeds imperialism and intercapitalist conflicts. In his last published report to the party in 1952, Stalin predicted that there would be yet another intercapitalist war for redivision of a shrunken colonial domain. The task for the Soviet Union was to deflect the imperialist drives of the capitalist powers into intercapitalist wars and prevent an accommodation among capitalist powers by which the Soviet Union might be divided. Stalin's pact of non-aggression with Hitler in 1939 proved to be the diplomatic catalyst that unleashed the intercapitalist war. The attack on the U.S.S.R. by Germany was not part of the calculation, but the end result was to spread Communist influence. World War II had scarcely terminated when Stalin reaffirmed the Leninist belief that war was implicit in the capitalist system and that the Socialist bloc must consolidate its internal power to ward off an attack by the imperialist bloc. Only by building up the military strength of the U.S.S.R. and its Socialist allies could imperialist aggression be deflected into another intercapitalist war.

It is a fundamental tenet of Marxism-Leninism that "socialism in one country" can be made militarily secure only by assisting the spread of socialism in the world. The sea of capitalism that surrounds socialism in one country must become a sea of socialism, and the capitalistic encirclement of the first Socialist state must be broken and replaced by a Socialist encirclement of the island remnants of capitalism before the Socialist system can be made secure. The Communists are not averse to military intervention by Socialist states against imperialist states and their economic colonies when there is tangible hope that this policy will extend socialism. But the Socialist states must not imperil their security in order to provide hasty liberation for subject peoples from imperialist rule. According to Marxist theory, eventual Socialist triumph is assured in all countries because of the internal contradictions of capitalism, but since the security of the Socialist nations is linked to the international liquidation of capitalism, it is in the interest of the Socialist bloc to encourage the progressive withering away of imperialist rule.

Lenin viewed international capitalism as a series of chains linking a few imperialist powers with their economic colonies. The weak links in each imperialist chain were formed by the economic colonies. Here there were no moral or political restraints upon capitalistic exploitation. Outside of the tiny class of native oligarchs who benefited from the imperialistic exploitation of their people, the colonial population was opposed to foreign capital. Social dissatisfaction could be easily diverted into national hatred of imperialist rule. A unitary nationalist movement would serve the interests of Socialist countries by weakening the imperialist powers through costly colonial conflicts. The newly liberated national states could become allies of the Socialist countries.

SOCIALIST CONSTRUCTION

Lenin also formulated the basic theory of Socialist development for the Communist movement. Stalin and Khrushchev have clung tenaciously to the Leninist program in their elaboration of Socialist domestic policies within the U.S.S.R. Although communism must await the liquidation of residual capitalism throughout the world, Lenin held that socialism must be constructed with haste in the Soviet Union for the defense of the first Socialist revolution as well as to assist the spread of socialism. Not only must military power be created to defend Socialist institutions from imperialist attack, but the foundations of the economy of abundance must be created. Lenin regarded socialism as a long and difficult period of transition from capitalism to communism.

Erection of a Socialist economy demanded that land and capital be placed in the hands of the state and that the peasants, artisans, merchants, and entrepreneurs be transformed into workers. Centralization of the instruments of production under the state would permit more effective planning of economic development. The entire population would be mobilized into a work force, whose standard of consumption could be regulated by the state. The surplus value that the labor force produced could be directed into those industries that would contribute most effectively to the defense of the state and to the creation of capital goods. The Socialist state must be freed as rapidly as possible from economic dependence upon the capitalist nations. Basic industries must be built first and Socialist technicians trained; then uninterrupted expansion of consumer goods industries and social services would take place within the limits of military security and capital requirements.

This long and arduous blueprint of economic growth meant that the population must be taught to accept years of toil and sacrifice. It must be trained and taught to respond to labor discipline and efficiency. For many years, the only satisfactions that the state would be able to provide the people would be pride in collective achievements. The use of nonmaterial rewards, such as medals and honors, admission to the party's ranks and to the exercise of leadership, elevation from the ranks of manual to intellectual labor, etc., have been emphasized. Due to human frailties that carry over from capitalistic to socialistic society, the Socialist state has had to provide material incentives in the form of differential wages to maximize labor efficiency. Recently, for the same reason, luxury items have been made available; but these luxuries have not diverted substantial wealth from the Socialist investment program.

THE WORKERS' STATE

Lenin devoted substantial treatment to the political institutions of the Socialist state. In his study of the *State and Revolution,* which he wrote on the eve of the March revolution, Lenin elaborated on the Marxian concept of the workers' state or dictatorship of the proletariat. Once having carried out a successful revolution against the capitalistic order, the proletariat must establish its own political institutions in order to protect the revolution from counterrevolution by the remnant forces of the capitalists. The workers' state must crush all internal resistance to its authority and create a powerful military force to resist imperialist attack by predatory capitalist powers. As it turned out, the Bolsheviks had to contend also with insurrectionary bands of armed peasants (the so-called "Green Armies") and with numerous secessionist forces that were mobilized by various national minority groups.

Lenin's concept of the workers' state was more authoritarian than that of Marx, just as his conception of the Communist party left little place for democracy, except perhaps among the top echelon or supreme leadership. The success of the proletarian struggle for liberation from capitalism and that of its revolution required maximum concentration of power in the hands of the dedicated proletarian elite. Lenin centralized all authority within the Bolshevik party in the hands of a Central Committee; later, a further concentration of authority occurred when a Political Bureau was created. Decisions of these supreme party organs were reached more or less democratically as long as Lenin lived. Once adopted, however, these decisions were absolutely binding upon the party membership. A military-type code of party justice was established to punish wayward members; under Stalin, the purge became a dread weapon of extermination against those who refused to conform to the will of the party chief, a practice that destroyed all semblance of democracy within the Central Committee and its Political Bureau. The democratic principle of election of party delegates and officers from the bottom up was never strictly adhered to among the Bolsheviks; under Stalin, co-option of the leaders from the top became the rule, and bureaucratic selection of delegates replaced democratic election. Democratic centralism degenerated quickly into mere centralism within the party structure. The leaders appropriated all power, including the right of self-perpetuation; under Stalin, all power was concentrated in the hands of the party chief. There was little difference between this form of authority and Tsarist autocracy as propounded by Pobedonostev, except the hereditary rule of succession.

THE PARTY DICTATORSHIP

The Leninist motto of all power in the hands of the party meant that the workers' state was to be a party dictatorship over the proletariat and not a workers' democracy as Marx and Engels had originally prescribed. The dictatorship of the proletariat was to be exercised by the party of the proletariat, not by the proletariat. The reasons for Lenin's preference of elitism over workers' democracy included a temperamental predisposition for aristocracy (in the Platonist sense) and a paternalistic attitude toward the masses. Leadership within the Socialist state could not be subordinated to the control of an untrained, undisciplined, inexperienced mass without endangering the revolution. Having guided the proletariat in the revolutionary struggle against capitalism so as to have "engineered" the revolution, the party could not turn over to the proletariat the even more difficult task of constructing the Socialist society in the face of so numerous and varied enemies. The proletariat must be led, guided, and controlled by the party if the dictatorship of the proletariat was to succeed in its task of liquidating the remnants of capitalism in one country, beating off the imperialists, and transforming the society first into socialism and then into communism. Lenin believed that the proletariat should be content to remain the docile instrument of party rule. Eventually, when the capitalistic encirclement would be broken and replaced by a Socialist encirclement and the phase of Socialist construction advanced to the point of the economy of abundance, the party would gradually restore authority to the workers themselves. As the state began to wither away, the party too would commence to vacate leadership and wither away.

STALINISM

Stalin's theoretical contributions to the doctrines of Marxism-Leninism were limited to elaborations of Lenin's ideas, not to the addition of a systematic body of thought to the philosophy of revolution, socialism, or communism. What is significant is that Stalin remained theoretically loyal to Marxism-Leninism throughout his long autocratic domination of the Communist party. He justified his policies as logical applications of Leninist principles to practice. In his report to the Eighteenth Party Congress in 1939, Stalin reasserted the party's goal as the creation of a Communist society, in which the workers' state would wither away and the Communist party would cease to act as the vanguard of the working people. In answer to a query, he indicated that the state and party would commence to wither away when the capitalistic encirclement would be broken and replaced by a Socialist encirclement of the remnants of capitalism. The party dictatorship would operate in Socialist countries so long as there remained a security problem. The problem of equality in a Socialist society was dealt with by Stalin in the same way St. Paul once handled the question for Christians: "He who does not work, neither shall he eat," and "From each according to his ability, to each according to his work" (Article 12, Constitution of the U.S.S.R.). In his report on the "Economic Conditions in the U.S.S.R." prepared for the Nineteenth Party Congress in 1952, Stalin reaffirmed the Leninist thesis that an intercapitalist war could be expected over the division of world markets. Despite the condition of American preponderance, the former capitalist powers (England, France, Germany, and Japan) would seek to break the hegemony of the United States and to re-establish new spheres of interest. Not to see this logic was to believe in miracles, according to Stalin, who concluded therefore that "the inevitability of wars between capitalist countries remains in force."

KHRUSHCHEV ON MARXISM-LENINISM

Khrushchev, a colorful, ingenious, and dynamic political leader, as a faithful disciple of Marxism-Leninism has not changed the theory appreciably. Indeed, Soviet leaders do not consider it either necessary or right to introduce changes in the theory. In his interpretation of the application of the theory, he has, however, introduced original features, such as his emphasis on the importance of the Communist example for winning adherents to the Marxist-Leninist approach to society. The doctrine of peaceful coexistence, though not original with him, has been stressed. By rectifying many of the mistakes made by Stalin, he has done much to strengthen the Communist cause. Perhaps his greatest contribution has been a vigorous practical approach to the solution of problems, which has brought results in increased productivity, increased support from the Soviet people, and a more sympathetic attitude on the part of some other nations.

At the Twentieth Party Congress, Khrushchev repeated the Leninist theme that as long as capitalism survives the monopolists would be tempted to unleash war, and that the Socialist states must build formidable power to discourage aggression against themselves. At the Twenty-first Party Congress, he added that when the Socialist bloc establishes its military preponderance in the world, it would be able to "compel the militant circles of imperialism to abandon plans for a new world war." [3] But as long as capitalism has the power to unleash war, the Socialist states must maintain powerful security forces and a vigilant police to combat counterrevolution. Should the Socialist countries attain the economy of abundance and enter the threshold of communism before the liquidation of capitalism is complete, the workers' state institutions would continue to function under communism. In no case would communism be inaugurated in one country or several countries while others were still struggling to develop a Socialist society; "it would be more correct to assume that by successfully employing the potentialities inherent in socialism, the

[3] This and subsequent quotations are from Khrushchev, "Report to the Congress," in *Current Soviet Policies,* Vol. III, *The Documentary Record of the Extraordinary 21st Communist Party Congress,* ed. Leo Gruliow (New York: Columbia University Press, 1960), pp. 41–72.

socialist countries will enter the higher phase of communist society more or less simultaneously."

An indication of the nature of Communist political institutions was given by Khrushchev in his report to the Twenty-first Party Congress:

> Marxism-Leninism teaches that under communism the state will wither away and that the functions of public administration will lose their political character and will turn into management of society's affairs directly by the people. But one cannot oversimplify and conceive of the process of the withering away of the agencies of state as something like the turning of leaves in autumn, when the branches are left bare as the leaves fall.
>
> If we approach it dialectically, the question of withering away of the state is a question of evolution of the socialist state toward communist public self-government.

Khrushchev listed several examples of public self-government that were being gradually developed alongside the institutions of the state administration while still in the phase of Socialist development toward communism. Just as a Federation of Public Sports Societies to replace the State Committee on Physical Culture and Sports was being formed outside of the regular state administration, so similar "public organizations" should be formed to administer certain functions: cultural and health services, resort facilities, public order and justice, and others eventually. In fact, "matters are approaching a situation in which public organizations, alongside and parallel with such state agencies as the militia and the courts, will perform the functions of safeguarding public order and security." The militia as well as the Procurators and courts would be required for a long time to come "in order to exert influence on persons who maliciously refuse to submit to socialist society's standards of behavior and are not amenable to persuasion." However, side by side with these state agencies have emerged comradely courts whose competence should be extended beyond their present jurisdiction. The comrades' courts are designed to "prevent and subsequently completely preclude individuals' commission of acts harmful to society." Publicly delegated persons (presumably Communists) would be authorized to denounce before the comrades' courts persons who manifested antisocial tendencies, so that these tribunals might salvage the wayward individual before he tumbled into crime. In time, as the more serious types of crime ceased to be committed (such as political crimes, which had become practically nonexistent according to the Communist Party First Secretary), state tribunals would be closed down and their tasks transferred to a constantly dwindling number of courts. Voluntary detachments of people's militia will eventually displace the police in the task of maintaining order locally, while public delegates will assume more and more the functions of the

Procurators. The public institutions of Communist society develop gradually within the structure of the Socialist order by a process that might be described as "the utmost unfolding of democracy, the enlisting of the broadest strata of the population in the management of all affairs of the country, enlistment of all citizens in participation in the management of economic and cultural construction."

The final stage of communism, in which society will be able to satisfy the needs of all persons (while the latter, in turn, willingly contribute their work time and talents to productive creation of goods and services) without the need to regulate work as a legal duty, will not be reached until work is regarded as a moral and social duty and an inner compulsion to perform socially necessary labor motivates all persons. By that time, technology will have conquered labor drudgery through the perfection of automation; and labor "will become a source of joy and pleasure for the healthy, rounded man." The economy of abundance will permit the distribution of goods and services to all persons in accordance with their needs. A condition of equality will be reached in the treatment of individuals by society that will reflect the disappearance of essential distinction between mental and manual labor. In 1961 the party promised that the present generation of Soviet people will live under communism.

IDEOLOGICAL IMPORTANCE OF MARXISM-LENINISM

Marxism-Leninism ends on a note of optimism. The working people may look forward to total liberation from all forms of subjugation when communism has been attained and to gradual improvement of their lot throughout the period of Socialist progress toward communism. For more than forty years, the Soviet people have been fed promises of social betterment through difficult and tragic times. The ideology has played an important role in motivating the Soviet people to perform constant drudgery and to accept iron discipline during an entire lifetime of toil and sacrifice. It has provided them with a rational explanation of the future and a belief in a system of rewards. It has served to justify the formation of new political and social elites and to attract popular consensus to the policies of the party and state.

Many people, including even a few Communists, are not able to accept the optimism of Marxism-Leninism. For example, Milovan Djilas, a lifelong Yugoslav Communist, in his book *The New Class* criticized the Soviet system. Djilas proposes that to the Communist party, Marxism-Leninism serves the same ends as other religions; that the Communist utopia that is dangled before Soviet citizens is the promised land that may never be attained. By propagating the myth of the equal and abundant land of freedom that lies ahead, the Communist party has sought to drug the people. He maintains that an autocratic and totalitarian state has been created along with a new social hierarchy of bureaucratic and professional elites that are permitted to exploit the working people in the name of social justice. By paying constant lip service to the ideology, the party leaders, according to Djilas, mask social reality in an effort to buttress their autocratic power and the privileged status of the class from which they now draw most of their following: the intelligentsia or new ruling class of the Soviet Union.

Marxism-Leninism performs an important function in the interest of the Communist party and of the bureaucratic politicians who derive absolute power over Soviet society from their control of the party apparatus. Just as the priesthood or other religious guides monopolize power in theocratic societies by serving as the human agents of the deity, the Communists insure their monopoly of political power in the U.S.S.R. by convincing the people that the ideal of communism can be engineered only by the party. The party is the indispensable vanguard of the working people during the long and arduous struggle to achieve complete liberation from injustice. Only through its infallible leadership can the working people build the perfect society. The road to utopia can be opened solely by the Communist party, which interprets the science of revolutionary progress (Marxism-Leninism) and applies its teachings to the laws of dialectical development.

By propagating the ideology, the party has built a powerful sustaining force in the minds of the Soviet working people. Power is identified with the party and not with would-be alternative elites, such as the military, the managerial caste, and the police bureaucracy. Any attempt by such alternate elite groups to overthrow party rule would be met by popular hostility. Through the ideology, the party has become the supreme legitimate institution of Soviet society. Its status has come to resemble that of the institution of monarchy, in much the same manner as this institution is respected in Japan. This ideological-institutional role of the Communist party as the legitimate source of authority in Soviet society gives the men of the party apparatus the character of a ruling caste or priesthood. The growth of Marxist-Leninist dogma resembles the process by which Christian theology developed during the Middle Ages. Mastery of the ideology and its dogma has become an indispensable tool of the Soviet politician. The struggle for personal exercise of power must be waged within the party, not outside. Power circulates entirely within the party. By controlling the admission and expulsion of party members, the tiny elite that directs the party has built for itself an edifice of power that is the envy of other oligarchies.

SELECTED READING

HOOK, SIDNEY. *Marx and the Marxists: The Ambiguous Legacy.* Princeton, N.J.: D. Van Nostrand Co., Inc., 1955.
LENIN, V. I. *Selected Works.* 2 vols. London: Lawrence & Wishart, Ltd., 1936–38.
MARX, KARL. *Selected Works.* 2 vols. New York: International Publishers Co., Inc., 1942.
MEYER, ALFRED G. *Marxism: The Unity of Theory and Practice; a Critical Essay.* Cambridge, Mass.: Harvard University Press, 1954.
———. *Leninism.* Cambridge, Mass.: Harvard University Press, 1957.
SHAPIRO, LEONARD. *The Communist Party of the Soviet Union.* New York: Random House, Inc., 1960.
STALIN, JOSEPH. *Foundations of Leninism.* New York: International Publishers Co., Inc., 1932.
———. *Problems of Leninism.* New York: International Publishers Co., Inc., 1934.

40

The Communist Party of the Soviet Union

CHARACTERISTICS

The Soviet Union is a one-party state in which the Communist party monopolizes all political power and prerogatives. After the Bolshevik Revolution, Lenin, supported by a majority of the Communist leaders, decided in favor of excluding all other parties from participation in the government and from further legal activity inside Russia. Despite the pleas of such Bolsheviks as Kamenev and Zinoviev that the Socialist parties be allowed to continue as allies of the Communists, the Soviet Communist party (in 1952 officially designated Communist party of the Soviet Union) has maintained a tight monopoly over all political life in the country. This position remains legitimated by the 1936 Constitution.

In defense of this party dictatorship, Stalin explained that multiple parties are necessary only in a society that is divided into antagonistic social classes, so that each class may be represented through its chosen elite. Since the Soviet Union had by 1936 abolished antagonistic social classes and Soviet society consisted only of two "friendly classes," the workers and peasants, both of which were represented in the Communist party, there was no need for the existence of another party in the U.S.S.R. In answer to Western criticism that one-party rule was undemocratic, Stalin asserted that the Communist party represented the majority of the people and governed in its interest, while Western bourgeois parties all represented merely the propertied minority and governed in the interest of the bourgeoisie and middle class. What Stalin failed to see was that unless competition is allowed among political parties, the majority of the people can have no way to express its consensus; and to assert that the majority of workers and peasants in the U.S.S.R. freely support the rule of the Communists remains an untested opinion, certainly not a verified fact.

By no stretch of the imagination can the Communist party of the Soviet Union be considered a democratic party, either in its relationship to the Soviet people or in the relationship between the leadership and the membership. Even though the party has permeated Soviet society and is omnipotent in all organized groups, and despite the fact that it has established close ties with the people so as to understand their desires and aspirations as well as their complaints, it functions as an elitist vanguard. The Communist party imposed its absolute rule upon the people of the Soviet Union by right of conquest in a bloody civil war and maintains its monopoly of power by military might. The people have no choice but to submit to its authority, since the state is the exclusive agency of the party. Soviet citizens are permitted to register favorable opinions of the party, but the expression of an unfavorable opinion is not permissible.

As the people's vanguard, the party knows better what is good for the country than the people. To quote Stalin:

> The Party cannot be a real party if it limits itself to registering what the masses of the working class feel and think, if it drags at the tail of the spontaneous movements, if it is unable to overcome the inertness and the political indifference of the spontaneous movement, if it is unable to rise above the momentary interests of the proletariat, if it is unable to elevate the masses to the level of the class interests of the proletariat. The Party must stand at the head of the working class; it must see farther than the working class; it must lead the proletariat.[1]

Not only does the party lead the people by the hand toward justice as a father would lead his children, but the tiny core of leaders who are perched atop the party's pyramid of power likewise treat the membership much the same as a general staff would treat the ranks of officers and troops who are subject to its commands. Party decisions and policies are made by a handful of leaders and very often by one supreme leader alone. The membership has no voice in the deliberations of the party elite and is not permitted to voice criticism against those decisions and policies. Rigid discipline is imposed by the party apparatus upon its membership through a centralized chain of command. In contrast to Western democratic parties, most of which permit considerable nonconformist individual expression of opinion by the membership and spokesmen, the Soviet Communist party does not tolerate nonconformism within the organization. Under Stalin, deviationism was brutally suppressed by means of the blood purge. The nonconformist was declared to

[1] Joseph Stalin, *Problems of Leninism* (Moscow: Foreign Languages Publishing House, 1940), p. 73.

be an "enemy of the people" and was liquidated after torture had succeeded in extracting a confession of guilt. Khrushchev has been more humane in his treatment of antiparty members, contenting himself with demotion and expulsion in most instances.

The Communist party of the Soviet Union is not only authoritarian and elitist, but totalitarian as well. It commands total loyalty of its members, who are not permitted to have divided loyalties or interests that conflict with party obligations. Party members must submit to personal hardships and sacrifices in the performance of their assignments. Service to the party must take precedence over all other commitments. The sweep of party authority over the lives of the Soviet people is also total. Every social, economic, political, cultural, scientific, or other problem is within the scope of party control and guidance. All forms of human behavior come under the scrutiny of the party, which may act independently of the governmental administration as well as through it to regulate private as well as public life.

MEMBERSHIP

Party membership has seldom exceeded 3.5 per cent of the population in the U.S.S.R. Admission is open to persons over eighteen years of age who are sponsored by three party members having three or more years of standing in the party. The sponsors must assume personal responsibility for the protégé, whose application is deliberated by the general meeting of the primary organization. If it is approved, the application is referred to the party district committee or to the party city committee for ratification. Currently, persons who once held membership in some other political party (viz., before the 1917 revolution, or perhaps in a foreign country prior to having become a citizen of the U.S.S.R.) must be sponsored by five party members and their applications must be ratified by the Central Committee of the party. If the recently published draft of changes in the party rules is adopted by the All-Union Party Congress to be held in the fall of 1961, ratification in the future will be by the province or territory party committee or by the Central Committee of the Union Republic. Soviet citizens who are under twenty may seek admission to the party only if they hold membership in the Young Communist League (Komsomol). This rule postpones but does not prohibit the application for party affiliation by youths who are not members of the Komsomol.

The novice to the party ranks must serve at least a year as a candidate before he can be admitted to full membership status. He must become familiar with the doctrine, dogma, program, rules, and activities of the party and prove his aptitudes and qualities. Candidates who show promise are recommended for full membership; those who are less promising may be granted an additional year of apprenticeship, while the ones who prove to be unfit for membership are dropped. Candidates are not permitted to vote on deliberations within the primary organization or to serve as officers or delegates. The standards for membership are rigidly maintained to prevent infiltration of the party by opportunists or careerists as well as by enemies of the people and antiparty elements. Even after one has been made a full member, the threat of expulsion is always real and imminent for those who fail to maintain the party's standards of loyalty and efficiency. The average Soviet citizen is not eligible for party membership, while many who are have little desire to become party activists.

OBLIGATIONS OF PARTY MEMBERS

Reluctance to join the Communist party of the Soviet Union is due to several reasons. Many Soviet citizens have no interest in politics or in the ideology of the party. Others find the obligations too exacting on their personal freedom and leisure or fear the consequences of expulsion. Membership in this elite group is fraught with great risk to the family as well as to the individual. Unless one has the ambition to become a leader and to exercise power over others or wishes to fill a position of some responsibility in the administrative bureaucracy, for which party membership is often a prerequisite, there is little to be gained from party membership.

The duties of the party member are explicitly enumerated in the Statute of the Communist party. He must promote unity within the ranks of the party by supporting the leadership and unmasking deviationists and antiparty persons. He owes strict obedience and discipline to party rules and policies, and he must fight for the defense of the party line. He must spy on his comrades and report their shortcomings and errors to his and their superiors, even though personal risks are involved. According to Khrushchev's report of 1956 to the Twentieth Party Congress, many loyal comrades were purged by Police Chief Beria for reporting his activities and those of his agents to the Central Committee. Party members must develop self-criticism to correct their own errors. Rule 3 of the Party Statute provides that, "He who silences criticism and substitutes ostentation and boastfulness in its place cannot remain in the ranks of the Party." Neither Stalin nor Khrushchev has engaged in much self-criticism while in command of the party, thus setting a poor example for the membership. This rule is apparently intended only for subordinate members. The party expects its membership to be truthful and honest toward the party and to select its cadres on the basis of individual qualifications rather than for reasons of friendship, personal ties, kinship, or ethnic origin. The individual Communist must set an example of labor efficiency and devotion to work, so as to improve general working norms and increase productivity among the working class. He must distinguish himself among the workers as a leader and thus strengthen the image of the party in their eyes. He must be prepared to volunteer for the most difficult tasks in his work at the factory, on the farm, or on the battlefield, so as to inspire heroism among the masses. The party faithful must spread knowledge, understanding, and belief in the values and science of Marxism-Leninism among the masses in order to preserve the role of the party as the vanguard of the people. Comrades must participate actively in regular party functions: meetings, campaigns, Socialist competitions, and volunteer work. They must accept extraordinary assignments irrespective of personal hardships that may be involved to themselves or to their families. The party member is required to assist the law-enforcement authorities in the protection of Socialist property, in combating antisocial behavior, in enforcing Socialist legality, and in promoting the interests and policies of the Soviet state against its enemies. This includes voluntary service in the people's militia and on the comrades' courts. The comrade must not abuse his party status for personal rewards or advantages, and he must remember that he belongs to a corps of select persons who have a mission to perform and that his greatest reward is the satisfaction of serving the working class.

Communists in the Soviet Union are assessed 2 per cent of their monthly income upon admission to the party and thereafter must contribute anywhere from 0.5 to 3 per cent of their monthly income as dues. Failure to pay dues is a common cause for expulsion. For very minor infractions against the law, a comrade may be reprimanded or demoted to candidate status, but members who are convicted of a crime are expelled. Expulsion for any reason may be followed by other sanctions, such as dismissal from a job, transfer to an undesirable location, and sometimes by police sanctions: exile, deportation and confinement, imprisonment. Reasons and evidence are not difficult to find for the purpose of harassing former Communists who have proved disloyal, untrustworthy, disreputable, disgraceful, negligent, or incompetent. The turnover in party membership is fairly high; some members find the obligations and duties too exacting and take the easy way out by failing to pay their dues.

Persons join the Communist party for different reasons. Many believe in the ideology sufficiently to want to belong to the vanguard elite and build the Communist utopia. Opportunists join because of the desire to qualify politically for high-ranking positions of power, responsibility, prestige, and reward, most of which are reserved for Communists. A large number of successful persons in management or the armed forces feel that they must accept party membership when this is offered to them; the pressures that can be applied are often convincing arguments in favor of assuming "social responsibilities" toward the working class.

Party membership does provide definite rewards for ambitious persons. It may offer a political career in the apparatus to those who seek the exercise of power and leadership and do not fear the risk of being purged. By rising within the ranks of the party to positions of responsibility and decision making, the party member may some day hope to penetrate the power elite. If he has greater technical or managerial skills than political acumen and fortitude, he may prefer a bureaucratic career within the state administration, where the risks are slightly less and the tenure prospects somewhat greater. Not all the positions in the state administration demand party membership, but those that carry prestige and responsibility generally do. The party offers persons of unusual personal qualities a vehicle of rapid upward social mobility as well as a medium to attain high professional status.

SOCIAL COMPOSITION OF PARTY MEMBERSHIP

The Communist party seeks to be "represented" as every social level and within every significant social unit (factory, office, collective farm, school, soviet, military formations, store, etc.), so that it will be informed of the activities of the population and of its state of mind. In the absence of democratic forms of expression, the population's wishes and feelings must be communicated to the party leadership; and the latter must have a network of agents to create social consensus in its policies and to maintain effective control over mass expression and behavior. To achieve this omnipresence of the party within Soviet society, members must be recruited from all social strata, occupational groups, nationalities, and geographic areas of the U.S.S.R. The tendency for overrepresentation of the intelligentsia or educated stratum of the population holding managerial positions has been checked somewhat in recent years by the drive to recruit new members for the party from the laboring classes.

More than one-half of the party members are Great Russians. This corresponds to the numerical strength of the Great Russians in the total population. Although some nationalities have been "overrepresented" and others "underrepresented" at certain times, all nationalities are represented in the party.[2] There is a trend that indicates an increasingly closer approximation of the percentage of members from a given nationality to the percentage of that nationality in the total population. Soviet leaders do not seem to commit the blunder of refusing to admit new members on the basis of national or racial origin.

[2] For example, Georgians were overrepresented while the Ukrainians and Moldavians were underrepresented.

In 1939, rural areas with almost 68 per cent of the total population had only 20 per cent of the party membership. This discrepancy is gradually decreasing, although the farm workers are still less well represented than any other group. There are now about three million party members and candidates in rural districts. Also, the percentage of the total population living in urban areas has increased from thirty-two in 1939 to forty-eight in 1959. It is likely that this trend will continue.

Although women are granted complete equality with men, women are latecomers in politics. The current figure of almost one and one-half million women party members represents a rapid increase since the pre-World War II period. Although the top-ranking party positions are held by men, women are becoming increasingly important in Soviet politics. Mme. Furtseva is the first woman member of the Presidium and formerly of the Secretariat of the Central Committee. The Twentieth Party Congress elected four women (including Mme. Furtseva) as full members and six women as candidates of the Central Committee. Several women have important posts as regional first secretaries.

Since the educational level of the entire population is improving rapidly, increasing numbers of party members are educated. In 1936, over two and one-half million members had completed the rigorous secondary school curriculum, higher institutions, or their equivalent, while two million more had partially completed such educational preparation. The party encourages its members to obtain a complete secondary and higher education, since it prefers to entrust leadership roles in administration and the economy to well-trained persons. The party operates a Higher Party School in which members are given training in organizational, administrative, and propaganda methods and procedures to increase their efficiency as political functionaries. The Academy of Social Sciences (formerly the Marx-Engels Institute) is also maintained by the Central Committee and directed by its Agitation and Propaganda Department; its task is to provide intensive training in Marxism-Leninism and the social sciences for party specialists who are to assume important roles as editors, journalists, research writers, and teachers. Graduates of the Academy are awarded higher degrees that carry great prestige value.

The Communist party caters to a fairly youthful membership. After World War II, some 63 per cent of all members were under thirty-five years of age. The principal source of new members is the Komsomol, which is expected to supply a steady stream of new candidates to fill the shoes of older members whose age precludes effective party service. Positions of leadership within the party are filled by considerably older persons, since experience is considered a more valuable asset among the leaders and functionaries than for ordinary members. Despite the frequent purges of older leaders, the average age of the top echelon of the party elite is above sixty years.

PARTY GROWTH

The Communist party of the Soviet Union has grown from a mere 23,000 conspirators against tsarism in January 1917 to 8,239,000 members and candidates in January 1959 on the occasion of the extraordinary Twenty-first Party Congress. The drastic purges of the middle 1930's weeded out more than half the membership and left the party in a weakened condition. Ideological standards were lowered during the war, thus enabling the size of the membership to treble. Persons who distinguished themselves in battle were gathered into the ranks of the party as patriotic examples, and heroism became the ideological value symbol of the Communist party in its greatest struggle for survival. Following the war, those who failed to perfect their ideological preparation were dropped from the membership roles; normal recruitment again was made through the Komsomol.

The normal turnover of party membership that occurs regularly because of substandard performance of members or non-payment of dues must be distinguished from its periodic purges of "antiparty" members, which are used to eliminate factionalism and personal rivalries from within the party. The purge is an institutionalized form of terrorism by which the supreme party leadership destroys its potential opposition and preserves its absolute monopoly of authority within the organization. Purges occurred as early as 1921, when the first mass purification campaign against opportunists and class enemies who had infiltrated the ranks of the Communist party took place under Lenin's direction. Stalin institutionalized terrorism for the purpose of consolidating his personal autocratic power over the party apparatus. Khrushchev has used the purge to eliminate his rivals from the Central Committee and Presidium and to re-establish internal party unity. The strength of the dominant leader and the collective leadership of the party are dependent upon the elimination of personal rivalries and factionalism from within the party.

COMMUNIST YOUTH ORGANIZATIONS

The profound influence of the party over Soviet society is supplemented by a number of mass organizations that are completely dominated by the party. Ever since Lenin's days, the party has paid special attention to the ideological preparation of the youth. The Young Communist League (Komsomol) is composed of approximately nineteen million youths aged fourteen to twenty-six. Though officially a non-party organization, the Young Communist League carries out its work under the guidance of the Communist party. The governing body of the Young Communist League is its Central Committee, which is subordinate to the

Central Committee of the Communist party. The local organizations of the Komsomol also resemble those of the parent and are guided and controlled in their work by the respective republic, territory, province, city, and district party organizations.[3] Members of the Young Communist League who join the party and do not occupy executive posts in the League must leave the Komsomol. The League has no "right" to be considered a party organization, but it has all the corresponding obligations. The Komsomol is the active aid of the party in all state and economic work.[4] The right of the League organizations listed in Rule 63 of the Party Statutes reads:

> Young Communist League organizations have the right of broad initiative in discussing and submitting to the appropriate Party organizations all problems in the work of industrial enterprises, collective farms, state farms and offices connected with the aim of eliminating shortcomings in their operations and rendering them help needed to improve work, organize socialist competition, carry out mass campaigns, etc.

The Komsomol is an effective training organization for future party members. An active Young Communist is likely to become a party member. All Young Communists are indoctrinated in the Marxist-Leninist ideology and in the values of Soviet patriotism; whether they become party members or not, they are likely to be politically conscious citizens.

Soviet children between the ages of nine and fourteen are recruited into the Young Pioneers, while those from age seven to nine are eligible to enroll in the association of Little Octobrists. Though each of these organizations has a different task, all of them are used to provide a political education. Since most of the young people participate in one or more of the youth organizations, most of the Soviet population receives active political indoctrination and training during the formative years of their ideological development.

Party groups are formed at all congresses, conferences, and meetings of the soviets, trade-unions, cooperatives, and the other mass organizations. The task of these *ad hoc* party groups is to intensify the party's influence in every way, to impose the party's ideals and policies on the non-party representatives of the people, and to see that the party line is understood and appreciated.

PARTY ROLE AND FUNCTIONS

The Communist party is defined by the U.S.S.R. Constitution (Article 126) as "the vanguard of the working people" and "the leading core of all organizations of the working people, both public and state"; its role in

[3] Party Statutes, Rule 60.
[4] Party Statutes, Rule 62.

Soviet society is described as that of uniting "the most active and politically conscious citizens in the ranks of the working class, working peasants and working intelligentsia" for the purpose of building a Communist society. The functions that the party performs within Soviet society are numerous and include the following: selection of the political or power elite and governing class of the Soviet state and society; formulation of the policies of all state and public institutions, agencies, and organizations; direction of all branches of the state administration; management of the major sectors and enterprises of the Socialist economy; formulation of the normative content of the legal order, morality, and social behavior, interpretation of the Marxist-Leninist ideology; guidance and control of the soviets; education and indoctrination of the masses; supervision and control of all state and public institutions, agencies, and organizations; and recruitment and training of the power elite and governing class.

Party rule in the U.S.S.R. is based upon the monopolization of the power of appointment by responsible organs of the party apparatus to all positions of any importance in the state administration; the economy; and so-called "public organizations" such as trade-unions, cooperatives, youth groups, defense (e.g., militia)organizations, and technical, scientific, and cultural societies. Although professional and technical proficiency are highly desirable qualities at all levels of Soviet administration, party loyalty remains the prime prerequisite for appointment to responsible positions. This does not necessarily mean that only party members and candidates are eligible to hold responsible positions in Soviet society, but that non-party persons must be as equally loyal to the Communist party as the most zealous members if they are to qualify for decision-making positions.

Within the soviets, the party has the duty of guiding, educating, informing, and supervising the workers' representatives but not to monopolize the leadership and so alienate the non-party representatives. Only in the event of some dire emergency would party organs be justified in imposing their authority over the soviets. Many party secretaries have been reprimanded for assuming personal direction over the executive committees of local and intermediate soviets, but most of these party functionaries have discovered that it is often more difficult to supervise than it is to govern or control. The party leaders who govern the state, rather than advising or supervising others, set a bad example. In the Supreme Soviet of the U.S.S.R., which, according to the Constitution, is "the highest organ of state power," almost all the deputies are party members. Therefore, the party may be described as a "ruling" force in the higher state organs and as a "guiding" force in the lower ones. Although non-party people may have an opportunity to participate in the government, the party is the decisive factor.

Government and the economy in the U.S.S.R. are inseparable, and the party is fully responsible for the economic progress of the country. The party task is complicated because political and economic goals are fused. In an attempt to accomplish this difficult task, the party has recruited large numbers of economic and industrial captains into its ranks. Party members who were experienced managers have been put into vital posts. Other talented plant managers have been invited to join the party. Thus, the party constantly attempts to absorb the most talented people, regardless of nationality, sex, or religion. Furthermore, in numerous party schools, the party trains its members in a wide variety of professions, so that the supply of industrial, technical, and agricultural specialists within the party may be increased. By having party members everywhere, in lower and managerial positions, a complete system of economic and political party checks is provided.

Although most party members are employed in administration and production, some do party work exclusively.[5] These paid officials of the party operate independently of the state machinery. They are the most trusted supervisors over the Soviet economy, the public administration, and the soviets. Under the interlocking system of controls, these paid officials act as additional checks. While reports from individual party members and primary organizations are transmitted to the Central Committee, additional direct checks by the upper echelons of the party are made in all enterprises. Under such a system, it would seem that anything other than superior performance, honesty, and diligence would be impossible. Yet, in spite of the careful supervision and intricate system of checks, Soviet newspapers frequently report incidents of maladministration and dishonesty involving production managers, state officials, and party functionaries.

The party is supposed to supervise rather than "run" the economy in the same manner as it is supposed to supervise the lower soviets. Party officials who are responsible for the economy have the duty of supervising management, but they are not supposed to intervene directly in economic decision making. However, since the manager and most persons in lower managerial positions are party members, the party functionaries do interfere indirectly in plant supervision; local party secretaries keep careful watch over economic enterprises in their district.

The party is responsible for the selection of personnel in governmental and economic organizations. The factory manager, or the personnel de-

[5] Estimates of the number of party officials range from 150,000 to 240,000. In most cases, besides having a good education, they have to possess an organizational talent, to be builders of enthusiasm in order to get results without antagonizing people, and to have good speaking ability and to demonstrate talent in any position that the party may ask them to fill. Most party officials fail to live up to these high standards of expectation and are dropped from the apparatus. Those who succeed are often promoted rapidly in the party hierarchy.

partment, subject to the approval of supervisors in the corresponding ministry or Regional Economic Council, may hire a man for a relatively important position in a factory. However, the District Party Secretary is held co-responsible for the hiring. The reason for this relatively expensive and clumsy procedure is distrust, and this complicated system of checks often produces undesirable results. It is probable that Soviet enterprises would be more efficient, and certainly the administrative machinery could be simpler, if the party leadership trusted party men in responsible positions. However, this would increase the power, prestige, and independence of the managerial personnel, though the check by party members within the plant would remain. The party cannot as yet part with the swollen party bureaucratic apparatus, although it is aware of the associated disadvantages and concurrently is attempting to increase production efficiency and to introduce labor-saving devices.

Political work within party ranks and among the non-party people is an indispensable task of the party. The teaching of ideology is considered vital. The one-party system leads to uniform political thinking. Differences have to be ironed out within the party. Party decisions are accepted by all party members and are spread by them throughout the nation.

The first task is, therefore, a thorough indoctrination of party members. This is being done regularly in meetings of primary party organizations and at party conferences. Here, the party member is informed about current party business and changes in the party line. In addition, numerous courses in ideology are offered by the party, which members may attend. Finally, they may study a correspondence course independently. The universities present Marxism-Leninism to thousands of students, including party members, members of youth organizations, and non-party people. Finally, newspapers, magazines, and other informational media in party hands make the indoctrination complete. This effective indoctrination is not opposed by any competing ideology. Yet the party leadership often warns against the danger of infiltration by foreign ideologies. Taking into consideration thc limited circulation of foreign information in the U.S.S.R., such as newspapers, periodicals, books, films, and broadcasts that are available to Soviet citizens, one cannot but wonder why the party leaders are so afraid. Insecurity after four decades of party work is surprising.

All party members, regardless of their position, have the task of educating non-party people. All organizations in the Soviet Union have been infiltrated by the party. The party members always introduce a program compatible with the party line and oppose programs contrary to it. Actually, there are few, if any, citizens in the U.S.S.R. who are not indoctrinated in the official ideology, which is taught in every school, in the armed forces, in trade-unions, in all other associations, and by all information media. A non-party man may be a Communist without ever joining the party. The party leadership has a high regard for such individuals and calls them non-party Bolsheviks. The party is responsible for the political education of the masses, and the lower party organizations are often reprimanded for neglect of this fundamental duty.

The system of forcible indoctrination in one ideology has several associated disadvantages. Non-party people often distrust the official ideological pronouncements. Passive resistance or outright disinterest in party ideology has been observed in Soviet universities, schools, professional associations, and elsewhere. The ideology has been presented in a repetitious and unimaginative manner, since party ideologists have been fearful of committing heresy. Courses on Marxism-Leninism are compulsory in all Soviet schools. Under such conditions, much of the enthusiasm that prevailed in the early years of the Soviet regime among students has been lost. Even convinced party members attempt to avoid the dull and monotonous indoctrination sessions that are devoted to political education, and interest centers on the study of subjects of non-ideolgical significance.

The party, aware of the slackening of interest in ideology, seems to be diverting the attention of the population to matters that are of much greater interest to the population, though not retreating from its ideology. The important matters where the interest of the whole population and government, and that means the party, coincide are the economy and increased standards of living. And this to the average Soviet citizen means more than what Karl Marx had to say.

PARTY LEADERSHIP AND INTRAPARTY DEMOCRACY

The Party Statutes, in prescribing the structure of the party and its democratic operation, make it clear that "the guiding principle of the organizational structure of the Party is democratic centralism." This is taken to mean:

(a) Election of all Party governing bodies from bottom to top;
(b) Periodic accountability of Party bodies to their Party organizations;
(c) Strict Party discipline and subordination of the minority to the majority;
(d) The decisions of higher bodies are unconditionally binding upon lower ones.[6]

Should these provisions be implemented, the party would indeed function democratically. Although elections are held more or less regularly and in accordance with the letter of the Party Statutes, it is a well-established custom that all officers and delegates to higher party conclaves who are to be elected must first be passed on for reliability and suitability by the higher party organizations. The latter exercise a veto power over the

[6] Party Statutes, Rule 21.

"free election" of party officers and delegates; and, wherever necessary, the higher party organs may actually designate the officers and delegates of inferior organizations. In such cases, the lower party organizations are expected to "ratify" the selections. Thus, Stalin and Khrushchev have been able to "pack" important positions in the party apparatus with their trusted followers. A similar condition applies to the exercise by inferior party organizations of their statutory power to remove their own officers and delegates. Approval by a higher party organ is mandatory before any apparatus officer may be removed.

The provisions of the Party Statutes that guarantee the right of free discussion and self-criticism among all party members and seek to insure majority control over the life of the Communist party are impossible to reconcile with the conformism that in fact characterizes party affairs. Fear of being purged has destroyed most initiative and pluck among Soviet Communists; critical freedom has become the right only of those in command of the party apparatus. Why do the Soviet leaders allow such an incongruous situation to persist between theory and practice? Is it not dangerous to cultivate the charge of hypocrisy? Cynicism would be impossible to reconcile with the idealistic demands of the party upon its members. The discrepancy between theory and practice has been rationalized by means of the excuse of the permanent threat of the capitalistic encirclement, wartime emergency, and more recently by the exigencies of the cold war. The Soviet state and its Communist party have been endangered continuously for over forty years. Each five- and seven-year plan and every policy to achieve the plans has been a battle of survival. In the do-or-die struggle to construct a viable Socialist economy and build the survival power of the Soviet state against the implacable enemies of progress, the Communist party has justified its deviation from principles respecting party organization and operation.

CENTRAL PARTY ORGANIZATION

The Congress of the Communist Party of the Soviet Union

Figure 40–1 presents the organization of the Communist party of the Soviet Union. The highest organ of the Communist party is the All-Union Party Congress of delegates elected by the Union Republican Party Congresses in the non-Russian areas and in the Russian Soviet Federated Socialist Republic (R.S.F.S.R.) by the territorial and regional party conferences. The Central Committee determines the basis of representation, presently one delegate per 6,000 members, and allots the number of delegates to the various party organizations. At the extraordinary Twenty-first Party Congress held in 1959, there were 1,269 voting delegates and 106 alternates. The Party Congress is supposed to meet once every four years

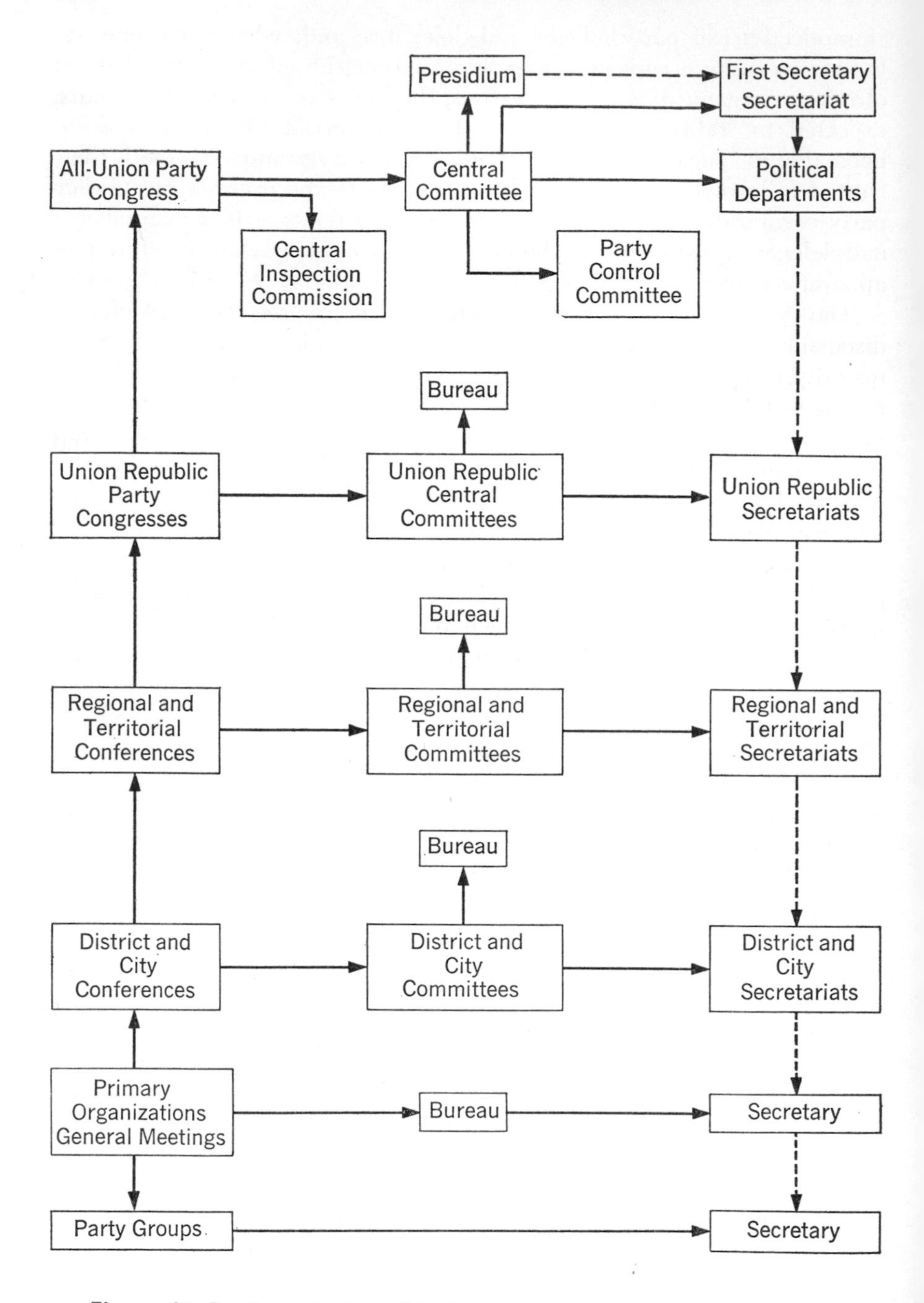

Figure 40–1. Organization of the Communist party of the Soviet Union.

or sooner at the discretion of the Central Committee. Stalin's successors have been more scrupulous than he was in ordering the convocation of the Party Congress.

The Congress hears the reports of the permanent central organs of the party and must approve them. It revises the Party Statutes and Program, elects the central permanent organs of the party, and adopts resolutions concerning ideological matters and policy. In theory, the delegates are free to criticize the leadership and its policies, to adopt new ones, and to elect whom they choose to lead the party. In practice, the delegates are convened to be informed of the party line and of the decisions of the leadership. Since the Fifteenth Party Congress, when Stalin wrested absolute power over his rivals and established his dictatorship, free debate and spontaneous discussion have fallen into desuetude and all decisions have been adopted by unanimity. The Congress has become a rubber stamp sounding board for the supreme party leadership.

The Central Committee

Between sessions of the All-Union Party Congress, the Central Committee functions as the supreme organ of the Communist party. The Party Statutes vest extraordinary authority in the Central Committee:

> In the intervals between Congresses the Central Committee of the Communist Party of the Soviet Union directs the whole work of the Party; represents the Party in its relations with other parties, organizations, and institutions; organizes various Party institutions and directs their activity; appoints editorial boards of central organs of the press, which function under its control, and confirms the editorial boards of Party publications of large local organizations; organizes and directs undertakings of social significance; distributes the manpower and resources of the Party; and administers the central fund.
>
> The Central Committee guides the work of the central Soviet and public organizations through the Party groups within them.[7]

Regular meetings of the Central Committee are to be held at least once every six months, and extraordinary meetings may be called by the Presidium or by the First Secretary. It was at an extraordinary meeting of the Central Committee in June 1957 that Khrushchev succeeded in purging the Presidium of its hostile "antiparty" majority after the latter group had attempted to remove him from power. The Central Committee has met far more frequently and made decisions of greater importance under Khrushchev than it was accustomed to under Stalin. The membership of the Central Committee is fixed by the Party Congress: in 1959, the Party Congress elected 123 members and 111 candidates to the Central Committee, which represented a reduction in size from 1956. Most of the members of the Central Committee are party functionaries: members of

[7] Party Statutes, Rule 36.

the central Secretariat, secretaries of the principal party organizations throughout the U.S.S.R., leading editors of the party press and publications, and the leaders of the Young Communist League and the trade-union organization. The others are high officials of the state bureaucracy: the Chairman and Vice-Chairmen of the Council of Ministers of the U.S.S.R., leading members of the Presidium of the Supreme Soviet, leading ministers of the Union and of the Union Republics, military leaders, and diplomatic leaders. There is usually a sprinkling of intellectuals among the membership of the Central Committee.

The Central Committee is responsible for all party actions taken by its subdivisions—i.e., by the Presidium, the Secretariat, and the numerous departments of party administration that permeate all public organizations in the Soviet Union. Article 37 of the Party Statutes empowers the Central Committee to "set up political sections and assign Party organizers of the Central Committee to individual sectors of socialist construction which may assume a special importance for the national economy." The Central Committee also elects the Presidium, Secretariat, and Control Committee and delegates specific responsibilities to each of these organs, reserving the power to reverse their decisions and change their membership. It is called upon to resolve internal disputes within these organs or between them. Finally, the Central Committee issues general directives and resolutions that assume the character of legal ordinances when they are signed by the Chairman of the Council of Ministers or the Presidium of the Supreme Soviet.

The Presidium

The Presidium of the Central Committee of the Communist party acts as the permanent executive organ of the Communist party and directs the other organs of the party in the name of the Central Committee in all matters of policy. It is responsible only to the Central Committee. The Presidium replaced the Political Bureau and Organizational Bureau of the Central Committee in 1952, but its powers are substantially the same as those of the former Politburo. There is no fixed membership, and the number of members has varied from twenty-five voting members and eleven candidates in 1952 to fifteen members and seven candidates in 1960. The Presidium generally meets once a week or oftener at the discretion of its Chairman, who is presently Khrushchev. Decisions are by majority vote, but consensus is usually obtained in the interest of party unity. Matters of high policy affecting the state as well as the party are deliberated by the Presidium, whose communiques are considered to be politically binding on the government as well as on all party organs and organizations. The extent to which the Presidium exercises real power depends largely upon the personality of the First Secretary and Chairman. Under Stalin, members of the Presidium were occasionally forbidden to attend its meetings, not invited to attend, instructed when to speak, admonished, berated, and threatened. Decisions were never based on the consensus of the members or upon the will of the majority; Stalin announced his plans to his colleagues, and they meekly agreed even when they disapproved of them. During the period of "collective leadership," which ended in June 1957 with the triumph of the First Secretary, real power was exercised by the Presidium. Since then, real power has again become highly concentrated in the hands of the First Secretary, although there is no evidence that Khrushchev has become as arbitrary as Stalin. It seems more likely that Khrushchev enjoys the support of most or all of the members of the Presidium and that he is able to persuade them without having to browbeat them.

The Control Committee

The Control Committee is the successor of the Central Control Commission. It no longer has the responsibility of checking the members of the Central Committee, since it is now responsible to the Central Committee instead of to the Party Congress. The Control Committee has two principal functions:

> (a) Verifies the observance of Party discipline by Party members and candidates; calls to account Communists guilty of violating the Party program and Statutes or of breaches of Party and State discipline, as well as violators of Party ethics (those guilty of deception of the Party, dishonesty and insincerity in relation to the Party, slander, bureaucracy, moral turpitude, etc.); and (b) Examines appeals against decisions of the Central Committee of the Communist Parties of Union Republics and of territory and province Party committees concerning expulsions from the Party and Party disciplinary measures.[8]

The Central Inspection Commission

The Central Inspection Commission is still elected by the Party Congress and has limited control powers over the Central Committee as well as the subordinate organs of the Central Committee. This control is merely formal and not substantive, since the Party Statutes (Rule 39) limit the Commission's functions to inspecting "(a) the speed and correctness of the conduct of affairs in central bodies of the Party and the organizational conditions of the apparatus of the Secretariat of the Central Committee" and "(b) the treasury and institutions of the Party Central Committee." The Central Inspection Commission reports to the Party Congress but has no power to interfere in the operational activities of the Central Committee, its Presidium, or Secretariat.

[8] Party Statutes, Rule 35.

The Secretariat

The functions of the Secretariat are described briefly and modestly in Rule 34 of the Party Statutes, which belies the tremendous influence of this "subordinate" organ of the Party Central Committee. The Secretariat is officially empowered "to direct current work, chiefly as concerns verification of the fulfillment of Party decisions and selections of cadres." After the 1952 reorganization of the central organs of the party, the Secretariat assumed the powers that had once been discharged by the Organizational Bureau and gave up none of the tremendous power that it had developed under Stalin's long tenure as Secretary-General.

The Secretariat was created in 1920 to discharge administrative functions for the Political and Organizational Bureaus of the Central Committee and insure that the decisions of these organs as well as those of the Central Committee were properly executed by the subordinate branches of the Communist apparatus. Stalin's appointment in 1922 to the post of Secretary-General was intended to coordinate the actions of the Political and Organizational Bureaus, since he was a member of both. Stalin gradually used his power to pack the subordinate branches of the party apparatus with his henchmen and, through these, to hand pick the delegates to the Party Congress, or a majority of them, which gave him control of the composition of the Central Committee. The secret police came under his direction as well; and after using it to liquidate the "enemies of the people," Stalin turned it into an instrument of terrorism against his personal enemies within the central party apparatus. Khrushchev's appointment as First Secretary in 1953 has enabled him to duplicate the feat of his predecessor: to eliminate his personal rivals and concentrate all power in his hands.

The principal functions of the Secretariat are (1) formation of party cadres, or selection, training, and appointment of the vast force of full-time party functionaries who manage the far-flung party apparatus; (2) direction of the party apparatus; (3) supervision and control over governmental organs, agencies, and offices; over non-governmental "public organizations" or voluntary associations; and over mass organizations (trade-unions, women, youth, and children's organizations) and cultural, scientific, and educational institutions and societies; and (4) administration of public opinion media. These tasks are administered through twelve major departments that function directly under the Secretariat. The First Secretary is the responsible head of the Secretariat. There is no problem of coordination, particularly when one considers that at present, Khrushchev, the First Secretary, is likewise Chairman of the Presidium, Chairman of the Central Committee, and Chairman of the Council of Ministers. The twelve departments that function under the Secretariat are headed by either the First Secretary himself or one of the other secretaries.[9] The departments are presently grouped as follows: party, trade-union, and Komsomol affairs; propaganda and agitation; cultural and scientific affairs; cadres or personnel; women's affairs; educational affairs; building, trade, finance, and planning groups; light industry; heavy industry; agriculture; foreign affairs; and armed forces political administration. Some are based upon the "functional" approach, while others are organized by economic sector. The former are centralized, while the latter administer their functions on a decentralized basis. To prevent overlapping operations by the functional and production-branch-type departments of the party bureaucracy, the production-branch units carry out all party administration within their exclusive sectors of the economy.

Subordinate Organizations

Below the central party organs are the intermediate and primary party organizations. The intermediate party organizations are organized geographically so as to correspond to the major political-administrative divisions of the country. Each Union Republic, except the Russian Soviet Federated Socialist Republic (R.S.F.S.R.), which maintains no party organization of its own, relying upon the Central Committee of the Communist party of the U.S.S.R. and its Bureau for the R.S.F.S.R. to handle party affairs on the all-Russian level, maintains a party organization similar to that of the All-Union organization. The Union Republic party organization consists of a Congress of delegates representing the territorial and regional party organizations; a Central Committee elected by the Congress; and an executive committee and an inspection committee, both elected by the Central Committee. The executive committee is responsible to its own Central Committee and to the Secretariat of the Central Committee for direction of the party apparatus within the Union Republic. The Union Republic Central Committee selects members of the executive committee, subject to the approval of the All-Union Central Committee, which also has the power to suspend and replace its members.

Union Republic party organizations are the principal instruments of party control and leadership over the Union Republic governments. The principal leaders of the Union Republic governments are generally members of the executive committee of the Union Republic party organizations. The Union Republic organization also publishes or supervises the publication within its jurisdiction of newspapers and periodicals by appointing the editorial boards of all press organs.

[9] In May 1960, these were Brezhnev, Kozlov, Kuusinen, Mukhitdinov, and Suslov. On July 16, 1960, Brezhnev, who replaced Voroshilov as the Chairman of the U.S.S.R. Supreme Soviet, asked to be relieved from the Secretariat of the CPSU because of his inability to handle both positions. Thus, the number of secretaries in 1961 is five including Khrushchev.

The regional and territorial party organizations are identical to those of the Union Republic except for terminology: the meeting of delegates is called a "conference," and the permanent committee of this body is shorn of the adjective "central." The executive committee of regional and territorial party organizations may not exceed eleven members, including paid party secretaries; all the members must be acceptable to the All-Union Central Committee. The regional and territorial party organizations are subordinated to the Union Republic and All-Union organizations. Below the territories and regions are the city and district party organizations, with a simpler apparatus consisting of an annual conference of delegates from the primary organizations, a committee not to exceed nine members (including paid secretaries), and an inspection committee. The election of the committees and secretaries is subject to the sanction of the higher party organizations, any of which may veto such designation or suspend and remove such officials from their party responsibilities.

The city and district party organizations supervise the activities of the primary organizations within their geographic areas, maintain active records of the party membership, direct and control the activities of the local soviets, assume the initiative in nominating competent persons for election to the soviets, direct the election campaigns so as to foment popular consensus in the party's leadership of the state, appoint local editorial boards of press organs, select and train local party leaders, and organize and direct mass propaganda and agitation campaigns and Socialist competitions among the workers and peasants.

The lowest level of party organization is found in places of employment, such as factories, state farms, collectives, repair and technical stations (RTS), offices, military units, and educational institutions. Once known as cells, these primary party organizations consist of a general membership meeting that is supposed to hold monthly sessions and a committee or bureau or secretary, depending upon the size of the membership. As few as three party members may form a primary organization with the consent of the city or district committee. Memberships that exceed 300 may be divided into separate primary organizations. An enterprise such as a collective farm or factory having over 50 party members may be subdivided into shop, sectional, or departmental party groups within the same primary organization. The subdivisions are designed to facilitate meetings and to intensify party activity. Primary organizations that have less than 15 members elect a part-time secretary to direct their activities and maintain ties with the city or district organization. Larger organizaions are entitled to appoint a bureau of from 3 to 11 members or, in the case of organizations that exceed 300 members, to elect a committee headed by a permanent (salaried) secretary, provided the city or district committee approves.

There are over 350,000 primary party organizations in the U.S.S.R. performing a multiplicity of functions that makes them the chief instrument of party domination over Soviet society. They supervise the work of all managerial personnel in every enterprise, office, farm, educational institution, public organization, and state institution. The party primary organization may criticize decisions or lack of decisions of managerial personnel through opinions, recommendation, and censures, reports of which are sent to the appropriate party organs. They report on the errors and shortcomings of government officials to the latter's administrative superiors as well as to the appropriate party organs. In the event of disputes between the trade-union officials and the management within any productive unit, the primary party organization will act as mediator. Primary party organizations direct Socialist competitions among the workers in order to improve production norms and quotas and stimulate labor efficiency and discipline. They publish shop and office newspapers, conduct political orientation meetings among the workers, recruit and train new party members, and promote the social and cultural interests of the workers. In a word, the primary party organizations are charged with the task of guiding the masses in their everyday labor toward the achievement of the party's goals of perfecting socialism and advancing toward communism. They form the link between the party elite and the masses. They also function as the eyes and ears of the party within all groups and at every level of social organization and ferret out the wrongdoers, the incompetents, the antisocial, and the criminal elements and keep the leadership informed.

Particular attention has been given by the Communist party to organizational control and agitation-propaganda activities by its cadres within the military forces. Party organizations correspond to the military units, with primary organizations functioning at the company level and party groups at lower levels. To assist the party organizations, political officers are attached to each unit from the company level to the army corps. The political officers are selected by the Central Committee's Main Political Administration of the Armed Forces, which functions also as an autonomous agency within the Defense Ministry. The political officers hold the equivalent rank to the military unit commanders at each level, and they exercise supervision and control powers over the military commanders. At times, they have been authorized to countermand the orders of the military commanders and to arrest them if necessary. The political officers direct the party organizations in the armed forces in propaganda efforts to maintain the morale and loyalty of the troops, in educational and cultural activities to improve the social consciousness of the military forces, and in agitational measures to promote discipline and efficiency among combatant and non-combatant personnel.

DRAFT OF THE STATUTES OF THE COMMUNIST PARTY

The new draft of the Statutes of the Communist party of the Soviet Union of 1961 differs from the previous statutes (rules) adopted at the Nineteenth Party Congress in 1952 and subsequently amended. The party member is now "to master Marxist-Leninist theory," while according to the old statute he was "to raise his level of political understanding and to broaden his knowledge of the principles of Marxism-Leninism."

Rule 25 of the new statutes includes a new principle of systematic turnover of the membership of party bodies combined with continuity of leadership. Accordingly, at all regular elections of the Central Committee of the Communist party of the Soviet Union and its Presidium, not less than one-quarter of the membership shall be newly elected. Presidium members shall as a rule be elected for not more than three successive terms (twelve years). However, particular party workers may (by virtue of their recognized authority and high political, organizational, or other abilities) be successively elected to executive bodies for a longer period. In such cases, election requires a majority of at least three-quarters of the votes cast by secret ballot.

At least one-third of the members of the Central Committees of the Union Republic Communist parties and of territory and province committees chosen at each regular election and one-half of the members of region, city, and district party committees and the committees and bureaus of primary party organizations shall be new members. Furthermore, members of these executive party bodies may be elected for not more than three successive terms. The secretaries of primary party organizations may be elected for not more than two successive terms.

A party organization may, in consideration of the political and work qualities of an individual, elect him to an executive body for a longer period. In such cases, election requires that not less than three-quarters of the Communists participating in the voting cast their ballots for him. Party members who are not re-elected to an executive party body on the expiration of their terms may be re-elected in subsequent elections. Although Rule 25 represents a degree of democratization, it may not result in the removal of the top leadership who are covered by the clause of work quality.

Rule 26 of the new statutes states that the question of removing a member or a candidate member of the Central Committee of the Communist party of the Soviet Union from membership in the Central Committee is decided at a plenary session of the Central Committee by closed (secret) ballot. The decision is regarded as adopted if at least two-thirds of all the members of the Central Committee of the CPSU vote for it. The secret voting is an improvement. Only the future will tell how effective this provision will be.

Rule 28 stresses that "the highest principle of Party leadership is collectivity" and that "the cult of the individual leader and the violations of inner-Party democracy connected with it cannot be tolerated in the Party." This rule, of course, refers to and is designed to counteract violations such as those committed by Stalin.

Rule 56 indicates that "full-time paid Party posts are as a rule not set up in primary Party organizations embracing fewer than 150 Party members." Thus, the number of paid party officials will be reduced. Rule 70 adds to the previous provisions on dues that party members whose monthly earnings are up to fifty rubles pay a due of ten kopeks only. For all incomes above fifty rubles, monthly dues are the same as they were previously.

The post-Stalin leadership is introducing limited but urgently needed democratization of the party to revitalize the activity of party members whose initiative was paralyzed under Stalin's leadership.

SELECTED READING

AVTORKHANOV, ABDURAKHMAN. *Stalin and the Soviet Communist Party.* New York: Frederick A. Praeger, Inc., 1959.

BRZEZINSKI, ZBIGNIEW K. *The Permanent Purge: Politics in Soviet Totalitarianism.* Cambridge, Mass.: Harvard University Press, 1956.

FAINSOD, MERLE. *How Russia Is Ruled.* Cambridge, Mass.: Harvard University Press, 1953.

KULSKI, WLADYSLAV W. *The Soviet Regime: Communism in Practice.* 3d. ed. Syracuse, N.Y.: Syracuse University Press, 1954.

MEISSNER, BORIS. *The Communist Party of the Soviet Union: Party Leadership, Organization and Ideology,* ed. John S. Reshetar, Jr. New York: Frederick A. Praeger, Inc., 1956. Includes chapter on the Twentieth Party Congress.

RESHETAR, JOHN S., JR. *A Concise History of the Communist Party of the Soviet Union.* New York: Frederick A. Praeger, Inc., 1960.

SCHAPIRO, LEONARD. *The Communist Party of the Soviet Union.* New York: Random House, Inc., 1959.

41

Soviet Federalism

TSARIST IMPERIALISM

The empire of the Tsar consisted of 180 different nationalities speaking over 150 distinct languages and dialects. About half of the total population of imperial Russia was Russian. No other country, with the possible exception of the British Empire at its zenith, contained such a diversity of ethnic groups and cultures. The Tsarist Empire was heterogeneous in religion as well; while more than half of the people were members of the Russian Orthodox faith, there were large numbers of Muslims, Jews, Roman Catholics, and a smattering of Protestants. The minority nationalities clung to their languages, cultures, and religious practices with zeal and determination, despite the discrimination and political pressures to which they were subjected by the officials. The empire was dominated politically, economically, and socially by a tiny minority of Russian aristocrats and upper middle-class groups who formed the elite. The mass of people were subjugated by an absolutistic bureaucracy that recognized few, if any, restraints upon its arbitrary powers in dealing with the non-privileged classes and nationalities.

The aim of Tsarist policy toward the non-Russian groups was total cultural and religious assimilation into the dominant culture. The Russian language and the Orthodox faith were to be imposed by persuasion or persecution. Russification stirred up strong resentments among the minority groups of the empire against the Tsar and his government. As a result, national particularism and hostility against the state increased in intensity and eventually produced separatist revolutionary movements whose aim was secession from the empire. The policy of discrimination against such partially assimilated subjects as the Jews fostered a burning resentment that drove many youth into revolutionary politics against the Tsarist regime.

BOLSHEVIK VIEWS ON NATIONAL SELF-DETERMINATION

As a revolutionary party dedicated to the overthrow of the Tsarist regime and the establishment in Russia of a dictatorship of the proletariat, the Bolshevik wing of the Russian Social Democratic Labor party took advantage of the widespread anti-Russian sentiments that prevailed among the minority nationalities of the Empire to win allies and adherents to its revolutionary goal. The Russian Marxist Plekhanov was instrumental in inserting the principle of national self-determination in the program of the Socialist International in 1896 and in the original program of the Russian affiliate in 1898. At that party's 1903 Congress, Lenin, the leader of the Bolshevik wing of the party, accepted the principle of national self-determination as an ideological slogan to weaken and overthrow the Tsarist state. Lenin and Stalin, who became the Bolshevik expert on nationality problems, believed that local nationalism would contribute to the disintegration of Tsarist authority and hasten the proletarian revolution in Russia.

Opposition to the principle of national self-determination was strong among the Polish and Russian Marxists. Rosa Luxemburg, Bukharin, and Piatakov spearheaded the antinational line with the argument that the growth of national independence movements would split the unity of the proletariat and turn the proletariat of each nationality into an appendage of its bourgeoisie. National secessions from the Russian Empire would be a setback for the Socialist cause. They favored the growth of a united proletarian movement that would combat national particularism. The views of Lenin prevailed, and the Bolsheviks made national secessionism a major principle in their revolutionary program.

Lenin's advocacy of the principle of national self-determination was not entirely opportunistic. He realized that proletarian internationalism could not be imposed by the Russian proletariat upon the non-Russian masses through compulsion. The Russian proletariat must recognize the cultural equality of the minority nationalities of the empire in order to win their trust and friendship. He regarded nationalism as a normal reaction by subject nationalities against imperialistic oppression. By recognizing the national aspirations of the non-Russian peoples of the empire, it would be possible to disarm the anti-Russian sentiments of the minority nationalities of all social classes and encourage the growth of proletarian solidarity between the oppressed groups among the non-Russians and the Russian proletariat.

Advocacy of the right of national self-determination did not prevent the Bolsheviks from building a united proletarian party. Lenin combated those revolutionary groups that sought to organize the party along federal lines. A confederation of nationality-based proletarian parties was incompatible with proletarian internationalism. The vanguard must be unified into a highly centralized party structure, since it constituted the core of the future Socialist society. Through the united proletarian party, the masses were to be organized and educated in accordance with the ideals of proletarian internationalism. The united party organization would transcend national divisions and work among the masses to diffuse internationalist values. Tactically, a centralized party would be able to act in a more concerted fashion to promote the common revolutionary aims of overthrowing the Tsarist state and building a federation of Socialist states among the nationalities of the empire and eventually of the world. A federated party structure would, in Lenin's opinion, have bred national estrangement and isolation between the autonomous units of the proletarian vanguard.

The success of the Bolshevik seizure of political power in Russia forced Lenin to come to grips with the problem of national particularism. He was torn between a desire to extend the area of Bolshevik power and the expediency of recognizing the national secessionist drives of many non-Russian territories of the former empire. The rule of thumb that the Bolsheviks adopted was realistic. Those territories that could be militarily subjugated by the Red Army were prevented from seceding, and the regions that came under the effective power of nationalist forces were recognized as independent states. Various arguments were used to justify these apparently paradoxical policies. The Bolsheviks recognized the right of any nationality to secede from the empire, but they also felt that the proletariat of any national group must be militarily aided to seize power and exercise its right to unite its people with the Russian proletariat. The interests of the proletariat of any nation took precedence over the national interest to establish an independent state, and the international proletariat owed an obligation to its national units to assist these in the consolidation of socialism. The Bolsheviks attempted without success to aid their party confreres in Finland, Poland, and the Baltic region. The power of the nationalists and their foreign allies proved too strong for the Bolsheviks and their supporters within these countries. The Bolsheviks bowed to reality in recognizing the secessionist states. By making peace with these states, it was hoped that their proletarians would improve their class consciousness and forge an internationalist movement that might overthrow the rule of their bourgeois nationalist elites.

THE POLITICAL BASIS FOR SOVIET FEDERALISM

The conclusion of military operations in 1921 left the Bolsheviks in control of most of the former Tsarist Empire. They held most of the subject nationalities in the grip of their military power just as their imperialist predecessors had. In some regions, this power was nominally vested in autonomous-type states controlled by the unitary Communist party organizations of the area and supported by units of the Red Army, most of which were composed of Russian soldiers. In other regions, Russian Bolsheviks exercised nominal as well as real power because of the absence of a native Communist elite. The apparent continuity of Russian rule proved to be a source of tension between the party and the local population, which was thus drawn toward its traditional elite groups in opposition against the Bolsheviks. It was necessary to break down this hostility and win over the workers and peasants to the new Socialist ideals of the revolutionary state if this state was to succeed in building up its power and to realize its political goals. To accomplish this feat, it was necessary to recruit local cadres into the Communist party who could exercise local power in the name of the people. Socialism could not be imposed by Russian administrators in the non-Russian areas, since active collaboration by the masses was essential to develop labor efficiency and productivity.

From 1918 until 1923, the Communist party governed the slightly shrunken Russian Empire through the decentralized system of state authority. The Russian-peopled regions and the territories that lacked a native Communist elite were governed through a unitary system of legal bodies (soviets) and a number of centralized administrations (commissariats). The supreme governing organs of the Russian Soviet Federated Socialist Republic were the Central Executive Committee of the All-Russian Congress of Soviets, which exercised legislative powers, and the Council of Commissars, which directed the administration of public policies through the commissariats and the hierarchy of soviets with their executive committees. The more advanced non-Russian regions of the empire that had adequate native Communist cadres, such as the Ukraine and the Caucasus, were allowed to remain during this period under nominally independent state organizations, although the Communist party and Red Army units preserved unitary control on behalf of the R.S.F.S.R. Governmental authority was in theory decentralized by means of an alliance between these nominally independent states and the R.S.F.S.R. An effort by the Georgian Mensheviks, who controlled the soviets in their region of the Caucasus, to secede and establish an independent national state free from all Russian Bolshevik controls (party and Red Army) was crushed by force in 1922.

The decision to federalize the organization of state power among the nominally independent Soviet Socialist Republics (R.S.F.S.R., Ukraine, Georgia, Armenia, and Azerbaidzhan) was made in 1921 by Lenin, who sent a directive in the name of the Central Committee of the Russian

Communist party to the Communist leaders in the three Caucasian republics that a federation of these republics be formed. Despite the resistance of the Georgian leaders, which had to be curbed by the Red Army, the three republics were united into the Transcaucasian Soviet Socialist Republic. In 1923, this federation and the Ukraine were admitted into a federal union with the R.S.F.S.R., which in 1924 became the Union of Soviet Socialist Republics.

The federalization of power strengthened central authority over those non-Russian areas that had been formally independent until 1923 and effectively blocked any further temptations to undertake secession. The new Union Constitution of 1924 continued to recognize the right of national self-determination and secession of the constituent republics, but no legal provision was ever made for the exercise of this right by any individual republic. As with the American federal experiment, the basic motivation was to strengthen the political bonds between the various new republics by means of an institutional unification of power. The federal structure was selected in preference to a unitary state organization of authority for two reasons. First, national animosities toward the Russians were too strong in the Caucasus to permit complete integration. If a Socialist culture was to evolve here, it would have to be constructed under the leadership of native Communist cadres. Second, the appeal of socialism to the Asian peoples had to be fostered through their national aspirations. If the Communist party was to succeed in revolutionizing the masses of Asia, which was the road to the complete victory of socialism under the Leninist analysis of imperialism, the national aspirations of these peoples had to be championed. They had to be given an example of how they might be able to attain national self-government within a Socialist system of economic development. By creating self-governing national republics within the Socialist federation, the Communist party might attract the masses of Asia and hasten their revolution against Western imperialism. Soviet federalism was to become the banner of liberation for the oppressed peoples of Asia, who held the key to the collapse of international capitalism and the world triumph of socialism.

The architect of Soviet federalism and its nationality policy was Stalin, the offspring of a Georgian father and an Ossetian mother. As Commissar of Nationalities in the first Bolshevik government of Russia, and later as the supreme leader of international communism, Stalin forged a policy that reconciled the unitary interests of the Communist movement with the diversities of national folkways. He coined the slogan that was descriptive of this policy: "national in form, socialist in content." He realized that national sentiment was deeply rooted in the folkways of people and that they could not be rudely torn away from their language, customs, and group culture without causing irreparable damage to the unity of the

Soviet state and the Communist party. National characteristics must be handled constructively by the proletarian state during and after the initial period of Socialist construction. Only after the transition from socialism to communism commenced would nationalities begin to wither away concurrent with the beginning of a process of universal assimilation into a single nationality of the diverse peoples of the Soviet Union.

CULTURAL ASPECTS OF SOVIET FEDERALISM

Stalin's nationality policy provided for the flowering of national cultures among all the peoples of the Soviet Union. Backward ethnic groups who had never developed a written language, but only a spoken one, were aided by cultural anthropologists and philologists to express themselves in a literate manner through their own language. Native music, dancing, theater, literature, and art forms were encouraged. Soviet policy aimed at fostering a sense of pride among all nationality groups of the country in their folkways. The Tsarist policy of banning the use of non-Russian languages in the schools, courts, and administrative offices was reversed. Stalin made each native language the official medium within its region, thus requiring Russians who resided there to learn the local language. In compensation, Russian became the second language throughout the non-Russian areas of the Soviet Union and thereby the common medium of expression between the different nationalities. By legalizing and defending the primacy of the local language among each non-Russian nationality group and making Russian the universal second language, Stalin succeeded far more deftly than the Tsars in diffusing Russian language and culture among the heterogeneous peoples of the empire. Russian will certainly become the universal language of the Soviet Union, but it will be enriched by the absorption into its vocabulary of many words and expressions from the non-Russian languages. Assimilation of cultures will take place, not by one-way integration of non-Russians into the majority culture, but by gradual synthesis and fusion of those customs, folkways, and characteristics that are vibrant and meaningful contributions to the Communist conception of internationalism. Stalin also removed all legal discriminations against minority nationalities and sought to eliminate social abuses by means of punishments and re-educational policies.

Although he gave full play and freedom to national cultural values within the Soviet Union, Stalin demanded that these cultures become proletarian and Socialist in content. He brooked no expression of bourgeois nationalism or national deviationism by nationality groups. Local Communist cadres and the governing elites that emanated from them in the non-Russian regions of the Soviet Union were expected to develop the proletarian consciousness of the masses and infuse them with Socialist values. A relentless effort to achieve assimilation on the basis of Socialist internationalism was directed by Stalin. The national cultures were required to adapt to the needs of Socialist construction and accept the fact that they must one day become fused into an evolving unitary culture. Assurance that Socialist assimilation would take place among the minority nationalities as well as among the Great Russians was provided by the centralization of the party, the trade-unions, the Procuracy, the police and military forces, and by the centralized institutions of the Socialist economy.

ECONOMIC FOUNDATIONS OF SOVIET FEDERALISM

Economic planning has fostered national integration among the people of the U.S.S.R. in three major ways. First, it has resulted in the transfer of millions of people from one region to another. Western Siberia, the central Asian regions, and the Far East, because of extensive economic development, have received a particularly large influx of population. This, of course, has resulted in increased intermingling of all nationalities, an important factor in removing nationality barriers. Since the Great Russians are more numerous than the other nationalities, the increased intermingling should result in the gradual Russification of the Soviet people, even if this goal is not being fostered deliberately by the party. Second, economic planning has increased the interdependence of the national regions. Planned industrialization has made the Union Republics less self-sufficient economically than before. If they were to be permitted to secede from the Union, most of the Union Republics would have to reorganize their economies so drastically that great hardship would result. Finally, although economic planning has already brought personal suffering to many, many more have benefited from it in terms of higher living standards. The vast majority of the Soviet people attribute to socialism their improved economic and social status relative to that of their parents and grandparents under capitalism.

Because of centralized economic planning by the Communist party and All-Union government, the economically underdeveloped regions of the Soviet Union have been industrialized and urbanized to the point where they are no longer economic colonies of Russia. Their populations have been raised economically and socially to levels that are comparable to those of the Russians. Economic and social integration of the Russian and non-Russian peoples of the U.S.S.R. has been accomplished without ethnic discrimination. The resultant equalization of status and living standards among the various nationalities of the U.S.S.R. has done much to reduce national resentments and to develop a unitary loyalty on the part of the diverse peoples of the country to the Soviet state and the Communist party.

EMERGENT SOVIET NATIONALISM

The goal of Soviet nationality policy and federalism was not to create viable national cultures or truly autonomous Union Republics, but to integrate, assimilate, and unify a multinational society into a proletarian Socialist culture. The leveling up process in living standards, education, and civic participation among the people of the U.S.S.R. has greatly abated national jealousy and tensions. The concept of Soviet nationality has gradually replaced particularist nationality sentiments. While the process of assimilation is far from complete, the federal approach to the administration of public policies through national Communist cadres and the recognition of national cultural autonomy within a centralized Socialist structure of power has won over the mass of the people to the Communist party and the Soviet state. Loyalty to the Soviet Union has gradually supervened particularist identifications among most of the peoples of the U.S.S.R. The stubborn resistance of the Soviet peoples to the German invaders cannot be attributed entirely to their maltreatment by the Germans. The relatively small proportion of defection and collaboration with the Germans that occurred among the Soviet peoples during World War II and the heroism of the Soviet fighting units lend credence to the view that a Soviet people has emerged.

THE STRUCTURE OF SOVIET FEDERALISM

Soviet federalism has been developed within the context of Stalin's nationalities policy and resembles its basic characteristic: it is federal in form and unitary in content. The obvious reason for this is that federalism was designed to serve as a transitional form of state organization until a unitary Socialist consciousness had evolved. Federalism in the U.S.S.R. has served as an organization device to spread the Communist value system, develop a new patriotism to the Soviet state, and build a Socialist economy.

Several criteria have been followed to determine the status of nationality groups within the U.S.S.R. in terms of how much self-administration and representation each was to enjoy. Four categories were established by the 1936 Constitution: Union Republics, Autonomous Republics, Autonomous Regions, and National Areas. The former were to enjoy maximum autonomy and greater representation in the Union government, while the latter were placed under greater guidance and tutelage. Population, geographic location, cultural development, political reliability, and the size of Communist cadres have all determined whether a nationality group was to enjoy first, second, third, or fourth status.

With the exception of the Karelo-Finns, who number less than 300,000 but were elevated to Union Republic status from 1940 to 1956 initially to pressure the Finnish Republic into territorial concessions and subsequently into a neutralist foreign policy, all the Soviet Union Republics contain over a million inhabitants. There are a number of nationalities who have the requisite numerical size to constitute Union Republics but which have been denied this privilege because of geographic dispersion or for political reasons—these are the Tatars, Jews, Germans, Chuvash, Poles, Mordovians, and Bashkirs. Stalin attributed major importance to geographic location in determining whether a nationality should enjoy Union Republic status. As he explained it, nationalities who resided in territories surrounded entirely by another nationality were not in a position to claim Union Republic status because they could not exercise the right of secession. Only those nationalities who were located along the external periphery of the U.S.S.R. could theoretically secede and, therefore, claim the privilege of becoming Union Republics.

The lesser nationalities have been grouped together, with certain exceptions, into Autonomous Republics, Autonomous Regions, and National Areas, depending again upon their numbers, cultural development, political reliability, the size of their Communist cadres, and their geographic compactness. Of the present nineteen Autonomous Republics, all but four are located within the R.S.F.S.R., while six of the nine Autonomous Regions are also within the R.S.F.S.R. There are at present ten National Areas.

FEDERAL REPRESENTATION OF NATIONALITIES

Although Article 13 of the U.S.S.R. Constitution describes the Soviet Union as a federation of Union Republics, direct representation in the Council of Nationalities of the Supreme Soviet is also provided, on a more modest scale, to the lesser nationalities formed into Autonomous Republics and Autonomous Regions as well as National Areas. Article 35 of the Constitution fixes representation in the Soviet of Nationalities at twenty-five deputies for Union Republics, eleven deputies for Autonomous Republics, five deputies for Autonomous Regions, and one deputy for National Areas. There is no legal requirement that the deputies to the Soviet of Nationalities be of the nationality of the major group within the territory that they are to represent. If this were true, the Russians would be entitled to only 25 seats; they occupy 147 seats out of a total of 640. Although there seems to be some indication that the Communist party wishes to have every nationality represented in the Soviet of Nationalities, it has not applied any proportional rule in the allocation of seats or in the selection of deputies. Relative to their numbers, some of the lesser nationalities enjoy substantial representation in the Soviet of Nationalities of the Supreme Soviet; while the Russians, with over one-half of the total population, have less than one-fourth of the seats. Representation of the smaller national groups in the Soviet of Nationalities counteracts the preponderance of deputies of Russian origin in the Soviet of the Union, which is selected on a different basis.

Besides being represented in the Soviet of Nationalities of the Supreme Soviet, the nationalities of the U.S.S.R. are also represented indirectly in the Presidium of the Supreme Soviet by the Chairmen of the fifteen Presidia of the Union Republic Supreme Soviets. These representatives hold the rank, ex officio, of Vice-Chairmen of the Persidium of the Supreme Soviet of the U.S.S.R. These Vice-Chairmen are seldom able to participate in the deliberations of the Presidium, since they are not often present in Moscow, and their membership is largely symbolic. Much the same is true of the membership, ex officio, which the Chairmen of the Union Republic Councils of Ministers possess on the U.S.S.R. Council of Ministers. In theory at least, the Union Republics, and the major nationality groups of the U.S.S.R., are given nominal representation on the higher state organs that are responsible for the issuance of most legislation and the principal administrative decisions of the federal government..

If the formal organs of state power in the U.S.S.R. exercised effective authority as provided in the Constitution, instead of merely nominal deliberating functions to formalize the decisions made by the supreme party organs, the representatives of the Union Republics within the federal government might acquire greater significance. Then, the federalist character of the Soviet regime might be expressed by a clash between the Russian and non-Russian interests. It is perhaps indicative of the caution of the party that of the 640 members of the Council of Nationalities, over 75 per cent are party members; while most of the members of the Presidium and Council of Ministers at the All-Union level are high-ranking party members. Coordination between the party's will and the formal acts of the government is achieved by having the same persons in the decision-making positions within both the party and the government. The largely symbolic value of Union Republic representation in the federal organs of government of the U.S.S.R. serves to affirm the constitutional principle of equality among the major nationalities and the federative character of their "voluntary union." It camouflages the reality of Russian hegemony over the party and the government of the U.S.S.R. that results naturally from their numerical preponderance and makes association between Russians and non-Russians more palatable to the latter.

Federalism does not operate even in theory in the decision-making organs of the Communist party. The Leninist principle of democratic centralist organization bases membership upon strict ideological conformism and absolute discipline and loyalty to the decisions of the higher party organs. The central, intermediate, and local apparatus of the Communist party, staffed by professional party functionaries who are trained and appointed from the center, rules the party organizations with ironclad authority. This party elite, in turn, is responsible for the nomination of reliable bureaucratic officials at each level of administration that is nominally operative under an elected soviet, which is in turn a carefully recruited institution that is manipulated by the party. The result of this is that responsible officials of the Union Republic and subordinate units of administration are members of a unitary structure of power. Irrespective of their national orgins, they are first Communists and second loyal servants of the Soviet state.

If the various nationality groups were permitted real autonomy in the exercise of their constitutional powers, instead of being shackled by the overriding powers of the central government and the unitary party machine, and if the locus of decision-making power at the central level really operated as the Constitution prescribes, instead of being subordinated to the party leadership, federalism might acquire some significance in the Soviet Union. However, since the entire territory of the U.S.S.R. is governed by the centralized apparatus of the Communist party, nationality representation within the elective organs of government is meaningful only in terms of public morale. The people of the U.S.S.R. can be told that a deputy from Moldavia has an equal voice in the government as one from the R.S.F.S.R., which might be the truth, since the vote of neither significantly affects public policies. The Communist party of the Soviet Union is using particularistic national sentiment to the advantage rather than to the detriment of party goals and is allowing the nationalities equal opportunity to become Socialist and internationalist. Given the numerical preponderance of the Great Russians within the party, the state bureaucracy, and the working class of the U.S.S.R., it is more than likely that the content of the internationalist culture of the U.S.S.R. will be heavily accented with Great Russian overtones.

FEDERAL DIVISION OF POWERS

Governing powers under the U.S.S.R. Constitution are federally divided between the All-Union government and the fifteen Union Republican governments. The Constitution prescribes by enumeration the scope of the All-Union's legislative, executive, administrative, and judicial competence on the basis of carefully defined subjects. It also prescribes the scope of Union Republic rights and competences with much less precision; but in compensation, the Union Republics are left with all residual powers not expressly reserved for the central government. The sweep of the powers that are vested by enumeration in the central government is extraordinary for a federal state. They include the following:

1. War and peace
2. Foreign relations
3. Foreign trade
4. State security and national defense
5. Guarantee of the constitutional order
6. Admission and dissolution of Union Republics, Autonomous Republics, and Autonomous Regions and confirmation of their territorial boundaries
7. Economic planning, budgetary determination and taxation, and allocation of revenues
8. Banking, industry, agriculture and commerce, money and credit, insurance, transportation, and communications
9. Land tenure, minerals, forests, and water resources
10. Public education and health
11. Statistics
12. Labor legislation
13. Legal codes and judicial organization and procedure
14. Citizenship, aliens, marriage, and family
15. Amnesties

Although there is no implied-powers clause in the U.S.S.R. Constitution, there is no states' rights tradition limiting the power of the All-Union government in the interpretation of its powers. In practice, therefore, the central government may legislate in practically any field, since the Union Republics have no material sphere of competence that is exclusively theirs.

The Constitutions and all constitutional legislation of the Union Republics must conform with the provisions that are prescribed in the U.S.S.R. Constitution. The judge of such conformity is the central government. The All-Union Constitution guarantees that each Union Republic must consent before its territory is altered and allows the Union Republics freedom to secede. There has been only one example of the dissolution of a Union Republic; in 1956, the Karelo-Finnish S.S.R. was reduced in status from a Union Republic to an Autonomous Republic by act of the Presidium of the U.S.S.R. No mention was made of whether the authorities of that Republic had been consulted. As previously indicated, no legislation has provided for the exercise of the right of secession. Many Communist leaders have been purged for high treason and conspiracies against the integrity of the state because they favored the idea of secession. Mere mention of the idea of secession is branded "national deviationism" and constitutes a political offense. Apparently the right to secede must be authorized by the Communist party of the Soviet Union and consented to by the Supreme Soviet; under existing penal legislation, there is no possibility for Union Republic leaders to petition for such permission without fear of punishment.

Union Republics are granted the constitutional right to conduct their own foreign relations and to maintain their separate military defense forces, subject to U.S.S.R. legislation, which prescribes the scope of such rights and the form and manner in which they may be exercised. When Stalin demanded that all Union Republics be permitted to exercise this right by maintaining diplomatic missions at the United Nations headquarters and participating in United Nations activities, Roosevelt and Churchill agreed to allow separate representation and voting rights to the Ukraine and Belorussian Republics. It would have been a distinct advantage for the Soviet Union if separate representation in the United Nations had been allowed the other republics in addition to the U.S.S.R., since the voting record of the Ukrainian and Belorussian delegates has never once differed from that of the Soviet delegate. Thus far, neither the Ukraine nor Belorussia has been permitted to establish diplomatic relations with any government, not even within the Communist bloc. No Union Republic has been allowed to establish separate military units.

Article 28 of the U.S.S.R. Constitution provides the only enumerated power that the Union Republics may exercise, concerning "the solution of problems pertaining to the administrative-territorial structure of the regions and territories of the Union Republics." This too must be exercised within the limitations fixed by U.S.S.R. legislation concerning the defense of constitutional forms of government. Again, the central government, acting through its Presidium of the Supreme Soviet, exercises exclusive right to interpret the exercise of this power.

In the event the Union Republics should violate the provisions of law through the improper exercise of their powers, their acts would be null and void, since U.S.S.R. laws take precedence over Union Republic laws. The Presidium of the U.S.S.R. Supreme Soviet has the power to nullify Union Republic legislation. The titular membership of fifteen Union Republic Presidium Chairmen on the Presidium of the Supreme Soviet of the U.S.S.R. has not provided any real check of the latter organ, since it is empowered to act without the participation of the Union Republic representatives. The Union Republics have no legal recourse against the central government in the event the former attempted to oppose U.S.S.R. interference in their functions. The Supreme Court is not empowered to implead the central government or to inquire into the "constitutionality" of its legislative and executive decisions. Like the Presidium and Council of Ministers, it too is an emanation of the Supreme Soviet; and its competence is limited to enforcement of federal laws and decrees in accordance with the interpretations laid down by the Presidium.

The Union Republic executives (Councils of Ministers) are equally subordinated to the U.S.S.R. Council of Ministers, just as their legislative organs are subservient to the All-Union legislature. The Council of Ministers of the U.S.S.R. may suspend decisions and orders of the Councils of Ministers of the Union Republics and of the regional Economic Councils of administration, to which management of the industrial sector has been delegated. Actual annulment of suspended decrees and orders is performed by the Presidium of the U.S.S.R. Supreme Soviet. Decisions and orders of the Council of Ministers of the U.S.S.R., made on the basis of and in pursuance of the laws in operation, are binding upon all Union Republic organs of government. Again, the judge of the propriety or legality, or both, of such acts is vested in the Presidium of the U.S.S.R. Supreme Soviet.

The consequence of this wholesale subordination of Union Republic organs to the U.S.S.R. Presidium and Council of Ministers is to reduce the Union Republic governments to the status of regional subdivisions of the central government. The relationship is not unlike that which exists between the central authorities and the locally constituted authorities of a unitary state. Even so important a function as constitutional revision is vested exclusively in the Supreme Soviet of the U.S.S.R., although here, in theory at least, the Union Republics are permitted to exercise a veto through their properly elected delegates to the Soviet of Nationalities. The Soviet of Nationalities is the only potentially "federal" institution in the U.S.S.R., since it might employ its legislative and constitutive powers to obstruct the unitary organs of the U.S.S.R. from imposing central authority upon the Union Republics and their territorial subdivisions. However, the Presidium of the U.S.S.R. Supreme Soviet is empowered to dissolve the Supreme Soviet in the event of a disagreement between the two houses, to conduct a direct popular referendum, and to exercise legislative authority itself. Thus, the Soviet of Nationalities could not effectively curb the exercise of power by the central government over the Union Republics.

In practice, such constitutional conflicts are precluded by the political monopolization of leadership at all levels of government by the highly centralized Communist party. The central leadership of the party is in command of the central government, while its carefully picked subordinates in the Union Republics are equally in command of the Union Republic governments. Should a "constitutional conflict" between the U.S.S.R. and the Union Republics ever occur, the central leadership of the Communist party would be able to remove from office the governing personnel at the Union Republic level without difficulty. Only a revolution within the party itself could sustain any effort by the Union Republics to "federalize" power within the U.S.S.R.

SELECTED READING

BARGHOORN, FREDERICK. *Soviet Russian Nationalism.* Fair Lawn, N.J.: Oxford University Press, 1956.

DMYTRYSHYN, BASIL. *Moscow and the Ukraine, 1918–1953: A Study of Russian Bolshevick Nationality Policy.* New York: Bookman Associates, Inc., 1956.

GOODMAN, ELLIOT R. *The Soviet Design for a World State.* New York: Columbia University Press, 1960.

McCLOSKY, HERBERT, and TURNER, JOHN E. *The Soviet Dictatorship.* New York: McGraw-Hill Book Co., Inc., 1959.

PIPES, RICHARD. *The Formation of the Soviet Union: Communism and Nationalism, 1917–1922.* Cambridge, Mass.: Harvard University Press, 1955.

STALIN, JOSEPH. *Marxism and the National and Colonial Question.* Moscow: Foreign Languages Publishing House, 1940.

TOWSTER, JULIAN. *Political Power in the USSR, 1917–1947: The Theory and Structure of Government in the Soviet State.* Fair Lawn, N.J.: Oxford University Press, 1948.

VYSHINSKY, ANDREI Y. *The Law of the Soviet State.* New York: The Macmillan Co., 1948.

42

Elections and Representative Organs

ELECTION PRACTICE BEFORE 1936

The Russian people gained very little experience in the art of representative self-government during the period of Tsarist rule. The autocracy limited popular participation in the exercise of civic responsibilities to direct election by the peasants of village assemblies and indirect election of county and provincial councils (zemstvos) and, after 1906, indirect election of a national assembly (Duma). Although neither the zemstvos nor the Duma exercised significant powers, the Tsar's government took exceptional pains to insure that their composition was socially and politically reliable. Property qualifications were emphasized and representation was fixed by social class or estate in such a way as to insure the hegemony within these bodies of conservative representatives. In the 1912 election of the Duma, the right of suffrage was restricted to 15 per cent of the population; and the representation of the nobility and upper middle class was heavily weighted through the operation of the indirect system of voting by *curia*. Even so, the Tsarist bureaucracy employed coercive pressures to influence the voters to "vote right." Honest and equitable elections to the impotent representative bodies of Tsarist Russia were never realized, and the Russian people received no civic training in democratic responsibilities.

EARLY SOVIET ELECTORAL PRACTICES

After the Communists seized power in 1917, they disenfranchised all persons whom they considered class enemies of the proletariat, which included all former landowners, capitalists, rentiers, exploiters of labor, priests and monks, officials of the Tsarist regime, members of the Tsarist police, etc. To allow the former exploiters and oppressors equal rights and liberties with the proletariat or its peasant allies would not have been compatible with Lenin's theory of the workers' state. Oddly, foreign proletarians and members of the Communist International who resided in Soviet Russia were enfranchised and permitted to be elected to the soviets.

Representation in the soviets was weighted in favor of the urban proletariat as against the peasantry. At each level, the workers were accorded a five to one ratio of representatives over the peasants. Furthermore, workers received double representation in the higher soviets, since the city soviets were permitted to elect direct representatives as well as to participate in the indirect election of additional representatives through the provincial soviets. In this way, the Communists were able to assure their hegemony within the higher soviets to the disadvantage of the various Socialist parties that derived their electoral support from the peasantry. Weighted representation for the workers continued to be practiced even after competitive parties had been dissolved in order to assure the Communists of hegemony within the higher soviets over any non-party elements who might attempt to turn the representative system of the proletarian state into a tool of counterrevolution.

Another feature of the electoral system that operated under the pre-Stalin Constitution was the indirect election of representatives to the soviets above the village, town, and city levels. Indirect election of the delegates to the intermediate and higher soviets made it possible for the Communist minority within the country and in the village and town soviets to utilize their superior organization and draw upon those towns and cities where they had a decisive electoral influence to secure control over the intermediate and higher soviets. During the formative decades of the new Soviet state (1917–1936), the people could not be trusted to elect "good" representatives above the local level of soviets. Indirect elections facilitated the tasks of the party at the intermediate and higher levels.

Soviet elections during the first two decades of Communist rule were by open show of hands. The voters were convened at designated centers on election days where they responded openly to the tabulation of their votes. Those who opposed the candidates sponsored by the party ran the risk of being persecuted, but on occasion this ancient method of "direct democracy" succeeded in developing considerable popular interest in the electoral process, and the party cells were forced to keep on their toes by supporting locally strong candidates.

On Stalin's initiative, the seventh Congress of Soviets of the U.S.S.R. adopted a resolution (February 6, 1935) to amend the existing Constitution and electoral system by "democratizing the electoral system . . . replacing not entirely equal suffrage by equal suffrage, indirect elections by direct elections, and the open ballot by the secret ballot."[1] In an interview that he granted to Roy Howard of the Scripps-Howard newspaper chain on March 1, 1936, Stalin expressed the opinion that: "Universal, equal, direct and secret suffrage in the U.S.S.R. will be a whip in the hands of the population against the organs of government which work badly."[2] As leader of the Communist party, Stalin was dissatisfied with the increasing "bureaucratism" of the state administration. He hoped that by arming the people with electoral freedom to reject candidates who did not enjoy popular approval, the local party apparatus throughout the U.S.S.R. might locate better candidates who knew how to exercise control through the soviets over the administrative apparatus and check such vices as "careerism" and bureaucratism.

CURRENT SOVIET ELECTORAL PRACTICE

The electoral norms of the Soviet Union are contained in Articles 131–142 of the U.S.S.R. Constitution and the Electoral Law of January 9, 1950. All citizens of the U.S.S.R. over the age of eighteen who have not been legally disqualified as voters by a court because of criminal offenses or insanity are enfranchised. No discrimination is practiced against any group (other than convicted criminals and lunatics), and the suffrage is supposed to be conducted equally (one vote per voter) by direct and secret ballot. Registration of voters is handled by the localities through their executive committees and by the unit commanders of all military forces. Registration lists are posted thirty days before all elections so that citizens may have recourse to the executive committee and the People's Court in the event their names are not included on the election rolls. Voters who move after compilation of the voting lists, or who plan to be traveling, or otherwise are absent from their residence on election day, may secure a voting certificate, which may be presented to the polling authorities at any place on election day. In this way, passengers may vote on trains, patients may vote in hospitals, and merchant seamen may vote aboard their ships. Few, if any, Soviet citizens are deprived of the right to cast a ballot. Election precincts are established by decree of the executive committee of the locality not later than forty-five days prior to the election. Precincts are never to exceed 3,000 voters in size or be inferior to fifty registered voters. There is no excuse for Soviet citizens to absent themselves from voting,

[1] Joseph Stalin, *Leninism: Selected Writings* (New York: International Publishers Co., Inc., 1942), p. 379.

[2] *Izvestia*, March 5, 1936, as reproduced in James H. Meisel and Edward S. Kozera (eds.), *Materials for the Study of the Soviet System: State and Party Constitutions, Laws, Decrees, Decisions and Official Statements of the Leaders in Translation* (Ann Arbor, Mich.: George Wahr Publishing Co., 1953), p. 223.

so that voters' turnout is exceedingly high. While voting is not legally compulsory, there are strong social pressures upon the voter to cast his ballot. Non-voters might be forced to justify their negligence before comradely courts, thus exposing themselves to possible penalties for being considered "antisocial" by their outraged comrades.

The election law requires that separate rooms or voting booths be provided at each voting precinct, where the voters may avail themselves of the right to mark their ballot without being observed. Soviet ballots are printed with only one candidate per office, and a vote in favor of the nominee requires no marking of the ballot but simply that it be folded and deposited in the ballot box. On occasion, persons who availed themselves of their legal right to enter the booth for the purpose of marking out the name of the nominee that appears on the ballot have been dealt with as antisocial deviants.

The Electoral Law regulates the procedures for the nomination of all candidates for elective offices in the Soviet Union. Nominations are made within each electoral district by separate nominating committees consisting of the representatives of the Communist party, trade-unions, cooperatives, youth organizations, and cultural societies. The nominating committees conduct prenominating mass meetings among the workers and employees of enterprises and institutions, peasants, state farm workers, and employees of agricultural collective and state farms. The names of all proposed nominees are carefully considered by the nominating committee of each electoral district so as to select a candidate who will strengthen the ties between the party and the electorate. The nominee need not be a member of the party, so long as he recognizes the role of the party in the Soviet society as the elite vanguard of the people and submits to its guidance. Such persons are referred to as "non-party Communists." Since the main purpose of Soviet elections is to elicit popular consensus in the party, it is essential for the nominating committees to select candidates who will be acceptable to the voters. If a non-party nominee demonstrates greater popularity than a party member, he will very likely be selected as the candidate, provided his political reliability is satisfactory. Such persons may be eventually induced to join the party. The nominating procedure serves as a method for distinguishing grass-roots leaders among the masses and presenting them for recognition by the party as membership material. This is one of the many ways by which the Communist party strengthens its ties with the masses.

After the nominating committee has made its selection of a candidate, the electoral commission of the appropriate election district must register the nomination. The names of the sponsors, their organizations, together with the number of persons who participated in the nominating discussion must be filed with a statement by the candidate of acceptance of the nomination. Should the electoral commission fail to make the registration, appeal may be made to a higher electoral commission. Although the Electoral Law provides for the registration of more than one candidate for each elective office, current practice is for only one candidate to be registered, since it is felt that rivalry among candidates would invite the growth of factionalism, which might endanger party unity or pit non-party groups against the party, thus alienating the party from the people. Soviet ballots, therefore, include only one candidate for each elective office, and the election has the character of a plebiscite. The voter has the right to approve of the nominee by dropping the ballot unmarked into the ballot box, or he may disapprove by canceling the name appearing on the ballot.

Few dissenting ballots are cast; usually 98 per cent or more of the voters support the official candidate. On occasion, the Soviet press reports the electoral defeat of certain candidates, either because a majority of those who voted canceled the name on the ballot or because a majority of the registered voters in the district failed to cast ballots. In either case, the electoral commission must reconvene the nominating groups and proceed again within two weeks with a new election. The degree of popular support will indicate to the party whether the electorate is pleased or dissatisfied with the locally selected candidates.

Although great care is taken by the party organizations and the electoral commissions to insure that only politically reliable candidates are nominated, and that no nominee is allowed to be registered who might subsequently cast discredit upon the party, Soviet election norms provide for the popular recall of elected representatives for reasons of incompetence, violations of Socialist morality, or legal offences. Recall elections may be ordered by the appropriate electoral commission at any time on request by any recognized nominating group or notification by the Procuracy. Further control is exercised by all soviets over newly elected representatives through a credentials committee, which may recommend that the soviet refuse to seat the representative; refusal to seat or expulsion requires that a new election be held to fill the vacancy. For the Supreme Soviet of the U.S.S.R., all vacancies are reported by the Presidium to the electoral commission, which must hold a new election within two months.

Verifications of all voting tabulations are made by the district electoral commissions and again by higher electoral commissions, although the results are officially proclaimed by the district electoral commissions. Interference with the right of Soviet citizens to cast their ballots freely is punishable by as much as two years of imprisonment, and election frauds by officials are punishable by as much as three years of imprisonment.

Soviet elections serve a multiplicity of purposes. They are intended to develop civic consciousness and political consensus among the people toward the Communist party and the Soviet state. As a member of the electorate that ratifies the party's choice of candidates for representative public offices, the Soviet voter is given a voice in the selection of the formal governing organs of the state. As a participant in the mass nominations of candidates, the Soviet citizen is likewise made to feel that he shares responsibility with the elite groups in the selection of the candidates. The Soviet electorate is permitted in this manner to believe that it really elects its own public representatives and that through these representatives it participates in the exercise of public power. Identification of the masses with the party and the Soviet state is fostered by the appearance of democracy, while the substance of leadership remains elitist.

Soviet elections also provide the party with an opportunity to conduct active political indoctrination of the masses at regular intervals, since the pre-election "campaign" period is accompanied by a deluge of propaganda pointing out the successes of the party in the solution of domestic and international problems. The party uses the election as a convenient excuse to focus favorable attention upon its accomplishments. This is intended to convince the Soviet people that the party is a blessing and that they are, indeed, fortunate to be governed by so capable a leadership. The millions of party members and candidates, aided by the youth groups and mass organizations, are enlisted as agitators and demonstrators to build up popular enthusiasm in support of the party and the candidates. While their ostensible role is to "get out the voters" to the polls, the real function of these volunteer party workers is to inspire the Soviet people with a sense of awe in the monolithic unity and massive power of the Communist party and its subsidiaries.

Another officially endorsed defense of mass elections in the U.S.S.R. is the view that they serve to educate and train the people in tasks of democratic self-government. Under communism, the role of the party as vanguard will gradually recede; and the people will take up the reins of power directly through their elected representatives. The present transition phase of democratization of power will form a bridge between the earlier regime of party dictatorship and the eventual workers' democracy. During the transition phase, it is necessary to train millions of persons to assume administrative responsibilities as members of the soviets and their committees, whose tasks are to supervise and control the acts of the bureaucratic functionaries; eventually, these people's committees will apparently be expected to assume active administration from the professional bureaucracy. By allowing limited popular participation in a controlled electoral process, the Soviet leadership satisfies an ideological demand of Communist dogma. It also strengthens the moral status of the Soviet Union among foreign Communists and their sympathizers and facilitates the tasks of the Communist parties in Western democratic countries. Finally, the apparent enthusiasm and active voters' response to

Communist leadership provides some indication that the Soviet regime enjoys considerable if not overwhelming consensus from its population, which may build up the legitimacy of the Soviet Union among non-Communists in the Western world.

To the non-Soviet world, Soviet-style elections may appear to be rigged and fraudulent because of the controlled manner of nominating the candidates and the plebiscitary form of the electoral consultation. To the Communist mind, however, they are regarded as eminently equitable and democratic. Communists do not question the vanguard conception of their party; they accept as a basic value the legitimacy of Communist hegemony over the state. The party's status as the real sovereign, however, becomes legitimated only through the expression of consensus by the people in its leadership. The role of the Communist party is not at issue in Soviet elections in a direct sense; but rather the election serves as an instrument by which the masses are permitted to corroborate and to assist the party in its responsible task of selecting competent and honest representatives who will be able to collaborate effectively with the party in furthering the ideals of the Marxist-Leninist ideology, which form the value system of the Soviet state. The Communists would never admit that there is any conflict between their party and the masses in the Soviet Union. If there are faults with the Soviet administration, these are the result of individual failures within the bureaucracies of the party and the state. The party is as interested as the people in eliminating these incompetents from their responsible positions and replacing them with more capable officials. The electorate is supposed to correct the errors of the bureaucracy by staffing the soviets with the most competent citizens and through these develop a systematic check against bureaucratism in the Soviet administration. The only way in which mass discontent against the regime can be manifested in the U.S.S.R. is by mass abstention or rejection of the candidates. Such a form of civil boycott has never occurred. The active interest that Soviet citizens take in elections would seem to indicate that the majority of people interpret their role in the same manner as the party does.

In many precincts and election districts, voting turnout is complete; and official statistics reveal that less than 2 per cent of eligible voters are remiss. Election procedure in the U.S.S.R. makes it difficult for a voter to neglect his civic responsibility. Voting always takes place on a work holiday; and precincts are established in hospitals, clinics, resorts, trains, military units, and ships. Social pressures are carefully organized to stimulate individual participation. The propaganda line is also cleverly designed to motivate voters' interest. The psychological pressure to conform is extremely high. If the Soviet citizen has any doubts concerning the regime, he is reminded of the lot of the masses under tsarism and of the tremendous progress that the people have made under the Communist rule. If moral suasion and social pressures fail to prompt the Soviet citizen, the uncomfortable fear of being singled out by the party vigilantes as a non-spirited citizen invariably stimulates even the most retrograde, and these would seem to constitute a small minority, to make a show of interest in the elections.

It is customary in the Soviet Union to reward civic-minded citizens and heroes of Socialist labor by nominating and electing them to one of the many levels of soviets. The manipulation of elections makes it possible to provide a highly cherished reward system for the masses. It is also customary for a fairly large turnover to occur among the elected representatives from one election to the next, thus permitting as many as a million new representatives to be selected every few years. There is no doubt that the incentive to become a member of a soviet has encouraged many citizens to improve their labor performance records and raise the level of their social and moral conduct, so as to attract favorable attention to themselves.

While the Soviet electoral system is formally far more democratic than it was during the initial phase of the Communist dictatorship, it is lacking in freedom of choice of both candidates and alternative programs and policies, which, to Western traditions and values, underlies a political democracy. It is interesting to note that the Soviet election law does not preclude the eventual development of competitive elections. Once the basic value system of socialism is securely established and the threats to the survival of the Socialist social and economic order are removed, it is conceivable that competition within the Communist system itself may evolve in the selection of the political elite and in the choice of alternative programs and policies. If the ideological pronouncements of the Soviet leaders are to be believed, when the process of gradual withering away of the state and party apparatus has made substantial progress, the soviets will inherit the primary political responsibilities that the party has thus far exercised, and the electorate will inherit the sovereignty that the party has held in trust.

REAL POWER AND FORMAL AUTHORITY

Under the monolithic power structure of Communist society, all significant decision-making powers are monopolized by the party, which is the source of all authority by the formal organs of the government for the exercise of their legally delegated functions. The Constitution is the gift of the party to the people and is the legal instrument through which the party legitimates its power. It provides the formal structure of institutionalized power (the state) through which the party exercises real power over Soviet society. In this manner, the party may play its stated role of mere guide to the state, so that the onus of public resentment can always be deflected onto the bureaucratic minions of the state administration. Through the representative soviets, the party enlists popular participation among a wider stratum than the party membership in the vital task of eliciting public approval and consensus on behalf of party-conceived programs and policies. The soviets also assist the party in developing a system of controls over the administrative bureaucracy, which is responsible for the actual government of the citizenry. The soviets thus form the juncture between real power, which proceeds from the top echelon of the party in a downward direction, and nominal authority, which proceeds upward from the people through its elected representatives. Figure 42–1 illustrates the convergence between real and formal authority in the Soviet Union.

THE SUPREME SOVIET OF THE U.S.S.R.

Under the prevailing Constitution of the U.S.S.R., the legislative powers of the Union are vested in the Supreme Soviet, which is described in Article 30 as "the highest organ of state power." The Supreme Soviet consists of two chambers: the Soviet of the Union and the Soviet of Nationalities, each of which is elected normally for a term of four years. The Soviet of the Union is elected by the citizens of the U.S.S.R. voting by election districts on the basis of one deputy for every 300,000 of the population (Article 34). The Soviet of Nationalities is elected by citizens of the U.S.S.R. voting by Union Republics, Autonomous Republics, Autonomous Regions, and National Areas on the basis of twenty-five deputies from each Union Republic, eleven deputies from each Autonomous Republic, five deputies from each Autonomous Region, and one deputy from each National Area (Article 35). The number of representatives to the Soviet of Nationalities is not affected by the size of the area or population of the republic or region. Originally, both chambers had almost the same number of deputies. However, the increasing population of the U.S.S.R. has resulted in a corresponding increase of the number of deputies in the Soviet of the Union. In 1958, the Soviet of Nationalities had 640 deputies while the Soviet of the Union had 738.[3]

Membership

Who are these exclusive legislators, what are their rights, and how is their constitutionally granted power exercised? Soviet sources state that of the 738 deputies who were elected to the Soviet of the Union in 1958,

[3] *SSSR-Kak on est'*, (*The U.S.S.R.—As It Is*), (Moscow: Gosudarstvennoe izdatelstvo politicheskoi literatury, 1959), p. 63.

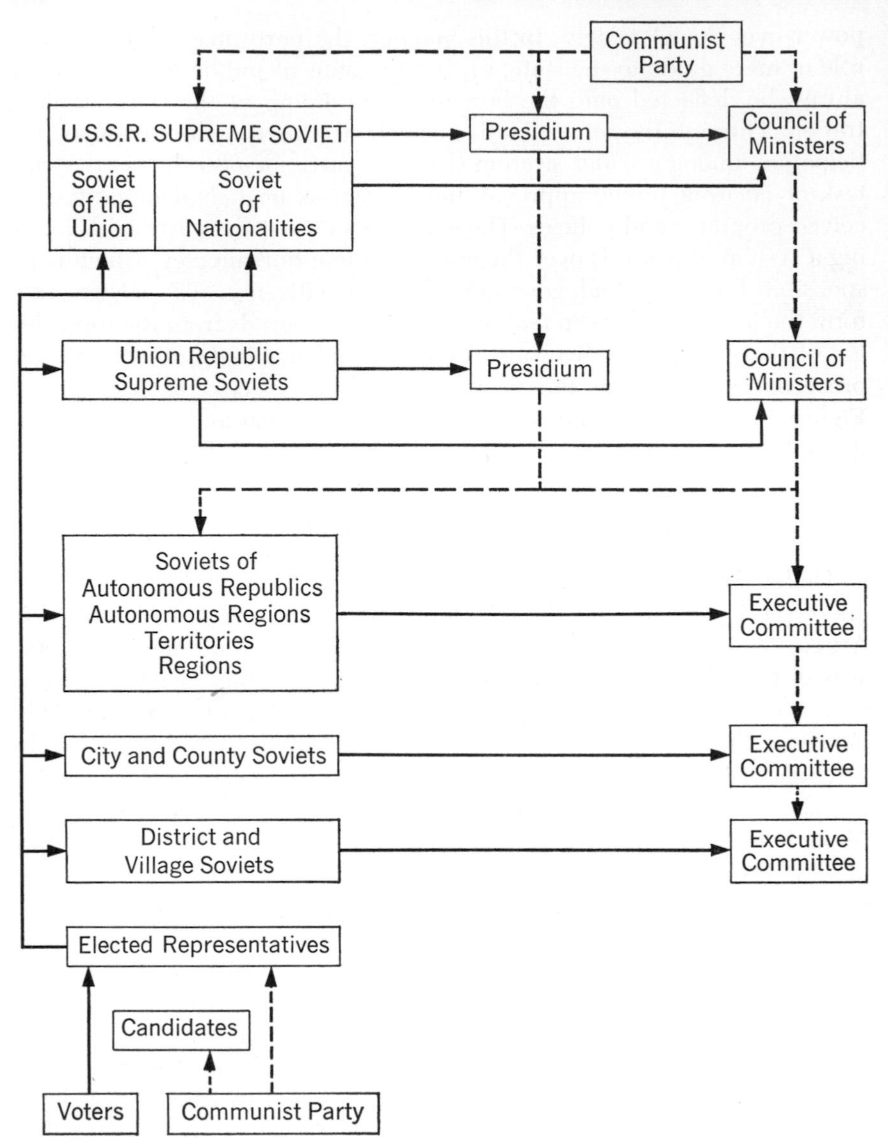

NOTE: Solid lines denote direction of formal authority. Broken lines indicate direction of real authority.

Figure 42–1. Soviet legislative and executive organs.

465 were workers and peasants, of whom some 327 were production workers. The remainder of the deputies are representatives of the working intelligentsia.[4] In the Soviet of Nationalities, of the 640 deputies, 366 are workers and peasants, of whom 287 work directly in production.

[4] *Ibid.*

Among the deputies of the Soviet of Nationalities are 77 workers of science, culture, and literature, including 9 academicians, 16 directors of scientific institutes and scientific workers, 17 teachers, and 11 physicians.[5] Non-Soviet sources indicate that in the 1954 Supreme Soviet, 83.3 per cent of the deputies belonged to the intelligentsia, 10.5 per cent were workers, and 6.2 per cent were peasants.[6] The discrepancy between Soviet and non-Soviet sources can be accounted for at least partially by different bases of classification. To become a deputy is considered a great distinction in the U.S.S.R. Hence, deputies are mostly members of the Soviet political and economic elite. Delegates referred to as "working deputies," are primarily concerned with their work in factories, schools, farms, hospitals, and the like. Deputies are expected to be directly involved in production; they are not expected to consider their functions as deputies as a profession. After the 1958 elections, the Soviet of the Union had 563 deputies who were members or candidate members of the Communist party. Only 175 deputies were non-party supporters of the party program. In the Soviet of the Nationalities, the numbers of party and non-party deputies were 485 and 155, respectively.

The Status of Deputies

The deputies have certain privileges as well as duties. The deputy enjoys immunity from arrest and prosecution and cannot be held to legal responsibility without the consent of the Supreme Soviet or, when the Supreme Soviet is not in session, without the consent of the Presidium of the Supreme Soviet (Article 52). He is granted free rail and water transportation within the U.S.S.R., a daily allowance during sessions of the Supreme Soviet, and a larger sum each month as reimbursement for the expense of carrying out a deputy's duties. The deputy is considered to be the servant of the people whom he represents in the Supreme Soviet. It is his duty to participate in the work of the Supreme Soviet and its committees and to ascertain that the laws that he approves are enforced in his own constituency. He has the right to address inquiries to the government or to a particular minister and to receive an answer (Article 71). He may, if this is considered by the party as appropriate, report on the application of a particular law in his district. He is expected to keep his electorate informed about his own work and the work of the Supreme Soviet. Between sessions, in spite of the fact that he is engaged in full-time employment, he is expected to visit enterprises, collectives and state farms, and to answer either orally or by mail numerous questions posed by his electorate. The deputies are overworked.

[5] *Ibid.*

[6] "Boris Meissner in Osteuropa," *Deutsche Gesellschaft fur Osteuropakunde,* No. 3 (1954), p. 216.

Sessions

Sessions of the two chambers begin and terminate simultaneously (Article 41). Each chamber elects a Chairman and four Vice-Chairmen (Articles 42 and 43). The Chairmen preside at the meetings of the respective chambers and have charge of their business and proceedings (Article 44). In actuality, the two chambers meet jointly on many occasions. Joint meetings are presided over alternately by the Chairman of the Soviet of the Union and the Chairman of the Soviet of Nationalities (Article 45). Sessions of the Supreme Soviet of the U.S.S.R. are convened regularly twice a year by the Presidium of the Supreme Soviet, while extraordinary sessions may be convoked by the Presidium on its own initiative or at the request of any Union Republic (Article 46).

Powers and Functions

The two chambers of the Supreme Soviet of the U.S.S.R. have equal rights and powers to initiate legislation (Articles 37 and 38). A law is considered to have been legally adopted following approval by simple majority of both chambers (Article 39). Such legislation is published, following certification by the Chairman of the Presidium of the Supreme Soviet and its Secretary (Article 40), in the languages of each of the Union Republics. Should the two chambers disagree, something that has not happened and is unlikely to occur, the disagreement would have to be resolved by a joint conference commission of the two chambers representing each equally. If the report of the commission were not approved or the commission was unable to agree on a compromise, the Presidium would be required to dissolve the Supreme Soviet and order new elections (Article 47). Elections must be held no later than two months after the term of the Supreme Soviet has been dissolved or expired (Article 54).

In addition to being given the constitutional right to exercise exclusive legislative power, the Supreme Soviet of the U.S.S.R. is charged with the following functions:

1. Verification of the credentials of deputies elected by the voters
2. Appointment of commissions of investigation and audit
3. Amendment of the Constitution
4. Election of the Supreme Court and special courts of the U.S.S.R.
5. Appointment of the Procurator-General of the U.S.S.R.
6. Appointment of the Chairman and members of the Council of Ministers of the U.S.S.R.[7]

Organization and Procedures

The Constitution of the U.S.S.R. has provided for a legislature that is strikingly similar in outward appearances to the parliamentary bodies of

[7] Articles 50, 51, 56, 102, 105, 114, and 146 of the Soviet Constitution.

the Western democracies. However, even to the uncritical observer, doubts about the democratic character of the Supreme Soviet must inevitably develop after comparing election procedures and from the fact that Soviet sources invariably report that all decisions in the Supreme Soviet are approved by unanimity or near unanimity. It is also true that most laws are issued as legislative decrees by the Presidium or by the Council of Ministers of the U.S.S.R. and are subsequently ratified by the Supreme Soviet. What does the Supreme Soviet, with its large and unwieldy membership and short and infrequent sessions, actually do? The first item of business on the agenda of each chamber of the newly elected Supreme Soviet is to appoint a mandates commission of seventeen members to examine the credentials of the deputies. Then permanent Chairmen and standing commissions must be elected by each house. The principal standing commissions consist of (1) a commission of legislative bills of nineteen members, (2) a budget commission of twenty-six members, and (3) a commission of foreign affairs of eleven members. Other commissions on matters such as education and public health have been established on an *ad hoc* basis from time to time. The two chambers meet in joint session to select the Presidium, the Council of Ministers, and the Supreme Court and Procurator-General of the U.S.S.R.

The activities of the second session of the Supreme Soviet during 1959 are representative of other sessions.[8] The Supreme Soviet approved the state plan for the development of the national economy in 1960, the state budget for 1960, and a law on the procedure for recalling U.S.S.R. Supreme Soviet deputies. It ratified the decrees of the Presidium of the U.S.S.R. Supreme Soviet of the formation and reorganization of the U.S.S.R. ministries and on the formation of state committees and the State Scientific and Economic Council of the U.S.S.R. Council of Ministers. It approved amendments to Articles 70, 77, and 78 of the Constitution. It approved a decree broadening the composition of draft commissions formed to assist in the drafting of citizens for active military service and various amendments and additions to Articles 21 and 22 of the U.S.S.R. Law on Universal Military Duty. Examples of discussion by the Supreme Soviet deputies included reports on the law concerning the recall of deputies; electrification in agriculture; the cultivation of virgin and idle lands; the mechanization of lumber procurement operations; the improvement of city transportation, sewage, and water mains; the storage of railroad cars; the erection of a new tractor plant, including comments about what is being done or should be done for improvement; and the overfulfilment of the quota in a factory managed by a deputy, along with statements about the need for modernization and the replacement of obsolete equipment. The activities of this session, which are more or less typical, indicate

[8] Cf. *Current Digest of the Soviet Press,* IX, No. 46 (December 16, 1959).

that the Supreme Soviet of the U.S.S.R., in fact, performs little original legislating.

Far more important as an initiator of legislation is the inner body of the Supreme Soviet—its Presidium. During the major part of the year, when the Supreme Soviet is not in session, the Presidium issues decrees that have binding force. In the subsequent sessions of the Supreme Soviet, the decrees are unanimously approved and become "laws." For Soviet citizens, there is no difference between a decree having binding force and a law. Only because the Presidium is selected by and accountable to the Supreme Soviet is it possible to say that the Presidium legislates by means of decrees on behalf of the Supreme Soviet.

The major deliberations and debates over matters that are presented to the Supreme Soviet occur in the commissions. Here, too, any legislation that originates in the Supreme Soviet is prepared. The commissions convene several weeks prior to the session of the Supreme Soviet. Much of their work is carried out by subcommittees. Members of the commissions are specialists on matters dealt with by the commission; other deputies are not. Most of the legislation is proposed by the Council of Ministers. The commission is fully informed, has the right to call officials, discusses proposed legislation with individual ministers, submits counterproposals, and may propose new legislation. In practice, the commissions take little initiative in the introduction or preparation of legislation. They do examine the drafting of proposed legislation and occasionally suggest amendments. There is no evidence that legislation proposed by the Council of Ministers and sanctioned by the Communist party has ever been rejected by a Supreme Soviet commission. The Supreme Soviet receives all information from its commissions, considers the application of the new bill, and approves it unanimously. Since both chambers of the Supreme Soviet work together and receive the same information, there is little likelihood of disagreement between the chambers. Most of the legislation is initiated not by the Supreme Soviet, but by the party, the Council of Ministers, or the Presidium; it is true that all legislation must be formally approved by the Supreme Soviet, but the approval is always given. In no Western Parliament has near unanimity been the rule. Reasons for the lack of dissenting votes are worth considering. First, a considerable amount of debate apparently does occur in the commissions. There, differences are ironed out and a program for concerted action is selected. The Soviet press covers the meetings of the Supreme Soviet and reports on the unanimity. Little attention is paid by the press to the debates that occur within the commissions. The unanimous decisions of the Supreme Soviet, which are criticized in the West, are prized highly in the U.S.S.R. because, like the elections, such decisions are a manifestation of support for the party program. Second, no legislation is proposed in the

Supreme Soviet unless it has the official sanction of the party. The majority of the deputies are party members or candidates, and all are supporters of the party program. The approval by such deputies of legislation sanctioned by the party is to be expected. Third, when a bill is presented in the Supreme Soviet, the deputies do not construe their duty to involve deciding whether or not the bill should pass. Why should they? The bill has the sanction of the party that is in power because of a victorious revolution; it has been considered carefully by specialists in the commission. Their duty, as members of a "working body," is to consider the application of the bill in their places of work. Although differences may arise, such differences are not concerned over whether the bill should be passed, but rather over how to make the bill more workable. Such differences can be resolved without difficulty.

Though theoretically the Supreme Soviet is the sole legislating organ in the governmental machinery of the U.S.S.R., it operates primarily as a body that ratifies legislation proposed by the party through the Council of Ministers or the Presidium of the Supreme Soviet. It has symbolic importance in that the U.S.S.R. is able to demonstrate to both its own citizens and foreign countries that the laws of the U.S.S.R. are made by the elected representatives of the people. It serves as a platform for the announcement of national policies. And periodically, or as the occasion demands, it provides the formality of approval by a representative assembly of governmental policy.

SELECTED READING

CARSON, GEORGE B. *Electoral Practice in the USSR.* New York: Frederick A. Praeger, Inc., 1955.

KARPINSKY, V. *The Social and State Structure of the USSR.* Moscow: Foreign Languages Publishing House, 1950.

———. *How the Soviet Union Is Governed.* Moscow: Foreign Languages Publishing House, 1950.

McCLOSKY, HERBERT, and TURNER, JOHN E. *The Soviet Dictatorship.* New York: McGraw-Hill Book Co., Inc., 1960. Chap. 11.

VYSHINSKY, ANDREI Y. *The Law of the Soviet State.* New York: The Macmillan Co., 1948.

———. *The Soviet Election Law: Questions and Answers.* Moscow: Foreign Languages Publishing House, 1955.

43

The Executive and Administration

THE PRESIDIUM OF THE SUPREME SOVIET

The Presidium of the Supreme Soviet of the U.S.S.R. is a miniature Supreme Soviet that is in continuous session. This smaller governmental organ is deemed necessary for two reasons. First, the Supreme Soviet is composed of nearly 1,400 deputies and is too large a body to deal with many of the legislative details. Second, the Supreme Soviet is required to convene only twice a year unless an extraordinary session is called. In general, each session is of approximately one-week duration. It is necessary for the Supreme Soviet to delegate some of its authority so that its duties can be performed during the approximately fifty weeks that it is not in session. Consequently, at a joint meeting of the two chambers, the Supreme Soviet of the U.S.S.R. elects a Presidium of the Supreme Soviet of the U.S.S.R., which is accountable to the Supreme Soviet for all its activities.

The Presidium retains its powers until a newly elected Supreme Soviet forms a new Presidium (Article 53). Article 49 of the Constitution lists the rights and duties of the Presidium of the Supreme Soviet of the U.S.S.R., as follows:

a. Convenes the session of the Supreme Soviet of the U.S.S.R.;
b. Issues decrees;
c. Gives interpretations of the laws of the U.S.S.R. in operation;
d. Dissolves the Supreme Soviet of the U.S.S.R. in conformity with Article 47 of the Constitution of the U.S.S.R. and orders new elections;

e. Conducts nationwide polls (referendums) on its own initiative or on the demand of one of the Union Republics;
f. Annuls decisions and orders of the Council of Ministers of the U.S.S.R. and of the Council of Ministers of the Union Republics if they do not conform to law;
g. In the intervals between sessions of the Supreme Soviet of the U.S.S.R., releases and appoints Ministers of the U.S.S.R. on the recommendation of the Chairman of the Council of Ministers of the U.S.S.R., subject to subsequent confirmation by the Supreme Soviet of the U.S.S.R.;
h. Institutes decorations (Orders and Medals) and titles of honor of the U.S.S.R.
i. Awards Orders and Medals and confers titles of honor of the U.S.S.R.;
j. Exercises the right of pardon;
k. Institutes military titles, diplomatic ranks and other special titles;
l. Appoints and removes the high command of the Armed Forces of the U.S.S.R.;
m. In the intervals between sessions of the Supreme Soviet of the U.S.S.R., proclaims a state of war in the event of military attack on the U.S.S.R.; or when necessary to fulfill international treaty obligations concerning mutual defense against aggression;
n. Orders general or partial mobilization;
o. Ratifies and denounces international treaties of the U.S.S.R.;
p. Appoints and recalls plenipotentiary representatives of the U.S.S.R. to foreign states;
q. Receives the letters of credence and recall of diplomatic representatives accredited to it by foreign states;
r. Proclaims martial law in separate localities or throughout the U.S.S.R. in the interests of the defense of the U.S.S.R. or of the maintenance of public order and the security of the state.

The Presidium of the Supreme Soviet is often called a collegiate or "Collective President" of the U.S.S.R. The Chairman of the Presidium is considered the titular head of the state, and in foreign countries it is not uncommon for him to be referred to as the President of the Soviet Union. This office was held from 1921 to 1946 by Kalinin, who had been a peasant and worker and was an active Bolshevik before and during the revolution. Shvernik, a trade-union official, succeeded to the post of Chairman upon the death of Kalinin, giving way in 1953 to the old Bolshevik metal worker and soldier Voroshilov. At the age of seventy-nine in May, 1960, Voroshilov requested the Supreme Soviet to relieve him of his responsibilities for reasons of health; whereupon the Supreme Soviet elected, on Khrushchev's nomination, Leonid I. Brezhnev to the post of Presidium Chairman. The Chairman of the Presidium, an important figure in the party hierarchy, is a member of the Presidium of the Central Committee of the Communist party of the Soviet Union. As Chairman of the Presidium of the Supreme Soviet, he must sign all the legislative decrees that are deliberated by the Presidium. His signature is, in turn, countersigned by the Secretary of the Presidium to attest to its authenticity. As the titular chief of state, the Chairman receives all foreign diplomatic envoys and officiates at state ceremonies. His powers as Chairman are purely formal, since the Presidium does not delegate its powers to the Chairman.

The membership of the Presidium is elected by the Supreme Soviet in a joint meeting of the Soviet of the Union and the Soviet of Nationalities and consists of a Chairman or President, fifteen Vice-Chairmen, a Secretary, and sixteen members (Article 48). The fifteen Vice-Chairmen are, by custom, always the Chairmen of the Union Republic Presidia, so that, in fact, these may be said to hold membership on the Presidium of the Supreme Soviet of the U.S.S.R. ex officio. This practice insures each Union Republic equal representation on the collegiate executive body of the U.S.S.R. Supreme Soviet. Most of the sixteen members of the Presidium are high party functionaries—members of the Presidium of the Central Committee of the Communist party, candidate members, members of the Secretariat, or members of the Central Committee. Before assuming the post of Chairman of the Council of Ministers in 1958, Khrushchev was a member of the Presidium of the U.S.S.R. Supreme Soviet. Neither the Chairmen of the Soviet of the Union and Soviet of Nationalities nor members of the Council of Ministers of the U.S.S.R. are eligible to serve on the Presidium of the Supreme Soviet. There is to this extent a notion of separation of powers operative in the Soviet system. Since the Presidium of the Supreme Soviet functions with a quorum of one-third of its membership (i.e., eleven out of thirty-three) and since the fifteen Vice-Chairmen are usually unable to attend its meetings because of pressing duties in the Union Republics, the working membership of the Presidium consists of the high party functionaries who reside in Moscow. Although it is referred to as a daily working organ, it is not known generally how often and how regularly the Presidium meets. Neither is it apparent by what rules of procedure the Presidium functions, since its deliberations are never published and its official decrees that are published carry only the signature of the Chairman (sometimes that of a Vice-Chairman) and the countersignature of the Secretary.

In practice, the Presidium has made full use of all of its prerogatives with the exception of items (d) and (e) (see pp. 644–45) of its enumerated powers. Since disagreement between the Soviet of the Union and the Soviet of Nationalities is virtually impossible under the existing procedure, the Presidium has not had to dissolve the Supreme Soviet nor has it had the occasion to conduct nationwide referenda. It convokes but does not conduct the sessions of the Supreme Soviet. It calls for or postpones elections and establishes electoral districts. The Presidium, rather than the Supreme Court of the U.S.S.R., interprets the laws of the U.S.S.R. in action. It has annulled orders of the Council of Ministers and appointed and removed ministers of the U.S.S.R. on the recommendation of the Chairman of the Council of Ministers, such appointments being subject to ratification by the Supreme Soviet. Numerous ranks, decorations, and titles of honor have been established and awarded. The right of pardon has been exercised; appointments, promotions, and demotions in the armed forces have been made. The Presidium has ordered general or partial mobilization, declared martial law, ratified and denounced international treaties, received diplomatic representatives of foreign states, and appointed and recalled the diplomatic representatives of the U.S.S.R.

Of the prerogatives and powers that are exercised by the Presidium, perhaps the most important is the issuance of legislative decrees. Since the Presidium functions continuously, while the Supreme Soviet meets seldom and briefly, the former decrees most of the legislation, which is converted subsequently into permanent statutes by resolution of the two houses of the Supreme Soviet with little or no discussion of the merits of such legislation. Representative decrees of the Presidium would include such items as changes in the composition, organization and functions of the ministries and other administrative agencies, modification of the legal codes (criminal, civil, and procedural), amendment of the provisions of the pension system and salary and wage scales, etc. These decrees have the same binding character as statutes, and no court is competent to annul or ignore them. There is no time limit on the conversion of decree legislation into statutory law; until and unless the Supreme Soviet has rejected such measures, they are considered to be legally binding on the courts.

THE COUNCIL OF MINISTERS OF THE U.S.S.R.

The Council of Ministers, or Government, of the U.S.S.R. is described by the Constitution as the "highest executive and administrative organ" of the state. It usually consists of about sixty members: the Chairman of the Council; the first Vice-Chairmen and a number of Vice-Chairmen (the number being unfixed by law); all the ministers of U.S.S.R. and persons holding the rank of minister, such as the heads of State Boards and chairmen of State Committees; and finally, ex officio, the chairmen of the Councils of Ministers of the Union Republics.

The Chairman of the Council of Ministers is appointed to an unfixed term of office by the Supreme Soviet in joint meeting. He is responsible to the Supreme Soviet at all times for the actions of the Council. Constitutionally he may be removed from office only by the Supreme Soviet. In fact, the Chairman of the Council of Ministers is selected by the Presidium of the Central Committee of the Communist party of the Soviet Union on the recommendation of the First Secretary. When the First

Secretary himself occupies the position of Chairman of the Council, as was true of Stalin from 1941 until his death and is true of Khrushchev from March 1958 to the present, nothing short of a successful conspiracy can force the Chairman from office. Of the three recognized "supreme party leaders" in the Soviet Union (Lenin, Stalin, and Khrushchev), all of whom held the post of Chairman of the Council, none has ever been removed from office. The others who have held the position of Chairman of the Council (Rykov, 1924–1930; Molotov, 1930–1941; Malenkov, 1953–1955; and Bulganin, 1955–1958) were eventually removed either because of suspicion of their loyalty by the supreme party leader or because the latter had decided to assume the position himself.

The first Vice-Chairmen and the Vice-Chairmen may be appointed by the Presidium of the Supreme Soviet on the request of the Chairmen of the Council, although their appointments are generally confirmed by the Supreme Soviet subsequently. The first Vice-Chairmen are invariably members of the Presidium of the Central Committee of the Communist party, while the Vice-Chairmen usually are either members of this high party organ or candidate members. They are the most influential members of the Council next to the Chairman; and they seldom are burdened with administrative responsibilities, such as direction of a ministry. Instead, the first Vice-Chairmen and the Vice-Chairmen assist the Chairman of the Council in supervising and coordinating the work of the numerous administrative agencies of the central government and in planning and formulating top-level policy for the government. Together with the Chairman of the Council, they form the "inner Cabinet" of the Council of Ministers, which compares with the Cabinets of most other governments in the world. The membership of the "inner Cabinet" or Bureau of the Council of Ministers seldom exceeds ten and thus far has never exceeded thirteen members.

The ministers and others holding equivalent rank are appointed either by the Supreme Soviet or its Presidium on nomination by the Chairman of the Council of Ministers; they hold office at his pleasure, although formal removal is vested in the Presidium of the Supreme Soviet or the Supreme Soviet itself. These ministers are generally not influential party leaders but rather highly experienced and competent administrators and technicians or experts. Some of them are eventually selected to membership or candidacy on the Central Committee of the Communist party if their performance is extremely good, and a few may be elevated to the inner circle of power if they obtain the favor of the supreme party leader. Ministers are not legally required to be deputies in the houses of the Supreme Soviet, although they may appear before the chambers during legislative sessions to speak. Although administrative and technical competence is the major qualification for appointment to the position of minister, very few of the technically or administratively competent in the

U.S.S.R. can aspire to such appointments on the basis of sheer ability. Political loyalty to the party is essential, and the personal favor of a party leader is indispensable. It is somewhat hazardous to accept ministerial rank in the Soviet Union because of the constant threat of personal disgrace and ruin that generally follows in the wake of any error, whether it be administrative, technical, or political. The turnover has been considerable. It is not unusual for persons who have held ministerial rank to be assigned to relatively insignificant posts in undesirable places.[1]

There is little published information concerning the internal organization and operation procedures of the Council of Ministers and of its inner Bureau. It is presumed that the Council has regular weekly meetings that are presided over by the Chairman occasionally, and more often by a first Vice-Chairman or simply a Vice-Chairman. These meetings are devoted to informing the ministers of high policy, criticizing ministers for their shortcomings, hearing the problems confronting the ministers, coordinating their actions, and correcting ministerial decisions and actions. The Council is presumed to have a number of interministerial committees, headed usually by a Vice-Chairman and established on an *ad hoc* basis to study controversial problems and report to the Council.

The competence of the Council of Ministers of the U.S.S.R. is defined constitutionally in Article 68, as follows:

a. Coordinates and directs the work of the All-Union and Union-Republic Ministries of the U.S.S.R. and of other institutions under its jurisdiction, exercises guidance of the Economic Councils of the economic administration areas through the Councils of Ministers of the Union Republics;
b. Adopts measures to carry out the national-economic plan and the state budget, and to strengthen the credit and monetary system;
c. Adopts measures for the maintenance of public order, for the protection of the interests of the state, and for the safeguarding of the rights of the citizens;
d. Exercises general guidance in the sphere of relations with foreign states;
e. Fixes the annual contingent of citizens to be called up for military service and directs the general organization of the Armed Forces of the country;
f. Sets up, whenever necessary, special Committees and Central Administrations under the Council of Ministers of the U.S.S.R. for economic and cultural affairs and defense.

Execution of the constitutionally defined competence of the Council of Ministers in practice endows the Council with extensive executive-administrative power along with significant legislative functions. It has direct or indirect control over the entire administrative apparatus in accordance

[1] After having been Chairman of the Council for years and then Foreign Minister for over a decade and a half, Molotov served briefly as Chairman of the Committee of State Control before he was assigned as Soviet Ambassador to Outer Mongolia. Shepilov had to take a teaching position when he was removed as Foreign Minister in 1957, while Malenkov and Bulganin were given minor technical posts.

with section (a) of Article 68. Direct control is exerted over both All-Union and Union-Republican Ministries.

The ministries of the U.S.S.R. are either All-Union or Union-Republican Ministries. Each All-Union Ministry directs the branch of state administration entrusted to it throughout the territory of the U.S.S.R. either directly or through bodies appointed by it. The Union-Republican Ministries, as a rule, direct the branches of state administration entrusted to them through corresponding ministries of the Union Republics; they administer directly only a definite and limited number of enterprises according to a list confirmed by the Presidium of the Supreme Soviet of the U.S.S.R. During recent years, the Union-Republican Ministries have had their jurisdiction extended considerably; although they are still subject to supervision and control from the All-Union Council of Ministers. Among the All-Union Ministries are Foreign Trade, Merchant Marine, Railways, Medium Machine Building, Transport Construction, Chemical Industry, and Construction of Electric Power Stations. Among the Union-Republican Ministries are Internal Affairs, Higher Education, Geological Survey and Conservation of Mineral Resources, Public Health, Foreign Affairs, Culture, Defense, Communication, Agriculture, and Finance (Articles 74 to 78). The Council of Ministers organizes and supervises the work of each of the ministries and Councils; it exercises the right to annul the orders of any individual minister. Although the ministers are appointed or released by action of the Supreme Soviet or its Presidium, such action is seldom taken without recommendation by the Chairman of the Council of Ministers. Since the Council of Ministers has the right to overrule the decisions of the Republican Councils of Ministers and Economic Councils, its jurisdiction is very extensive, encompassing regulation of the entire economy, national defense, internal security, foreign affairs, education, health, and culture. No aspect of life within the U.S.S.R. is unaffected by the actions and decisions of the U.S.S.R. Council of Ministers.

Much of the work of the Council of Ministers is associated with the organization and activity of subordinate administrative organs. It appoints the heads and deputy heads of chief administrations as well as deputy ministers and confirms the collegia of the ministries. It establishes and abolishes committees, commissions, and chief administrations, and issues statutes and regulations concerning the structure and function of these organs and of various bureaus, ministries, and industrial administrations. All important orders issued by the ministers are examined and accepted or annulled by the Council.

Section (b) of Article 68, which refers to the competence of the Council of Ministers in the economic sphere, somewhat understates the reality of the situation. The functioning of the planned economy will be discussed in detail in Chapter 44; therefore, brief comments will be sufficient at this point. The central planning agencies, which have immediate responsibility for preparing and enforcing the economic plan, work under the supervision of the Council of Ministers. Although the Supreme Soviet has constitutional authority over economic planning, it has invariably merely confirmed the plan as submitted to it. Therefore, the Council of Ministers not only exercises its constitutional authority to administer the plan, but since it is very active in the formulation of plans, it, in fact, regulates all phases of economic life. In conjunction with the preparation and administration of the economic plan, the Council of Ministers, and especially the Ministry of Finance, exert practical control over the state budget, including both sources of revenue and expenditures. Before the budget is submitted to the Supreme Soviet for approval, individual aspects of the budget, and the budget as a whole, are studied and revised by the Council of Ministers. As the "exclusive legislative organ," the Supreme Soviet should, according to the Constitution, exert considerable control over the budget. In practice, major financial policies are determined by the party; the detailed preparation of the budget is handled by the Council of Ministers; and after occasional minor changes suggested by the Budget Commission of the Supreme Soviet, the budget is approved by the Supreme Soviet and administered by the Council of Ministers. Thus, the Council determines rates of taxation and other assessment rates and, moreover, allocates the revenue for the budget of each Union Republic and its subdivisions and for various segments of the economy such as agriculture, industry, national defense, education, and health. Wage rates, prices, social insurance benefits, and the like also come under the jurisdiction of the Council of Ministers.

The effect of section (c), Article 68, has been to give the executive branch of the government, the Council of Ministers, control over not only the police force, but over many of the regulations that the police are required to enforce. The Council of Ministers has, by decree, defined what constitutes a crime against Socialist property and fixed the associated penalty. Among the very numerous decrees issued in accordance with constitutional right have been decrees pertaining to tardiness, absenteeism, inefficiency, poor management, defective commodities, petty theft, defacement of Socialist property, and sabotage. The activities of police agencies, in general, are supervised by the Council, although the relationship of the secret police to the Council, or to any other agency with the exception of the higher echelons of the Communist party, has typically been nebulous.

The Council of Ministers is actively involved in foreign affairs, more so, in fact, than the Presidium of the Supreme Soviet, to which the treaty power is constitutionally assigned. Most of the treaties are prepared by the Council, which, in addition, confirms treaties and agreements not requiring ratification and enters into agreements with other states. Foreign-trade organs act under its supervision, and it may appoint or replace trade representatives. It may order acts of reprisal and withdraw recognition and sever relations with other states, and it operates embassies and consulates.

All agencies related to national defense, such as the Ministries of Armed Forces, Armaments, Munitions, Shipbuilding, and Aviation Industry, are supervised and coordinated by the Council. In addition, it likewise controls the annual draft quota, the organization and training of the military forces, as well as the appointment of high-ranking military officers.

In spite of the fact that according to the Constitution the Council of Ministers is an executive-administrative organ rather than a legislative one, many of its activities may be described most appropriately as legislative. Some constitutional sanction is provided by Articles 66 and 67, which specify that the Council of Ministers of the U.S.S.R. may issue decisions and orders on the basis of and in pursuance of the laws in operation and verify their execution, and that, moreover, these decisions and orders are binding throughout the territory of the U.S.S.R. In principle, such measures are supposed merely to amplify the existing laws. However, the laws are few and vague; and the decisions and orders of the Council of Ministers are more numerous and, in general, more precise. Many of the ministerial decrees are, of course, associated with the operation of ministries or agencies under the supervision of the Council. Others are not. In fact, the Council of Ministers has almost unlimited power in the issuing of decrees, both with regard to subject matter and to laws in operation. Theoretically, a check on the legality of decrees in relation to statutes is available in that the Constitution specifies that the decrees of the Council of Ministers may be annulled by the Supreme Soviet or its Presidium. However, since the inner body of the Council of Ministers is composed of members of the Central Committee of the party, the decrees issued by the Council are seldom annulled by the superior organs of state authority. Courts have occasionally not upheld the legal status of an order issued by one of the lower administrative organs; but judicial rulings against the decrees of the Council of Ministers are unknown and, it seems, would be highly impermissible. Although Soviet writers do refer to the acts of the Council of Ministers as inferior to laws passed by the Supreme Soviet, in practice, such acts are equally binding on the Soviet citizen. A Soviet source states: "The decrees and dispositions of the Council of Ministers are not subject to oversight in respect to their legality by any organ except superior organs of state authority. Acts of the Government are obligatory for unconditional application by all, including the courts."[2]

[2] A. A. Askerov, N. D. Durmanov, M. P. Kareva, V. K. Kotok, I. D. Levin, and I. P. Trainin, *Sovetskoe gosudarstvennoe pravo* (Soviet State Law) (Moscow: Gosudarstvennoe izdatelstvo yuridicheskoi literatury, 1948), pp. 295–96.

Thus, checks on the legality of decrees of the Council of Ministers are in practice almost non-existent.

It is of interest that many of the decrees of the Council of Ministers are cosponsored by the Central Committee of the Communist party or by the Council of Trade Unions, neither of which has legal authority to issue binding decrees. Cosponsorship by the party may be expected to add significance and strength to the decree, while cosponsorship by trade-unions permits the trade-unions to be described as a regulating force in the labor field and, moreover, may create the illusion that unpopular labor measures are self-imposed.

Finally, with reference to the legislative practices of the Council of Ministers, it should be reiterated that most of the statutes that are introduced before the Supreme Soviet's Commissions are initiated and formulated by the Council of Ministers and presented to the Commissions for consideration and adoption. The legitimate rationale for this practice is that the ministries, in their executive-administrative capacities, are cognizant of problems requiring legislative action and, because of their specialized knowledge, are well equipped to draft detailed legislation. However, the fact that this does occur, combined with the decree issuing rights, indicates that the Council of Ministers, not the Supreme Soviet, is, *de facto,* the major legislative organ of state machinery in the U.S.S.R. Consequently, the Council of Ministers may be described as the leading executive-administrative, legislative, and managerial organ of the state and of the Communist party.

SOVIET ADMINISTRATIVE MACHINERY AND PRACTICE

Like the Communist party, the Soviet administration is purported to be organized according to the principle of democratic centralism. As in the former case, democratic practices are supposedly represented by such features as the responsibility of administrative organs to elected bodies (i.e., the Council of Ministers to the Supreme Soviet, the participation of the Soviet people in designating and achieving state goals, and the role of collegia in advising policy-making administrators). Centralism, the more important or realistic of the descriptive terms, indicates that the decisions of the higher organs of central authority are absolutely binding on all lower organs. Centralism, as a major feature of Soviet administration, is certainly a reality; i.e., the U.S.S.R. Council of Ministers directs and supervises the work of the Union Republic Council of Ministers. However, the use of the term "democratic" is less justifiable unless one interprets democracy as the clever utilization by the regime of "mass participation" to more readily achieve the goals set by the central administrators. Just as there is a flow of orders and directives from the top of the administrative hierarchy to the lower organs, a flow of information from the lower to the higher organs is indispensable. Insofar as possible, upper-echelon administrators are willing to capitalize on local information and local initiative to achieve the centrally designated goals. However, each administrator is held solely responsible for all aspects of the conduct of agencies or enterprises under his supervision.

Soviet administrative personnel constitutes a vast, constantly growing, and cumbersome bureaucracy. Although accurate figures are not available, current estimates indicate that approximately thirteen million managerial, administrative, and technical officials fall into the category of public employees or civil servants. This figure, of course, excludes all persons engaged directly in production, since millions of employed persons in the U.S.S.R. are state employees. The excessively large bureaucracy would seem to be, in the main, the result of attempts on the part of the state to maintain firm control over all instruments of power: economic, military, ideological, and political. Bureaucrats supervise, inspect, report on, and exert control over all aspects of life within the state.

The Civil Service

The regime has paid specific attention to the training, selection, and placement of public employees, since their function in the smooth attainment of party goals is fully recognized. Among the most important of the regulative agencies is the State Commission on Civil Service, which operates under the joint guidance of the Council of Ministers and the Communist party. This Commission administers employee codes and recommends procedures related to the recruitment and utilization of personnel, salary scales, and job classifications. It may inspect governmental agencies with the goal of detecting waste and duplication of functions and may recommend reductions of overstaffed units and place limits on the number of officials who may be employed by a particular agency.

The U.S.S.R. only occasionally uses competitive examinations in the selection of civil servants. Most administrative employees are recruited directly from the universities or technical institutes that have trained the candidates according to specifications outlined by the hiring ministry or agency. Some of the bureaucrats have been trained in institutes not associated with a particular ministry; but these persons, during their training period, have no assurance of future employment in public administration. Very high-ranking officials are selected directly by the Council of Ministers or, if associated with a particular ministry, by the involved ministry. The Communist party, as always, exercises guidance and control over such appointments. Each ministry typically has a "cadres section" that keeps rosters of personal information about present and potential officials, the need for new officials, and the like. This information is available to the minister or department head, who is responsible for the selection and appointment of new officials. Since, in general, members of the administrative hierarchy earn higher salaries, are the recipients of a disproportionately high number of bonuses and awards, and are accorded higher social status than persons of corresponding training and competence in non-administrative positions, administrative positions are eagerly sought by Soviet citizens.

Administrative Responsibility

The administrative hierarchy is headed by the Council of Ministers of the U.S.S.R. Immediately subordinate to the Council are the ministries, whether All-Union or Union-Republican, each of which is headed by a minister, appointed by the Supreme Soviet or its Presidium on the recommendation of the Chairman of the Council of Ministers. Each minister is formally responsible to the Council of Ministers and to the Supreme Soviet. The ministers, unless they are important party members, cannot be described appropriately as policy makers. Rather, they are administrators of the party policy and expert technical advisors. They can advise, make suggestions, and submit tentative plans to their political superiors, who in turn make the policy decisions to which the ministers must adhere. Each minister is provided with a collegium of deputy ministers and other advisors, who are appointed by the Council of Ministers, with a technical council for advice on technical matters, and a chief inspection office that investigates the fulfillment of administrative decisions. In addition, some ministries have had attached to them large advisory councils composed of representatives from enterprises directed by the ministry and representatives from local organizations. Representatives of the party offer both advice and criticism to the minister. None of these advisors or advisory bodies are elected, or even appointed, by elected organs. On the other hand, their function is merely to advise, not to decide. The principle of "one-man responsibility" is maintained. Only the minister himself has the legal authority to issue directives for the operation of the ministry. If these directives are not condoned by his superiors, he is held personally responsible.

Each minister is an important and powerful administrator even if the over-all policy decisions are made by the party and the inner Cabinet of the Council of Ministers. He is appropriately described as the "sole director" of his ministry. He is permitted to issue, within the limits of the jurisdiction of his department, orders and instructions on the basis of and in pursuance of the laws in operation, as well as decisions and ordinances of the Council of Ministers (Article 73). He also supervises the execution of the orders and instructions. Although many legal and extra-legal controls, which will be discussed in detail later and which include party supervision and the right of the Council of Ministers to annul his orders, do limit his administrative power, the minister's power is extensive; and he does bear responsibility for numerous and important decisions.

Since the coordination and direction of the activities of a ministry constitute a mammoth task, the minister necessarily delegates some of his responsibility to subordinates. In general, each ministry is subdivided into a number of chief administrations, whose heads are held personally responsible by the minister for decisions and for the activities of all subordinates. Typical of a ministry's chief administrations are such general divisions as personnel, planning and supply, and production units such as ore refining, smelting, and pig iron production.

The Council of Ministers of each Union Republic is controlled by the Council of Ministers of the U.S.S.R., and each Republican ministry is supervised by the corresponding U.S.S.R. ministry. The organizations of the economic administration will be elaborated in Chapter 44. Here it is sufficient to say that the U.S.S.R. is divided into over one hundred Economic Regions or Sovnarkhozy, each administered by an Economic Council that is supervised by the Council of Ministers and by the Union Republic in which the Economic Region is located. Each Sovnarkhoz is in turn subdivided into a number of chief administrations, some of which are subdivided into several combines or trusts, which are given supervisory control over factories or other production units. At the head of each factory is a director who, subject to various controls and the supervision of all superior administrative officers in the administrative hierarchy, is given "sole responsibility" for the administration of the factory.

Administrative Controls

Regardless of the explicitness of directions issued by the party and by superior administrative officers, it is inconceivable that all exigencies can be anticipated. Therefore, it is inevitable that all administrators from the U.S.S.R. minister to the director of a factory are required, on occasion, to make independent decisions. It is likewise inevitable that in a totalitarian system such as exists in the U.S.S.R., numerous controls are required to insure that the decisions conform to the party policy and the over-all state plan, and that the opportunities for administrators to use their positions for personal aggrandizement be sharply curbed.

Some control over administrative activities is exercised by the governmental machinery. The Council of Ministers has the right to annul the orders of individual ministers and even of the Councils of Ministers of the Union Republics. It can moreover recommend the dismissal of individual ministers, an action that may be followed by more dire legal consequences. Both the Supreme Soviet and its Presidium have the constitutional right to pass on the legality of decisions made by the Council and by individual ministers. Although this has seldom happened, the possibility of its occurrence may tend to limit the extravagance of administrative action. One of the chief duties of the Procurator-General of the U.S.S.R. and his subordinates is to insure strict observance of the law by all ministries and institutions subordinated to them and by officials and citizens of the U.S.S.R. generally (Article 113). The Procuracy has, not infrequently, initiated criminal procedures against government officials, particularly local ones, for illegal activities. Likewise, as previously mentioned, the courts can, but rarely do, rule against administrative action.

The most important controlling agency is, of course, the Communist party. Among the party's control weapons are the following: the issuance of directives that affect over-all administrative policies; the appointment of none but trusted party members to all-important administrative positions; the infiltration of loyal party members into every administrative and production unit so that all infringements may be reported to party officials; rewards for officials who faithfully administer policies according to the party line and demotions for those who stray from it, either intentionally or inadvertently.

The Commission of Soviet Control, an organization that is formally responsible to the Council of Ministers of the U.S.S.R. but in fact cooperates very closely with the party Control Committee, is empowered to oversee the administrative fulfillment of directives and can investigate the activities of almost all administrative and economic units.[3] Its very numerous investigators have the right to examine the records of governmental, economic, and even cultural and social agencies or societies. Along with the Ministry of Finance, it supervises the expenditure of state funds and has the right to audit financial records and to supervise accounting techniques. Irregularities and administrative violations are reported to higher administrative authorities, party officials, and to the courts.

A number of other organs have, in the interest of their own efficiency, investigatory and supervisory powers over administrative and economic units. Among these organs are the State Planning Committee, which oversees the fulfillment of its quotas; the State Bank, which investigates the financial status of a unit to determine whether credit should be granted; and the Ministry of Finance, which exercises control over financial and budgetary considerations. The secret police are empowered to investigate possible sabotage, treason, mismanagement, and any other economic or political activity that might be detrimental to the welfare of the state.

Since each administrative official is held responsible for all actions and decisions of his subordinates, it is to be expected that careful supervision and control is exercised by him. Moreover, sections within enterprises,

[3] Andrei Y. Vyshinsky (ed.), *The Law of the Soviet State* (New York: The Macmillan Co., 1948), p. 379.

such as the accounting section, for self-protection are constantly on the lookout for irregularities. On the other hand, all citizens are encouraged to participate in "criticism from below" as well as in "self-criticism." The possibility of criticism of supervisors and officials by the workers is expected to decrease the number of violations, and the criticism itself may serve as an expedient reason for removing administrative officials for inefficiency or for political reasons. Not infrequently, the press publishes letters from "ordinary citizens" who complain about mismanagement, maladministration, misappropriation of funds, etc. It is likely that some of these letters are genuine and voluntary expressions of distaste for unsalutary practices, but that even more letters are sponsored by the party for reasons such as informing the public that the party is cognizant of all misdemeanors, keeping administrators on the alert, and justifying the removal of officials. Organizations and groups that provide additional checks on the activities of administrative officials include commissions assigned to the lower soviets; the Komsomols and other youth organizations; the trade-union; professional organizations; and particularly the activists; who are, in general, expected to help implement the decisions of the regime, to submit proposals to improve output, and to uncover shortcomings.

In spite of these very numerous and seemingly foolproof techniques for administrative control, frequently leading party and governmental officials complain about such things as inefficient translation of decisions into action, misappropriation of funds, faulty products, excessive and unnecessary paper work, unreliable officials, overstaffing in higher administrative categories, along with insufficient numbers of workers. Obviously, all of these complaints could be made legitimately about the bureaucracy of most countries and even most economic organizations. It is difficult to judge whether the administrative setup of the U.S.S.R. is less adequate than that of other countries, especially when one considers the fact that state control and ownership of the economy increases manifold the necessary number of administrators. However, the numerous complaints and criticisms do suggest that the extensive system of administrative checks and controls in the Soviet Union falls far short of meeting its objectives. A few of the many possible reasons for failure or, rather, semifailure will be mentioned. First, the Soviet administrative system may be appropriately described as overorganized. Each enterprise and agency is subject to supervision, inspection, and spying from such a multitude of external and internal officials, agencies, and individuals that, in spite of the regime's attempts to establish clear-cut lines of administrative command, individual administrators and workers may well be unable to determine exactly what their designated functions are and to whom they are responsible. Likewise, the very multiplicity of checks and counterchecks may blur the lines of responsibility. Moreover, the restrictive nature of some of the controls may enhance inefficiency by minimizing initiative on the part of any but the highest administrators and by causing them to use non-productive and sometimes illegal techniques to mask unsalutary situations that could be rectified if openly analyzed.

That the techniques of administrative control used by the Soviet regime are costly and not as efficient as they are intended to be is beyond dispute. The expenditures involved in paying the control and checking agents, the overswollen bureaucracy, combined with the inhibiting of local initiative and the use of non-productive techniques costs the regime an unknown number of millions of rubles per year. All states have, of course, corresponding expenses; but it seems reasonable to estimate that on a per capita basis, such expenses in the U.S.S.R. are higher than in most countries. Soviet leaders are fully aware of the problem, but at present are unable to deal with it in all its complexities. The recent economic decentralization policy, discussed in Chapter 44, is one attempt, and reportedly a relatively successful one, to improve efficiency by relaxing some of the rigid controls from the center. Experimental maneuvers designed to increase efficiency are constantly in progress. And in spite of the expense and cumbersomeness of the over-all system, the Soviet administrative system may be described as relatively successful. On the credit side, from the Soviet point of view, it may be pointed out that, under this system, administrators and workers alike have remained subservient to the party, productivity has increased very substantially, standards of living are higher than ever before, and the U.S.S.R. has been one of the victors in a devastating world war and emerged as one of the two greatest world powers.

THE UNION REPUBLICS AND AUTONOMOUS REPUBLICS

As previously stated, the U.S.S.R. is a federal union of fifteen Soviet Socialist Republics or Union Republics, some of which contain Autonomous Soviet Socialistic Republics. The federal Constitution provides that each Republic has its own Constitution that conforms to the Constitution of the U.S.S.R. It further specifies that each Republic should have a Supreme Soviet, a Presidium of the Supreme Soviet, and a Council of Ministers, all of which in structure and function parallel the corresponding organs in the federal government. The essential structural difference is that the Supreme Soviet of the U.S.S.R. is bicameral, while the Supreme Soviets of the Union and Autonomous Republics are unicameral.

A detailed discussion of the operation of the governmental organs of the Republics will be omitted, since it would constitute a repetition of the preceding discussion. Each Republic Supreme Soviet, composed of the elected representatives of the people, functions primarily as a ratifying board and a platform for the announcement of governmental policy; only in terms of ratification does it act as the highest legislative organ. The Presidium is, in reality, more powerful than the Supreme Soviet, since it performs both executive and legislative functions. The Council of Ministers is a legislative, executive, and administrative body that, in addition, directs or manages the economy of the Republic. The Council of Ministers of the Autonomous Republic is responsible to the Council of Ministers of the corresponding Union Republic, which is, in turn, responsible to the Council of Ministers of the U.S.S.R. The superior Council may annul acts of the subordinate Council or of any of the ministers of the subordinate Council. All republican governmental organs are responsible to and controlled by the party organization in the Republic and by the Central Committee of the Communist party of the U.S.S.R. and its Presidium.

Among the constitutionally guaranteed rights of the Union Republics, two merit particular consideration and comment. First, every Union Republic is given the right to freely secede from the U.S.S.R. There have been no secessions. Should such an attempt be made, it is highly unlikely that it would be tolerated. During the 1937–1938 purge, many of those charged with treason were accused of working "to dismember the Soviet Union." The national anthem, which refers to "the unbreakable union," no doubt depicts more accurately than the Constitution the nature of the bonds between the U.S.S.R. and its Union Republics. Second, each Union Republic is given the right to enter into direct relations with foreign states. This right, which is an extremely unusual one in the federal union, has been used to the advantage of the U.S.S.R. The Soviet government has arranged, on the basis of this constitutionally granted right, that the Ukranian S.S.R. and the Belorussian S.S.R. be given membership in the United Nations. In this manner, the U.S.S.R. has in actuality three votes in the United Nations, while other nations have only one. The Union Republics are permitted to use the constitutional right of having direct relations with foreign states when the purposes of the party are served. Unless this crucial condition is met, the constitutionally guaranteed rights and privileges of the Union Republics are waived in favor of the central government and the party. It is probable that in the future the purposes of the state and the Communist party may be served by permitting more of the Union Republics to exercise this right more extensively.

LOCAL GOVERNING BODIES

The Constitution provides that Soviets of Working Peoples' Deputies, elected for a term of two years, shall be the organ of state power in Territories, Regions, Autonomous Regions, Areas, Districts, cities, and rural localities (stanitsas, villages, hamlets, kishlaks, auls) (Articles 94 and 95). The Soviets of Working Peoples' Deputies direct the work of the organs of administration subordinate to them; insure the maintenance of public order, the observance of the laws, and the protection of the rights of citizens; direct local economic and cultural affairs; and draw up the local budgets (Article 96). Such soviets are permitted to adopt decisions and issue orders, within the limits of the powers vested in them by the laws of the U.S.S.R. and the Union Republics (Article 98). An executive committee, consisting of a chairman, vice-chairman, secretary, and members is the executive and administrative organ of the Soviet of Working Peoples' Deputies (Article 99). The size of the executive committee depends on the size and population of the area; in small areas or subdivisions, such as villages, the chairman, vice-chairman, and secretary perform the functions of the executive committee. The executive committee is responsible to both its own soviet and to the executive committee of the superior Soviet of Working Peoples' Deputies. In most of the constituent republics, city or village soviets are responsible to district soviets, which, in turn, are responsible to the territorial or regional organs. In 1957 there were, including autonomous regions and national areas, 59,097 soviets with a total membership of 1,549,460. Some deputies serve simultaneously on soviets at different levels. Membership in the soviet varies with the size of the area and is known to have been as low as 9 and as high as 2,100. Since 1936, the deputies to all soviets have been elected directly.

The frequency of meeting of local soviets is prescribed by the republic constitutions; in general, between two and twelve meetings a year are specified. Evidence that not all of the local soviets meet as frequently as demanded may be indicative of lack of local interest or of recognized lack of the meaningfulness of such meetings.

The chairman of the executive committee is appointed by the Party Committee at the immediately superior level. With the approval of the superior party and soviet executive committee, the chairman appoints and dismisses other members of the executive committee, with the exception of the vice-chairman and the secretary, who are selected by the Party Committee at the level of the soviet. Important departmental heads of local administrative units are usually made members of the executive committee; almost always the secretary of the local Party Committee is included in the membership. The soviet ratifies the executive committee membership; and, as might be expected, the ratifying vote is almost always unanimous. Not infrequently, the members, and even the chairman of the executive committee, are not elected deputies, in spite of constitutional directions to the contrary. Reasons for the constitutional violation are not known, since the party is able to arrange for the election of the persons it designates. The violations may reflect the indifference of the people and their elected deputies to the work of the soviets and also the indifference of the party to the constitutional guaranties.

In practice, the chairman seems to exert a fair amount of control over his colleagues on the committee. The heads of departments who are members of the executive committee apparently have a role analagous to that of those ministers in the Council of Ministers who are not high-ranking party members. That is, the heads of departments are experts in health, communications, roads, and the like and direct local activities pertaining to their departments in accordance with the policy of the party.

The Constitution of the Union and Autonomous Republics provide for the organization of departments and administrations in the executive committee of the Soviet of the Working Peoples' Deputies with the exception of the village soviets. Obligatory departments or administrations for the territorial and regional soviets may include land, finance, trade, health, popular education, local industry, communal economy, social security, roads, arts, administration of the industry of construction materials, administration of automobile transport, administration of the local power industry, a planning commission, internal affairs, and the sector of cadres under the office of the chairman of the executive committee. Other departments may be formed, subject to the approval of the appropriate Union-Republican Ministry, if deemed necessary. In general, the number of obligatory departments and administrations for districts and cities is somewhat smaller than that for territorial and regional soviets. Variations include a militia (general police) department instead of an internal affairs administration, and departments of municipal economy, commerce, or agriculture may be included. Each department is subordinate to the appropriate ministry.

The executive committee of the local soviet is accountable to the soviet as its agent. It is also accountable to the executive committee at the next level in the hierarchy and, in fact, to all higher organs. Higher authorities may intervene or direct, rather than merely supervise, the activities of lower organs. If the immediate superior to an executive committee does not exercise appropriate supervision, his superior is expected to intervene.

The executive committees of districts and cities meet, in general, two or three times a month. Although the meetings are private, there are indications that a certain amount of debate does occur, certainly more than occurs in the Supreme Soviet and in the Soviets of Working Peoples' Deputies. The chairman is expected, by his superiors, to consider the opinions of his colleagues on the Committee but at the same time is held personally responsible for fulfilling the plans provided or approved by the higher authorities.

The competence of the Soviets of Working Peoples' Deputies consists of matters of a local nature. Included among the reported activities of local soviets are the following: reporting local needs and the neglect of local interests to the appropriate ministry, supervising the supply and marketing of consumer goods and the conduct of industries and collective farms, directing the fulfillment of the economic plan and of the budget, determining the distribution of personnel and the issuance of certificates for state assistance, supervising educational programs and preventive medicine programs, issuing internal passports, supervising cultural and social matters, considering claims for housing accommodations and various social service benefits, supervising military callup and other defense obligations, and administering privileges to the dependents of veterans. As in all levels of government of the U.S.S.R., the local soviets are concerned primarily with matters of an economic nature.

Local soviets are expected to have standing commissions composed of interested citizens or "activists" who are not members of the soviet. Village soviets are expected to have three to five such commissions, while larger soviets may have ten to fifteen. These commissions, which have a chairman, secretary, and perhaps a vice-chairman, may specialize in education, health, social services, the budget, or branches of industry. Activists may study the functioning of their respective agencies or services and submit a co-report, along with that of the executive committee, to the superior authorities. The executive committee is expected to invite the commission or its chairman to participate in discussions of the appropriate agency or service. In many cases, the activists are ignored by the executive committee. Encouragement of activists, of which there are about 2,000,000, by the party is but another attempt to develop public support, to keep the official goals constantly before the people, and to have still another source of information about, and check on, the workings of the local authorities and the enterprises under their supervision.

As is true of all other branches of the governmental apparatus, the Soviets of Working Peoples' Deputies have, according to the Constitution, fairly extensive jurisdictional rights. Like all other governmental agencies, the activities of the soviets are subject to supervision, direction, and interference from the higher authorities. Like the higher organs, the soviets are controlled by and subservient to the party. The chief functions of the local soviets would seem to be: first, they are convenient tools to implement the economic policy of the party in local areas, industries, and enterprises; and second, the local soviets provide an opportunity for numerous citizens to participate in governmental activities and, consequently, to admire and support the party that provides such rights. Rigorous centralized control by the Communist party, combined with limited local initiative, is the pattern of all governmental agencies within the U.S.S.R.

The Constitution of the U.S.S.R. is a document that would seem to provide opportunities for self-government equal to those enjoyed by the citizens of any nation. In practice, although Soviet citizens go through the forms and motions of governing themselves, they are ruled by the leadership of the Communist party. These are the facts. The interpretation of these facts varies with the interpreters. Western observers, steeped in democratic traditions, tend to conclude that Soviet citizens are victims of deception—that their leaders deliberately foster the impression that the common man has a voice in the government while in reality his participation is, and will continue to be, nothing more than a series of meaningless actions. The Soviet interpretation is colored by the realities of the imperial past and the hopes for the Communist future. The present situation is interpreted as a training period. The masses, considered to be insufficiently versed in governmental activities to be permitted to exert a significant effect on the operation of the government, are being given limited experience so that, ultimately, the form of self-government indicated in the Constitution may be achieved.

SELECTED READING

FAINSOD, MERLE. *How Russia Is Ruled.* Cambridge, Mass.: Harvard University Press, 1953.

KARPINSKY, V. *The Social and State Structure of the USSR.* Moscow: Foreign Languages Publishing House, 1950.

———. *How the Soviet Union Is Governed.* Moscow: Foreign Languages Publishing House, 1950.

MCCLOSKY, HERBERT, and TURNER, JOHN E. *The Soviet Dictatorship.* New York: McGraw-Hill Book Co., Inc., 1960. Chap. 12.

SCOTT, DEREK J. R. *Russian Political Institutions.* New York: Holt, Rinehart & Winston, Inc., 1958. Chap. 3.

VYSHINSKY, ANDREI Y. *The Law of the Soviet State.* New York: The Macmillan Co., 1948.

44

Soviet Planned Economy

CONSTITUTIONAL AND IDEOLOGICAL FACTORS

The Soviet Union is described in its Constitution as "a socialist state of workers and peasants." Private ownership of the instruments and means of production has been replaced by Socialist ownership (Article 4). Socialist property is divided into state property and the property of collective farms and cooperative societies (Article 5). State property includes the land, its mineral wealth, waters, forests, mills, mines, rail, water and air transport, communications, state farms, municipal enterprises, and most of the dwelling houses in the cities and industrial areas (Article 6). The Socialist property of collective farms and cooperative enterprises includes common buildings, implements, livestock, and products (Article 7). Every household on a collective farm, in addition to its basic income from the common, collective farm enterprise, has for its own personal use a small plot of household land, and as its personal property, a subsidiary husbandry on the plot, a dwelling house, livestock, poultry, and minor agricultural implements (Article 7). The law also permits a small private economy of individual peasants and handicraftsmen, who are allowed to employ members of their own family, but who may not hire other labor, since that would be interpreted as the exploitation of the labor of others. Although a few individual peasants and many more handicraftsmen do exist, they are exceptional cases. Almost the entire Soviet population is employed within the Socialist economy.

In the Soviet Union, the state and the economy are inextricably interwoven. The Soviet state is the largest enterpreneur in the world and directs almost all of the production, distribution, and consumption of goods within its territory.

Marxist theory calls for nationalization of the means of production and for economic planning in order to avoid "exploitation" and "anarchy of production." Capitalist enterpreneurs are said to be motivated by profit alone and, consequently, in their desire to maximize profits, are accused of exploiting workers. An economic and political system based on the private ownership of the means of production, they claim, necessarily results in "anarchy of production," which includes periodic overexpansion followed by a depression that throws millions of workers out of work. In order to prevent such periodic crises, the Marxists say it is necessary to nationalize the means of production and to follow a comprehensive economic plan prepared by technical experts and public minded statesmen, who have intimate knowledge of the country's needs and resources and who are motivated by the desire to serve their fellow men rather than to accumulate private fortunes. In a capitalist society, the economy is regulated in the main, albeit imperfectly, by the more or less free interaction of supply and demand, the interaction being made possible by competition among enterpreneurs. In a Socialist state, which controls the production and consumption of almost all commodities, competition among enterpreneurs, and hence the interplay between supply and demand as a regulator of the economy, is eliminated. The Soviet Union has substituted economic planning as the regulator of the economy. However, the goals of Soviet economic planning are social and political as well as economic. Article 11 of the Constitution states: "The economic life of the USSR is determined and directed by the state national-economic plan, with the aim of increasing public wealth, of steadily raising the material and cultural standards of the working people, of consolidating the independence of the USSR and strengthening its defensive capacity." It is claimed by Soviet economists that, to be feasible, economic planning requires the nationalization of the means of production and unified leadership, namely, the leadership supplied by the Communist party.

HISTORICAL FACTORS

The extent of economic planning in the U.S.S.R., the techniques of planning, and the success or failure associated with economic plans have varied greatly throughout the years. It is not within the scope of this account to present the historical development. Only a few of the background factors will be mentioned.

When the Bolsheviks gained control of Russia, after World War I and a revolution, they inherited a backward, ruined, and exhausted country. Because the proletarian revolution did not succeed in other countries, Russia was politically and economically isolated. The Bolshevik leaders were conscious of both the military and economic weakness of the territory that they controlled. They realized that the peasantry constituted an uncertain ally that was prepared to feed the workers only if supplied with manufactured goods. It was obvious to them that their hope for victory in the struggle between capitalism and socialism lay in the economic sphere, even more than in ideology. But their handicap, the low productivity of the workers, estimated by Soviet economists to be less than one-fifth that of American workers, was equally obvious.

Rapid industrialization, which required the nationalization of the existent means of production, along with the accumulation of vast additional supplies of producer goods, appeared to be an absolute necessity. The source of producer goods typically used by backward countries in the process of industrializing, that is, foreign loans, was neither available nor acceptable. Individual capitalists and capitalist governments were not willing to risk their funds with a seemingly unstable revolutionary government that advocated the overthrow of capitalism. And the Bolshevik leaders feared that the independence of their system would be lost if they became indebted to antagonistic foreigners. Consequently, the capital required for the reconstruction and industrialization of the new Socialist state had to be derived from internal sources, namely, by the sacrifices of the Soviet peoples. Economic planning became a practical necessity as well as a theoretical prerequisite.

At the beginning, Soviet planners had at their disposal a huge country with rich resources and a large population. However, instead of sufficient numbers of qualified workers, technicians, and engineers, they had millions of peasants, many of whom were illiterate. The resources were widely separated, and transportation facilities were woefully inadequate. They lacked the necessary capital for expansion and development. Moreover, the planners lacked experience and had no model to use as a guide. On the other hand, the planners did have some advantages; they were able to exert their influence over all branches of the economy. Total planning, complex as it is, is in some respects simpler than partial planning, which is existent in countries like Britain and France. Planning in the U.S.S.R. was supported and indeed, controlled, by one unopposed political party; hence, there was unified leadership. In spite of the odds against the success of economic planning, and in spite of numerous blunders by the planners and immeasurable suffering on the part of the peoples of the U.S.S.R., in two short decades of relative normality, 1930–1940 and 1950–1960, the country was transformed into an industrial power.

The price for the rapid transformation was high. The masses had to fight, starve during the famine, and learn to perform in jobs that were new to them and often demanding. Many had to accept positions far away from their homes, often to live in worse housing than the poor housing to which they were accustomed. They were denied all luxuries and conveniences of modern living and frequently had barely enough essential food and clothing. When the material situation began to improve somewhat, the U.S.S.R. was attacked by Germany and her allies. New sacrifices and incredible destruction in lives and property followed. Factories, villages, and cities were leveled from the western border as far inland as Leningrad, Moscow, Stalingrad, and the Caucasus. Reconstruction had to be paid for by the peoples of the U.S.S.R. However, after World War II, the recovery was amazingly rapid. By 1945, the U.S.S.R. had a staff of planners who, although far from being omnipotent, had more experience than planners in any other country. The people, proud of their victory, were willing to support the government and the system that had made the victory possible. Furthermore, a new Soviet intelligentsia had developed, and skilled technicians and professional people were available. During the war, many industrial enterprises had been transferred behind the Ural Mountains and these were not destroyed. The planners capitalized on the advantages, and the people continued to live at subsistence standards to overcome the disadvantages. The war damage was repaired, and the U.S.S.R. has, at present, a booming economy, which is steadily growing at an unprecedented rate. The people have tolerated the excessive deprivations partly because they were forced to and, perhaps even more, because they were promised great improvements in the future. Finally, the promises began to materialize. During the 1950's, economic conditions improved considerably. Greater improvements have been promised for this decade (1960–1970).

SOURCES OF REVENUE AND MAJOR EXPENDITURES

Table 44–1 presents the major sources of revenue and major expenditures in the U.S.S.R. for the years 1938, 1948, and 1959. Several features in this table are worthy of note. First, total public revenue and total public expenditures have increased more than five times during the twenty-one-year time span. Second, almost 30 per cent of the total expenditures has been devoted to social and cultural services, including education, social insurance and security, public health and physical culture, maternal welfare, and the like. Third, individual income taxes have consistently contributed a relatively minor portion of the total revenue. Fourth, more than 40 per cent of the total state revenue has been used to support the economy. The Soviet economy receives its capital from public revenue; the billions of rubles required for capital investment have come from the population, which has had to produce more and consume less. The profit tax, which is levied with differential severity on different industrial enterprises, contributed in 1959 approximately one-half as much revenue to public funds as the amount transferred from public funds to the national economy. In 1938 and 1948, the revenue derived from the profit tax was approximately one-fifth of the amount spent by the state on the national economy. Finally, the most significant source of revenue has been the turnover tax, which in 1959 provided almost one-half, and in the past has provided as much as two-thirds, of the public revenue of the U.S.S.R.

Table 44–1. Sources of State Revenue and State Expenditures for Selected Years (In billions of rubles)

Item	1938		1948		1959	
	Amount	% of Total	Amount	% of Total	Amount	% of Total
Total revenue	127.5	100.0	410.5	100.0	722.7	100.0
Turnover tax	80.4	63.1	247.3	60.2	332.4	46.0
Profit tax	10.5	8.2	27.2	6.6	159.9	22.1
Social insurance	7.2	5.6	16.2	3.9	148.4*	20.5
Individual income tax	5.1	4.0	33.2	8.1	56.0	7.8
Other	24.3	19.1	86.6	21.9	26.0	3.6
Total expenditures	124.0	100.0	370.9	100.0	707.6	100.0
National economy	51.7	41.7	149.6	40.3	308.9	43.7
Military defense	23.1	18.6	66.3	17.8	96.1	13.6
Social and cultural services	35.3	28.5	105.6	28.5	232.2	32.8
Other	13.9	11.2	49.4	13.9	70.4	9.9

* The 1959 figure for social insurance includes income from forestry and from foreign trade organizations.

SOURCES: Harry Schwartz, *Russia's Soviet Economy* (Englewood Cliffs, N.J.: Prentice-Hall, Inc., 1954), p. 487; A. G. Zverev, "Report to the Supreme Soviet," *Pravda*, December 23, 1958 (translated in *CDSP*, X, No. 52 (1959), 9; "Budget Law," *Pravda*, December 24, 1958 (translated in *CDSP*, XI, No. 2 (1959), 27.

The turnover tax merits special attention as a major source of revenue. This tax is an addition, over and above profit, to the cost price of commodities. It is a type of sales tax that is levied on goods when they leave the producer and upon the agricultural deliveries from the farms. Thereafter, the tax is included in the price of the commodity. The turnover tax, which is usually computed as a percentage of the retail price, varies from commodity to commodity and has almost invariably been high for consumer goods and low for producer goods. For example, the turnover tax on cotton dresses has varied around 75 per cent of the sales price. This means that if the cost of the dress without the tax were 50 rubles, the retail price would be 200 rubles. Fifty rubles would pay for the cost and profit for the production of the dress, and 150 rubles would go to the State Treasury. Thus, a turnover tax listed as 75 per cent of the sale price is, in fact, 300 per cent of the cost price, a high tax indeed. However, Soviet sources deny that the turnover tax is a tax at all and claim that it is merely a technique for transferring part of the industry's net profit to the budget.[1] To Western economists, such a claim seems unwarranted. If the receipts from the turnover tax represent economic profit, then most of the production units producing consumer goods in the U.S.S.R. are realizing well over a 200 per cent profit, since the cost price prior to the imposition of the turnover tax includes a planned profit. As previously indicated, the turnover tax, plus a portion of the planned profit, is diverted to the budget. Although in other countries, certain enterprises have, for short periods of time, realized profits as high as 200 per cent, in all existent economies, continuous and generalized profits of over 50 per cent have not been achieved. Although there is evidence that the Soviet economy is growing in efficiency, there is certainly no evidence to support the notion that it is many times more efficient than that of the U.S.A. or Britain. Moreover, one could legitimately question why consumer industries would be able to earn a 200 per cent profit, while industries specializing in producer goods earn a very significantly lower profit, since the latter pay little or no turnover tax. The Soviet statements that label the turnover tax as earned profit must be rejected as propaganda. Khrushchev, of course, interpreted the turnover tax as economic profit rather than a tax, when he stated on an American television program, "In the near future we are going to abolish, I repeat, to abolish—all taxation of the people."[2] His promise, however, pertains only to the abolishment of income taxes, which at present provide somewhat less than 8 per cent of the annual budget. Income tax rates in the U.S.S.R. are, in fact, extremely low in comparison to income tax rates in Western countries. However, the combined impact of direct and income taxes, the turnover tax being the most important in the latter category, is such that the Soviet citizen returns to the state over one-half of his income in taxes. There is no indication that the turnover tax will be abolished.

The turnover tax provides the government with an indispensable source of revenue with which to subsidize industry and to meet other expenses. In addition, it has served as a useful technique for equating demand and supply. There has been, because of the tremendous emphasis on industrialization and the development of capital investments, a perpetual shortage of consumer goods. Both wages and the number of wage earners in the U.S.S.R. have increased much more rapidly than the production of consumer goods. Discontent with the shortage of consumer goods would increase if workers had ample funds lying idle; in addition, non-utilization of funds would not be economical from the government's

[1] M. Postolovsky, *Why Taxation of the People can be abolished in the USSR* (Washington, D.C.: Embassy of the Union of Soviet Socialist Republics, Press Department, January, 1960), p. 3.

[2] *Ibid.*, p. 1.

point of view. The government has used the simple expedient of setting the turnover tax rate at such a level that the worker can afford to buy little more than is available. Thus, supply and demand are equated; and, at the same time, the difference between the cost of production and the consumer's purchasing power is acquired by the State Treasury.

As a source of revenue, the turnover tax is considered to be both reliable and flexible. The yield from it depends on the volume of production, the price of goods, and the tax rate, all of which are controlled by the government. The tax may be levied on a percentage of the selling price, a percentage of the cost price, or as a fixed sum per unit of goods. The severity of the tax on the same goods may vary from region to region or even selling place to selling place.[3] The government can, within limits, increase its source of revenue by increasing any one of the tax rates, which have been modified from time to time by the Minister of Finance; the production of goods; or the price of goods. Likewise, it can permit an increase in consumption by lowering the price, the tax rate, or by increasing production. The tax must be paid immediately after the goods are produced; thus, the government has a steady source of revenue and, in addition, a technique for checking on the output of enterprises. Since the bulk of the revenue from the turnover tax is derived from consumer goods, chiefly the basic necessities, and not from luxuries that, until recently, have been much too rare to provide much revenue, it has caused great hardship to the lower-income groups who, in comparison to the higher-income groups, have a disproportionately high percentage of their income diverted to the Treasury in this way. However, in recent years, it is most probable that the better-paid groups pay a higher tax, since they are able to buy luxuries that are now available. The turnover tax on luxuries is very high.

Profits from economic enterprises yielded approximately 21 per cent of the state revenue in 1959. The rate of the profit tax varies from industry to industry and has been as low as 10 per cent on certain heavy-goods industries and as high as 90 per cent on consumer-goods industries. The profit tax on given industries has varied from time to time in accordance with the state plan for expansion. If, according to the plan, an industry is to grow and expand, the rate of the profit tax is set at a relatively low level, so that money will be available for capital expenditure. On the other hand, industries that are not expected to develop forfeit to the state almost the entire planned profit, plus a goodly share of unplanned profits, if any. In this way, the government is able to obtain funds from industries that are operating at a profit but whose expansion is not crucial

[3] A. K. Suchkov, *Dokhody gosudarstvennogo byudzheta SSSR* (*Revenue of the State Budget of the U.S.S.R.*), (Moscow: Gosplanizdat, 1945), p. 22 ff.

to the entire economy at a given time. Such funds have been used to subsidize other industries, which operated at a loss, but which were considered crucial to the economy.

All industries are permitted to retain some of their profits. Each enterprise has a fund based on from 1 to 5 per cent of planned profits and from 15 to 45 per cent of the unplanned profits. Fifty per cent of this fund must be spent for capital investment and for unplanned construction and repair of houses for the workers. The remainder is to be used to improve living conditions for the workers and to provide bonuses and other rewards for outstanding workers. Thus, the government attempts to motivate individual workers and managers to cooperate in maximizing profits.

PLANNING AND INDUSTRIAL ORGANIZATION

Economic planning in the U.S.S.R. has been directed toward two objectives, one political and the other economic. The first objective is to control the economy as a means of increasing political power and insuring political loyalty. Second, planning is used as an instrument of economic growth with the goal of increasing productivity and economic capabilities and "the ever more complete satisfaction of the rising material and spiritual needs of the people."[4] The party leaders contribute the political aspects and the over-all objectives, while the economic aspect is said to be based on "plans worked out directly by the collectives of enterprises and construction projects, economic councils, ministries and departments."[5]

The major organs involved in preparing and carrying out the economic plans are presented diagramatically in Figure 44–1. As in all aspects of Soviet life, it is appropriate to indicate the controlling role played by the party. The Gosplan or State Planning Commission of the U.S.S.R. is the central planning agency of the Soviet Union. The chief duty of the Gosplan is to prepare a unified plan for the entire country based on the general directives issued by the party leadership and the Council of Ministers. This requires the compilation and recording of detailed information about all aspects of the economy in all parts of the country. The required information is supplied through the channels indicated in Figure 44–1 from the individual enterprises to the trusts or combines, to the Sovnarkhozy, to the Republic Gosplan and Council of Ministers, and finally to the State Gosplan. In addition to preparing the plan, the Gosplan must supervise the performance of assignments by subordinate agencies and rectify unsatisfactory situations.

[4] N. S. Khrushchev, Twenty-first Congress of CPSU.

[5] A. Kursky, "Some Problems in the Improvement of National Economic Planning," *Voprosy ekonomiki* (*Problems of Economics*), II (June, 1959), 43–45.

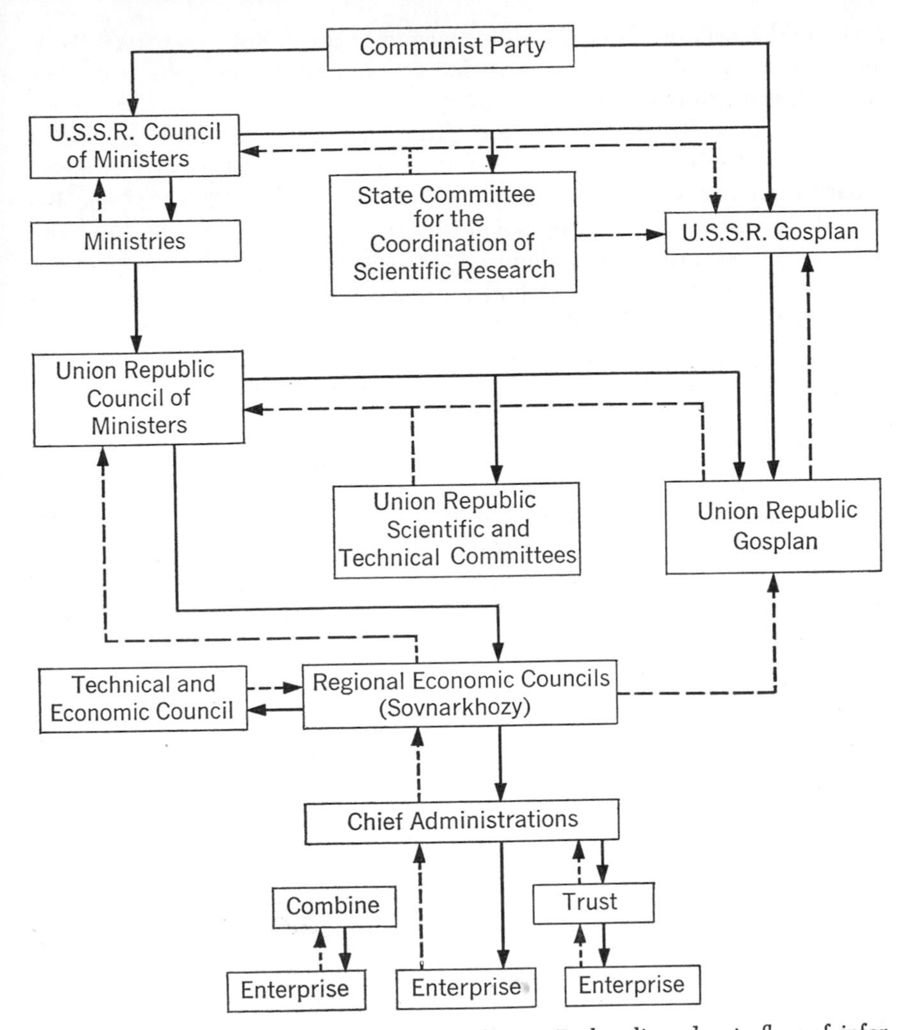

NOTE: Solid lines denote direction of authority. Broken lines denote flow of information.

Figure 44–1. Organization of Soviet industrial system.

Numerous subordinate planning institutions share the responsibility for planning with Gosplan. Attached to each major planning and administrative organ is a scientific and technical advisory board. At the All-Union and Republic levels, these boards are called the "State Committee for the Coordination of Scientific Research" and the "Scientific and Technical Committees," respectively; the Sovnarkhoz is advised by Economic and Technical Councils, while research institutes are attached to the combines and trusts. Each of the ministries of the U.S.S.R., the State Bank, and other All-Union organizations has its own planning agency, as does each of the ministries in the constituent republics. Sovnarkhozy, combines, trusts, collective farms, and even individual factories and enterprises have their own planners. Among the most important of the subordinate planning agencies are the Gosplans of the republics and the Regional Economic Councils or Sovnarkhozy. The planning agencies form a hierarchy, as indicated in Figure 44–1, with each of the lesser agencies being subordinate to the next highest one, and each being subject to directions from the high officials in Moscow if the supervision from regional or republican officials appears to be inadequate.

The specific agencies involved in the planning procedure and in industrial administration have varied from time to time. On July 1, 1957, the bulk of the industrial and building enterprises were transferred from the control of the various central ministries to the newly created Sovnarkhozy.[6] Local soviets are still responsible for purely local industry within these Economic Regions. Each Sovnarkhoz is under the jurisdiction of the Council of Ministers of its republic, which appoints the members of the Sovnarkhoz. The Council of Ministers of the U.S.S.R., and especially the State Gosplan and party leadership, in turn give directions to the republican Council of Ministers; thus a central unifying force is provided.

The 1957 reorganization provided for increased decentralization of planning and industrial management. Prior to the reorganization, approximately forty ministries were responsible for Soviet industries. Each ministry was predominantly interested in reaching and surpassing its own targets. Consequently, there was a wasteful lack of cooperation among enterprises under the jurisdiction of different ministries. Moreover, it was observed that since there has never been a perfect plan, in some factories resources lay idle or spoiling while other factories were unable to operate because of lack of crucial ingredients for their products. The authority of local officials was curtailed; and decisions that could have been made on the spot were made, sometimes less wisely, in Moscow. The delays were expensive, and the fact that all important decisions were made by the central authorities adversely affected local initiative.

The reorganization removed some of the disadvantages of highly centralized planning and administration, including the objectionable "departmentalization" of the industrial ministries. Within each economic region there can be a more effective cooperation among enterprises and certainly a great saving in transportation costs. Because of proximity, the

[6] In 1957, there were 105 of these Economic Regions distributed as follows: the R.S.F.S.R.–70, the Ukrainian S.S.R.–11, the Kazakh S.S.R.–9, the Uzbek S.S.R.–4, each of the other Union Republics–1. Recent reports in the Soviet press indicate that some of these regions are being consolidated.

Sovnarkhoz is in a better position to maximize the utilization of local resources. Likewise, crucial decisions can be made much more quickly than previously, when the authorities in Moscow had to be contacted. Necessary modification of plans within each region can be made more readily and more rationally; and consequently, there is increased flexibility in planning. However, the decentralization perpetuates some of the disadvantages of the previous organization. Just as each separate ministry attempted to fulfill its planned quota with relatively little consideration for the needs of other ministries, so each economic region attempts to maximize its own production, often to the disadvantage of other regions. Examples of giving priority in the supply of needed industrial ingredients to enterprises within one's own economic region, and simultaneously depriving enterprises in other regions, are common. The primary goal of each region is to fulfill the regional plan, with a resultant trend toward autarchy. Yet the nature of the dependence between regions is such that close cooperation is an absolute necessity. Quite naturally, the central government initiates action to combat local sectionalist tendencies. Factories that do not deliver the required quotas to other regions, regardless of how much over the quota they have delivered within their own region, are considered to have not fulfilled the plan. If an enterprise fails to carry out the conditions of an agreement to deliver goods of a specified quality at a given time to an enterprise in another region, the delinquent enterprise is liable to financial penalties, such as fines and forfeits.[7] Planners in any capacity, including heads of Regional Economic Councils and top officials in the republics, are removed from their positions for placing local interest before the interest of the entire country. The welfare of the Union must be given priority. This is more difficult than under more highly centralized planning, since the regional planners, regardless of good intentions, may have intimate knowledge of only their own regions. What they may consider to be good for the Union and for the specific region may, in fact, not be to the advantage of the entire country. Should sectionalism become obstructive to central planning, centralization would doubtless be intensified.

The decisive power remains in the hands of the party, and the Council of Ministers of the U.S.S.R. Decisions still made at the national level are very numerous. These decisions include the rate of expansion of production and the scale of development of the various branches of activity, the division of labor in the national economy, the territorial distribution of the forces of production, the distribution and utilization of the national income, the size and location of large-scale construction projects, price

[7] Ch. Touretski, "Regional Planning of the National Economy in the USSR and its Bearing on Regionalism," *International Social Science Journal,* UNESCO, XI, No. 3 (1959), 382.

reductions, the strengthening of the country's defenses, the extension of trade relations with foreign countries, and the development of science.[8] Thus, the index figures (plan) prepared by Gosplan, and approved by the Council of Ministers of the U.S.S.R. and the Central Committee of the Communist party, fix the rate and scale of the development of the national economy, the scales of production in key industries, the main directions of technical progress and scientific development, the national income and its distribution, the amount of investment, and the degree of improvement in the worker's standard of living.[9] Plans made by each economic region and lower planning organ are required to conform to the national plan. The reorganization is an attempt by the government to utilize the combined advantages of centralized planning and local initiative. Soviet authorities consider the reorganization to be highly successful. The reports of economic growth in 1959 and 1960 support the Soviet claim.

Each Sovnarkhoz is subdivided into a number of administrations, some of which supervise particular types of production such as machine building, clothing industries, and television industries; others supervise operations such as purchasing, marketing, and planning. There are also service departments in charge of finance, accounting, and transportation. Subordinate to the administrations are combines and trusts, which, in turn, may be composed of several enterprises. Individual enterprises may be responsible to either a combine, trust, or Sovnarkhoz administration. At the head of each enterprise is a director.

The director, subject to the supervision of his superiors, has full administrative power over the enterprise. He has the right to reorganize the enterprise to increase efficiency; to adapt the central plan when necessary; to hire and dismiss personnel; to enforce labor and financial discipline; and, within the limits of his allotted wage fund, to set wage rates and award bonuses. His orders are binding on all subordinates. Depending on the size of the enterprise, the director is likely to subdivide his administration into departments for planning, sales, supplies, personnel, and the like; to have a chief engineer and other assistants; and to have a number of work shops, each with its own chief and foremen. The chiefs of each of these sections are empowered to issue binding orders to their subordinates.

The extent of the director's seemingly great control is, however, severely limited. First, he has to adhere to the principles set forth for him in the economic plan. He cannot decide what to produce or the quantity or quality of his products. He has little control over the numbers of workers, their pay scale and hours of work, the prices he can charge, to whom he must sell, and from whom he must buy, ad infinitum. Second,

[8] *Ibid.*, p. 383.
[9] *Loc. cit.*

all financial transactions between enterprises and all short-term credit have to be handled by the State Bank, which has the right to investigate the functioning of the enterprise and to refuse credit. Thus, the State Bank functions as a financial supervisor, and not always a sympathetic or reasonable one; the Soviet press has published many complaints about the Bank refusing credit when the shortage of funds within the enterprise was due to the delinquency of another enterprise. Finally, the activities of the director are subject to a complex system of controls. His activities may be carefully watched and interfered with by the local party, or even by high-ranking party officials from Moscow. The Procuracy, the secret police, special inspectors from Gosplan, the Ministry of Finance, and the trade-unions are on the alert for irregularities, improper use of machinery and materials, and the manufacture of goods of inferior quality. The director is held personally responsible for any violations, including nonfulfillment of the plan. However, the difficulties encountered by the director have apparently decreased appreciably as a result of the 1957 reorganization. Because his superiors, the chief of the trust or combine, or the members of the Sovnarkhozy are more readily available and closer to the scene of action, decisions relayed to him are presumably faster and more appropriate. Equally important, his own right to make decisions has been expanded. Previously excessive delays, the inability to modify plans when other enterprises did not meet their obligations, and the like, had a detrimental effect on productivity. The result was that, not infrequently, the frightened director resorted to unproductive or illegal techniques, such as limiting cooperation with other enterprises, forcing workers to work overtime, and even falsifying accounts.

The preparation of an economic plan begins with a thorough analysis of the existing resources, including the material, financial, technical and labor potentialities, and the realized level of production. The planners take into consideration the relationship between various branches of production, the number of employees, the cultural level and output of the workers, the amount of wages, the cost of production, the total working capital, profits and reserves, the utilization of existing resources, and recent achievements in science and technology. Concurrently, the needs of the national economy during a specified period are analyzed. The proportions that will be formed during the plan's action are then determined by coupling resources and needs.

Individual branches of the national economy prepare, independently, on the basis of directives from the Communist party and the superior planning and administrative organs, an optimal estimate of development for a period of years. Their deliberations are supposed to be based on economic importance with reference to the entire economy, recent scientific and technical advances, available resources, and previous experience.

Concurrently, the superior planning organs prepare their own estimates; and this is followed by the essential and complex task of coordination. The Regional Economic Councils, and finally Gosplan, have to harmonize the responsibilities of the individual branches, adjust optimal proposals for development with concrete possibilities, and coordinate planned proportions for the national economy, thus attempting to establish the required balance.[10]

Communist planners state that the fundamental characteristics of a planned economy are proportional development of the economy according to a plan prepared in advance; planning must cover all spheres of social reproduction, that is, production, distribution, and consumption; economic development must be planned for the benefit of the working people.[11] Proportionality refers to harmony between the production of goods and the needs of the national economy. For the smooth functioning of the economy and the satisfaction of the needs of society, it is necessary for the planners to implement the proportional development of all branches of the economy. It is no small task to make plans that will guarantee that the production of agricultural products will be sufficient, but just sufficient to meet the needs of the population and trade commitments; that the production of steel will be just sufficient to meet the needs of all industries using steel, and will moreover be properly distributed at the appropriate time; and that the required amount of steel be utilized to produce the number of ball bearings needed in the economy; and so on. It is obvious that proportional development requires a complex balance in the utilization of material resources, both skilled and unskilled labor, capital investments, housing, consumer goods, transportation facilities, ad infinitum. A disproportion in any aspect of the economy can cause disproportions in numerous branches. Planners and administrative agencies must be ever on the alert to prevent the incidence of disproportions and to remove disproportions immediately when they do occur. That the methods of insuring proportional development and of removing disproportions immediately upon their occurrence have not been perfected is obvious from reports in the Soviet press. Soviet economists write freely about the need for improvement in all stages of planning.[12]

[10] A. Kursky, "Some Questions of the Improvement of Planning in the USSR," *Voprosy ekonomiki* (*Problems of Economics*), I (January, 1959), 9–13.

[11] Vysoká škola ekonomická v Praze, Kolektiv katedry národohospodárského plánování, *Plánování národního hospodářství,* University of Prague, Department of Economics, Collective of the Chair of National Planning, Planning of the National Economy, (Praha: Státní pedagogické nakladatelství, n.p.), p. 5.

[12] E. G., E. Manevich, "The Principle of Personal Incentive and Certain Wage Problems in the USSR," *Voprosy ekonomiki* (*Problems of Economics*), II (May, 1959), 20–26; L. Berri and A. Efimov, "Current problems of Planning Specialization in Machine Building," *Voprosy ekonomiki* (*Problems of Economics*), I (January, 1959), 15–21; V. Koltsov, "Some Problems in the Improvement of Economic Planning," *Voprosy ekonomiki* (*Problems of Economics*), II (June, 1959), 43–45.

Proportionality demands the utilization of all material, financial, and labor resources and their distribution in optimal proportions. Proportionality, however, does not demand equality of development, since the specified objectives and optimal utilization of resources might require that certain branches of the economy develop more rapidly than others. This is known as the principle of the major link. For example, industrial development was emphasized while agriculture temporarily was almost completely neglected; the proportion of capital goods was maximized while, for many years, only essential consumer goods were produced. The principle of the major link requires that the situation be thoroughly analyzed to determine which sphere of production is, at a given time, of greatest importance for the fulfillment of given political and economic tasks.

Plans have to meet two requirements—complexity and reality. The requirement for complexity results from mutual relationships and causality of economic processes. Plans for individual economic branches must be coordinated. For example, industrial production plans presuppose a certain growth in agriculture, construction, and transportation. Reality requires that the plan be an effective tool for transforming objectively existing economic potentialities into reality. Minimalism and maximalism, two possible mistakes, must be avoided. Minimalism leads to the non-utilization of all potentialities, demobilization of workers, and consequent reduction in production and consumption. Maximalism in the U.S.S.R. has led to gigantomania, i.e., the tendency to build very large industrial enterprises and power stations regardless of need and economic feasibility. Unrealistic maximalism, of course, results in wasted materials, disproportions, and retarded economic development, and thereby discredits plans.[13] A realistic plan uncovers unused reserves and "mobilizes the working people to make optimal use of production potentialities in order to reach the highest degree of productivity of labor." [14]

Economic planning is carried out in two stages—perspective and current plans. The perspective plans cover a period of several years, usually five but sometimes seven, ten, or fifteen. Current plans are yearly operational plans that may be divided into half years, quarter years, or months.

Long-term perspective plans are necessary because technical progress, the growth of the scale of capital construction, and the expansion of economic cooperation among Socialist countries require considerable time. Furthermore, they are used as morale-maintaining devices. Lenin wrote, "It is necessary to inspire the masses of workers and staunch peasants with a great program which extends for ten to twenty years." [15] Knowledge of the perspectives is supposed to become "a powerful factor which

[13] Collective, *op. cit.*, p. 60.
[14] *Loc. cit.*
[15] V. I. Lenin, *Spisy* (*Works*) (Praha: Svoboda, 1952), p. 65.

strengthens the revolutionary initiative of the masses of workers, peasants and working intelligentsia."[16]

Perspective plans are usually prepared for five-year periods, a time unit long enough to put into operation large economic projects such as industrial enterprises and canals, to effect considerable reconstruction of other industrial branches, to change proportions within the national economy, and to train specialists. The five-year period also allows for determination with sufficient exactness the directions and results of technical progress; and this, in turn, makes it possible to execute blueprints for a definite production program. The long-term perspective plans are also convenient for coordinating the economic plans for all Communist countries.

Current plans, which are prepared on the basis of perspective plans, are used to materialize the goals specified by the perspective plans, thus permitting the planners to deal with present economic problems while considering the goals for the future. Current plans reveal existing reserves and disproportions, and thus enable the perspective plans to be more precise. At the same time, current plans are used as tools for the removal of disproportions.[17] Current plans that are not coordinated with perspective plans are considered undependable and may well lead to mistakes.[18]

In the execution of the plan, new and unexpected reserves may be discovered and unforeseen difficulties encountered. Disproportions may be caused by international trade, by non-fulfillment of the plan in a certain branch, or even because of overproduction of quotas. The planning organs have to make immediate proposals to rectify such situations.[19] Systematic control and concrete direction for the execution of the plans are absolute necessities.[20]

FINANCING THE PLAN

As previously indicated, the financial support, provided by the government, for the economic plan is derived chiefly from the turnover tax, the profit tax, taxes on collective farms and the like, and the income tax. Several months before the beginning of the year, the Ministry of Finance of the U.S.S.R. informs the planning agencies of available budgetary resources. On the basis of the state plan, a general state budget is prepared by the Finance Ministry and submitted to Gosplan and the Council of

[16] Collective, *op. cit.*, p. 65.

[17] A. Kursky, "Some Questions of the Improvement of Planning in the USSR," *op. cit.*, pp. 9–13.

[18] Collective, *op. cit.*, p. 48.

[19] M. Ippa, "A Higher Level of Industrial Specialization," *Voprosy ekonomiki* (*Problems of Economics*), II (May, 1959), 69–70.

[20] Collective, *op. cit.*, p. 92.

Ministers of the U.S.S.R. After being approved by the Council of Ministers, the budget is submitted to the budget commissions of the Supreme Soviet and finally to the Supreme Soviet for unanimous approval. In addition to providing the necessary financial support for economic, defense, social, and cultural spheres under the jurisdiction of the federal government, the state budget makes available to the lower organs in the system the funds necessary for their budgets; and this process is repeated, with each agency allocating funds to the next lower agency.

The national budget handles the basic features of the financial aspects of the economic plan, in that it arranges the transfer of funds from one branch of the economy for investment in another branch, the most important transfer of funds being from the consumer-goods sector to the producer-goods sector. This transfer is one of the indispensable factors in the establishment of the complex economic balance. When the plan authorizes capital expenditure such as the construction of or additions to a plant, the purchase of additional machinery, etc., investment banks supply the necessary funds. The plant is then obliged to pay the bank a depreciation charge and 10 per cent of its profits. The payments above may be considered as repayment of a loan; however, it is of importance that the plant is not obliged to pay interest. In free enterprise systems, enterprises that borrow money to make capital improvements are almost invariably required to pay interest on the loan. If the enterprise is not sufficiently profitable to meet the interest payments, it is forced out of business. Enterprises in the U.S.S.R., unburdened by interest charges, do not have to meet this profits test. Moreover, until the recent introduction of the cost accounting system, if the enterprise was considered indispensable to the economy, government subsidies were supplied to keep it in operation, although it may have been operating at a very considerable loss.

Short-term financial transactions between enterprises are handled by the State Bank and its regional head offices, which act as clearing houses. At the completion of a transaction, the State Bank reduces the outstanding loan of the seller by the appropriate amount and increases that of the buyer by a corresponding amount. Industry, agriculture, and other economic units are thus partially financed by bank credit on goods in the process of production or distribution. The State Bank is supposed to certify that the buyer has funds to pay for goods prior to their release by transportation authorities. Furthermore, if there is any reason to doubt the existence in the production process of goods for which credit is being asked, the Bank is obliged to investigate the assets of the debtor. Thus, the Bank acts as an agency through which the government supervises and inspects the operation of enterprises. In the transactions between enterprises handled by the State Bank, no money is involved; the transaction is merely that of bookkeeping; the appropriate credit and debit are recorded in the accounts of the seller and buyer. However, prices expressed in monetary terms are assigned for bookkeeping purposes to all commodities. Also, the Bank supplies cash for wage payments and for retail transactions.

PRICES

In the Soviet economy, price and value have important functions. In general, wholesale or industrial prices are based on the planned cost of production, plus a commission or profit for every enterprise that handled or processed the goods, plus the turnover tax. The prices are set on the basis of average costs of the whole of a given industry, within a given region, and not on the costs of a particular enterprise. Thus, certain enterprises may not realize the costs of production and, at least theoretically, can be forced out of business by the financial bank, if additional government subsidies are not forthcoming. Prices are fixed for certain standard qualities only. For goods of other qualities, the price may be negotiated between enterprises on the basis of the fixed standard.

Retail prices are supposed to be uniform within specified regions but may vary from one part of the country to another. A guiding principle governing price setting for retail goods is that demand and supply must be more or less equated. Consequently, as previously indicated, the prices of consumer goods have, in general, been very high. High prices for consumer goods are necessary because their supply is limited; and if their prices were set relatively close to the cost of production, the workers would have surplus money. Of course, the government could remedy that situation by reducing wages but would hesitate to do so because the higher wages have been used as an incentive for increased work. Moreover, since the high price of consumer goods is due to the high turnover tax, the government acquires substantial revenue and simultaneously equates demand and supply. The high price of retail goods and low price of producer goods is one of the most significant techniques used to establish financial balance within the plan. Moreover, the government manipulates prices to attain the desired proportional development of the economy; for example, if increased production of certain agricultural products is deemed important, prices are raised to increase production.

WAGES

The general wage policy is set by the central government in the process of economic planning. The principle guiding the determination of wage scales is the role of wages in achieving goals, particularly production goals, which is determined by the party. If more workers are required to increase production in a particular industry, wages in that industry may be raised, while wages in other industries remain unchanged. Governmental agencies employing workers are governed by the over-all government wage policy. The influence of pressure from the workers and trade-unions on wages is negligible.

The great majority of workers in the U.S.S.R. are paid on the basis of piecework, in accordance with the principle "to each according to his work." Progressive piece rate systems are common, whereby the worker is given a fixed payment per unit of product for all production until his norm is reached, and beyond that a higher rate, the rate per unit increasing progressively with additional production beyond the norm. Collective piece rates, whereby a team of workers is paid according to its output, are also used. The piece-rate system and bonuses represent attempts to increase productivity by adding monetary incentives. Bonuses are paid for achieving or exceeding certain quantitative or qualitative goals, for showing special initiative, for the suggestion of technical improvements, for work beyond the line of duty, and for innovations that lower the cost of production. To bonuses and other forms of recognition for outstanding work, special privileges, such as preferred housing, are frequently added.

Because base pay is determined with reference to the needs of the national economy, and varies widely from industry to industry, and because of the piece-rate and bonus systems, wages in the U.S.S.R. are highly differentiated. The practice in the Stalin period of maximizing wage differentials is, at present, being somewhat tempered. Nevertheless, outstanding differences do exist. In 1956, a minimum wage law was adopted with 270 rubles per month in the country and 350 rubles per month in the urban areas as the specified minimum wage. This law had a beneficial effect on many persons such as rural workers, janitors, cleaners, shop assistants, messengers, and low-grade railroad workers. Several steps up the economic ladder, most of the skilled workers, technicians, engineers, teachers, physicians in general practice, minor bureaucrats, directors of kholkozy, and a few collective farmers were earning from 800 to 2,000 rubles per month. Most of the top engineers and technicians, scientific workers, architects, professors, pilots, and some physicians, journalists, and lawyers received from 2,000 to 4,000 rubles monthly, while army marshals, Cabinet ministers, and some lesser executives earned at least 5,000 rubles per month. Moreover, top industrial managers received from 6,000 to 10,000 rubles; and it was not uncommon for popular actors, musicians, and novelists to receive from 20,000 to 40,000 rubles per month in stipends and royalties. Thus, in comparison to the lowest paid workers, many others received monthly incomes twice as high, and a goodly number six to twelve times as high, while a few of the intelligentsia were paid more than fifty times as much per month as their less fortunate fellow citizens. Standards of living varied accordingly, with the lowest paid workers able to buy only the most urgent essentials, while the "rich" could afford excellent food and clothes, comfortable apartments, and even servants and a car.[21]

The most recent trend in the U.S.S.R. has been to reduce the wage differential. The present Seven Year Plan provides for increasing the minimum wage from 400 to 450 rubles per month during 1959 to 1962, and from 500 to 600 rubles during 1963 to 1965. Concurrently, the middle-grade workers are to receive a proportionately smaller increase. Since the plan calls for an average increase in wages of only 26 per cent, it seems that most of the increase will be given to the presently lower-paid workers. Also, reforms pertaining to the more extreme practices in progressive piece-rate systems are being introduced and will tend to reduce disparities. Some collective farms are now paying skilled workers only three times as much as unskilled workers, instead of the previously recommended practice of paying five times as much. There is some evidence that recently there have been reductions in very high salaries, such as those of some bureaucrats, professors, and government officials. Although there is no evidence that the U.S.S.R. is returning to a system of equal pay for all, it does seem that some of the excessive differences of the Stalin era are being eradicated.

In 1928, the average *annual* income in the U.S.S.R. was 703 rubles. At present, the average *monthly* wage is approximately 700 rubles; therefore, the average monetary income has increased twelvefold since 1928. It is appropriate to question whether real earnings increased correspondingly. Detailed information is not available. However, there is ample evidence to indicate that after 1928, real earnings in the U.S.S.R. decreased appreciably, and that in the early thirties, and during and immediately following World War II, the Soviet citizen could buy only about half as much with his earned income as he did in 1928. During 1948, real earnings began to rise significantly; and the upward trend has been steady and extensive. Soviet sources claim that the average real income of workers increased by 57 per cent between 1947 and 1957 and that of peasants

[21] The reader may be interested in determining for himself the approximate amount of goods that could be purchased with a monthly salary of 350 rubles or 600 rubles. Below is a list of official Soviet prices taken from: Lynn Turgeon, *Levels of Living, Wages and Prices in Soviet and United States Economies* (Washington, D.C.: Joint Economic Committee of the U.S. Congress, U.S. Government Printing Office, 1959), pp. 335–36. Prices are listed in rubles; and for food, the amount involved is one kilogram unless otherwise stated: beef (stewing), 12; port, 19.5; chicken, 16.5; average fish, 11; butter, 28; milk, 2.2 per liter; rye bread, 1.24; potatoes, 1; coffee, 40; eggs (10), 7.5; cotton print dress, 200; shoes, 200; wool dress, 475; man's overcoat, 720; man's all wool suit, 2,000; toilet soap (bar), 2.2; washing machine, 2,250; radio, 400.

was more than doubled between 1940 and 1958.[22] It seems safe to say that standards of living are, at present, higher than ever before in the Soviet Union. More consumer goods are available at lower prices, and the constantly reiterated promises for improved standards of living are being at least partially realized.

TRADE-UNIONS

Discussions of factors determining the monetary and real earnings of workers in countries other than the U.S.S.R. would necessarily include reference to the role of the trade-unions. Mention has already been made of the fact that pressure from workers and from trade-unions in the U.S.S.R. does not affect wage scales. However, since trade-union membership includes approximately 90 per cent of the workers, it is certainly appropriate to inquire into their role in the total economy. In capitalist countries, one of the chief functions of the trade-unions is to protect labor against management, particularly with reference to the division of profits and to working conditions. In the U.S.S.R., this function is reputed to be unnecessary, since the workers are "the owners" of the national economy and since what is good for the economy is, *ipso factor,* supposed to be good for the workers. Trade-unions, like all other organizations in the U.S.S.R., are controlled by the party. The goals espoused by the unions must be those sanctioned by the party. According to the statutes and by-laws of the trade-unions, they are officially permitted to "participate in planning and regulating wages of workers and employees, in devising a system of wages guided by the socialist principle of pay according to amount and quality of labor."[23] However, the total wage fund is set by the state as part of the general economic plan. Trade-unions can do nothing to alter the fixed amount, but what they can do is to discuss the distribution of the total. Their part in the discussion is to help devise wage scales that will have maximum incentive value and consequently increase production. The primary function of the unions, stated as the first point in the union statutes, is to "organize socialist competition of workers and employees for fulfilling and overfulfilling state plans, increasing the productivity of labor, improving the quality and lowering the cost of production." The trade-unions have been described, not inappropriately, as "cheer leaders" for the party program in industry. Furthermore, they are pledged to "help workers and employees to raise their production and business qualifications; spread the work experience of

[22] *SSSR Kat on est'* (*The U.S.S.R.—As It Is*), (Moscow: Gosudarstvennoe izdatelstov politischeskoi literatury, 1959), p. 245.

[23] The full text of *1949 Statutes and By-Laws* of Soviet trade-unions is available in the *Current Digest of the Soviet Press,* May 31, 1949, pp. 26–32. Only minor amendments have been made since that time.

leading workers and employees, the innovators in production and science, and assist in introducing progressive techniques in industry" and to "help members of trade unions to raise their ideological-political and general-educational standards, spread political and scientific knowledge . . ." In the above and other functions, it is obvious that the unions are designed to be the handmaiden of the party and that their services to the membership are significant only insofar as the goals of the membership and the party coincide. However, they do have many other functions, some of which are outlined in the quotation from a Soviet author that follows:

> Soviet trade unions and their local committees enjoy rights guaranteed by law. Trade union committees in particular closely supervise the enforcement of labor laws and safety rules and regulations by management. Management cannot discharge workers or set piece rates or production quotas without consulting the trade union. Trade unions consider questions of social insurance and have a decisive voice in providing housing for their workers. Trade union committees have the right to raise before the appropriate authorities questions of punishment or replacing executives if they fail to live up to their commitments under collective agreements, if they display bureaucratic tendencies or violate labor legislation. The trade union's opinion is always sought when new executives are being appointed in offices, construction sites or camps.[24]

Available evidence indicates that most of the rights outlined above can be practiced some of the time. Collective agreements do not, of course, pertain to wages or hours of work, which are set by law, but rather to commitments by the management to install certain safety devices or to make specified improvements in the housing of the workers and the like.

Among the most important functions practiced by the unions is the administration for the state of social insurance legislation, including old age pensions, disability payments, building and operating rest homes and sanitoriums, organizing medical aid for workers, and helping to distribute housing. Although some of the funds for these activities come from union dues, more of the funds are allocated from the state budget. The unions are expected to exercise control over safety measures in enterprises and to "form clubs, houses and palaces of culture, Red Corners and libraries and develop among workers and employees mass amateur art participation, physical culture, sports and touring." The diligence and efficiency of the unions in carrying out these activities has been highly variable.

Unions are organized on the basis of industries, with one union for coal miners, another for workers in chemical plants, a lumbering union, and so on. Their structure is in the form of the pyramidical hierarchy so prevalent in the U.S.S.R. The primary unit is the shop or factory group, the branches of which are combined into district, regional, republican, and U.S.S.R. organizations. The members of the lower organization elect dele-

[24] Vladimir Nikolayev, *The Development of Soviet Democracy* (Washington, D.C.: Embassy of the Union of Soviet Socialist Republics, Press Department, January, 1960), p. 2.

gates to the next higher organization, and the decision of a higher organization is binding on all subordinate organizations. At all levels, the unions are controlled by the party.

Trade-union membership is voluntary. The members pay a small initiation fee and thereafter a small monthly fee, the fee being amply compensated for by the additional privileges enjoyed by the union members. Members receive larger sickness and disability payments and enjoy priority in the use of rest homes, sanatoriums, and recreational and cultural facilities; they are entitled to loans and grants from funds supervised by the union and to free legal aid. Nevertheless, approximately 10 per cent of the Soviet workers have refrained from joining a trade-union.

The union plays an important role in the Soviet society but can take no credit for the steady increase in wages. In fact, no techniques are available for them to force an increase in wages. Although strikes are not forbidden by law, the party considers strikes unnecessary, since the welfare of the worker and the state, which is the employer, are considered synonymous. On rare occasions, minor strikes have occurred; but many Western observers are of the opinion that these rather feeble demonstrations were staged by the party to inform the world that Soviet workers have the right to strike but are so well satisfied with employment conditions that they have no desire to strike. It seems likely than an attempt to call a major strike would be ruthlessly suppressed, because a strike would seriously disrupt the fulfillment of the economic plan and would, moreover, be an unwanted indication of lack of solidarity. Increases in wages have been introduced by the government in relation to its over-all policy, and the increases have been completely unrelated to union activities. It should be borne in mind that in countries other than the U.S.S.R., strikes by governmental employees are rare and in some countries are expressly forbidden.

LABOR PRODUCTIVITY

One might question whether increased monetary wages have been associated with increased productivity of labor. At the beginning of the Five Year Plans (1928), the productivity of Soviet industrial workers was much below that of workers in comparable occupations in the West and, according to Soviet economists, was less than 20 per cent of that of workers in the U.S.A. The shortage of equipment, transportation facilities, and technical experts, combined with outdated methods, severely hampered productivity. Much of the work that was being done by machines in other countries was done by hand in the U.S.S.R., and many of the machines that were available were operated by novices. During the intervening years, concerted efforts have been made to increase productivity. In almost every enterprise, modern machinery has been introduced.

Industrial experts and human engineers concentrated on effecting the most efficient use of time and energy. Cajolery and enticing incentives were used in an attempt to get workers to work more diligently and to improve their skills and the quality of their output. The effect of these various techniques was offset by the devastation of the labor force and of equipment during the war and by the necessary assimilation of millions of untrained workers, predominantly women, into the industrial labor force. Naturally, the mistakes and general lack of efficiency of the new unskilled workers lowered the over-all productivity per worker. Nevertheless, Soviet officials claimed that the productivity per worker increased by more than three and a half times from 1928 to 1940, or about 11 per cent per year, and that it rose another 40 per cent during the war.[25] After the war, the productivity of labor fell, not unnaturally, and in 1946 was considerably lower than in 1940. Only by 1949, did labor productivity exceed the prewar level, although the reported increase from 1946 to 1949 was 43 per cent. By 1950, it was claimed officially that the output of the average worker in heavy industry was five times that in 1928. Non-Soviet writers, while admitting substantial increases in productivity, make much more conservative estimates of the extent of the increase and consider that by 1950, Soviet productivity was approximately 40 per cent of that of the U.S.A.[26] The non-Soviet estimates are confirmed by the comparison of annual output per worker in the U.S.S.R. and U.S.A., which is presented in Table 44–2 and which is based on an analysis prepared by

Table 44–2. Comparison of Annual Output per Worker in the U.S.A. and U.S.S.R.

Industry	Annual Output per Worker U.S.A.—1954 (tons)	U.S.S.R.—1956 (tons)	% of U.S.A.
Ferrous metallurgy			
Iron, steel, rolled metal	443.8	217.8	49.1
Steel and rolled metal	316.0	149.5	47.3
Steel	178.1	86.8	48.7
Rolled metal	137.9	62.7	45.5
Iron ore	2,622	1,151	43.9
Coke	1,898	932	49.1
Coal	1,346	515	38.3
Underground mining	1,077	434	40.3
Strip mining	2,791	2,735	98.0
Oil refining	1,510	655	43.4

SOURCE: *Sotsialistichesky trud* (*Socialist Labor*), No. 1 (January, 1959), 42–55.

[25] Sh. Turetsky, *Proizvoditelnost truda i snizheniye sebestoimosti v novoy pyatiletke* (*Productivity of Labor and the Lowering of Production Costs*), (Moscow: Gosudarstvennoe izdatelstvo politicheskoi literatury, 1947), p. 49.

[26] Walter Galenson, "Industrial Labor Productivity," in *Soviet Economic Growth,* Abram Bergson (ed.) (Evanston, Ill.: Row, Peterson & Co., 1953), p. 195.

Soviet economists. That significant increases are being made in the productivity of workers is indicated by officially reported increases in 1959 in comparison to 1958.[27] The following increases were reported: 5 per cent in ferrous metallurgy, 12 per cent in the oil refining industry, 5 per cent in the chemical industry, 10 per cent in machine building and metal working, 10 per cent in the lumber procurement industry, 6 per cent in light industry, 10 per cent in the food industry, and only 2 per cent in the coal industry because of the shorter working day. Despite a shorter working day in a large number of industries, the reported average gain during 1959 was 9 per cent for construction and 7.6 per cent for industry.

INDUSTRIAL OUTPUT

A consistent goal of the Soviet leaders has been to maximize industrial productivity. To this end, they have nationalized industry, introduced economic planning, diverted enormous capital funds to industry, and made numerous organizational and procedural changes throughout the years. The state has used all resources at its command to enhance industrial efficiency. Promising workers have been transferred from agriculture to industry to such an extent that the rural-urban population ratio has changed from 85:15 in 1914 to 52:48 in 1959. Differential incomes and privileges have effected a significant increase in the number of managerial, technical, and engineering experts. Universities and institutes are currently supplying well over 120,000 new scientists and engineers of all types each year.[28] As the result of planning, there is no shortage of trained experts in any field; and in the post-Sputnik era, few doubt the quality of Soviet experts. Continuous efforts have been made to improve the skill of all levels of workers in Soviet industry. Soviet authorities have not permitted industrial progress to be hindered by wage disputes and strikes. Competition between plants for increased efficiency and lowered costs is encouraged, and various awards and privileges are accorded to successful plants. Managers, engineers, and even workers are amply remunerated for suggestions, innovations, or inventions that favorably affect productivity and efficiency. Beneficial modifications developed in one plant are introduced in similar plants. Much working time has been saved by having physicians associated with each large plant and scheduling appointments that do not interfere with work output. These and numerous other policies have been introduced by the state to achieve higher efficiency and productivity goals.

[27] *Pravda,* January 22, 1960.

[28] Soviet Technical Schools were reported to have graduated 106,000 engineers in 1959. At the beginning of 1960, the U.S.S.R. had 900,000 engineers plus 300,000 scientific workers in research and educational institutions. On July 5, 1961, *Pravda* reported the number of engineers to be 1,116,000 and the total number of persons with a higher education employed in the national economy to be 3,600,000.

What has been the result of these efforts? Since 1917, the U.S.S.R. has moved from fifth place in the ranking of nations according to industrial production to second place. Before the revolution, machinery and almost all technical and scientific instruments had to be imported. In the 1950's, the U.S.S.R. astonished the world with its advanced scientific and technical achievements. However, the recent successes in the exploration of the cosmos are no more interesting than the actual and anticipated industrial growth of the U.S.S.R. Contrary to the predictions of Western economists, the rate of industrial growth in the U.S.S.R. did not slacken as soon as most of the extensive war damage was repaired. The U.S. Department of State admits that the Soviet Union is developing more rapidly than the United States but rejects the Soviet claim that by 1970 or earlier the U.S.S.R. will lead the world in both absolute and per capita production and predicts instead that the Soviet Union will have achieved 60 to 75 per cent of United States industrial output.[29] There is no doubt that the U.S.A. currently has a significant but steadily declining lead. The continuous Soviet concentration on the development of producer goods has paved the way for increased production of consumer goods, and it is probable that the recent trend in improved standards of living will be accelerated. The Soviet people, who have long been required to increase productivity at a rate disproportionate with increases in consumption, are beginning to reap rewards for past sacrifices. Their support for the regime can be expected to parallel increased production.

AGRICULTURE

As early as 1901, Lenin had plans to form large, highly mechanized farms. His goal could be accomplished by making the peasant an employee of the state or by an extensive cooperative movement. However, he realized that an important preliminary requirement to his over-all plan was the acquisition of the support of the peasants. Thus, in 1917, he encouraged the land-hungry peasants to appropriate the land of the large land owners, though he urged the local soviets to redistribute the land equitably and preferably to establish collective farms. Lenin realized that the transfer from small individual farms to common tillage could not be effected instantaneously. According to the New Economic Policy (NEP) of 1921, private farming was legalized. The NEP was a tactical retreat based on the realities of the situation. During the disruption associated with the Revolution and the period of War Communism, industrial output was severely limited. The cities and the armies expected and, not

[29] The Department of State, External Research Division, Office of Functional and Biographic Intelligence, *Report,* November 25, 1959.

infrequently, took food from the farmers, who were not able to obtain in exchange the manufactured goods that they demanded. Furthermore, the Bolsheviks had nationalized industry and were preoccupied trying to operate industry efficiently and successfully. Their inexperience was too great for them to attempt to reorganize agriculture concurrently. Thus, the NEP, which legalized private enterprise in agriculture, although absolutely contrary to Marxist dogma, served to pacify the peasants, to maintain agricultural production during a difficult time, and to permit the inexperienced Bolsheviks to concentrate on industry temporarily.

The NEP, a temporary expedient, had mixed effects. The small, often ill-shaped holdings of the peasants would have prohibited the use of machinery, had the machinery been available. Industry was unable to supply machinery and other manufactured goods that the peasants demanded in exchange for their products; and on many occasions the peasants withheld their produce, rather than exchange it for money that was meaningless when the goods they desired were not available. A vicious circle developed; industrial production was hindered by the minimum supply of food, and agricultural development was hindered by the lack of machinery and the lack of manufactured goods that would motivate the peasant to increase production or to part with his goods. The fate of communism seemed to depend on the capacity to produce cheaper goods. But at the same time, internal pressures demanded the import of cheaper goods from capitalist countries. Capitulation to such pressures would, however, have been tantamount to abandoning the Communist program. On the other hand, at least one result of the NEP was advantageous to the Bolsheviks. Under the NEP, without the interference of the government, agricultural production grew because of private initiative. At the same time, the more well-to-do peasants grew richer while poor peasants grew poorer. Class antagonisms in rural areas were maximized; and the poor peasant, who had to borrow animals, implements, and money at exorbitant rates from the rich kulak, was discontented with his own lot and eager to share the material well being of his more prosperous neighbor. The prospect of forceful collectivization, in which the property of the well-to-do would be pooled with that of the poverty stricken, seemed less dire to the very numerous subsistent farmers.

Action by the government was inevitable. A reliable and adequate supply of food was indispensable to progress in industrialization. The peasants were not only using less efficient methods of farming, but in addition, the government had increasing difficulty in appropriating farm produce for use in industrial centers. Industry had already been nationalized, and the existence of agriculture as a large free enterprise segment in the economy was not feasible. Furthermore, the U.S.S.R. was in the 1920's moving toward a planned economy; and planning of the type envisaged by the Bolshevik leaders could not have been effective had there been millions of small and relatively inefficient entrepreneurs in agriculture.

In January, 1930, the government announced the goal of complete collectivization within three years, combined with the liquidation of the kulak. Within a relatively short time, approximately five million of the well-to-do farmers were dispossessed of their property, and most of them were dispersed to other parts of the country. The land and property of the dispossessed kulaks was, in most cases, assigned for use by the collectives. Millions of the poor peasants willingly associated themselves with the collectives; their willingness was, no doubt, affected by jealousy or hatred for the kulak and the desire to share the property confiscated from him. Anarchy prevailed. The ingenuity and plans of the state officials were entirely inadequate to cope with the confusion and chaos resulting from the drastic changes in policy. Zealous officials took stern measures to force unwilling peasants to join the collectives and to pool all property including garden plots and domestic fowl. Peasants killed much of their livestock—some because they naïvely believed that the government would supply animals for the collectives, some because they wanted to make whatever profit they could from their property prior to pooling it, some because of a deliberate attempt to undermine the collective movement, and some because they feared that they might be labeled and treated as kulaks if they possessed livestock. The effects of the wholesale slaughter of animals, which drastically reduced the supply of meat, milk, wool, draft power, and manure, were felt for many years. The detrimental effects of the lack of organization and confusion were enhanced by other non-salutory factors. While it was true that the enlargement of farms did facilitate the introduction of mechanization, an adequate supply of machinery was not immediately forthcoming. With the dispossession and dispersion of the kulaks, the government had done more than to remove the last major free enterprise segment from the society; at the same time, it removed from the agricultural scene the best farmers. The majority of the peasants who joined the collectives had not been successful farmers; had little education; and knew little about agronomy, business administration, and the operation of machinery. The need for expert guidance was crucial.

The Soviet government utilized a rather ingenious technique in the attempt to cope with the numerous problems resulting from a too rapid collectivization. A new institution known as the Machine Tractor Station (MTS) was established throughout the country. The MTS was designed to serve in both economic and political capacities. The total supply of machinery was inadequate; and, moreover, the peasants were unfamiliar with the operation and servicing of machines. Consequently, the available machinery was allocated to the MTS, which supervised the use and distribution of the machines on the various collectives served by each MTS. Centralized control of the machinery was designed to maximize its use and to minimize damage. Also assigned to each MTS were trained agronomists, veterinarians, and other experts who guided, instructed, and served the personnel on the collective farms. The MTS rendered these services to the collectives for stipulated fees paid partly in money and partly in kind. Thus, the MTS, in addition to acting as a state supervisor of collective farming with the goal of increasing production, acted as an instrument for the procurement of farm products by the Soviet government. Furthermore, the MTS acted as the agents of the Communist party. Initially, the peasants were little versed and little interested in the party dogma. Consequently, associated with each MTS were party workers who were instructed to provide a political education for the inhabitants of the collective farms.

In 1958, the role of the MTS was modified considerably. The merging of collective farms into larger units made it more feasible for party organizations directly on the farm to supply the political education. No doubt the members of the collectives had become much more skilled in the use of machinery. At any rate, the government decided that the dual management imposed on the collective farm by the director of the farm and by the MTS was not efficient. Arrangements were made for the collectives to purchase machinery from the MTS and to absorb the MTS specialists and workers directly on the collectives. Modified versions of the MTS now called Repair and Technical Stations (RTS) are still existent and supply the collectives with spare parts, major repair services, new machinery, fertilizer, fuel, and other production supplies.

As previously indicated, the collectivization process was by no means smooth. Gradually steps were taken to decrease the confusion and to limit the excessive and sometimes brutal zeal of some of the organizers. In March, 1930, it was decreed that 5 per cent of the surplus product of the farms was to be distributed to the members in proportion to the value of the property contributed to the farm and also that no more than 3 per cent of the peasantry were to be described and treated as kulaks. Members were not to be forced to pool their living arrangements and their incomes and were to be remunerated in accordance with the number of days of work done by each. Individual household plots of land were permissible. The collectives were given the right to sell surplus products on the open market after the government quotas had been satisfied. Slowly and painfully, the administrators have been groping toward an organization and a system of regulations that will maximize production and will contribute to the over-all goals of the Soviet regime. Although both the mistakes and the modifications have been numerous, a fairly steady progress is reported, especially in Khrushchev's era.

By the beginning of 1933, fourteen and a half million peasant households had been collectivized with the collectivized segment ranging from 43 to 80 per cent in different regions of the country. By July 1, 1935, and July 1, 1936, 83 and 90 per cent respectively of the peasants had joined the collectives. By the end of the second Five Year Plan (1937), almost 100 per cent of the farming was done by the collective (kolkhoz) or state (sovkhoz) farms. Pressures, such as differential taxation and the non-availability of machinery, so necessary for competition, have virtually eliminated the independent farmer; and those few who remain play an inconsequential role in Soviet agriculture. State farms, which are supervised by the appropriate federal and republican ministries differ from collective farms in that state farm workers are paid fixed wages, while the income of collective farm workers is dependent on the production of the farm. State farms have been established in new agricultural areas, close to large industries as "grain factories" and "meat factories" and, also, as model farms.

The number and size of the kolkhoz and sovkhoz has varied from time to time. On January 1, 1958, there were 76,500 collective farms and 5,900 state farms in the U.S.S.R.[30] In 1957, the average sown area per collective farm was 4,200 acres,[31] and the average number of peasant households per collective farm was 245. Some collective farms that contain 375,000 acres (about 586 square miles) are considered by Soviet experts to be rather large. About 18 per cent of the collective farms contain less than 1,240 acres. On the average, the state farms are larger than collective farms; Soviet statements about the sown acreage vary between 20,000 and 25,200.

Theoretically, the administration of the collective farm is based on equality and democracy. The chairman, the executive board, and the control committee, which constitute the management of the collective, are elected by a general assembly of the members. However, the chairman, who is the chief executive officer, seems to be selected by the government officials or by the local party leaders who propose a candidate to the general assembly, which in turn admits him to membership of the collective if, as frequently happens, he is an outsider and duly elects him. It might well seem that the imposition of an outsider as chairman of the collective is a serious breach of guaranteed democratic rights. However, it should not be forgotten that the chairman assumes major responsibility for the operation of a very complex economic institution and, as such, needs special qualifications and training. Since the economic well-being of the collective members depends largely on the efficiency of the operation of

[30] In comparison to the total of 82,400 farms in the U.S.S.R., the United States had approximately 4.8 million farms at the same date.

[31] The average acreage in U.S. farms is approximately 310.

the farm, they may prefer to have a well-qualified outsider rather than a less well-qualified member in this position. Whenever the government has to choose between efficiency and principles of democracy, efficiency is preferred. On the other hand, since the position is, in general, highly remunerative, it has been used as a reward for loyal party members.

The chairman shares some of his responsibility with an executive board of five to nine members who, though elected for two-year terms by the general assembly, are commonly in fact selected by the chairman. The executive committee is required to meet at least twice a month with the chairman of the farm acting as the chairman of the committee. The control committee, elected by the general assembly and confirmed by the executive committee of the local soviet, inspects the financial and economic activities of the chairman and the executive board and is expected to intervene when necessary with reference to the fulfillment of the plan and meeting of the farm's obligations to the state.

The executive board appoints from among the members brigadiers for a term of not less than two years; the length of the term varies with the nature of the work; for example, on grain farms, the term is for the full period of crop rotation. Each brigadier is in charge of a brigade, which usually varies from forty to sixty workers, and is given responsibility for production on a specified acreage, or segment of the farm economy. Sometimes the brigades are subdivided into smaller units called squads (zveno) each with its own squad leader. Brigadiers and squad leaders assign specific duties to their members and are responsible for the fulfillment of subplans.

Prior to 1958, farms were required to make compulsory deliveries to the state, the size of the quotas being determined by such factors as the number of hectares of tillable land. For these compulsory deliveries, the state paid low fixed prices. Higher prices were paid for extra-quota purchases. In addition, farm products were paid to the MTS in exchange for services. In 1958, compulsory deliveries were abolished, although quotas per unit of land have been retained. The prices paid by the government for farm products were raised, and the policy of paying higher prices for extra-quota produce is no longer in effect. Cash payments are made for the services rendered by the RTS.

After fulfilling obligations to the government, the collective farm is required to set aside seed grain, feed for livestock, and emergency reserves. The remainder of the produce may be sold on the so-called kolkhoz market, which is almost the only competitive market in the U.S.S.R., since in this market prices are not fixed by the state and are determined largely by supply and demand. However, except in times of scarcity or overabundance, prices in the kolkhoz market correspond closely to those set by the state. The sale of the products in the market constitutes an important source of revenue for the kolkhoz. A portion, usually between 20 and 30 per cent of the gross sales of the products must be allocated to the "indivisible fund" or capital fund, which is used to finance capital construction, and for various educational and cultural purposes. For the next few years, a large part of this fund will be used to make payments to the state for machinery purchased from the MTS. Also, kolkhoz administrative personnel must be paid. After all these commitments have been met, the remaining cash and produce is distributed to the collective members in proportion to the number and value of workday credits accumulated by each member.

The system of remuneration on the collective farm is based on an arbitrary unit called the workday. The workday refers to a certain output and quality of work. For example, thinning ½ acre of sugar beets or milking eighteen cows may each be the equivalent of one workday. A skilled mechanic or a tractor driver may receive two workday credits for each day of work performed, while a messenger may receive only one-half a workday credit for working the same number of hours. Bridages that exceed their production plans are given supplementary credits, which are divided among the brigade members in proportion to the annual total of workdays that each accumulates. Deductions are made when plans are not fulfilled. The complicated system of remuneration is illustrated by considering the computation of the salary of the kolkhoz chairman. His basic pay consists of a monthly cash payment plus a specified number of workday credits, based on the size and type of farm and his seniority. Furthermore, the higher the annual cash income of the kolkhoz, the higher his basic cash income. If the kolkhoz overfulfills the plan, the chairman receives a bonus, which may be as high as 25 per cent of his basic workday credits. If the plan is underfulfilled, the chairman is penalized by a deduction of 1 per cent of his workday credits for each percentage of underfulfillment. Obviously, the incomes of both chairmen and workers may vary widely from farm to farm and from year to year. The system of remuneration is designed to motivate higher productivity and efficiency and increases in skill among all levels of agricultural workers. Although it has been reported to be in the main a satisfactory system, it has its drawbacks. The Soviet press has cited many instances of kolkhoz chairmen who have dared, in spite of the supposed vigilance of bookkeepers, to appropriate for their own use money belonging to the farm. In the assignment of duties and, hence, workday credits, and in the evaluation of work by the brigadier and squad leaders, there is ample room for discrimination. Furthermore, since the bonuses and the distribution of surpluses are based on earned workday units, the net result is that the individual who earns a smaller income receives a smaller bonus and vice versa. Although this may be just, it increases inequalities within the collectives. However, the previously mentioned policy of reducing wage differentials will have a mitigating effect, since skilled laborers are now allowed correspondingly fewer workday units in comparison to unskilled laborers.

The income of the collective farm worker is derived from three sources. First, his portion of the cash income of the kolkhoz; second, his portion of the surplus produce of the kolkhoz; and third, the produce grown on his own individual plot of land. Each household is permitted to use from ½ to 2½ acres, usually adjacent to the dwelling place, as a privately operated garden plot. Usually, livestock, as well as gardens, are raised on these plots. Individual holdings account for almost a half of all cattle, a third of hogs, and a fourth of sheep and lambs in the U.S.S.R. Surplus produce awarded to the peasant by the kolkhoz provides much of the feed for the livestock. Farm workers are permitted to sell in the kolkhoz market any remaining surplus product, plus products from their own holdings not required for individual consumption. On many collectives, the incomes derived from such sales constitute the major portion of the cash income of the workers. It is perhaps not surprising that government officials have, on occasion, complained that too much time is spent on the cultivation of individual plots at the expense of work on the kolkhoz. Measures have been introduced to penalize those members who do not devote sufficient time to the work of the collective.

State farm workers are paid fixed wages based on the skill required for the work done, with bonuses added for outstanding quantity or quality. They are permitted to use individual plots and to rent state-owned houses for a minimal fee. They do not, however, receive payments in kind as the collective workers do. Incomes on state farms appear to correspond closely to those of industrial workers of comparable skill or training and are higher than those of the average collective workers.

Like all branches of the Soviet economy, agriculture is directed by the national economic plan. However, because the planners have no control over climatic conditions, and less control over the widely dispersed agricultural units than over the more concentrated industrial units, agricultural production has not always corresponded closely to planned production. Nevertheless, the effect of planning has been significant.

Five and Seven Year Plans specify objectives pertaining to acreage, yields, construction, irrigation, mechanization, and drought and disease control. Yearly plans are more specific. The plan, formulated in Moscow on the basis of party directives and information submitted by lower administrative and agricultural units, is subdivided and transmitted through channels until it reaches the kolkhozy and sovkhozy with specific directives. The planners aim to have each farm producing those products important for the national economy for which it is most suited, but numerous errors of judgment in allocating tasks are to be expected. Recently, collective farms, subject to the approval of regional authorities, have been granted greater autonomy in the formulation of the production plan.

Current plans call for very significant increases in agricultural production; and powerful factors, which only a totalitarian Socialist government can control, are being manipulated to effect the increase. Industry has been directed to produce the machinery required for increased mechanization in agriculture. The state, as the owner of the land and employer of most of the population, can decide that previously untilled land be cultivated and can supply the necessary manpower. Prices, established by the state, are manipulated to effect production changes. Prices, however, are not the sole criterion in the distribution of production resources, since the plan specifies minimum production quotas for all products. Steps have been taken to increase the educational and skill level of agricultural workers. The effort expended in agricultural research can be manipulated, and currently attempts are being made to develop grain and livestock strains especially suited to the available climatic and soil conditions. Authorities on Soviet agriculture, both within and without the U.S.S.R., realize that there is ample room for improvement. For example, storage facilities and processing plants on the farm are, in general, inadequate. Waste results from the spoilage of grain piled on the ground and the discard of milk that could be powdered for city consumption. Maximum utilization of both time and produce requires extensive improvement in transportation facilities. The agricultural labor force, which averages one worker per 15 acres of sown area in comparison to one worker per 60 acres in the U.S.A., is not used efficiently. During slack periods, farm workers are required to engage in relatively unproductive tasks. With improved mechanization and transportation facilities, fewer workers will be required; and the large labor reserve, available when necessary for industrial expansion, will be increased. It is expected that some of the labor reserve will be used in processing plants on the farm and to increase productivity per acre. Since the Plan calls for higher production at lower cost, the keynote of agricultural operation must be efficiency. Farms are required to operate on a strict cost accounting system and are not provided with government subsidies. However, generous ten-year loans at a low interest rate are available for building construction and other capital improvements. The Ministry of Agriculture provides the farms with plans for new buildings or for the adaptation of old buildings, as well as with expert advice on numerous technical and procedural matters. Promises of great improvements in standards of living in the future, combined with the new procurement and pricing system, which has permitted an increase in the kolkhoz income, are used by the government to encourage greater productivity.

Thus, the Soviet government has at its command a multitude of factors that it does or may use to modify and increase agricultural production.

CONCLUSION

The purpose of Soviet planning has been to transform a backward agricultural country into a leading industrial power and, at the same time, to provide for the defense needs of the Soviet state and increase the standard of living of the people. It would be a mistake to assume that the methods of Soviet planning have been perfected and that the Soviet economy is operating at peak efficiency. Mistakes, bottlenecks, supply deficiencies, and underfulfillment of production quotas are still major problems that the planners must resolve. Furthermore, such progress as has been made toward optimum industrialization and productivity has been accomplished at the expense of the consumers' interests. Many foreign observers have accused the Communist party of undue exploitation of the people in the interest of the party elite. Although the party has placed its retention of power above every other consideration, it must not be presumed that the stated goal of attaining the highest living standard in the world is only propaganda. Strenuous efforts toward actual attainment of this goal are already being made. By achieving the economy of abundance, the Soviet leadership intends to make life in the U.S.S.R. so attractive that the masses in every country will demand that their governments adopt socialism. Should the Soviet regime achieve this economic goal, the Communists would have a powerful weapon for influencing world opinion.

SELECTED READING

BALZAK, S. S., VASYUTIN, V. F., and FEIGIN, YA.G. (eds.). *Economic Geography of the USSR.* New York: The Macmillan Co., 1949.

BARANSKY, N. N. *Economic Geography of the USSR.* Moscow: Foreign Languages Publishing House, 1956.

BERGSON, ABRAM (ed.). *Soviet Economic Growth.* Evanston, Ill.: Row, Peterson & Co., 1953.

BERLINER, JOSEPH S. *Factory and Manager in the USSR.* Cambridge, Mass.; Harvard University Press, 1957.

EMMET, W. H. *The Marxian Economic Handbook.* London: George Allen & Unwin, Ltd., 1925.

HOLZMAN, FRANKLYN D. *Soviet Taxation: The Fiscal and Monetary Problems of a Planned Economy.* Cambridge, Mass.: Harvard University Press, 1955.

STALIN, JOSEPH V. *Economic Problems of Socialism in the USSR.* Moscow: Foreign Languages Publishing House, 1952.

VARGA, EUGENE. *Two Systems: Socialist Economy and Capitalist Economy.* New York: International Publishers Co., Inc., 1939.

45

The Judicial System

Marx and Engels did not provide an adequate guide for the development of a judicial system in a Communist society, or a society that is approaching communism. They regarded law as an instrument of state power designed to enforce the dominance of the ruling class. Their prediction was that following a proletarian revolution and the abolition of classes, asocial behavior would gradually disappear and, along with it, the need for laws and legal coercion. Since the classless society could not be achieved immediately, the Bolshevik leaders, after some exploratory modifications, accepted law, revolutionary expediency, and even terror as instruments to be used by the new dominant class, the proletarians, against counterrevolutionary enemies. According to a postrevolutionary authority, "Law is a system of social relations which corresponds to the interests of the dominant class and is safeguarded by the organized force of that class."[1] With the liquidation of the exploiting classes, Soviet law is now claimed to be an embodiment of the will of the entire population.[2] However, the will of the entire population means, in fact, the will of the party leaders, as indicated by the following statement: "The meaning of the law must therefore be explained by reference to the most important works and documents expressing Soviet ideology—the works of Lenin and Stalin and the programs, decisions and resolutions of the all-union Communist Party."[3] Soviet law is used as a weapon of the party. Soviet authorities make no pretence about the political neutrality of their legal system. The courts are declared to be instruments of state power, whose major

[1] P. I. Stuchka, "The Revolutionary Part Played by Law and the State: A General Doctrine of Law," trans. Hugh W. Babb, *Soviet Legal Philosophy* (Cambridge, Mass.: Harvard University Press, 1951), p. 20.

[2] Academy of Sciences of the USSR, Institute of Law, *Istoria gosudarstva i prava* (*History of State and Law*), (Moscow: Gosudarstvennoe izdatelstvo yuridicheskoi literatury, 1949), p. 112.

[3] Academy of Sciences of the USSR, Institute of Law, *Osnovy sovetskogo gosudarstva i prava,* (Principles of the Soviet State and Law, Moscow, 1947), p. 63.

purpose is to further the cause of communism. In democratic nations, legal systems are considered to be apolitical, a basic prerequisite for the maintenance of justice, order, and stability in society, and very definitely not the tool of any political party. Democratic nations consider binding rules necessary because of the inevitability of social conflict, socially deviant behavior, and the propensity of humans for self-gratification. Communist leaders consider laws to be devices that can be manipulated, as the party leaders deem necessary, to effect the establishment of a society in which social conflict, socially deviant behavior, and greed are not expected to occur.

The Soviet constitution provides a judicial apparatus that in many respects resembles the judicial apparatus of Western democracies. However, coexisting with the relatively respectable legal system is an extra-legal system, operated by the secret police and characterized by irregularity; arbitrariness; and, at least in the past, by cruelty. In order to prevent a biased impression of the administration of justice in the U.S.S.R., both legal and extra-legal systems must be examined. The legal judicial apparatus provided by the Constitution of the U.S.S.R. consists of two hierarchical arrangements, which are outlined in Figure 45–1.

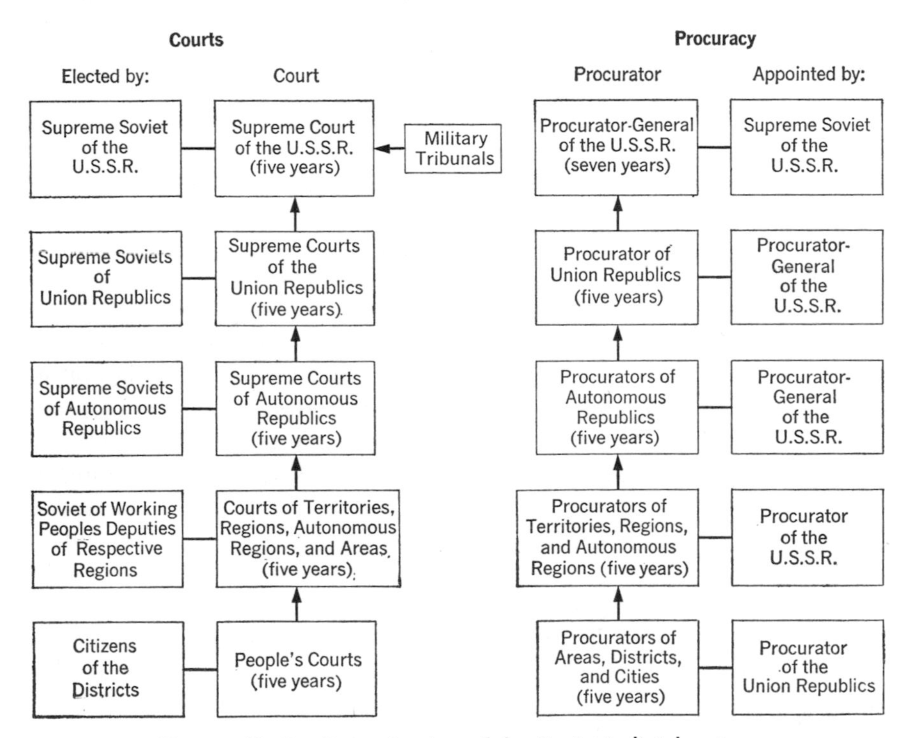

Figure 45–1. Organization of the Soviet judicial system.

THE COURTS

The Supreme Court of the U.S.S.R., the highest judicial organ, is charged with the supervision of all judicial organs of the U.S.S.R. and of the Union Republics within the limits established by law (Article 104). Thus, although each Union Republic has its own Supreme Court, which is able to exercise supervisory functions over lower courts operating within the republic, all Soviet courts are subordinate to the Supreme Court of the U.S.S.R. That the system of courts throughout the nation is specified by the U.S.S.R. Constitution and supervised by the federal Supreme Court has the obvious advantage of a standardized system. Since the laws of the U.S.S.R. are applicable in every Union Republic (Article 19), a standard organization of courts is important.

The Peoples Courts, the lowest courts in the hierarchy, are, like most Soviet courts, collegial. The bench of a Peoples Court is composed of one judge and two "peoples assessors." The judges are "elected" for five years by the electorate of the area of the court's jurisdiction. Until recently, judges often lacked legal training, which is not required. At present, the majority of judges have legal training or experience, and it seems safe to predict that in the future all judges will be trained jurists. The "people's assessors" are elected for a two-year term from among Soviet citizens eligible to vote. Legal training is not a prerequisite, although, lately, short courses have been conducted to increase the legal knowledge of assessors. Candidates are nominated by factories, kolkhozes, sovkhozes, scientific institutions, etc. The assessors, who act as cojudges and not as jurors, since the jury system is not used in the U.S.S.R., are expected to represent the community with the common sense approach of the layman. Furthermore, the purposes of the party leadership are furthered by the impression of mass participation in the administration of justice, which is effected by the people's assessors. Each judge has a panel of about fifty to seventy-five assessors from which to draw. No assessor is permitted to function in court more than ten days per year. While acting as an assessor, he is paid the same daily salary as he would earn on his permanent job. Should, for some reason, the full-time judge not be available, an assessor is called upon to assume the role of judge and, under those circumstances, is paid the same salary as the judge for the ten-day period. Both judges and people's assessors are subject to recall at any time by their electorate. While on duty, the assessor has the same rights and duties as a judge. However, since the legal training and experience of the judge is usually superior to that of the assessors, the assessors usually defer to the professional judge.[4]

[4] Cf. John N. Hazard, *The Soviet System of Government* (Chicago: University of

The People's Courts, which are exclusively courts of original jurisdiction, deal with the majority of civil cases and many of the less serious criminal cases. Civil cases include disputes between individuals with regard to property, alimony, and inheritance, as well as disputes between enterprises, and labor relations cases. Criminal cases include theft, tax evasion, violation of the electoral law, failure to meet state obligations, and embezzlement. Crimes with important political implications, such as counterrevolutionary acts or theft of Socialist property, and crimes that carry the death penalty or imprisonment for more than ten years are not entrusted to the People's Courts.

The courts of the Autonomous Republics, Territories, Autonomous Regions, and Areas each have a collegial bench consisting of a president, several vice-presidents, ordinary judges, and people's assessors. All members of the bench are elected by the appropriate soviet for a five-year term. These intermediate courts have original jurisdiction in civil cases dealing with disputes between state and public institutions; enterprises and organizations; and in criminal cases such as counterrevolutionary crimes, theft of Socialist property, and crimes against state administration. Moreover, the intermediate courts supervise the work of and hear appeals from the People's Courts. A case of original jurisdiction is heard by a judge and two assessors, while appeals are heard by three judges.

The Supreme Court of the Union Republic is the highest judicial organ in the republic. The composition of the collegial bench of this court is the same as that of the intermediate courts. It has original jurisdiction in both civil and criminal cases of extreme importance, such as might be brought before it by the Procurator or the Presidium of the Supreme Soviet of the Republic, or crimes committed by important republican governmental officials, or cases of great political significance. All lower and intermediate courts within the republic are supervised by the Supreme Court, which can reverse verdicts, hear appeals, and remove cases from lower courts to assume jurisdiction itself.

Permanently established military courts exist as special courts under the direct supervision of the Supreme Court of the U.S.S.R. These courts deal in a summary manner with important political as well as military crimes. They have jurisdiction over all military personnel accused of committing any crime whatsoever; all espionage cases; and, in territories under martial law, over all crimes, regardless of the offender, committed against public order and the security of the state.

The Supreme Court of the U.S.S.R., the highest judicial organ in the nation, has had since 1957 twenty-seven professional judges, including a

---

Chicago Press, 1957), p. 160. For an interesting commentary by Soviet citizens on the role of the assessor see Ye. Rozanova and N. Shtanko, "Three People on the Judges' Bench," *Izvestia,* August 30, 1960, p. 3.

chairman, two vice-chairmen, nine members, and the fifteen chairmen of the Supreme Courts of the Union Republics, the latter being a concession to both federalism and the rights of the various nationalities. In addition, it has twenty people's assessors. All members of the bench are elected for a five-year term by the Supreme Soviet of the U.S.S.R. The judges are divided into collegia specialized in military, civil, or criminal cases. Although the Supreme Court of the U.S.S.R. functions primarily as an appellate court, only the Procurator-General of the U.S.S.R. and the Chairman of the Plenum of the Supreme Court of U.S.S.R., not private individuals, have the right to present cases for appeal. The Supreme Court takes original jurisdiction over only those cases of exceptional military, legal, or political significance, as, for example, when a very-high-ranking government official is involved. When functioning as a court of the first instance, it has, as all Soviet courts under similar circumstances, only one professional judge and two people's assessors. When it functions as an appellate court, the bench consists of three professional judges. The Chairman of the U.S.S.R. Supreme Court may preside in any case dealt with by a collegium of the Supreme Court.

Plenary sessions of the Supreme Court are held at least four times a year and are attended by the Procurator-General of the U.S.S.R. and sometimes by the Minister of Justice of the U.S.S.R. At the plenary sessions, the decisions of the separate collegia of the U.S.S.R. Supreme Court and of the republican Supreme Courts are considered; and sometimes protests are heard. General principles and directives aimed at guiding the work of the lower courts in conformity with the decisions of the U.S.S.R. Supreme Court are issued.

Although the Supreme Court of the U.S.S.R. is expected to issue guiding principles and explanations of laws and legislation, it most definitely does not have the right to declare unconstitutional a law or a decree, whether issued by the Supreme Soviet or its Presidium or by the Council of Ministers. The right to interpret statutes and decrees is given to the Presidium of the Supreme Soviet rather than to the Supreme Court. It has never possessed the power of judicial review of legislation. The concept of separation of powers has been rejected by the Soviet leaders, and the courts cannot act as a check against violation of the Constitution by the executive and legislative branches of the government. The party, which controls all branches of the government, could not tolerate a judicial system that would interfere with its activities.

According to the Constitution, Soviet judges are independent and subject only to the law (Article 112). However, no court and no judge in the U.S.S.R. can be apolitical. A judge, like all other Soviet officials, must be a "builder of socialism"; hence, his independence cannot lead to disagreement with governmental policy directed by the Communist party. Perhaps it would be appropriate to say that judges can be independent of local interests when these are in conflict with the law. The mere indication of concern about the independence of judges is, however, an improvement, since early Bolshevik jurists rejected *in toto* the concept of impartiality and independence of judges.

THE PROCURACY

The Procurator-General of the U.S.S.R. is vested with "supreme supervisory power to ensure the strict observance of the law by all ministries and institutions subordinated to them as well as by officials and citizens of the USSR" (Article 113). The Procurator-General appoints Procurators of Republics, Territories, Regions, Autonomous Republics, and Autonomous Regions, while area, city, and district Procurators are appointed by the Procurators of the Union Republics, subject to the approval of the Procurator-General (Articles 115 and 116). The term of the Procurator-General is seven years and for all other Procurators, five years.

The Procurator-General is appointed by the Supreme Soviet of the U.S.S.R. and is legally responsible only to the Supreme Soviet and its Presidium, although *de facto* he is responsible to the party leadership. He is in no way subordinate to or supervised by either the Council of Ministers or the Supreme Court of the U.S.S.R. The office of the Procurator forms a single federal apparatus with the Procurator-General at its head, since all branches of the Procuracy are subordinate to the Procurator-General of the U.S.S.R. (Article 117). The Procurator's office functions in complete independence of all local organs including local party organizations. For example, the Union Republics are not consulted about the choice of a republican Procurator.

The supervisory powers of the Procurator-General, which include the supervision of economic as well as judicial organs, are very broad and exceed those of the Supreme Court of the U.S.S.R., which supervises only the activity of the courts. The Procuracy, a highly centralized office, is charged with the responsibility of achieving uniformity in law enforcement and adherence to Soviet statutes by both courts and administrative organs. Acting as the state prosecutor in criminal matters, it ferrets out misdemeanors. In this activity, the Procuracy is aided by a large group of "activists," who are required to be on the alert for criminal conduct and to inform the appropriate authorities. The activists, or "groups of aid," include approximately three million members[5] and, in addition to providing the Procuracy with information that might otherwise be overlooked, add impetus to the mass participation movement. At the same time, the Proc-

[5] Samuel N. Harper and Ronald Thompson, *The Government of the Soviet Union* (2d. ed.; Princeton: D. Van Nostrand Co., Inc., 1949), p. 237.

uracy knows about and deals with the complaints of the ordinary citizens. The apprehension of any person suspected of criminal activities may be ordered by the Procurator. The approval of the Procuracy is required before an arrest can be made; even the secret police are supposed to obtain permission,[6] although it is most doubtful that this regulation is adhered to with regularity. Since the Procurator-General is required to "ensure the strict observance of the law by all Ministries and institutions subordinate to them," he has, technically at least, some power over the activities of the Ministry of Internal Affairs (MVD) and State Security Board (KGB) and their subordinates, the secret police. Reports of the activities of the secret police would seem to indicate that the Procurator-General has not always demanded strict observance of the Soviet statutes, a deviation easily explained by the fact that both the Procurator-General and the secret police are required to be subservient to the Communist party.

The Procurator-General or his subordinates may interfere at any level of court proceedings. Most criminal actions are initiated by the Procuracy, and even civil action may be initiated without the consent of the involved parties. A Procurator may intervene in civil action if it seems that state interests are involved. In criminal cases, the Procurator acts as the prosecuting attorney. Appeals can be initiated by the Procuracy even in cases where the court's decision is regarded as final or when the defendant does not indicate a desire to appeal. The Procurator can interfere if he thinks court decisions are either too severe or too lenient. Higher Procurators can intervene in the activities of lower Procurators. Of considerable interest is the fact that Procurators can and do, on occasion, act as defending attorneys. Persons accused of committing crimes against the state may not be able to obtain adequate defense counsel, since lawyers, like other Soviet citizens, must observe the party line. Procurators, in their role of insuring uniform enforcement of the law, may act as counsel for the defendant.

THE OPERATION OF JUSTICE

Does the complex apparatus provided by the Soviet Constitution mete out justice to Soviet citizens, or even to the majority of Soviet citizens? Any attempt to provide a meaningful answer to this question requires consideration of diverse factors such as what is and what is not provided as the constitutional right of Soviet citizens, the training and orientation of judges and lawyers, the conduct of investigations and trial procedures, and finally the role of the secret police.

[6] S. A. Golunsky and D. S. Karev, *Sudoustroistvo S.S.S.R.*, (*The Judicial System of the U.S.S.R.*), (Moscow: Gosudarstvennoe izdatelstvo yuridicheskoi literatury, 1946), p. 169.

The Soviet Constitution makes the following provisions:

1. Judicial proceedings are conducted in the language of the Union Republic, Autonomous Republic or Autonomous Region, persons not knowing this language being guaranteed the opportunity of fully acquainting themselves with the material of the case through an interpreter and likewise the right to use their own language in court (Article 110).
2. In all Courts of the U.S.S.R. cases are heard in public unless otherwise provided for by law, and the accused is guaranteed the right to defense (Article 111).
3. Judges are independent and subject only to the law (Article 112).
4. Citizens of the U.S.S.R. are guaranteed inviolability of the person. No person may be placed under arrest except by decision of a court or with the sanction of a procurator (Article 127).
5. The inviolability of homes of citizens and the privacy of correspondence are protected by law (Article 128).

These provisions, insofar as they go and insofar as they are upheld, seem quite reasonable. Available evidence indicates that the language of the territory is used in court and that in court, defendants do have the use of an interpreter when required. Although in most instances, public hearings are held, the "unless otherwise provided by law" clause permits Soviet authorities to exclude the public from cases of extreme political or military importance or for a number of other reasons. Defendants are guaranteed the right to counsel during the actual court procedure; but, during the most important phase of the investigation, the pretrial investigation, the defendant is not permitted to have counsel and the investigation is not open to the public. Moreover, until 1956, defendants accused of certain counterrevolutionary crimes were denied counsel during the trial. There is ample evidence that in the recent past, the pretrial investigation for political offenses has consisted of harsh and continuous interrogation and that physical abuse has been used. The public is not permitted to witness such investigations, which have not infrequently resulted in public confessions of crimes that the defendant could not possibly have committed. Until 1956, persons accused of certain crimes, such as counterrevolutionary conspiracies, were not even informed of the indictment until twenty-four hours before the trial and, of course, had totally inadequate time to prepare a defense. However, since in such cases it has been customary to consider the defendant guilty before the trial begins, the lack of time for defense preparation would not affect the outcome of the trial. On occasion, trials with important political implications have been conducted in the absence of the defendant and of the defense attorney. Prepared documents providing evidence of guilt have been sufficient for conviction. Beria, for example, was not present at his own trial and was denied the right of appeal. The death penalty was carried out almost immediately. There is some evidence, however, of improvement since 1956.

According to the 1958 revision of the legal code, a defendant has the right to know the charges against him and to present a defense. That judges are necessarily agents of the party, and as such are not independent, has already been mentioned.

Theoretically, no arrest can be made without the sanction of a Procurator or by decision of a court. In practice, this guaranty has been violated frequently, especially by the secret police. Soviet jurists as late as 1958 have argued for the need to enforce this rule.[7] An order authorizing arrest and subsequent detention for months can be issued if there is reason to merely suspect that a crime has been committed or contemplated. Although inviolability of homes and correspondence is guaranteed, the militia has the right to enter private dwellings in pursuit of suspects or escapees and to seize documents and letters, all without judicial warrant. The Procurator's office is able to instruct the post office and telegraphic office to deliver to an investigator the private communications of a suspect. It should be pointed out that violations of the constitutionally guaranteed rights of citizens, such as those mentioned above, are relatively uncommon with reference to civil and ordinary criminal cases. Only in cases with political implications is it likely that the rights of citizens will be blatantly violated. Moreover, the number and seriousness of such infractions has decreased in the post-Stalin era.

Certain glaring omissions in the constitutional rights of Soviet citizens must be considered in evaluating Soviet justice. Only outstanding examples will be mentioned. The Soviet Constitution does not provide for a writ of habeas corpus. The preliminary investigations conducted by the Procurator's office may take weeks or even months, during which time the defendant is imprisoned. Although higher authorities or the party may intervene against dilatory and unfair practices, if it suits their purposes, there is no way that a private individual may force the authorities to bring the accused to court for a legal decision.

Second, no legal statute in the U.S.S.R. proclaims the presumption of innocence until guilt is proven. Although Soviet jurists claim that the presumption exists but has not been formalized, the Supreme Soviet refused to formalize the principle in the 1958 revision of the legal code. In civil and ordinary criminal cases, the defendant may, indeed, be presumed innocent until proven guilty. In most political cases, an arrest is tantamount to a conviction; and the defendant is most definitely presumed guilty prior to his trial and ultimate conviction. There is ample evidence that the purpose of many political trials is not to determine whether the defendant is guilty. Rather, such trials may be used to provide warnings to would-be deviationists; to inform the public that the party is fully aware

[7] *Byulleten Verkhovnogo suda SSSR* (*Bulletin of the Supreme Court of the USSR*), No. 4 (1958), pp. 1–20.

of the activities of the citizens; to pin the responsibility for economic failure on a few officials; to remove personal rivals of a party leader; and, of course, to punish those who are actually guilty of espionage, treason, or other crimes.

The rule of analogy, a particularly reprehensible feature of Soviet law that has been abolished recently, deserves mention. According to this rule, a person who had not violated any known law could, nevertheless, be punished for doing something that bore some resemblance to an act prohibited by law. Thus, an act by a citizen who had no intention of breaking the law could be condemned by a Soviet judge, acting on the basis of his "Socialist conscience." Soviet citizens could be imprisoned for not adhering to laws passed by the Supreme Soviet, to orders issued by the Council of Ministers and other non-legislative governmental bodies, to orders issued by non-governmental agencies such as the party, such orders being subject to erratic changes with changes in the party line, and could, moreover, be punished for doing something vaguely related to one of the modifiable orders. Furthermore, the definition of some offenses has been extremely vague; and in the past, a Soviet citizen could be arrested and imprisoned on "suspicion of espionage" or because he represented a "socially dangerous element." Under such circumstances, it was next to impossible to be sure that one was "on the safe side of the law." Recent revisions in the Soviet legal code have had salutary effects on the vagueness of the law.

Another recent improvement is the acceptance of a statute of limitations of sentences. Even so, the severity of the imposed sentence varies considerably with the party line. The party hands down orders to judges to punish certain crimes more severely at a particular time. The judge who would dare to ignore such directives from the party, which has no constitutional right to instruct the judges, would be inviting trouble.

Court action in civil cases is initiated by a written complaint, and in criminal and political cases, by an arrest. The most important phase of investigation for criminal and particularly political cases occurs prior to the trial. This is alleged to be an impartial hearing conducted by a civil servant under the administrative control of the Procurator's office. Evidence provided by the defendant and his witnesses is supposed to bear equal weight with that provided by the police and the Procurator. The investigator, on the basis of his records of the investigation, prepares a conclusion from which the Procurator may issue an indictment. All records are sent to the court for the use of the judge. For civil cases and ordinary criminal cases, it may well be that most preliminary investigations are conducted in an unbiased manner. For political cases, there is ample evidence that unfair means have been used to expedite confessions, whether the accusation was just or otherwise. During the post-Stalin era, the party leaders have expressed abhorrence of such tactics; and some mitigating influence has resulted.

The court session, particularly if the case is heard by a People's Court, is surprisingly informal and is designed to be educational. The courtroom may for special cases be situated in a factory or kolkhoz so that factory or farm workers may be instructed in the nature and consequences of the crime. Speeches glorifying the regime or expressing extreme distaste for the crime under consideration are not uncommon, though the propaganda value of such speeches is much more apparent than their role in insuring justice. The Soviet judge has responsibility for the political and legal education of the masses; and in some cases, it seems that the courtroom is used more effectively for these purposes than for the administration of justice. The political reliability of the judge must, of course, be guaranteed; all judges in the higher courts are party members, as are approximately three-quarters of the judges in the People's Courts. The reliability of the non-party judges is insured by the fact that, as in other Soviet elections, the electorate is supplied with only one name on the ballot. As previously pointed out, the judges may indeed be relatively independent of local pressures; but as they hear a case, reach a verdict, and pronounce sentence, they must be continually aware of the party line and the effect of their speeches and decisions on the strengthening of the Socialist society.

The defendant is in most cases permitted to have a defense attorney during the actual trial though may be denied counsel during the pretrial investigation. Previously, anyone with a "revolutionary conscience" could serve in such a capacity; but there has been of late increasing emphasis on legal training and licensing of lawyers. A defense lawyer in an ordinary civil or criminal case may be free to serve the needs of his client. However, in a case with political implications, he is required to "think first of all of the interests of the people, the interests of the state."[8] To argue against the policy of the party in a case where the defendant is presumed guilty before he stands trial would put the attorney in grave personal jeopardy. In political cases, it is therefore customary for the defense attorney to do little more than to ask for clemency for his client. As previously indicated, the Procurator may, under certain circumstances, come to the defense of such an otherwise undefended person.

During the court session, the judges may participate actively. The court may, on its own initiative, call witnesses in support of the accused, or in civil cases, in support of either litigant. The Soviet judge may use his own discretion about what may be considered relevant evidence and may introduce witnesses to provide information about the defendant's political views, past and present, and even those of his relatives and as-

[8] P. Kudryantsev, in *Literaturnaya Gazeta*, June 8, 1951.

sociates, his class origin, his service to the party, his contact with foreigners, his work record, etc. In cases where the verdict of guilty is predetermined, the breadth of admissible evidence serves important educational and explanatory functions. The evidence can be selected and interpreted to "prove" that a crime against the state cannot be attributed to a weakness in the Soviet system but rather is the result of incomplete eradication of capitalist influences transmitted from non-Bolshevik forbears or by the contaminating influence of foreign capitalist contacts. Yet, in spite of the selection of evidence in cases with political implications, it seems that in other cases, an attempt is made to produce witnesses and to collect evidence that will have a bearing on a just decision.

Political crimes in the past have been very broadly defined; in fact, no Soviet citizen could be absolutely certain that he would not be accused and punished. Any act considered by the authorities to endanger the security of the state is punishable. Included, as might be expected, are acts of treason, espionage, armed revolt, anti-Soviet propaganda, sabotage, etc. Moreover, any act that "leads to a disturbance of administration of the national economy" [9] is considered "especially dangerous." Economic blunders, falsifications of production figures, violations of labor discipline, damage to Socialist property, and innumerable other acts, which in most nations would not be considered politically significant, are considered acts against the state and are punished severely as political crimes.

A Soviet citizen may be sentenced by bodies other than regular courts. In addition to state institutions, such as the militia and the courts, public organizations operate simultaneously to maintain public order and security. "Popular justice" is exercised under the antiparasite laws by comrades' or social "courts" and people's guards. The antiparasite laws are directed against antisocial and parasitical elements who avoid socially useful labor or live on unearned income.[10]

The "trial" is a simple one. The majority of the adults of a village or of an apartment block in a city meet and by simple majority vote by open ballot may sentence the offender to two to five years' exile with compulsory labor at a specified location. The sentence has to be confirmed by the executive committee of the local soviet. The accused is not protected by the normal rules of evidence and proof. He has neither the right to defense nor the right to appeal.

The task of "comrades' or public courts" is to maintain discipline and to settle disputes among workers, utilizing the force of public opinion and social pressure to accomplish their function. These "courts" are set up in factories, apartment houses, collective farms, and other organizations.

[9] Criminal Code of the R.S.F.S.R., Article 59.
[10] This law has been enacted in the Kirghiz S.S.R.

The "court" consists of a president and two members appointed by the president from an elected group. Cases are heard in public. Decisions made by majority vote are pronounced publicly. There is no right of appeal. The effectiveness of the "sentence" is supposed to lie in the shame felt by the defendant. However, the "comrades' courts" are empowered to apply "corrective measures," including not only public reprimands and fines of up to 100 rubles, but even the demotion or dismissal of a worker, or in apartment houses cases, eviction from the flat. In the latter two cases, the "court" brings up the question of dismissal or eviction before the head of the enterprise or, for apartment houses, the People's Court.

The "court" may try petty offenses, e.g., minor poaching, petty profiteering, and petty misappropriation of state or public property. Persons may be brought before a "comrades' court" for tardiness or absence from work without valid reason; for delaying production because of carelessness; for shirking socially useful work; for insults, beatings, drunkenness, bad language; and for "failure to fulfill the duties of bringing up children."

People's guards, known under various names, e.g., "people's squads," "volunteer squads," "voluntary people's guards," are groups of citizens formed to assist public organs in maintaining public order and social discipline. Reports from many cities indicate wide participation, e.g., the city of Kiev reported in February, 1960, that it had more than 22,000 squad members. The squads take action against amoral and antisocial acts such as drunkenness and holliganism.

The antiparasite laws, the comrades' courts, and the people's guards are described by the party as an aspect of the transition to communism, the inclusion of the widest strata of the population in the management of all the affairs of the country, and the ultimate withering away of the state. Popular justice is praised in the Soviet Union but criticized in the West, since it is controlled and manipulated by activists and skilled agitators of the party.

THE SECRET POLICE

Ever since the Bolsheviks seized power, the secret police under various labels (CHEKA, GPU, OGPU, NKVD, MGB, and currently MVD and KGB) have had broad powers, which they have often overstepped, to ferret out "enemies of the state." Not infrequently, they have on their own authority arrested, imprisoned, and executed persons. The secret police played a leading role in the Red Terror, the Great Purge, all lesser purges, and in forcibly eliminating opposition to the regime by eradicating opposition elements and by terrorizing the population into submission.

Currently, the secret police are subdivided into the Committee on State Security (KGB) and the Ministry of Internal Affairs (MVD), both of which are nominally subordinate to the Council of Ministers. During the post-Stalin era, it has been claimed that arrests can be made by the secret police only if authorized by the Procuracy and that the police are required to transfer certain cases to the courts for trial and sentencing. Although it is most likely that some of the activities of the secret police have been limited, and moreover that many of their activities are legally sanctioned, the police still constitute a threat to the security of the Soviet citizen. The party, which uses terror as a powerful weapon to maintain control over its subject peoples, still needs the secret police. With dossiers full of potentially incriminating information on millions of citizens, with control over the movement of citizens from one part of the country to another, with memories of secret arrests and the eventual disappearance of individuals, with rumors about the horrors of interrogation and the forced labor camps, the secret police are able to engender sufficient terror to safeguard party control. And the party, having gained and retained power by force and by prohibiting the emergence of any oppositional tendencies that might weaken its absolute control over the populace, needs the secret police and the terror it inspires.

Not uncommonly, important victims of secret police investigations have been brought to public trial where they admitted all accusations, incriminated others, and apologized for their crimes against the Communist regime, about which at their trials they made glorifying speeches. Although it is possible that a few of the most ardent Communists had, in spite of their personal humiliation, retained devotion to the Communist cause, it is likely that most of the public confessions were the result of cruel interrogation procedures or were based on the hope of clemency. Soviet authorities make much of the need to rehabilitate or retrain those who have committed political crimes; in the past, the most important aspect of the retraining seems to have been the public confession, during which the victim told the Soviet citizens and the world in general that he, not the system that caused his downfall and perhaps ordered his execution, was wrong and expressed gratitude that his errors were brought to his attention so that he might repent.

A large percentage of the citizens sentenced by the courts or by the secret police were sent to forced labor camps. Reports of persons who have been inmates of forced labor camps and have since escaped to the West indicate that the emphasis has been on work rather than retraining, even political retraining. Like all other branches of the Soviet economy, the prisoners were given production quotas, usually unreasonably high ones. Food rations were restricted if output did not meet minimum requirements. In general, common criminals were treated better than political prisoners. Although sickness and death resulted from undernourishment, overwork, and unsanitary conditions, there are no indications of the deliberate brutality that characterized the Nazi concentration camps.

Thousands of prisoners have been released after the successful completion of a major economic task, but other prisoners have had their terms of imprisonment extended. Although the party leaders have claimed recently that the forced labor camps have been abolished, most Western observers are skeptical. The Soviet system, even if supported by the majority of the population, still needs the methods of terror to eliminate expressions of opposition. Conviction for political crimes is an integral part of maintaining terror and, hence, control. Furthermore, no society has been successful in eradicating all crime. The Soviet Union still has prisoners—the majority of whom may have been imprisoned for criminal offences. And in a society where great efforts are made to maximize production, it is unlikely that the prison population is permitted to be non-productive.

It is entirely possible that because demands made on the Soviet citizens are decreasing, and the rewards are increasing, their support for the regime may be much more genuine and the need for terror tactics might be diminishing. As popular support for the regime grows, the number of arrests for political crimes will decline correspondingly. Furthermore, it would be erroneous to assume that foul play predominates in all aspects of Soviet administration of justice.

The Soviet Union, like all other nations, needs the stability resulting from certain rules of conduct that are enforced. And Soviet society, like all other societies, would suffer dire consequences if habitually the innocent were punished or if many of the guilty went unpunished. The party leaders are fully cognizant of the need for stability and for fair play between individuals and for the protection of society against asocial behavior. There is no reason to suspect that the administration of justice, in cases without political implications, is inferior to that of other countries. However, because of political considerations, some citizens have been treated unjustly.

SELECTED READING

Babb, Hugh W. (trans.) *Soviet Legal Philosophy*. Cambridge, Mass.: Harvard University Press, 1951.

Berman, Harold J. *Justice in Russia: An Interpretation of Soviet Law*. Cambridge, Mass.: Harvard University Press, 1950.

Gsovski, Vladimir, and Grzybowski, Kasimierz. *Government, Law and Courts in the Soviet Union and Eastern Europe*. 2 vols. New York: Frederick A. Praeger, Inc., 1959.

Hazard, John N. *Law and Social Change in the USSR*. Toronto: The Carswell Co., Ltd., 1953.

Konstantinovsky, Boris A. *Soviet Law in Action: The Recollected Cases of a Soviet Lawyer*. Cambridge, Mass.: Harvard University Press, 1953.

Schlesinger, Rudolph. *Soviet Legal Theory*. London: Kegan Paul, Trench, Trubner & Co., Ltd., 1945.

Starosolski, Iurii. *The Principle of Analogy in Criminal Law and Aspects of Soviet Legal Thinking*. New York: Research Program on the U.S.S.R., East European Fund, 1954.

VI

POLITICS AND INSTITUTIONS OF EUROPEAN UNION

0 100 200 300 400 500
Miles
ARCTIC
ICELAND
Reykjavik
ATLANTIC OCEAN
NORWAY
SWEDEN
Oslo
Stockholm
Helsi
NO. IRELAND
Belfast
GREAT BRITAIN
IRELAND
Dublin
DENMARK
Copenhagen
Kalining
London
NETH.
The Hague
Elbe
Berlin
Danzig
POLAND
Warsaw
Oder
Brussels
BELG.
GERMANY
Bonn
LUX.
Rhine
Paris
Prague
CZECHOSLOVAKIA
FRANCE
Berne
SWITZ.
Vienna
AUSTRIA
Budapest
HUNGARY
Danube
RU
Belgrade
YUGOSLAVIA
PORTUGAL
Andorra
Lisbon
Madrid
SPAIN
CORSICA
(Fr.)
ITALY
Rome
Tirana
ALB.
Balearic Islands
(Span.)
SARDINIA
(It.)
Corfu
(Gr.)
GREE
Tangier
Gibraltar
(Br.)
MEDITERRANEAN
SICILY
(It.)
Malta
(Br.)
MOROCCO
ALGERIA
(Fr.)
TUNISIA
KOTSCHAR

EUROPE
= 1962 =
CEAN
PETSAMO
Archangel
Leningrad
UNION OF SOVIET SOCIALIST REPUBLICS
Moscow
Dvina R.
Don R.
Kiev
Donetz R.
Volga R.
Dnieper R.
ARAL SEA
CASPIAN SEA
Baku
BLACK SEA
Ardahan
Kars
Ankara
TURKEY
IRAN
SYRIA
IRAQ
CYPRUS
LEBANON
Athens
CRETE (Gr.)
Dodecanese Is. (Gr.)
SEA

46

The European Community

THE STIMULUS TO EUROPEAN UNITY

The ideal of a unified Europe is as ancient as the demise of the universal state of Rome. For centuries, political publicists have urged Europe's leaders to restore the unity of law and authority to the war-ravaged continent. Humanitarian appeals to end war and establish perpetual peace in Europe were never seriously considered by European princes and politicians. The movement to unify the states of western Europe gathered force after World War II because it served the power and status interests of the European elites. The idealism that accompanied the diplomacy of European union has served as an ideological garnish to win popular consensus for the project of federalizing the states of western Europe.

What were the conditions that prompted the hard-headed statesmen of western Europe to formulate the goal of federation and to devise as steps to its creation the establishment of a series of supranational institutions endowed with far-reaching administrative powers? The statesmen of postwar western Europe faced an appalling situation of economic breakdown, social disunity, and political unrest. Belief in the traditional value system of private property and capitalism was at low ebb and revolution was latent. The upper- and middle-class elites no longer commanded the deference of the poorer classes, who were undergoing rapid conversion to Socialist ideals. In 1945, all of Europe seemed to be heading toward a revolution in social relations, political leadership, and institutions.

The economic vitality of European capitalism had been sapped by the depression and the war. Most of the productive plant in industry was destroyed, damaged, or badly deteriorated. Huge amounts of new equipment were required before the factories and farms could again produce the goods for even minimal consumption needs. Capital to finance the construction of the European economy had to be acquired by means of austerity programs at home and loans from abroad. Imports of raw materials and foodstuffs had to be financed before the wheels of industry and agriculture could be set in high gear. Europe was devoid of goods to trade and of foreign exchange. Instead of finding comfort from their colonies, the colonial powers were forced to expend their fragile resources in a futile effort to preserve their overseas empires from the pressures of national liberation.

Caught between the impending threat of social upheaval at home and colonial rebellion abroad, and lacking the military power, the political prestige, and the economic resources to restore health to their national economies, Europe's statesmen turned in desperation to the United States for help. The United States financed UNRRA and various interim aid programs and provided large-scale loans as immediate methods of succor to western Europe. Rising demands for economic assistance from Europe and the prospect that the aid programs and loans might become a permanent economic crutch for the Europeans and a burdensome drain on American resources prompted the United States to formulate the European Recovery Program in 1947. The United States agreed to supply the economies of the European countries with the capital goods and resources necessary for their rehabilitation as a donation of the American people in the interest of healing the ravages of the war and preventing the seeds of future war from being sown.

Among the conditions that the United States prescribed to the recipients of its largesse were that they work out in concert an acceptable program to utilize American supplies and that they form a permanent economic organization to harmonize their economic policies, maximize their exchanges, and draw their economies together into a multilateral free-market structure. It was the hope of the United States to regenerate the vitality of European capitalism. If the formerly self-contained economies of the European states could be joined in a multilateral market economy, the free movement of goods, capital, and labor could be expected to release vast competitive powers and generate tremendous initiative. The profit system of incentives could be employed in a vast market of three hundred million persons to rationalize production and distribution in emulation of the American experiment with free enterprise. It was the belief and hope of American policy makers that Europe's economic malaise might be remedied by amalgamating the several national economies into a larger, more coordinated economic system. The cooperative efforts that the United States offered to underwrite in order to stimulate the economic recovery of Europe constituted the first serious impulse toward the creation of common institutions on that continent.

The second propulsive influence in the direction of European union was the political threat of communism and the military awe of Soviet power that were undermining the viability of the European states. The feeling of national insecurity was very acute throughout western Europe, particularly after the Communist coup in Czechoslovakia in February, 1948. In Greece, the Communist guerrillas were waging open warfare against the monarchy. The presence of preponderant Soviet military forces in central Europe and the slender line of American and British forces generated fears among European statesmen that Stalin might order the Communist parties and the Soviet Armed Forces into coordinated action to conquer all of Europe.

The immediate reaction of the insecure governments of western Europe was to expel all Communists from positions of power and to seek American commitments to buttress their defenses. Truman's containment pronouncements were the first indication that the United States had reversed its historic peacetime policy of non-alignment in world politics and that it intended to oppose the Soviet bid for world hegemony. In order to spur the United States to ally itself formally with western Europe, Britain, France, and the three Benelux countries concluded the Brussels Pact early in 1948. This alliance elicited a promise of unqualified American military assistance and was the nucleus about which NATO was formed in 1949.

A third factor to spur the unification of western Europe was the importance of rehabilitating conquered and subjugated Germany into a reliable ally. It was not the first time in European history that a defeated power had to be raised to its feet in order to check the expansionism of one of the members of the victorious coalition. As the Western powers set about to reconstruct a viable balance of power system in Europe, it suddenly became obvious that German collaboration was essential to NATO. By wedding fifty million Germans to the Western coalition, the only dangerous vacuum of power in Europe would be eliminated, and an important accretion of power could be obtained. The price that the Germans demanded was high. They wanted the prompt restoration of independence, substantial if not complete sovereignty, a diplomatic pledge to assist Germany in the recovery of her prewar frontiers, and massive economic assistance to restore the German economy. The Ruhr and the Saar would have to be handed back to Germany, and the restraints on German power removed—both measures bound to encounter French opposition.

The idea of a union of western European states to contain German nationalism and check the resurgence of authoritarianism and militarism helped to disarm French suspicions and fears of their neighbor. By placing

Germany under the wraps of a supranational authority, she might be guided toward democratic institutions, purged of her dreams of European hegemony, and transformed into a loyal partner of the Western coalition. Western European union provided an institutional device through which a powerful German state could be restored to help prop up the balance of power without endangering the vital interests of France.

Perhaps the most persuasive argument in support of western European unity is the appeal among Europeans for their return to great-power status and influence in the world. The demise of Europe as the center of world power is largely the consequence of the concentration of vaster power in the hands of the superpowers. The United States and the Soviet Union have dwarfed the individual states of Europe to such an extent that these once proud powers have been reduced individually to small-power status in the world. They have been stripped of imperial status in great measure because both the United States and the Soviet Union have encouraged their colonies to rebel. The states of Europe have no power individually to defend their vital national interests except as dependencies of either the United States or the U.S.S.R.

Despite their admiration for the United States, the Europeans are extremely sensitive to the fact that they must depend upon American power and goodwill for their national survival. They find it galling not to be masters of their own destinies. National inferiority in terms of power has deprived the European states of equal partnership status in the Western coalition and made NATO essentially an American institution with European associates. The decline of national power has damaged the prestige of the Europeans, undermined their prosperity, endangered their morale and internal unity, and sapped their vitality as nations. What is the likely future of western Europe under permanent conditions of bipolarity in the world? Most politically conscious Europeans see either total Americanization of their way of life at the end of this process or a violent end of their civilization from the clash of interests between the United States and the Soviet Union. To arrest this course of development toward national extinction, some Europeans propose a union of three hundred million persons comprising the nations that lie outside the Soviet orbit. Such a union of European states, if welded together by federal ties, could become an independent superpower. It would be able to strengthen the peace of the world by serving as a balancer between the United States and the Soviet Union. It could then also become an independent force of attraction for the underdeveloped nations of the world and arrest the extension of bipolarity to the continents of Asia, Africa, and now Latin America.

American interest in promoting greater unity among the western Europeans has been motivated by a desire to increase their contribution to NATO and strengthen the internal cohesion of the Western alliance.

Western European rivalries could seriously endanger the strength of NATO and Balkanize Europe, thus re-establishing a dangerous power vacuum and loosening a competitive struggle for the repartition of Europe between the United States and the Soviet Union. The United States has sought to eliminate the traditional rivalries of western Europeans by encouraging their efforts to unite in order to make western Europe a secure bulwark against the further advance of Soviet influence and power.

Added to the weighty political purposes are the economic goals of European unity. The most significant economic objective of the supranational community experiment that has taken place in western Europe has been the creation of the Common Market. A Common Market to free the movement of goods, services, capital, and labor from legal barriers and discrimination between nations means that a competitive market economy might be created in western Europe. By aiming at the removal of all national trade barriers and personal impediments, it is hoped that Europeans will be able to utilize their existing resources more economically. This should help to increase labor efficiency, reduce production costs, and increase wealth and living standards. By achieving optimum utilization of their available resources and greater productivity, the countries of the Common Market should be able to fulfill the rising level of expectations of their citizens, particularly the lower-income groups that have been attracted to communism, without having to destroy the capitalistic system or uproot private property. It might thus be possible to win back the loyalty and deference of millions of underprivileged western Europeans to traditional values and institutions and restore their faith in the liberal conservative elites that have emanated from the upper and middle classes.

There can be little question but that an economic union of western European countries will stimulate capital investments in the more efficient mass production enterprises and that submarginal enterprises will be eliminated. This will mean better utilization of capital resources and greater labor efficiency, which is still less than half as efficient as American labor when averaged out. Lower costs and more competition will result in reduced prices and expanded consumption. As market demand rises, production will expand and more capital and labor will be required. The stimulus to ever greater consumption will in turn stimulate more investment, output, and employment. Competitive pricing of European goods and services will also expand external demand for exports from Europe and provide the solution to postwar Europe's exchange problems. The actual results of the initial phase of Common Market economics have proved extremely successful. Employment and consumption have risen sharply, and European monetary reserves have increased to such an extent that Europeans have again become creditors in the world of trade.

Economic integration of the national economies of western Europe will cause many social problems, and measures will be required to protect displaced workers and their families from hardship and suffering. Vocational retraining programs will require large outlays of funds as will low-cost housing facilities and relocation of workers' families. Social discrimination will create tensions as migrant workers and their families are shifted from labor-saturated areas to labor-deficient areas. The rationalization of industry and commerce and the industrialization of agriculture will release a vast horde of persons from poorly paid forms of employment and increase unemployment. Millions of Italians will press into northern Europe in search of jobs and cause social tensions. Many lower middle-class persons will face a loss of status and security as the myriad of small retail shops are forced to give way to chain stores. The phenomenon of cutthroat job competition may restore conditions favorable to capital investments, industrial rationalization, export trade, and monetary stability. However, it may not be easy to reconcile with the aspirations and expectations of the working class or the declassed lower levels of the old middle class. Substantial amounts of wealth will have to be spent by the governments on social welfare programs until the transition to full employment can be carried through if the appeal of communism is to be contained among the workers and if neofascism is to be forestalled among the declassed.

European economic unity is designed to do more than raise living standards. While this is the major goal of the Common Market experiment, the governments of the European Community have other broader aims in mind as well. There is a strong desire to make western Europe more self-sufficient so that the loss of national colonies will not cause irreparable dislocations of trade requirements. Economic union is viewed as a means to improve the competitive quality of European goods in international trade and draw western Europe more firmly into the Western trade bloc. Americans hope that this will lead to the establishment of a multilateral free market throughout the non-Communist world and cement an interdependent community of interests. This should strengthen the cohesion of the alliance system of the Western bloc. Another consequence of rising European prosperity should be the development of an effective partnership among the European Community, the British Commonwealth, and the United States in funneling capital for developmental purposes into the emergent nations and the capital deficient countries to save them from more costly forms of experimentation and from Soviet influence. Finally, the success of economic integration is calculated to disarm all effective opposition to the projected federation or political community of European states. If cooperation and limited centralization of authority can produce lasting economic benefits, think what might be accomplished by a federal state of western Europe.

By placing the nations and governments under a common political authority, there should be greater assurance of compliance with Community interests and policies by the national authorities. The Community agencies would have more adequate instruments of enforcement at their disposal. Evasion of responsibilities and obligations could be corrected. Federal organs of government based on popular suffrage and direct representation could be expected to develop a unitary outlook in support of social legislation, the protection of consumer interests, and the elimination of inequalities. A political community would be capable of enforcing individual rights and liberties more effectively than certain national governments. Such a positive role for the political community is particularly attractive to organized labor, which would like to mold the evolving European Community into a social welfare state. The votaries of laissez faire are likewise politically oriented toward a federal state structure in western Europe because they believe that it would provide more secure defenses to private property, capital investments, and free enterprise than certain national states would.

The decision of the six countries (France, West Germany, Italy, and the Benelux trio) to form an integrated Community without Britain made possible the experiment in supranational institutions. Had the six listened to the British, a much looser and less effective form of cooperative association might have been attempted. Now, Britain and the other nations of the European Free Trade Area (EFTA) are being forced to seek membership in the stronger European Community market. Whether this enlargement of the European Community will hasten the process of political centralization of authority under a federal power structure or delay it remains to be seen.

EUROPEAN INSTITUTIONS

Of the numerous international organizations that have functioned in western Europe to promote cooperation since the end of World War II, only a few are included in this account. These are the Council of Europe, the Western Union, the European Coal and Steel Community, the European Economic Community, and the European Community for Atomic Energy. Other important organizations operating in western Europe, such as NATO and the recently established Organization for Economic Cooperation and Development (OECD), are not discussed because they represent the larger Atlantic community of interests with the United States and Canada and are extra-European in their scope. The Organization for European Economic Cooperation (OEEC) is not discussed because it was essentially also an instrument of Atlantic cooperation and has been succeeded by the OECD. The European Free Trade Area (EFTA) is not included either since it is a loose association of states pledged to certain reciprocal policies that seem to be headed toward a merger into the European Community. There is no mention of the many technical agencies that operate in western Europe to assist and coordinate national policies in economic, social, and cultural fields of endeavor, since they are not engaged in making policy and lack the quality of political institutions. The five European institutions that have been selected for consideration here are the principal examples of the practical achievements toward the goal of a United States of Europe that have been made since the end of World War II. See Figure 46–1 for the structure of the European Community.

THE COUNCIL OF EUROPE

The drive behind the creation of a European union was launched in 1946 by Winston Churchill. His proposal that a "Council of Europe" be formed gave impetus to the efforts of the pressure groups that were agitating for the unification of Europe. The Brussels Treaty states (Britain, France, Belgium, The Netherlands, and Luxembourg) sponsored a conference of ambassadors in 1949 to which Norway, Sweden, Denmark, Ireland, and Italy sent representatives. The product of this conference was the Statute of the Council of Europe, which was signed on May 5, 1949. The original ten signatory states (mentioned above) have since been joined by Greece, Iceland, Turkey, West Germany, and Austria.

The Statute of the Council of Europe restricts membership to the states of Europe that adhere to the rule of law and respect the basic human rights and fundamental freedoms of democratic society. States that seek membership in the organization must first be invited to adhere to the Statute by vote of two-thirds or more of the members acting through the Committee of Ministers. An indication of what is expected of member states was set forth in 1950 when the Council of Europe adopted the European Convention of Human Rights. A protocol to the convention was added in 1952 to make more explicit the ideals that the Council of Europe intends to promote.

The aims of the Council of Europe are to promote greater cooperation between the states of Europe by inducing their governments to further the ideals of freedom and democracy and to work for economic and social progress. The Council of Europe has no independent legislative prerogatives, but it is empowered to draw up treaties and conventions for adoption by the member states. Among its advisory functions are the recommendation of common policies on all matters except national defense. The Council of Europe supplies its members with a friendly forum where criticism of national policy may be made freely and where sugges-

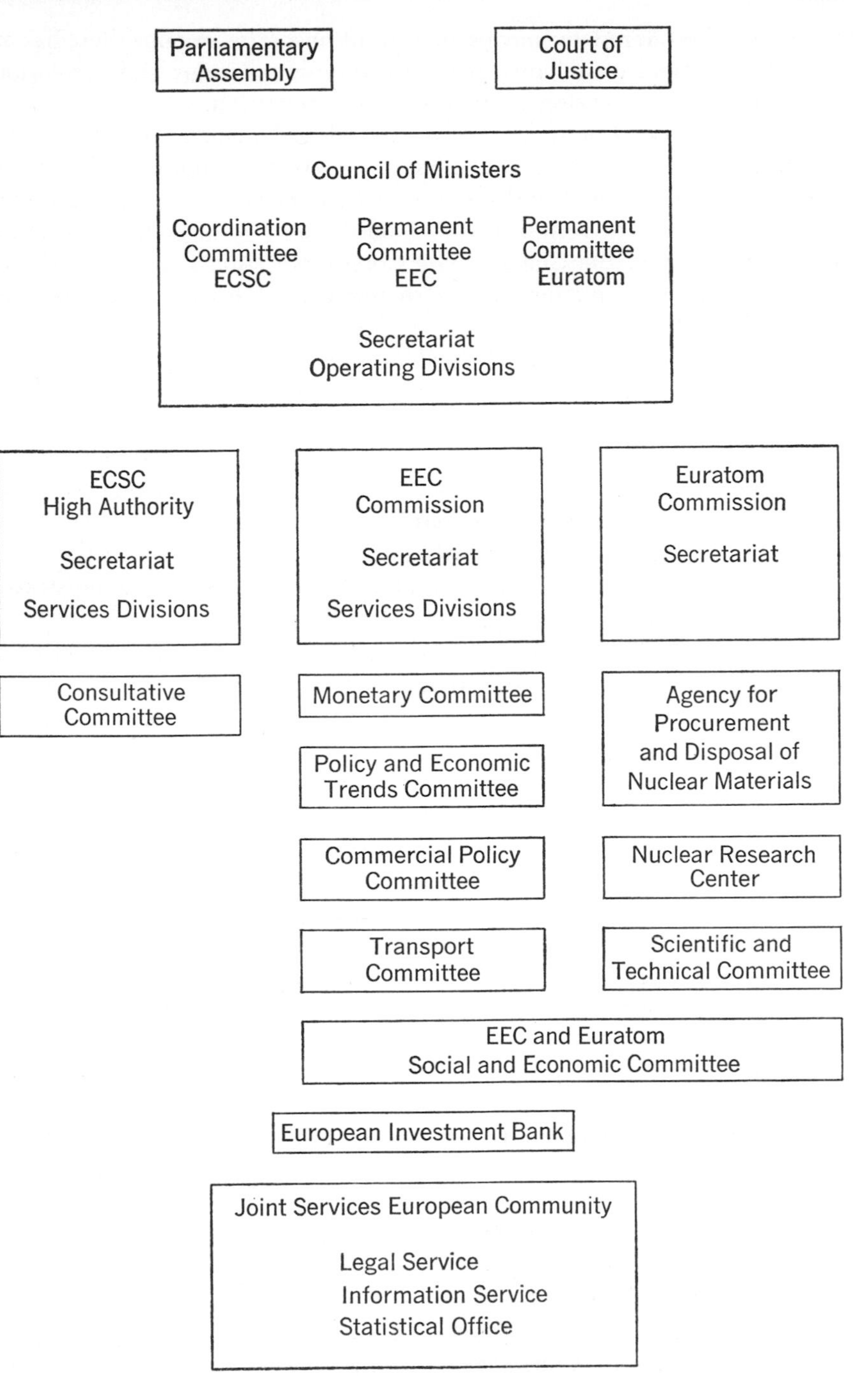

Figure 46–1. Structure of the European Community.

tions may be offered by means of resolutions. The organization has no power to compel compliance with its recommendations and resolutions except through suspension of membership or expulsion.

The Council of Europe functions through a Committee of Ministers, a Consultative Assembly, a Commission of Human Rights, a European Court of Human Rights, and a secretariat. All decision-making powers of the organization are vested in the Committee of Ministers, which is the executive organ of the Council. The Committee adopts treaties and conventions, makes recommendations to member states, and verifies compliance by the governments with their legal obligations. It also passes on the eligibility of new members and applies the sanctions of suspension and expulsion to members. The Committee of Ministers consists of one minister delegate from each member state. He is generally the Foreign Minister or Deputy Foreign Minister, although other Cabinet officials sometimes represent their governments in this capacity. Decisions by the Committee of Ministers are by unanimity on some items of business. In other cases, they are by two-thirds of the membership; or in the interpretation of the rules of procedure and the financial and administrative regulations, by simple majority.

The Consultative Assembly of the Council of Europe is competent to discuss any matter except questions of defense policy. It may compile reports and make recommendations to the Committee of Ministers containing suggestions and criticisms for transmission to member governments. It may ask for information or explanations from the Committee of Ministers or any member of this body. The Consultative Assembly also debates questions and makes recommendations to the Committee of Ministers on the latter's request. Representation in the Consultative Assembly is fixed by the Statute. The larger states have eighteen seats and the smallest state has three seats. The representatives to the Consultative Assembly are appointed by the national governments in accordance with the wishes of their legislatures. Most of the representatives are members of national legislatures. However, they must not hold ministerial positions. All political parties are represented except the Communists and the neo-Fascists.

Sessions are held annually for one month unless the Committee of Ministers authorizes an extension. The agenda is prepared by the Assembly's Bureau, which consists of the president and seven vice-presidents. After preliminary debate, matters are referred to a permanent committee by a two-thirds vote. There are eleven permanent committees: political, economic, social, legal, cultural, rules, agriculture, local authorities, nonmember states, budget, and population and refugees. Special committees may also be formed. The committees compile reports on matters that have been referred to them for presentation to the plenary Assembly. A Standing Committee composed of the officers of the Bureau, the chairmen of the permanent committees, and other members representing gographic areas and parties acts as coordinator between the committees and the Assembly. The committees conduct their work between sessions of the Assembly. They may utilize the services of specialists from the secretariat, other international agencies, or independent consultants. A Joint Committee of members of the Assembly and the Committee of Ministers may be formed by the president of the Assembly to coordinate action between the Assembly and the Committee of Ministers.

The secretariat serves the Committee of Ministers and the Consultative Assembly. It is divided into five directorates: political, research, human rights, press and information, administration; three departments: legal, external, general services; and two offices—one for the Assembly clerk and one for the secretary-general. The secretary-general and his deputy are elected by the Assembly on nomination of the Committee of Ministers. The staff is professionally recruited from competent nationals of the member states.

The Commission on Human Rights consists of a national of each of the countries that have ratified the Convention on Human Rights and its protocol. The Committee of Ministers selects the individuals who serve on the Commission from lists submitted by the national delegations to the Consultative Assembly. The Commission investigates alleged breaches of the Convention or its protocol by the government of any signatory state. It attempts to remove the breach through the mediation of a subcommission. Should this fail, the Commission reports its findings to the Committee of Ministers for further action.

The European Court of Human Rights adjudicates controversies that are referred to it by the Committee of Ministers involving alleged breaches of the Convention and Protocol on Human Rights. On it are a national of each signatory state, selected in the same manner as the members of the Commission. The Court has jurisdiction only where the state concerned has agreed in advance to submit to its authority. Cases are heard by a panel of seven judges, one of whom is a national of the respondent state, while the others are selected by lot.

While the Council of Europe is essentially an intergovernmental organization designed to promote the greater unity and cooperation between the member states, it contains *in nuce* the organs of a supranational confederation. The Consultative Assembly is a rudimentary parliament representing the national parliamentary groups (other than Communists and neo-Fascists) and indirectly the electorates. The Commission and Court that are attached to the Council of Europe have little more than moral authority, but they constitute the first step in the direction of a uniform conception of the rule of law in Europe.

THE WESTERN EUROPEAN UNION

Western European Union (WEU) is the organization for defense planning and weapons control of the United Kingdom, France, West Germany, Italy, and the three Benelux countries. It was established in pursuance of four protocols concluded in 1954 and 1955 by the seven governments and represents an enlargement of the Brussels Treaty Organization of 1947. This organization was devised as a substitute for the abortive European Defense Community. Its main purpose was to enable West Germany to be made eligible for full membership in NATO by placing limitations on future German military power and vesting control powers in this supranational organization. As further assurance to France, the United Kingdom assumed a permanent obligation to maintain the equivalent of four combat divisions on the continent.

West Germany is not permitted to produce atomic, biological, or chemical weapons; guided missiles; large warships; or heavy bombers without the express consent of two-thirds of the members of the WEU Council. An Agency for the Control of Armaments was created to enforce these restrictions through the exercise of inspection powers. The organization also aims to achieve standardization of weapons. It has the task of discussing any aspect of defense policy affecting the members and to assist in coordinating military planning. Its major organs, the Council and the Assembly, are empowered to consider any political or other general problems affecting the goal of European unity and to make recommendations to the governments of the member states concerning their further integration.

The decision-making organ of the Western European Union is the Council, which consists of the Foreign Ministers or the ambassadors of the seven member states. Some of its decisions require unanimous agreement, while others are made by either a two-thirds or simple majority vote. The member states are bound by the protocols to submit in good faith to the decisions of the Council. The seat of the Council is in London.

The Assembly of the WEU consists of parliamentary delegates from the member countries. They are the same persons who serve as representatives to the Council of Europe's Consultative Assembly, since the meetings of both organizations are held in Strasbourg. The WEU Assembly meets twice a year and has a small administrative staff to assist it. The Assembly elects a Bureau of officers (the president and six vice-presidents), a Presidential Committee (the officers and chairmen of the permanent committees), and four permanent committees: defense and armaments, general affairs, budget and administration, and rules and privileges. Coordination between the Assembly and the Council is achieved through a joint meeting between the Presidential Committee and the Council of Ministers.

The secretariat of the WEU is divided into separate staffs that serve the Council in London and the Standing Armaments Committee and the Agency for the Control of Armaments in Paris. They are in theory subordinated to the secretary-general. The secretarial staff of the Assembly is under the authority of the Assembly clerk and operates on a separate budget.

The WEU has not developed a regional command structure for the armed forces of its members, nor has it formulated any defense policy. These organizational and technical matters have been delegated by the members to NATO.

THE EUROPEAN COAL AND STEEL COMMUNITY

The European Coal and Steel Community (ECSC) was established in 1951 by treaty between the governments of France, West Germany, Italy, and the three Benelux countries. It became operative in August, 1952. Unlike the many intergovernmental organizations that depend entirely upon national governments to execute their decisions, the ECSC has authority to enforce its decisions directly upon the individual subjects (both persons and corporations) of the six countries. Executive and administrative powers have been transferred from national officials to Community officials, and judicial review of Community acts has been vested in a Community court. Legislative powers are theoretically fixed by the Treaty. However, executive extensions of its scope through interpretation are possible by decision of the Council of Ministers. The ECSC represents a partial federalization of authority for the six member states. It is an experiment with federal institutions that is limited to one sector of the economy (coal and steel) and to certain social problems connected with that economic sector.

The major aim of the ECSC was to establish a common market for coal and steel within the territory of the six member countries. This was to be done by the gradual removal of all impediments and discriminatory practices involving the production and distribution of coal, coke, iron ore, scrap, pig iron, and steel. It meant the elimination of protective legislation, charges, quantitative restrictions, subsidies, monopolies, cartels, unfair transportation rates, as well as other devices that might impede competitive pricing of these products. Another aim was to provide capital loans to coal and steel industries for modernization and rationalization of production so that they might be able to survive in the competitive market. A third purpose was to improve living and working conditions among the labor force by supplying funds for the construction of low-cost housing, the retraining of displaced workers, the resettlement of workers' families, and the financing of unemployment compensation.

The object of the ECSC was to achieve lower prices for European coal and steel, expand market demand in the Community for these products, encourage exports, stimulate greater output and productivity, expand plant capacity and employment, and raise wages and profits. The marginal industries were to be assisted to survive competitive conditions, while the submarginal industries were to be closed. The workers and employees were to be assisted in finding new jobs and homes within the national territory or in other countries of the Community. To encourage labor migration, the member states concluded agreements that have facilitated movement across national frontiers, prohibited discrimination against foreign workers, and extended to non-nationals the benefits of social security legislation.

The ECSC functions through the following organs: the High Authority, the Council of Ministers, the Parliamentary Assembly (formerly the Common Assembly), the Court of Justice, and the Consultative Committee.

The High Authority is the executive and administrative organ of the European Coal and Steel Community. It consists of nine members who must be nationals of the states that form the Community, although not more than two must hold the nationality of any one state. Eight of the persons who form the High Authority are jointly appointed by at least five-sixths of the member states, while the ninth person is chosen by the first eight appointees and confirmed by the governments. The ninth member of the High Authority is selected by a majority of his eight colleagues. Members of the Authority normally serve the full term of six years. However, this term may be shortened by adoption of a vote of censure in the Parliamentary Assembly against the High Authority, since censure entails the resignation of all the members of the High Authority. Individual members of the High Authority are also subject to removal by decision of the Court of Justice of the European Community on petition of the Council of Ministers or of the High Authority. The ECSC Treaty also provides for the renewal of one-third of the High Authority every two years. This is accomplished by requiring the members to draw lots for a full term, a four-year term, or a two-year term whenever there is a complete turnover of the membership. Thereafter, the appointment of new members takes place every two years.

The president and two vice-presidents of the High Authority are designated from the membership by the governments every two years. A quorum on the High Authority is formed by five members; and all decisions, recommendations, and opinions are made by majority vote of those present. Meetings are held twice a week or oftener if necessary.

Preliminary deliberation of matters that require the attention of the High Authority is generally entrusted to one of the eight working groups to which the president assigns the members, each of whom serves on four working groups. The president of the High Authority directs the administrative staff of the secretariat, which is divided into services for press and information; personnel and administration; and into operating divisions such as economic, agreements and concentrations, finance, investment and productivity, market, production, labor problems, transport, statistics, external relations, and legal. The president is responsible for insuring that all decisions of the High Authority are properly executed.

The High Authority consults the Consultative Committee for opinions and advice on policy matters. The Consultative Committee is composed of representatives of national organizations of producers, consumers, and labor. A maximum of fifty-one persons are appointed by the Council of Ministers of the ECSC from the names recommended by the qualified national organizations. The High Authority is required to consult this body on certain matters before it makes decisions, and it may request advice on any other subject if it chooses. The opinions of the Consultative Committee are not binding.

The High Authority is required by the ECSC Treaty to enforce the obligations of the member states under the Treaty; formulate policy in pursuance of the aims and purposes of the ECSC; and issue directives, recommendations, and opinions to all enterprises whose operations fall under Community authority. It has the power to instruct governmental agencies of the member states to comply with its orders. The High Authority may impose fines upon enterprises and suspend certain payments to enterprises and governments. The courts of the member states are legally required to issue judicial orders of enforcement of the High Authority's fines unless the Court of Justice of the European Community should rule against the High Authority. Enterprises may appeal directly to the Court of Justice, as may the government of any member state. If the Court of Justice should uphold any order of the High Authority directed to a government and the latter should still refuse to comply, the High Authority may suspend payments to it. The High Authority may also invite the other governments of the Community to retaliate against the recalcitrant government. Should the violation of a government against the Community persist, the High Authority must refer the matter to the Council of Ministers for further persuasion or sanctions. The ECSC Treaty vests the High Authority with the power to levy a production tax on coal and steel producers for strictly revenue purposes. This taxing power has provided the High Authority with an independent source of revenue with which to initiate various social policies such as the construction of workers' housing.

The Council of Ministers of the ECSC consists of an officer of Cabinet rank from each of the member states. Meetings are held at the request of the High Authority or of a government. Monthly meetings are the rule. The Council of Ministers will generally hold its meetings jointly with the members of the High Authority. The voting procedures of the Council of Ministers are not uniform. Certain decisions require unanimous agreement, while other matters may be decided by a qualified majority. For example, whenever prior authorization by the Council of Ministers of the ECSC is required by the High Authority for the latter to act, the Council must vote by qualified majority. This qualified majority requires the consent of four ministers including either the French or the German minister; or should the French and German ministers vote together, the decision may be by a vote of three. The qualified voting procedure gives more weight to the French and German members of the Council because their countries are the major coal and steel producers of the Community.

Besides its power to confer or deny to the High Authority power to act on certain matters, the Council of Ministers of the ECSC may reverse some of the decisions already taken by the High Authority. Council disallowance of High Authority decisions requires the unanimous vote of all of the ministers. However, the Council of Ministers is not permitted to disallow specific items (i.e., item veto) or make modifications of such decisions of the High Authority. The Council of Ministers has only limited powers to initiate policy decisions, although it may make recommendations on such matters to the High Authority. Such recommendations are not legally binding, but they nevertheless carry great political weight. The role of the Council of Ministers of the ECSC is thus primarily one of checking the High Authority, not of directing it.

The Council of Ministers of the ECSC is assisted by two administrative bodies, a secretariat and a coordination committee. The secretariat is organized into divisions for general affairs, economic and financial affairs, legal affairs, exchange and commercial policy, and foreign economic policy. The coordination committee is staffed by senior civil servants from the ministries of the member states. These senior officers brief the ministers of the details and prepare reports and draft decisions for consideration by the Council.

The Court of Justice of the European Community serves the three sectors of the Community, viz., the ECSC, the EEC, and the Euratom. It was established by the ECSC Treaty with a total of seven judges. The judges are appointed by the governments of the member states jointly and by unanimous agreement. They serve for renewable terms of six years, with partial renewal taking place every three years. The president of the Court is selected by the judges themselves by majority vote, and he serves as presiding judge for three years. The Court is served by two advocates-general who are jointly selected by the governments of the member states. The Court has its own secretariat that is headed by the registrar.

The jurisdiction of the Court of Justice of the European Community may be invoked by the High Authority, the Council of Ministers, the government of any member state, producers' associations, and individual firms located within the territory of the Community and subject to the authority of the Community. The Court is competent to annual decisions of the High Authority and to award the payment of damages to appellants. It is also competent to annul decisions of the Council of Ministers and the Parliamentary Assembly on substantive or procedural grounds. Individual officers of the Community are personally liable to payment of damages in certain instances. The effect of Court annulment of decisions of the High Authority, the Council of Ministers, or the Parliamentary Assembly is to deprive these measures of legal validity.

The Parliamentary Assembly also serves the three sectors of the European Community. Representation in the Assembly is fixed by the Treaty of the ECSC. France, West Germany, and Italy are each allowed thirty-six seats; while Belgium and The Netherlands each occupy fourteen seats, and Luxembourg fills only six seats. Until the member states agree on the procedure for the direct election of representatives to the Parliamentary Assembly, the representatives will continue to be chosen by the national Parliaments annually. Each national Parliament prescribes the qualifications and procedures for the selection of its representatives to the European Parliamentary Assembly. Parties whose views toward the European Community have been hostile or unfriendly have generally been excluded from representation. As a result of this political discrimination, the membership of the European Parliamentary Assembly has not been representative of the electorates of the member nations, particularly of Italy and France. Individual representatives organize by political party instead of by nationality in the Assembly. Christian Democrats have invariably dominated the membership of the Parliamentary Assembly.

The Parliamentary Assembly is required to meet at least once every year in order to hear and vote for or against the report of the High Authority. Extraordinary sessions may be convoked by the president of the Assembly at the request of the High Authority, the Council of Ministers, or a majority of the representatives. In practice, the Assembly has met four times each year, dividing its session as follows: a brief meeting in the autumn to organize for business, a winter meeting to adopt its own legislative budget, a meeting in May for preliminary discussion of the High Authority's report, and a meeting in June for detailed examination and debate of the report.

The Assembly elects its own officers (a president and five vice-presidents) who form the Assembly Bureau. Each of the member states must be represented on the Bureau. The usual political composition of the

Bureau has been three Christian Democrats, two Socialists, and one Liberal.

The Parliamentary Assembly forms its own standing and special committees for each of the three sectors of the Community. The ECSC standing or permanent committees of the Assembly include the following: common market, investment, social affairs, political affairs, transport, accountancy, rules, industrial safety, and the working group. Other standing committees have been formed for the EEC and the Euratom. As a rule, a fixed ratio is followed in assigning the representatives to the committees by nationality, so that national representation on every committee is proportionally the same as it is in the Assembly.

The Parliamentary Assembly is served by its own permanent secretariat of Community employees. This secretariat is divided into various divisions such as committees, research and documentation, general services, and general administration, and into offices of control and coordination.

The principal function of the Parliamentary Assembly is to examine the annual report of the High Authority and vote approval or censure of it. A censure motion against the High Authority requires a vote of two-thirds of the representatives present. Should the High Authority be censured, it would have to resign. The possibility of *post facto* censure has caused the High Authority to respond to inquiries and suggestions from the committees of the Assembly and to questions from the representatives. The High Authority has developed the practice of keeping the Assembly informed of its policies by meeting with its committees and by appearing before its plenary meetings to listen to suggestions and to reply to criticism. On occasion, the Assembly as well as its committees have taken the initiative to propose important policies, such as the program for financing the construction of workers' apartments.

THE EUROPEAN ECONOMIC COMMUNITY

The European Economic Community (EEC) is a customs union in the making of the ECSC countries that became operative on January 1, 1958. The primary goal of the EEC is to unify the national markets of its member states by removing all barriers to the free flow of goods, services, capital investments, and labor. Its second aim is to establish a single and uniform set of regulations for trade with non-member countries. These objectives are to be achieved gradually and by stages over a period of from twelve to fifteen years. The EEC does not replace the ECSC. Regulation of the coal and steel sector of the European Community remains the responsibility of the ECSC.

Despite the fact that the EEC has not yet unified the national markets of the original six member states, its success in lowering internal tariffs and in removing other restrictions on internal commerce within the Community has stimulated trade tremendously among its members. The European Community has experienced a business boom that is attracting the interest of other European countries. The British and their partners in the European Free Trade Area are seeking admission to the European Economic Community.

The EEC shares with the ECSC the Parliamentary Assembly and the Court of Justice of the European Community. The Council of Ministers also serves both sectors of the Community, but it utilizes different subordinate administrative machinery in performing its functions, and its powers under the EEC Treaty are more extensive than under the ECSC Treaty. The executive organ of the EEC is entirely distinct from the ECSC High Authority and is called the Commission. The chief advisory body to the Council of Ministers and the Commission of the EEC is the Economic and Social Committee. Other advisory committees of the EEC are the Monetary Committee, the Policy and Economic Trends Committee, the Commercial Policy Committee, and the Transport Committee. Attached to the EEC as a specialized organ under the authority of the Council of Ministers is the European Investment Bank.

Basic policy decisions of the EEC are made by the Council of Ministers, not by the Commission. The Council of Ministers issues binding directives to the Commission on policy and sets the scope of administrative powers that are delegated to the Commission. The Council is the sole organ of the EEC that is competent to extend the powers and functions of the Community by interpretation of the EEC Treaty. Most of the significant decisions of the Council of Ministers under the EEC Treaty require the unanimous vote of the ministers, particularly during the earlier stages of transition to the fully integrated Common Market. An exception to the unanimity rule is followed by the Council when it considers proposals of the Commission. Such proposals may be adopted as policy by the Council by a qualified majority of twelve votes. For qualified voting, the ministers from Germany, France, and Italy each dispose of four votes; while the Belgian and Dutch ministers each possess two votes; and the minister of Luxembourg has one vote. On certain procedural matters, the Council of Ministers votes by simple majority of its members. The Council of Ministers meets regularly once every month and may be summoned by its chairman upon request of the Commission or any minister. The Council of Ministers is assisted on EEC matters by a committee of permanent representatives that is composed of senior civil servants from the member states. A secretariat, established originally by the ECSC Treaty to serve the Council of Ministers, also functions under the EEC.

The EEC Commission is formed of nine members who must be nationals of the states included in the European Community. Not more than two may hold the same nationality however. All nine commissioners are jointly selected by the governments of the member states for a term of four years. The president and the two vice-presidents of the Commission are chosen every two years from the commissioners by the governments of the member states. Individual commissioners are subject to removal by the Court of Justice for cause on petition by the Council of Ministers or by the Commission. The Commission is also required to resign in the event it is censured by the Parliamentary Assembly. All decisions by the Commission are made by majority vote.

Besides proposing policy matters to the Council of Ministers, the Commission of the EEC has certain independent powers of decision. It may authorize a government to apply certain safeguards in an emergency situation to resolve a balance of payments deficit or some serious economic problem. In such cases, the Commission fixes a time limit during which measures that are normally incompatible with membership in the Common Market may be applied. Such measures might include temporary restrictions on imports or subsidies to some group of producers or region. The Commission has no authority to issue binding orders to a government of a member state or to impose sanctions upon it in the event it should fail to observe its legal obligations under the EEC Treaty. It can only refer the matter to the Court of Justice.

The Court of Justice adjudicates legal disputes involving the Council of Ministers, the Commission, or the government of a member state. The jurisdiction of the Court may be invoked by either of these as well as by individuals and corporations. In contrast to the procedures prescribed by the ECSC Treaty concerning legal disputes between the High Authority and the government of a member state, the EEC Treaty requires the Commission to appeal to the Court for judicial enforcement of all governmental obligations. Governments of member states may sue one another before the Court of Justice. The Court has authority to annul all decisions of the Commission or the Council of Ministers except non-binding opinions and recommendations. The composition of the Court of Justice remains as prescribed by the ECSC Treaty.

The Parliamentary Assembly functions with the same representatives for the EEC as with the ECSC. Its powers under the two treaties are almost identical. The Assembly has the power to censure the Commission and force its resignation. The Assembly must be consulted by the Council of Ministers and by the Commission before these are empowered to promulgate certain decisions. However, the opinions of the Assembly on such matters are not legally binding. The committees of the Assembly may demand information and explanations from the Commission, and individual representatives of the Assembly may question members of the Commission. The Assembly has been authorized by the EEC Treaty to formulate a draft election law for the first direct election of its own membership by the voters of the member countries. This draft law is to be then approved by the Council of Ministers of the European Community and adopted by the governments of the member states. If and when the voters are permitted to elect representatives to the European Parliamentary Assembly, the latter is expected to gain prestige and influence in Community affairs. A directly elected Assembly that represented the European voters could be expected to demand considerably more legal powers than have been assigned to it by the existing treaties.

The Economic and Social Committee of the EEC is a consultative body of representatives from national organizations of producers, farmers, labor, businessmen, artisans, transport operators, the professions, and the general public. The Council of Ministers of the European Community is responsible for appointing the members of the Economic and Social Committee. It selects the most qualified persons from a list that is prepared by the governments of the member states and consults the Commission in making the appointments. Members of this advisory committee serve for a term of four years. France, West Germany, and Italy are each represented by twenty-four nationals, while Belgium and The Netherlands are assigned twelve apiece, and Luxembourg is allowed five seats on the Committee. The Economic and Social Committee elects its own officers and assigns its members to the working sections, which correspond to the major areas of activity of the EEC and the Euratom. Reports are presented by the Economic and Social Council on request to the Council of Ministers and to the Commission. Certain matters, such as agricultural, labor, and transport policy, require the previous advice of the Economic and Social Committee.

The EEC has established four specialized advisory committees to facilitate the work of the Council of Ministers and the Commission. These are the Monetary Committee, the Policy and Economic Trends Committee, the Commercial Policy Committee, and the Transport Committee. Each of these committees is staffed by experts from the member countries selected by the national governments. The Commission of the EEC designates two experts to serve on the fourteen-member Monetary Committee along with two from each national government. The Monetary Committee advises the Commission and the Council of Ministers on balance of payments problems, currency questions, and financial policies. The EEC Treaty also prescribes the establishment of an advisory committee to assist the Commission in negotiating agreements with foreign governments on tariff matters.

The European Investment Bank was established by a special protocol to the EEC Treaty. Its initial capitalization of one billion dollars has been subscribed by the member states in accordance with their national wealth. The Bank is permitted to raise additional financial resources by borrowing on the international capital market. The Bank is intended to provide loans and guaranties for developmental projects, modernization and conversion of enterprises, new enterprises, etc. The Board of Governors of the European Investment Bank is formed by the ministers of the Council of Ministers of the European Community. Acting as the Board of Governors of the Bank, the Council of Ministers appoints the Bank's Board of Directors on joint advice of the governments of the member states of the EEC and the Commission. General policy of the Bank is fixed by the Board of Governors. The latter makes decisions on such matters as increasing the capital subscription of the member states and dismissal of the Board of Directors. The twelve directors of the Bank (three French, German, and Italian, respectively; two from the Benelux nations; and one nominated by the Commission) act as a board of supervision over the Bank's Management Committee. The Board of Directors also approves all loans and guaranties as well as international borrowings proposed by the Management Committee. The latter consists of a chairman and two vice-chairmen that are appointed by the Board of Governors on nomination by the Board of Directors. The Management Committee proposes measures for adoption by the Board of Directors and executes the decisions of the latter. All Bank officials and employees are responsible to the chairman of the Management Committee.

The EEC Treaty established two funds that are administered by the Commission: a Development Fund for Overseas Territories and a Social Fund to retrain and resettle workers in the European Community. Most of the development funds were allocated by the Treaty to the Overseas Territories of France for the establishment of hospitals, vocational schools, and technical institutes, and also for economic development, viz., the construction of roads, etc. The EEC Commission was charged with responsibility for administering these funds. The Social Fund is to be administered by the Commission and an advisory body of governmental officials, union representatives, and delegates of employers' associations from the member countries. The Treaty limits the operation of the Social Fund through the period of transition to the fully integrated Common Market unless the Council of Ministers votes unanimously to continue it.

THE EUROPEAN ATOMIC ENERGY COMMUNITY

The European Atomic Energy Community (Euratom) is the third sector of the European Community. It became operative on January 1, 1958. Interest in an integrated program for the development of nuclear energy was prompted by a desire to ease the strain on western Europe's limited sources of fuels and hydroelectricity and to conserve foreign exchange. It was estimated that western Europe's import requirements for petroleum would impose a severe burden on available foreign exchange within a decade or two unless nuclear power were developed. The urgency has diminished somewhat as the result of the discovery of vast petroleum resources in the French Sahara and the expanded output of coal and gas. Nuclear generated electricity is still two and one-half times costlier to produce than conventional methods, but further research should make it commercially feasible in another decade or so. Western European planners foresee the importance of nuclear energy and are keen on developing it commercially as rapidly as possible. The Community approach to nuclear energy was logical in view of the costs of research and development.

The major purposes of Euratom are to promote research and training in the sciences related to the peaceful utilization of fissionable substances, to encourage investment projects in industries that utilize nuclear matter, to regulate the supply and distribution of these materials, to control their use, and to make available useful information on the utilization of nuclear energy. Euratom is not empowered by the Treaty of Rome to interfere in the national defense uses of fissionable materials, so the French are free to maintain a separate nuclear weapons program under their exclusive national control. Euratom is not designed to supplant national programs already under way for research, training, and development of nuclear energy for peaceful uses, but rather to supplement and coordinate such efforts.

Euratom has been vested with substantial authority and facilities to carry out its assigned role. Its primary organs are the Council of Ministers, the Commission, the Scientific and Technical Committee, the Commercial Agency for the Procurement and Disposal of Nuclear Materials, and a Joint Nuclear Research Center. Euratom utilizes the Parliamentary Assembly, the Court of Justice, and the Economic and Social Committee of the European Community.

The Council of Ministers of the European Community functions under the Euratom Treaty in much the same way as under the EEC Treaty. The unanimity rule is employed much less frequently, and decisions by qualified majority and simple majority are much more common. Unanimity of the ministers is required only to authorize extensions of the powers and functions of Euratom beyond those prescribed in the Treaty. Decisions that require the consent of the Council of Ministers are the adoption of new policies, the extension of Community functions, increases or modifications of the contributions required from the member states, agreements concluded with foreign governments, the establishment of joint enterprises, the adoption of research programs, the approval of public health regulations for industries employing fissionable materials, the adoption or amendment of the statute of the Agency for the Procurement and Disposal of Nuclear Materials, the fixing of prices for fissionable materials, and the issuance of directives to member states to exploit their available nuclear resources. The governments of the member states are obliged by the Treaty to adopt the necessary legislation to implement the decisions of the Council of Ministers and to provide Euratom with its financial requirements. The budgetary requirements of Euratom are determined by the Council of Ministers.

The Euratom Commission consists of five persons of different nationality from the member states. In practice, France, West Germany, and Italy are each represented; while the three Benelux countries share the remaining two seats. The commissioners of Euratom are appointed for a term of four years by joint agreement between the member governments. They are subject to removal for cause by the Court of Justice and may be forced to resign by a vote of censure passed by the Parliamentary Assembly. The president and single vice-president are selected by the governments of the member states every two years. The Euratom Commission adopts all of its decisions by majority vote.

The powers of the Euratom Commission are greater than those vested in the EEC Commission. The Euratom Commission is competent to decide on classifying information (including patents) related to nuclear research, on the dissemination of such data, on authorizing the sale and export of fissionable substances outside of the Community, on licensing imports of such matter, on allocations of financial support to companies engaged in prospecting for nuclear substances, on controlling the use of nuclear materials, on licensing the use of Community patent rights, on the establishment of training institutions, and on the issuance of instructions of the Joint Nuclear Research Center and the Agency for the Procurement and Disposal of Nuclear Weapons. All the remaining functions of the Euratom Commission require the approval of the Council of Ministers. The Commission is free to make policy proposals to the Council of Ministers.

The Commission carries out its functions largely through the Agency for the Procurement and Disposal of Nuclear Materials, the Nuclear Research Center, and such schools and institutes (including an institution of university level) as it may establish. It utilizes the Scientific and Technical Committee for expert advice and the Economic and Social Committee for general advice. The Commission maintains its own secretariat.

JOINT SERVICES

The three sectors of the European Community have combined their legal, statistical, and information services into a Joint Services operation. The European Community Information Service has established offices in the capital cities of many foreign countries, including the United States. Its function is to provide reliable information about the European Community and to promote its image abroad as well as within the Community nations. The Joint Services are part of the growing Community staff of supranational officials and employees.

SELECTED READING

BENOIT, EMILE. *Europe at Sixes and Sevens: The Common Market, the Free Trade Association, and the United States.* New York: Columbia University Press, 1961.

LISTER, LOUIS. *Europe's Coal and Steel Community.* New York: Twentieth Century Fund, 1960.

POLITICAL AND ECONOMIC PLANNING. *European Organisations.* London: George Allen & Unwin, Ltd., 1959.

ROBERTSON, A. H. *The Council of Europe.* New York: Frederick A. Praeger, Inc., 1956.

ZURCHER, ARNOLD J. *The Struggle to Unite Europe, 1940–1958.* New York: New York University Press, 1958.

Bibliography

Part I

POLITICS AND GOVERNMENT OF GREAT BRITAIN

General Works

AMERY, L. S. *Thoughts on the Constitution.* 2d ed. Fair Lawn, N.J.: Oxford University Press, 1953. An excellent introduction to British government with emphasis on the role of custom.

ANSON, SIR WILLIAM. *Law and Custom of the Constitution.* 2 vols. Fair Lawn, N.J.: Oxford University Press, 1935. A standard reference work.

BAGEHOT, WALTER. *The English Constitution.* World Classics ed. Fair Lawn, N.J.: Oxford University Press, 1933. A classic—still useful on the monarchy.

CHRIMES, S. B. *English Constitutional History.* 2d ed. Fair Lawn, N.J.: Oxford University Press, 1953. A short but valuable history.

DICEY, A. V. *Introduction to the Study of the Law of the Constitution.* 9th ed. New York: St. Martin's Press, Inc., 1939. A standard classic with emphasis upon the rule of law.

JENNINGS, SIR IVOR. *The British Constitution.* 3d ed. Cambridge: Cambridge University Press, 1950. One of the best standard texts.

———. *Cabinet Government.* 2d ed. Cambridge: Cambridge University Press, 1951. One of the best studies of the parliamentary system.

LASKI, HAROLD. *Parliamentary Government in England.* New York: The Viking Press, Inc., 1938. Written in Laski's neo-Marxist period, a good account from a particular point of view.

MATHIOT, A. *The British Political System.* Stanford, Calif.: Stanford University Press, 1958. An interesting and good account written by a Frenchman.

MORRISON, HERBERT. *Government and Parliament.* Fair Lawn, N.J.: Oxford University Press, 1954. A Labor party leader's examination of the parliamentary system.

STOUT, H. M. *British Government.* Fair Lawn, N.J.: Oxford University Press, 1953. One of the best texts.

WHEARE, K. C. *Government by Committee.* Fair Lawn, N.J.: Oxford University Press, 1953. An excellent account of the use of committees by the legislative and executive branches of government.

Chapter 1

BARKER, SIR ERNEST. (ed.). *The Character of England.* Fair Lawn, N.J.: Oxford University Press, 1948. A number of essays on the British people and their social characteristics.

COLE, G. D. H. *Studies in Class Structure.* London: Routledge & Kegan Paul, Ltd., 1956. A British Socialist scholar's thorough study of the class structure in Britain.

GLASS, D. V. (ed.). *Social Mobility in Britain.* London: Routledge & Kegan Paul, Ltd., 1954. A very good sociological study.
LEWIS, ROY and MAUDE, ANGUS. *The English Middle Classes.* New York: Alfred A. Knopf (a division of Random House, Inc.), 1950. One of the best studies of the British middle class.
MANLEY, G. *Climate and the British Scene.* London: William Collins Sons & Co., Ltd., 1952. A geographic study of Britain.
PEAR, T. H. *English Social Differences.* London: George Allen & Unwin, Ltd., 1955. An examination of the class structure—socioeconomic approach.
TREVELYAN, G. M. *English Social History.* New York: Longmans, Green & Co., Inc., 1942. A standard social history.

Chapter 2

BARKER, ERNEST. *Essays on Government.* Fair Lawn, N.J.: Oxford University Press, 1945. A delightful series of essays. Provides insight into the British system.
———. *Political Thought in England: 1848–1914.* 2d ed. Fair Lawn, N.J.: Oxford University Press, 1947. A concise account of leading political theorists of the latter part of the nineteenth century.
BURKE, EDMUND. *Burke's Politics.* New York: Alfred A. Knopf (a division of Random House, Inc.), 1949. Writings of the outstanding British conservative theorist.
COLE, G. D. H. *Fabian Socialism.* London: George Allen & Unwin, Ltd., 1943. A historical and analytical account of British socialism.
CROSSMAN, R. H. S. (ed.). *New Fabian Essays.* New York: Frederick A. Praeger, Inc., 1952. A series of essays by Fabian Socialists in which traditional Socialist principles are examined and new ones suggested.
DAVIDSON, W. L. *Political Thought in England: The Utilitarians from Bentham to J. S. Mill.* Fair Lawn, N.J.: Oxford University Press, 1947. An excellent short account of utilitarian thought.
HEARNSHAW, F. J. C. *Conservatism in England.* London: Macmillan & Co., Ltd., 1935. A critical evaluation of conservative thought.
HOGG, QUINTEN. *The Case for Conservatism.* Baltimore: Penguin Books, Inc., 1948. A contemporary conservative leader's interpretation of modern conservatism.
LASKI, HAROLD. *Political Thought in England: From Locke to Bentham.* Fair Lawn, N.J.: Oxford University Press, 1920. A good short analysis.
LOCKE, JOHN. *Of Civil Government.* New York: E. P. Dutton & Co., Inc., 1943. The best single work for Locke's political liberalism.
MILL, J. S. *Autobiography.* New York: Columbia University Press, 1948. Almost required reading for an understanding of the transitional period of British liberalism.
———. *On Liberty.* Fair Lawn, N.J.: Oxford University Press, 1944. The classic defense of individual freedom.
PELLING, HENRY. (ed.). *The Challenge of Socialism.* London: Adam and Charles Black, Ltd., 1954. Essays the effect of socialism on British society.
SAVASTANO, L. *Contemporary British Conservatism.* New York: Vantage Press, Inc., 1953. An excellent short treatise on modern conservatism.
STEPHENS, SIR LESLIE. *The English Utilitarians.* London: Peter Smith, 1900. An outstanding analysis of utilitarianism.

Chapter 3

ATTLEE, C. R. *The Labour Party in Perspective.* London: Victor Gollancz, Ltd., 1949. A Labor party leader's observations on the past and future of his party.
BAILEY, S. D. (ed.). *The British Party System.* London: Hansard Society, 1952. Essays on the organization and functions of the parties.
BOYD-CARPENTER, JOHN. *The Conservative Case.* London: Allan Wingate, Ltd., 1950. A Conservative presents his party's program.

COLE, G. D. H. A *History of the Labour Party from 1914.* London: Routledge & Kegan Paul, Ltd., 1948. A detailed history.

FINER, J. E. *Anonymous Empire: A Study of the Lobby in Great Britain.* London: Pall Mall Press, Ltd., 1958. One of the few good studies of pressure-group activity.

FYFE, H. H. *The British Liberal Party.* London: George Allen & Unwin, Ltd., 1928. An older study of the Liberal party when it was still a major party.

PELLING, H. M. *The Origins of the Labour Party.* London: Macmillan & Co., Ltd., 1954. An excellent historical study.

SLESSER, SIR HENRY. *A History of the Liberal Party.* London: Hutchinson & Co., Ltd., 1944. A good account of the development of the Liberal party.

STEWART, J. D. *British Pressure Groups: Their Role in Relation to the House of Commons.* Fair Lawn, N.J.: Oxford University Press, 1959. Examines the methods of pressure groups in Britain.

Chapter 4

BUTLER, D. E. *The British General Election of 1951.* London: Macmillan & Co., Ltd., 1952. An analysis of the 1951 election with detailed accounts of selected voting areas.

MACCALLUM, R. B., and READMAN, A. *The British General Election of 1945.* Fair Lawn, N.J.: Oxford University Press, 1945. Another in the series above on elections.

NICHOLAS, H. G. *The British General Election of 1950.* London: Macmillan & Co., Ltd., 1951. Another in the series above.

PARKER, F. R. *The Powers, Duties and Liabilities of an Election Agent.* London: Charles Knight & Co., 1950. An excellent account.

Chapter 5

CAMPION, LORD. (ed.). *Parliament: A Survey.* London: George Allen & Unwin, Ltd., 1952. Essays on the nature and function of Parliament.

HERBERT, SIR A. P. *Independent Member.* New York: Doubleday & Co., Inc., 1951. An interesting account of the role of the independent member.

RICHARDS, P. G. *Honourable Members.* New York: Frederick A. Praeger, Inc., 1959. One of the few studies of the composition of the House of Commons and the role of the individual member.

WHEARE, K. C. *Government by Committee.* Fair Lawn, N.J.: Oxford University Press, 1955. Excellent for the description of committees and their functions.

Chapter 6

ALLEN, C. K. *Law and Orders.* London: Stevens & Sons, Ltd., 1945. A critical study of the nature and extent of delegated legislation.

BEER, S. H. *Treasury Control.* Fair Lawn, N.J.: Oxford University Press, 1956. An excellent account of the Treasury as a coordinating agency.

DIMONT, C. *British Monarchy.* New York: The Macmillan Co., 1956. A good study of the role of the monarch.

HEWART, LORD. *The New Despotism.* New ed. London: Ernest Benn, Ltd., 1945. An older criticism of the increased power of bureaucracy.

SCHWARTZ, BERNARD. *Law and the Executive in Britain.* New York: New York University Press, 1949. A good study written by an American critic of delegated legislation.

Chapter 7

BRIDGES, SIR EDWARD. *Portrait of a Profession.* Cambridge: Cambridge University Press, 1950. A public servant looks at his own profession.

BRITTAIN, SIR HERBERT. *The British Budgetary System.* London: Macmillan & Co., Ltd., 1960. One of the few works on the budget system.

Finer, S. E. *A Primer of Public Administration.* London: Frederick Muller, Ltd., 1950. An excellent introduction to British administration.

GREAVES, H. R. G. *The Civil Service in the Changing State.* London: George H. Harrap & Co., Ltd., 1948. Emphasis upon the role of the civil servant in the welfare state.

HOULDSWORTH, SIR HUBERT, *et al. Efficiency in the Nationalized Industries.* London: George Allen & Unwin, Ltd., 1952. Critical analysis of nationalization.

ROBSON, W. A. (ed.). *The Civil Service in Britain and France.* New York: The Macmillan Co., 1956. A good comparative study.

ROYAL COMMISSION. *Report on the Civil Service, 1953–55.* London: Her Majesty's Stationery Office, 1955. The definitive study of the problems of the civil service.

WHITE, L. D. *Whitley Councils in the British Civil Service.* Chicago: University of Chicago Press, 1933. A good study by an American scholar.

Chapter 8

BURTON, J. H. *Local Rates.* London: Stevens & Sons, Ltd., 1950. An excellent study on taxation.

CHESTER, D. N. *Central and Local Government.* London: Macmillan & Co., Ltd., 1951. As the title suggests, a study of the relationship of the central government to the local levels.

CLARKE, J. J. *A History of Local Government.* London: Herbert Jenkins, Ltd., 1955. Good for the historical development of local government.

COHEN, E. W. *Autonomy and Delegation in County Government.* London: Institute of Public Administration, 1953. Examination of the extent of devolution.

FINER, HERMAN. *English Local Government.* 4th ed. London: Methuen & Co., Ltd., 1950. A standard text.

HART, W. O. *Introduction to the Law of Local Government and Administration.* 6th ed. London: Butterworth & Co., Ltd., 1957. Standard text with emphasis on administrative law.

ROBSON, W. A. *The Government and Misgovernment of London.* 2d ed. London: Macmillan & Co., Ltd., 1958. An excellent study.

SCHOFIELD, A. N. *Local Government Elections.* 3d ed. London: Shaw & Sons, Ltd., 1954. A very good study of local election law and procedure.

WARREN, J. H. *The Local Government Service.* London: George Allen & Unwin, Ltd., 1952. A good account of the civil service at the local level.

Chapter 9

AMOS, SIR MAURICE. *British Criminal Justice.* New York: Longmans, Green & Co., Ltd., 1957. A good account of criminal courts and procedures.

DENNING, LORD. *Freedom under Law.* London: Stevens & Sons, Ltd., 1949. A study of the liberties of the individual under English law.

GILES, F. T. *The Criminal Law.* Baltimore: Penguin Books, Inc., 1954. An excellent introduction to English criminal law and criminal courts.

HANBURY, H. G. *English Courts of Law.* 2d ed. Fair Lawn, N.J.: Oxford University Press, 1953. A standard text.

Part II

POLITICS AND GOVERNMENT OF FRANCE

General Works

The *Journal officiel de la République francaise* contains the parliamentary debates, laws, decrees, and administrative annexes of the Republic. *L'Année politique* lists chronologically events in national political life and useful documents. Many professional reviews contain specialized articles—important among these are the *Revue française de science politique, Politique étrangère, Revue du droit publique et des science, Droit social,* and the *Revue administrative. L'Express and France-Observateur* are weekly news periodicals and organs of social criticism. *L'Express* reflects the welfare orientation of Mendès-France. *France-Observateur*'s position is classical Left. Although the quality of *L'Express* varies, Siné's cartoons are gems of political expression. Despite its political sensationalism during the past two years, *France-Observateur* has evolved into a more serious, though not less partisan, journal of Left expression. Many popular journals contain social and political criticism. Among the most famous are *L'Esprit,* of Catholic Left orientation, and *Les temps modernes.* The best source of daily information is by far *Le Monde,* the great newspaper of the metropole whose staff is without parallel. Jacques Fauvet's articles are rich with insights, and much is to be said for the contributions of Pierre Viansson-Ponté and Maurice Duverger (even if the latter's articles reflect his anxiousness to orient the notables of the regime on "the right road"). The daily *Le Figaro* has a large budget and a staff that is less than that of *Le Monde's;* nevertheless, it does have Raymond Aron who writes lucidly and forcefully about political problems from a conservative point of view that is in the best of the English tradition (not the French). The other newspapers of the metropole are generally unrewarding. Some are sensational, all are partisan, and a few have a hard time keeping in touch with the realities of politics. (*L'Information,* for example, reacted to the American arms shipment to Tunisia in 1957 by suggesting that the United States should exercise caution due to the existence off of New York harbor of a French aircraft carrier!) The party press is in serious financial difficulty and almost dead. At the same time, the trend has not been in the direction of serious newspapers; the majority of "the children of Descartes" prefer the organs of sensational expression.

Chapter 10

ALAIN. *Le Citoyen contre les Pouvoirs.* Paris: Éditions du Sagittaire, 1925. Classical treatment of the meaning of authority in a country that has been rebelling against it for years. Old but absolutely fundamental.

BROGAN, D. W. *The French Nation: From Napoleon to Petain, 1814–1940.* New York: Harper & Bros., 1958.

———. *France Under the Republic.* New York: Harper & Bros., 1940. Stimulating and takes a great deal for granted concerning the reader's background.

EARLE, EDWARD M. (ed.). *Modern France.* Princeton, N.J.: Princeton University Press, 1951. Valuable essays that touch many aspects of French life.

FAUVET, JACQUES. *La France déchirée.* Paris: Librairie Arthème Fayard, 1957. Invaluable for identification of French political tendencies.

LUETHY, HERBERT. *France Against Herself.* New York: Frederick A. Praeger, Inc., 1955. Brilliant study of paradoxes in a country of paradoxes. A "must."

SCHOENBRUN, DAVID. *As France Goes.* New York: Harper & Bros., 1957. High style and insights that are the result of many years of reporting for the Paris branch of the *New York Herald Tribune.*

THOMSON, DAVID. *Democracy in France, The Third and Fourth Republics.* 3d ed. Fair Lawn, N.J.: Oxford University Press, 1958. Valuable for setting historical trends in proper perspective.

WERTH, ALEXANDER. *France, 1940–55.* New York: Holt, Rinehart & Winston, Inc., 1956.

———. *The Twilight of France.* New York: Harper & Bros., 1942. Partisan but extraordinarily developed treatment.

WYLIE, LAWRENCE W. *Village in the Vaucluse.* Cambridge, Mass.: Harvard University Press, 1957. Gets right to the heart of the village, that unit that is the "heart of France."

Chapter 11

ARON, RAYMOND. *La Tragédie algérienne.* Paris: Plon, 1957. Good explanation of the futility of the Fourth Republic's Algerian policy.

DUVERGER, MAURICE. *The French Political System.* Chicago: University of Chicago Press, 1958. Neatly packaged summarization of the Fourth Republic.

DUVERGER, M., GOGUEL, F., and TOUCHARD, J. *Les Élections du 2 janvier 1956.* Paris: Librairie Armand Colin, 1957. Worthwhile papers on the last general election held under the Fourth Republic (although the work is somewhat marred by several spotty graphs).

FAUVET, JACQUES. *La IVe République.* Paris: Librairie Arthème Fayard, 1959. Excellent job of summing up the end of a regime.

MACRIDIS, ROY, and BROWN, BERNARD. *De Gaulle's Republic; Quest for Unity.* Homewood, Ill.: The Dorsey Press, 1960. First-rate job. A "must."

PICKLES, DOROTHY. *The Fifth Republic.* New York: Frederick A. Praeger, Inc., 1960. Modest coverage of the first two years of the regime.

PRIOURET, ROGER. *La République des Députés.* Paris: Bernard Grasset, 1959. Brilliant essay on the Third and Fourth Republics by a writer of great insights.

SIRIUS. *La Suicide de la IVe République.* Paris: Les Éditions du Cerf, 1958. Consists of editorials published originally in *Le Monde* that trace the slow death of the Fourth Republic.

TILLON, GERMAINE. *Algeria; the Realities.* New York: Alfred A. Knopf (a division of Random House, Inc.), 1958. Lays bare the real meaning of the Algerian insurrection.

VIANSSON-PONTÉ, PIERRE. *Risques et Chances de la Veme République.* Paris: Plon, 1959. Helpful assessment by *Le Monde's* able journalist.

WAHL, NICOLAS. *The Fifth Republic.* New York: Random House, Inc., 1959. Brief account of the first months of the Fifth Republic.

WRIGHT, GORDON. *The Reshaping of French Democracy.* New York: Reynal & Hitchcock, 1948. The Constituent Assembly debates and the forces that shaped the Constitution of the Fourth Republic.

Chapter 12

BLUM, LEON. *For all Mankind.* New York: The Viking Press, Inc., 1946. Veteran politician's statement of personal values and his hopes for the emergence of a "new France."

BODLEY, J. E. C. *The Church in France.* New York: The Macmillan Co., 1906. Standard work.

EINAUDI, M., and GOGUEL, F. *Christian Democracy in Italy and France.* Notre Dame, Ind.: University of Notre Dame Press, 1952. Helpful.

KOHN, HANS. *Making of the Modern French Mind.* New York: D. Van Nostrand Company, Inc., 1955. Author's introduction plus valuable readings.

MARTIN, KINGSLEY. *French Liberal Thought in the Eighteenth Century.* London: Ernest Benn, Ltd., 1929.

MAYER, J. P. *Political Thought in France from the Revolution to the Fourth Republic.* Rev. ed. London: Faber & Faber, Ltd., 1949. Highly recommended.

RÉMOND, RENÉ. *La Droite en France de 1815 à nos Jours, continuité et diversité d'une tradition politique.* Paris: Aubier, 1954. Standard classic on the French Right.

SCOTT, J. A. *Republican Ideas and the Liberal Tradition in France, 1870–1914.* New York: Columbia University Press, 1951.

SÉRANT, PAUL. *Où va la Droite?* Paris: Plon, 1958. Helpful for differentiating among different types of rightism.

SOLTAU, ROGER. *French Political Thought in the Nineteenth Century.* New Haven, Conn.: Yale University Press, 1931. One of the best studies available for this era.

Chapter 13

BLOCH-MORHANGE, J. *Les Politiciens.* Paris: Librairie Arthème Fayard, 1961. Political profiles of important party personalities (e.g., Mendès-France, Guy Mollet, and others).

BOURRE, RAYMOND LE. *La Syndicalisme français dans la Ve République.* Paris: Calmann-Lévy, 1959.

DEPREUX, ÉDOUARD. *Renouvellement du Socialisme.* Paris: Calmann-Lévy, 1960. Conception of party and statement of personal beliefs of one of the leaders and founders of the PSU.

DUVERGER, MAURICE. *Les Partis politiques et Classes sociales en France.* Paris: Librairie Armand Colin, 1955. Dated but helpful information on all parties, including the now dead RPF, and the political tendencies of the social classes.

EHRMANN, HENRY W. *Organized Business in France.* Princeton, N.J.: Princeton University Press, 1957. Strong study of a phenomenon on which few authoritative works exist.

EINAUDI, M., DOMENACH, J. M., and GAROSCI, A. *Communism in Western Europe.* Ithaca, N.Y.: Cornell University Press, 1951.

FAUVET, JACQUES, and MENDRAS, HENRI. *Les Paysans et la Politique.* Paris: Librairie Armand Colin, 1958. Valuable essays on voting habits, organization, and political tendencies of the peasantry.

LAVAU, GEORGE. "Political Pressures by Interest Groups in France." In *Interest Groups on Four Continents,* Henry W. Ehrmann (ed.). Pittsburgh: University of Pittsburgh Press, 1958. Pp. 60–95. First-rate piece.

LORWIN, VAL. *The French Labor Movement.* Cambridge, Mass.: Harvard University Press, 1954. The best study of French labor organizations.

MALTERRE, JACQUES, and BENOIST, PAUL. *Les Partis politiques français.* Paris: Bibliothèque de l'Homme d'action, 1956. Survey of the parties from a Left viewpoint.

MAURICE, GASTON. *La Parti radicale.* Paris: Marcel Rivière, 1928.

MEYNAUD, JEAN. *Les Groupes de Pression en France.* Paris: Librairie Armand Colin, 1958. Pioneer effort to handle pressure groups systematically; definitely out of the traditional nineteenth-century rut of French political science.

MILHAUD, ALBERT. *Histoire du Radicalisme.* Paris: Société d'Éditions, 1951. Includes both some very helpful and some very misleading information on radicalism.

NICOLET, CLAUDE. *Le Radicalisme.* Paris: Presses Universitaires de France, 1956. Another of the *Que sais-je?* series; traces the Radical party from its birth to 1956.

ROSSI, A. *A Communist Party in Action.* New Haven, Conn.: Yale University Press, 1949. Important account of doctrinal and tactical zigzags of the French Communist party.

Chapter 14

CAMPBELL, PETER. *French Electoral Systems and Elections, 1789–1957.* London: Faber & Faber, Ltd., 1958. Highly recommended work by one of the ablest students of electoral institutions.

DUVERGER, MAURICE. *The French Political System.* Chicago: University of Chicago Press, 1958. Describes electoral laws briefly.

GOGUEL, FRANCOIS. *France Under the Fourth Republic.* Ithaca, N.Y.: Cornell University Press, 1952. By the foremost authority on French electoral laws.

———. *Géographie des Élections françaises, de 1870 à 1951.* Paris: Librairie Armand Colin. Brief commentary and many maps illustrating vote distributions.

MINISTÈRE DE L'INTÉRIEUR. *Les Élections législatives du 2 janvier 1956.* Paris: La Documentation française, 1957. Complete election returns.

WILLIAMS, PHILIP. *Politics in Post-War France; Parties and the Constitution in the Fourth Republic.* 2d ed. New York: Longmans, Green & Co., Inc., 1958. Contains an excellent chapter on the electoral laws.

Chapter 15

GOOCH, R. K. *Parliamentary Government in France; Revolutionary Origins, 1789–1791.* Ithaca, N.Y.: Cornell University Press, 1960. Precise, scholarly account.

———. *The French Parliamentary Committee System.* New York: Appleton-Century-Crofts, Inc., 1935. Dated but very helpful for trends.

HOWARD, J. E. *Parliament and Foreign Policy in France.* London: Cresset Press, Ltd., 1948. Dated standard work but still valuable for past political history.

LIDDERDALE, D. W. S. *The Parliament of France.* New York: Frederick A. Praeger, Inc., 1952. Best account of Parliament of Fourth Republic.

MAVRINAC, A. *Organization and Procedure of the National Assembly of the Fifth French Republic.* London: Hansard Society, 1960.

Chapter 16

FISHER, H. A. L. *Bonapartism.* Fair Lawn, N.J.: Oxford University Press, 1908.

FUNK, ARTHUR. *Charles de Gaulle: The Crucial Years, 1943–1944.* Norman, Okla.: University of Oklahoma Press, 1959.

FURNISS, EDGAR. *France, Troubled Ally; de Gaulle's Heritage and Prospects.* New York: Harper & Bros., 1960. Able description of the Gaullist regime.

GAULLE, CHARLES DE. *The Call to Honour, 1940–1942.* New York: The Viking Press, Inc., 1955.

———. *Unity, 1942–1944.* New York: Simon & Schuster, Inc., 1959. Absolutely necessary for understanding De Gaulle's approach to diplomacy.

———. *Salvation, 1944–1946.* New York: Simon & Schuster, Inc., 1960.

LIDDERDALE, D. W. S. *The Parliament of France.* New York: Frederick A. Praeger, Inc., 1952. See introduction for good discussion of past executive trends.

PRIOURET, ROGER. *La République des Députés.* Paris: Bernard Grasset, 1959.

REDSLOB, ROBERT. *Le Régime parlementaire, Études sur les Institutions d'Angleterre, de Belgique, de Hongrie, de France.* Paris: M. Giard, 1924. Old, wise, and too frequently neglected commentary.

THOMSON, DAVID. *Two Frenchmen: Pierre Laval and Charles de Gaulle.* London: Cresset Press, Ltd., 1951.

WERTH, ALEXANDER. *The Strange Story of Pierre Mendès-France and the Great Conflict over French North Africa.* London: Barrie Books, Ltd., 1957. Clever treatment of the former President of the Council of Ministers, one of the most difficult to assess figures of this century.

WILLIAMS, PHILIP. *Politics in Post-War France; Parties and the Constitution in the Fourth Republic.* 2d ed. New York: Longmans, Green & Company, Inc., 1958. Several good chapters on the executive.

Chapter 17

BARKER, ERNEST. *The Development of Public Services in Western Europe, 1660–1930.* Fair Lawn, N.J.: Oxford University Press, 1944.

BAUM, W. C. *The French Economy and the State.* Princeton, N.J.: Princeton University Press, 1958. Capable broad treatment.

CHAPMAN, BRIAN. *Introduction to French Local Government.* London: George Allen & Unwin, Ltd., 1953.

———. *The Prefects and Provincial France.* London: George Allen & Unwin, Ltd., 1955. Both studies are excellent.

EINAUDI, M., BYE, M., and ROSSI, E. *Nationalization in France and Italy.* Ithaca, N.Y.: Cornell University Press, 1955.

JEANNENEY, JEAN M. *Forces et Faiblesses de l'Économie française.* Paris: Librairie Armand Colin, 1956. By the famous professor and government official.

ROBSON, W. A. *The Civil Service in Britain and France.* London: Hogarth Press, Ltd., 1956. Especially recommended.

SCHWARTZ, BERNARD. *French Administrative Law and the Common Law World.* New York: New York University Press, 1954.

SHARP, W. R. *The French Civil Service, Bureaucracy in Transition.* New York: The Macmillan Co., 1931. Old but excellent.

Chapter 18

BLANCHET, ANDRÉ. *L'Itinéraire des Partis africains depuis Bamako.* Paris: Plon, 1958. Good for views favoring decolonization in the African territories.

CADY, JOHN F. *The Roots of French Imperialism in Eastern Asia.* Ithaca, N.Y.: Cornell University Press, 1956.

DELAVIGNETTE, ROBERT. *Freedom and Authority in French West Africa.* Fair Lawn, N.J.: Oxford University Press, 1950. Valuable for background.

GONIDEC, P. F. *L'Évolution des Territoires d'outre mer depuis 1946.* Paris: Pichon, 1958. Traces postliberation policies.

HAMMER, ELLEN. *The Struggle for Indo-China.* Stanford, Calif.: Stanford University Press, 1954. Valuable now for the effect on the French of that war that they could not win.

JULIEN, CHARLES A. *L'Afrique du nord en marche.* Paris: René Julliard, 1952. The impressions of one of France's best-known journalists.

MOUSSA, PIERRE. *Les Chances économiques de la Communauté franco-africaine.* Paris: Librairie Armand Colin, 1957. Important now for the economic positions of the former French territories.

PRIESTLEY, HERBERT I. *France Overseas: A Study of Modern Imperialism.* New York: Appleton-Century Crofts, Inc., 1938. Old standard work; good for background.

THOMPSON, V., and ADLOFF, R. *French West Africa.* Stanford, Calif.: Stanford University Press, 1958.

Chapter 19

AMOS, MAURICE S., and WALTON, F. P. *Introduction to French Law.* Fair Lawn, N.J.: Oxford University Press, 1935. Dated but still good for main outlines.

CAMPBELL, PETER, and CHAPMAN, BRIAN. *The Constitution of the Fifth Republic: Translation and Commentary.* Fair Lawn, N.J.: Oxford University Press, 1958. Brief, annotated translation; one of few available.

DAVID, RENÉ, and VRIES, HENRY P. DE. *The French Legal System.* New York: Oceana Publications, 1958.

ENSOR, R. C. K. *Courts and Judges in France, Germany and England.* Fair Lawn, N.J.: Oxford University Press, 1933. Standard work.

Part III

POLITICS AND GOVERNMENT OF ITALY

Chapter 20

BANCO DI ROMA. *Ten Years of Italian Economy, 1947–1956.* Rome: Banco di Roma, 1957. Studies on Italian economic development.

BATTAGLIA, ACHILLE, *et al. Dieci Anni Dopo, 1945–1955: Saggi sulla Vita Democratica Italiana.* Bari: Laterza, 1955. Studies on Italian politics and government.

BRAGA, GIORGIO. *Il Comunismo fra gli Italiani: Saggio di Sociologia.* Milan: Comunita, 1956. Analysis of causes for the spread of communism in Italy.

CARO, GIOVANNI. *Itinerari Sociali.* Naples: Rinascita Artistica, 1957. A study of social conditions in Italy.

CONGRESSO MONDIALE DI SOCIOLOGIA, IV. *Aspetti e Problemi Sociali dello Sviluppo Economico in Italia.* Bari: Laterza, 1959. Proceedings of the fourth international convention of sociology devoted to the social problems caused by economic development in Italy.

HUGHES, H. STUART. *The United States and Italy.* Cambridge, Mass.: Harvard University Press, 1953. A good introduction to the politics of contemporary Italy.

LUZZATTO, FEGIS P. *Il Volto Sconosciuto dell'Italia: Dieci Anni di Sondaggio D.O.X.A.* Milan: Giuffre, 1956. Public opinion studies on political, economic, and social questions.

ROSSI, DORIA, MANLIO. *Dieci Anni di Politica Agraria nel Mezzogiorno.* Bari: Laterza, 1959. Analysis of the policy of land reform in southern Italy.

SMITH, DENIS MACK. *Italy: A Modern History.* Ann Arbor: University of Michigan Press, 1959. A penetrating history of Italian national development.

VALERI, NINO, *et al. Lezioni sull'Antifascismo.* Bari: Laterza, 1960. Lectures on the origins of fascism, the anti-Fascist movement, and on the problems of Italian democracy.

Chapter 21

CANDELORO, GIORGIO. *Il Movimento Cattolico in Italia.* Rome: Editori Riuniti, 1953. Detailed study of political Catholicism in Italy.

CARRACCIOLO, ALBERTO, and SCALIA, GIANNI. *La Citta Futura.* Milan: Feltrinelli, 1959. Studies of the ideas of the Italian Marxist, Antonio Gramsci.

FOGARTY, MICHAEL. *Christian Democracy in Western Europe.* Notre Dame, Ind.: University of Notre Dame Press, 1957. The ideas and development of the Christian Democratic parties.

GASPERI, ALCIDE DE. *Discorsi Politici.* 2 vols. Rome: Edizioni Cinque Lune, 1956. Major political speeches by the Christian Democratic party leader.

GENTILE, PANFILO, *et al. Saggi Storici sul Liberalismo Italiano.* Perugia: Historia Editrice, 1954. Studies of the liberal tradition in Italian politics.

GRAMSCI, ANTONIO. *The Modern Prince and Other Writings.* London: Lawrence & Wishart, Ltd., 1957. Selections from the notebooks of the Italian Marxist.

HILTON YOUNG, WAYLAND. *The Italian Left: A Short History of Political Socialism in Italy.* New York: Longmans, Green & Co., Inc., 1949. Brief history of the Italian Socialist party.

ROMMEN, HEINRICH. *Lo Stato nel Pensiero Cattolico.* Milan: Giuffre, 1959. Detailed study of the political philosophy of the Catholic church.

TOGLIATTI, PALMIRO. *La Via Italiana al Socialismo.* Rome: Editori Riuniti, 1956. Statement of Communist policy in Italy by the party leader.

WEBB, LEICESTER C. *Church and State in Italy, 1947–1957.* Carlton, Australia: Melbourne University Press, 1958. Brief study of the influence of religion on Italian politics.

Chapter 22

ALMIRANTE, GIORGIO, *et al. Il Movimento Sociale Italiano.* Milan: La Nuova Accademia, 1958. Brief statement of the aims of the Italian social movement.

BASSO, LELIO. *Il Partito Socialista.* Milan: La Nuova Accademia, 1958. Brief statement of the aims of the Italian Socialist party.

D'ANTONIO, MARIO, and NEGRI, GUGLIELMO. *Raccolta degli Statuti dei Partiti Politici in Italia.* Milan: Giuffre, 1958. Texts of the party charters, together with a commentary on the legal regulations governing political parties in Italy.

DEGLI OCCHI, CESARE. *Il Partito Nazionale Monarchico.* Milan: La Nuova Accademia, 1958. Brief statement of the aims of the Monarchist party.

DEMOCRAZIA, CRISTIANA, LA. *Atti e Documenti della Democrazia Cristiana, 1943–1959.* Rome: Edizioni Cinque Lune, 1959. Documents of the Christian Democratic party.

FORLANI, ARNALDO. *Il Partito Socialista Italiano di Fronte al Comunismo dal 1945 al 1956.* Rome: Edizioni Cinque Lune, 1956. A critical account of the ties between the Socialists and Communists.

MAITAN, LIVIO. *Teoria e Politica Comunista nel Dopoguerra.* Milan: Schwarz, 1955. The theory and policy of the Italian Communist party since 1945.

NEUFELD, MAURICE. *Italy, School for Awakening Countries: The Italian Labor Movement in Its Political, Social, and Economic Setting from 1800 to 1960.* Ithaca, N.Y.: New York State School of Industrial and Labor Relations, Cornell University, 1961. A history of the conditions of Italian labor and its development and organization.

PARTITO COMUNISTA ITALIANO. *Atti del IX Congresso del Partito Comunista Italiano.* 2 vols. Rome: Editori Riuniti, 1960. Proceedings of the ninth congress of the Italian Communist party.

PARTITO LIBERALE ITALIANO. *Dati Sommari su Alcuni Problemi Politici ed Economici: La Campagna Elettorale.* Rome: Partito Liberale Italiano, 1958. Electoral campaign statement by the Italian Liberal party.

PARTITO SOCIALISTA ITALIANO. *Due Anni di Lotte Socialiste per la Democrazia e pet la Pace.* Rome: S.E.T.I., 1955. Policy statement by the Italian Socialist party.

Chapter 23

BIRON, GIOVANNI. *Codice Elettorale Politico.* Parma: Casanova, 1958. The laws regulating political elections in Italy.

CARANTI, ELIO. *Sociologia e Statistica delle Elezioni Italiane nel Dopoguerra.* Rome: Editrice Stadium, 1954. An analysis of political elections in Italy.

COMPAGNA, FRANCESCO, and DE CAPRARIIS, VITTORIO. *Geografia delle Elezioni Italiane dal 1946 al 1953.* Bologna: Il Mulino, 1954.

LUZZATTO, LUCIO. *Elezioni Politiche e le Leggi Elettorali in Italia.* Rome: Editori Riuniti, 1958. An analysis of the Italian electoral system.

MAZZAFERRO, LUCIANO. *Elezioni Politiche in una Zona di Riforma e di Emigrazione.* Bologna: Il Mulino, 1959. An analysis of the effects of land reform and emigration on Italian elections.

MINISTERO DELL'INTERNO. *Raccolta di Giurisprudenza in Materia Elettorale.* Rome: Istituto Poligrafico dello Stato, 1959. Laws, regulations, and court decisions on elections.

SCHEPIS, GIOVANNI. *Le Consultazioni Popolari in Italia dal 1848 al 1957.* Empoli: Caparrini, 1958. A study of elections in Italy from 1848 to 1957.

Chapter 24

CAMERA DEI DEPUTATI. *Manuale Parlamentare: Legislatura III.* Rome: Tipografia del Senato, 1959. Official manual of the Italian Parliament.

ESPOSITO, CARLO. *Saggi sulla Costituzione Italiana.* Padua: C.E.D.A.M., 1956. Essays on the Italian Constitution.

MOHRHOFF, FEDERICO. *Trattato di Diritto e Procedura Parlamentare.* Rome: Bardi, 1948. Treatise on parliamentary law and procedure.

MORTATI, COSTANTINO. *Istituzioni di Diritto Pubblico.* Padua: C.E.D.A.M., 1960. Definitive treatise on Italian government.

RUINI, MEUCCIO. *I Regolamenti Parlamentari.* Milan: Giuffre, 1953. The rules of parliamentary procedure in Italy.

Chapter 25

BALLADORE PALLIERI, GIORGIO. *Diritto Costituzionale.* Milan: Giuffre, 1959. Analysis of the Italian Constitution.

CONCI, F. *La Potesta Legislativa del Potere Esecutivo.* Milan: Giuffre, 1951. Study of the legislative prerogatives of the Italian executive.

PRETI, LUIGI. *Il Governo nella Costituzione Italiana.* Milan: Giuffre, 1954. Study of the position and powers of the executive branch of the Italian government.

SICA, VINCENZO. *La Controfirma.* Naples: Jovene, 1953. An analysis of the presidential power of countersignature.

Chapter 26

ALESSI, RENATO. *Sistema Istituzionale del Diritto Amministrativo Italiano.* Milan: Giuffre, 1958. Treatise on administrative law.

GUICCIARDI, E. *La Giustizia Amministrativa.* Padua: C.E.D.A.M., 1953. The system of administrative justice.

SANDULLI, ALDO. *Manuale di Diritto Amministrativo.* Naples: Jovene, 1957. Treatise on Italian administrative law.

SCUOLA DI PERFEZIONAMENTO IN SCIENZE AMMINISTRATIVE, UNIVERSITA DI BOLOGNA. *Problemi della Pubblica Amministrazione.* Bologna: Universita di Bologna, 1960. Studies on administration and personnel administration.

ZANIBONI, GUIDO. *Corso di Diritto Amministrativo.* 5 vols. Milan: Giuffre, 1956. Definitive treatise on Italian administrative law.

Chapter 27

AUSIELLO, ORLANDO. *Studi sull'Ordinamento e la Legislazione Regionale.* Milan: Giuffre, 1954. Studies on the organization and powers of the regions.

GIOVENCO, L. *L'Ordinamento Comunale: Struttura, Organi, Controlli.* Milan: Giuffre, 1958. The organization and powers of the Italian commune.

LENTINI, ANTONIO. *L'Amministrazione Locale.* Como: Nani, 1953. The organization and operation of local government in Italy.

PALADIN, LIVIO. *La Potesta Legislativa Regionale.* Padua: C.E.D.A.M., 1958. Study of the legislative powers of the region.

PRATELLI, DANTE. *Costituzione e Funzionamento degli Organi Istituzionali della Provincia.* Empoli: Caparrini, 1955. Study of the organization and operation of the province.

SOLMI, G. *La Provincia nell'Ordinamento Vigente.* Pauda: C.E.D.A.M., 1953. The organization and functions of the province.

Chapter 28

ABBAMONTE, G. *Il Processo Costituzionale Italiano.* Naples: Jovene, 1957. Trial procedure before the Italian Constitutional Court.

BATTAGLIA, ACHILLE. *Processo alla Giustizia.* Bari: Laterza, 1954. Critical description of police administration and criminal court procedures.

BELLAVISTA, GIROLAMO. *Studi sul Processo Penale.* 2 vols. Milan: Giuffre, 1953, 1960. Studies on criminal trial procedures.

CARNELUTTI, FRANCESCO. *Principi del Processo Penale.* Naples: Morano, 1960. Criminal trial procedure in Italy.

CURCI, P. *La Corte Costituzionale.* Milan: Giuffre, 1956. Study of the organization, functions, and procedures of the Italian Constitutional Court.

SABATINI, GIUSEPPE. *Il Pubblico Ministero nel Diritto Processuale Penale.* 2 vols. Naples: Jovene, 1943, 1948. Organization and procedures of the Public Ministry.

SANTOSSUOSSO, FERNANDO. *Il Consiglio Superiore della Magistratura.* Milan: Giuffre, 1958. The organization and functions of the Superior Judiciary Council.

Part IV

POLITICS AND GOVERNMENT OF GERMANY

General Works

Deutschland Heute. Published by the Press and Information Office of the Federal German Government, 1959. Includes statistical material and charts on every phase of German life.

Deutschland im Wiederaufbau. Published by the Press and Information Office of the Federal German Government, 1960. Official report of the German government for the period 1949–1959.

ESCHENBURG, THEODOR. *Staat und Gesellschaft in Deutschland.* Stuttgart: Curt Schwab, 1956. A comprehensive text on the development of German society and institutions.

Facts About Germany. Published by the Press and Information Office of the Federal German Government, 1960. A short illustrated book describing the German recovery and presenting the newest statistical data.

GOLAY, JOHN FORD. *Founding of the Federal Republic of Germany.* Chicago: University of Chicago Press, 1958. Excellent study of the politics and government of the Federal Republic.

HARTMAN, HEINZ. *Authority and Organization of German Management.* Princeton, N.J.: Princeton University Press, 1959. Systematic treatment of leadership and employer-employee relations in German industry.

LITCHFIELD, EDWARD H. (ed.). *Governing Postwar Germany.* Ithaca, N.Y.: Cornell University Press, 1953. Outstanding collection of studies on politics and government of the Federal Republic.

Meet Germany. Hamburg: Atlantik Bruecke, 1960. A non-partisan private group published this collection of essays to further better understanding between the United States and Germany.

POLLOCK, JAMES K. (ed.). *German Democracy at Work.* Ann Arbor: University of Michigan Press, 1957. Good study of election system.

VERMEIL, EDMOND. *The German Scene: Social, Political, Cultural, 1890 to the Present Day.* London: George H. Harrap & Co., Ltd., 1956. Good historical analysis.

———. *Germany in the Twentieth Century: A Political and Cultural History of the Weimar Republic and the Third Reich.* New York: Frederick A. Praeger, Inc., 1956. The second volume of the previous work.

Chapter 29

GEIGER, THEODOR. *Die Klassengesellschaft im Schmelztiegel.* Koeln Hagen: 1949. A critical study of the German middle class.

GREBING, HELGA. *Der Nationalsozialismus.* Munich: Isar Verlag, 1959. An attempt to explain the Nazi movement on entirely sociological grounds.

KOHN, HANS. *The Mind of Germany: The Education of a Nation.* New York: Charles Scribner's Sons, 1960. Good study of German cultural traditions.

MOMMSEN, WILHELM. *Groesse und Versagen des Deutschen Buergertums.* Stuttgart: Deutsche Verlagsanstalt, 1949. Deals with the aspirations and failure of the German middle class.

SNYDER, LOUIS. *German Nationalism: The Tragedy of a People.* Harrisburg, Pa.: Stackpole, 1952. Traces nationalistic trends in education, literature, music, arts, and philosophy.

Chapter 30

EPSTEIN, KLAUS. *Mathias Erzberger and the Dilemma of German Democracy*, Princeton, N.J.: Princeton University Press, 1959. An evaluation of the struggle for democracy during the empire and the Weimar period.

GOEHRING, MARTIN. *Bismarsks Erben 1890–1945*. Wiesbaden: Steiner Verlag, 1959. A treatment of the perversion of German conservatism.

HAMEROW, T. S. *Restoration, Revolution, Reaction, Economics and Politics in Germany 1815–1871*. Princeton, N.J.: Princeton University Press, 1958. A picture of nineteenth-century Germany.

KLEMPERER, KLEMENS VON. *Germany's New Conservatism: Its History and Dilemma in the Twentieth Century*. Princeton, N.J.: Princeton University Press, 1957. Good study of German political thought.

KREBS, ALBERT. *Tendenzen und Gestalten der NSDAP*. Stuttgart: Deutsche Verlagsanstalt, 1959. A history of the early Nazi party by a prominent member who broke away in 1932.

KRIEGER, LEONARD. *The German Idea of Freedom, History of a Political Tradition*. Boston: Beacon Press, Inc., 1957. Treats the topic in philosophical terms.

Chapter 31

BERGSTRAESSER, L. *Geschichte der Politischen Parteien in Deutschland*. Munich: Isar Verlag, 1955. A concise presentation of the history of German political parties.

FOGARTY, MICHAEL. *Christian Democracy in Western Europe*. Notre Dame, Ind.: Notre Dame University Press, 1957. Good presentation of the politics of the Christian Democratic Union.

HEIDEGGER, HERMAN. *Die deutsche Sozialdemokratie und der nationale Staat*. Goettingen: Musterschmidt, 1960. A complete history of German democratic socialism.

KAUTSKY, KARL. *Erinnerungen und Eroerterungen*. Gravenhage: Monton and Co., 1960. The last collection of writings of the chief theoretician of German social democracy.

MATHIAS, E., and MORSEY, R. *Das Ende der Parteien, 1933*. Düsseldorf: Droske Verlag, 1960. A collection of monographs dealing with the different parties from 1918–1933.

Chapter 32

KITZINGER, V. W. *German Electoral Politics: A Study of the 1957 Campaign*. Fair Lawn, N.J.: Oxford University Press, 1960. Describes the relationship between parties and interest groups during the 1957 Bundestag elections.

ZIEGLER, D. J. *Prelude to Democracy, A Study of Proportional Representation and the Heritage of Weimar Germany*. Studies No. 20. Lincoln, Neb.: University of Nebraska, 1958. Legalistic treatment of proportional representation.

Chapter 33

DECHAMPS, BRUNO. *Macht und Arbeit der Ausschuesse; der Wandel der parlamentarischen Willensbildung*. Heidelberg: 1954. A comparison of the parliamentary procedure and legislative committees in Great Britain, France, United States, and Germany.

KREMER, KLEMENS. *Der Abgeordnete*. Munich: 1953. A treatment of the position of the legislator in the Federal Republic.

SCHAEFER, HANS. *Der Bundesrat*. Berlin: Koeln, 1955. Describes structure, composition, and functions of the Federal Council.

Chapter 34

BRECHT, ARNOLD T. *The Art and Technique of Administration in German Ministries.* Cambridge, Mass.: Harvard University Press, 1940. Still useful study of the organization and procedures of German central administration.

HOFER, WALTER. *Der Nationalsozialismus, Dokumente 1933–1945.* Frankfurt: Fischer Buecherei, 1957. A collection of important speeches and documents of the Nazi period.

LUCAS, FRIEDRICH. *Hindenburg als Reichspraesident.* Bonn: L. Roehrscheid, 1959. Investigates the type and consequences of the presidency of Hindenburg.

SCHMITT, CARL. "Der Hueter der Verfassung," *Archiv des Oeffentlichen Rechts,* Vol. XVI, 1929. Exposition of the guardianship theory of the presidency.

Chapter 35

FISCHER, LORENZ, and HAUTEN, PETER VAN. "Cologne." *Great Cities of the World: Their Government Politics and Planning,* William A. Robson (ed.). London: George Allen & Unwin, Ltd., 1957. Good study of local government in a large city.

PETERS, HANS. *Handbuch der Kommunalen Wissenschaft und Praxis.* 3 vols. Berlin: 1955–1958. Principal treatise on local government administration.

Chapter 36

GIESE, FRIEDRICH. *Grundgesetz fuer die Bundesrepublik Deutschland.* Frankfurt: Verlag Kommentator, 1955. A short commentary of the Basic Law of 1949.

MANGOLDT, HERMANN. *Das Bonner Grundgesetz.* Berlin: Franz Vahlen Verlag, 1953. Commentary of the Basic Law by an outstanding constitutional lawyer.

MATTERN, JOHANNES. *Principles of the Constitutional Jurisprudence of the German National Republic.* Baltimore: Johns Hopkins Press, 1928. Highly scholarly introduction to German legal philosophy.

Chapter 37

CRANKSHAW, EDUARD. *Die Gestapo.* Berlin: Colloquium Verlag, 1959. A short history of the notorious Secret Police of the Hitler regime.

GROSSER, ALFRED. *Die Bonner Demokratie, Deutschland von draussen gesehen.* Duesseldorf: Karl Rauch, 1960. An evaluation of positive and negative trends in Germany by a French observer.

LEMBERG, E. (ed.). *Die Vertriebenen in Westdeutschland.* 3 vols. Kiel: Ferdinand Hirt, 1959. An extensive treatment of the whole refugee and expellee problem by thirty-six experts.

Part V

POLITICS AND GOVERNMENT OF THE U.S.S.R.

General Works

BERLIN, ISAIAH. *Karl Marx: His Life and Environment.* Fair Lawn, N.J.: Oxford University Press, 1959. A short but well-written biographical study.

BRZEZINSKY, ZBIGNIEW K. *The Permanent Purge: Politics in Soviet Totalitarianism.* Cambridge, Mass.: Harvard University Press, 1956. A study of the use of the purge as an instrument of enforcing conformity.

CHAMBERLAIN, WILLIAM H. *The Russian Revolution, 1917–1921.* 2 vols. New York: The Macmillan Co., 1935. The standard history of the revolution and civil war in Russia.

Current Digest of the Soviet Press. Published by the Joint Committee on Slavic Studies of New York, this weekly publication contains all the important laws, decrees, resolutions, declarations, etc. issued by the Soviet government, as well as significant articles taken from the Soviet press.

KHRUSHCHEV, N. S. *For Victory in Peaceful Competition with Capitalism.* New York: E. P. Dutton & Co., Inc., 1960. Speeches by the Soviet leader from 1958–1959.

KLIUCHEVSKY, VASILY. *A History of Russia.* 5 vols. New York: E. P. Dutton & Co., Inc., 1911. Monumental social and political history of imperial Russia.

LANDAUER, CARL. *European Socialism: A History of Ideas and Movements from the Industrial Revolution to Hitler's Seizure of Power.* 2 vols. Berkeley, Calif.: University of California Press, 1959. Huge study of the history of European socialism, including communism.

LENIN, V. I. *Imperialism: The Highest Stage of Capitalism.* New York: International Publishers Co., Inc., 1937. Famous study of monopoly phase of international capitalism and the inevitability of war doctrine.

MASARYK, THOMAS G. *The Spirit of Russia.* 2 vols. New York: The Macmillan Co., 1955. History of nineteenth-century Russian thought.

MAZOUR, ANATOLE G. *Russia: Past and Present.* Princeton, N.J.: D. Van Nostrand Co., Inc., 1951. A cultural history.

VERNADSKY, GEORGE. *A History of Russia.* New Haven, Conn.: Yale University Press, 1961. Brief history of Russian political development from the earliest times.

Chapter 38

BLACK, CYRIL. (ed.). *The Transformation of Russian Society: Aspects of Social Change Since 1861.* Cambridge, Mass.; Harvard University Press, 1961. Good collection of essays on Russian society and institutions.

CURTISS, J. W. *Church and State in Russia, 1900–1917.* New York: Columbia University Press, 1940. Describes the relationship between church and state under the Tsarist regime.

DALLIN, DAVID. *The Real Soviet Russia.* New Haven, Conn.: Yale University Press, 1944. An analysis of the class system of Soviet society.

MOORE, BARRINGTON. *Soviet Politics: The Dilemma of Power; the Role of Ideas in Social Change.* Cambridge, Mass.: Harvard University Press, 1950. Analysis of the class system.

ROSTOW, W. W. and LEVIN, ALFRED. *Dynamics of Soviet Society.* New York: Mentor Books, 1954. Good study of Soviet institutions and behavior.

WEBB, SIDNEY and BEATRICE. *Soviet Communism: A New Civilization?* 2 vols. New York: Longsmans, Green & Co., Inc., 1935. Friendly study by famous British Socialists.

Chapter 39

BERDYAEV, NICHOLAS. *The Origins of Russian Communism.* London: Geoffrey Bles, Ltd., 1937. A description of the historical antecedents of Russian communism.

BURNS, EMILE. *A Handbook of Marxism.* New York: Random House, Inc., 1935. A good selection of excerpts from the writings of Marx, Engels, Lenin, and Stalin.

CARR, EDWARD H. *Karl Marx: A Study in Fanaticism.* London: Macmillan & Co., Ltd., 1935. One of the best written biographies.

———. *A History of Soviet Russia: The Bolshevik Revolution.* 3 vols. New York: The Macmillan Co., 1951–53. One of the best and most detailed studies.

DEUTSHER, ISAAC. *Stalin: A Political Biography.* Fair Lawn, N.J.: Oxford University Press, 1949. Perhaps the best biography of the dictator.

HAIMSON, LEOPOLD H. *The Russian Marxists and the Origins of Bolshevism.* Cambridge, Mass.: Harvard University Press, 1955. Study of doctrinal sources of Soviet communism.

HOOK, SIDNEY. *Towards an Understanding of Karl Marx.* New York: John Day Co., Inc., 1933. Brief critical evaluation of sources of Marxism.

———. *From Hegel to Marx: Studies in the Intellectual Development of Karl Marx.* New York: Humanities Publishing Co., 1950. Good critical study of origins of Marxian thought.

HUNT, N. C. CAREW. *The Theory and Practice of Communism.* New York: The Macmillan Co., 1957. Analysis of sources and development of Communist doctrine.

KELSEN, HANS. *The Political Theory of Bolshevism.* Berkeley, Calif.: University of California Press, 1949. Analysis of philosophic assumptions and logic of Communist political philosophy.

LENIN, V. I. *State and Revolution.* New York: International Publishers Co., Inc., 1945. Classic study of the nature of the state and the necessity of revolution and dictatorship to establish socialism.

MARCUSE, HERBERT. *Soviet Marxism: A Critical Analysis.* New York: Random House, Inc., 1961.

MARX, KARL. *Capital.* 3 vols. Moscow: Foreign Languages Publishing House, 1959. Major work of criticism of capitalism and scientific basis for Marxism.

MAYO, HENRY B. *Introduction to Marxist Theory.* Fair Lawn, N.J.: Oxford University Press, 1960. Critical evaluation of Marxist doctrines.

TREADGOLD, DONALD W. *Twentieth Century Russia.* Chicago: Rand McNally & Co., 1959. Historical study of political development.

TROTSKY, LEON. *The History of the Russian Revolution.* 3 vols. New York: Simon & Schuster, Inc., 1937. Interpretation of the revolution by one of its leaders.

VENTURI, FRANCO. *Roots of Revolution.* New York: Frederick A. Praeger, Inc., 1960. Fine study of the nineteenth-century Russian Populist movement.

WOLFE, BERTRAM D. *Three Who Made a Revolution.* Boston: Beacon Press, Inc., 1955. Study of the three leaders who engineered the Bolshevik revolution.

YARMOLINSKY, AVRAHM. *Road to Revolution: A Century of Russian Radicalism.* London: Cassell & Co., Ltd., 1957. A study of the Populist movement and its outgrowth.

Chapter 40

BORKENAU, FRANZ. *European Communism.* New York: Harper & Bros., 1953. A study of the national Communist parties of Europe and the international tie among them.

Current Soviet Policies: The Documentary Record of the 19th, 20th and 21st Communist Party Congresses. 3 vols. New York: Frederick A. Praeger, Inc., and Columbia University Press, 1953, 1957, 1960. Complete report of the proceedings of three important party events.

History of the Communist Party of the Soviet Union: Short Course. New York: International Publishers Co., Inc., 1939. Stalinist account of the development of the Bolsheviks from a faction to a regime.

Vsesoyuznaya kommunisticheskaya partiya (B) v rezolyutsiyakh i resheniyakh s"ezdov, konferentsii i plenumov TsK (1898–1939) (All-Union Communist Party [B] in Resolutions and Decrees of Congresses, Conferences, and Plenums of the Central Committee, 1898–1939). 2 vols. Vol. I, Moscow–Leningrad: Partiinoe izdatel'stvo, 1932. Vol. II, Moscow–Leningrad: Politizdat pri TsK(b), 1941.

Chapter 41

MAYNARD, SIR JOHN. *Russia in Flux.* New York: The Macmillan Co., 1948. Historical analysis of social and political institutions.

Chapter 42

FAINSOD, MERLE. *How Russia Is Ruled.* Cambridge, Mass.: Harvard University Press, 1953. A detailed descriptive analysis of the structure of the Soviet dictatorship.

INKELES, ALEX. *Public Opinion in Soviet Russia.* Cambridge, Mass.: Harvard University Press, 1950.

KULSKI, W. W. *The Soviet Regime: Communism in Practice.* Syracuse, N.Y.: Syracuse University Press, 1954. Comprehensive study of political and governmental system based on Soviet sources.

Sbornik zakonov S.S.S.R. i ukazov Prezidiuma Verkhovnogo Soveta S.S.S.R. (Collection of the Laws of the U.S.S.R. and Decrees of the Supreme Soviet of the U.S.S.R.), Moscow: Izdanie Verkhovnogo Soveta SSSR, 1945.

SCOTT, DEREK. *Russian Political Institutions.* New York: Holt, Rinehart & Winston, Inc., 1958. Brief description and analysis of party and governmental system.

TOWSTER, JULIAN. *Political Power in the U.S.S.R., 1917–1947: The Theory and Structure of Government in the Soviet State.* Fair Lawn, N.J.: Oxford University Press, 1948. Analysis of structure and practice of the Communist party and the Soviet government.

Chapter 43

FLORINSKY, MICHAEL L. *Towards an Understanding of the U.S.S.R.* New York: The Macmillan Co., 1953. A brief and concise description and analysis of the Soviet regime.

HAZARD, JOHN M. *The Soviet System of Government.* Chicago: University of Chicago Press, 1957. Brief description of organization and operation of government in the U.S.S.R. and good analysis of political institutions and practices.

HENDEL, SAMUEL. *The Soviet Crucible: Soviet Government in Theory and Practice.* Princeton, N.J.: D. Van Nostrand Co., Inc., 1959. Selected excerpts of representative studies on the Soviet system of government.

MEISEL, JAMES, and KOZERA, EDWARD S. *Materials for the Study of the Soviet System: State and Party Constitutions, Laws, Decrees, Decisions and Official Statements of the Leaders in Translation.* Ann Arbor, Mich.: George Wahr Publishing Co., 1953. Good collection of source materials.

ROGERS, ELTON. *Recent Trends of Reform in Soviet Constitutional and Administrative Practice.* New York: St. Martin's Press, Inc., 1956. Brief study of reforms to restore Socialist legality to Soviet administration.

Chapter 44

AREKALIAN, A. *Industrial Management in the U.S.S.R.* Washington, D.C.: Public Affairs Press, 1950. A description of the administrative machinery of industry in the U.S.S.R. by a Soviet author.

BIENSTOCK, GREGORY, SCHWARTZ, SOLOMON M., and YUGOW, AARON. *Management in Russian Industry and Agriculture.* Fair Lawn, N.J.: Oxford University Press, 1944. A description of Soviet managerial systems and procedures.

DEUTSCHER, ISAAC. *Soviet Trade Unions.* London: Royal Institute of International Affairs, 1950. A study of the role of Soviet trade-unions.

DOBB, MAURICE. *Soviet Economic Development.* London: Routledge & Kegan Paul, Ltd., 1948. Descriptive analysis of the economic system and its development.

GRANICK, DAVID. *The Red Executive: A Study of the Organization Man in Russian Industry.* New York: Doubleday & Co., Inc., 1961.

JASNY, NAUM. *Socialized Agriculture of the U.S.S.R.* Stanford, Calif.: Stanford University Press, 1949. Description of the administration of the collective farm system.

KURSKY, A. *The Planning of the National Economy of the U.S.S.R.* Moscow: Foreign Languages Publishing House, 1949. Study of the planned economy by a Soviet author.

MAVOR, JAMES. *An Economic History of Russia.* 2 vols. New York: E. P. Dutton & Co., Inc., 1925. Description of social as well as economic development of Russia.

SCHWARTZ, HARRY. *Russia's Soviet Economy.* Englewood Cliffs, N.J.: Prentice-Hall,

Inc., 1954. A study of all aspects of Soviet economic life from planning to administration and organization.

Chapter 45

GSOVSKI, VLADIMIR. *Soviet Civil Law.* 2 vols. Ann Arbor: University of Michigan Press, 1948. Comparative law study of private rights in the U.S.S.R. and the court system.
SZIRMAI, Z. (ed.). *The Federal Criminal Law of the Soviet Union.* (*Law in Eastern Europe,* Vol. III.) Leyden: Sythoff, 1959. Complete text of the revised criminal code of the U.S.S.R.
VYSHINSKY, ANDREI Y. *The Law of the Soviet State.* New York: The Macmillan Co., 1948. Official textbook on Soviet Constitution and jurisprudence.
ZELITCH, JUDITH. *Soviet Administration of Criminal Law.* Philadelphia: University of Pennsylvania Press, 1931. Early study of Soviet courts and trial procedure.

Part VI

POLITICS AND INSTITUTIONS OF EUROPEAN UNION

Chapter 46

BALL, M. MARGARET. *NATO and the European Union Movement.* New York: Frederick A. Praeger, Inc., 1958. An informative study of the principal organizations of the Atlantic community and the European Community.
DIEBOLD, WILLIAM, JR. *The Schuman Plan.* New York: Frederick A. Praeger, Inc., 1959. A lengthy study of the European Coal and Steel Community.
FLORINSKY, MICHAEL T. *Integrated Europe?* New York: The Macmillan Co., 1955. A short critical evaluation of the effort to unify western Europe.
HAAS, ERNST B. *The Uniting of Europe.* Stanford, Calif.: Stanford University Press, 1958. A detailed study of the politics of European unification.
HAINES, C. GROVE. (ed.). *European Integration.* Baltimore: Johns Hopkins Press, 1957. A collection of informative essays by persons closely connected with the European Community.
HEISER, H. J. *British Policy with Regard to the Unification Efforts on the European Continent.* Leyden, The Netherlands: A. W. Sythoff, 1959. A study of British policy leading to the formation of the European Free Trade Area.
ROBERTSON, A. H. *European Institutions.* New York: Frederick A. Praeger, Inc., 1959. A brief study of the principal organizations of the western European countries.
SANNWALD, ROLF F., and STOHLER, JACQUES. *Economic Integration.* Princeton, N.J.: Princeton University Press, 1959. A complex economic analysis of the Common Market system.
SCITOVSKY, TIBOR. *Economic Theory and Western European Integration.* Stanford, Calif.: Stanford University Press, 1958. An economic analysis of the Common Market system.
STRAUSS, E. *Common Sense About the Common Market: Germany and Britain in Post-war Europe.* New York: Holt, Rinehart & Winston, Inc., 1958. A short critical study of the Common Market.

Index